NEW MUSEUMS

NEW MUSEUMS

Intentions, Expectations, Challenges

Musée d'art et d'histoire de Genève
May 11 – August 20, 2017

Edited by
Art Centre Basel,
Katharina Beisiegel

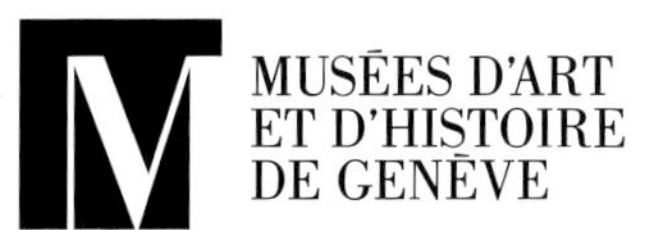

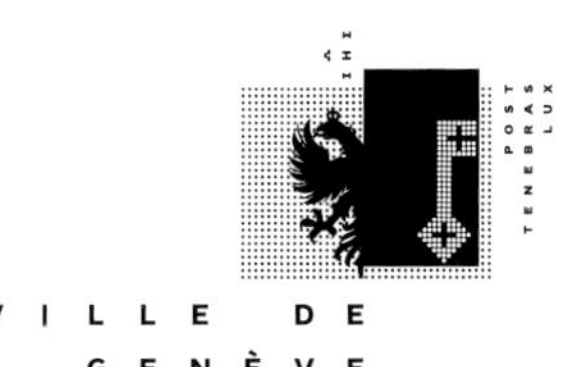

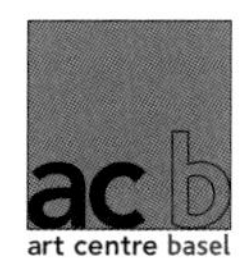

HIRMER

Contents

Museums of the 21st Century

Jean-Yves Marin

Whenever a museum is opened to the public, it brings with it a flood of images – many of them very impressive – in the media. It is an important moment, awaited by a curious public eager to discover a new cultural facility that will offer much more than just collections.

The success of the number of visitors is important and the reception is often enthusiastic. This social phenomenon – that still does not appear to have reached its pinnacle – was difficult to imagine half a century ago when the proclaimed death of museums seemed to be inevitable. Following May 1968, these backward-looking "temples" no longer had their place in society and their collections were deserted. The opening of the Centre Pompidou in 1977 and the enormous aesthetic and cultural shock that followed culminated in a swing to museums that rang in a new era. Hereafter, architecture placed itself at the service of museums and became inscribed in the urban landscape as a societal marker. Museum professionals were no longer merely scholarly conservers but had to become mediators, designers and communicators with the responsibility of making it possible for the largest number of people to participate in scientific achievements.

Today, these extraordinary monuments to knowledge are not only being constructed in occidental countries but throughout the world; each country, every community feels that it has to have a museum – and, if possible, one that is immediately distinguishable. The "Bilbao phenomenon" and its enormous economic and touristic consequences revolutionised the cultural vision of decision makers and major collectors. The very best architects would be needed to construct these new museums. The alchemy of the balance between the contents and container is the key to success and there is no way that the public can be deceived.

This exhibition, conceived by the Art Centre Basel on the initiative of the Musée d'art et d'histoire de Genève (MAH) is designed to reflect on this museum phenomenon. There have been many manifestations of this in Switzerland up to now and there can be no doubt that this will continue and even increase in the years to come.

In this period of uncertainty and reflection on the future of the MAH, the exhibition has the aim of making all aware of the factual elements of the evolution of museums in the world through the remarkable initiatives taken – most of them accomplished in recent years or in the course of being realized. Quite clearly, this panorama is not exhaustive but it does have the aim of showing the tendencies of understanding the main architectural, cultural, economic and social orientations that, today, shape the museum landscape.

Geneva is the first station of what is conceived as a travelling exhibition that will be presented in many countries in the years to come. It has only one objective: to make people aware of – and love – museums. Those of today and those of tomorrow.

My sincere thanks go to all the architects and museum professionals who agreed to take part in this project review. This also applies equally to the Art Centre Basel and to Bertrand Mazeirat, who guaranteed the commission for Geneva, and the teams of the Musée d'art et d'histoire who were entrusted with its production.

Foreword

Suzanne Greub

It is of great personal pleasure that the Musée d'art et d'histoire de Genève (MAH) is presenting with *New Museums: Intentions, Expectations, Challenges* the third architectural exhibition conceived by the Art Centre Basel. As in our first two exhibitions, this time we once again focus on buildings that protect our cultural heritage. It matters not whether a museum displays archaeological finds, features modern art or provides a home for a Chinese comics collection; they all provide us with new interpretations of the concept "museum", along with a recognition of all the demands imposed on the museum world at the beginning of the 21st century.

Nearly ten years after the conception of the Art Centre Basel's second architectural exhibition, *Museums in the 21st Century: Concepts, Projects, Buildings*, it is clear that, judging from current exciting new projects, the major social upheavals of the last decade have also led to a paradigm shift in museum architecture. With this publication we therefore discuss not only the most important trends in new museum design, but at the same time document how society's current concerns and challenges relating to urbanism, privatisation, globalisation and technological progress are reflected in new museum projects.

This exhibition could not have been realised without the trust and support of the participating architects. The Art Centre Basel is sincerely grateful to:

Adjaye Associates, Atelier Deshaus, Aires Mateus e Associados, Barozzi/Veiga, David Chipperfield Architects Berlin, Christ & Gantenbein, estudio Herreros, Fender Katsalidis Architects, Foster + Partners, Heatherwick Studio, Heneghan Peng Architects, Klaus Schuwerk of Kleihues + Schuwerk Architects, MAD Architects, Moreau Kusunoki Architectes, MVRDV, SANAA, Studio Libeskind, Tadao Ando Architect & Associates, and Zaha Hadid Architects.

I would also like to take this opportunity to express my personal gratitude to the many people who have helped on this exhibition: I thank my husband for his constant support, my colleagues for their untiring dedication, and most especially Deputy Director Katharina Beisiegel and Curatorial Assistant Marie Gaitzsch for curating and designing the show and producing the catalogue, as well as my colleagues from MAH – above all Director Jean-Yves Marin and Curator Bertrand Mazeirat, who helped make the exhibition a reality.

I am particularly grateful to the catalogue's authors for their scholarly and up-to-the-minute contributions: Karen van den Berg, Chris Dercon, Suzanne MacLeod, Kali Tzortzi and Wolfgang Ullrich. And I thank Anke Gröner for presenting her personal view of the nineteen museums that granted us special access to the very different projects. With this publication I am hoping that we are able to offer new stimuli for discussions relating to the tasks of today's museum buildings.

My special thanks to Hirmer Verlag, which as represented by Jürgen Kleidt, Gunnar Musan and Vanessa Magson-Mann produced this inspiring book in collaboration with the Art Centre Basel.

I hope the exhibition contributes to a better understanding of future-oriented museum architecture, and wish the Musée d'art et d'histoire much success and its Geneva visitors much enjoyment with *New Museums: Intentions, Expectations, Challenges*.

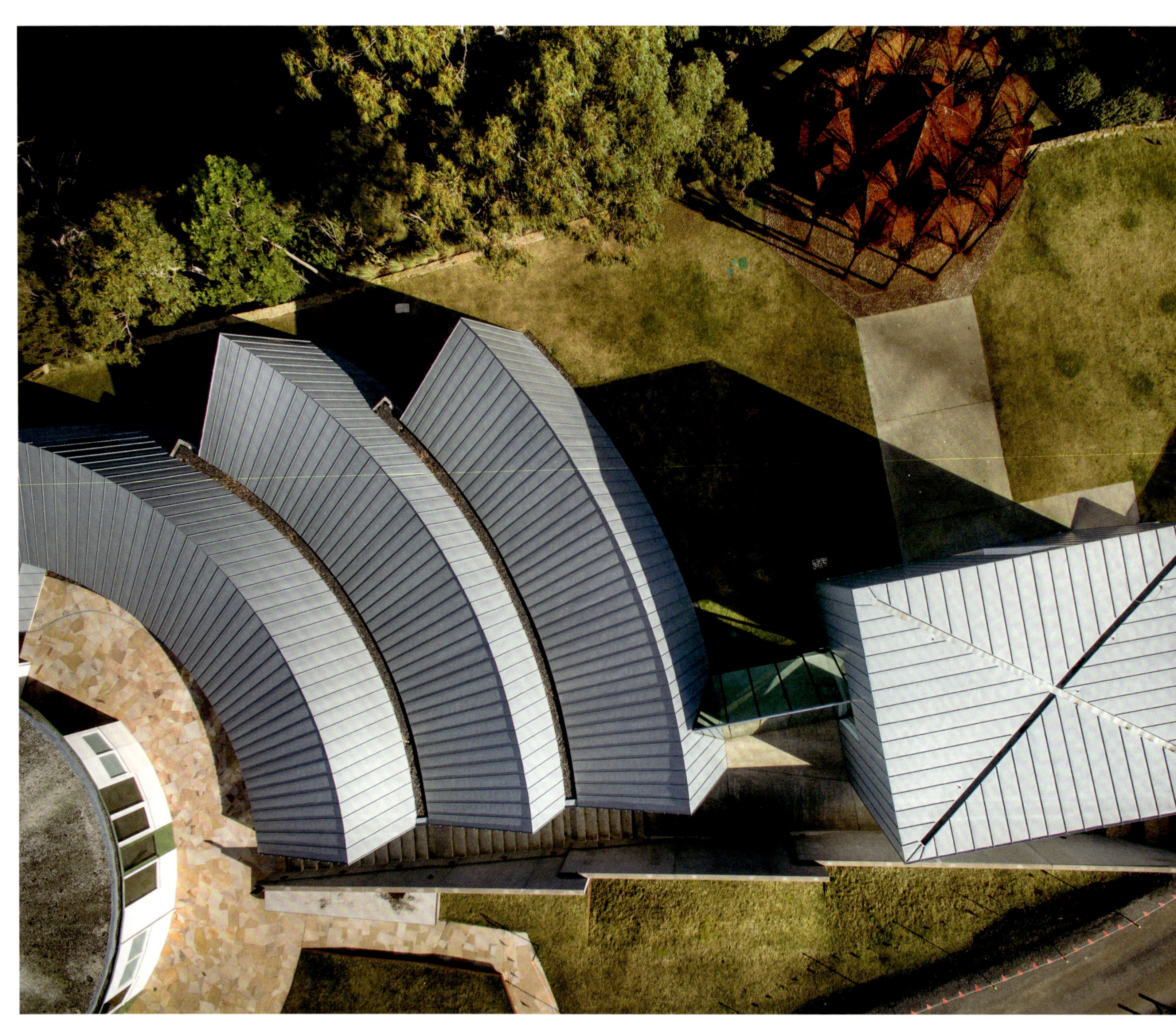

↑ MONA, Berriedale, Fender Katsalidis Architects.
View from above including the Library and Kiefer Pavilion.

Keeping the Past Alive in the Future:
A New Digital Museum Age

Katharina Beisiegel

Museums are important. They serve to preserve our history and reinforce our understanding of our own culture. It is possible that they even make us better, more creative and more tolerant people.[1]

It is therefore not very surprising that new museum projects frequently appear in the features pages of major newspapers,[2] where the state of today's museum is regularly addressed. New museums, whether only imagined, planned or already under construction, reflect current debate about sustainability, technology, consumption, research and the future significance of culture. The meaning of the term "new museum" has meanwhile continuously evolved, vaguely incorporating all the catchwords that have dominated discussion of museum concepts since the 1970s.[3] In this exhibition we consider the "new museum" to refer to the intersection of museology and museum architecture, as the embodiment of what the museum might look like in the future and what its functions will be.

Eleven years after the opening in 2006 of our last exhibition on museum architecture, *Museums in the 21st Century: Concepts, Projects, Buildings*, we once again note a paradigm shift in museum debate. After the financial crisis of 2008 it became clear that so-called mega-museums, Bilbao babies and satellites of the A-list institutions[4] are not necessarily models for success. A certain humility and return to the essentials have come to predominate. In addition to well-known, iconic mega-buildings, there are many smaller projects devoted to the specific task of redefining what objects of cultural value worthy of preservation might be.[5]

Fundamentally, the "new museum" is faced with the challenge of mitigating between the public's expectations and the aspirations of those involved in its foundation, construction, use and support – and at the same time serving as an attractive component for cultural education. The demands placed on the museum have become positively utopian: it is required to be a visitor magnet, a place for ambitious study and conservation of cultural treasures, a reflection of the socio-cultural pulse, an economic attraction helping to revitalise its urban surroundings and an iconic landmark. It must be both innovative and respectful of tradition. In addition, it is increasingly expected that museums should be partially or wholly self-supporting rather than relying on state or private funding. This has occasioned an inexorable commercialisation. Museums have become products, consumer goods that can be reproduced anywhere in the world. These days

nearly every major museum is experimenting with some form of expansion, either creating satellite museums, staging pop-up events,[6] or organising travelling exhibitions of world-famous masterworks to remote corners of the world.[7] Well-known museums increasingly function as brands, with determined business plans and the desire to be global players, yet in order to profit from globalisation they cannot avoid having to perceive its negative aspects.[8]

What does this mean for the future of the museum?

The noted economist David Throsby feels that the future of museums will be mainly influenced by two important issues: technological changes and the new abundance of private museums.[9] The increasing privatisation of the museum means that in place of being institutions ostensibly created for the good of society as a whole they are furthering the personal agendas of a few super-rich art collectors, while to an increasing degree privatisation is giving rise to new ideas about how the actual spaces, with regards to content, of the "new museum" can be filled. Self-confident private museums are now in dialogue with public institutions, with the result that museum practice is opening up to a new era of change.[10]

A prime example of this is the collector David Walsh's MONA Museum of Old and New Art. There established museum practices are being challenged with a wink of the eye: for 75,000 Australian dollars it offers a so-called "Eternity Membership",[11] which includes a post-mortem display in the museum in a "fancy jar" – an allusion to many a museum's marketing strategy of turning visitors into permanent (financial) supporters through memberships. Beyond such attention-getting schemes, MONA has developed since its founding in 2011 a programme that has attracted streams of visitors, despite its extremely remote location off the coast of Tasmania and its lack of similarity with traditional types of displays.[12] According to its founder, MONA is an anti-museum, a "secular temple and a subversive adult Disneyland",[13] and (yet) it is highly admired by museum critics.

Surprisingly, and regardless of the success of such unusual projects, visitors tend to have more conservative notions of what a museum ought to be. According to a British study in 2013, visitors are clearly less interested in new trends than had been assumed. They would mainly like to preserve the museum as they know it. Among the "essential purposes" to which museums even in the 21st century should remain committed, they identified such classic functions as "care and preservation of heritage, holding collections and mounting displays" and "creating knowledge for, and about, society".[14] Visitors expressed particular faith in the museum as a place where knowledge is accumulated and imparted, a "guardian of factual information".[15] At a time when we are inundated with a surfeit of information and trust in established media is declining while digitalisation proceeds unabated, this becomes an important museum responsibility.

In recent years the digital world has taken on increasing importance in museum operations. Along with now standard online communication through websites and newsletters, numerous new assignments have been added, ranging from content management and digital collection administration to digitalisation projects and the development of target-group-specific applications to branches of E-publishing. For a long time museum websites were mainly only digital brochures that could be consulted for such information as opening times and collection contents. With the arrival of the so-called "social media" and the attendant desire of users to be able to communicate with the museum faster and more directly, this has radically changed. Nearly every museum is now developing its own digital strategy, led by major houses like New York's Metropolitan Museum of Art,[16] which was quick to climb aboard. Of particular importance is the museums' professionalisation in their handling of digital media; staff must be trained, guidelines established[17] and experimental spaces created that make it possible to keep abreast of technological developments and, together with visitors, render possible new museum experiences.

Britain's Tate, which has helped to lead this discussion most decisively from the beginning, is pursuing an interesting approach. As early as 2012 the museum developed the concept of a "fifth gallery",[18] a virtual museum on an equal footing with its other houses, Tate Modern, Tate Britain, Tate Liverpool and Tate St Ives. Under the aegis of John Stack, then "Head of Digital", appropriate resources have been channelled into the creation of a progressive digital strategy: "Our ambition is to make Tate Online the most engaging and most social arts website, to match this with the richest, deepest arts content found anywhere on the web, and to pair this with an increased presence for Tate beyond our own website, so that we engage with Tate audiences wherever they are active online."[19]

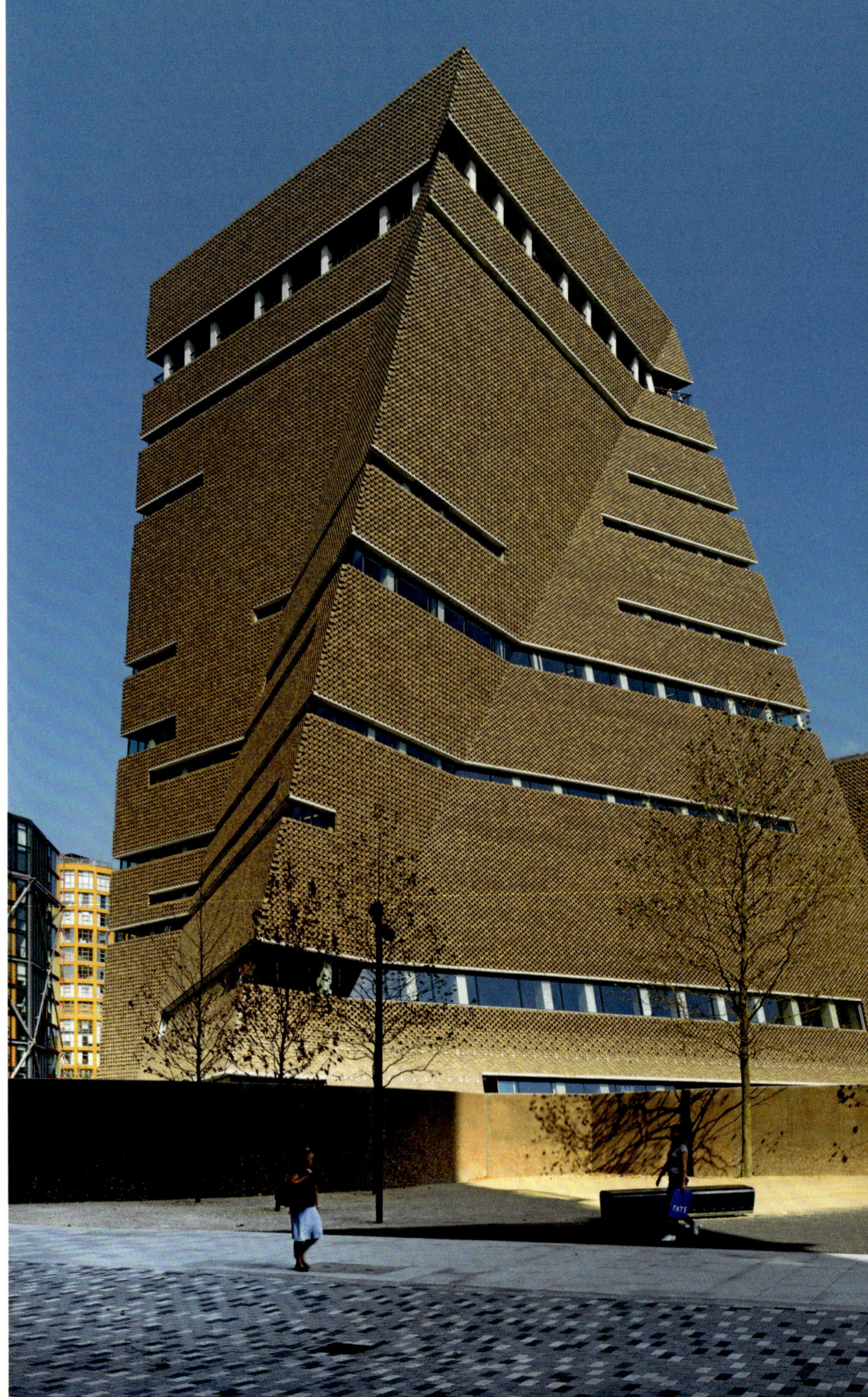

The institution of the museum's former sovereign claim to "knowledge" and "culture" has been transferred into a digital space partially created through a kind of swarm intelligence by visitors and users of the museum's online platforms. These include all types of online communities hosted on the museum's website, for example special forums on exhibitions, children's pages, curatorial blogs, "digitorials" and official Twitter, Facebook, Flickr and Instagram accounts managed by museum staff. In addition, there are livestreams, YouTube channels, virtual exhibitions, as well as apps and games for mobile devices, to name but a few of the manifold digital options. They all invite the user to actively communicate with the museum. Web 2.0 and its successors have established two-lane communication between museums as content providers and visitors as co-creators. Needless to say, this can be problematic. How can the museum continue to function as a place of knowledge when control over important areas of its web presence is turned over to its visitors? In its role as precursor even the Tate has been forced to experience some of the negative aspects of digital freedom, for example in that, through uncensored streams, inadvertent critical and inappropriate user commentaries appeared on picture screens within the Tate's galleries.[20] Another problem is the vast amount of users' personal data available to museums through such close networking. This has been recognised as an economic asset, one with which to better market the museum's own products and those of its sponsors or partners.[21] Digital strategy thus sooner or later becomes an important part of the business plan. But participation in the endeavours of the virtual museum means that as an aside a transparent visitor comes into being, whose interests and ways of using the site will not be the primary focus of the museum's efforts to improve their programme.

What does the digital future mean for museum architecture?

If one follows the logic of a virtual museum, it would at first appear that sooner or later the museum building will become obsolete. In 2014 Damien Whitmore, former Director of Programming at the Victoria and Albert Museum in London, made the provocative statement: "Museums of today are not buildings, because most people experience museums online … ."[22] This implies that the museum building is a relic from a time that is past and if it plays any role in the future at all it will have only a subordinate one as a mother ship.

I would here argue for the precise opposite: museum buildings are just as important and indispensable to the "new museum" as virtual museums or digital museum practice. In a future when all museums everywhere in the world make possible virtual access to exhibits, collections and general knowledge at all times, the museum building itself takes on much greater importance than we might assume today. It is appropriate to preserve the uniqueness of the museum building as the locus of the institution's identity, distinct from the levelling of Web 2.0 and its successors. Historically, the museum has always been a place where visitors experienced and studied things and engaged with them. The tangible experience

of objects has always been a central feature of the positive museum experience. This suggests that the museum building offers something that sets it apart, that cannot be replicated in a virtual museum, or "fifth gallery". The sociologist George Ritzer has advanced the concept of "glocalization" – "the interpenetration of the global and the local resulting in unique outcomes in different geographic areas" – that needs to be fostered as a partial alternative to the homogeneity resulting from globalisation.[23] As applied to the museum, this means creating added value for a relatively small public. Ritzer insists that various influences create an idiosyncratic mix that makes it impossible to reproduce an experience (including a museum experience) outside the original location. The "new museum" can accordingly become a "glocalisation of something" in that its architecture presents distinct characteristics – and this is what is important – at least in most cases as a result of decisions made locally. In contrast to its virtual sister, the museum's aim is not to satisfy a global hunger for information and encourage maximal participation but rather to make unique experiences possible for its building's visitors.

Museum architecture plays a crucial role in this. It illustrates how international projects are involved in the redefinition and realisation of the "new museum" in such a wide variety of ways. It is not the iconic buildings that will dominate, but rather intelligent ongoing strategies that tie the museum to its location[24] and thus make possible a singular, local visitor's experience. Almost all the museum projects portrayed here achieve this in very different ways. Two examples illustrate divergent approaches: one is Nicolas Moreau's and Hiroko Kusunoki's Guggenheim Helsinki. The architecture deliberately attempts to relate to its location by incorporating Finnish materials and taking into account Finnish social structures and living habits. The other is the Long Museum West Bund in Shanghai by Atelier Deshaus, which creates a dramatic connection between an old industrial structure and new architecture, recalling Shanghai's past as a port in the coal trade while serving as a hypermodern art museum. The old structural elements are central to the new architectural aesthetic, and provide a tie to the history of its site.

Upcoming decades will show what technological progress will mean for digital museum culture. From our present point of view, it would seem that a symbiotic link between the virtual museum and the actual museum building is ideal, for this provides room for experimentation and further evolution of the idea of the "new museum"

↓   Long Museum West Bund, Shanghai,
     Atelier Deshaus.

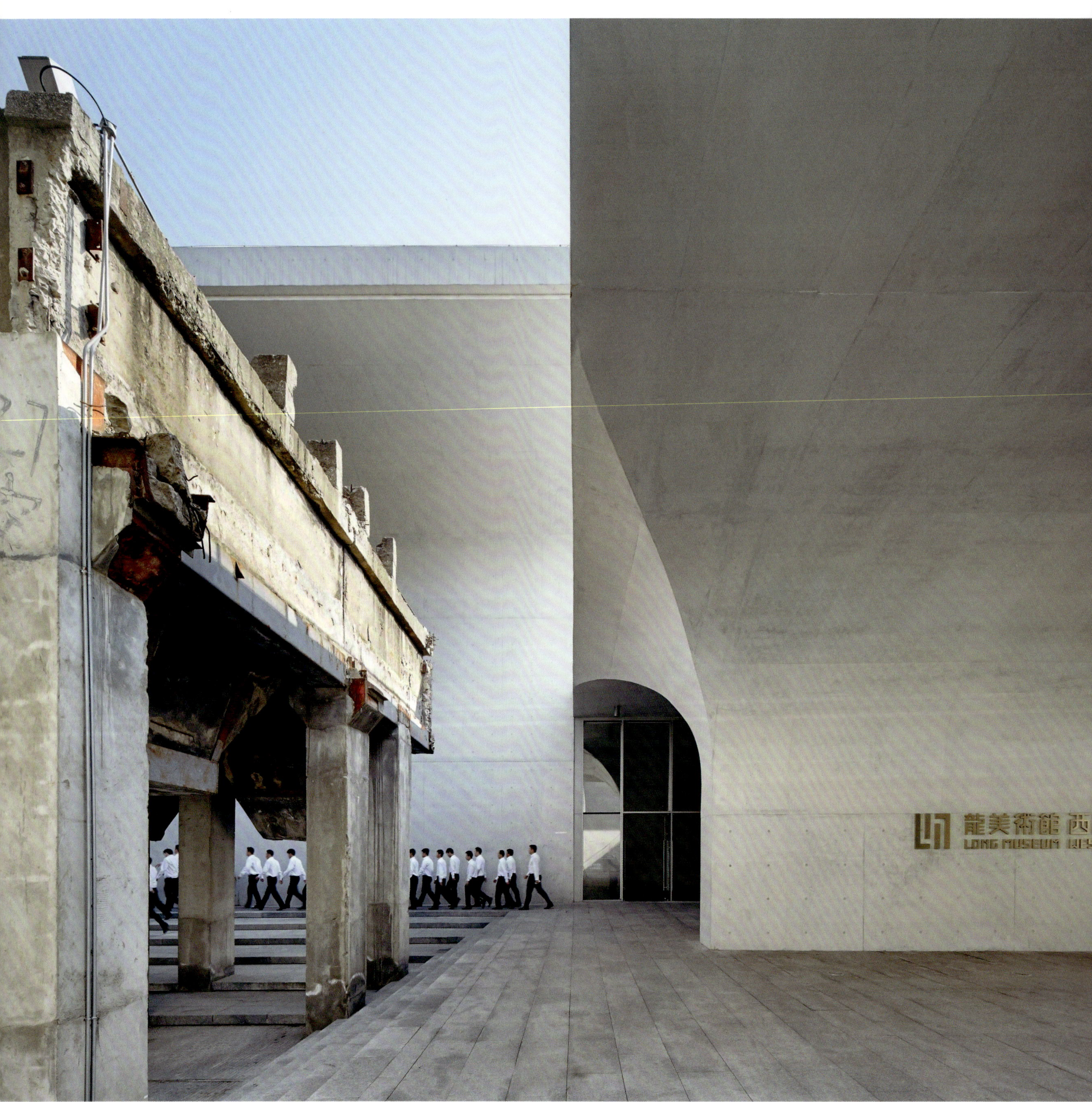

while at the same time retaining the physical museum as a traditional place to experience art or other cultural artefacts.

At the beginning of the 21st century "new museum" is proving to be an umbrella term covering many different developments – from the small museum of culture to the redevelopment of entire inner-city quarters. Localised projects in which the populace increasingly has the last word make the "new museum" an important topic of public discussion and an agent for the future.

1 See Suzanne MacLeod, "Image and Life: Museum Architecture, Social Sustainability and Design for Creative Lives" in the present volume, 175 ff.

2 See, for example, Joshua Rothman, "The Meaning of Culture", *The New Yorker*, December 26, 2014, accessed September 15, 2016, http://www.newyorker.com/books/joshua-rothman/ meaning-culture; Stephan Mann, "Die Lage der Museen. Neue Hierarchie Fallen", *Frankfurter Allgemeine Zeitung*, November 5, 2015, accessed September 15, 2016, http://www.faz.net/aktuell/ feuilleton/kunst/die-lage-der-museen-in-der-hierarchiefalle- 13891625.html; Felix Müller, "Historische Museen in der Krise. Die Eventfalle", *Neue Zürcher Zeitung*, June 3, 2016, accessed September 15, 2016, http://www.nzz.ch/feuilleton/akturall/ historische-museen-in-der-krise-die-eventkultur-fordert-ihren- preis-ld.86606; Ben Davis, "How the Rich Are Hurting the Museums They Fund", *The New York Times*, July 22, 2016, accessed September 15, 2016, http://www.nytimes.com/2016/ 07/24/opinion/sunday/how-the-rich-are-hurting-the-museums- they-fund.html?_r=0.

3 See Wolfgang Ullrich, "The Idea of the Open Museum: History and Problems" in this volume, 163 ff.

4 In addition to the Guggenheim Helsinki and the Louvre Abu Dhabi discussed in this book, there are, for example, the planned branches of the Victoria and Albert Museum in Dundee, Scotland, and Shekou, China, and the Centre Pompidou Metz, open since 2010.

5 David Chipperfield's Naga Site Museum in Sudan, Studio Libeskind's Kurdistan Museum, and Heneghan Peng Architects' Palestinian Museum are only three examples from our exhibition in which both well-known architects and rising younger firms have committed themselves to the protection and display of important cultural arte- facts without exalting the structure above the museum's mission.

6 For example, the BMW Guggenheim lab, a mobile think tank on urban issues, which from 2010 to 2013 made stops in New York, Berlin and Mumbai.

7 To this day visitors are willing to wait for hours to be able to see a selection of works from such museums as the Louvre or Paris's Musée Picasso in places like Shanghai or Sydney.

8 See Karen van den Berg, "Museum Buildings in the 21st Century: Major Projects and Notes on the Redefinition of the Museum" in this volume, 185 ff.

9 Keynote speech by David Throsby at ICOM Milan, July 6, 2016.

10 See Chris Dercon, "Why Bother? or, The Rise of the Private Museum" in this volume, 171 ff.

11 "Cemetery", Mona, accessed September 15, 2016, https://www.mona. net.au/mona/Cemetery.

12 Of the 1,153,300 travellers to Tasmania in 2015, 340,800 visited the museum, roughly 30 per cent of all tourists. "Mona Visitor Statistics, March 2016", Tourist Tasmania, accessed September 15, 2016, http://www.tourismtasmania.com.au/_data/assets/pdf_file/0010/ 39772/MONA-Visitor-Profile-YE-Dec-2015.pdf.

13 Richard Flanagan, "Tasmanian Devil", *The New Yorker*, January 21, 2013, accessed September 15, 2016, http://www.newyorker.com/ magazine/2013/01/21/tasmanian-devil.

14 Report by Britain thinks for Museums Association, March 2013, accessed September 15, 2016, https://www.museumsassociation.org/ download?id=954916, 4.

15 Ibid., 3.

16 In 2009 The Metropolitan Museum of Art established a Digital Media Department responsible for the museum's "public-facing digital profile".

17 Here published digital strategies define not only the museum's approach but also the way users are dealt with.

18 John Stack, "Tate Online Strategy 2010–12", *Tate Papers* 13 (Spring 2010), accessed September 15, 2016, http://www.tate.org.uk/research/ publications/tate-papers/13/tate-online-strategy-2010-12.

19 Ibid.

20 Jill Avery, "The Tate's Digital Transformation", *Harvard Business School Case* 314–122, April 2014, 10.

21 Ibid., 11. This is mainly tracked through DROI digital's return on investment. Jill Avery identified four main categories regarding how the Tate monetised its digital strategy: 1. online shop, 2. making use of the data for e-marketing, 3. philanthropic outreach and 4. charging users for additional content.

22 Full quote: "Museums of today are not buildings, because most people experience museums online, so the V&A may have 3.5 million people to its buildings but 25 million people use the V&A online, so museums are now content curators which are accessible anytime anyplace anywhere, and that's very important." See "Leading Art Expert Says Finland Too Coy about Its Visual Culture", *Yle*, October 4, 2014, accessed September 16, 2016, http://yle.fi/uutiset/ leading_art_expert_says_finland_too_coy_about_its_visual_cul- ture/7508772.

23 George Ritzer, "The Globalization of Nothing", *SAIS Review* 23, no. 2 (2004): 189–200.

24 See Kali Tzortzi, "The Museum, a Building in and for the City. An Exploration from a Spatial Point of View" in this volume, 195 ff.

CATALOGUE

All texts by Anke Gröner

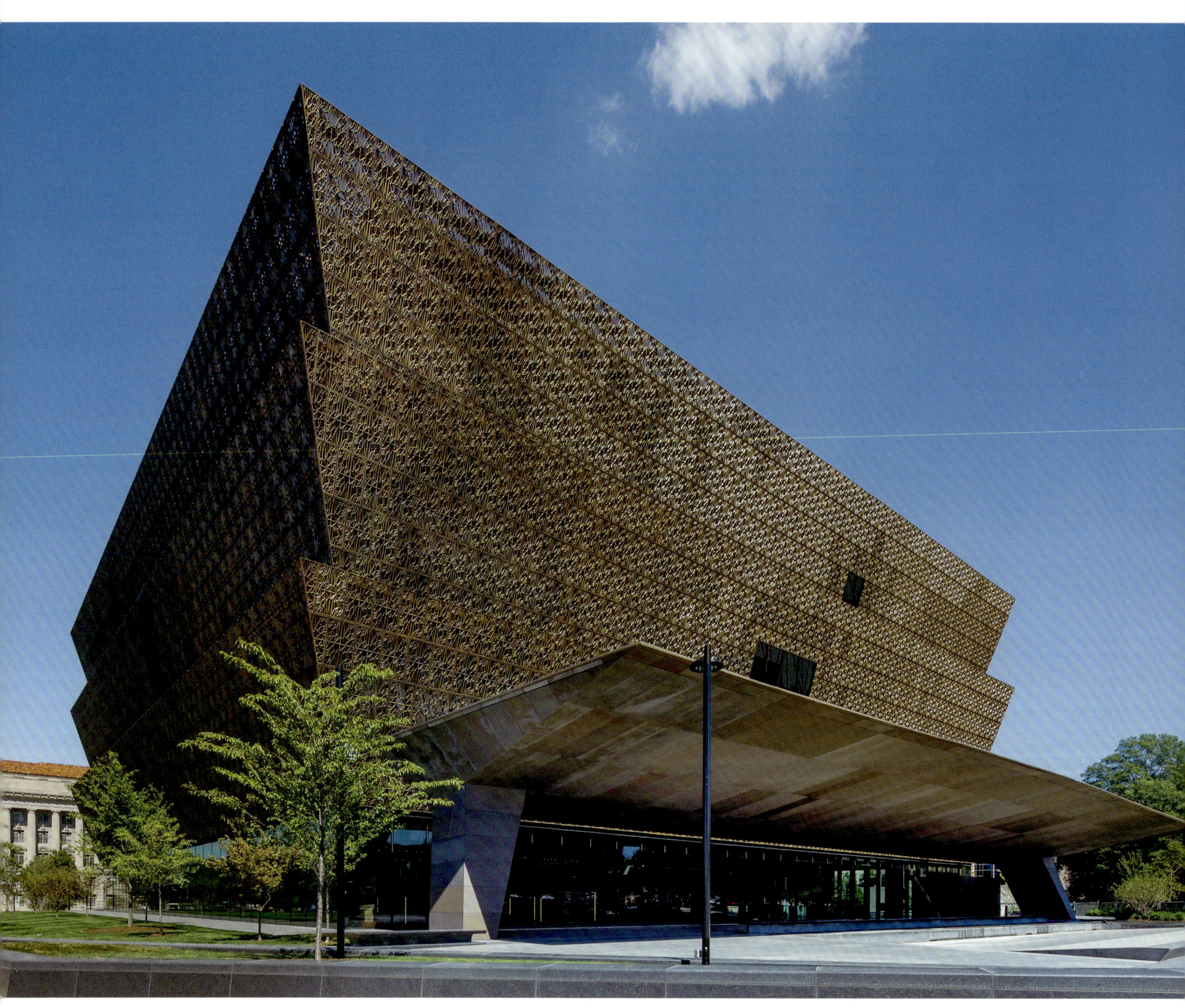

National Museum of African American History and Culture (NMAAHC)

Washington, D.C., USA

Adjaye Associates, New York / London
Construction 2009–2016, opened 2016
Building 39,000 sq. m
Permanent and temporary exhibitions about African American history and culture

David Adjaye's works are more than buildings, they are something between public spaces and social projects. Adjaye begins his structures with the hope that as long as future visitors linger in them, they will constitute a small civil society.[1] The National Museum of African American History and Culture, the newest branch of the Smithsonian Institution on the National Mall in Washington, intends to realise that hope.

Standing near a row of other branches of the Smithsonian, which serves as a national – predominantly white – archive, the NMAAHC, with its focus on the history of black America, sees its function as an urgently needed supplemental or competing archive.[2] Although its design is in distinct contrast to the architecture of the Smithsonian's other buildings, in subtle details it expresses the desire of America's ethnic minorities to belong. For example, the angles of the façade, the so-called corona that forms the above-ground portion of the museum, repeat that of the pyramidal tip of the Washington Monument next door.[3]

In various spots the design employs water as a symbol of African American history: the broad basin one has to cross before entering the building recalls the "middle passage", the transport of enslaved Africans across the Atlantic.[4] Inside, however, water stands for protection and catharsis. From the aboveground basin it flows through a circular opening into a smaller one in the lower floor. Here, in an underground court illuminated from above by this "eye", it creates a pleasant micro-climate that visitors find refreshing and invigorating. At the same time, it is an emotionally charged symbol of the tears shed by African Americans in centuries of pain, mourning and rage.

But the building is above all a celebration of their own special history and strength. The filigree metal shell of the corona recalls African handicrafts, and is expressive of self-confidence and pride. Inside, rough concrete and fine woods provide varied textures. These materials are also keyed to history: slaves were forced to survive with very little and everything which was of use was kept. The museum honours this tradition by incorporating recycled materials,[5] and plantings on the roof reduce the cost of insulation. The façade grille allows visitors to look outside, and passers-by on the National Mall can look in. A dialogue is created, and when you think of David Adjaye's notion of a museum fostering a civil society, there is the hope that thanks to this transparency people will feel encouraged to enter the museum and help to shape society anew.

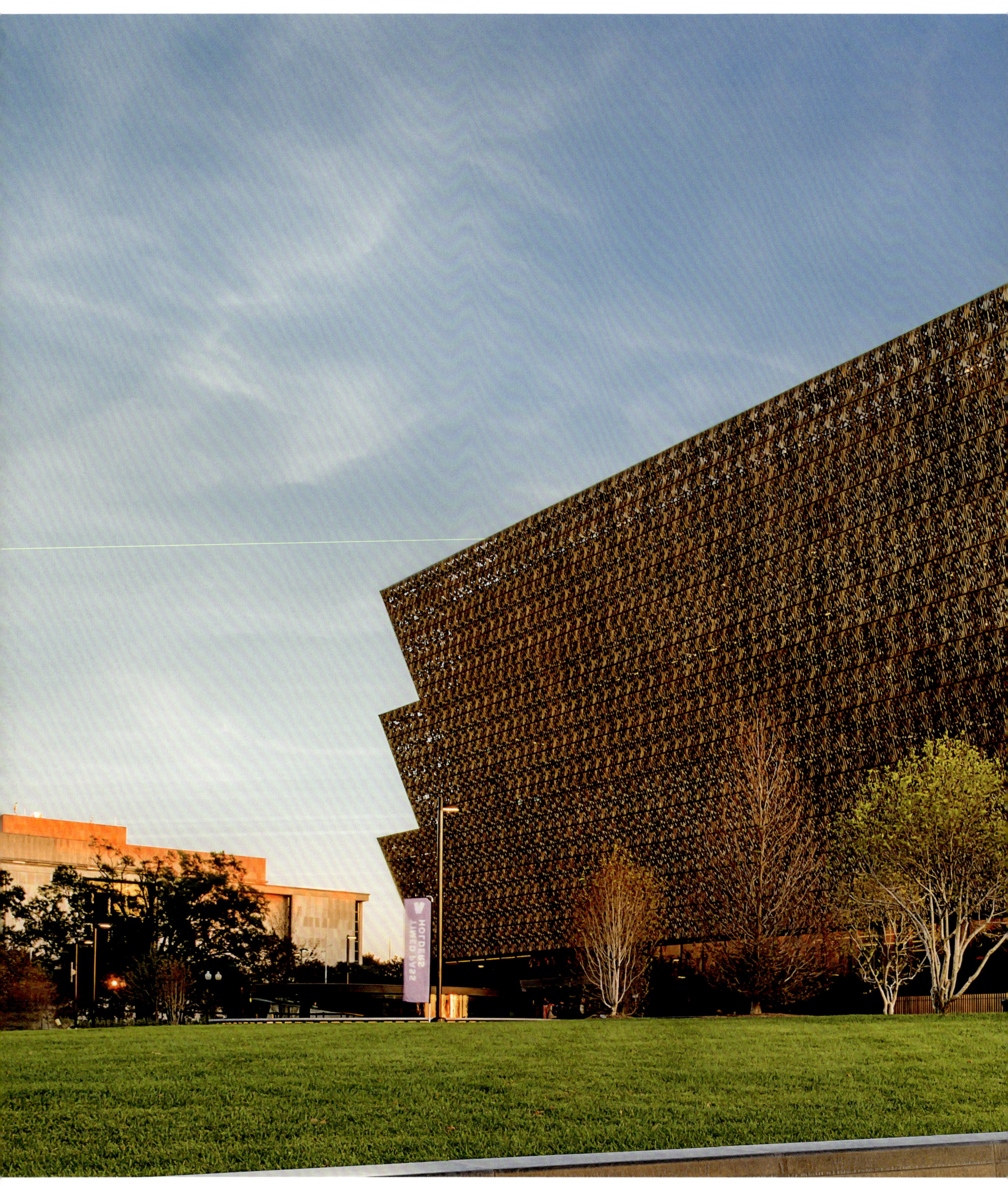

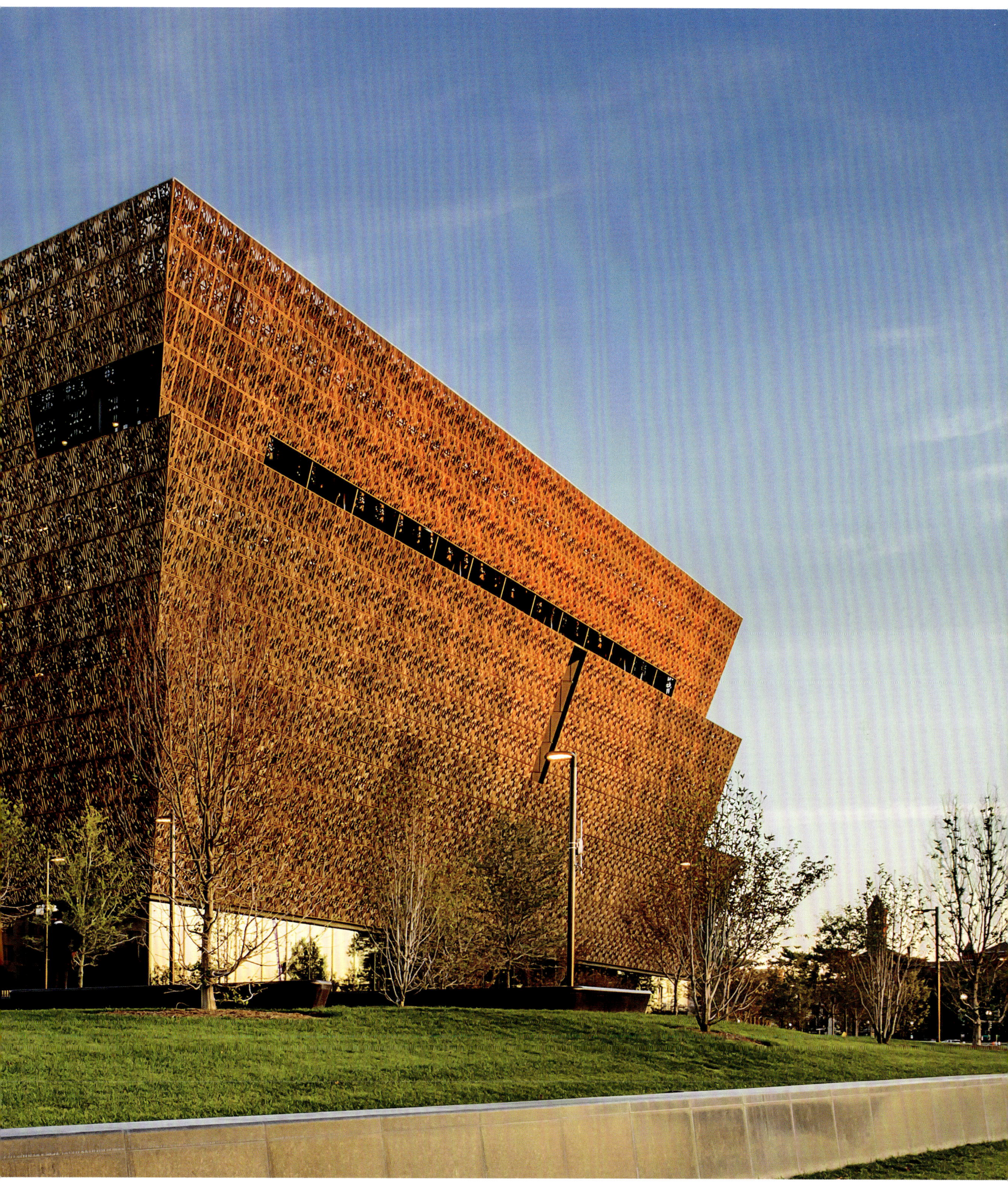

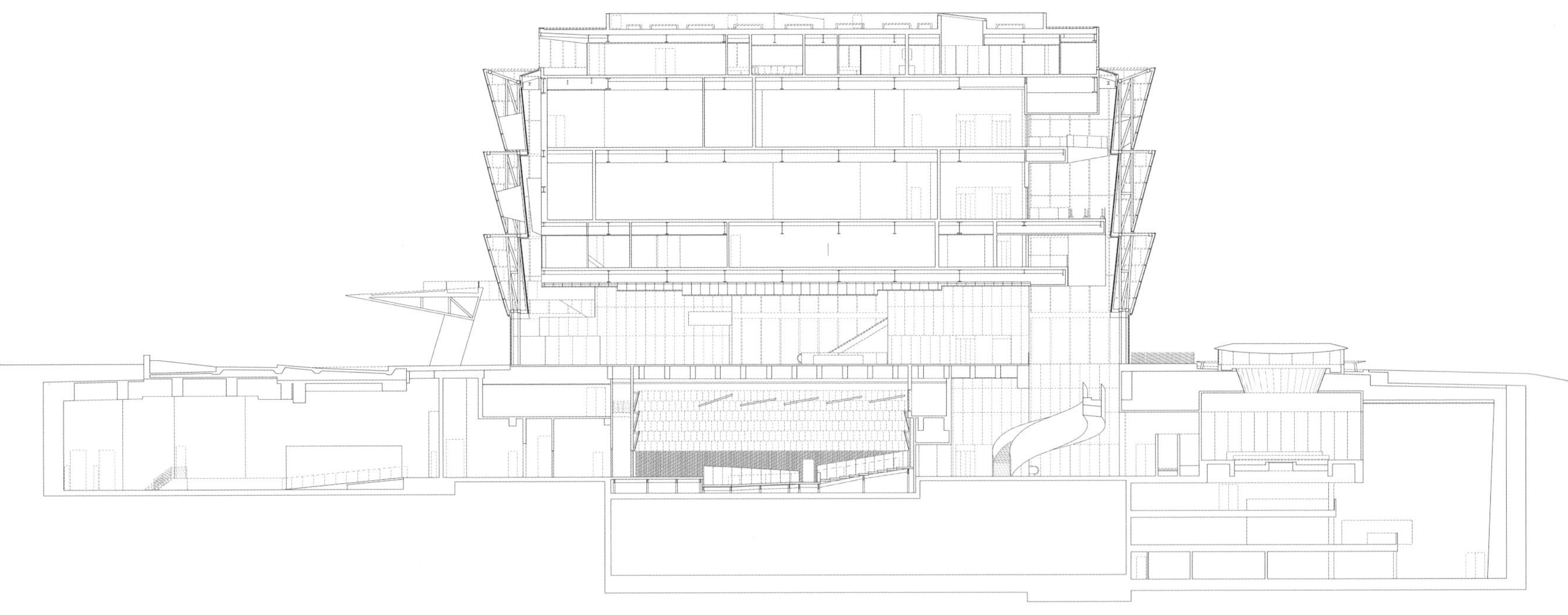

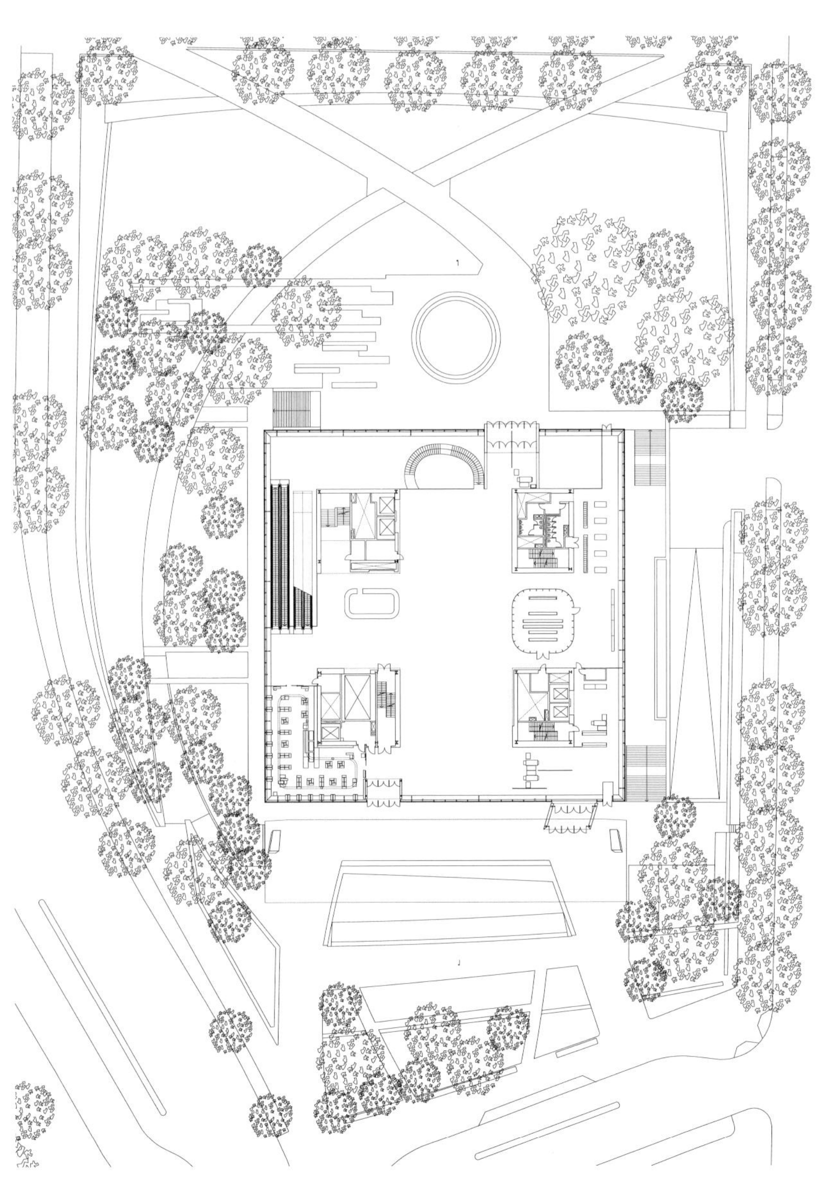

↑   Long section south–north.

←   Site and ground-floor plan.

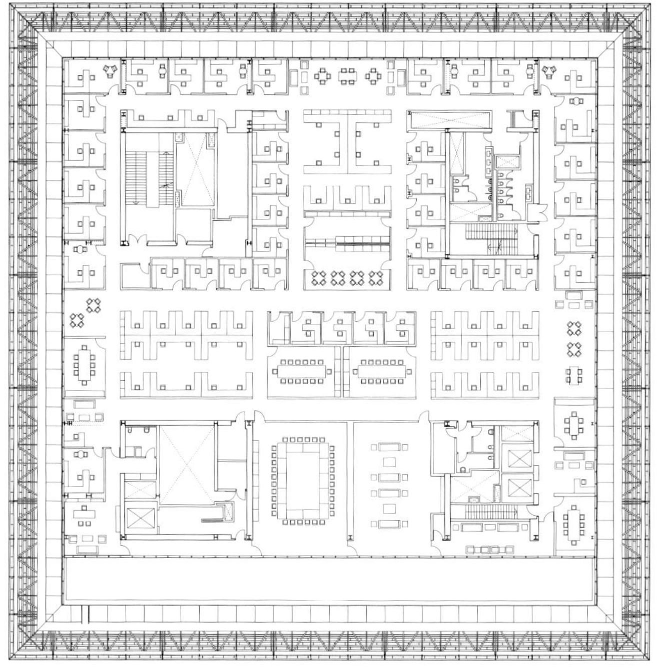
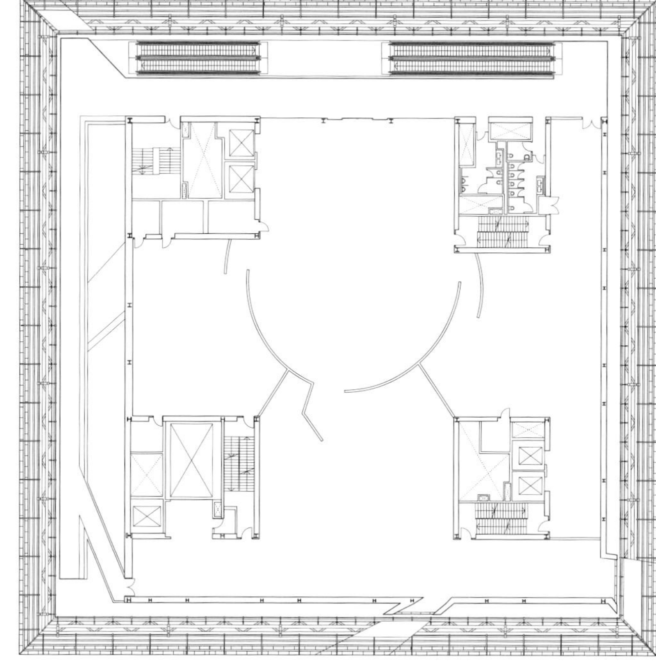
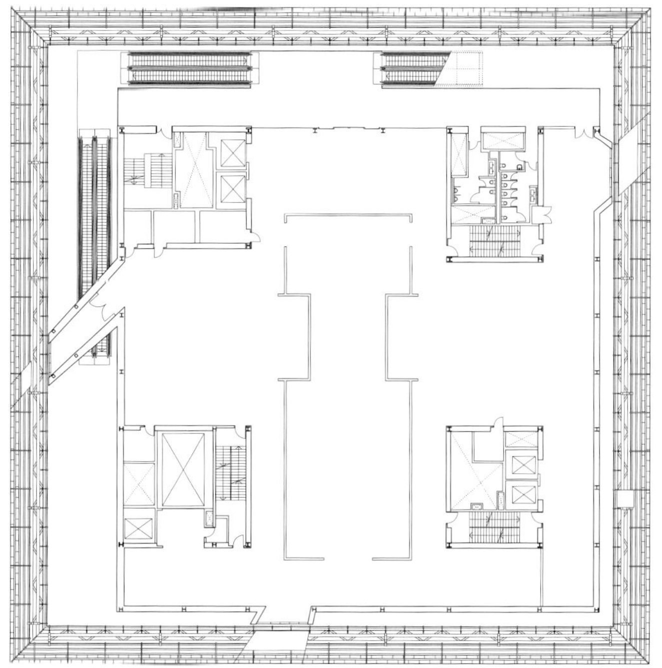
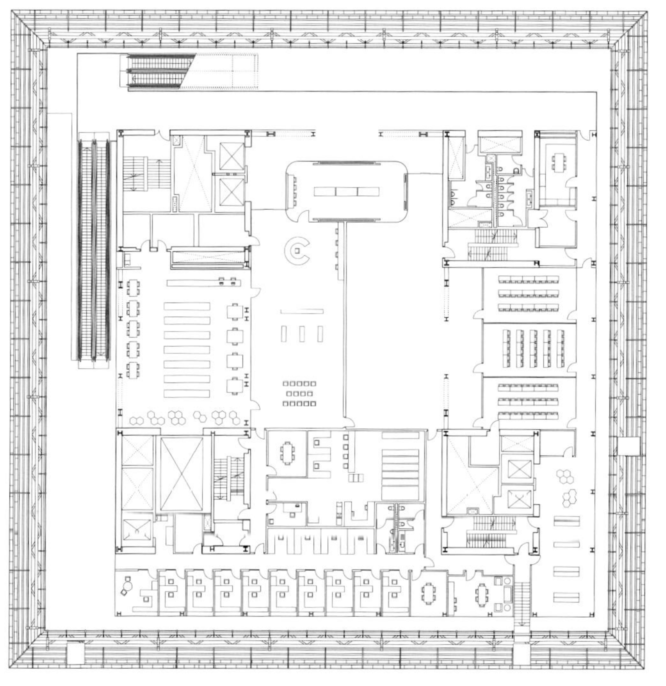

↑ Floor plans:
+4, +3, +2, +1.

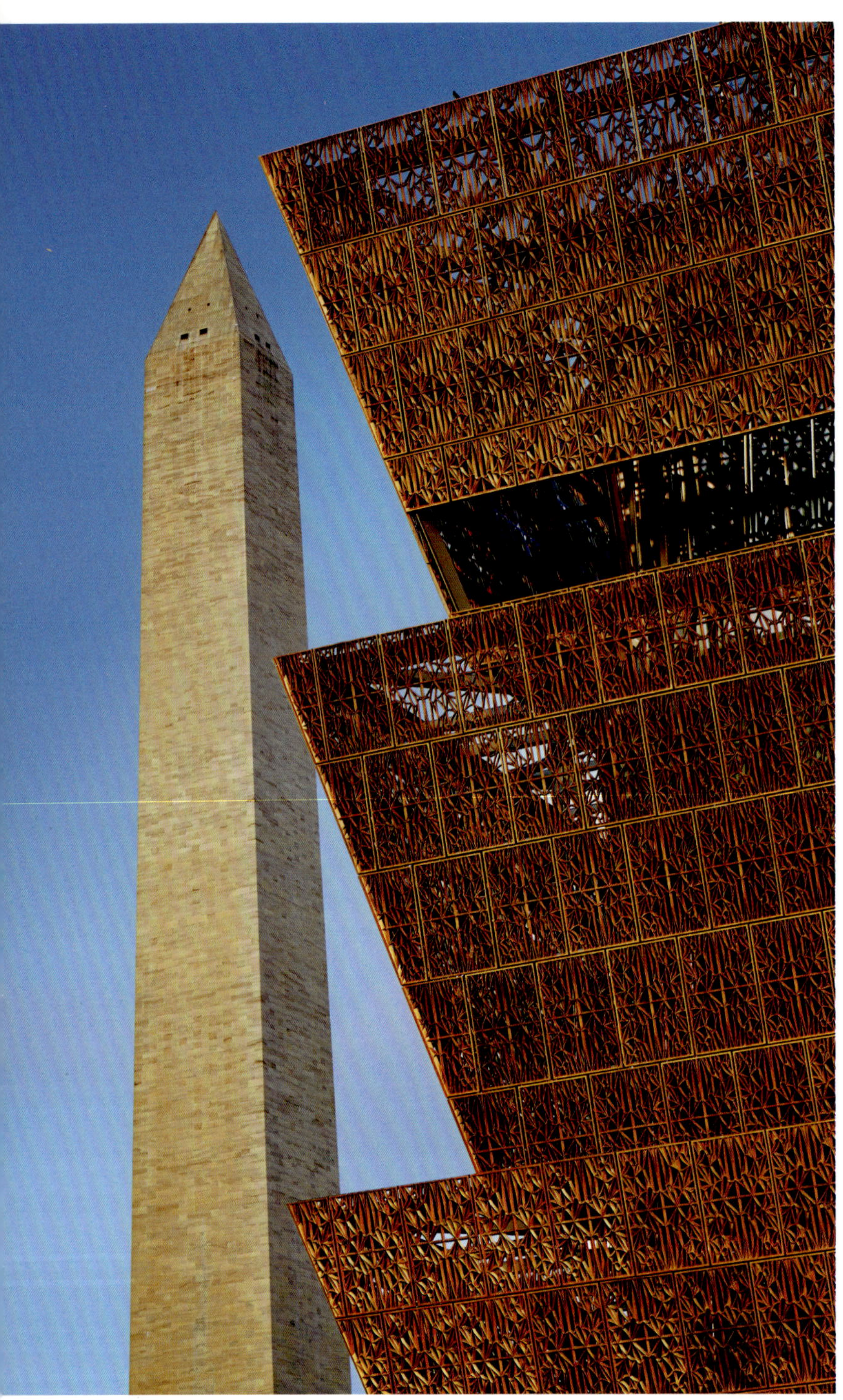

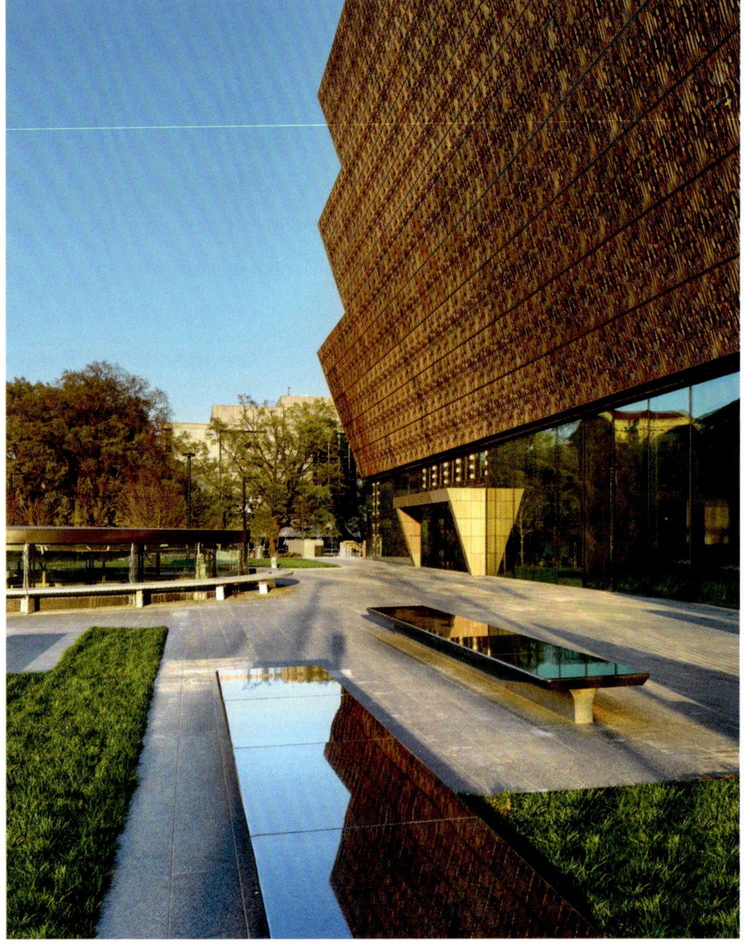

↑ Museum façade and
     Washington Monument.

↗ Exterior, northern façade.

↗ Interior, exhibition space.

→ Heritage Hall.

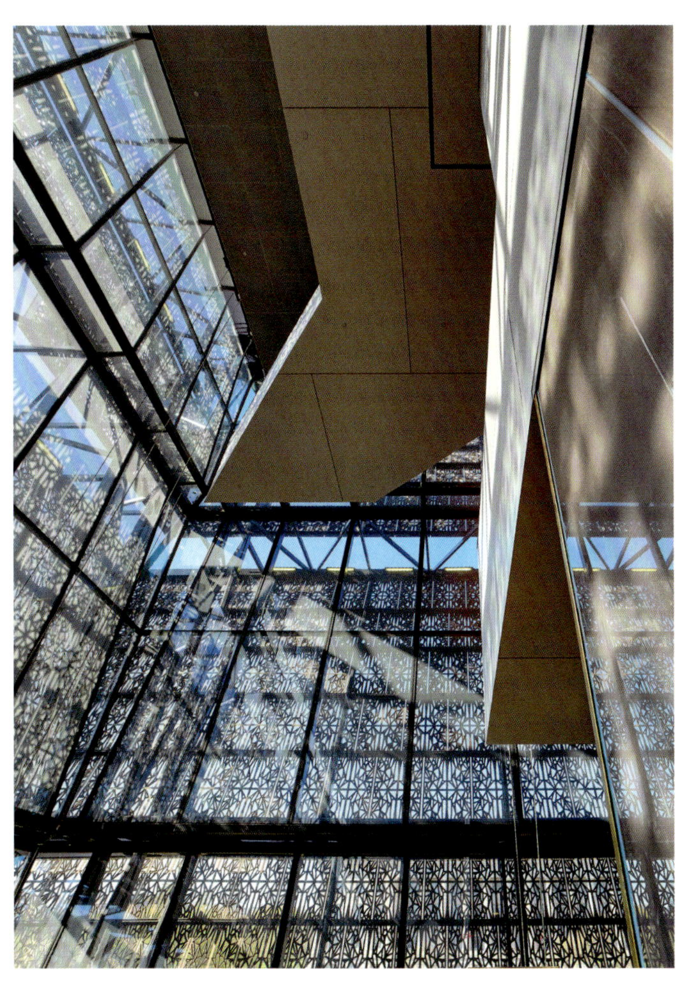

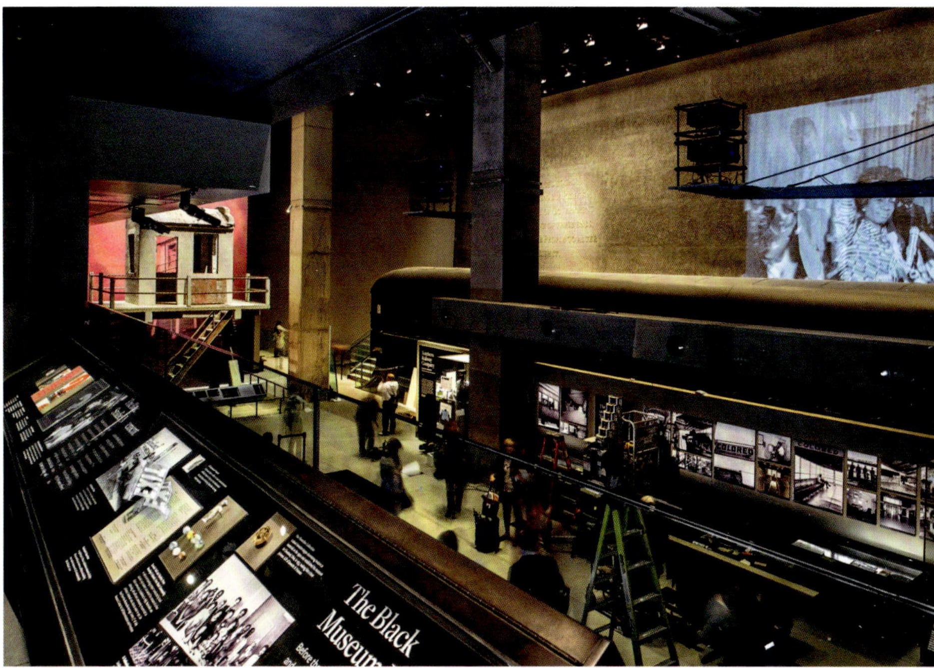

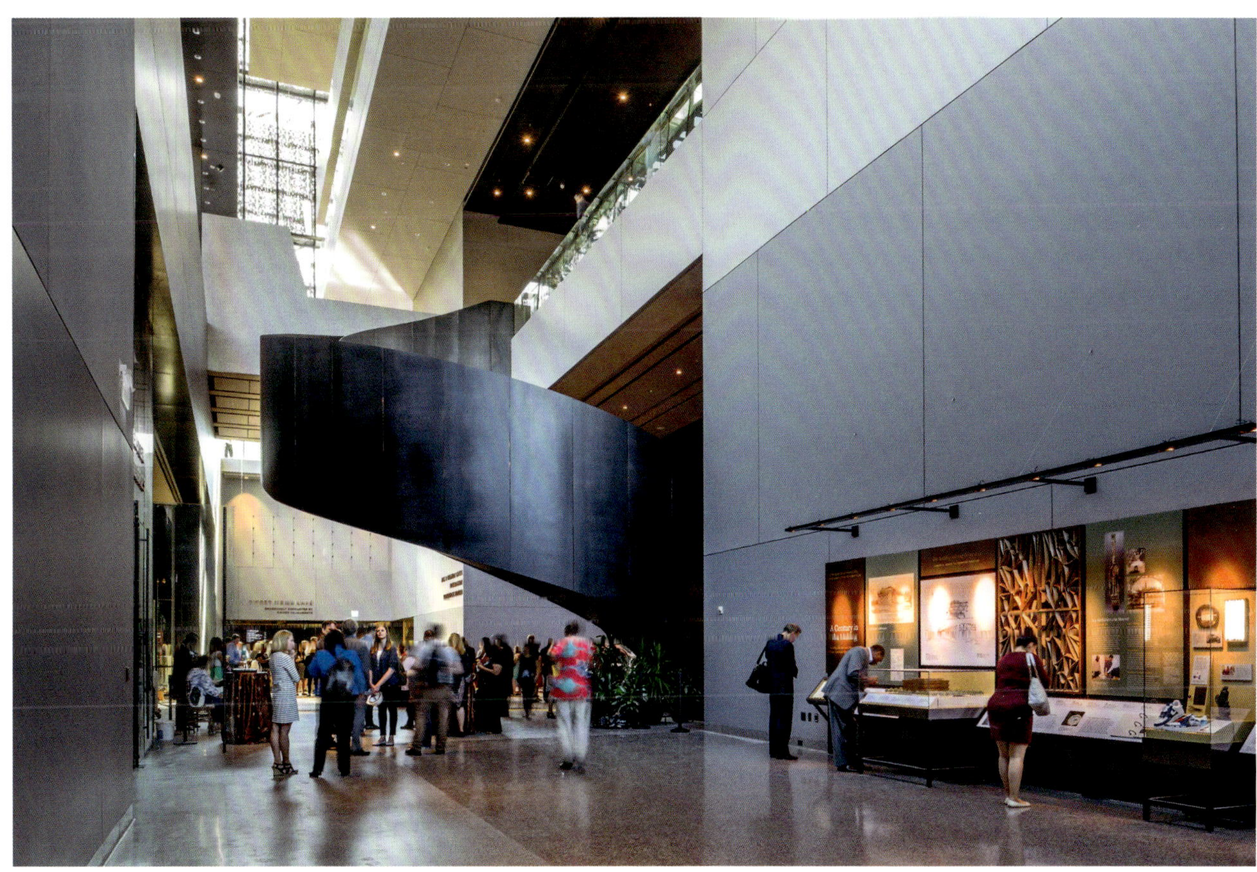

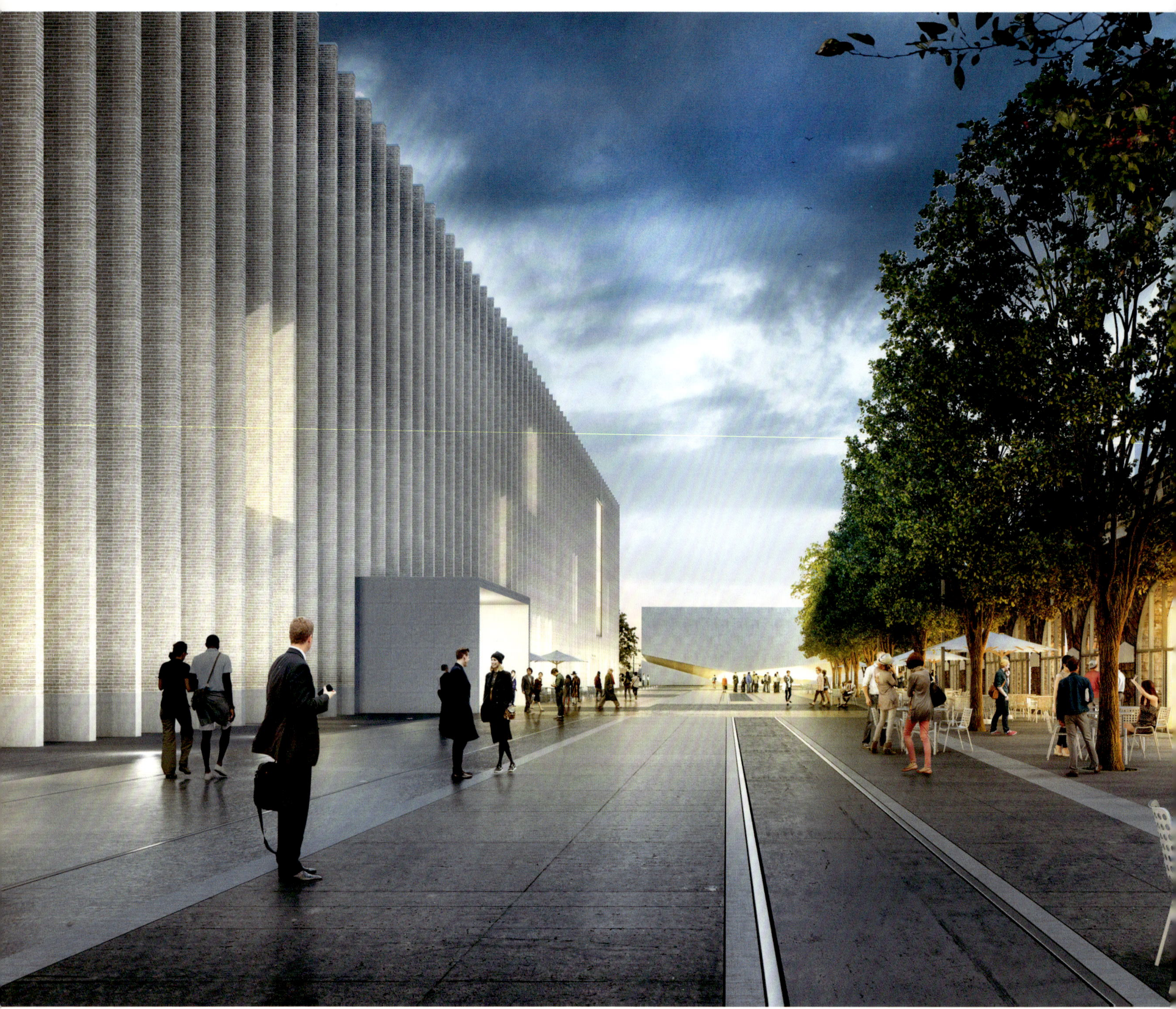

Plateforme 10

Lausanne, Switzerland

mcb-a:
Barozzi/Veiga, Barcelona
Construction 2016–2019, opening 2019
Building 12,450 sq. m
Permanent art collection and special exhibitions

mudac & Musée de l'Elysée:
Manuel Aires Mateus and Francisco Aires Mateus, Lisbon
Construction 2017–2021, opening 2021
Building 14,056 sq. m
Design and photography permanent collections
and special exhibitions

Collections grow or change, research focuses on something new, the mix of visitors changes – a museum that cannot flexibly respond to changes has no future. For this reason Lausanne's Musée cantonal des Beaux-Arts, (mcb-a), mudac (Musée de design et d'arts appliqués contemporains) and Musée de l'Elysée (Musée cantonal de la photographie) will create a new cultural hub called Plateforme 10: three museums with different collections housed in two new buildings designed by different teams of architects, Barozzi/Veiga for the mcb-a and Aires Mateus e Associados for the Musée de l'Elysée and the mudac.

The new district is being created right next to the present-day train station on the site of the former maintenance and repair hall for locomotives. Despite the site's repurposing, the switchyard that put locomotives on the right tracks by means of a turntable is to be preserved, and is incorporated into Plateforme 10's new corporate identity. It serves as the zero following the single "1". The "10" is a reference to the nine existing railway platforms of the nearby station of Lausanne. The simple form of these ciphers is in turn taken up by the straightforward façade of the new mcb-a building. A three-storey structure is rising above a slender rectangular ground plan parallel to the old tracks. The old engine shed was almost completely razed, though the turntable and some rails crossing the whole site will be preserved. Additionally, a few fragments like the nave of the historic hall were incorporated into the long façade, which is broken up by vertical trusses. Large windows and generous skylights ensure pleasant interior illumination.

To the west of the mcb-a is another building complex, the new home of the mudac, the Musée de l'Elysée and the institutions' administration. Facing the mcb-a, a structure on a square plot of ground mirrors the geometric precision of the neighbouring museum. On the side facing east towards the city, the complex breaks open: here jagged projections link the site to its surroundings. By standing in front of the construction, one can see that if these were models all the structures could be fitted together. Because of this, they communicate with each other without denying their independence and their different collections.

From the outside it is apparent that in the square building there are two museums. An angled crevice circles the structure, permitting views of the interior. It separates the upper and lower parts of the building and thus the two museums from one another, but at the same time it emphasises their unity – that one could not exist without the other or the building would be incomplete. The underground part houses the Musée de l'Elysée, on the openly visible ground floor are a café, a bookstore and the visitors' information desk, and finally on the top floor, which appears to float above the public ground floor, is the mudac. The administrative portion of the building lies in the jagged module that abuts the square on two sides and projects into the surrounding city.

This flexible building-block principle defines the total layout of Plateforme 10, which can be thought of as an extension of railway tracks 1–9 of the adjacent train station. A single museum turns into two that relate to each other but are still independent. Two museums have become one, whose architectural design both separates and unites. Three museums have become a whole complex, which despite its cubic construction suggests flexibility and dynamism. Just what the future museum requires.

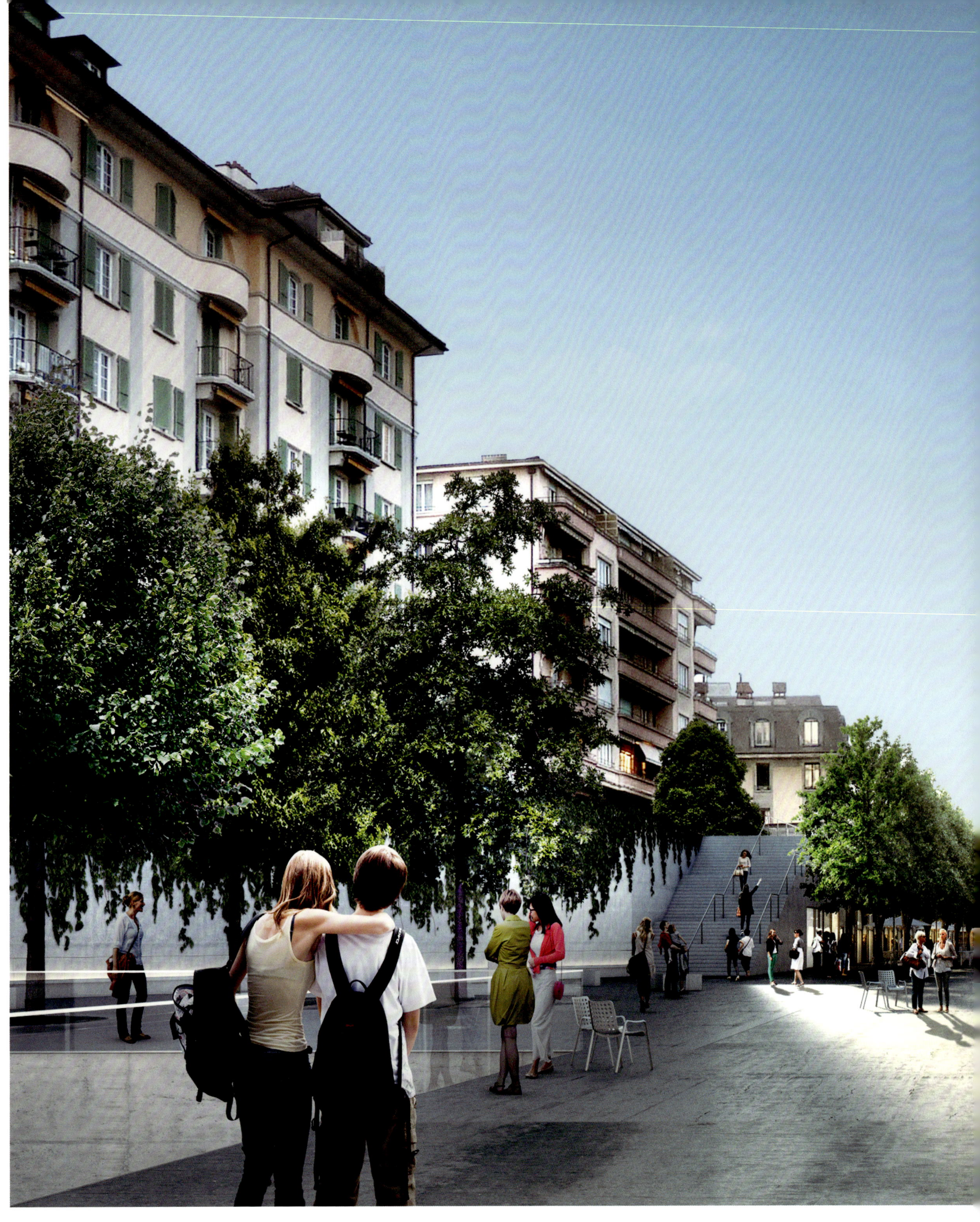

↑ View of the new urban district from the west.

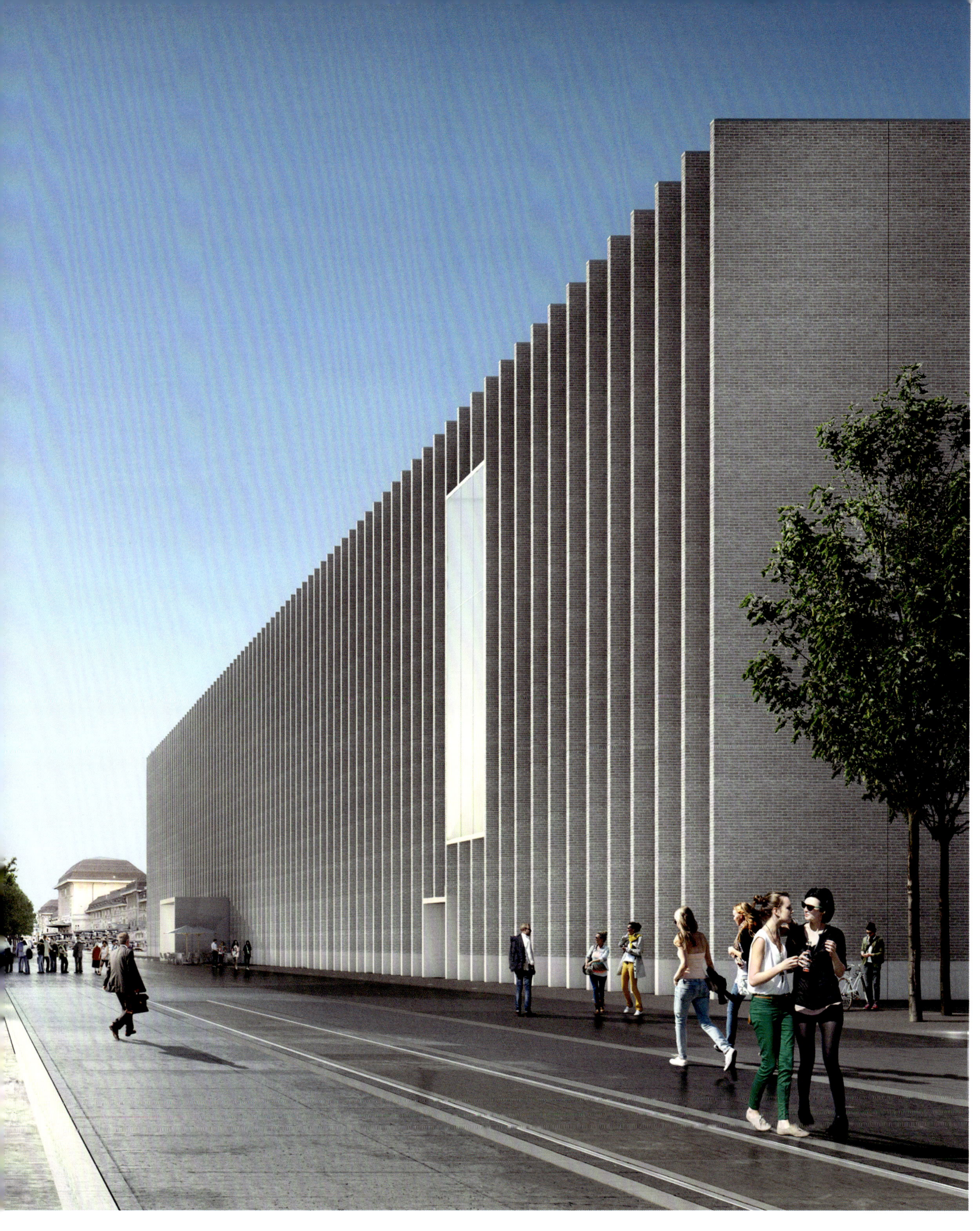

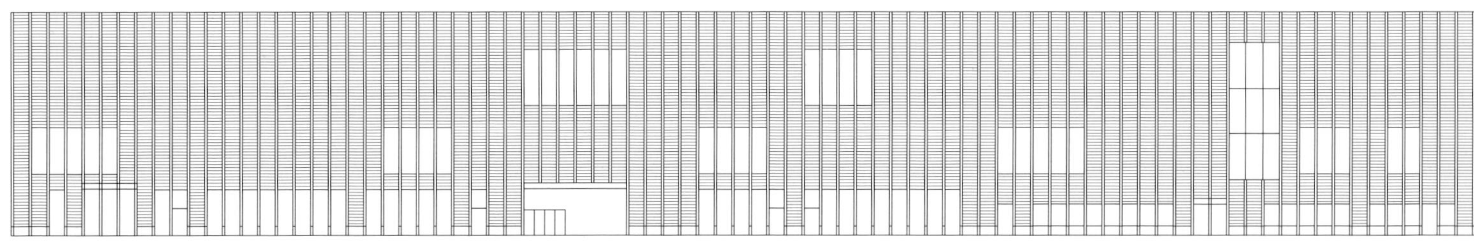

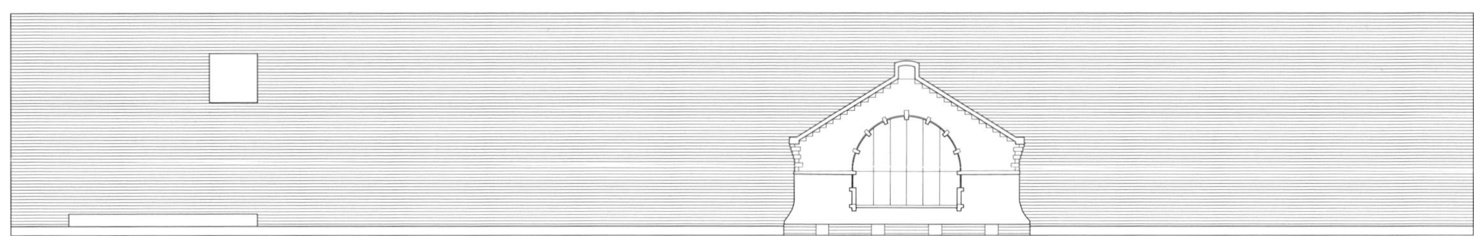

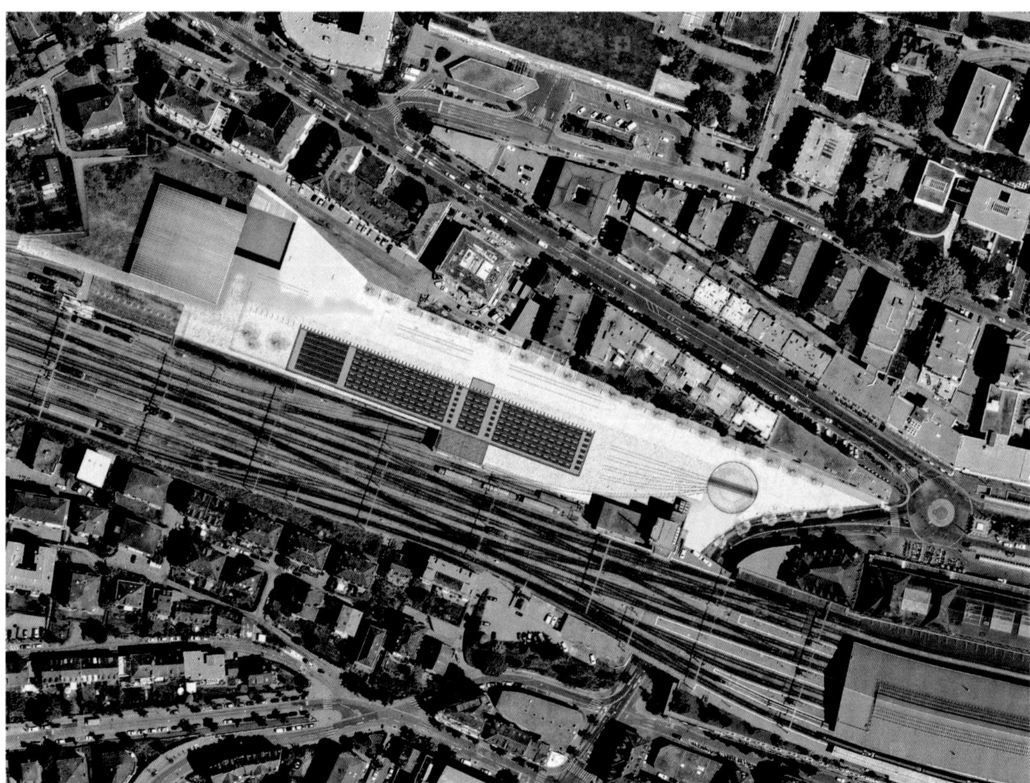

↑ Northern façade.
Southern façade.

→ Aerial view.

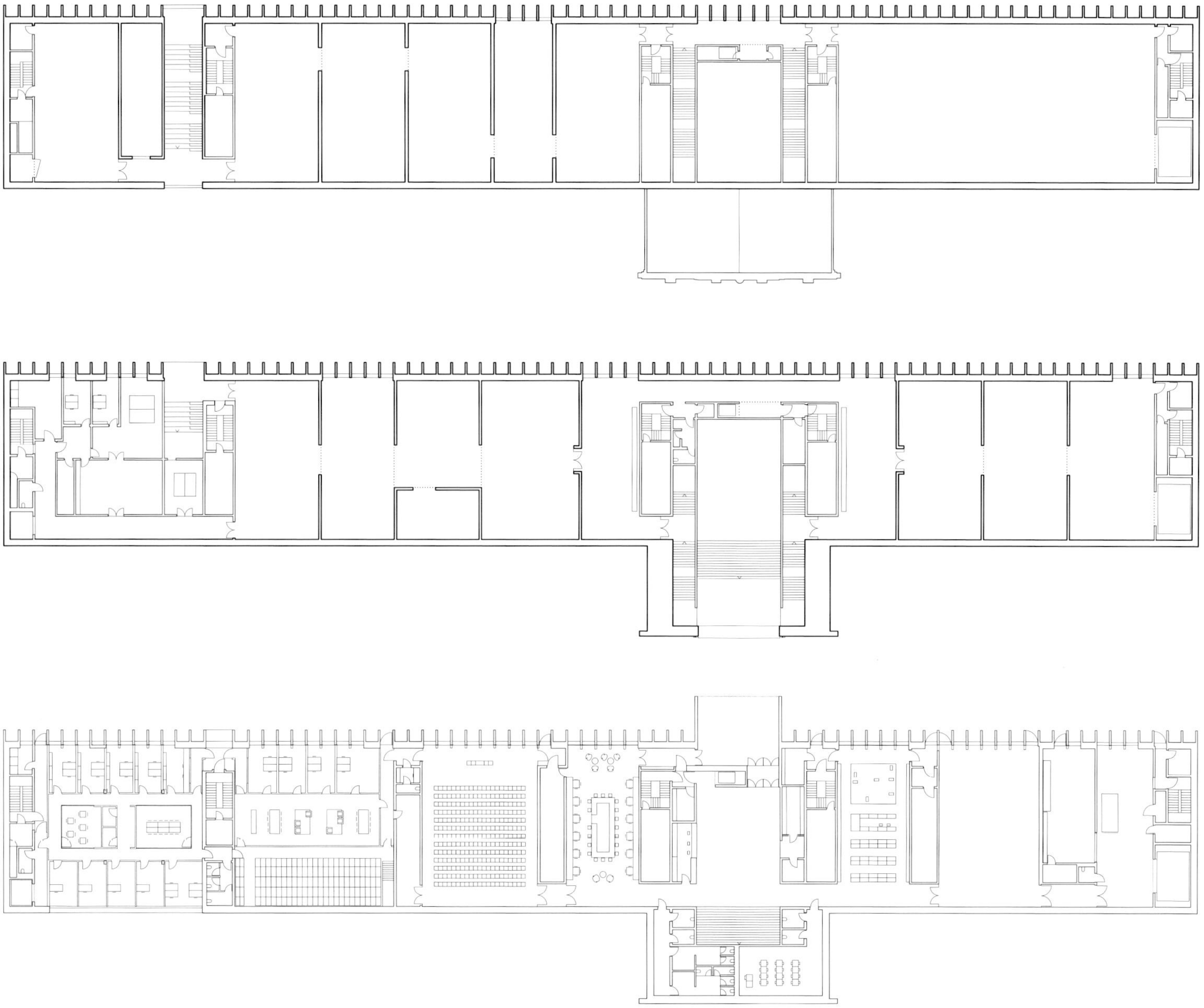

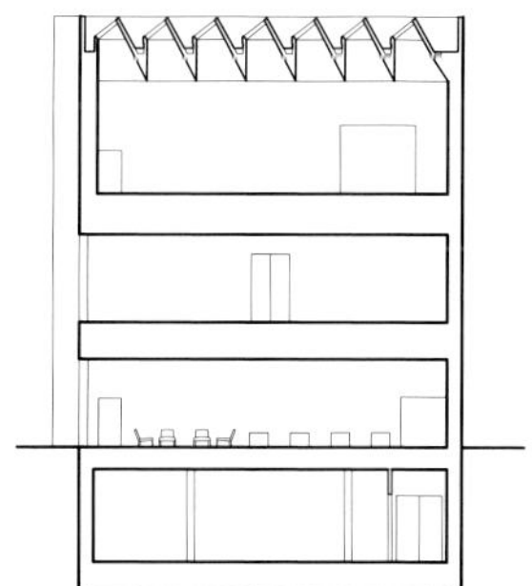

↑   Floor plans: +2, +1, 0.

→   Cross-section north–south.

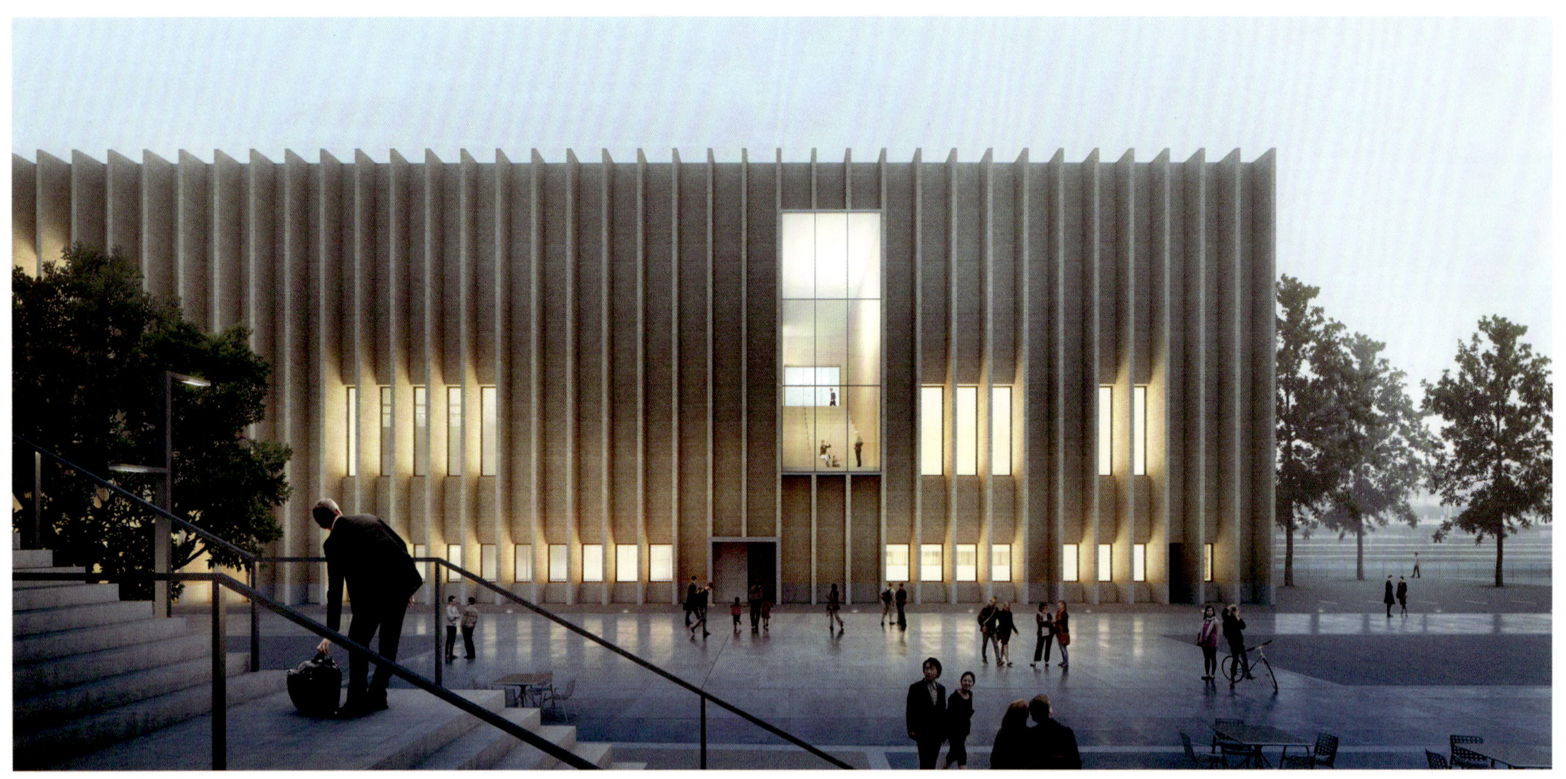

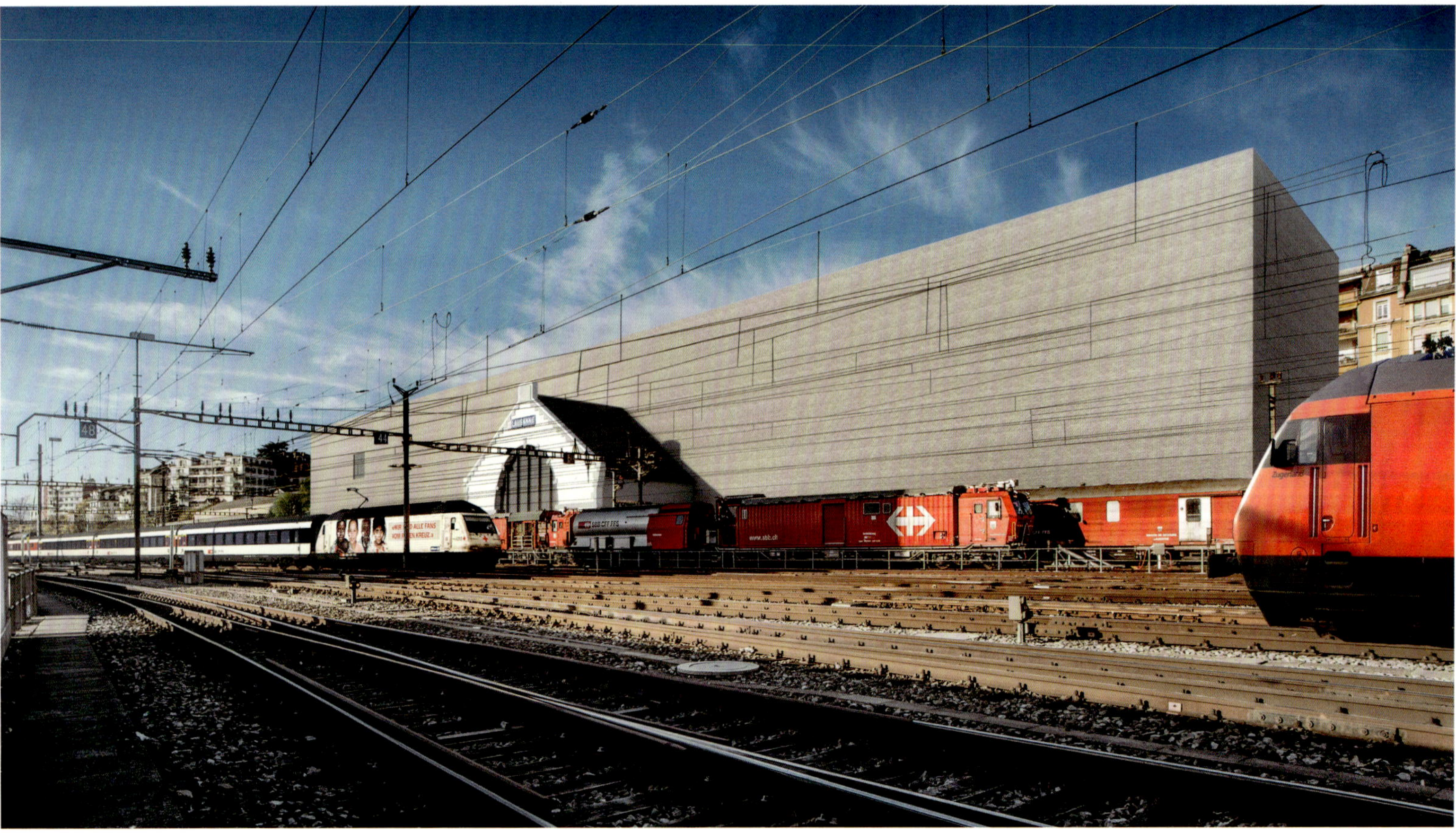

↑ Exterior, from the north.
Exterior, from the south.

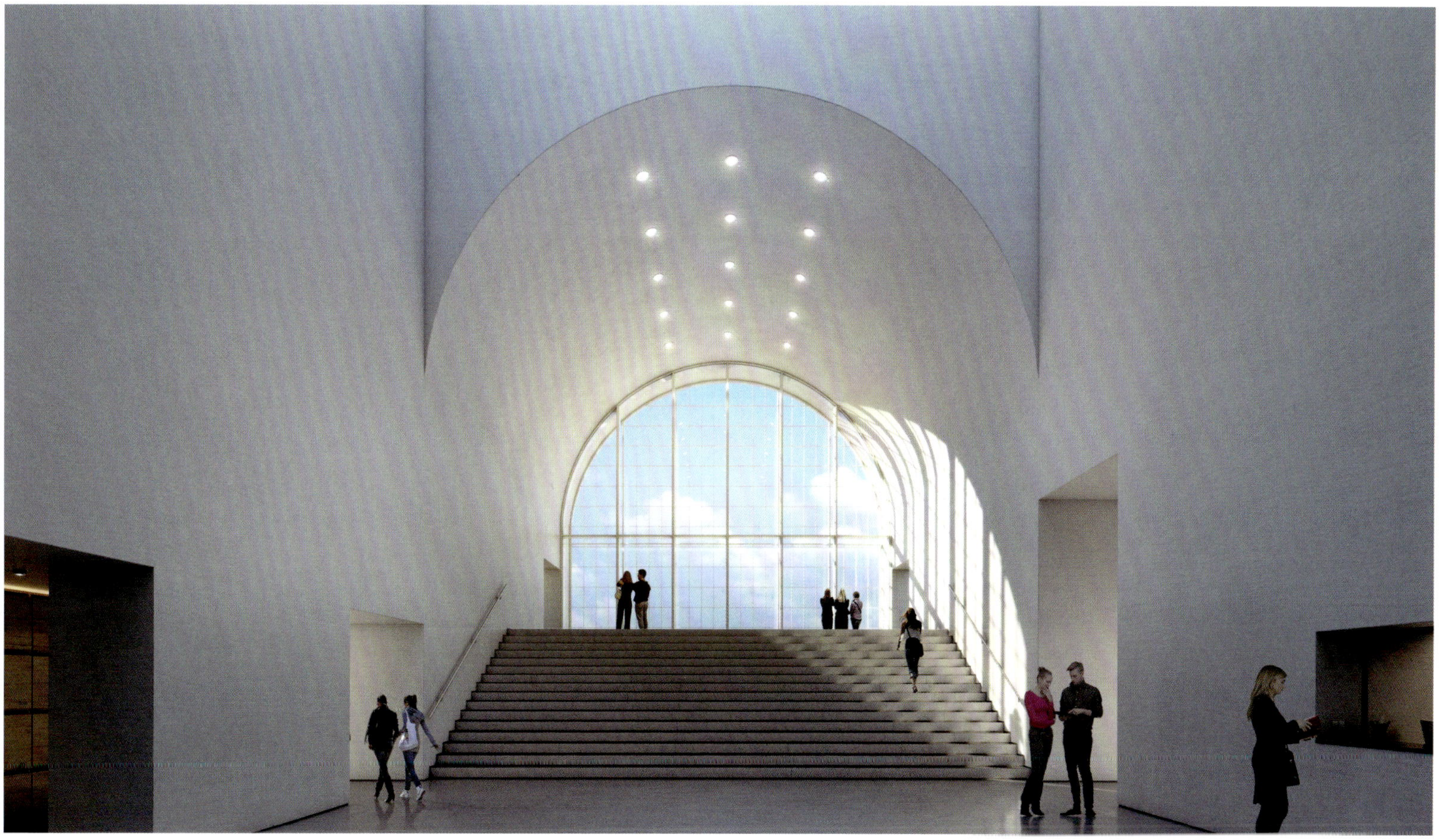

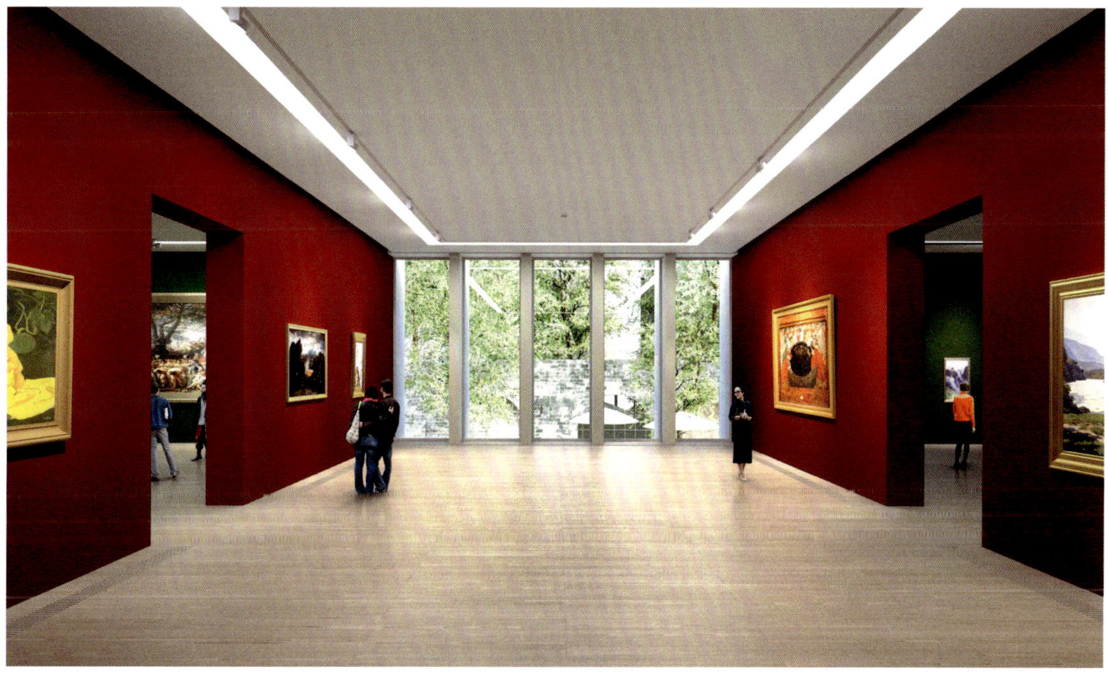

↑ Entrance.

↖ Permanent collection.

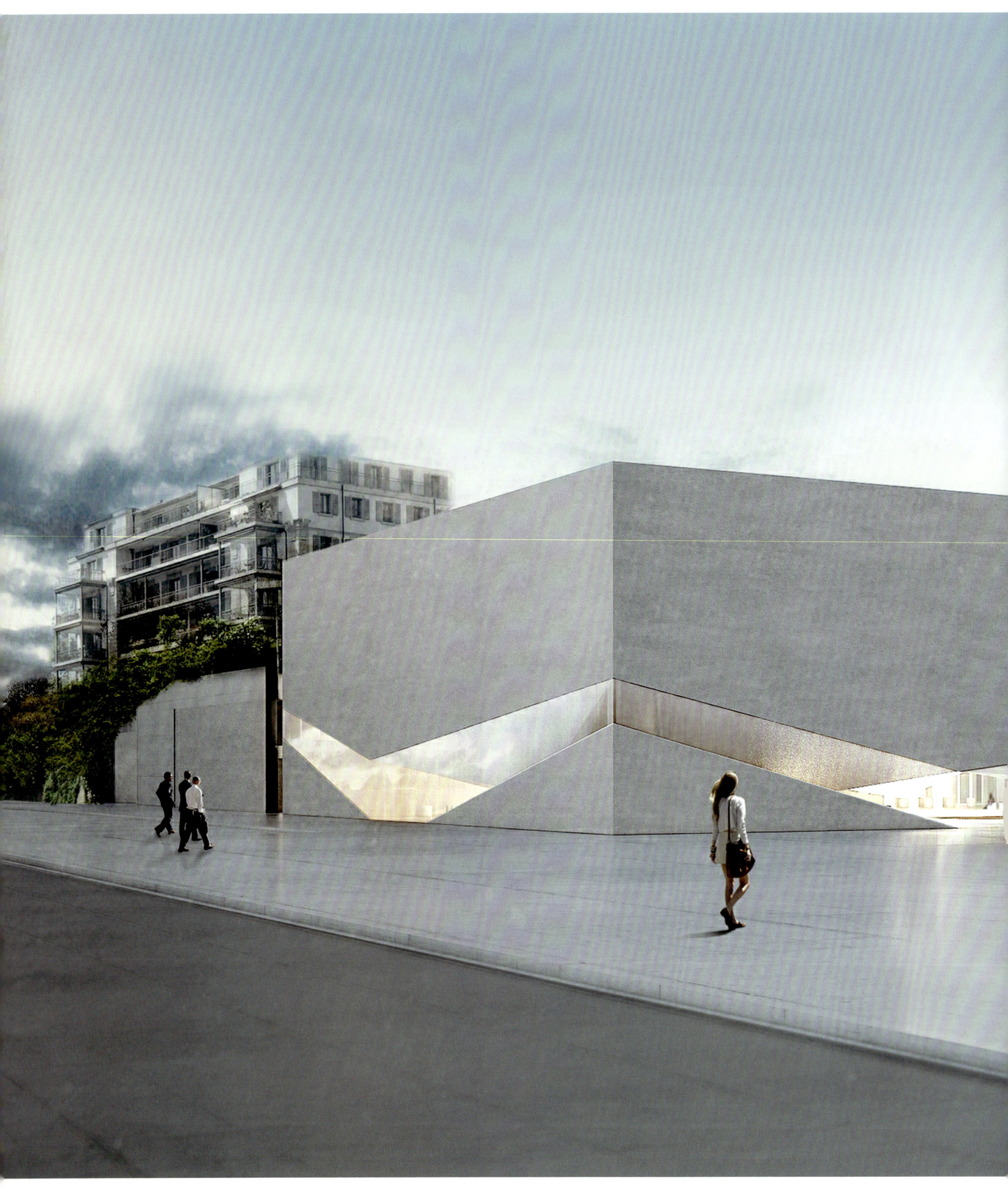

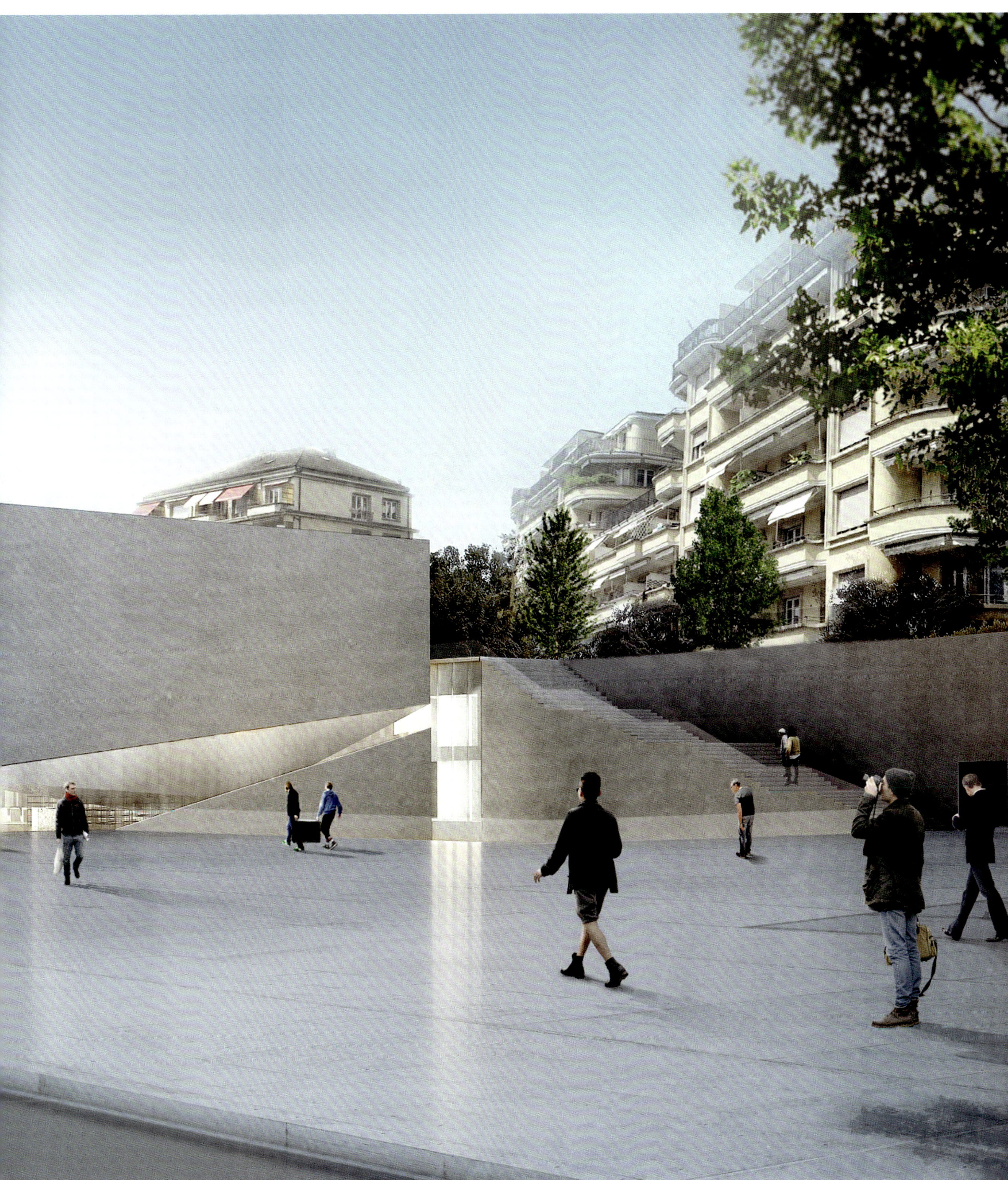

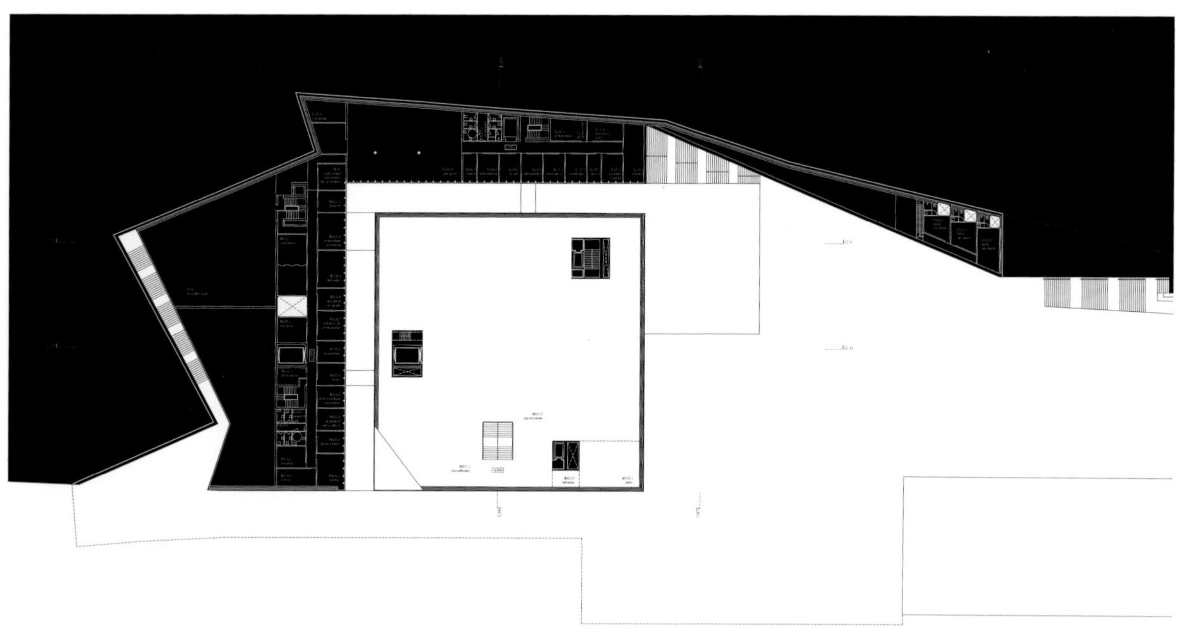

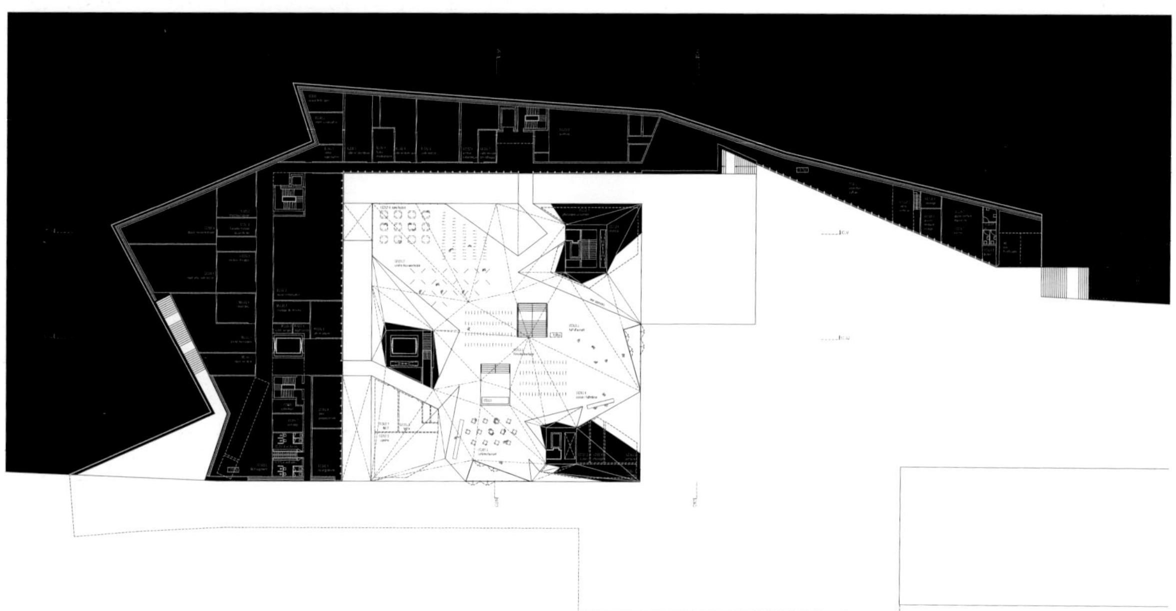

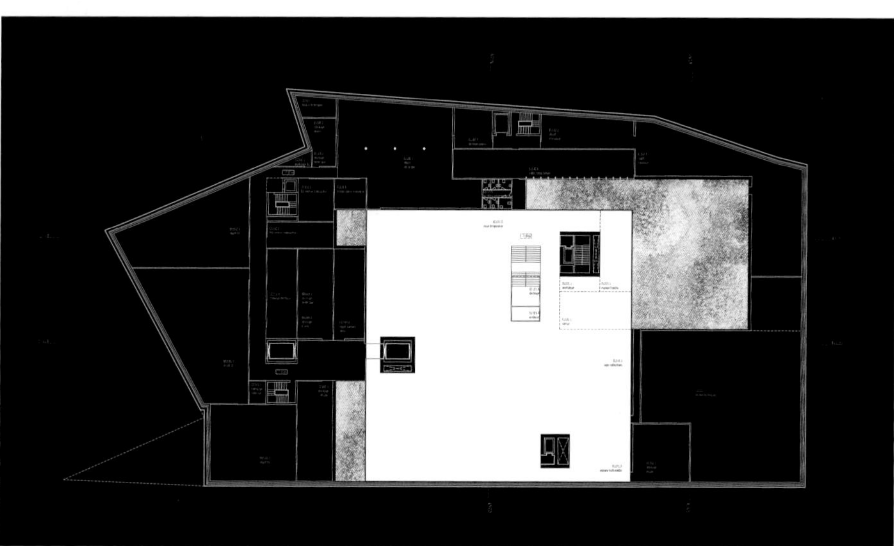

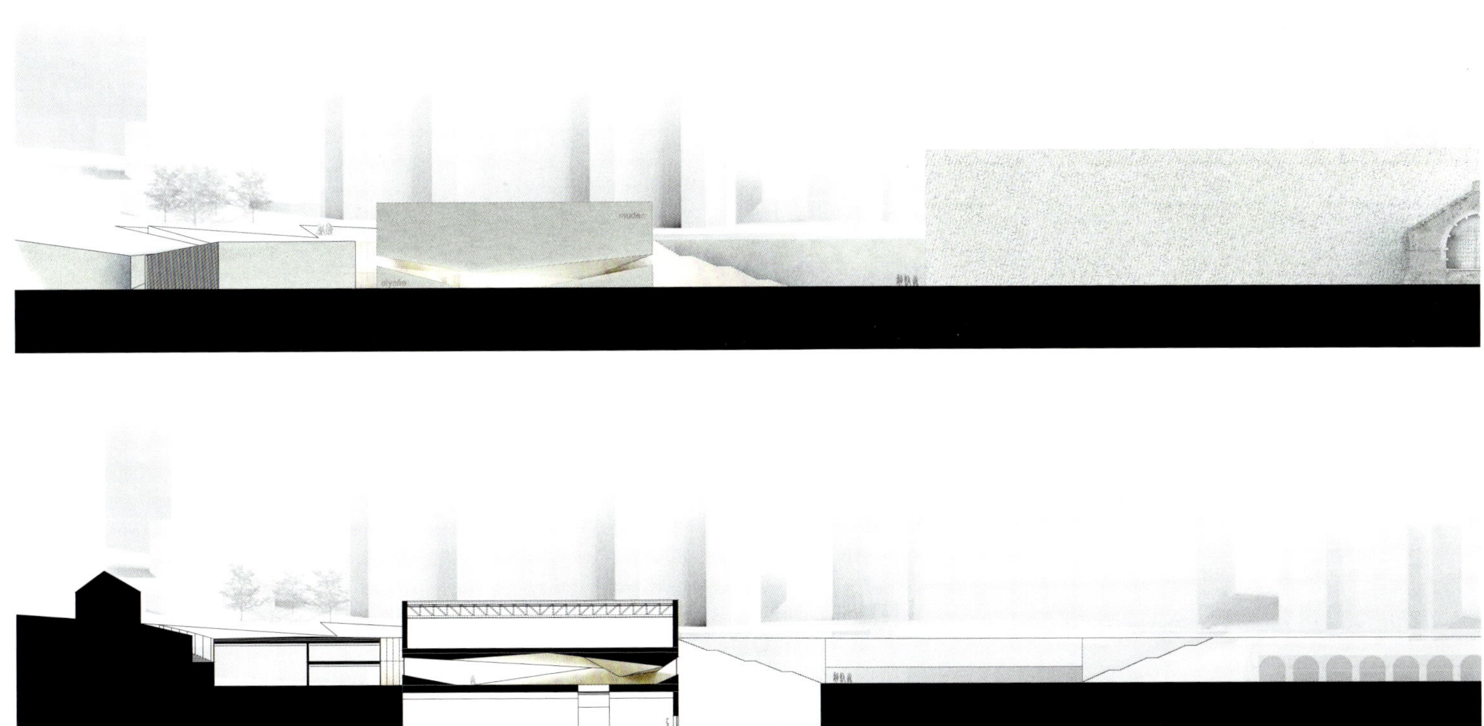

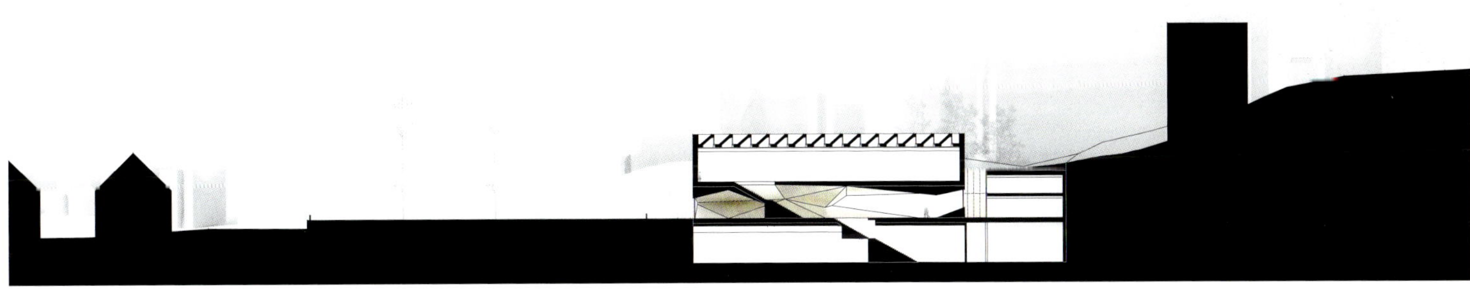

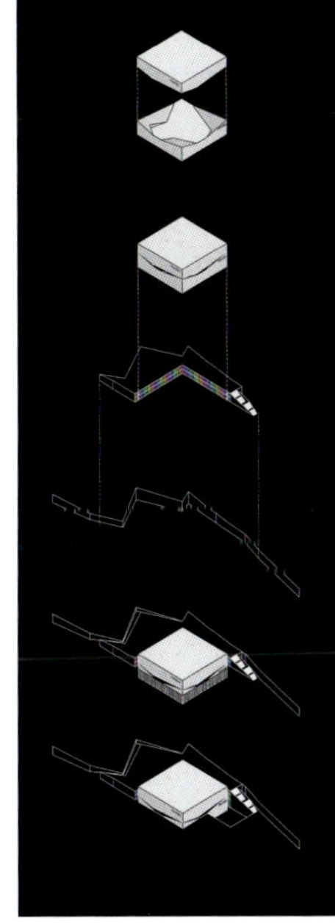

↑   Elevation, looking north.
Section, west–east.
Section, south–north.

→   Axonometric projection.

←   Floor plans: +1, 0, -1.

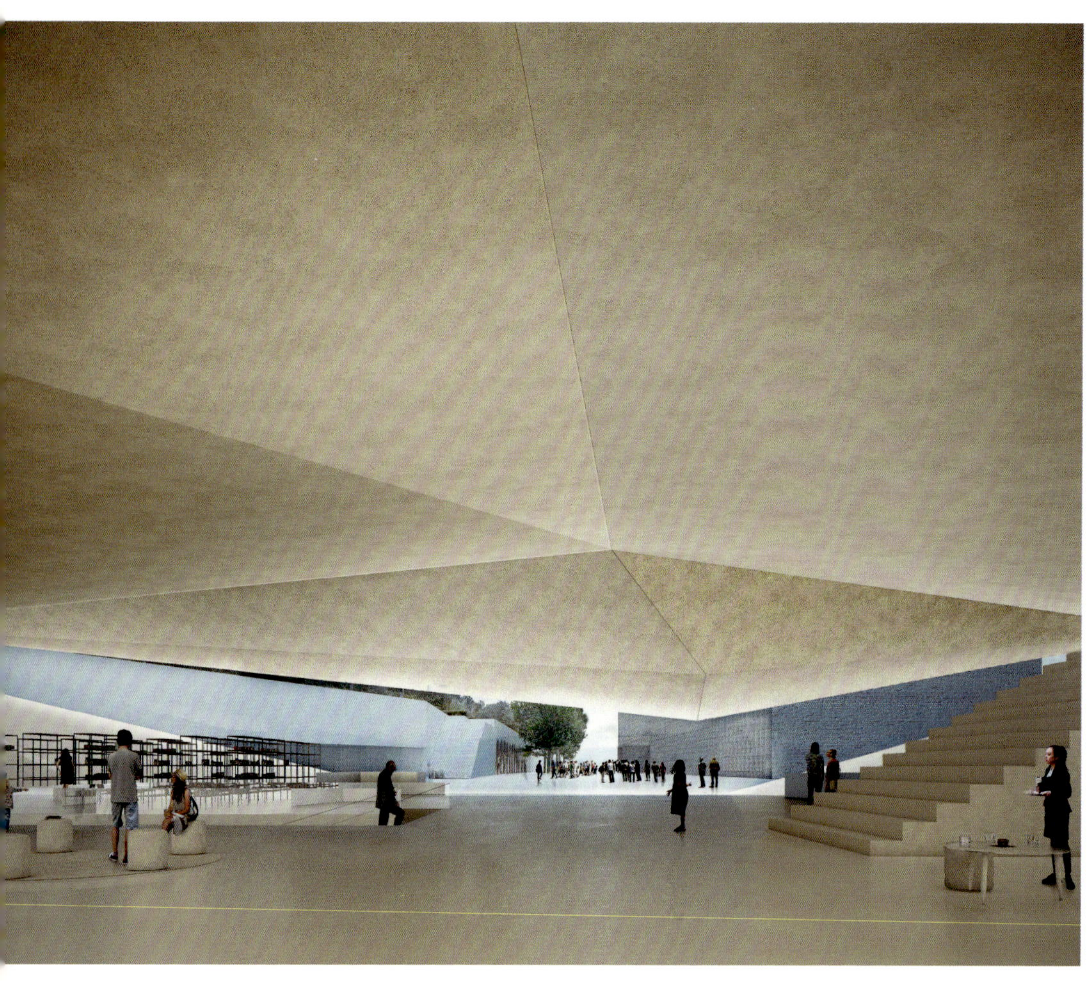

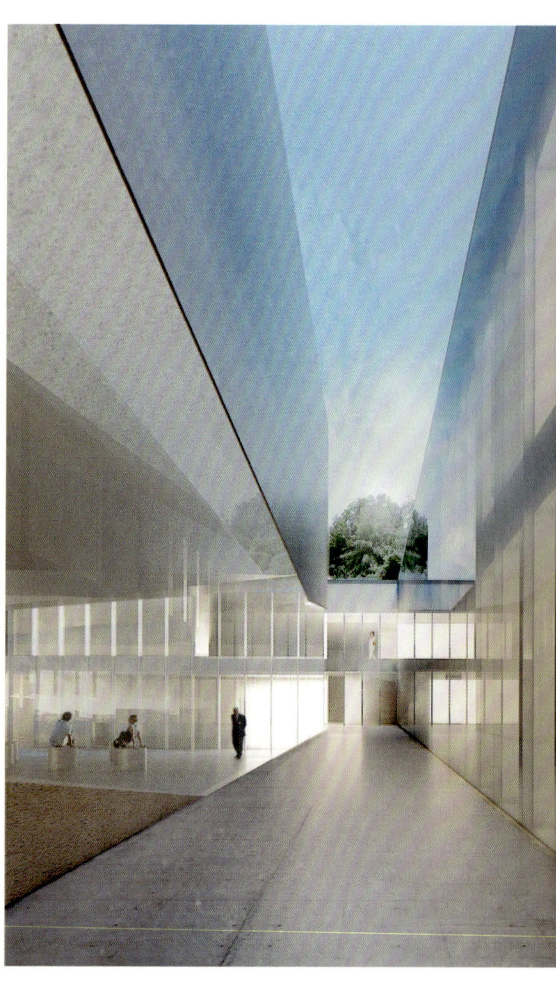

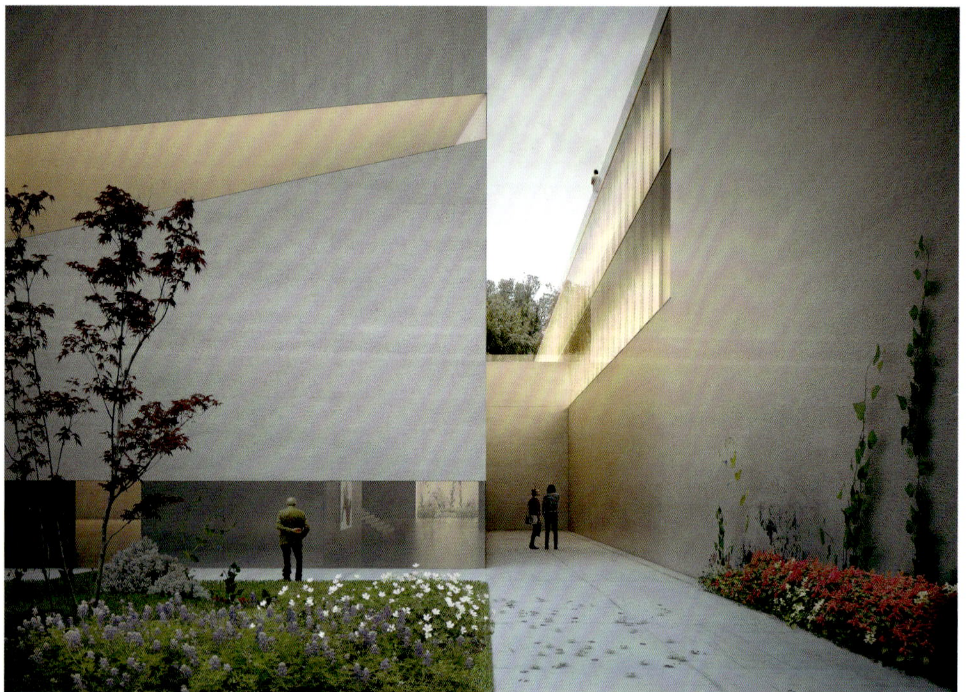

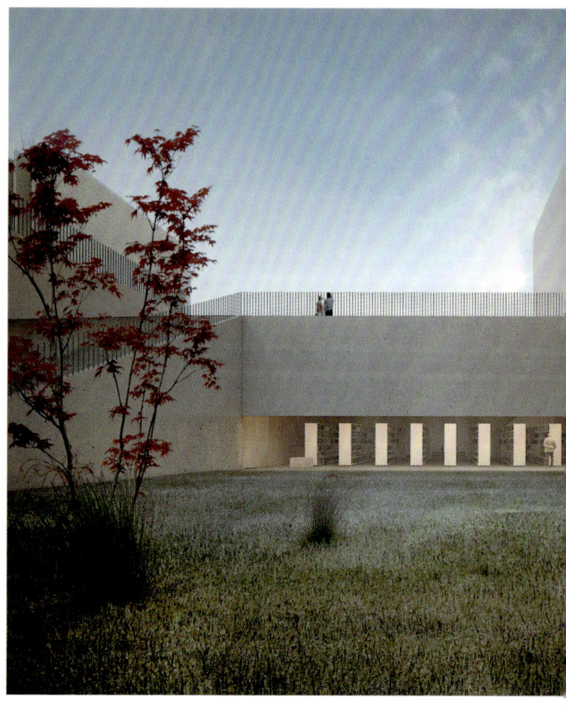

↑ Ground floor, entrance hall.
Underground floor,
patio and alley view.

↑ Alley between exhibition
and office building.
Underground floor,
patio and library view.

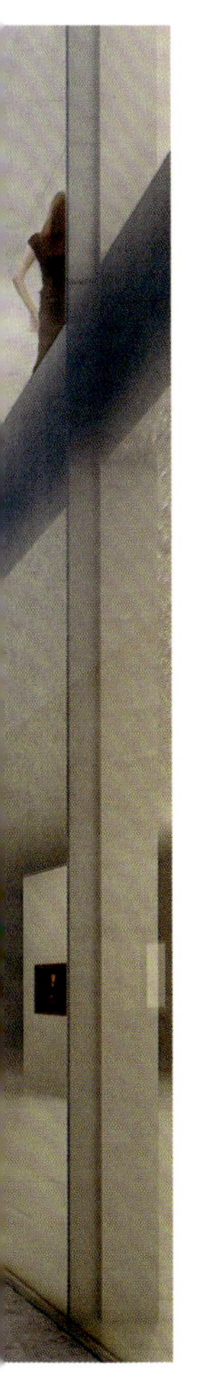

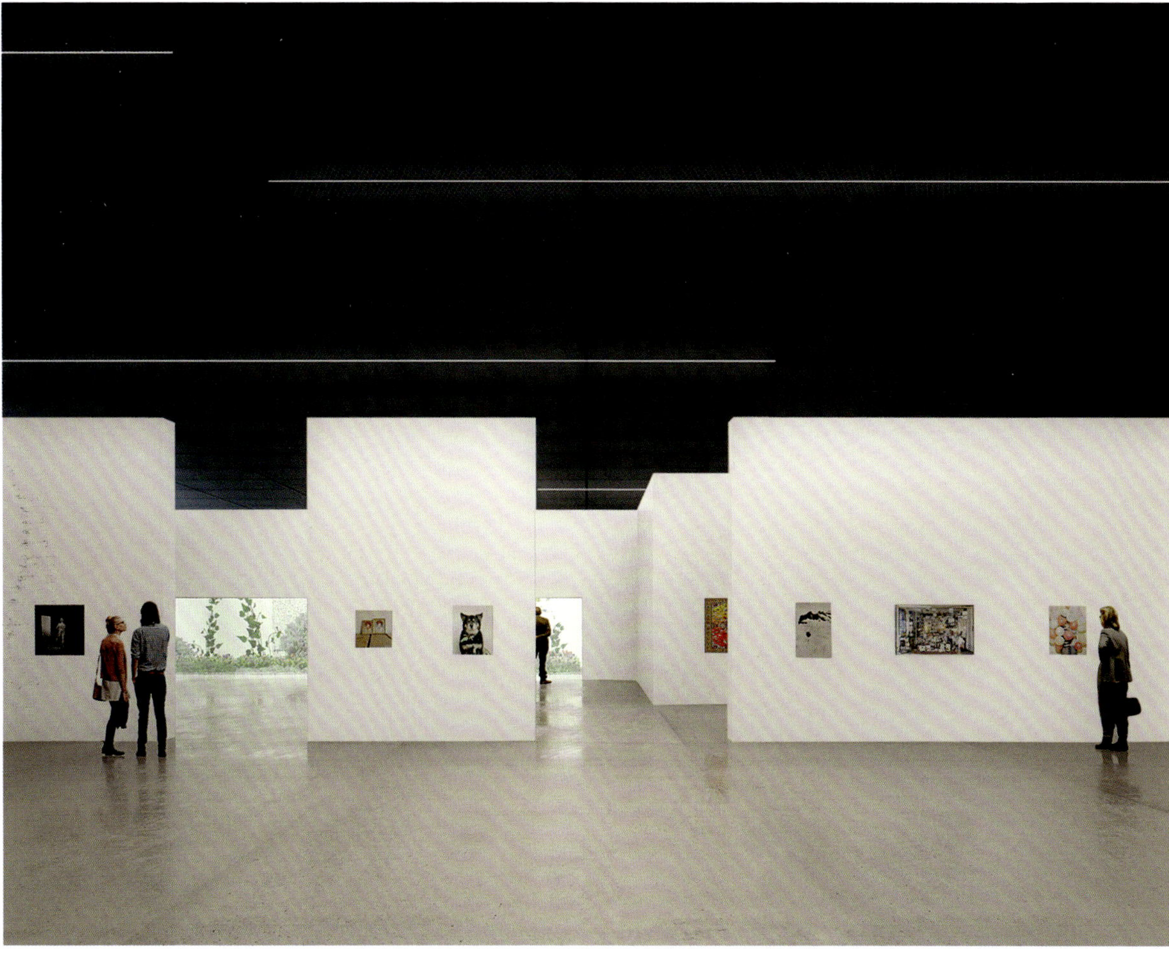

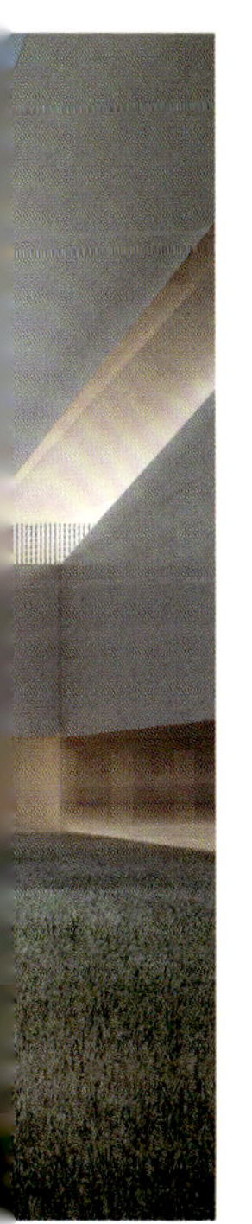

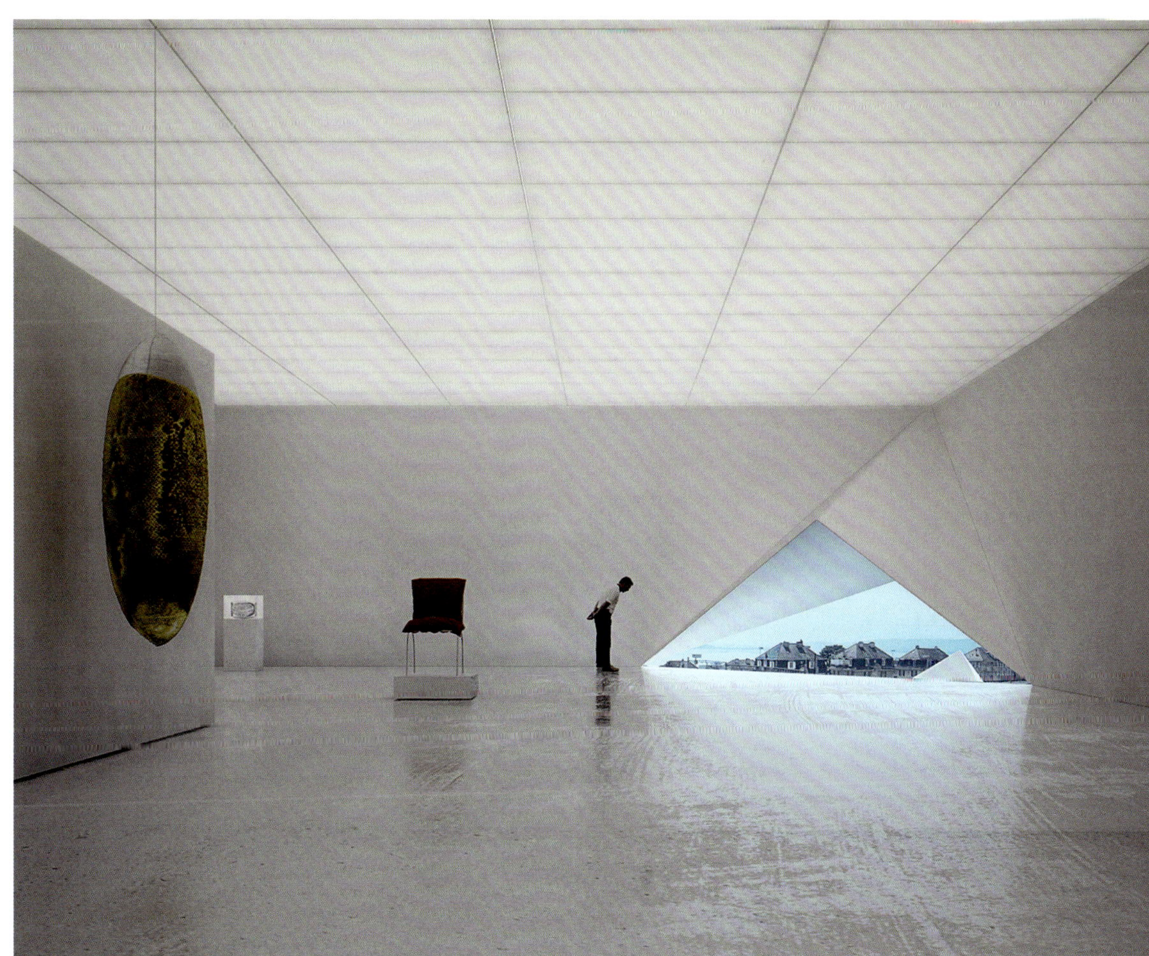

↗ Exhibition space,
underground floor.
Exhibition space,
first floor.

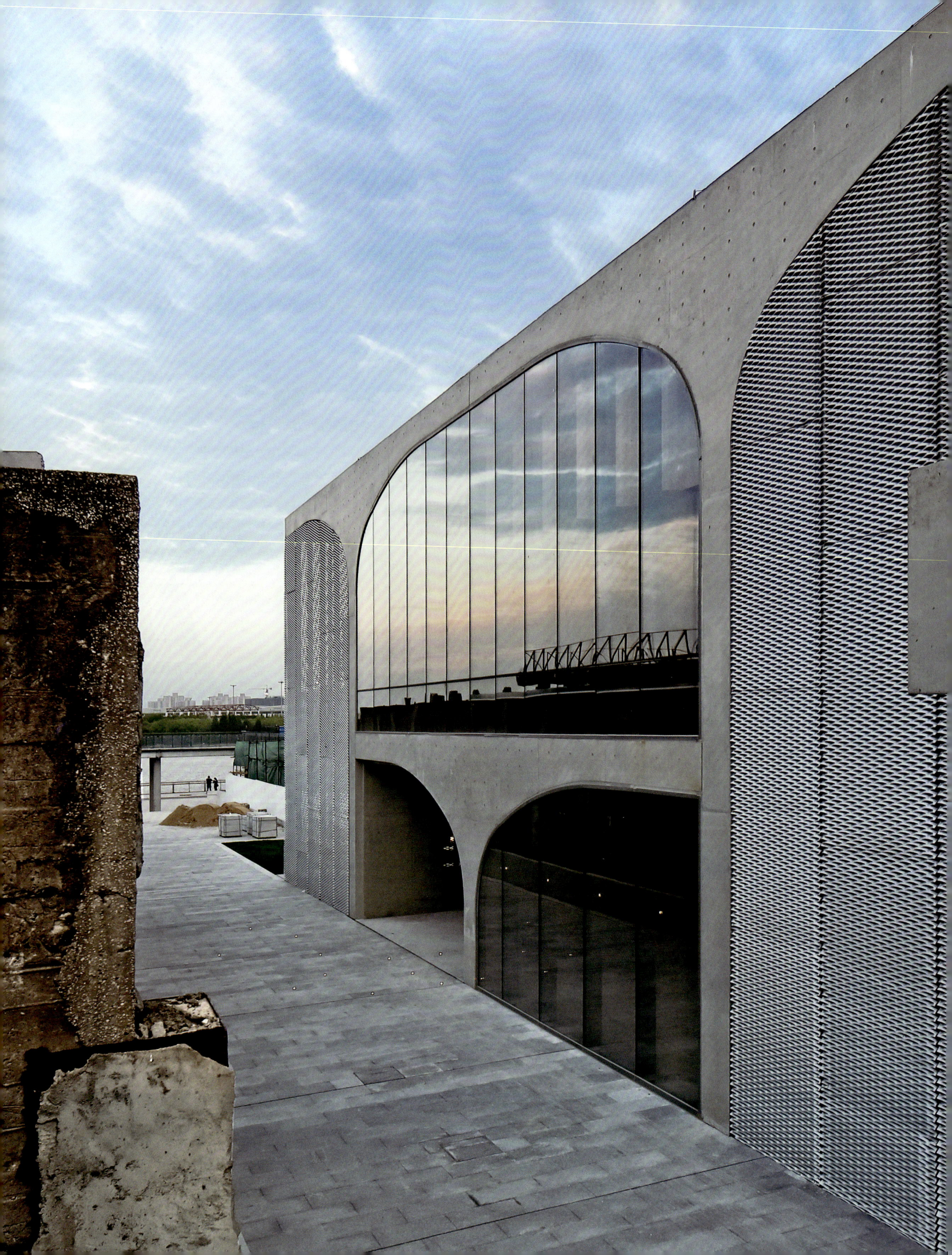

Long Museum West Bund

Shanghai, China

Atelier Deshaus, Shanghai
Construction 2012–2014, opened 2014
Building 33,007 sq. m
Contemporary art and Chinese ancient art

The architect Liu Yichun recalls: "The first time I arrived at the spot where the Long Museum now stands, it seemed surreal: I had just been in the throbbing inner city, and now, only a few kilometres away, I was standing in front of an old conveyor belt in an expansive, empty space with water in front of me and a world of decay all around me."[1] This world was once a wharf, and the conveyor belt, 110 metres long, once transported coal. Today it is the visual centrepiece of the largest private art museum in China.[2]

Ten metres tall, eight metres wide, erected in the 1950s of steel and concrete and showing its age – this is the structure that Liu used as an exciting point of departure for the museum. In addition, he had to integrate an already existing underground parking garage. He managed to do so with a simple yet ingenious solution of thin, movable concrete walls. The bearing walls are positioned in such a way that they align with the underground construction, and with them additional lightweight walls of metal grilles, glass and concrete comprise the new aboveground structure. The nearly square museum bridges the conveyor belt in one spot, otherwise it appears to acknowledge the primacy of the older structure and draws back from it. The belt is allowed to extend eastward unhindered before it is enveloped by the museum. But it not only serves as an excuse to spectacularly break through the new building's smooth outer shell, it also functions as outdoor exhibition space, and so has been given a new assignment without obscuring its original function.

Some of the walls bend forward at the top to form wide projections, creating a sort of umbrella structure that not only protects the contemporary art and its viewers but also the old conveyor belt. The structure does not want to deny its past or even destroy it, which is unusual in present-day China. The right of use of industrial buildings is fixed at fifty years – tearing it down would not have been a problem.[3]

Inside, the umbrellas cause a similar effect: among the massive fragments of suggested barrel vaulting and simple, grey concrete walls you never feel small, oppressed or uncomfortable. On the contrary: here, too, you feel enclosed and safe – and at the same time unexpectedly free. Liu considered this important: from the start his concept included a "free wall plan" – no inflexible rooms, but walls that penetrate each other, appear to overlap, interrupt a floor here, open up the view of another one there. "Viewing an art piece [then] is to allow the body to move with a consciousness, to realize a sense of freedom, which is the critical reason why we choose the free wall plan."[4]

When leaving the Long Museum, one looks afresh at the conveyor belt. It has become a harmonious component of the museum experience, part of the *Gesamtkunstwerk* that is the city.[5]

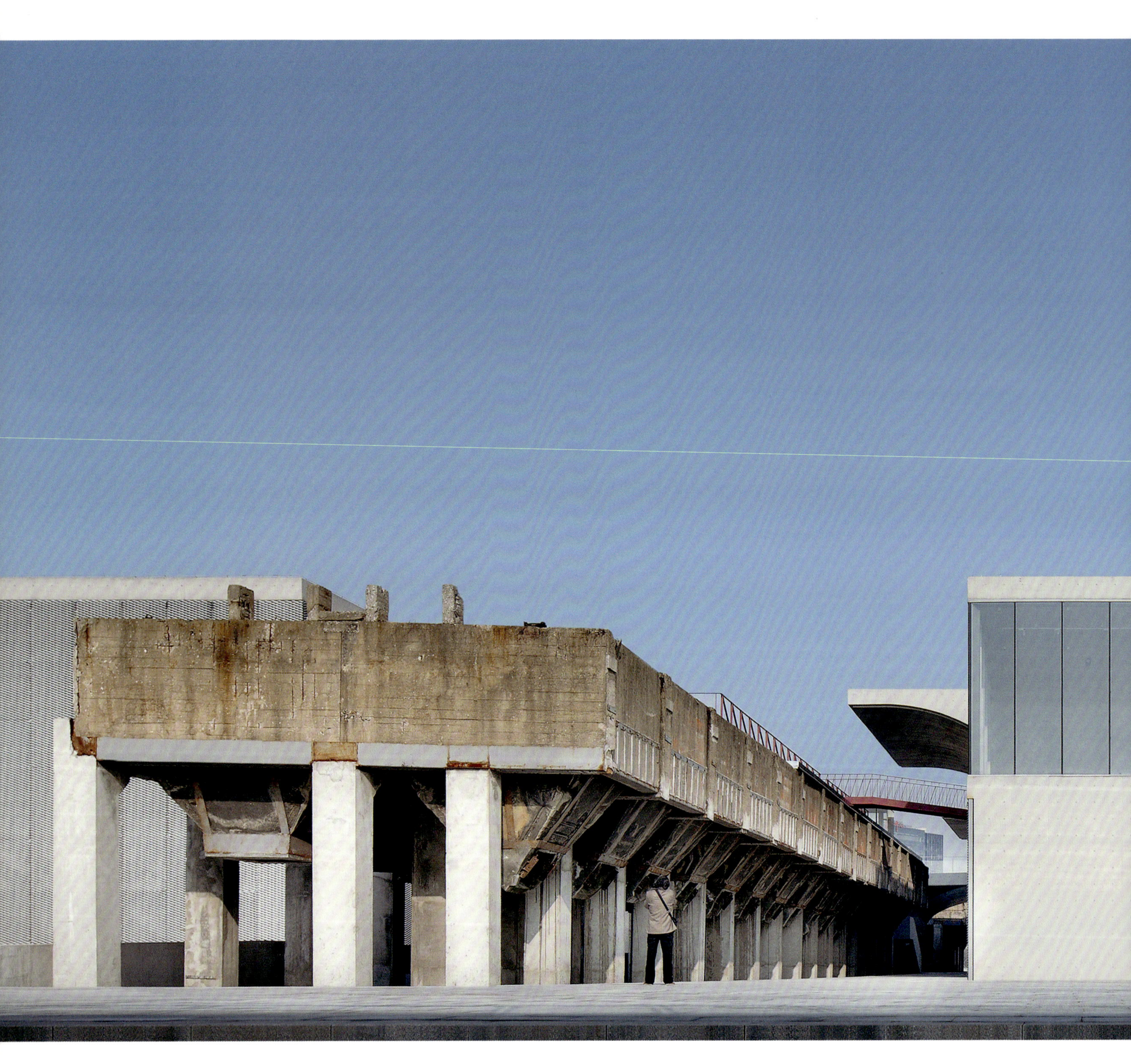

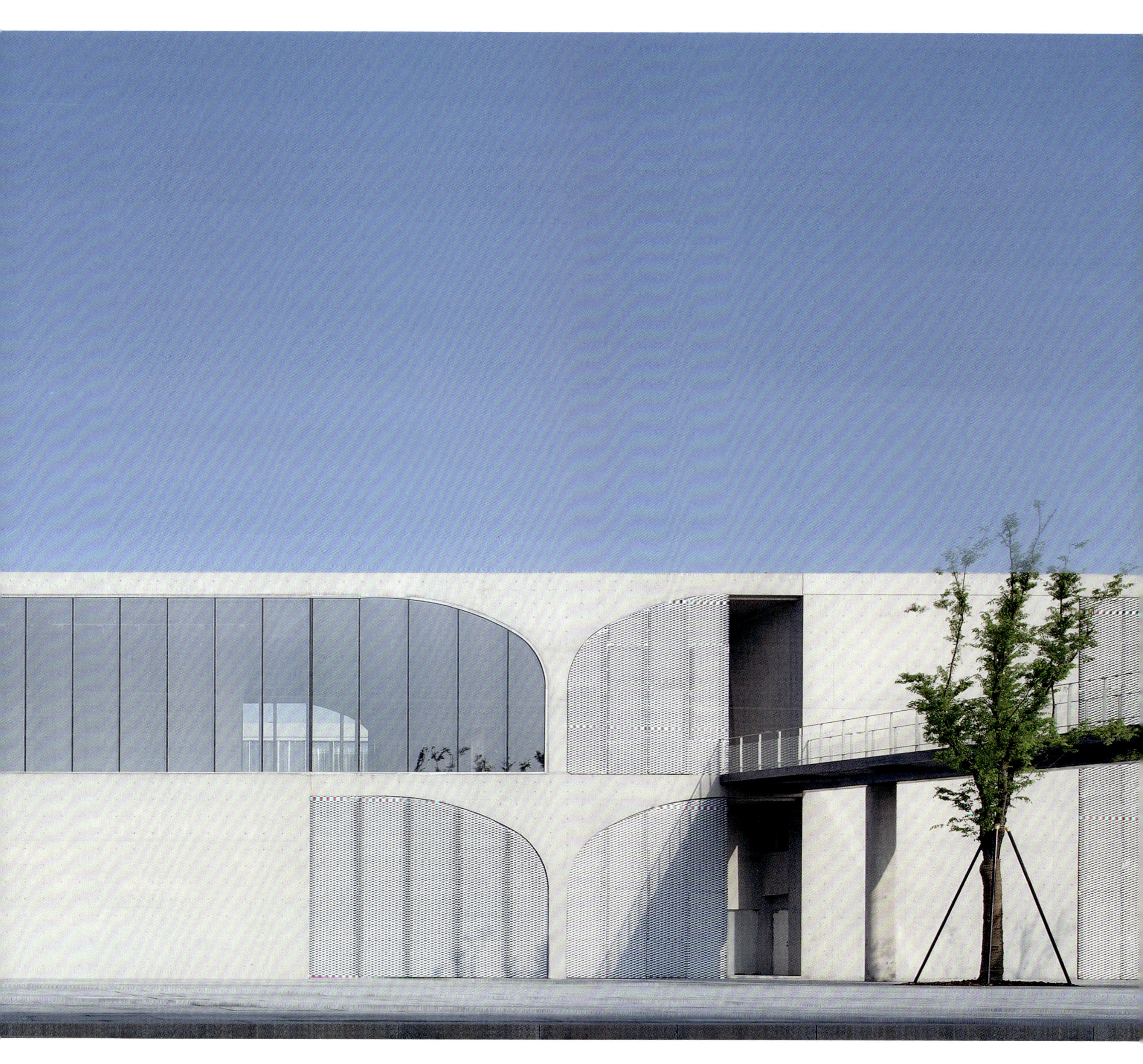

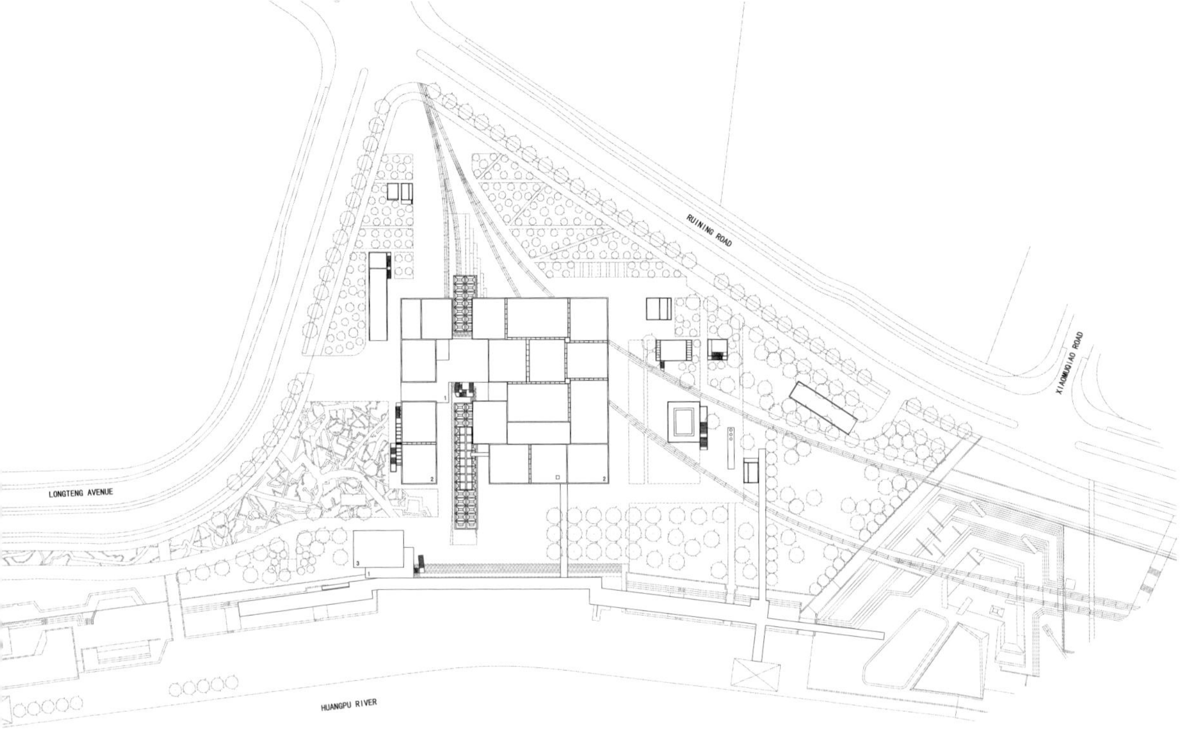

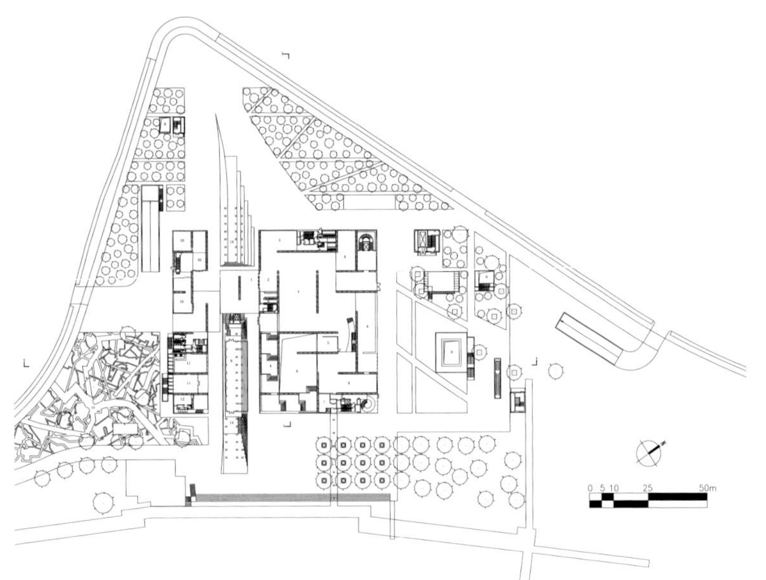

← Main plan.
  Ground-floor plan.

↓ Section, southwest–northeast.
  Section, southeast–northwest.

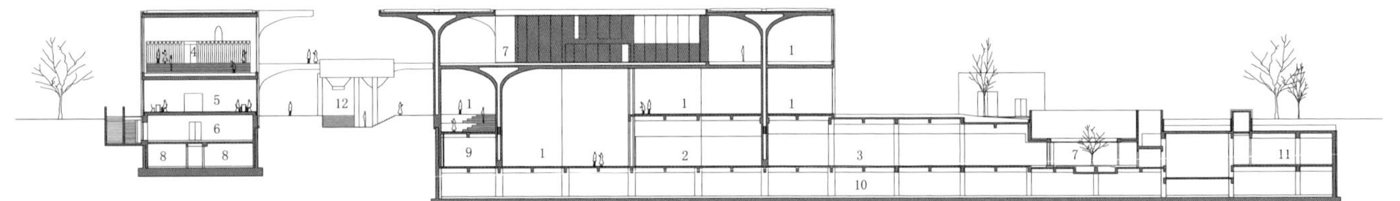

1   Contemporary Art Gallery
2   Corridor
3   Ancient Art Gallery
4   Auditorium
5   Restaurant
6   Kitchen
7   Courtyard
8   Office
9   Storage
10 Car Parking
11 Bicycle Parking
12 Coal-Hopper-Uploading-Bridge

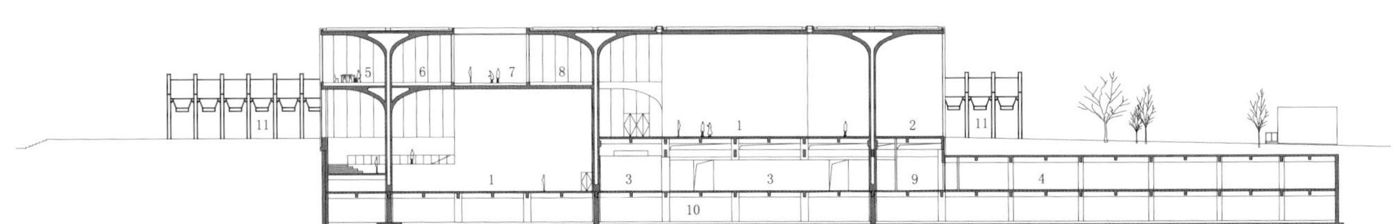

1   Contemporary Art Gallery
2   Shop
3   Modern Art Gallery
4   Warehouse
5   Riverview Restaurant
6   Café
7   Courtyard
8   Guest Reception Room
9   Car Parking
10 Coal-Hopper-Uploading-Bridge

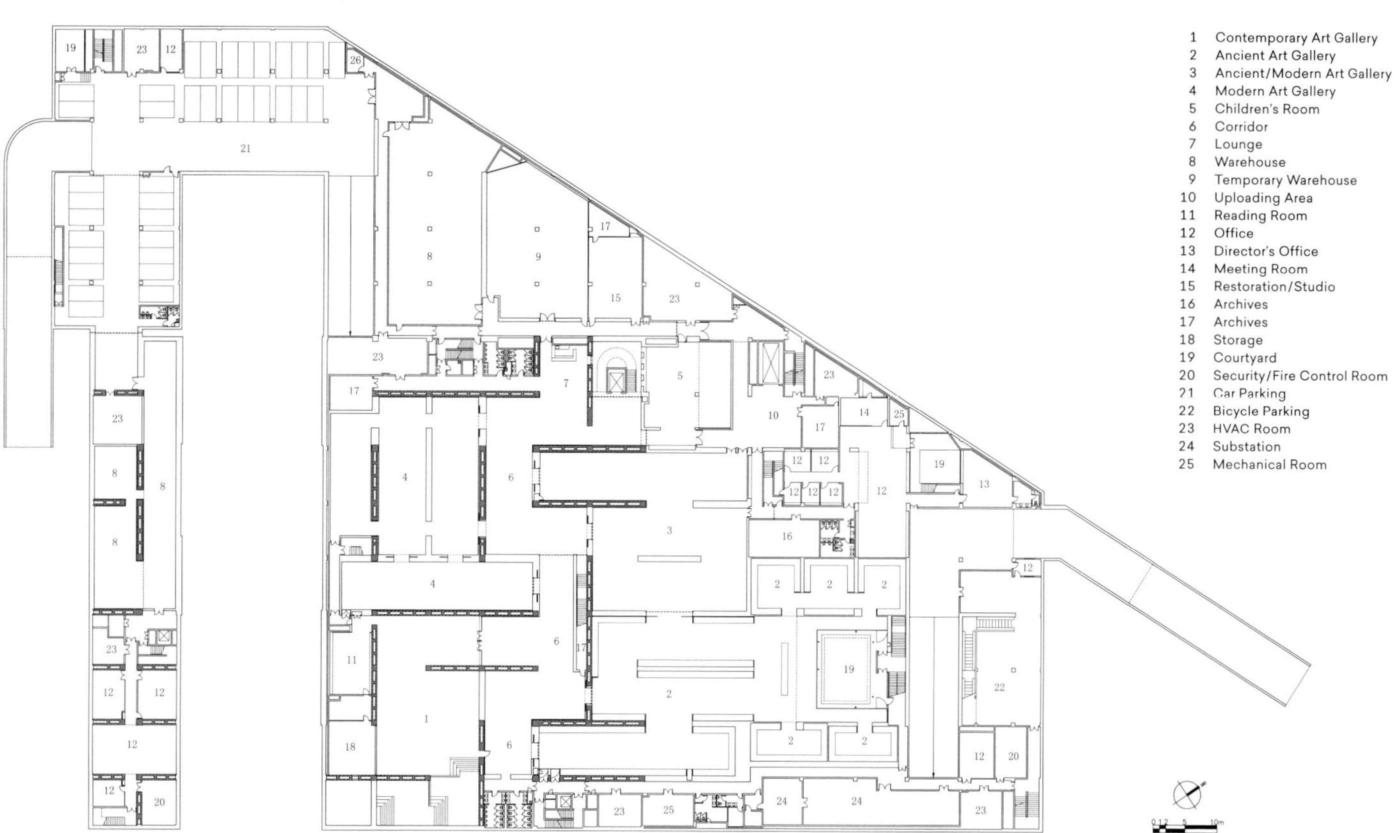

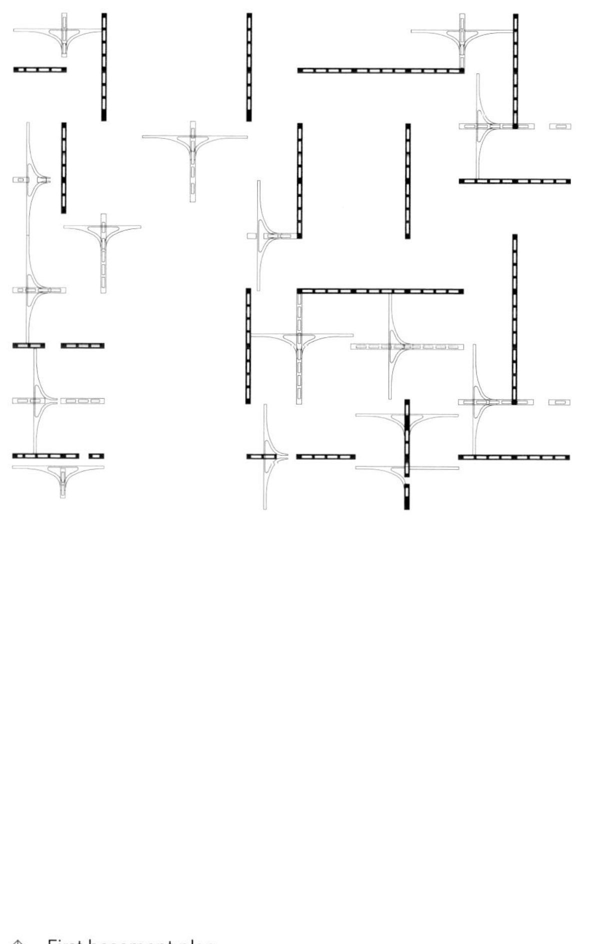

↑ First basement plan.
   Structure plan.

→ Cavity of the vault structure.

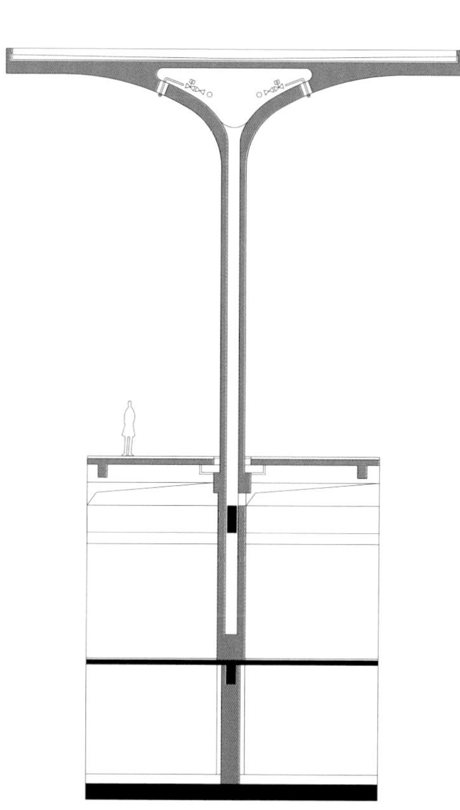

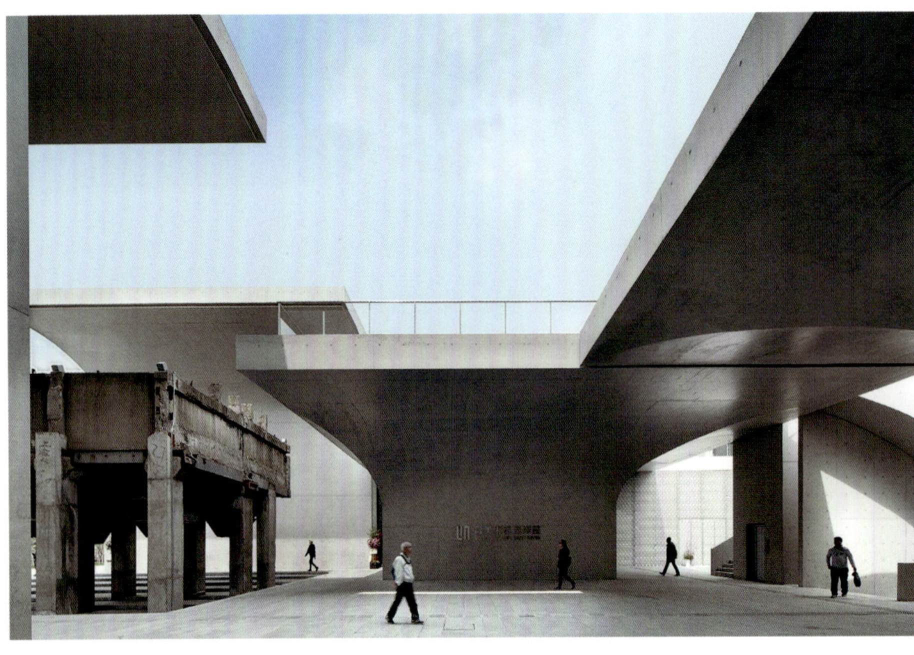

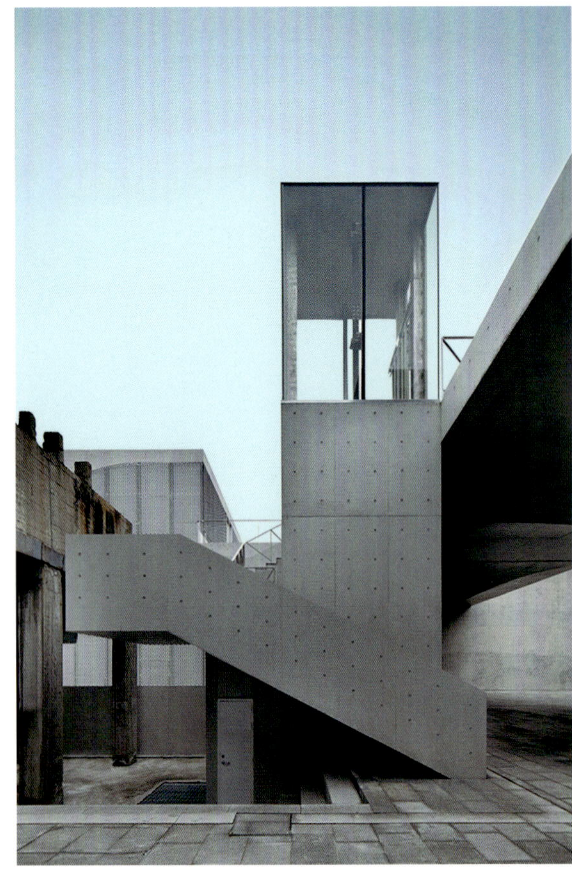

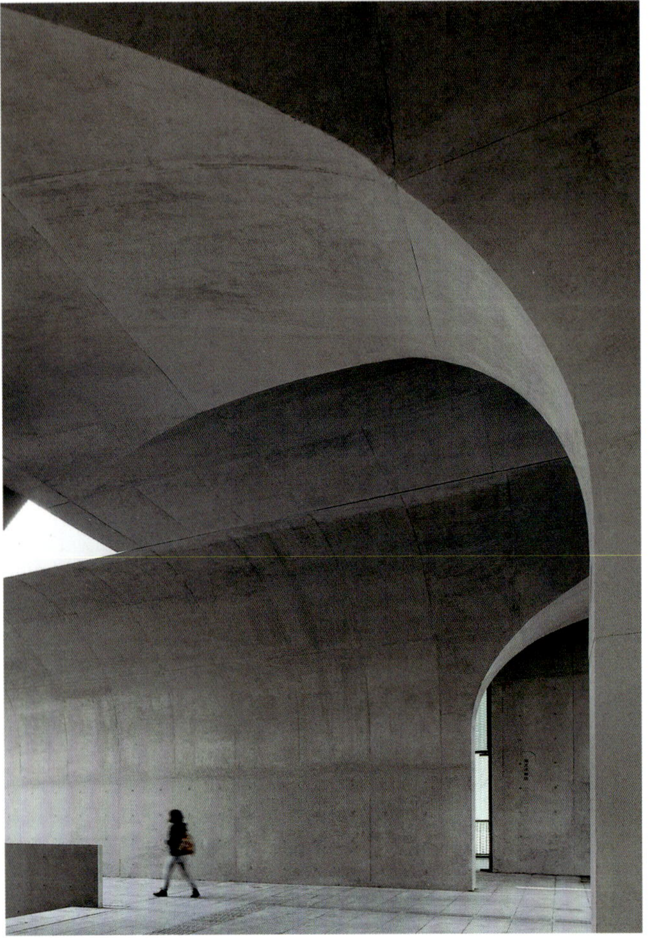

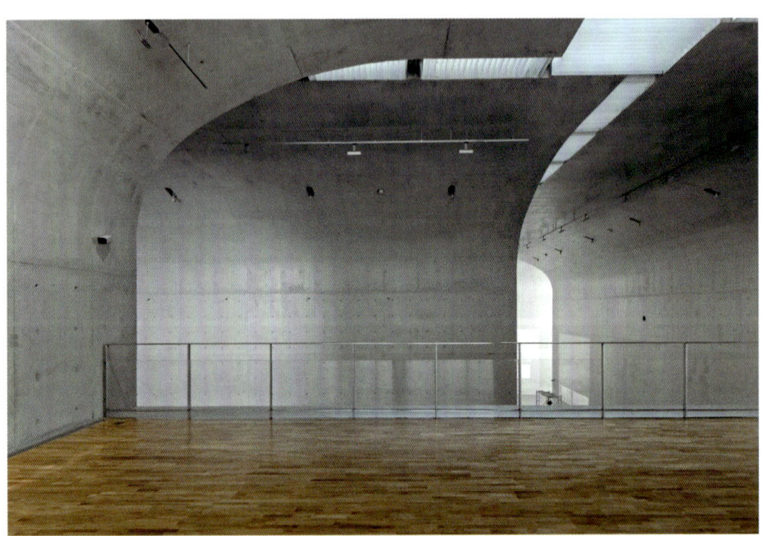

↑ Main entrance.
Lift and stairs.
Interior.

← Concrete vaults.

↗ Contemporary art gallery.

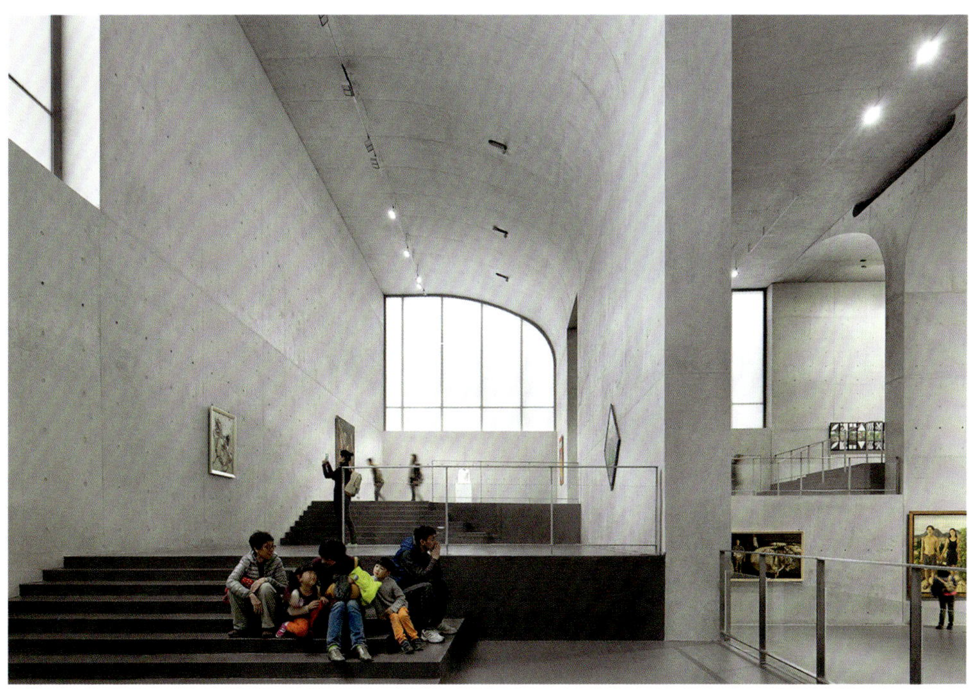

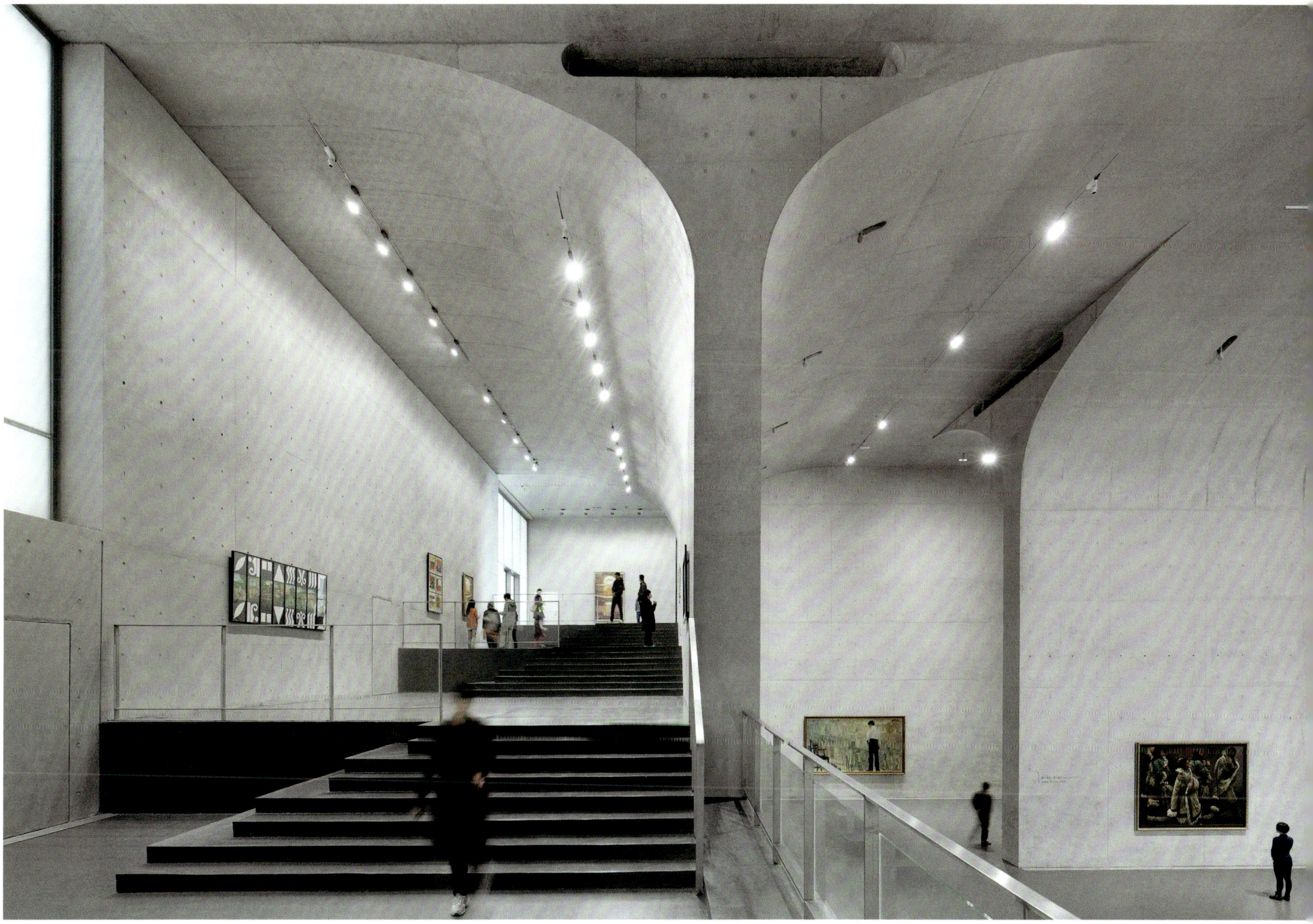

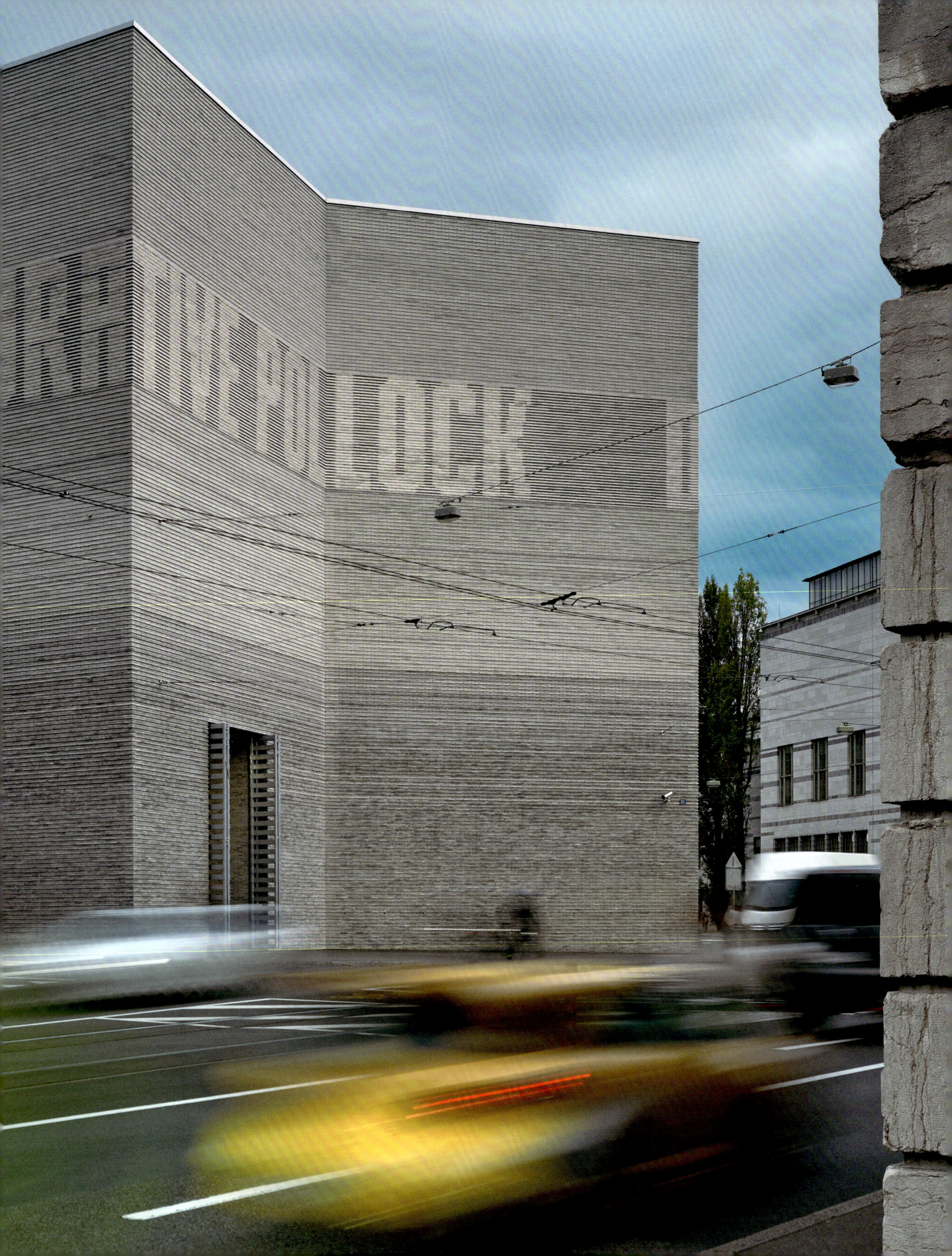

Kunstmuseum Basel Extension

Basel, Switzerland

Christ & Gantenbein, Basel
Construction 2012–2016, opened 2016
Building 11,481 sq. m
The museum's permanent art collection and special exhibitions

The new extension of the Kunstmuseum Basel, which is actually in fact an annexe, is a radical alternative to the many sensational, iconic new museum buildings. As you approach from the direction of Rittergasse it appears to be relatively unimpressive. Instead of burdening the intersection with a massive block, where two narrower streets debouch into the wider St. Alban-Graben, the building backs away from the streets. Rather than presenting an unbroken front, its façade is creased backward in the centre, giving it a playful lightness. The expanse of light grey water-struck bricks is interrupted by a galvanised steel entrance gate. What puts the simple structure in league with so many fantastic museum designs is the band of luminous LED lights set into the façade. They can be programmed with texts and graphics, so that the face of the museum constantly changes.

From the museum's old building one reaches the extension through an underground foyer linking the two without disturbing the intervening Dufourstrasse. The older museum was built by Rudolf Christ and Paul Bonatz in 1932–1936; its front, with its arcades with massive figural capitals, recalls Romanesque and Renaissance architecture, whereas the interior of the four-wing layout around an open atrium bears more modern features. Christ and Bonatz indulged in a variety of materials – some sixteen types of stone were built into the façade alone[1] – but the architects of the new building, Emanuel Christ and Christoph Gantenbein, limited themselves to a far more modest palette. This reduction is already visible on the façade, but in the interior the material minimalism is stunningly portrayed. The underground foyer, with a broad staircase leading to the upper floors, is completely clad in silver-grey Carrara marble; grey walls of rough scraped plaster are nicely set off by galvanised steel handrails. The rough scraped plaster is reminiscent of the old building, as is the broad staircase design. But where the latter curves elegantly upward in the older structure, the new building appears to project pure, almost brutal strength.

This force exuded by the architecture can also be sensed in the exhibition galleries, where it is absorbed by the exhibited artworks with no diminution of their own presence. Though deliberately plain, the spaces offer more to the viewer's eye than the often arbitrary white cube. The new building displays mainly art from the second half of the 20th century, though its spaces need to be able to house earlier art as well.[2] They perform this balancing act with aplomb. The floor of oiled oak recalls traditional building materials, though here joints of wood cement lend a contemporary accent. The ceilings are finished in grey exposed concrete. But they are not flat; they are divided into prefabricated beams suggestive of coffered ceilings. Bright white LED lamps sunk into these concrete recesses supplement the natural light entering from the side on the second floor and through skylights on the top floor to provide a pleasant illumination appropriate to the art. Christ & Gantenbein call their new building the older structure's "contemporary brother"[3] and with their architectural cross-over have created a contemporary space that has the potential of becoming timeless.

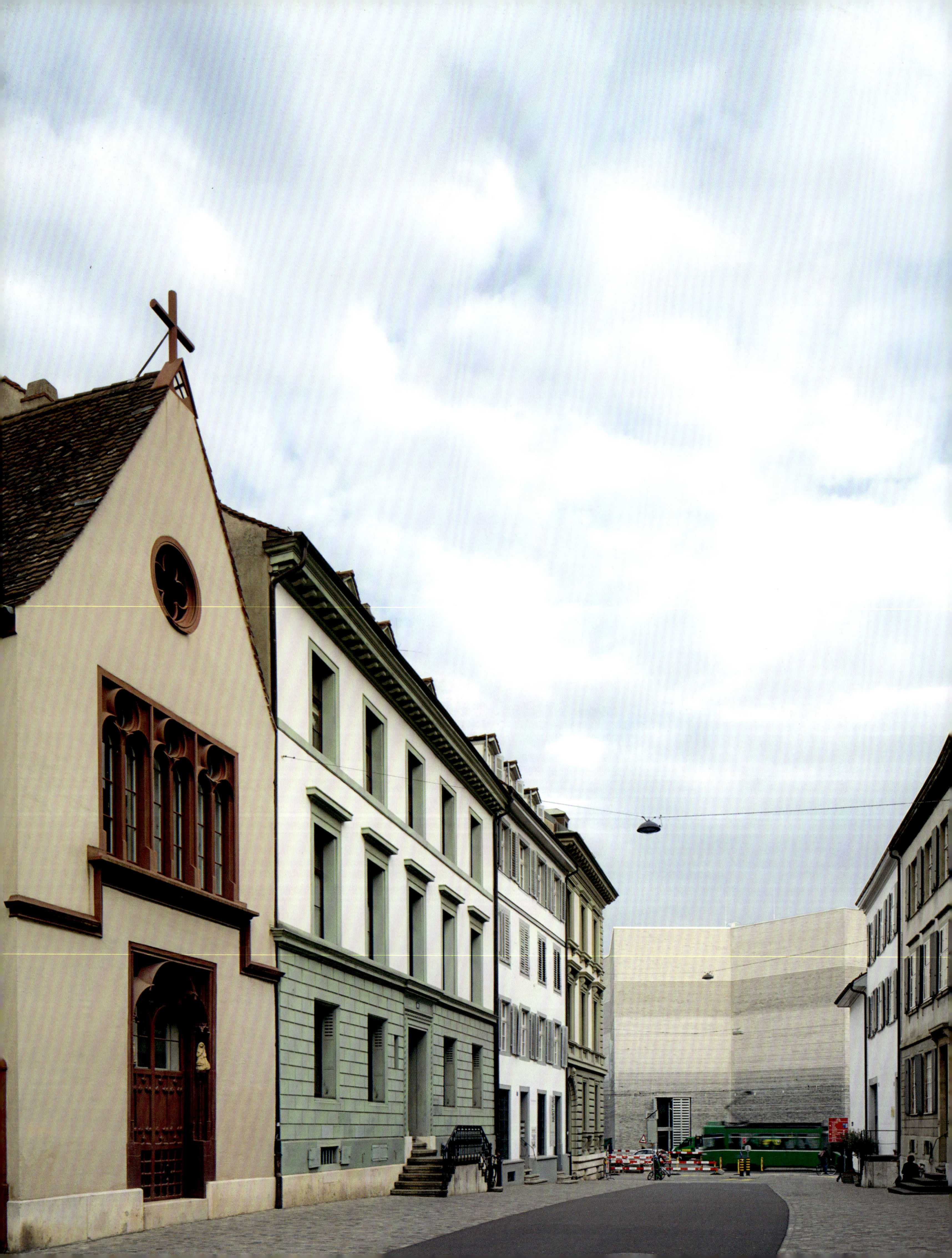

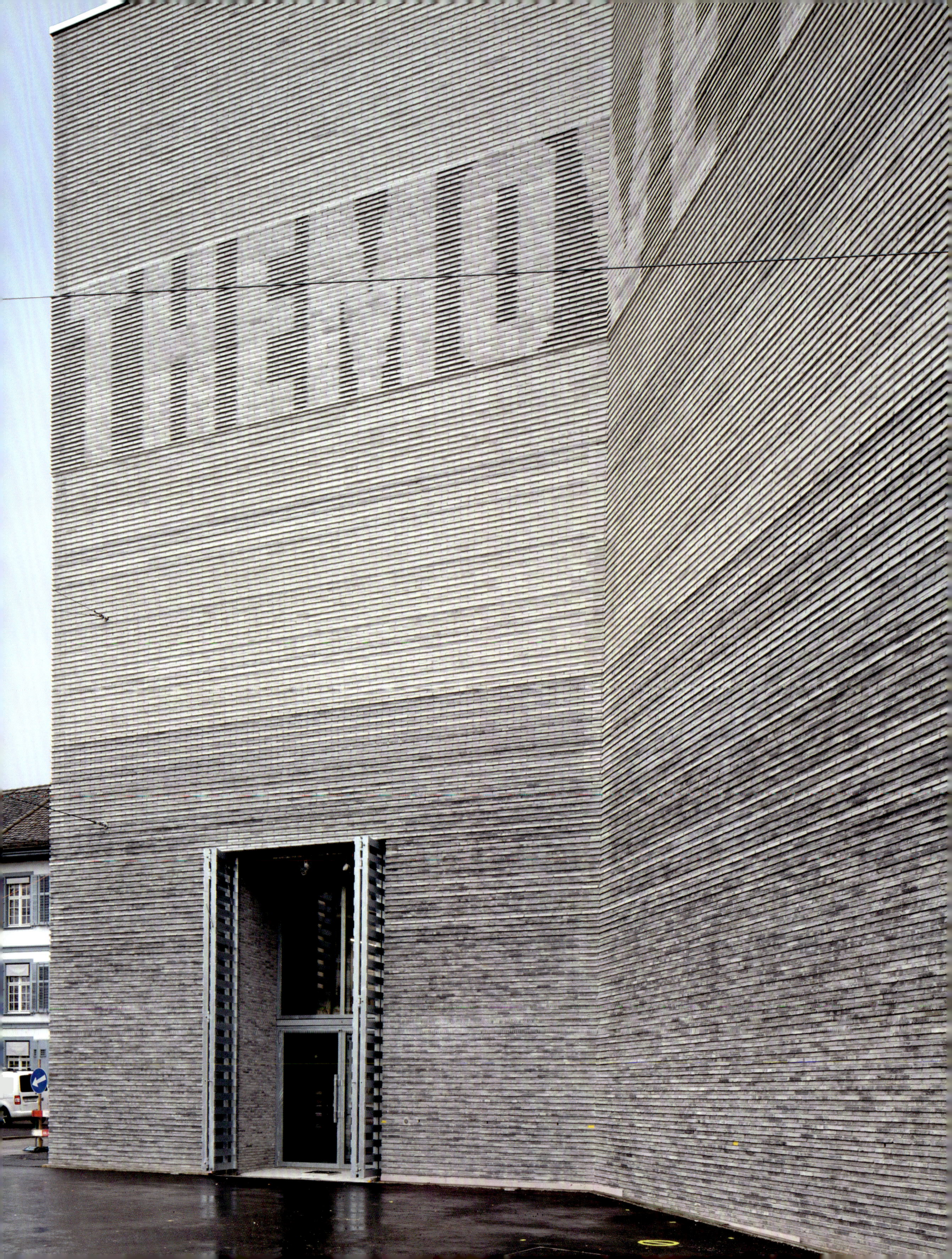

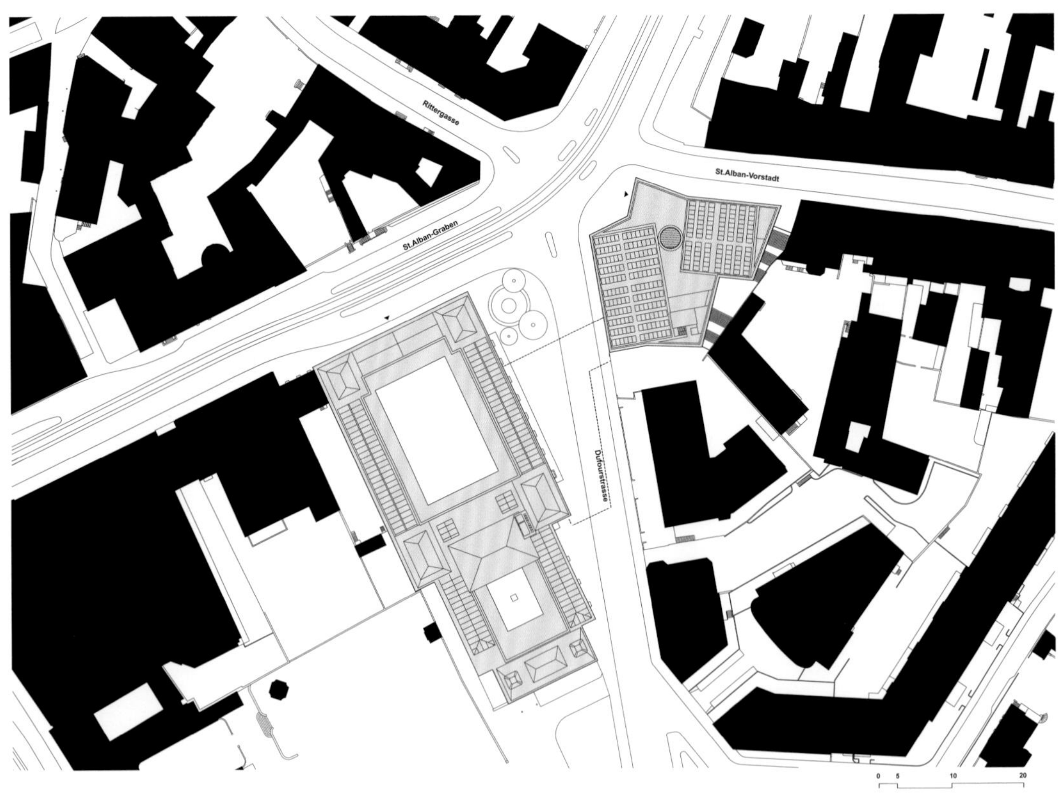

→ Site plan.

↓ Section, west–east.
Section, south–north.

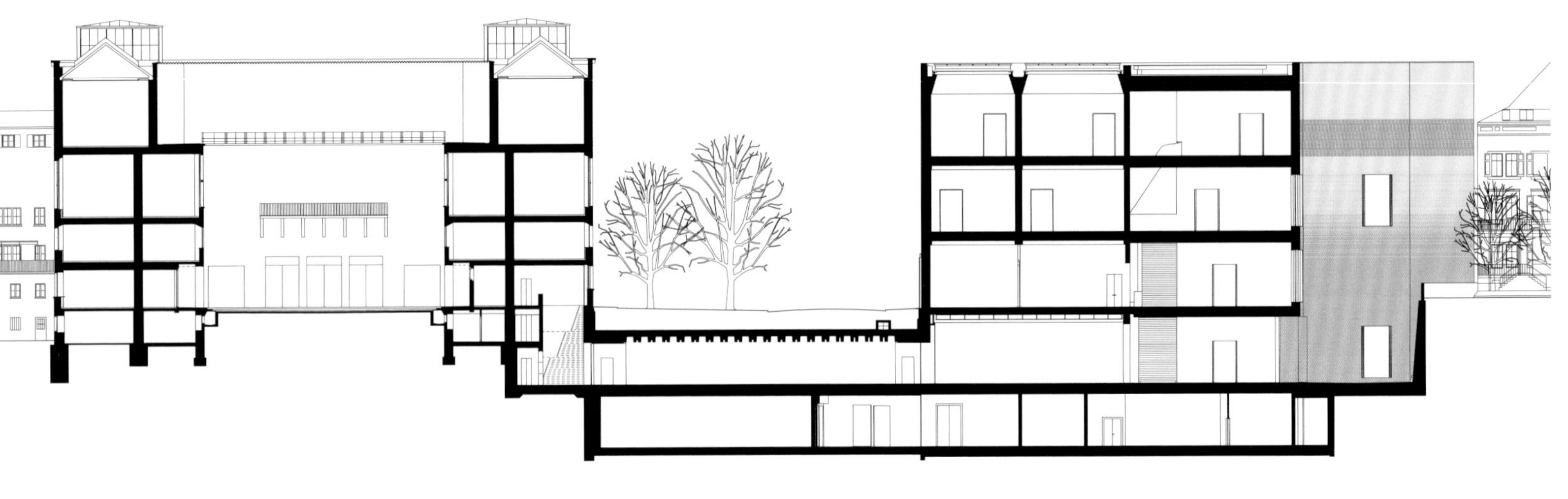

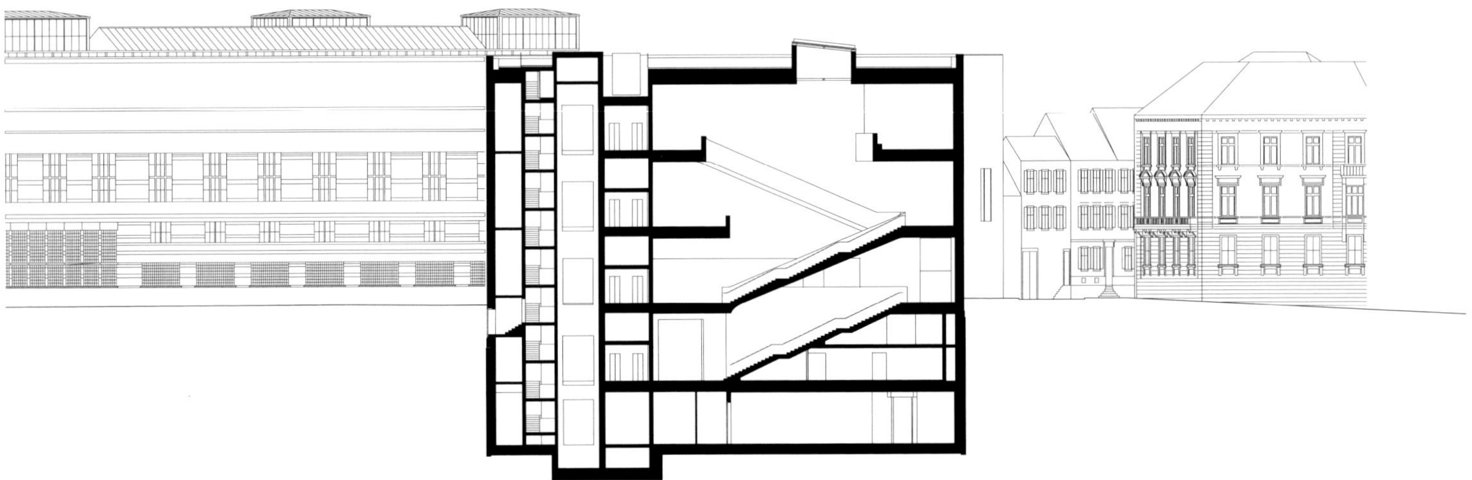

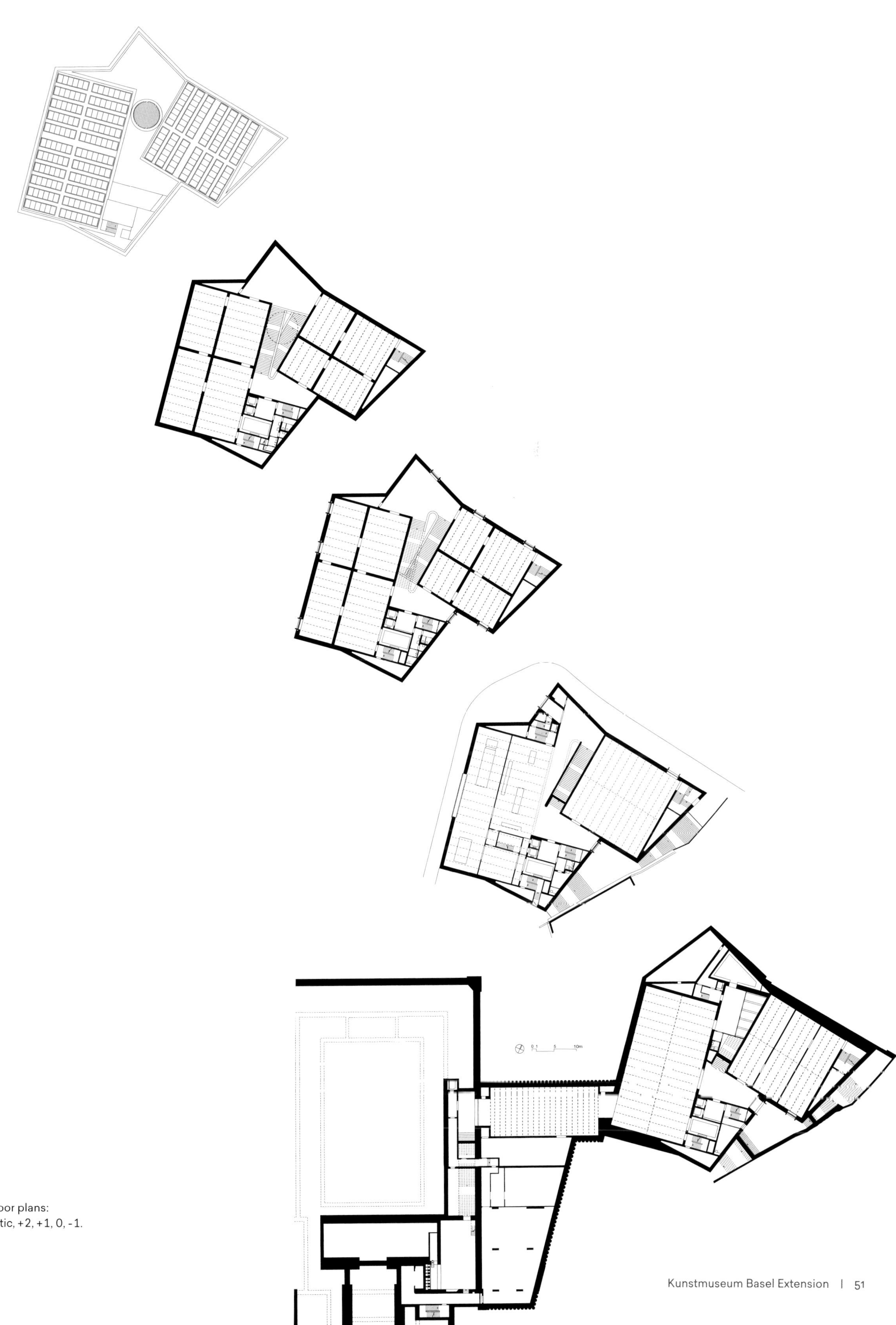

↗ Floor plans:
Attic, +2, +1, 0, -1.

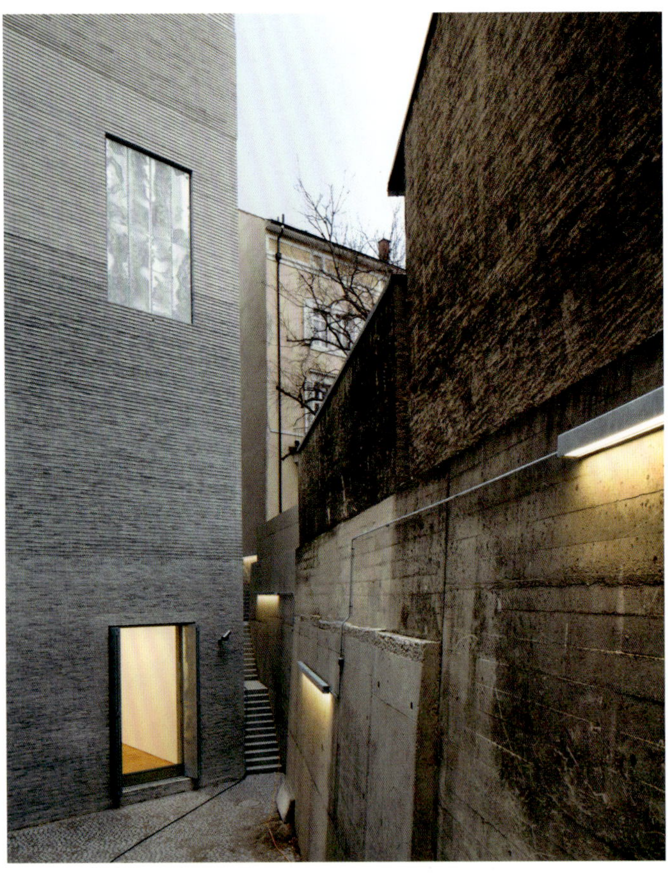

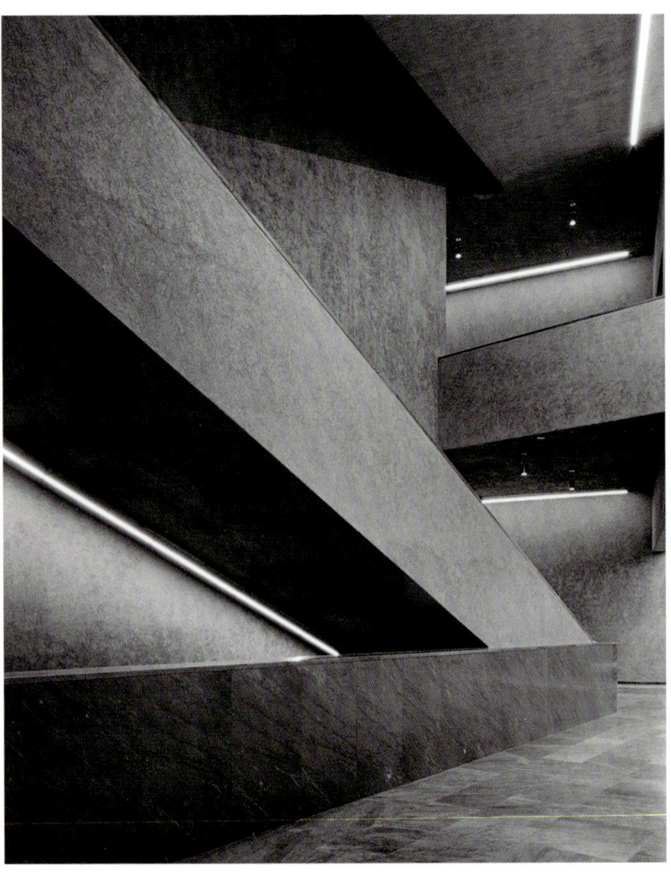

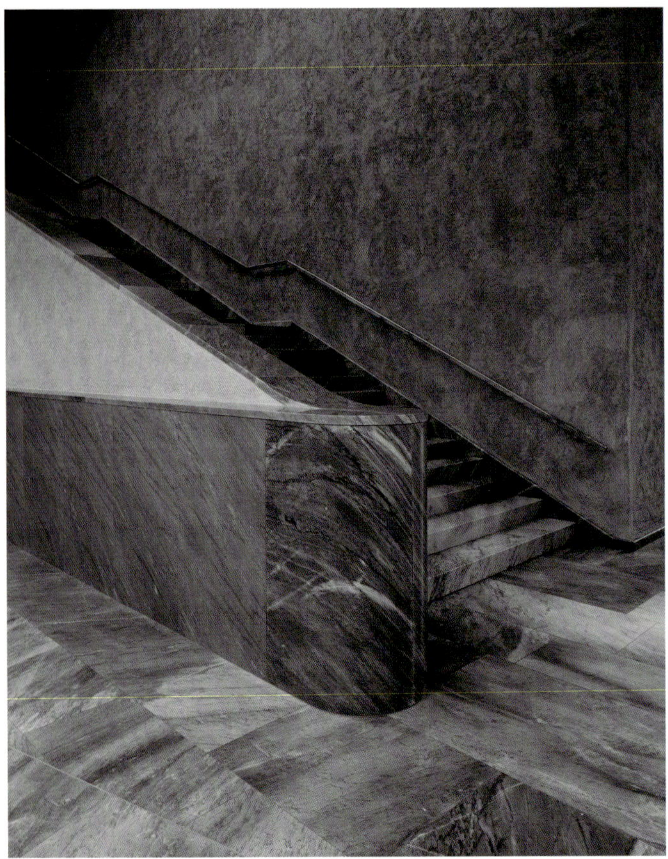

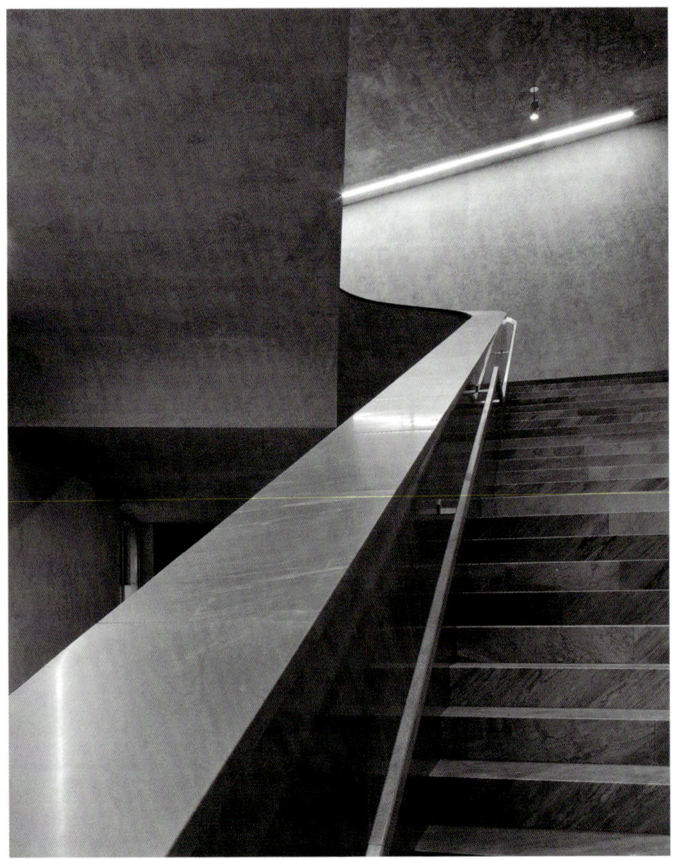

↑ Backyard.

↗ Staircase.

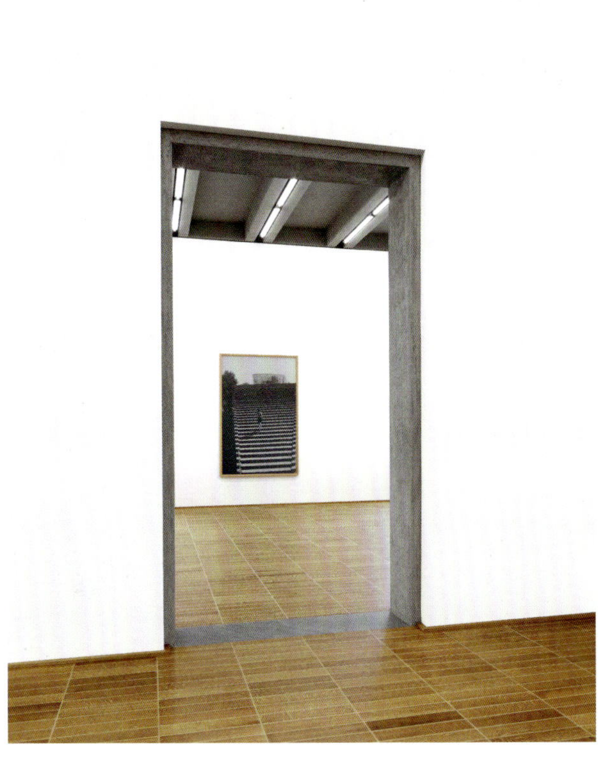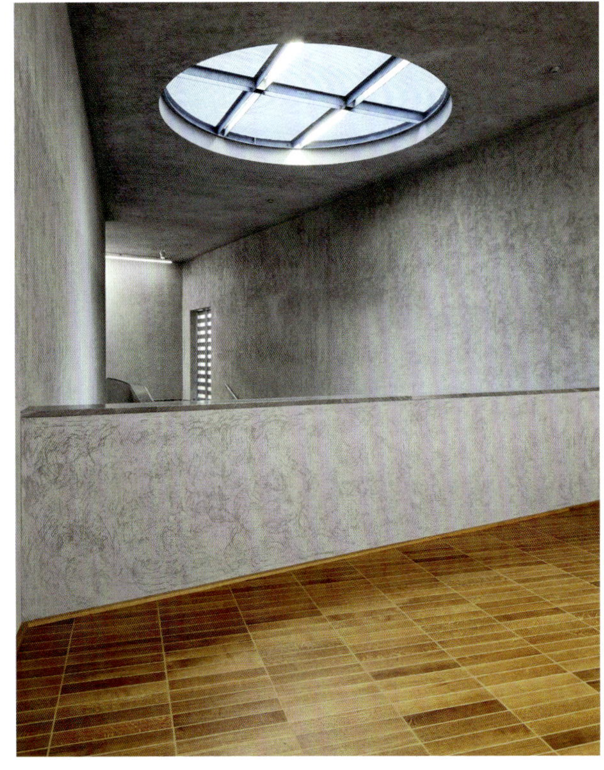

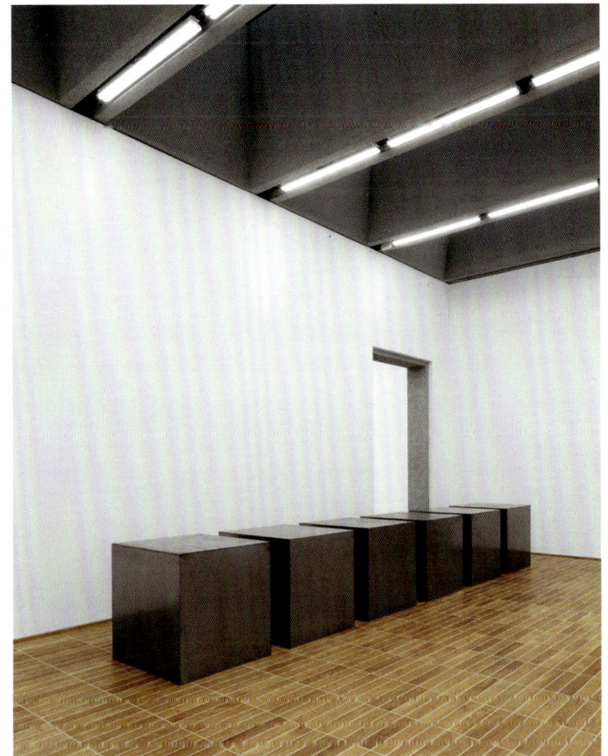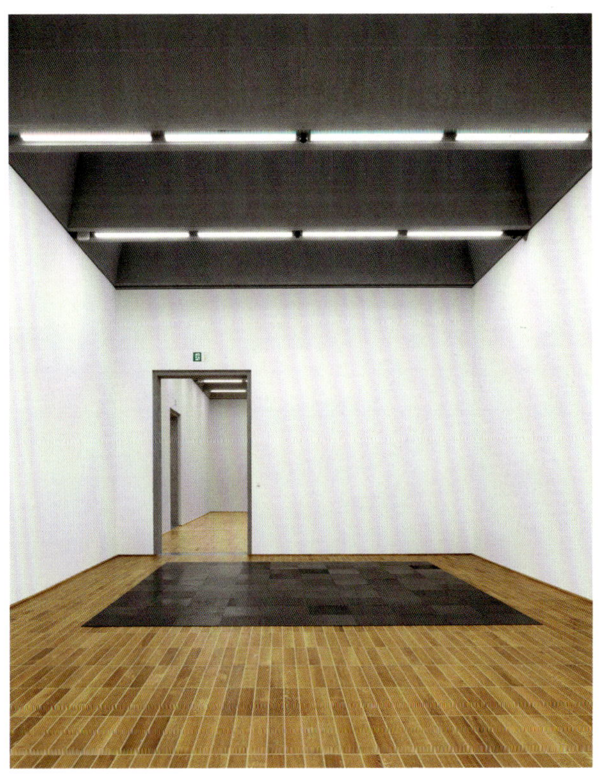

↑ Exhibition spaces.

↗ Oculus in the attic.

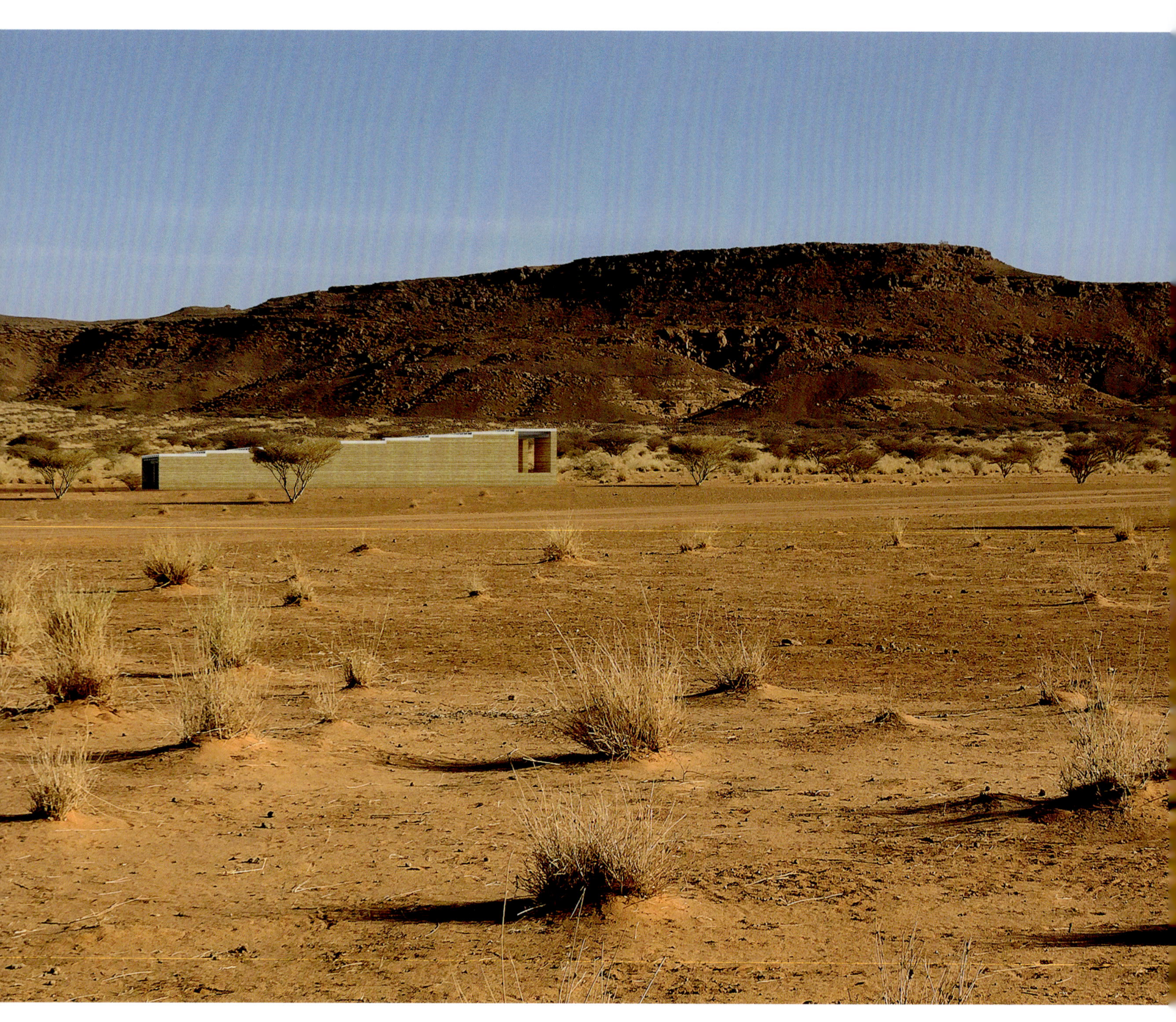

Naga Site Museum

Naga, Sudan

David Chipperfield Architects Berlin
In the planning phase
Building 1,400 sq. m
Excavations from the site

The museum in Naga in Sudan's Butana steppe will be small. Compared to most museums we know, even tiny. It will measure exactly twenty metres wide and sixty metres long, and will no doubt see very few visitors a week. But they are not what is most important. Most important are the excavated objects protected from the sun and disintegration in this museum.

The ancient city of Naga, which flourished around AD 250, encompassed a full square kilometre; today fifteen of its temples survive, including the Hathor Chapel and the Amun Temple with its avenue of rams, both UNESCO World Heritage sites since 2011. Since 2013 excavations have been under the patronage of Munich's Staatliches Museum Ägyptischer Kunst (Egyptian Museum). Archaeologists have measured the Hathor Chapel, which is threatened with collapse, with digital 3D scanning, and now portions that cannot be salvaged are being replaced with copies, while the originals are meant to remain on site.[1] These, along with other artefacts, will be found in the Naga Museum which will lie a good two kilometres north of the excavation site and barely interact with it. To the architects, David Chipperfield Architects Berlin, it was important that the historic site remains undisturbed, and many museum directors and caretakers of monuments have praised the practice's considerate treatment of ancient structures[2] as well as the architects' feeling for the landscape and surroundings.[3] The architects themselves see architecture as having a stabilising and protective function.[4]

The Naga Museum will be built of tamped concrete, using sand from its surroundings, and with its warm ochre tones blending with the hilly desert landscape. The roof will be constructed of prefabricated concrete slabs, forming a series of flat steps sloping downward from the entrance to the back of the building, and from the side simply looking like wind-blown sand. It is only when viewed from above that the roof's concrete-grey structure will be seen, and how it lets light into the interior.

The building design quotes the layout of the ancient Amun Temple, with its columned entrance and two rows of columns inside. In order to structure the building and in imitation of the Roman cella, the practice created a few separate spaces that serve as offices and storerooms. The building has no windows; light only enters from the side in the loggia in the entrance area and in the small central courtyard. Additional light streams down from between the offset roof slabs, whose slope is taken up by a ramp running through the building's interior. The museum does completely without glass.

The architects see their job as mediating between material and what can be done with it. They first consider a structure's surroundings, then draw on their accumulated knowledge to create something new.[5] Their respectful treatment of the terrain makes them less modern, less contemporary than many of their colleagues. But in return they can free themselves from the constraints of Modernism, and were able to design a tiny museum in the desert that almost looks as if it has stood there for 2,000 years.

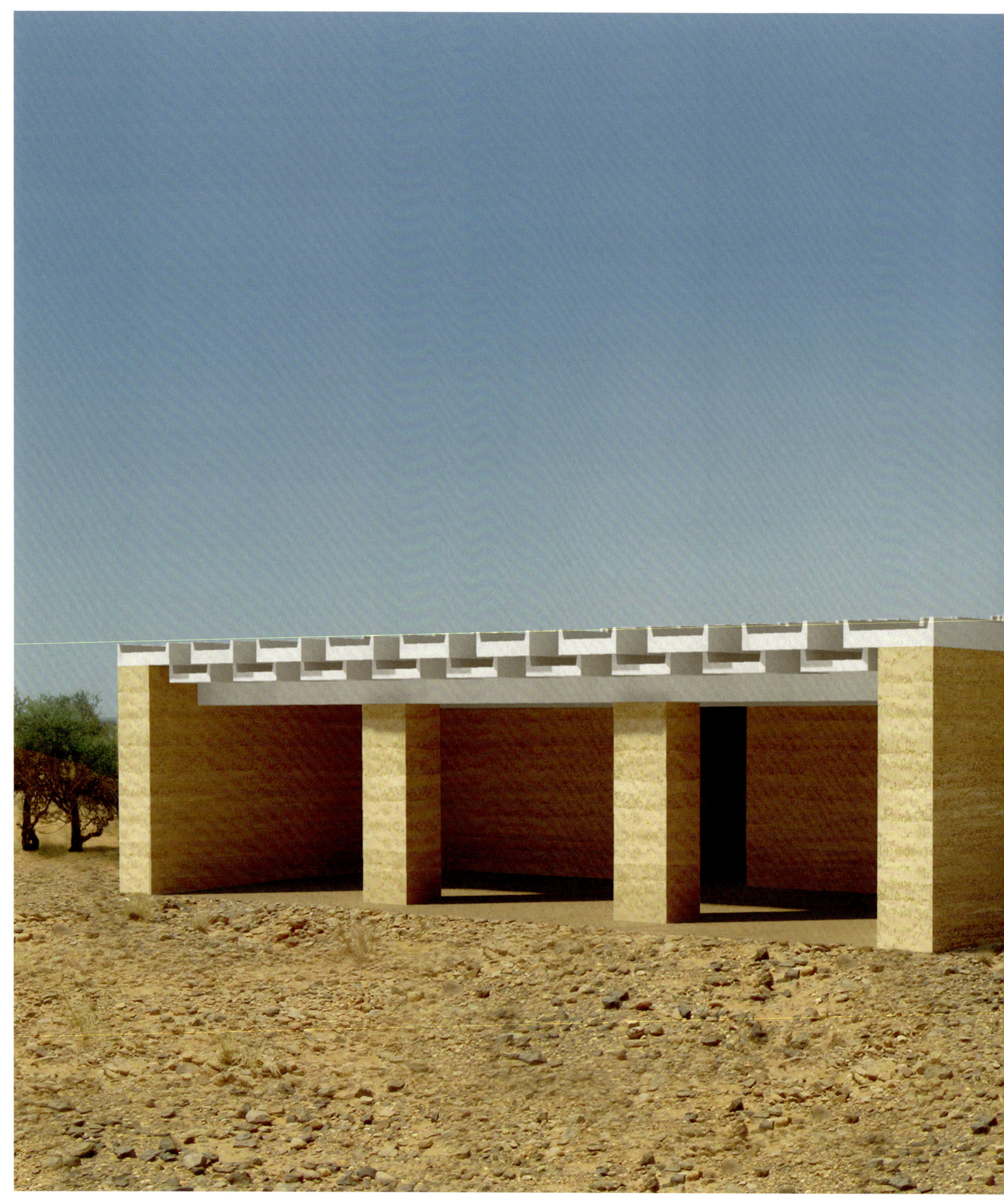

Exterior, looking south.

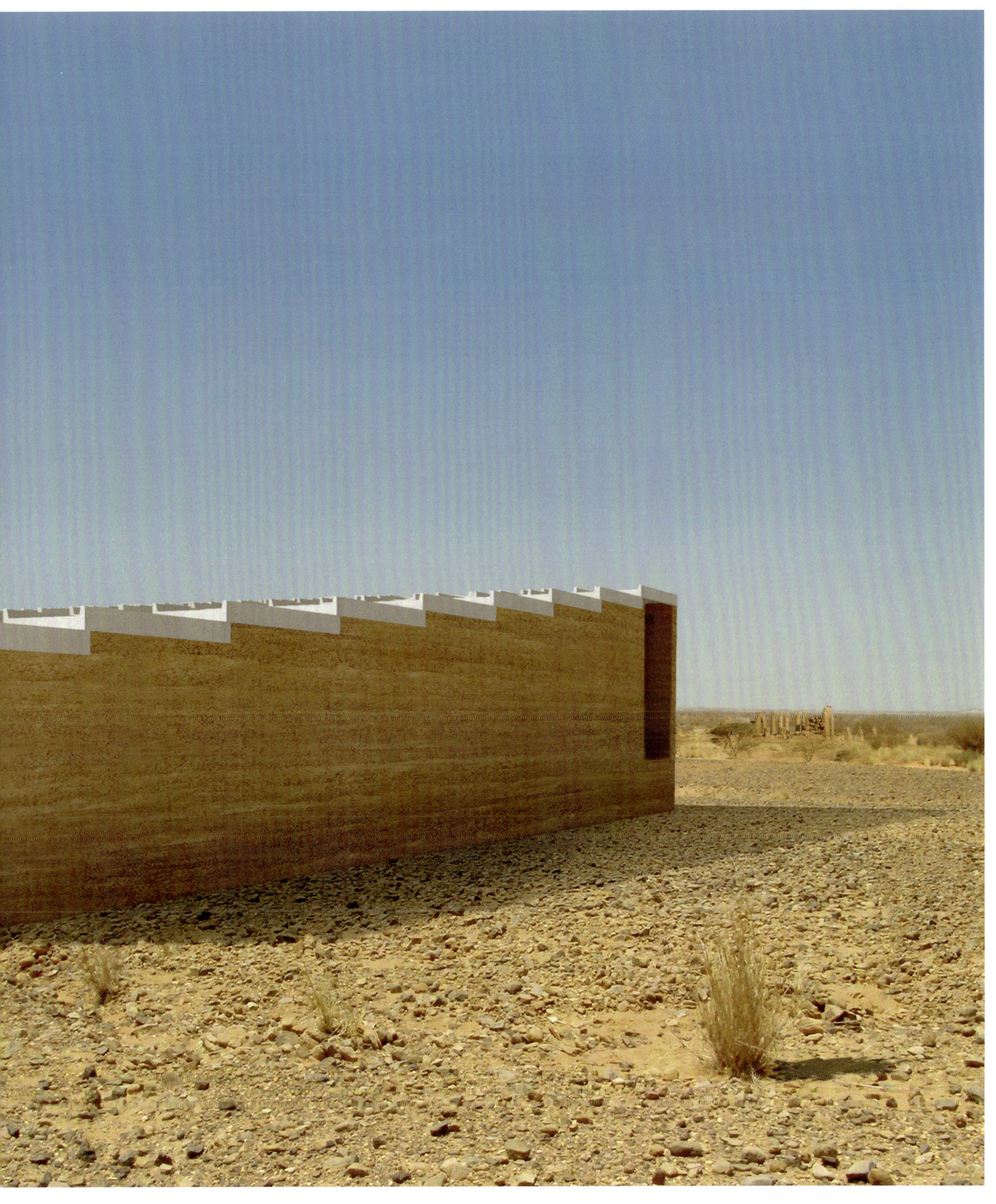

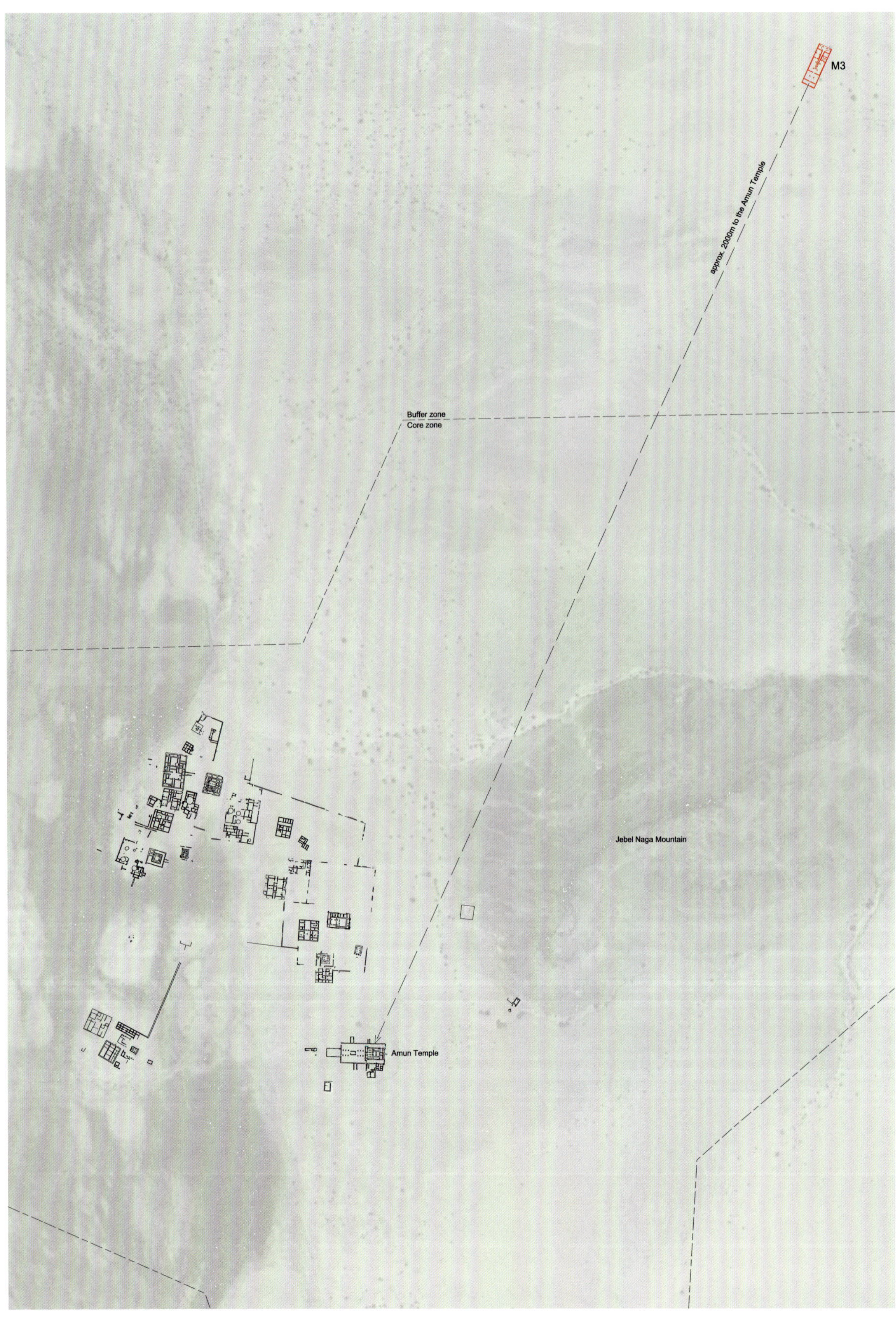

↑   Map with archaeological site.

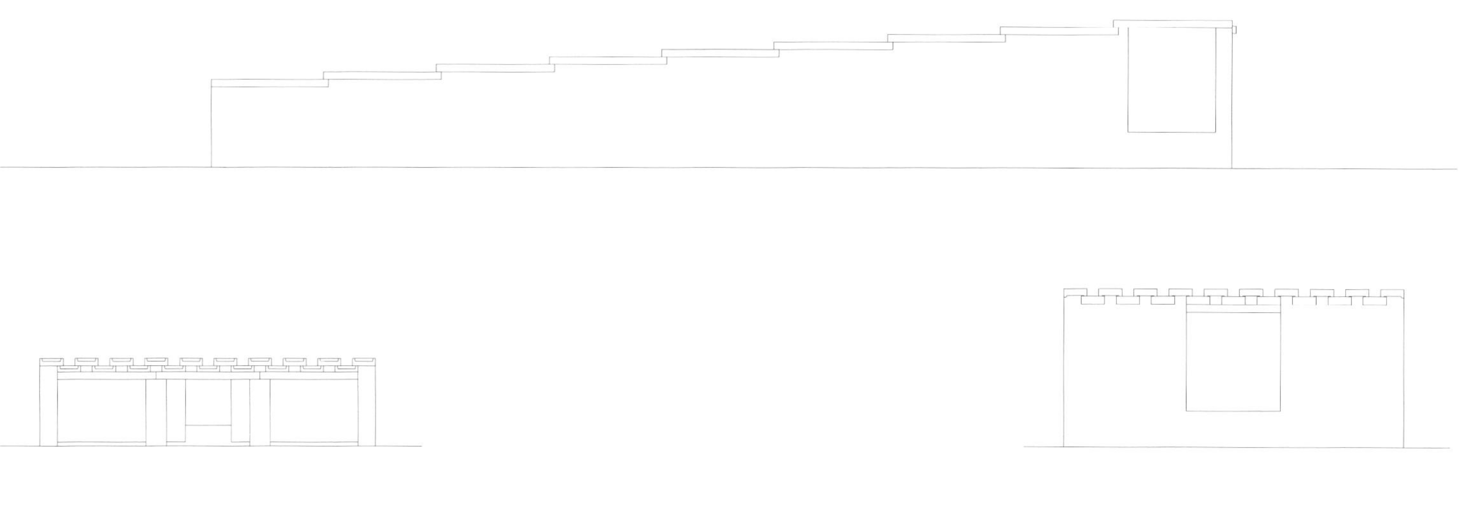

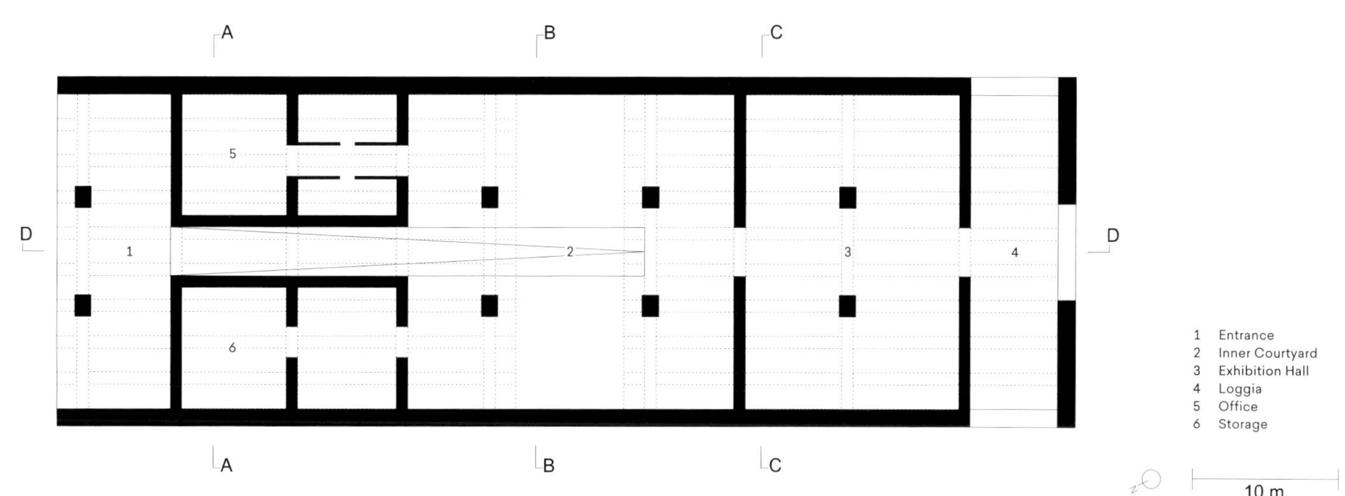

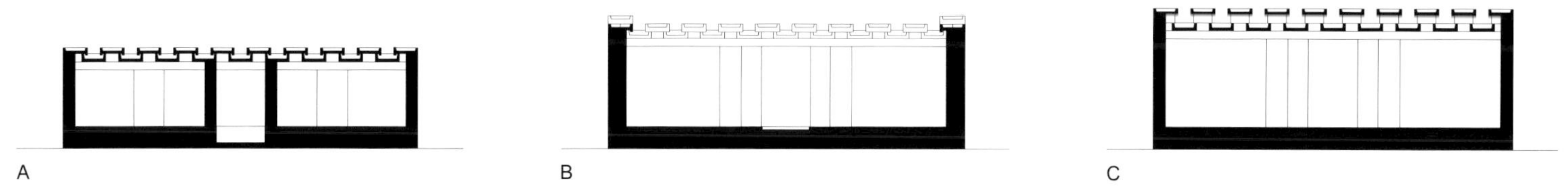

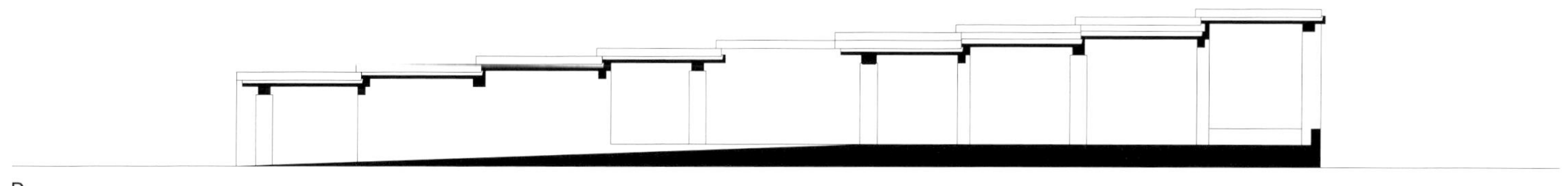

↑   Elevations.
Plan.
Sections A, B, C, D.

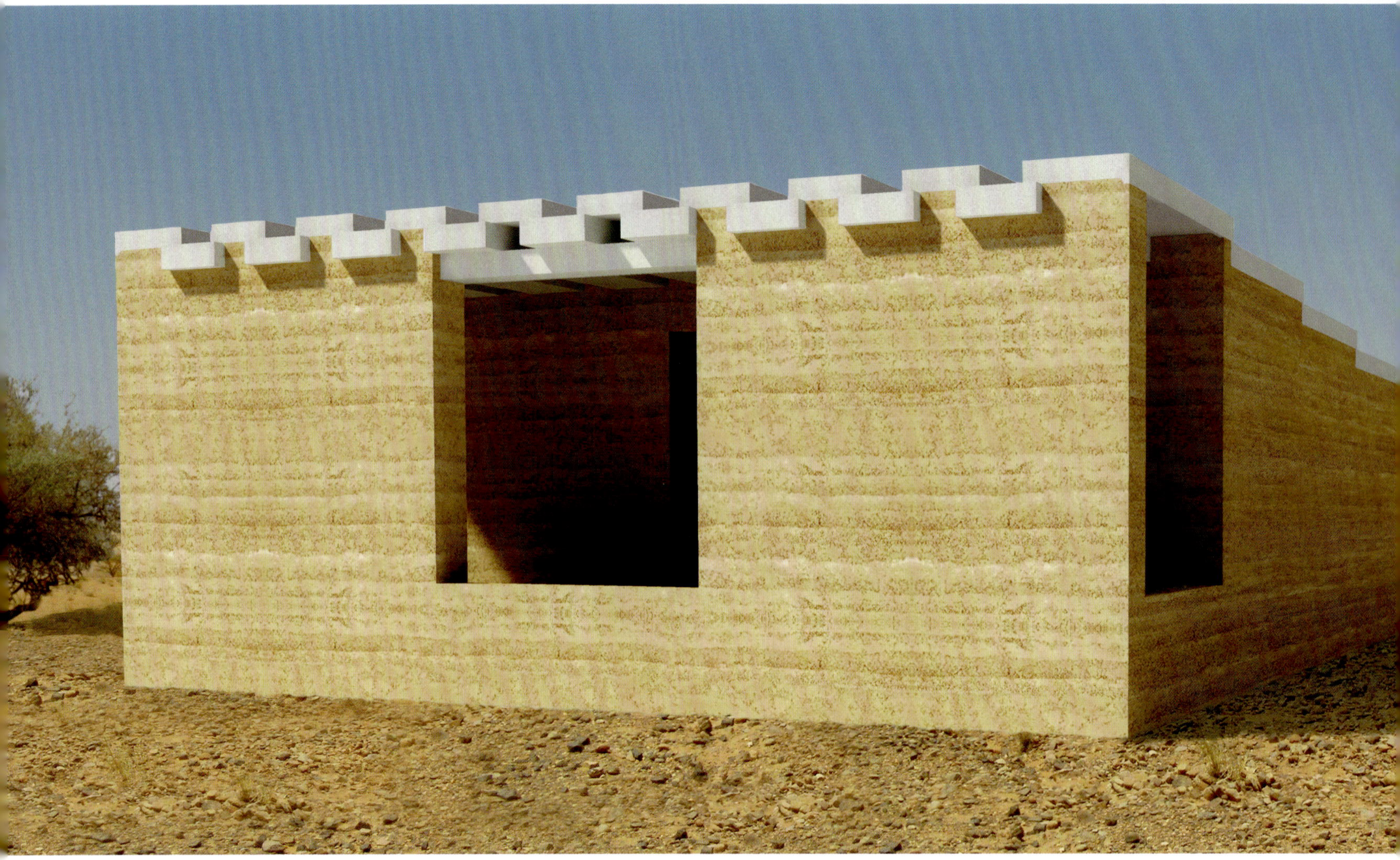

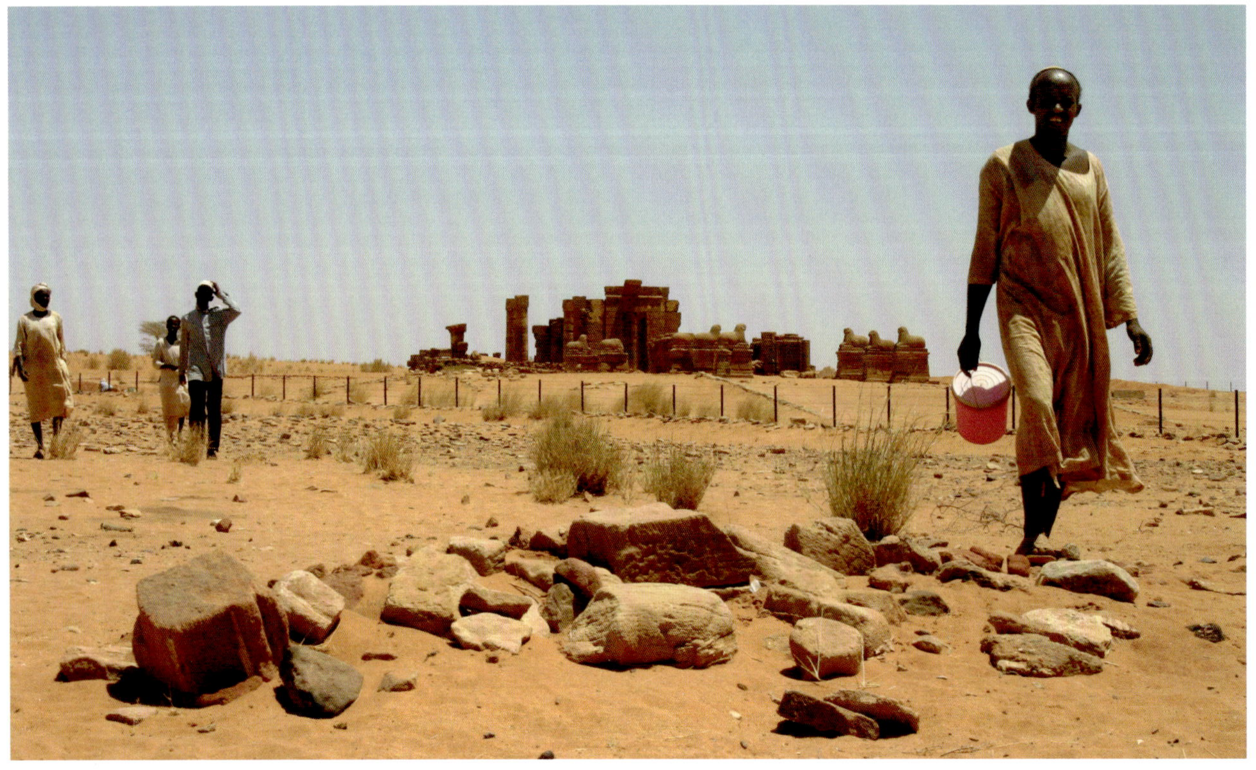

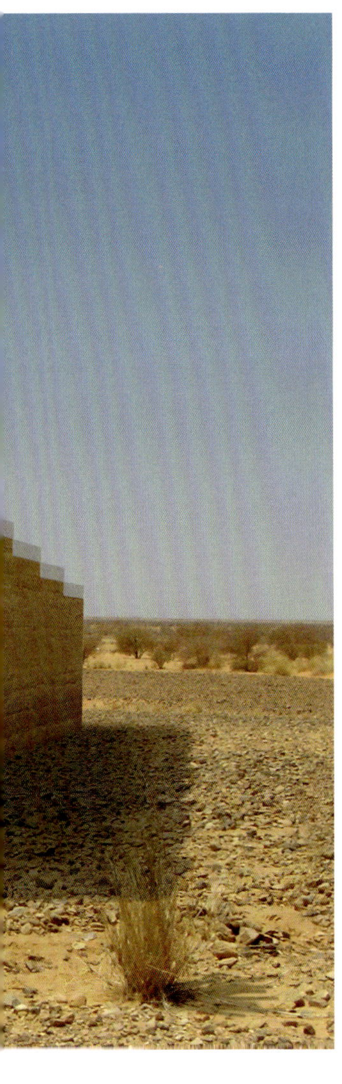

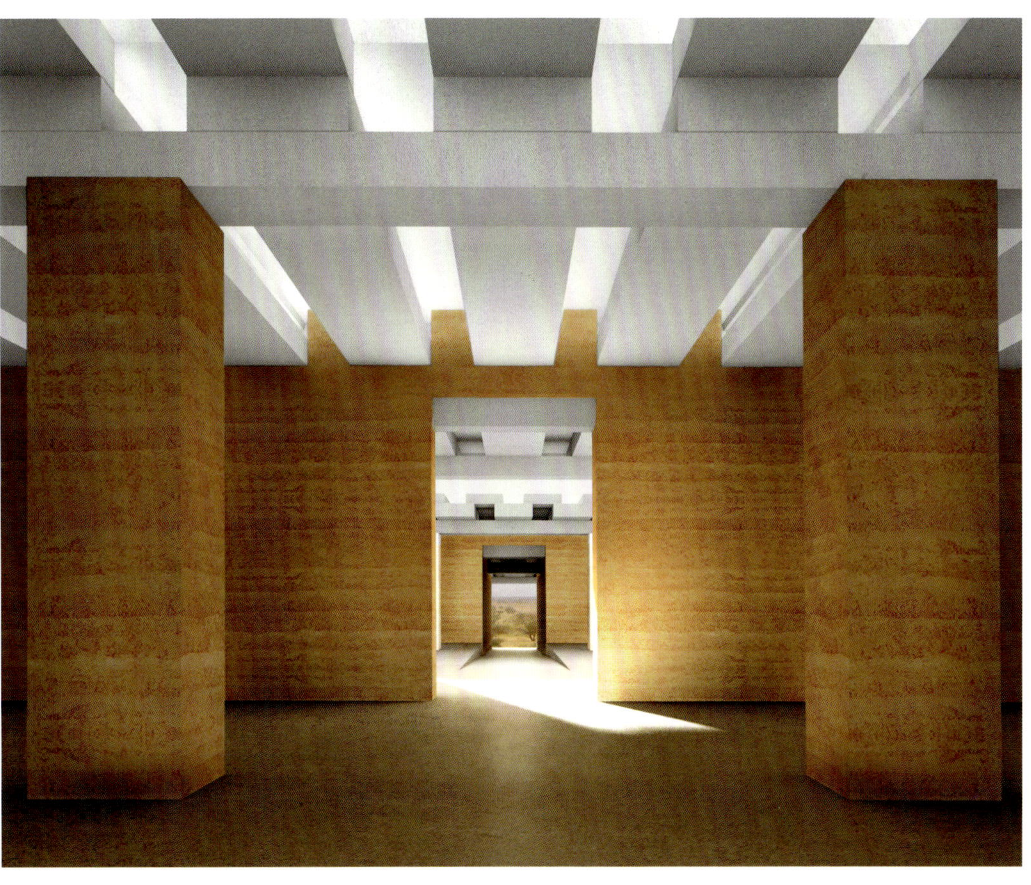

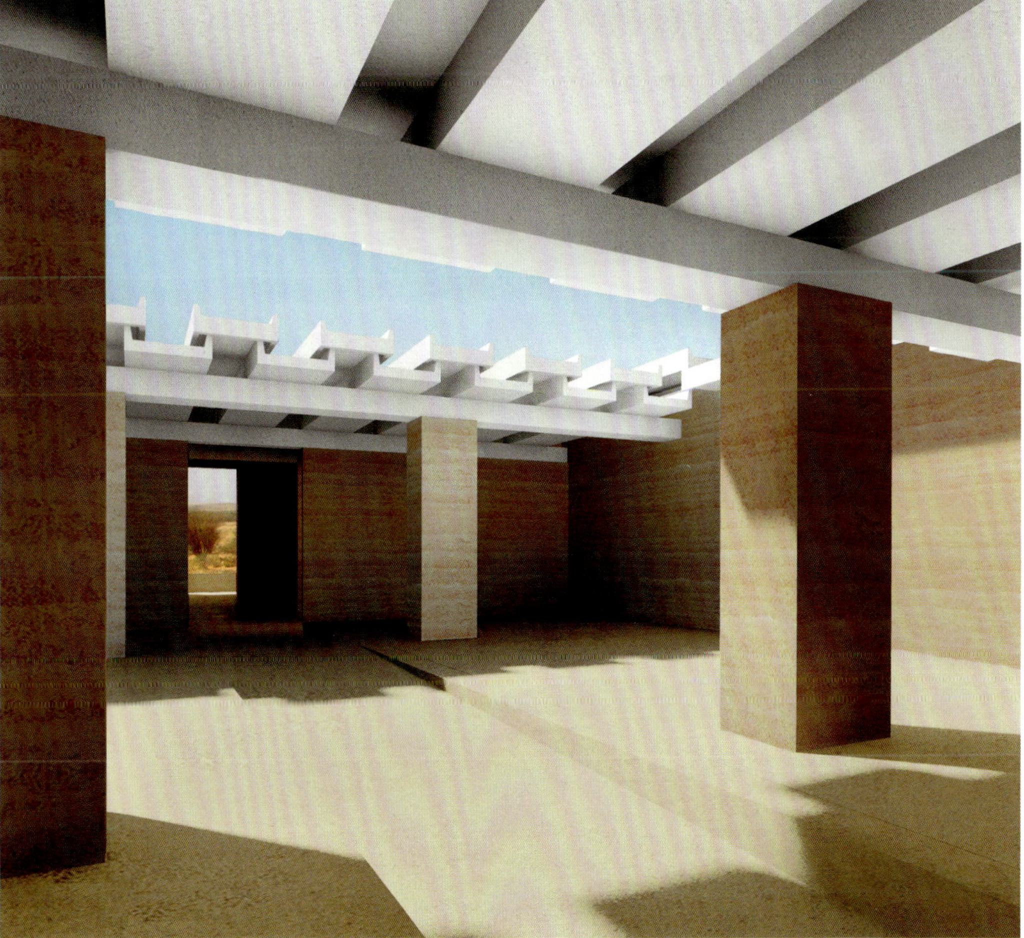

↖   Exterior, looking north.

←   Archaeological site.

↗   Exhibition hall,
    looking north.
    Inner courtyard,
    looking south.

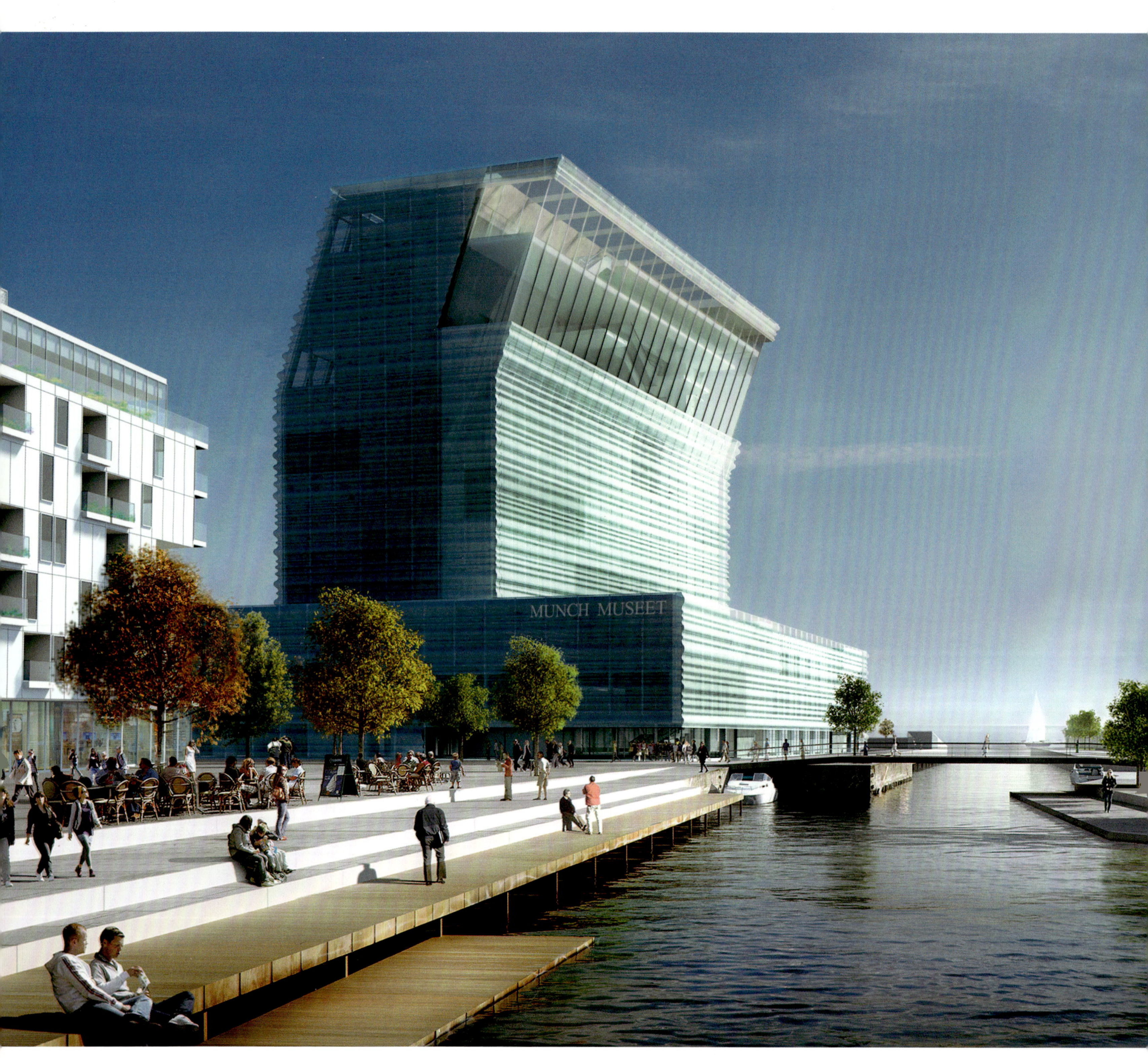
MUNCH MUSEET

Munchmuseet

Oslo, Norway

estudio Herreros, Madrid
Construction 2015–2019, opening 2019
Building 26,300 sq. m
The museum's permanent collection of works by Edvard Munch and special exhibitions

It was in 1940 that Edvard Munch bequeathed his artwork to the city of Oslo. More than 1,000 paintings, nearly 18,000 prints, close to 8,000 drawings and watercolours, as well as other objects, came into the city's possession after the artist's death in 1944. Since 1963 parts of the collection have been on display in the Munchmuseet. Now the collection is to be moved into a new building that offers modern technical equipment and more display space. For this assignment estudio Herreros designed a structure that wholly accords with Munch's wishes: it is accessible not only to museum visitors but to the entire city of Oslo.

The elegant structure, its top third tilting forward, towers eleven storeys above the harbour. A café on the top floor is also open outside of museum hours, and with its almost completely glazed frontage it offers an expansive view of the city. As visitors ride the escalators upward behind the glass façade they can see Oslo's history unfolding below: from the harbour, then and now an important trading post, the industrious town extended inland to become a lively metropolis that is the country's cultural and industrial centre. This new elevated point of view establishes a strong relation between the heritage of the art collection of Edvard Munch and his native city.

The new museum structure based on the "Lambda" design by estudio Herreros deliberately towers above the surrounding buildings and places a new visual accent above the harbour. The projecting upper third gives the otherwise plain façade an unmistakable, forward-thrusting dynamism. In his landscapes and city scenes Munch himself liked to work with an exaggerated perspective so as to direct the viewer's eye to what was essential.[1] Even if the painter was not their primary inspiration, estudio Herreros has managed to employ this same principle in architecture.

The project was initially received as controversial and was heavily debated by the public, especially because in Norway's highly egalitarian society it is considered improper for an individual to stand out too much. The architects entered into a dialogue with the city and its inhabitants, taking criticism of their initial designs into consideration, and further developing the building until it was approved by the authorities. Now, the Munchmuseet's eleven storeys are new to Oslo's largely horizontal architecture, and dominate the cityscape.

Over the bearing structure of concrete and steel a sophisticated, multi-layered curtain wall of glass and perforated metal masks the floors' irregular openings. In the museum itself light breaks through the glass front and pours into the building's interior public areas in contrast to the artificially lit exhibition rooms, while the ground floor is not only illuminated from the side but also from above. The building appears to consist of levels the visitor can enter and experience. The light streaming in through the translucent curtain wall of triple-layered glass and perforated aluminium lends the structure a new, almost magical quality,[2] making it seem more flexible and fluid.

This flexibility was desired; exhibition rooms are of different sizes and heights. Sculptures and large format paintings can be appreciated in the larger galleries, prints and drawings in the smaller, more intimate cabinets. Instead of the traditional, somewhat rigid enfilade of rooms through which visitors are forced, here spaces can be set aside or opened, depending on the given exhibition. Around these inner exhibition spaces the museum is a structure that is accessible at no cost, open to Oslo and the world.

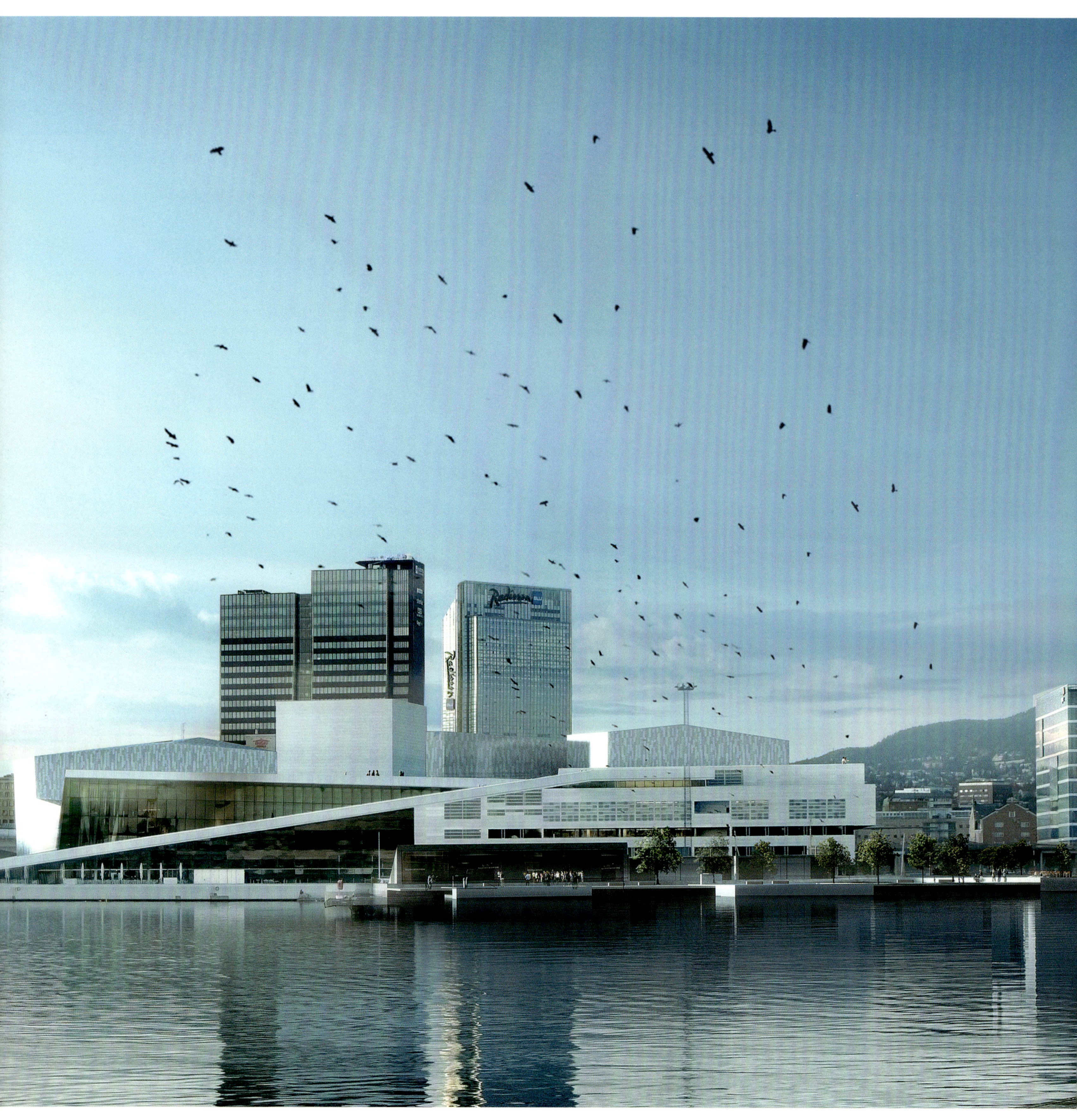

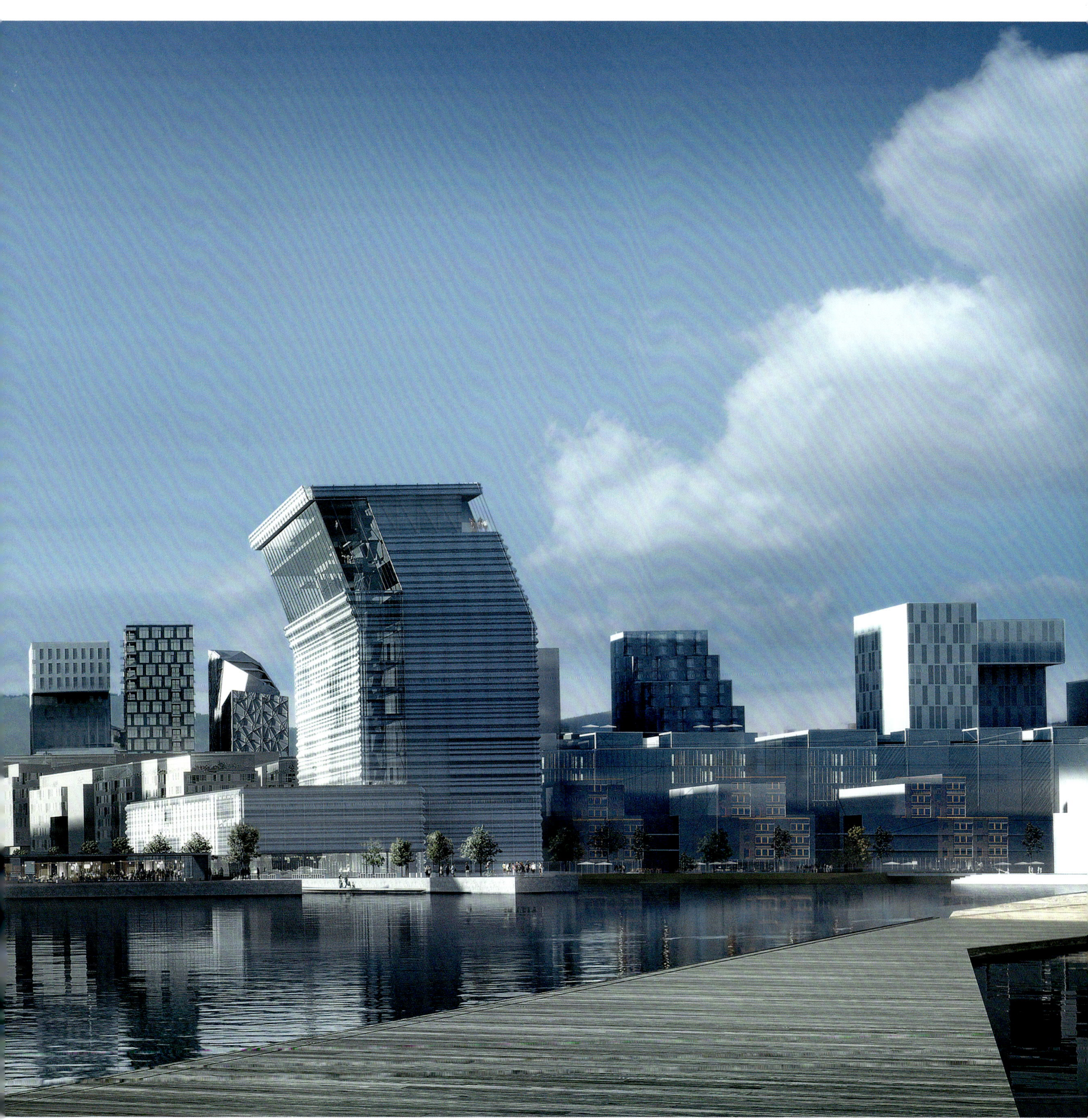

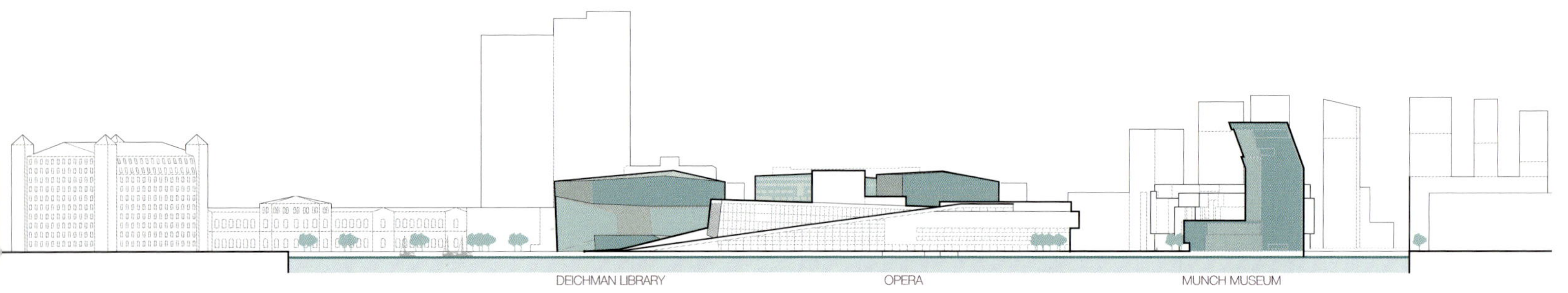

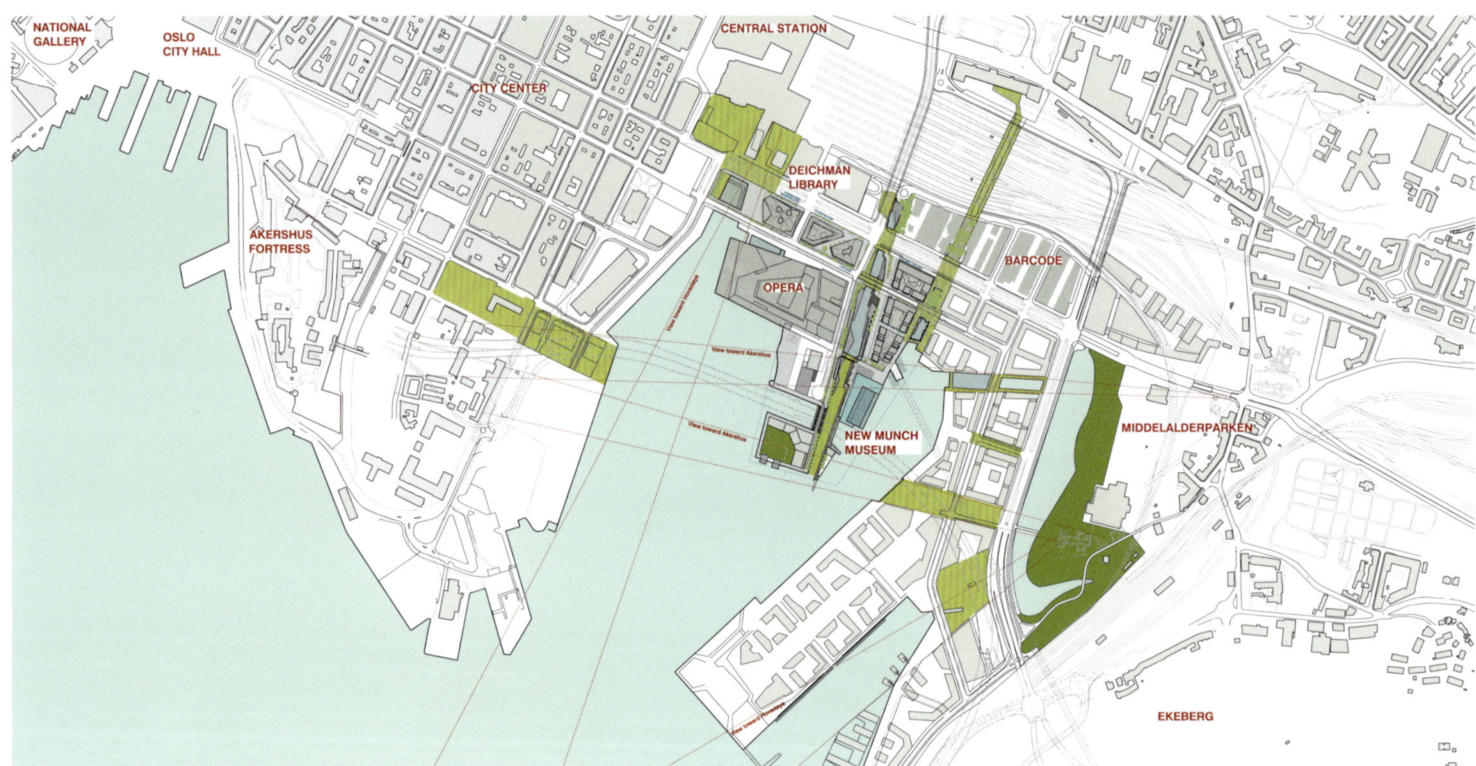

↑ Urban context, elevation
   from the south.
   Site plan.

→ Elevation, from the south.
   Section, west–east.

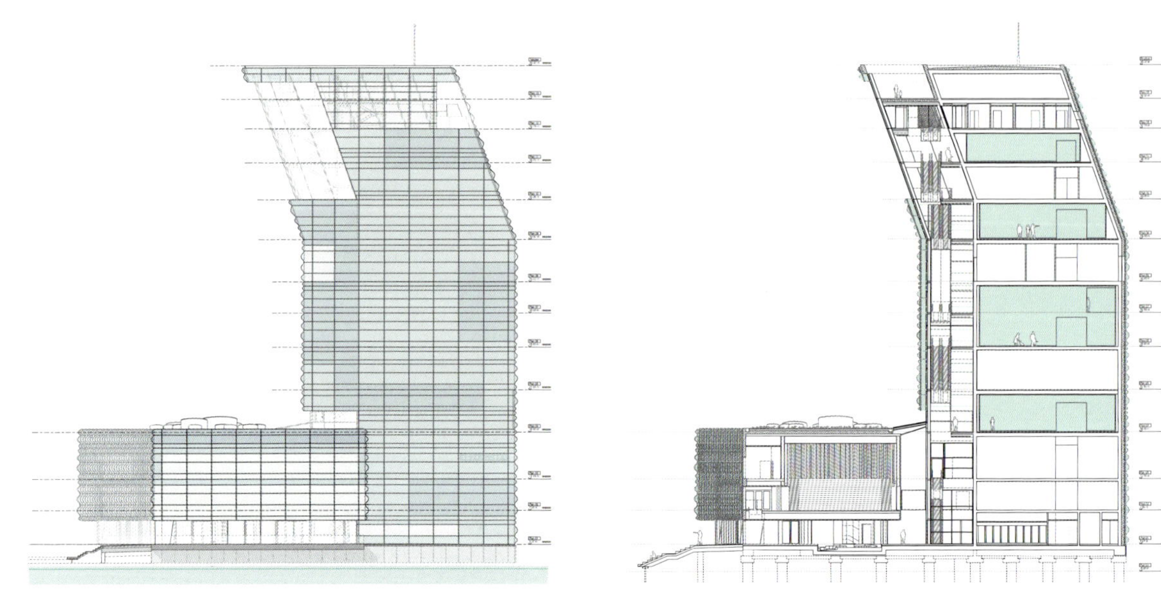

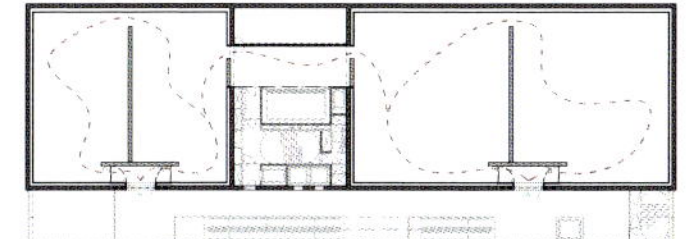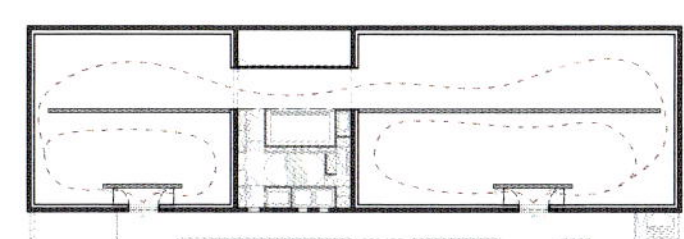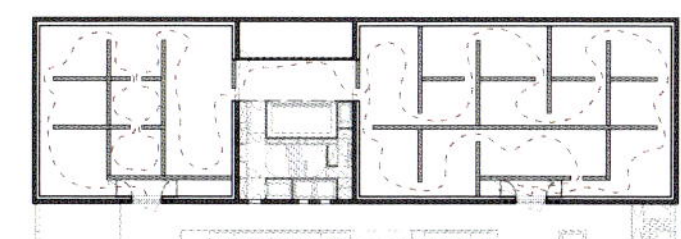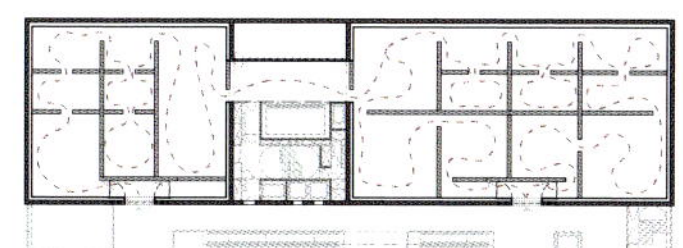

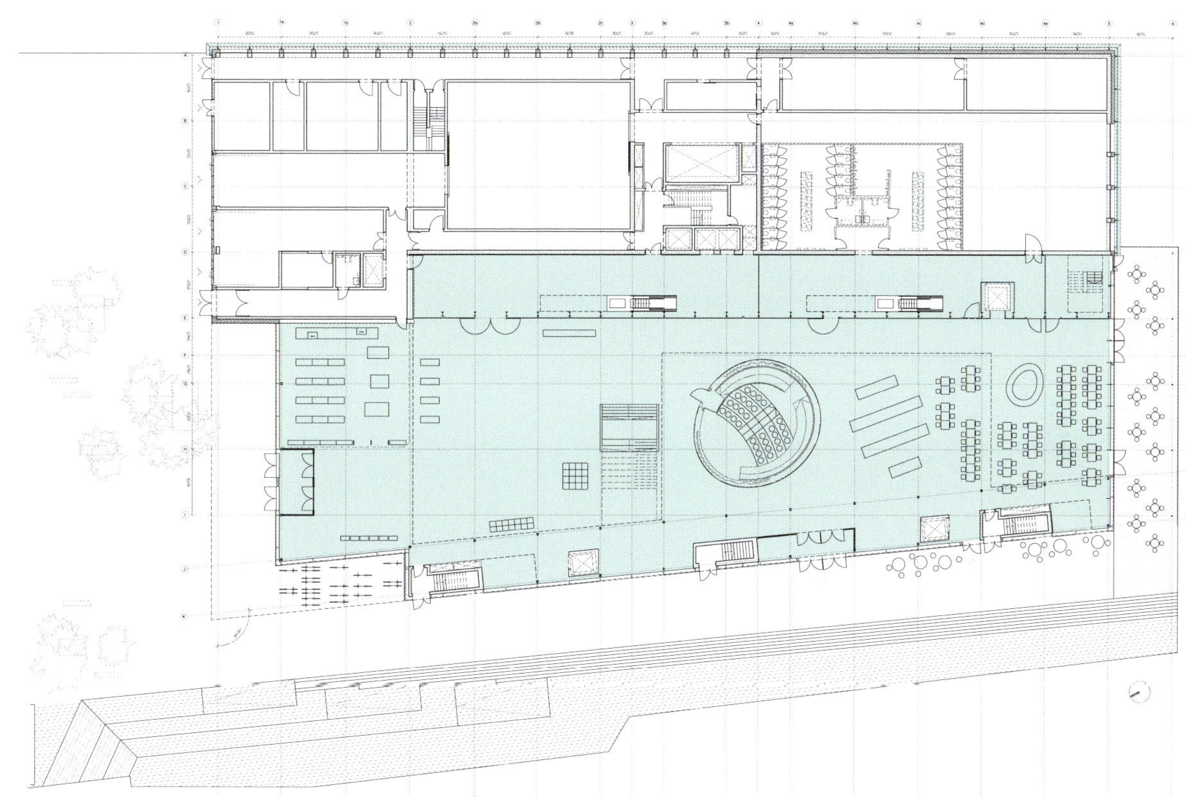

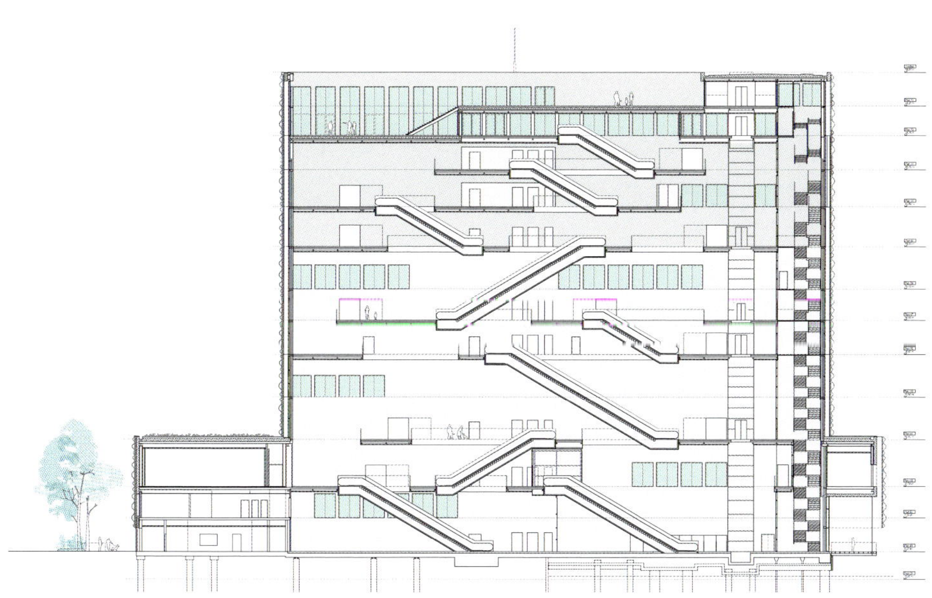

↑ Exhibition rooms:
layout examples.
Ground-floor plan.

← Section, north–south.

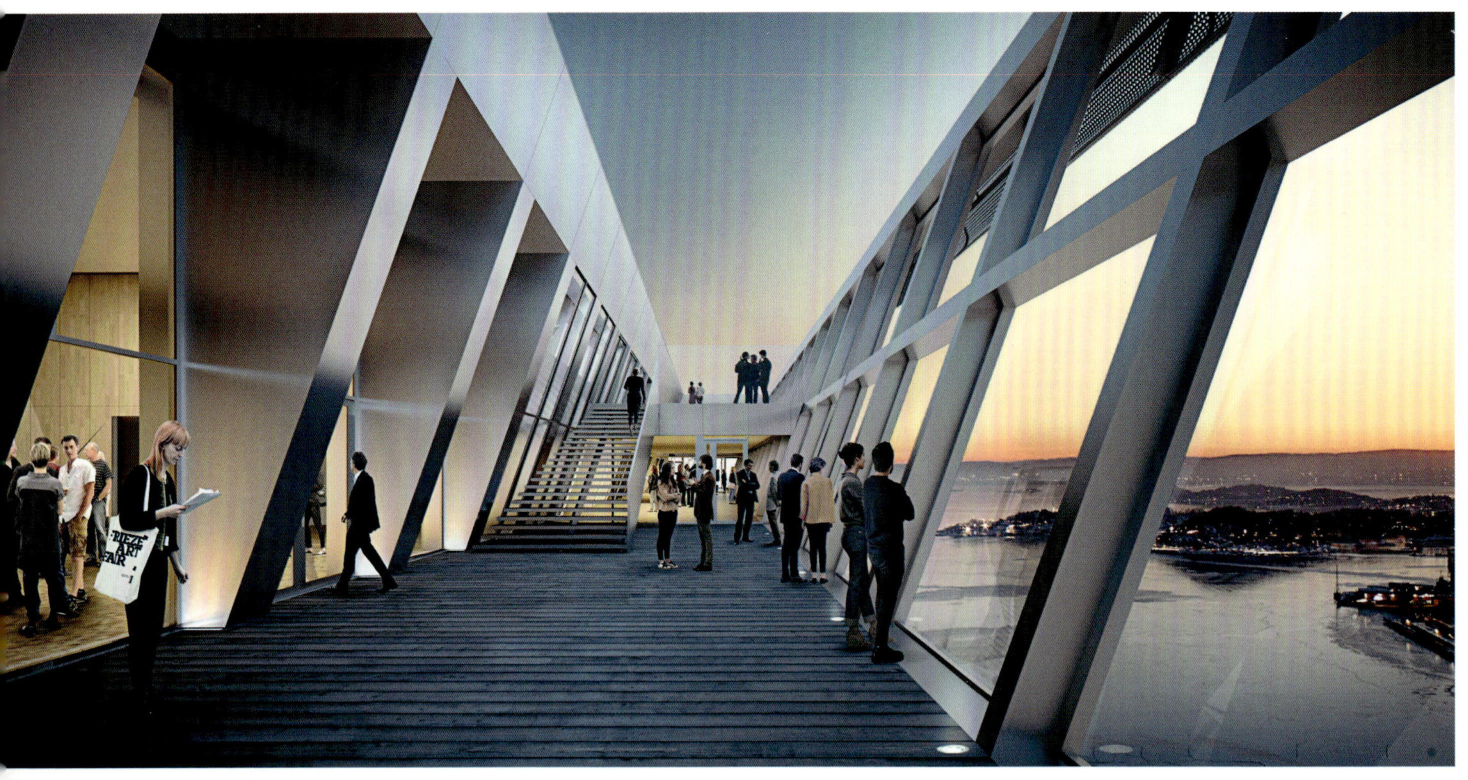

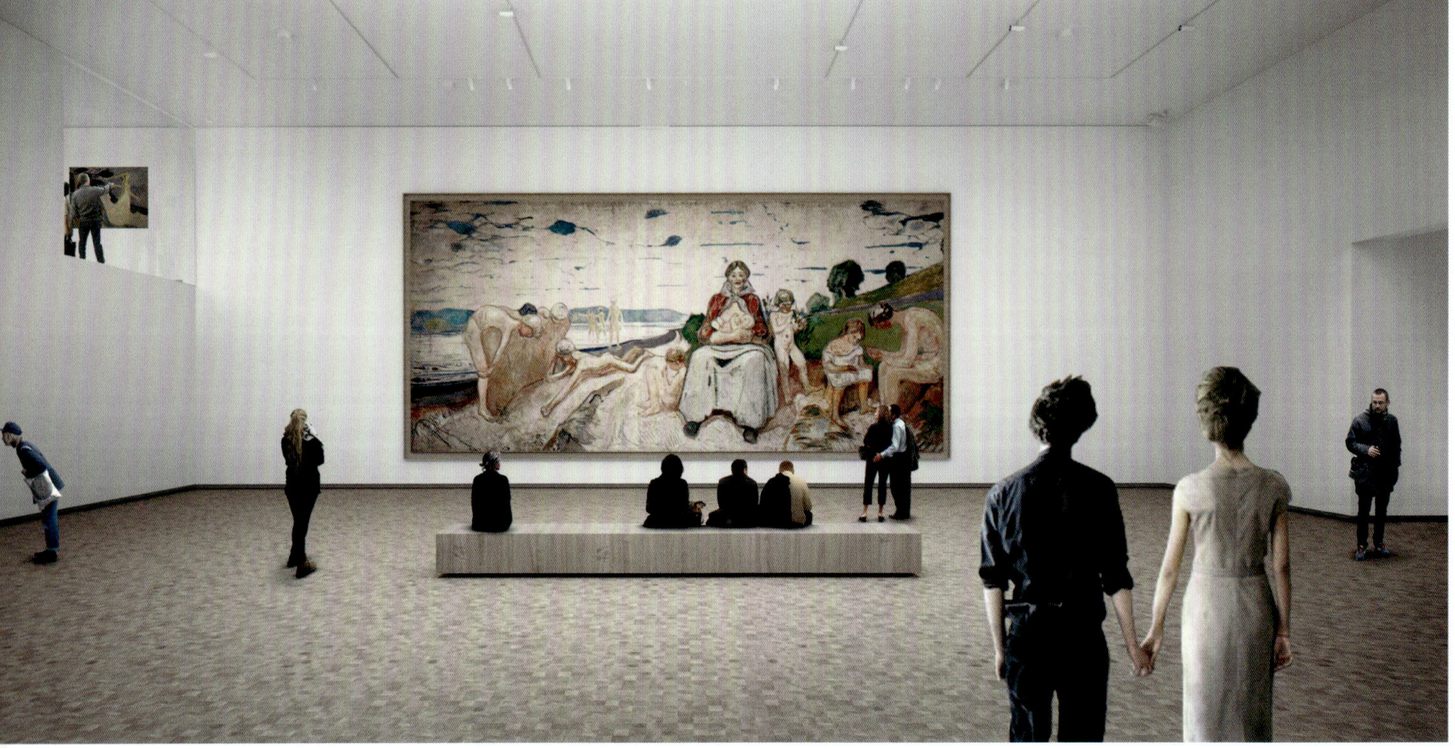

↑ Observatory terrace, western façade.
Monumental artwork gallery.

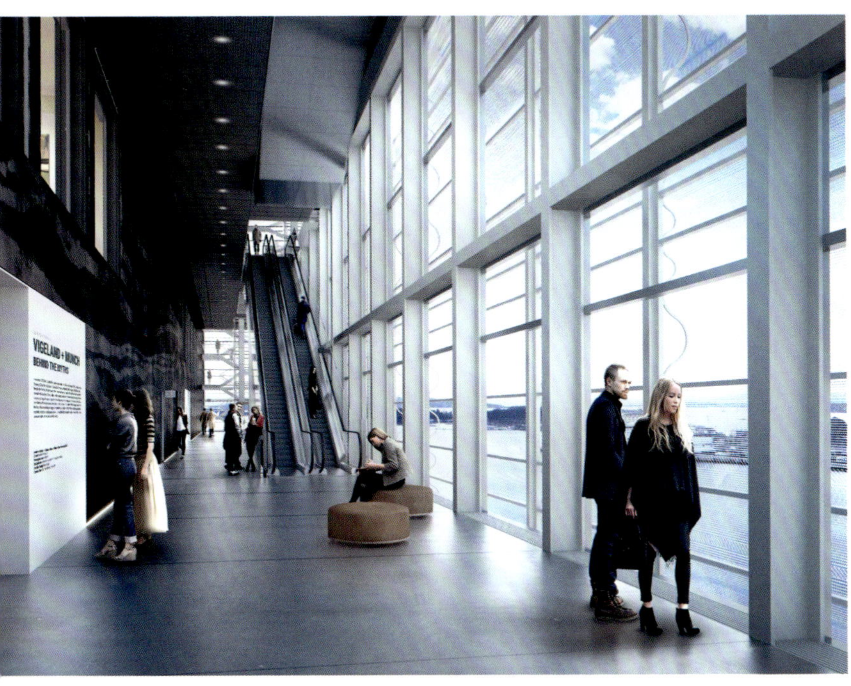

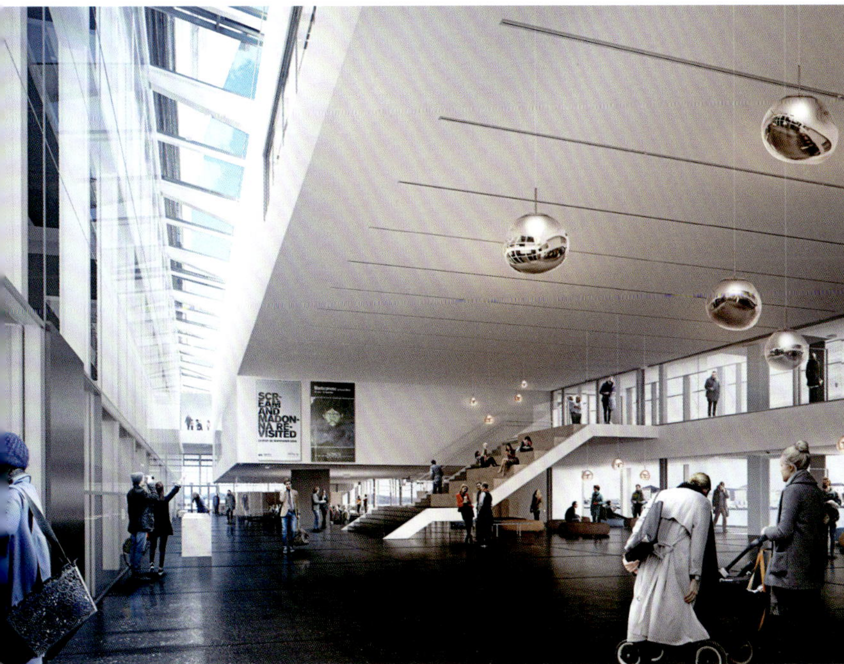

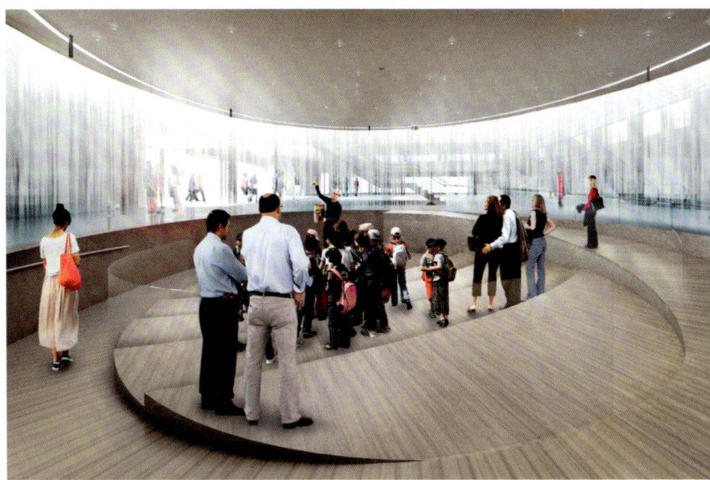

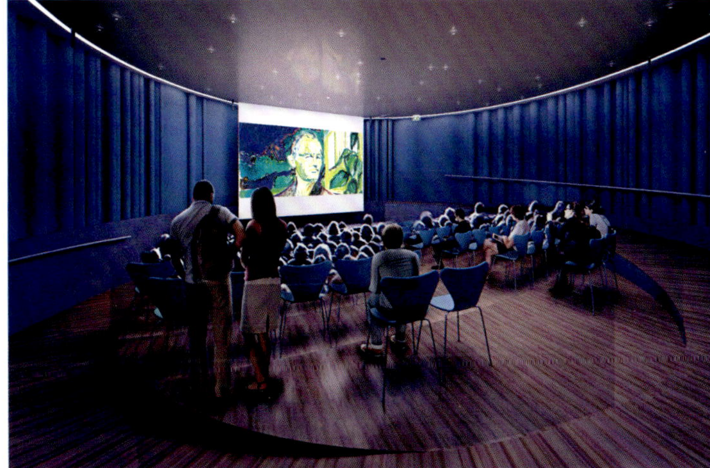

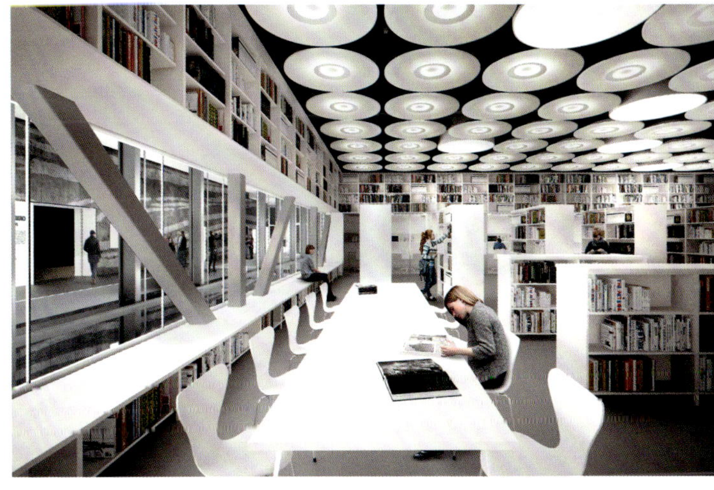

↑ Circulation space, "dynamic part".
Public access plaza.

↑ Cinema: open, closed.
Research library.

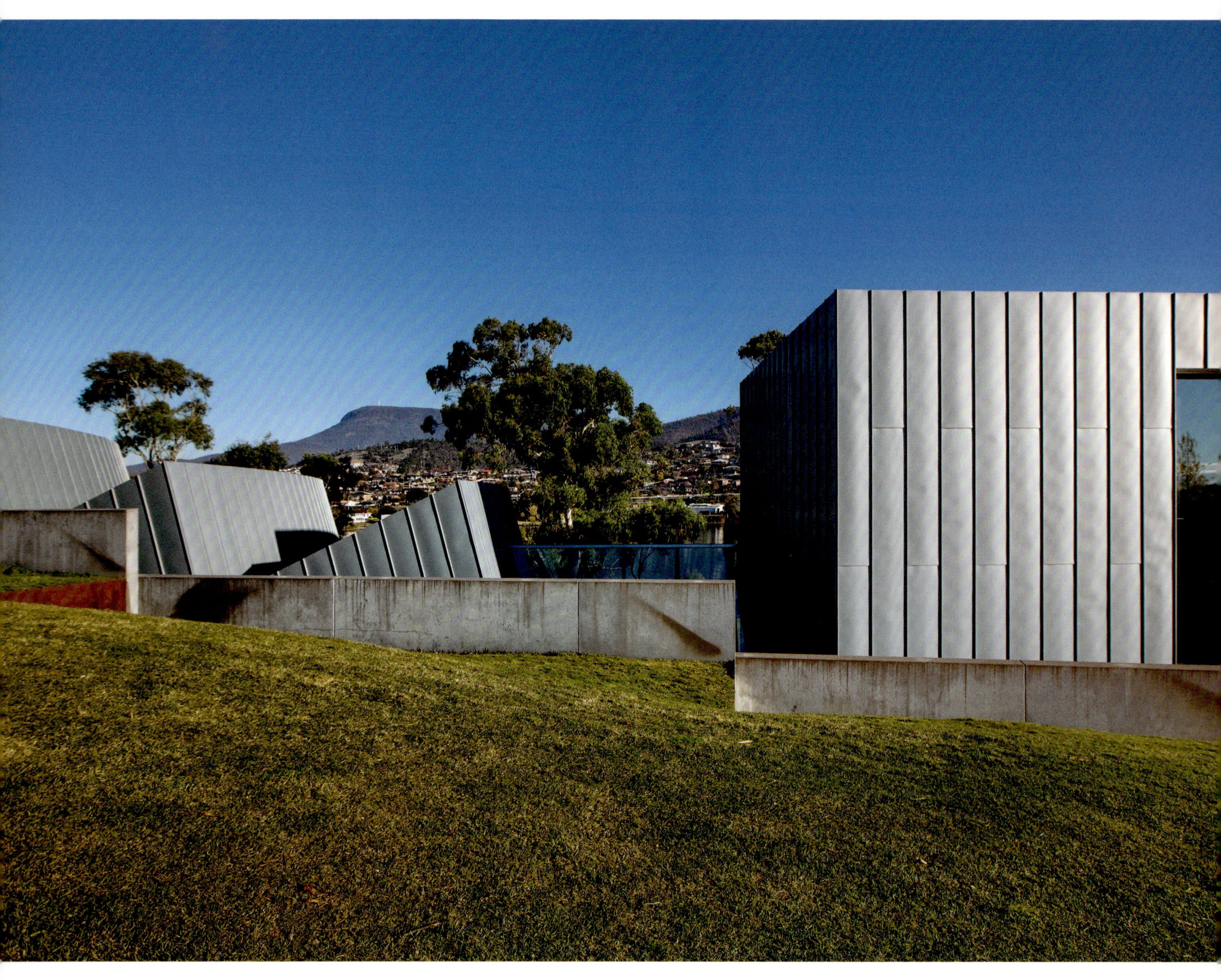

MONA Museum of Old and New Art

Berriedale, Tasmania

Fender Katsalidis Architects, Melbourne
Opened 2011
Building 9,500 sq. m
Antiquities and contemporary artwork from around the world

The architect Nonda Katsalidis recalls that David Walsh knew precisely what sort of building he wanted for his art collection: "a functional receptacle, not [an] architectural spectacle".[1] The aboveground portion of the building is certainly bland: with its red metal and grey concrete it is more reminiscent of an industrial plant than a temple of art. But the underground spaces, which amount to the greater part of the museum, are hardly banal storerooms. They are spectacular in the best sense of the word: exciting and sensational.

Visitors descend a steel spiral staircase past three floors to a depth of seventeen metres below the surface, into windowless, in part only dimly lit, rooms where Walsh, with help from his curators and advisors, exhibits the art he likes. It is not arranged by styles or periods – it is arranged the way Walsh prefers, which makes for unexpected, exciting combinations and represents a very personal engagement with art.[2]

The museum was placed underground so as not to compromise the aboveground, Modernist buildings from the 1950s designed by the Australian architect Roy Grounds. So the builders bored into the island's stone and created a space whose walls are raw, unworked rock, then capped it with a coffered concrete ceiling. Here the space itself reflects aspects of the collection: Walsh collects both ancient artefacts like mummies as well as contemporary art, so the natural stone evokes prehistoric times while the coffered ceiling can be associated with antiquity, the Renaissance and Modernism. The light installation *Amarna*, by James Turrell, which stands on the museum's roof and was an addition to the grounds in 2015, even suggests a timeless eternity. Every day at sunrise and sunset its square surface on slender supports shimmers in various colours and links the building and visitors with the elements. *Amarna* (2015) is the largest of the more than eighty so-called Skyspace installations Turrell has to date placed in high or remote spots around the world.

Fender Katsalidis Architects see their job as making art accessible through the spaces in which it is shown – and here they succeeded in an exemplary way.[3] A staircase of Corten steel, which looks more like a sculpture than a simple building amenity and that visually resembles the museum's outer shell in its rust-red colour, snakes between the rock, the concrete and the small number of walls that structure the giant cave.[4] It is one of a handful of elements that seem familiar; otherwise, you feel your way through this wild, cluttered, very personal museum as through a maze, suddenly discovering between solid walls simple wire stands reminiscent of museum storerooms on which art worth millions has been hung without ceremony as if flung there, become one with the space and the experience of art provided here with almost brutal force.

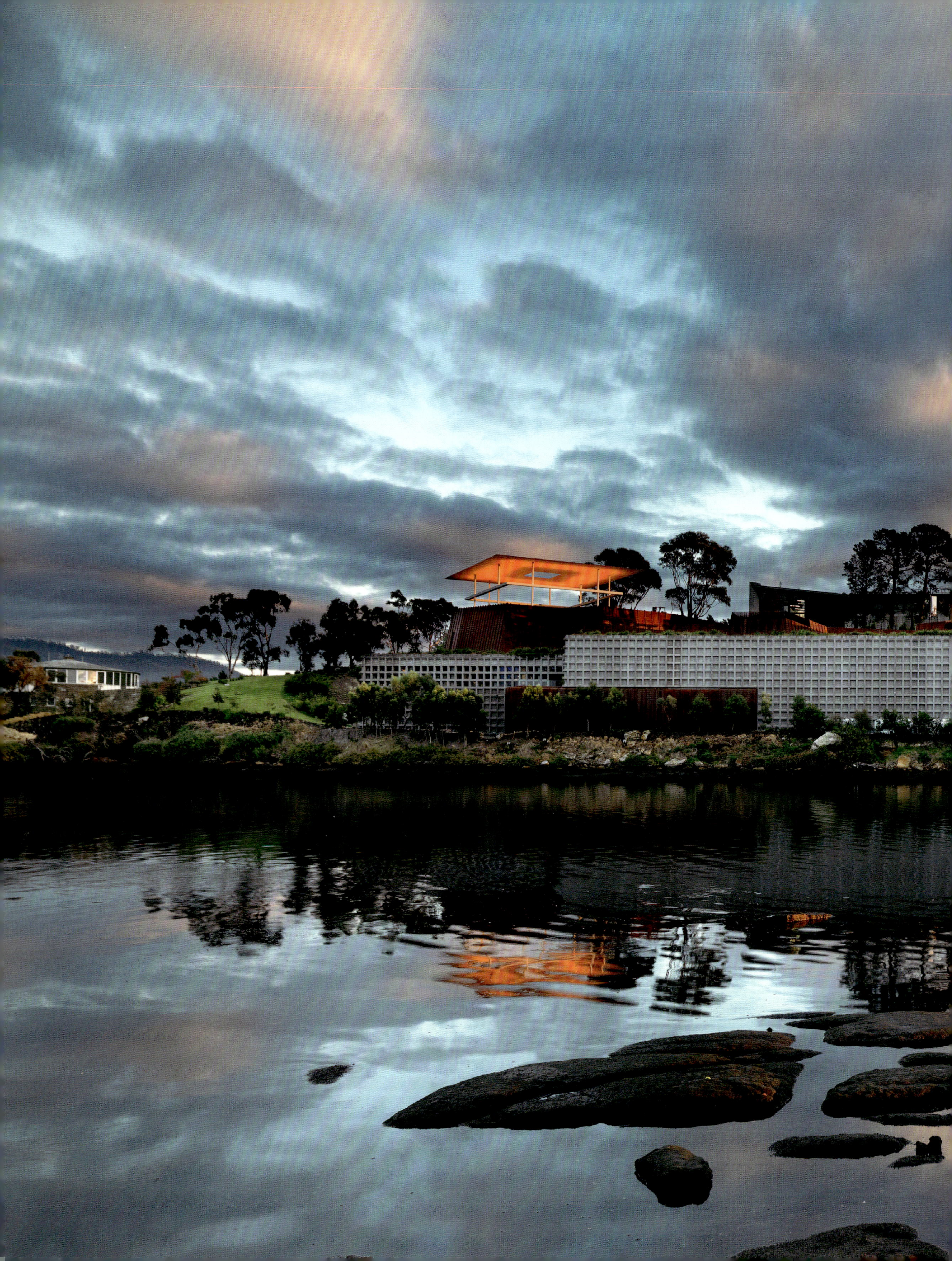

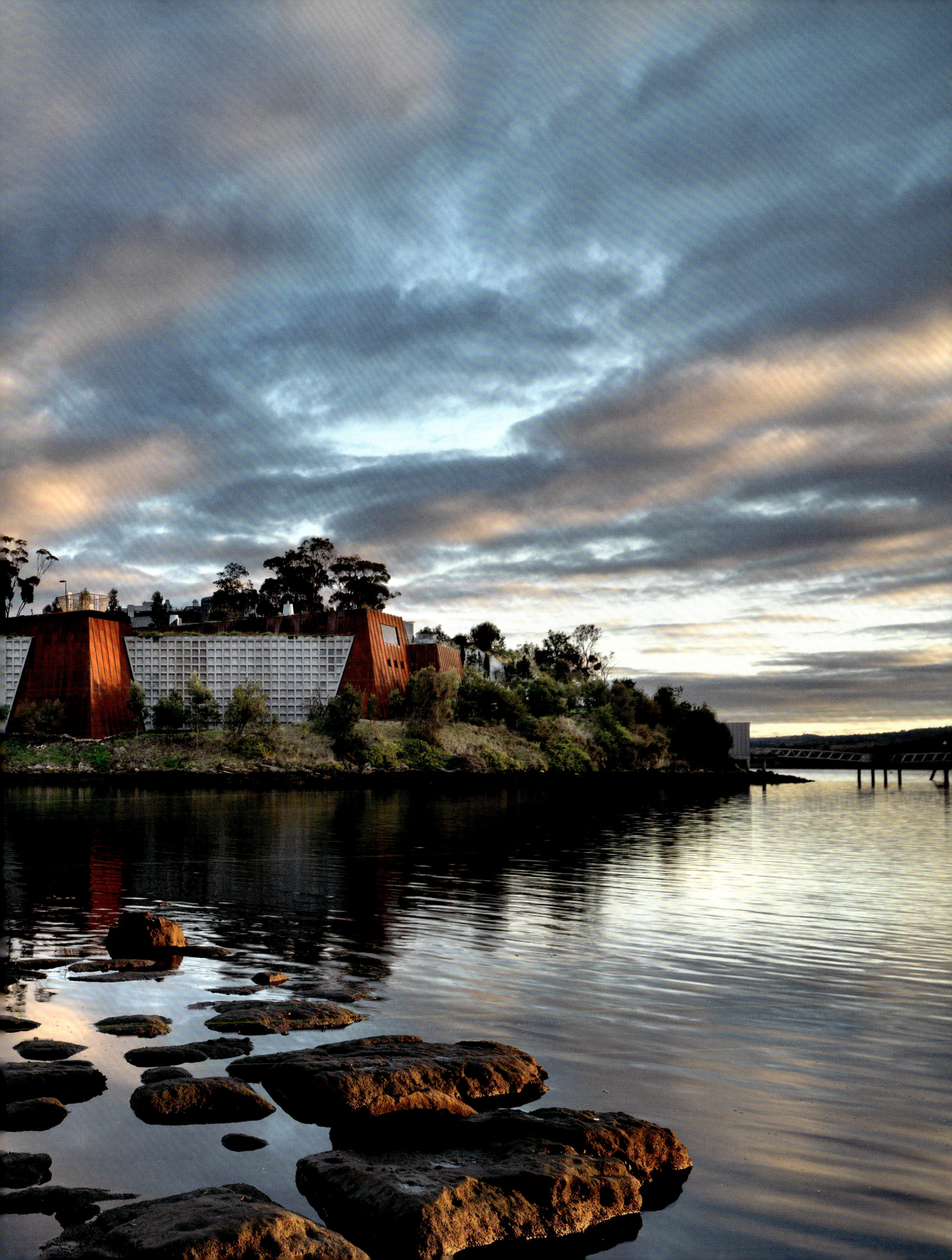

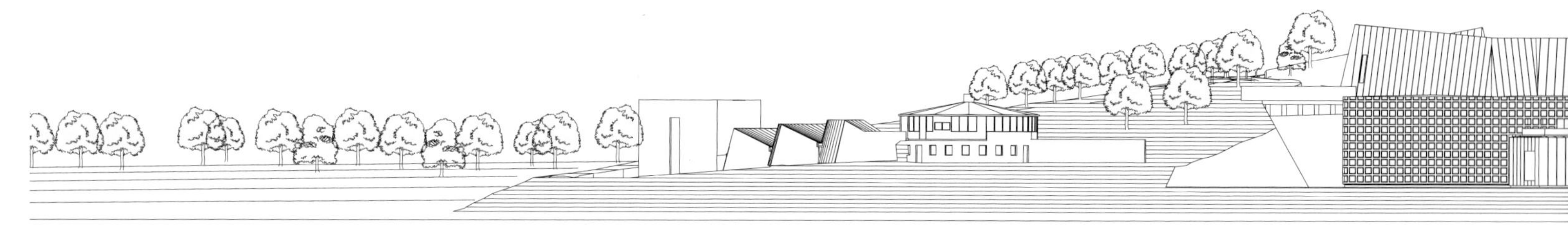

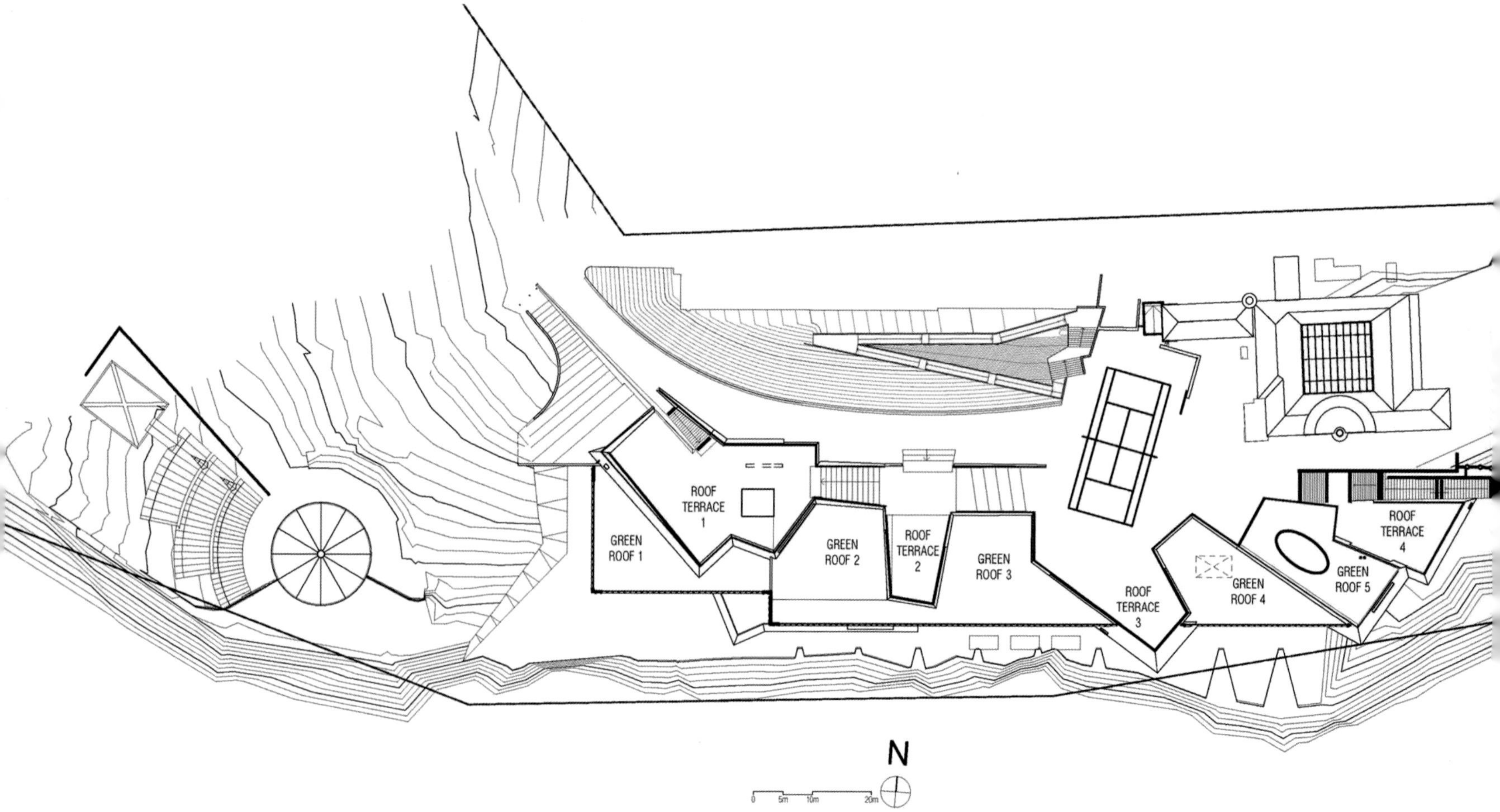

↑   Elevation, looking north.
Site plan.

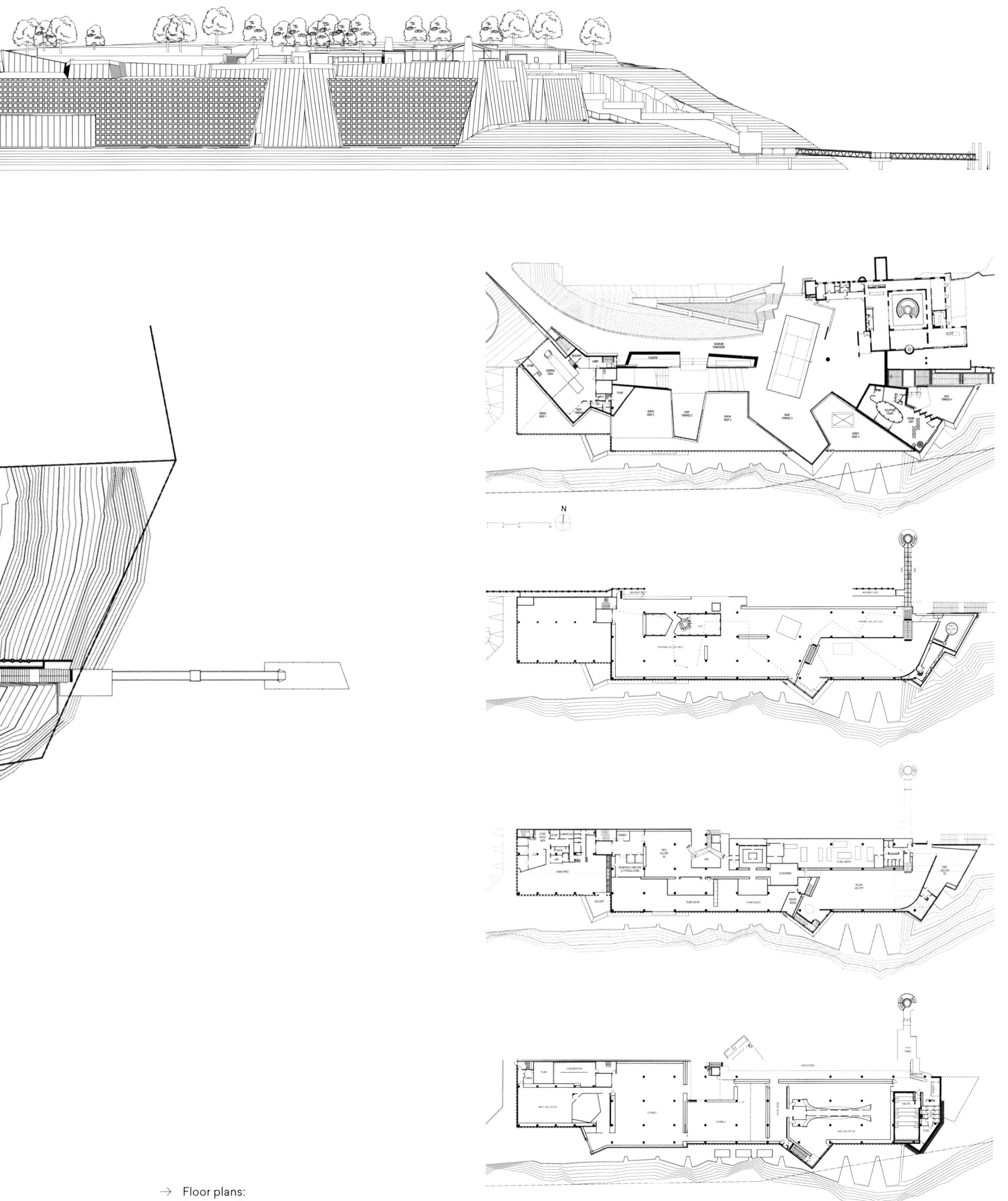

→ Floor plans:
 0, -1, -2, -3.

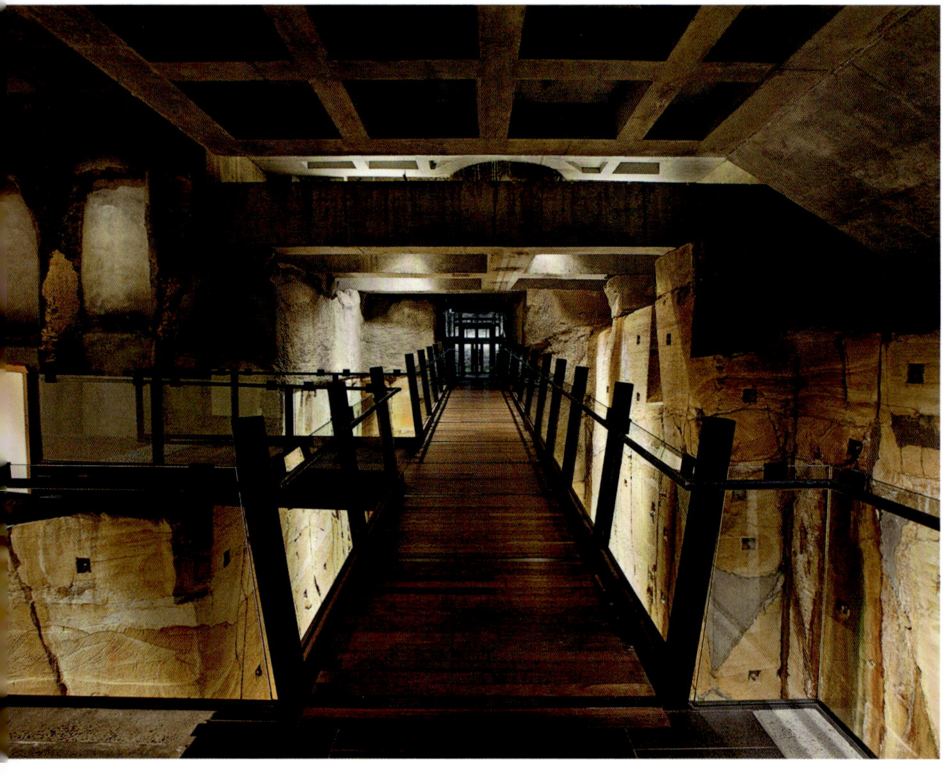

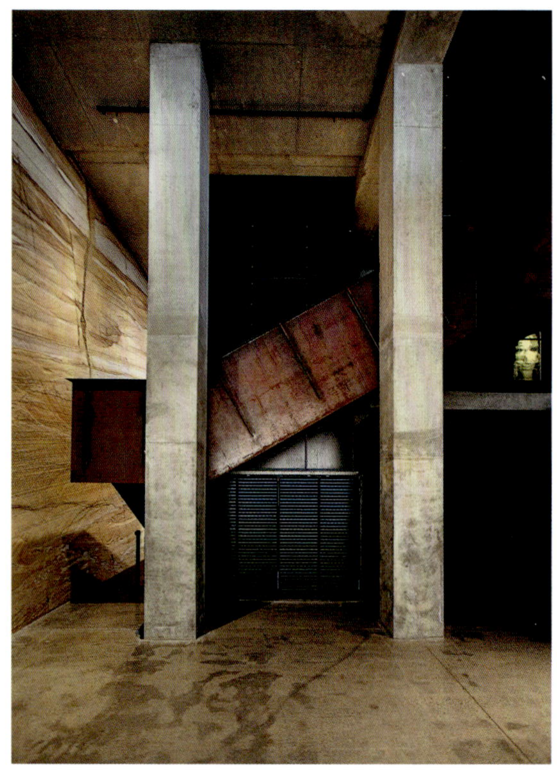

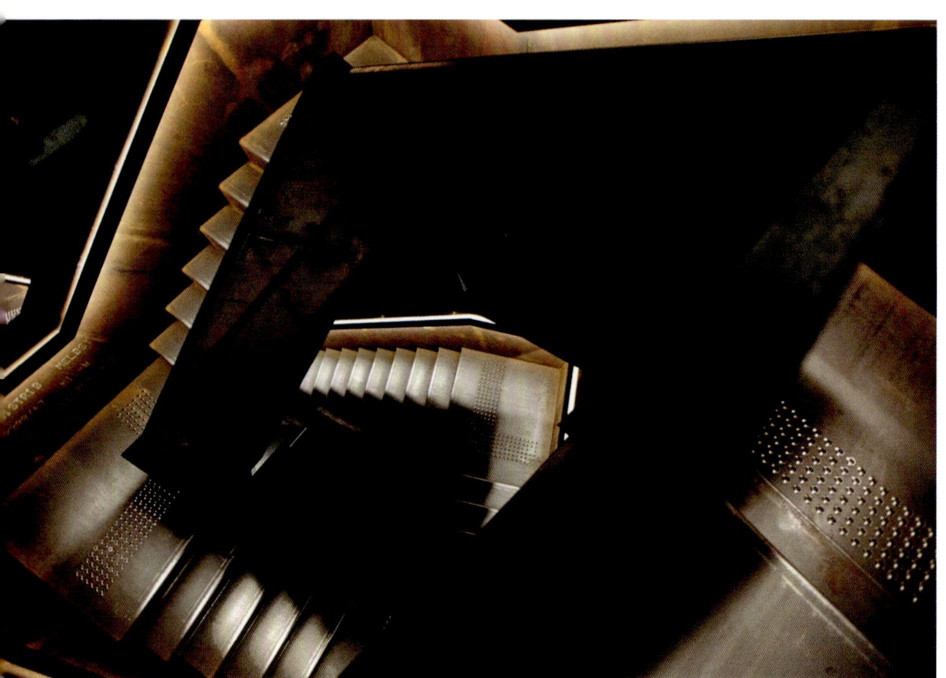

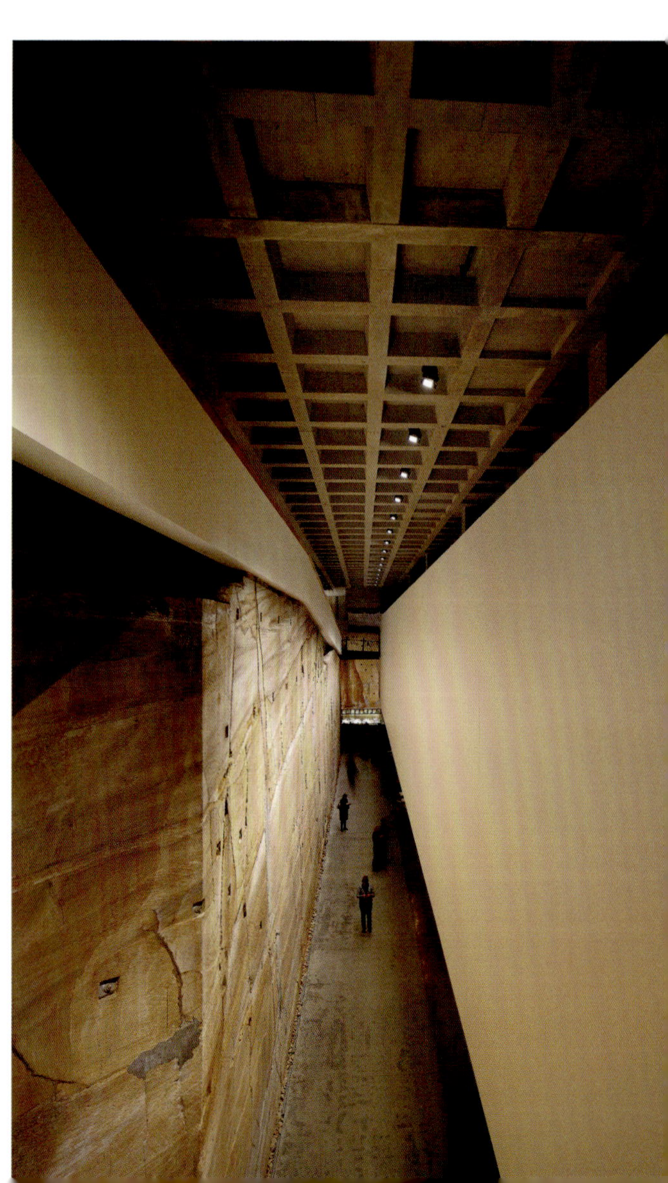

↑ Museum interior, detail.
Staircase.

↗ Museum interior of
steel, concrete and
sandstone, detail.

→ 'The Void'.

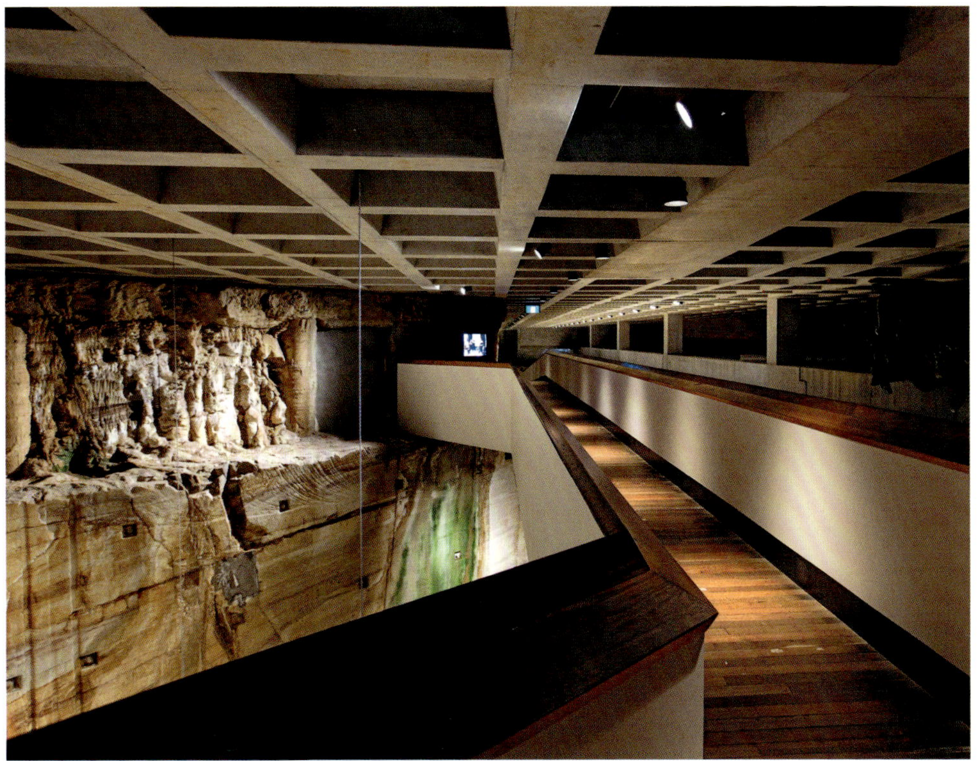

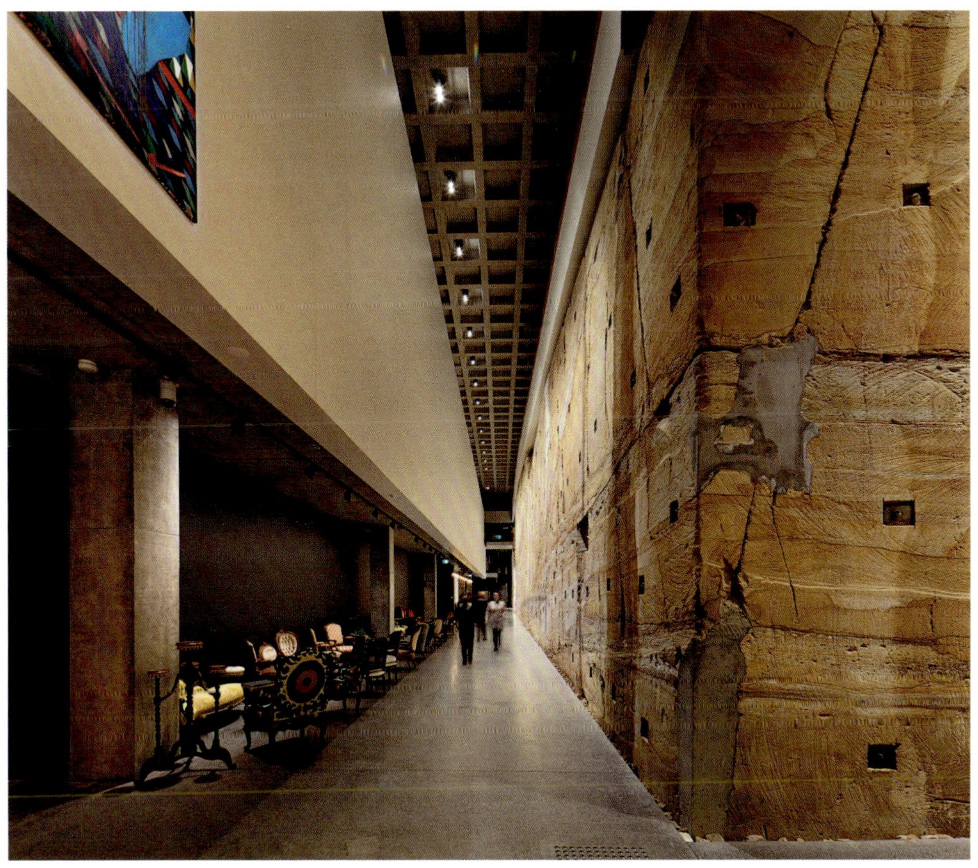

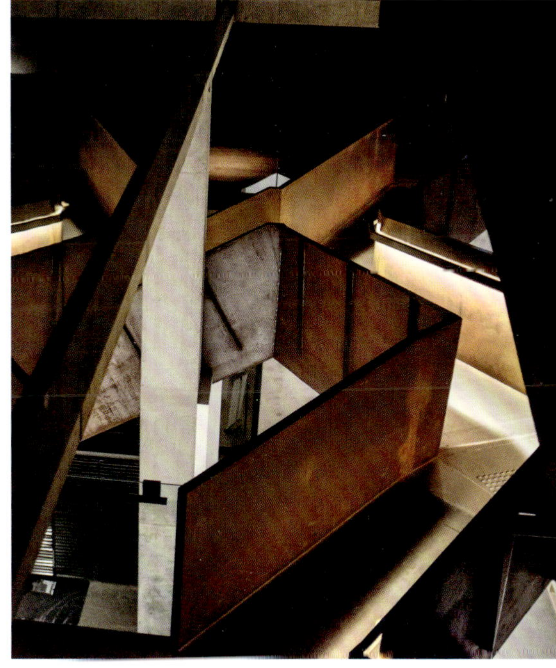

← Museum interior, detail.

↙ 'The Void'.

↓ Abstract reflections within the interior.

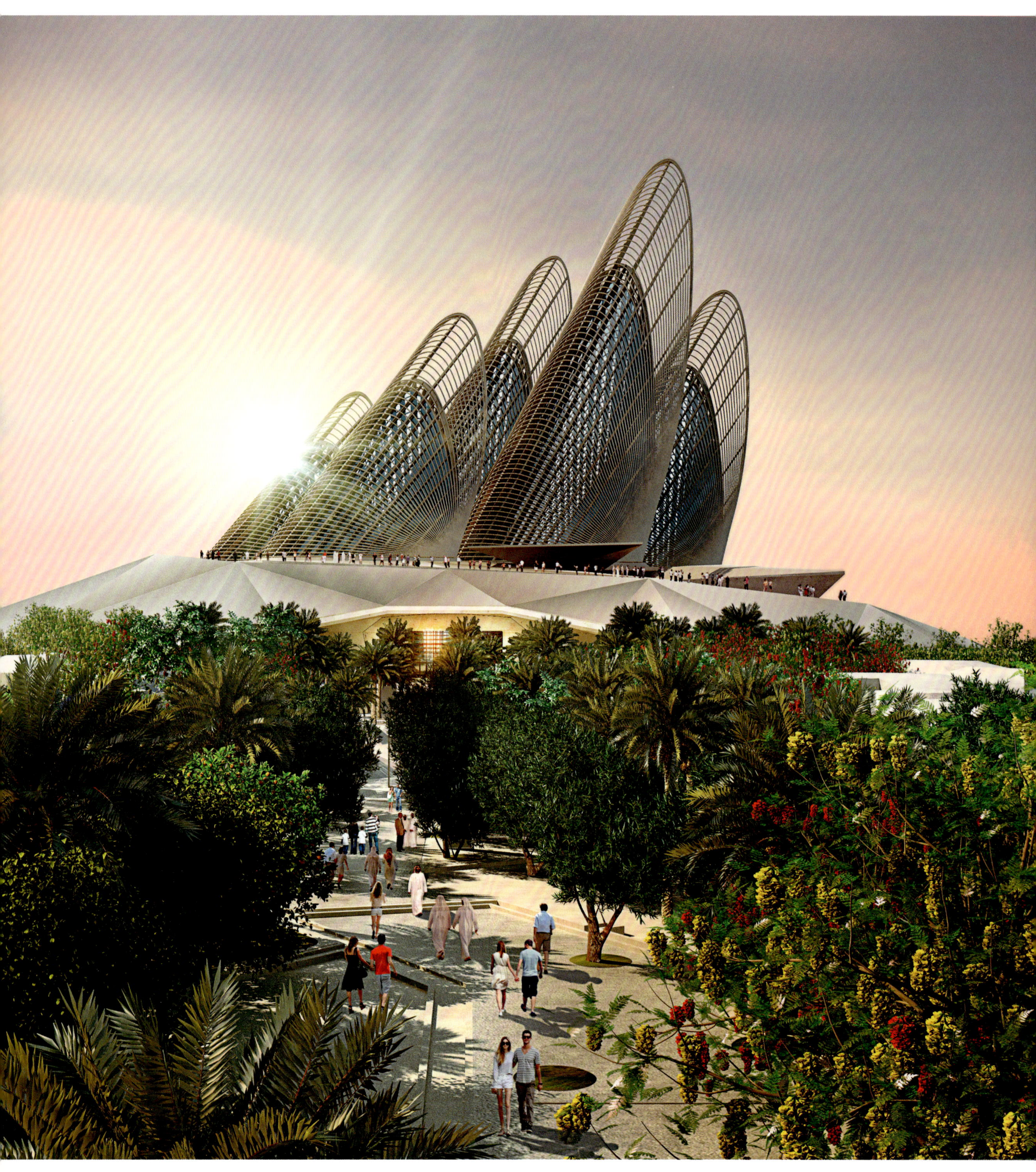

Zayed National Museum

Abu Dhabi, United Arab Emirates

Foster + Partners, London
Opening 2020
Building 38,000 sq. m
History, culture and the social and economic transformation of the Emirates

The United Arab Emirates' first national museum had major architectural competition from the start. It is to stand in the Saadiyat Island Cultural District just off the coast, where the Louvre and the Guggenheim are also creating their Middle East outposts. The difficulty for the designers was therefore adapting to surroundings only now being created and providing contrast to two iconic structures of which no plans were yet known. Foster + Partners met this challenge by creating a visible landmark that makes an abstract reference to the natural landscape of UAE with five aerodynamic profiles arising from an artificial mound.

The Zayed National Museum impresses at first sight with five elongated vertical elements. In front of the visitor, approaching the museum by way of a bridge, these steel structures, painted to match the colour of the coastal sand, loom up into the sky at an angle. They reach heights of as much as 125 metres, and serve as a natural cooling system for the museum on the ground floor. The hot air at the tips of the towers draws warm air upward out of the building owing to the chimney effect, while cooler air is drawn in from below.

The towers stand atop an artificial hill of interest for its geometric shape, which in abstract form traces the outlines of the United Arab Emirates. Jagged, angular, seemingly tumbled forms are penetrated by slender light shafts that serve to bathe the curved galleries inside the museum in natural sunlight. The large underground lobby with its skylight enjoys the same natural light. Like the towers, this space takes advantage of the prevailing thermal conditions.

A garden leads up from the coast to the complex of buildings, and is designed to retrace the life of Sheikh Zayed bin Sultan Al Nahyan. The first president of the United Arab Emirates after its independence in 1971 saw to it that there was a more equitable distribution of water in his country, planted 50,000 trees to make it green and was aware of ecological processes.[1] The museum celebrates his achievements with references to his person, his country and its history. Even its colours were selected to that end: its sandy, neutral shades are meant to reflect the Sheikh's calm, reflective nature … and his love of the desert. In every part of the museum and its surroundings it is made clear to visitors just where they are in the world. The atmosphere between the towers is meant to be peaceful and yet lively; looking upward the gaze sweeps across the aerodynamic profiles – the desert mound provides a unique point of view. Here one gets a sense of how the development of the architecture began with separate buildings before the area around them was designed. In its consistency the Zayed National Museum recalls the British Museum, where Foster + Partners made a previously sealed-off space accessible to the public and at the same time created an entirely new spatial experience.[2]

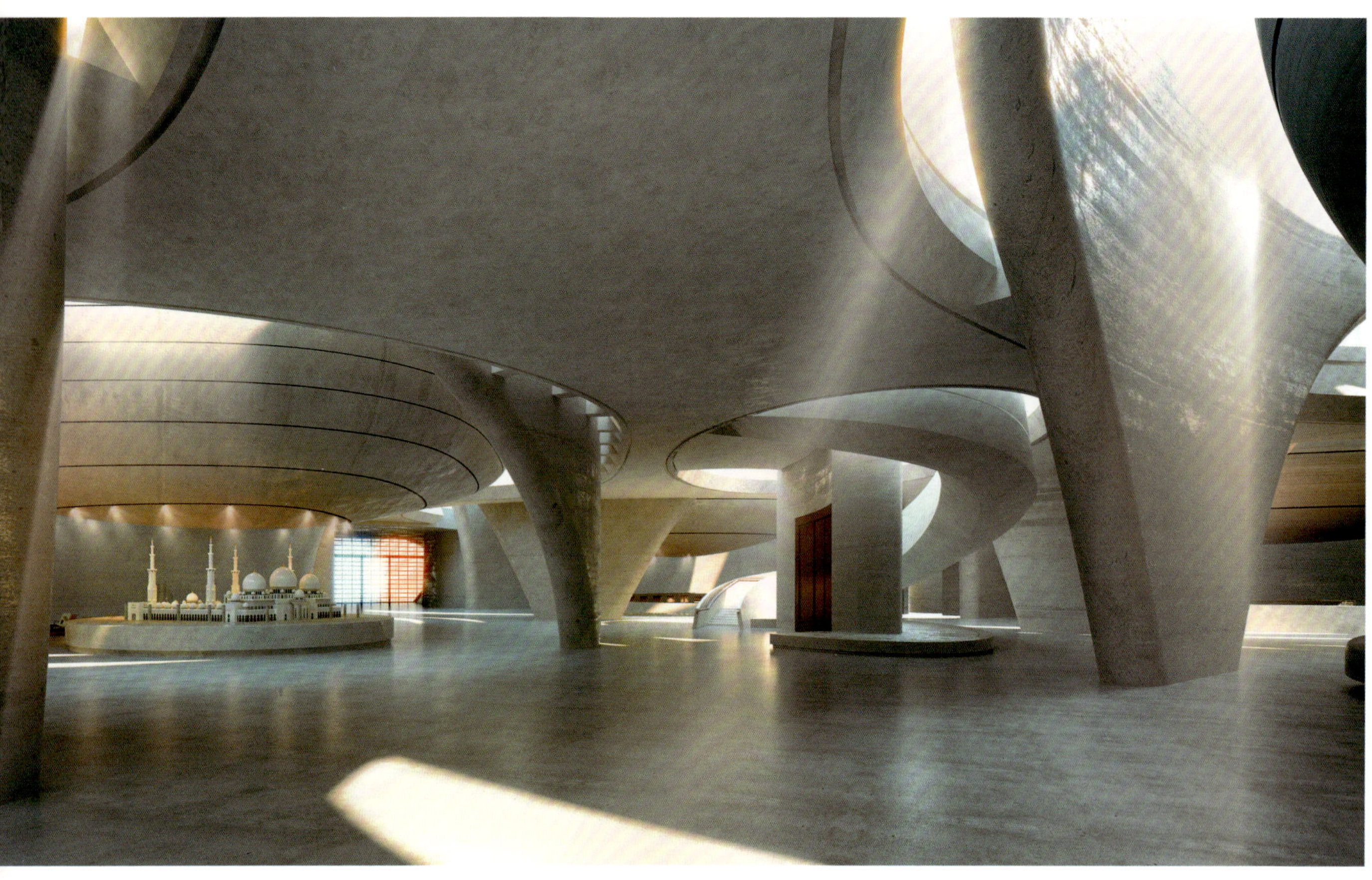

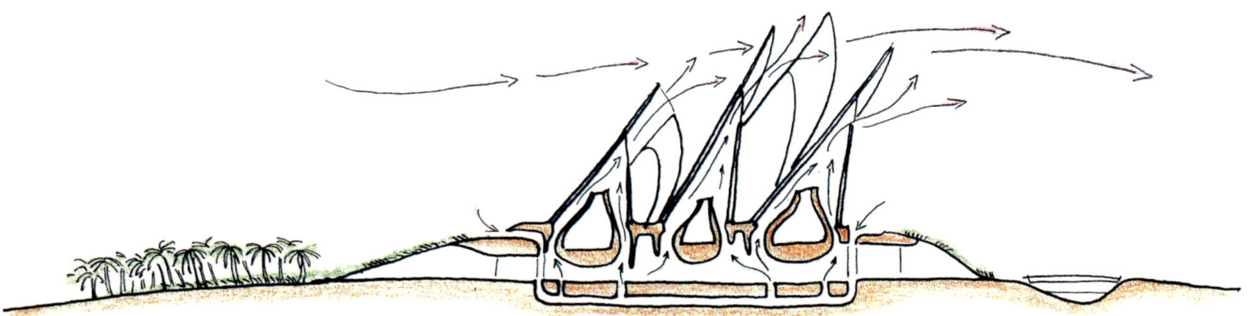

↑ Interior.
Air circulation.

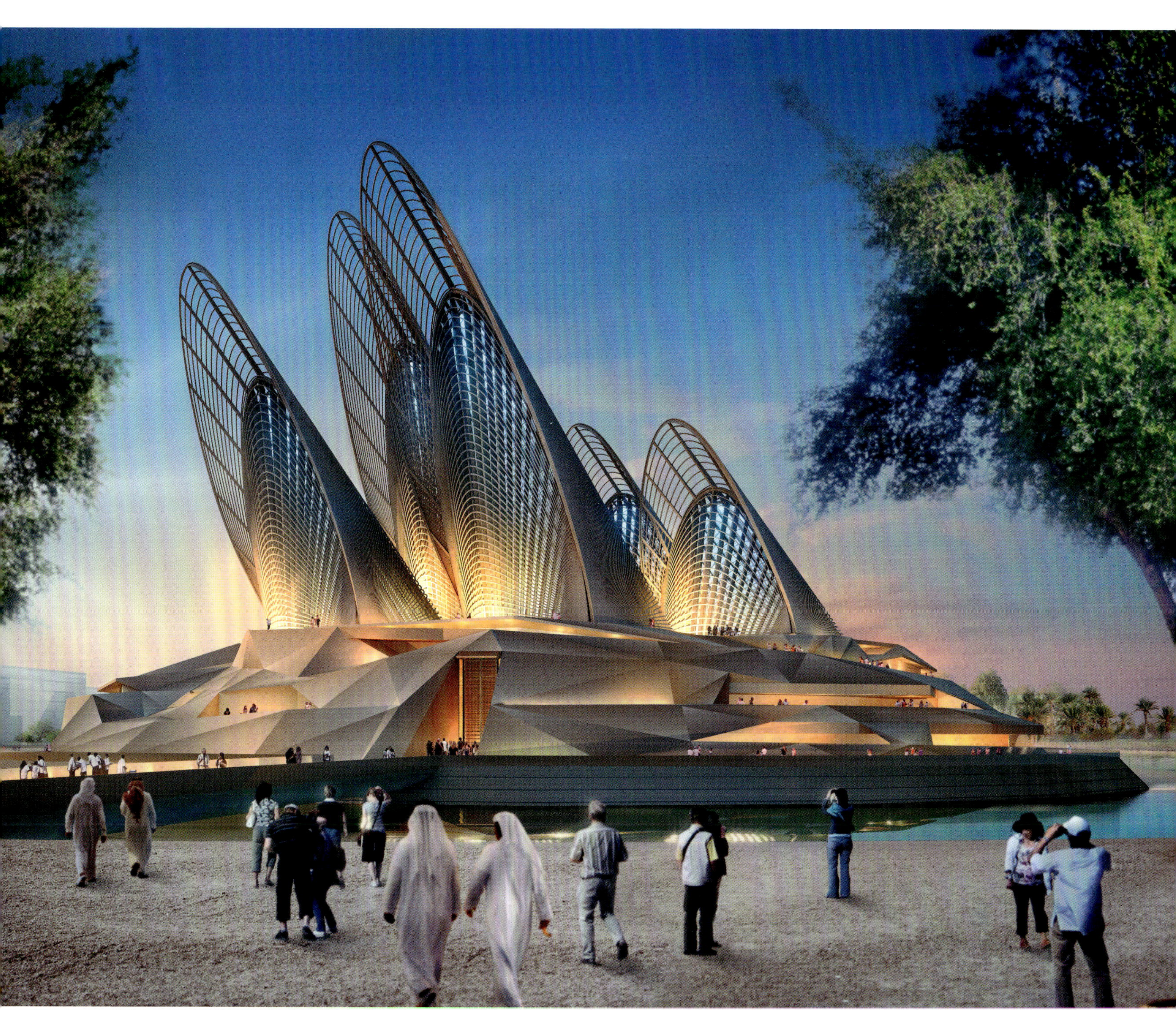

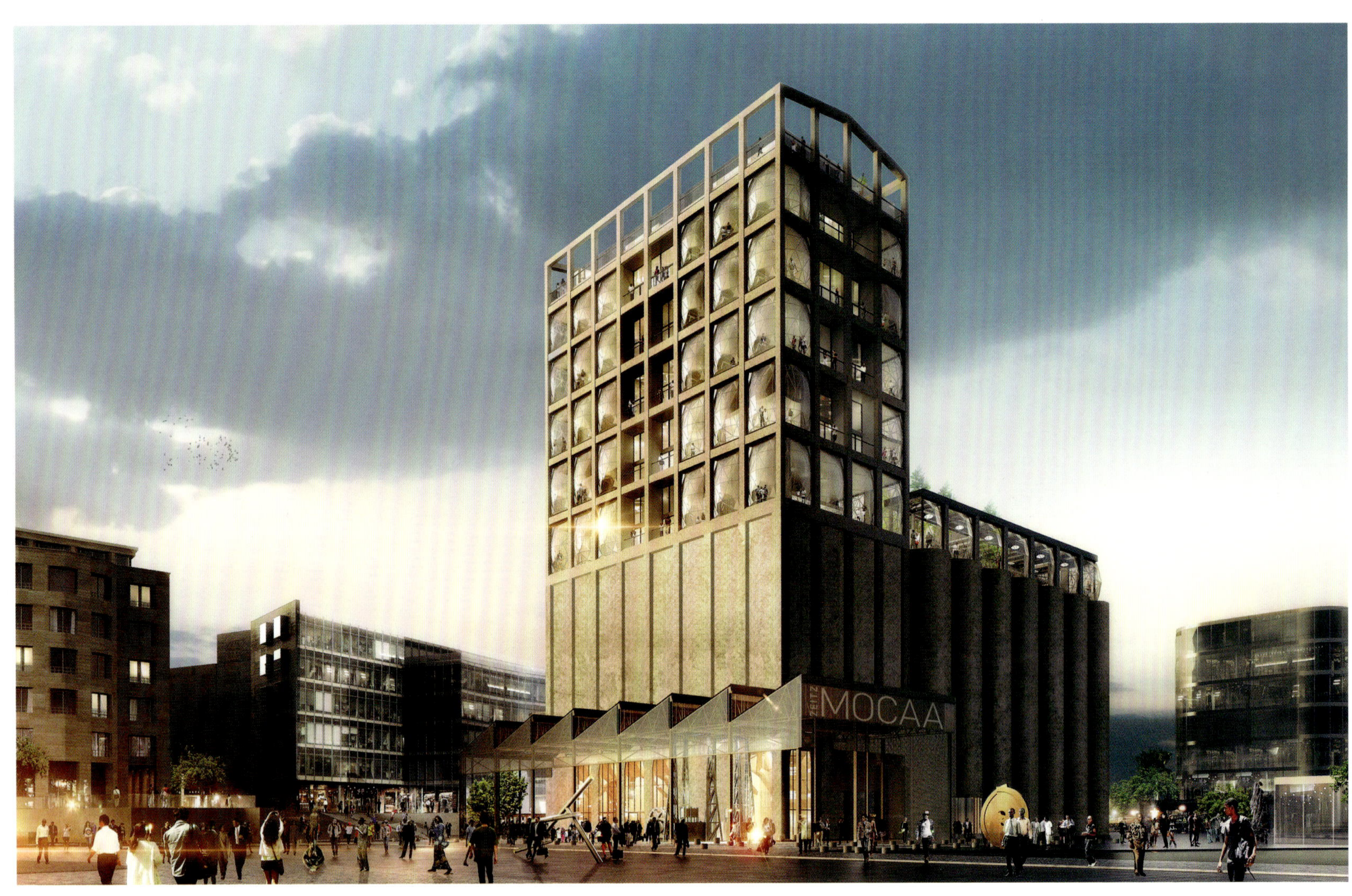

ZEITZ MOCAA

Zeitz Museum of Contemporary Art Africa (Zeitz MOCAA)

Cape Town, South Africa

Heatherwick Studio, London
Opening expected 2017
Building 9,500 sq. m
The Zeitz collection, the museum's permanent collection and special exhibitions

Heatherwick Studio designed the cauldron for the Olympic Flame in London 2012, which was not a bowl but made up of single rods; they designed a bridge that can roll up into an octahedron, and for a window display they broke through the glass surface and let the building's interior extend outward.[1] Heatherwick Studio appears to see every kind of material as a mass that can be formed at will – and always in an extraordinary manner. For Zeitz MOCAA, which is to display contemporary art from the collection of Jochen Zeitz, the former CEO of a German sporting goods manufacturer, Heatherwick Studio has transformed a grain silo into a cathedral-like building that fulfils a museum's two functions: presenting something to people – and filling them with awe.

Forty-two former silos are packed tight together on a rectangular ground plan. Until 2001 they were used to store the grain processed in the taller adjacent building. Instead of razing the silos and thus ignoring the history of the site on the Victoria and Alfred Waterfront, Heatherwick Studio decided to hull them. This provides visitors with the unique chance to look up at the sky through tubes thirty metres tall and five metres in diameter. By cutting away part of them, an atrium could be created in the bottom third of the block that is illuminated solely by daylight. It falls in through the new glass roofs Heatherwick Studio placed on the silo tubes and resembles the soft light in the choirs of Gothic cathedrals. As in a cathedral, the viewer has the impression of seeing something unique, almost transcendently beautiful. They should feel something similar before every work of art – and it is wonderful if museum architecture can have the same effect. The structure now celebrates its uniqueness and history: the carving produced the form of a giant ear of grain, and thus recalls the silos' earlier function. Around the glass roofs, which visitors can walk on and look down through, a sculpture garden has been created. Glass elevators have been installed inside some of the tubes, and in others winding metal stairs resemble drills that have eaten their way down through the concrete.

In the adjacent building, the former grain mill, the more conventional rooms have been redesigned as white-cube exhibition spaces; eighty rooms contain art displays, and a further eighteen rooms are available for the museum's education programme.[2] The massive outer walls were almost completely replaced by windows, not ordinary flat windows but rather convex ones, giving the building the appearance of a honeycomb. Little by little it appears to be arching outwards. At night the tower is also illuminated from within. Then it is no longer the voices of the visitors dispersed across the floors but only the light that turns the structure into a softly shimmering lantern lighting up the harbour.

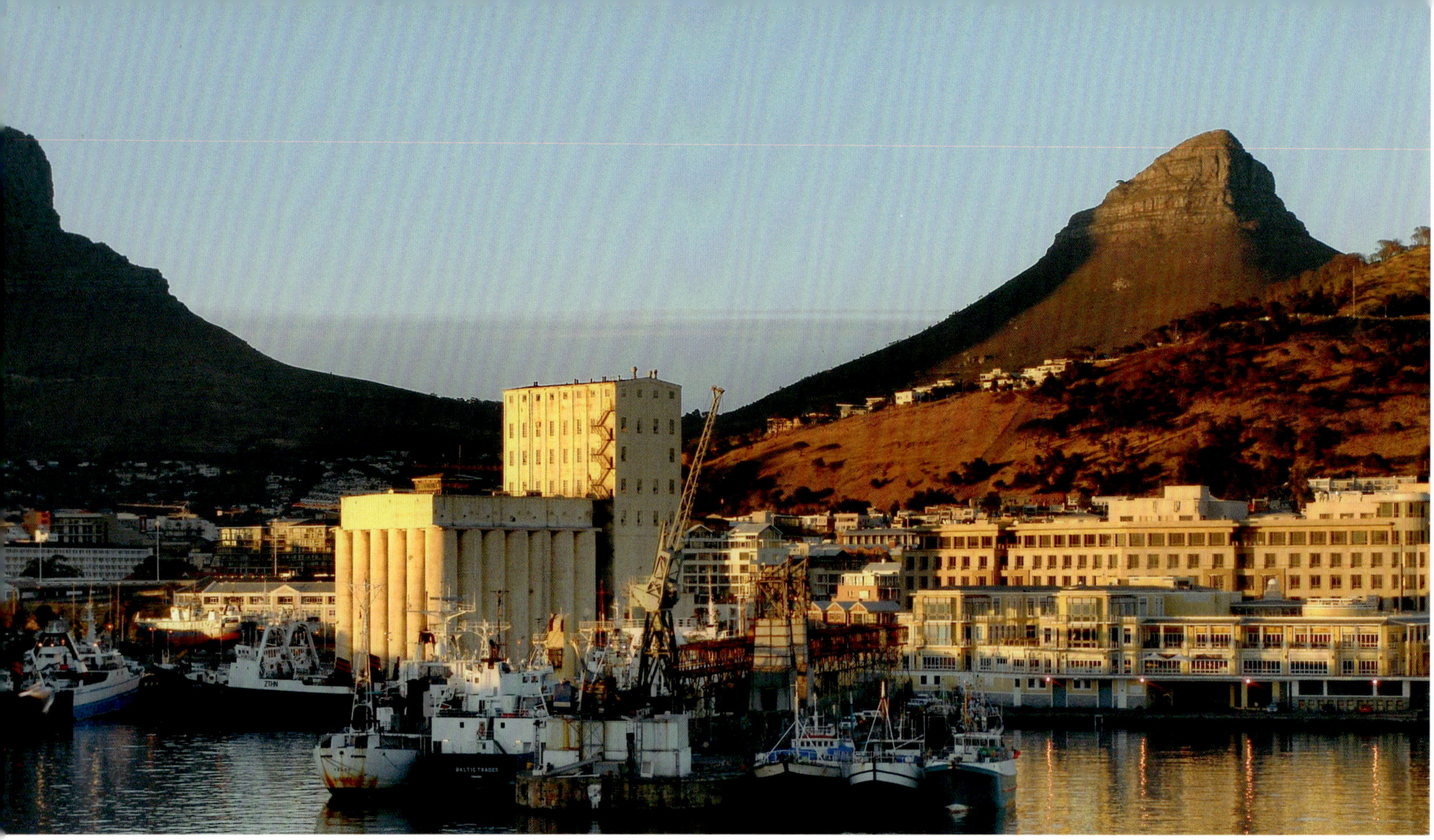

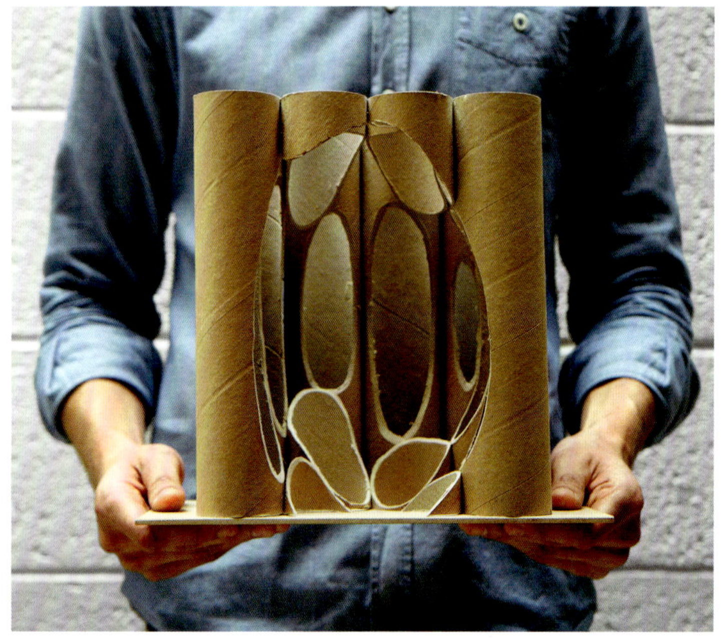

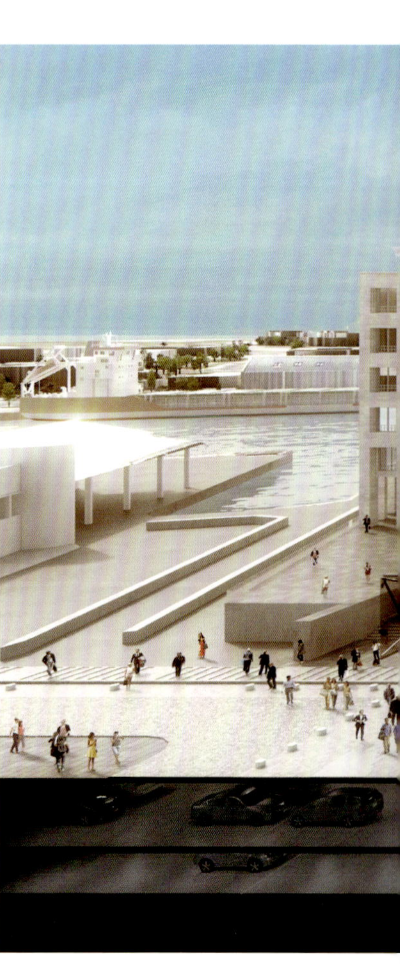

↑ Site view.

↗ Concept model.
   Design concept.

→ Section.

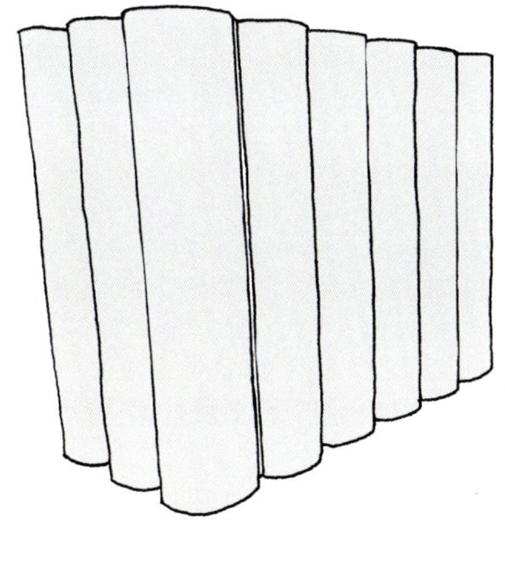

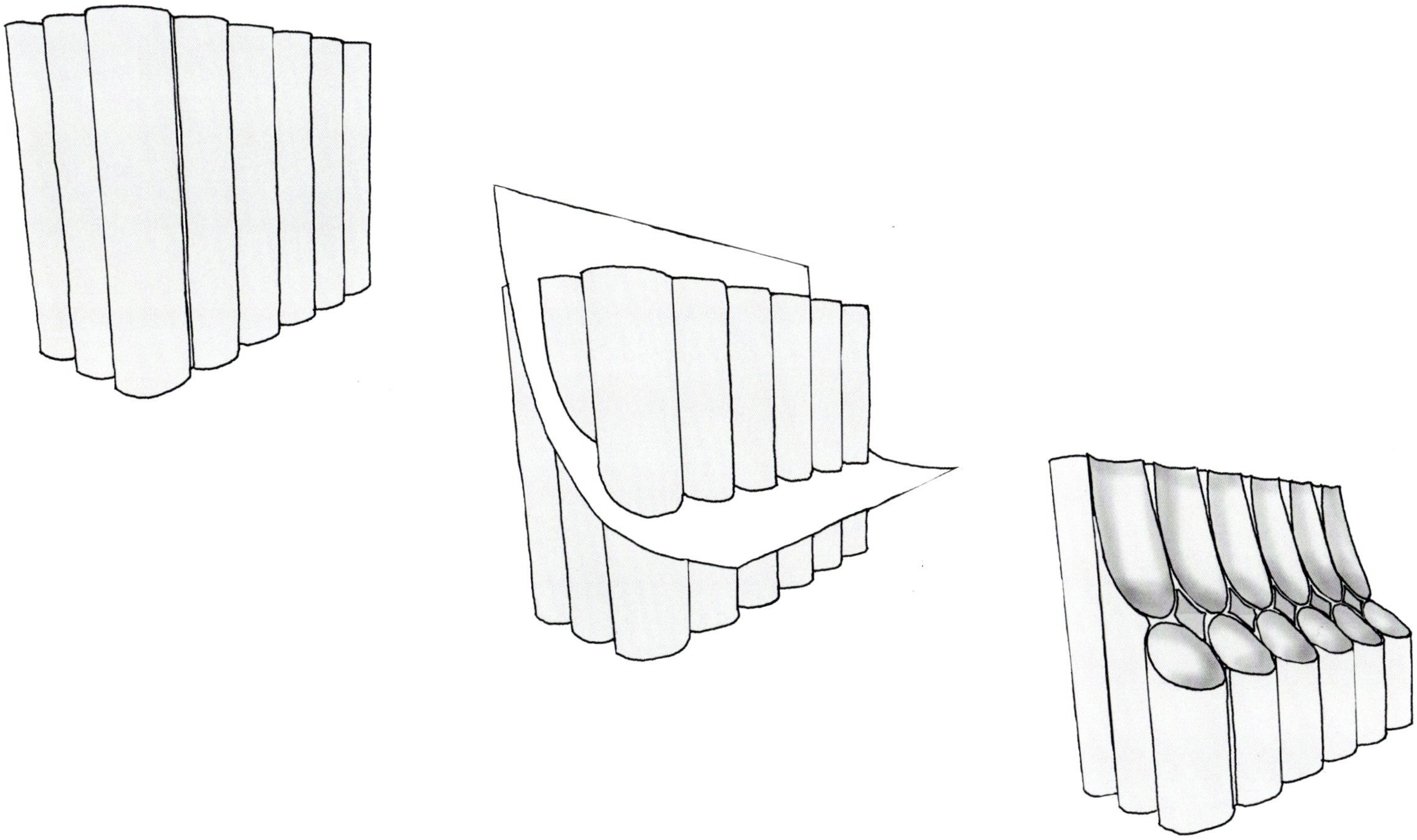

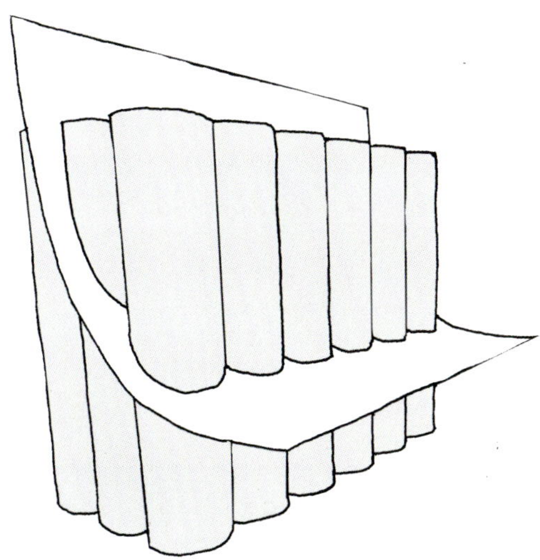

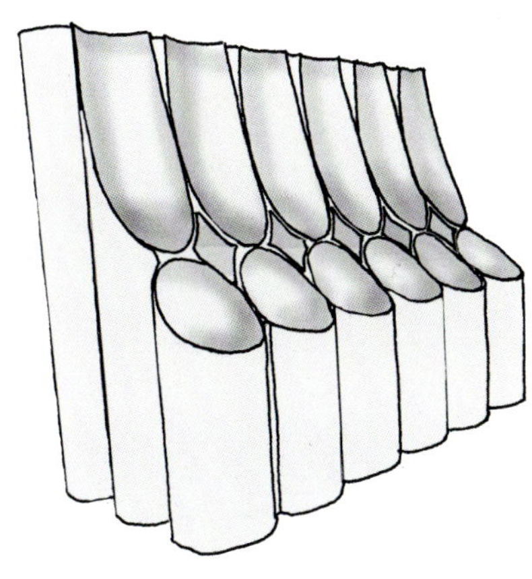

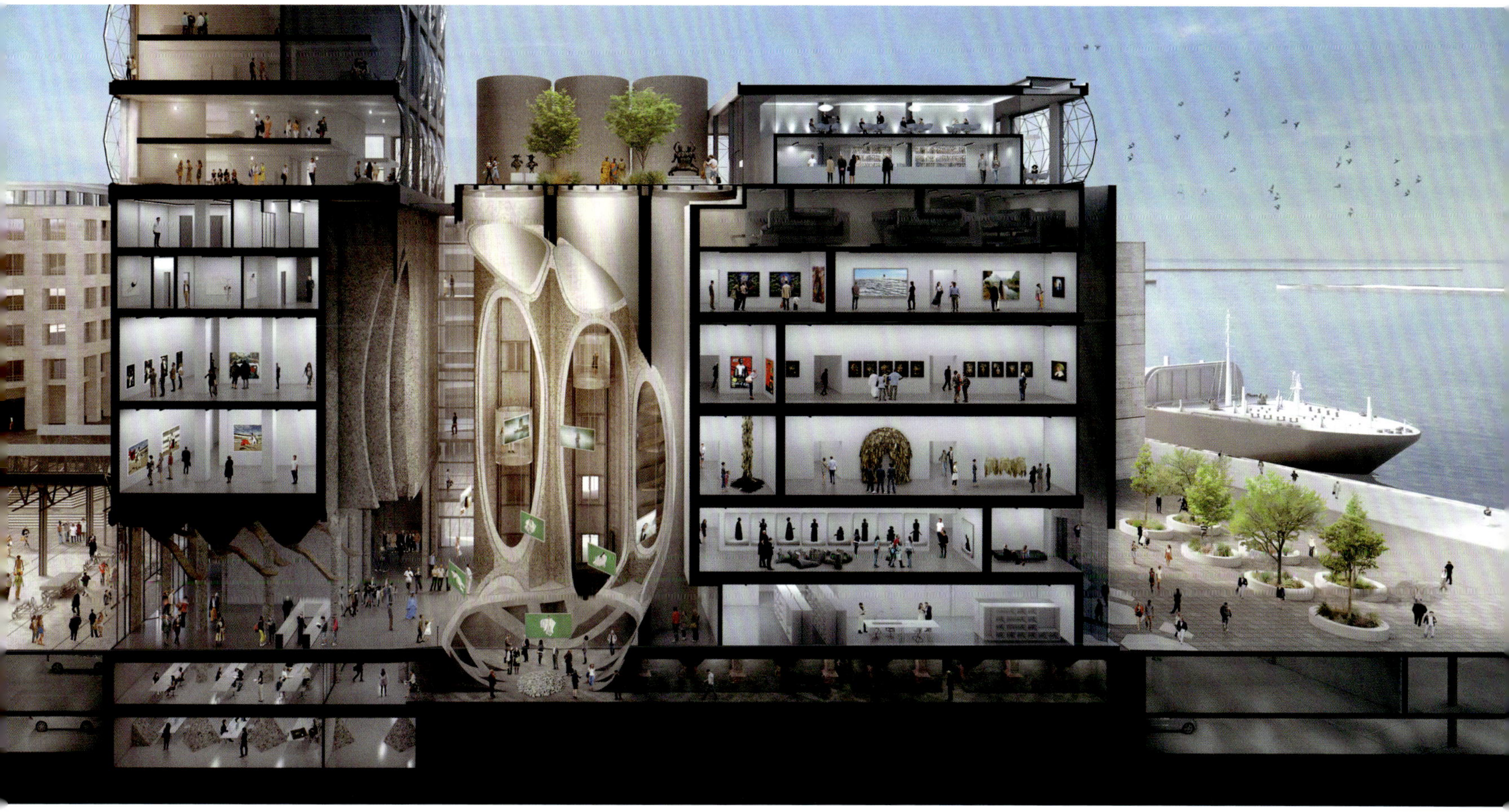

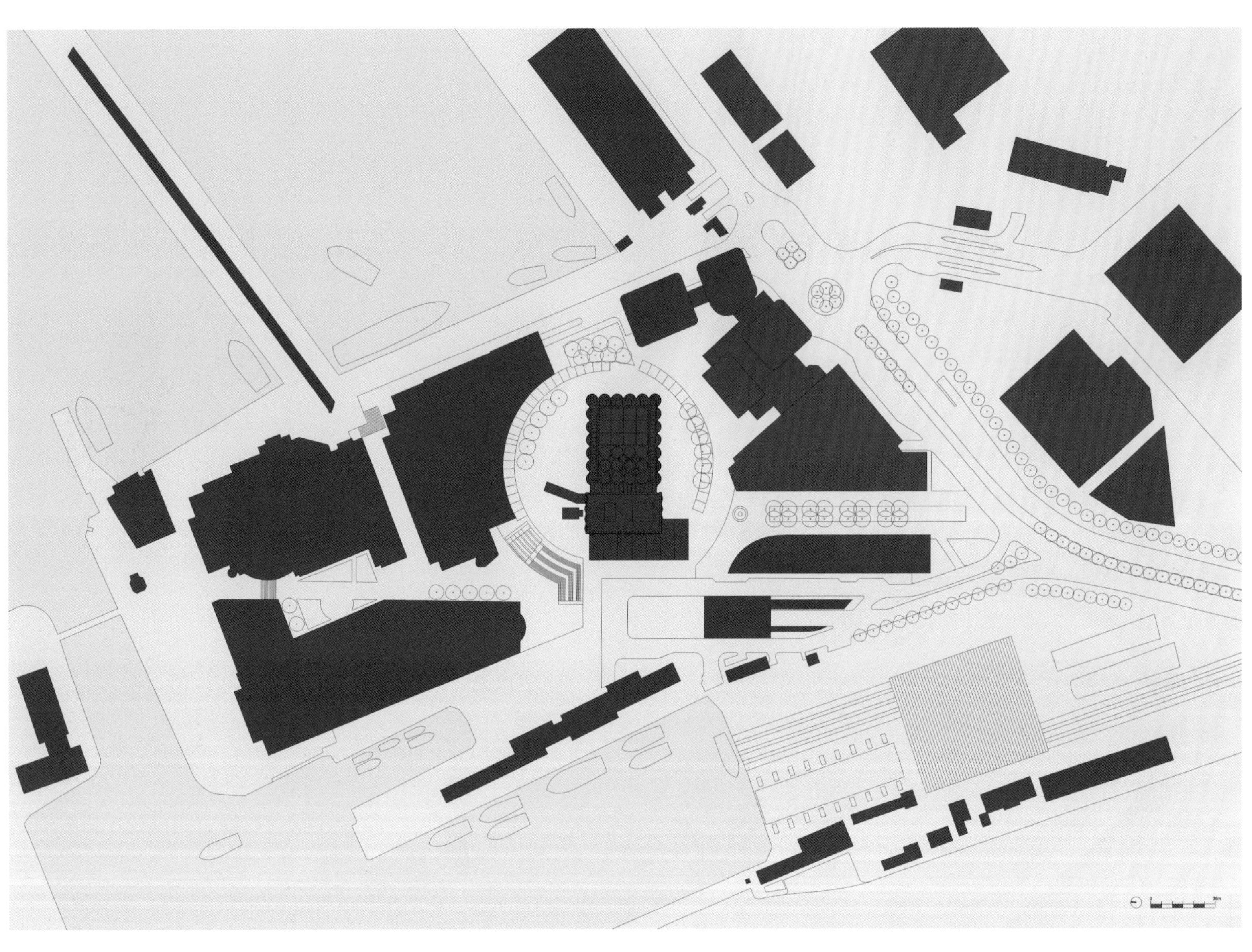

↑ Site plan.

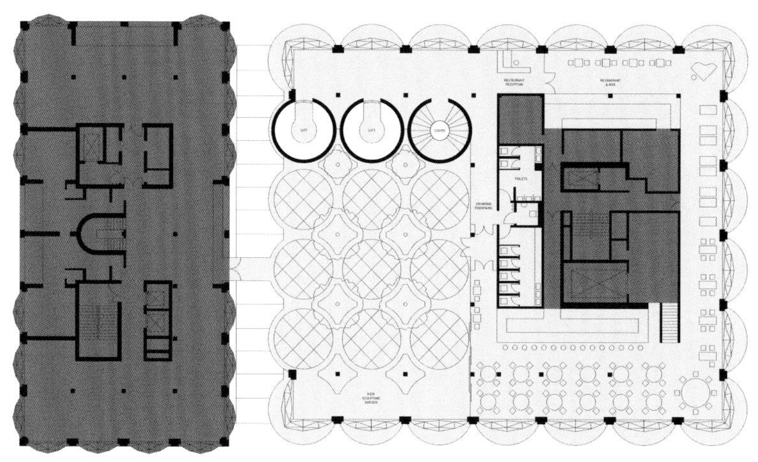

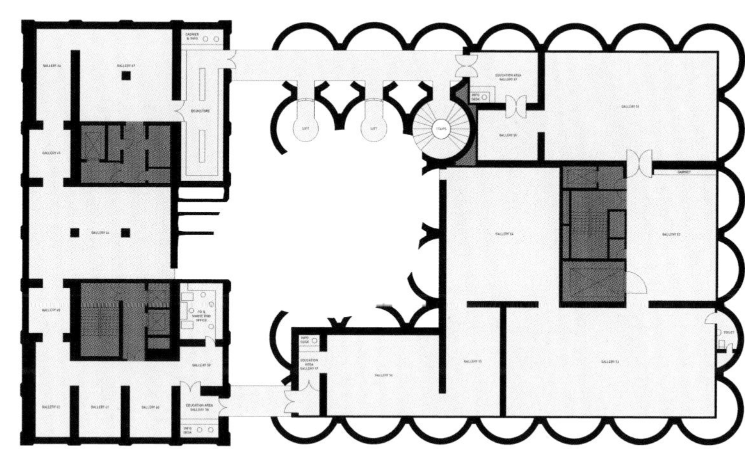

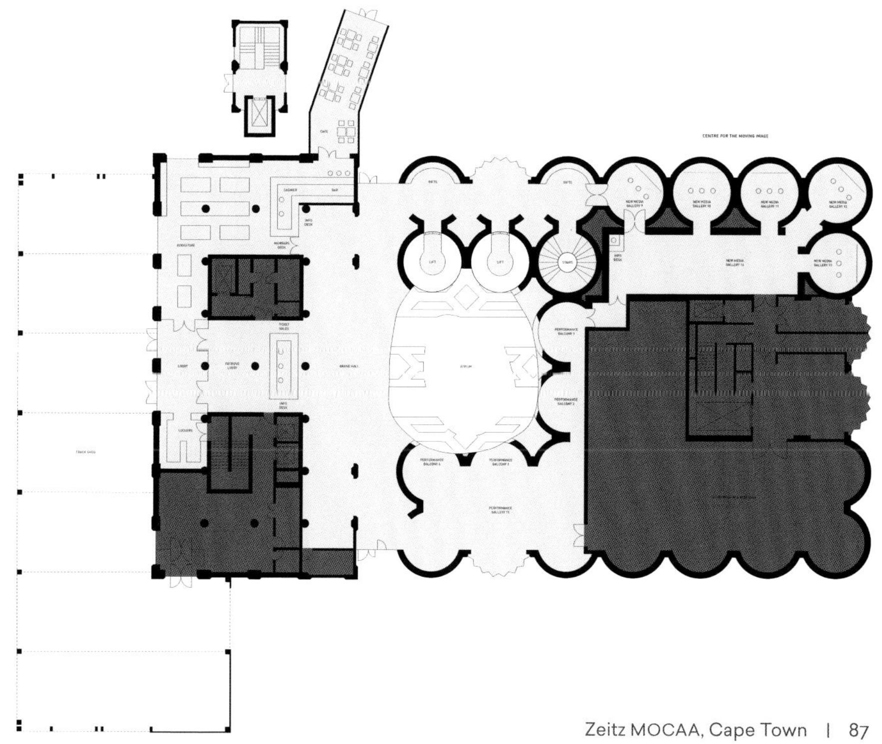

↗ Plans:
Roof, +4, ground floor.

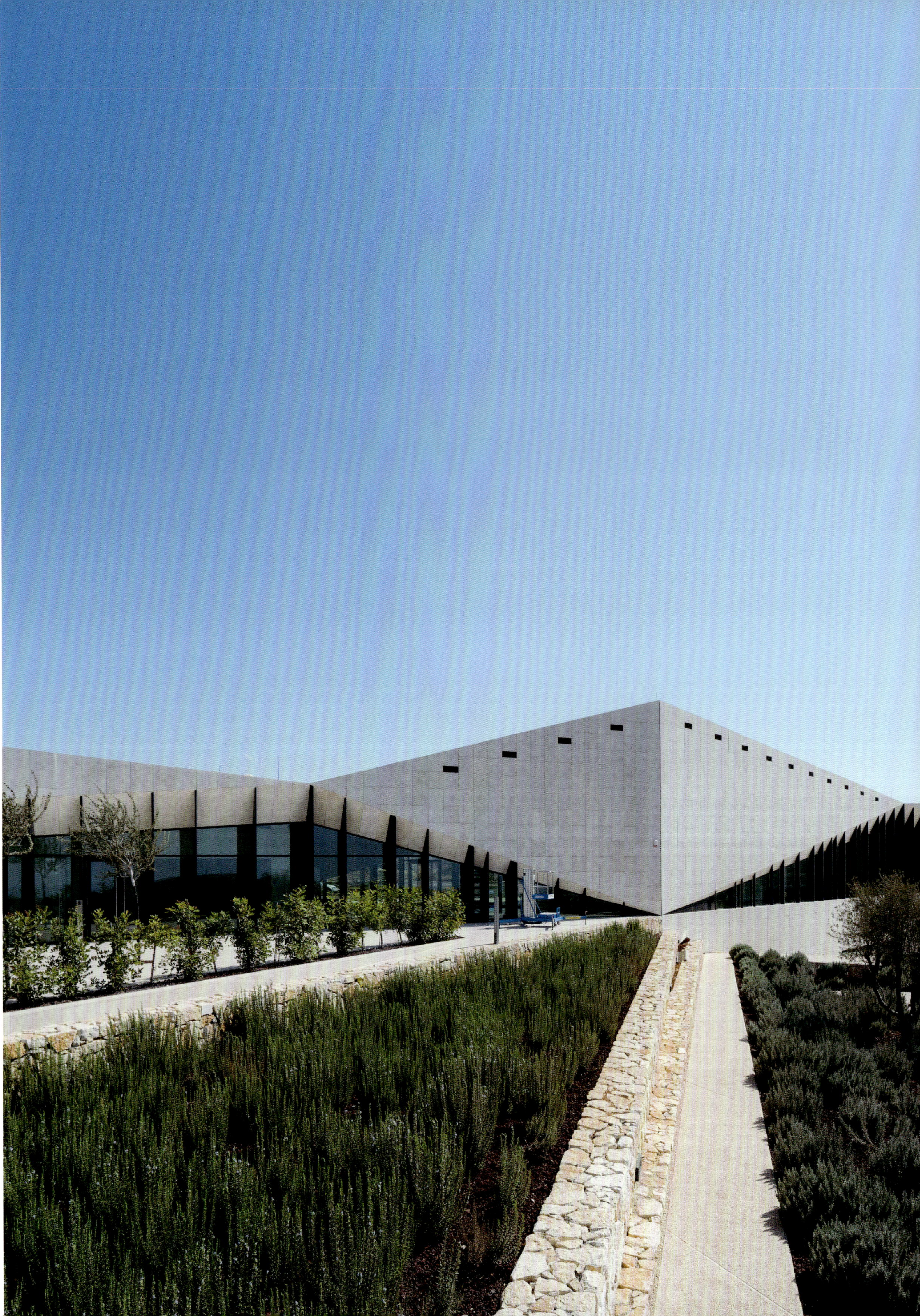

The Palestinian Museum

Birzeit, West Bank, Palestine

Heneghan Peng Architects, Dublin
Construction 2014–2016, opened 2016
Building 3,500 sq. m
Permanent and temporary exhibitions with archaeological, ethnographic
and contemporary art collections

The landscape north of Ramallah in the West Bank is gently rolling. Each hill follows the last with a strip of vegetation before it becomes green, flat, beige and hilly. Then your eye is drawn to a sand-coloured building nestled into the hills, mirroring their lines.

Heneghan Peng Architects' Palestinian Museum deliberately references its surroundings. It has no desire to seek attention, but rather subordinates itself, for it is precisely the landscape in which it stands, its past and that of its inhabitants, that it wishes to draw attention to. This is the first museum of this size in which the history of the Palestine people will be displayed. The future tense here is deliberate; at the moment the museum is empty. It stands in a country where statehood has not been recognised. It displays things that as yet have no home. It is not only an exhibition space; it is also a political gesture.

Nevertheless, the architecture refers to the historical country. The architects speak of the "worked city" as inspiration,[1] in which each element tells a story of culture, production and change. This strip of land can also tell a great deal, but for now everything is manifest in a building built above several terraces and crowning a hill. Each of the terraces is planted with something different, suggestive of the terrain's possible reclamation. On the top terrace stands the flat, elongated building clad in light-coloured limestone. With its angled ground plan, from above it resembles a Bedouin tent.

Apricot and pomegranate trees have been planted around the museum, and the scent of mint and rosemary hangs in the air[2] – the museum provides the visitor with a traditional Arabic welcome, though not with conservative architecture. Quite the opposite: the building is contemporary and bold. The roofs of the building's separate sections slant upwards and downwards in a visual nod to the undulating landscape. The long row of light-coloured exterior walls is broken up by black, slender roof supports that are more decorative than functional as well as wide glass surfaces that make the overall structure seem more modern than the traditional building materials would suggest.

Since the museum still has no displays, for now it is concentrating on digital programmes. An interactive timeline of the history of Palestine will be published on the museum's website.[3] At the same time, the collection continues to be assembled and exhibitions mounted by the museum in places with large Palestinian refugee populations. For example, samples of Palestinian embroidery from two superb private collections were featured in its first "satellite" exhibition in Beirut from May to July, 2016.

The Palestinian Museum already shows by its very existence the political will of a people. By way of its so-called satellite exhibitions it points to the presence of its culture, and its active use of the website and other electronic platforms is an expansion of the physical exhibition space into the digital world. It is therefore going beyond a purely architectural form of existence and indicating a remarkable viability for the future.

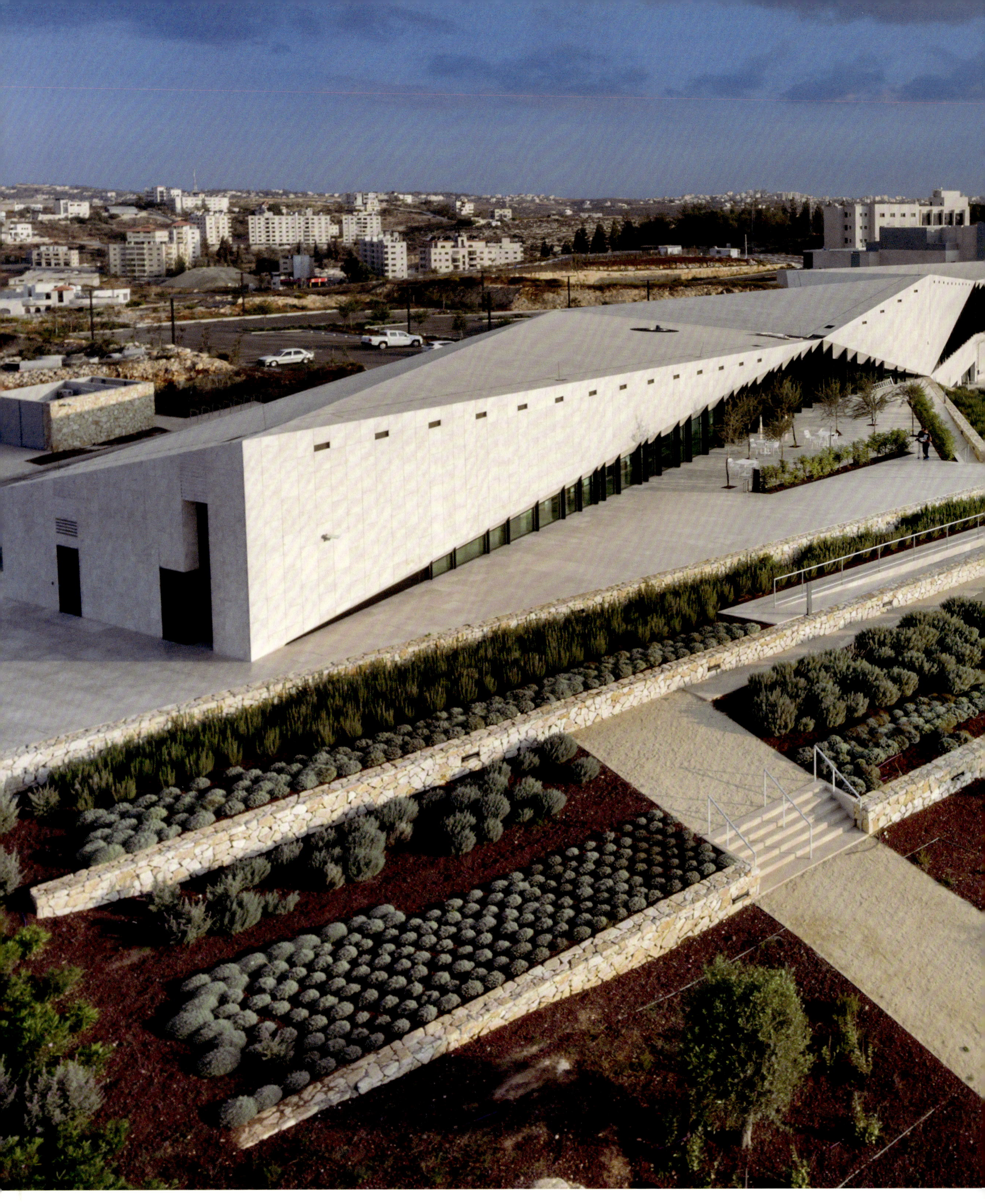

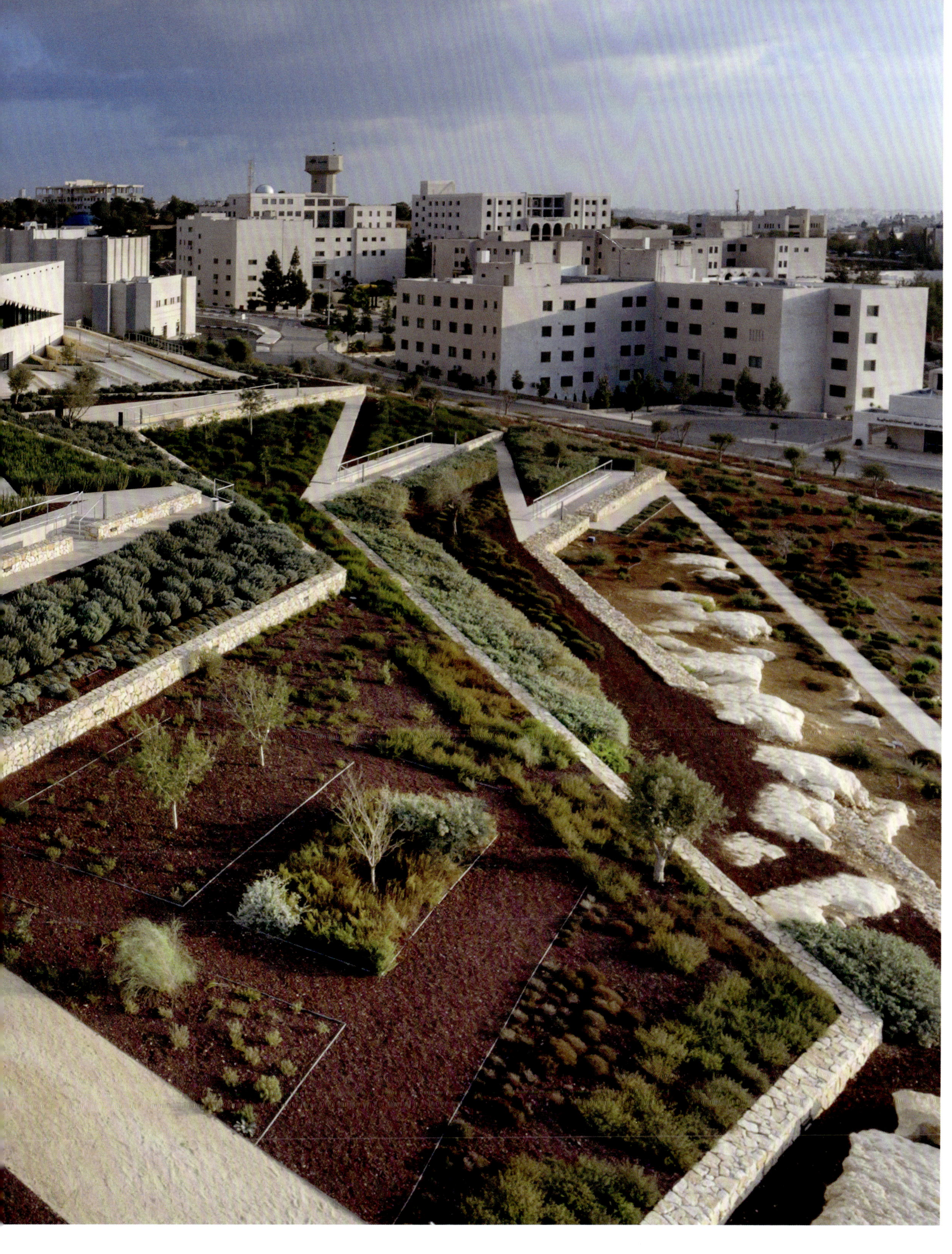

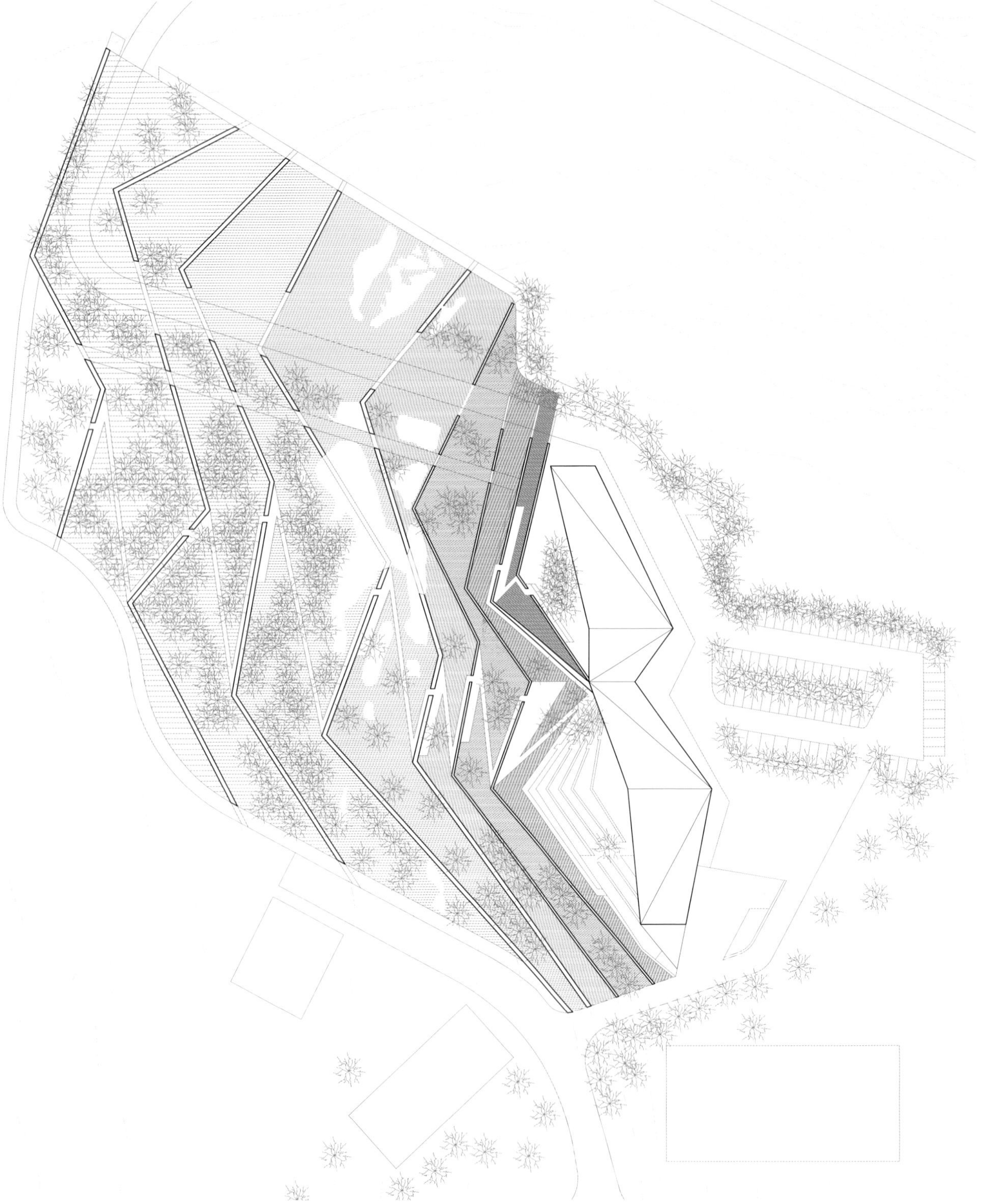

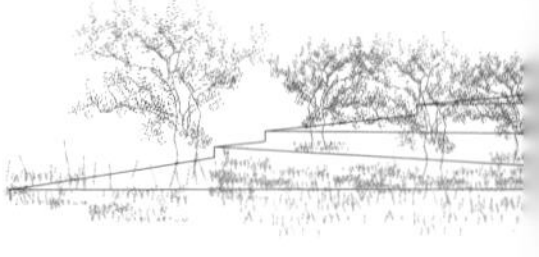

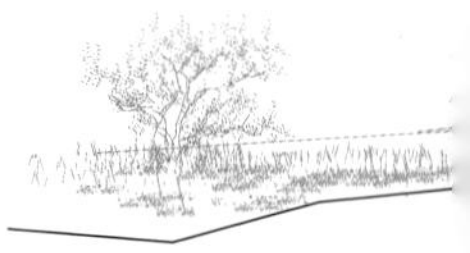

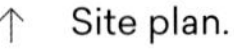

↑ Site plan.

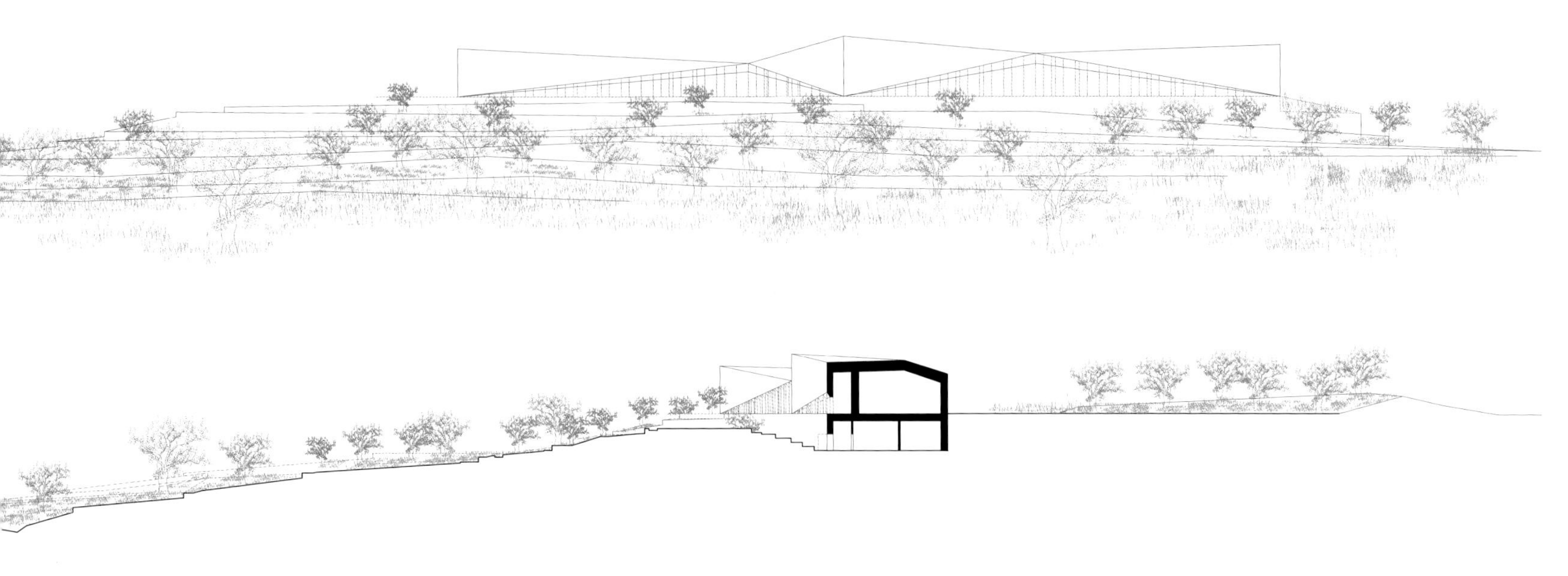

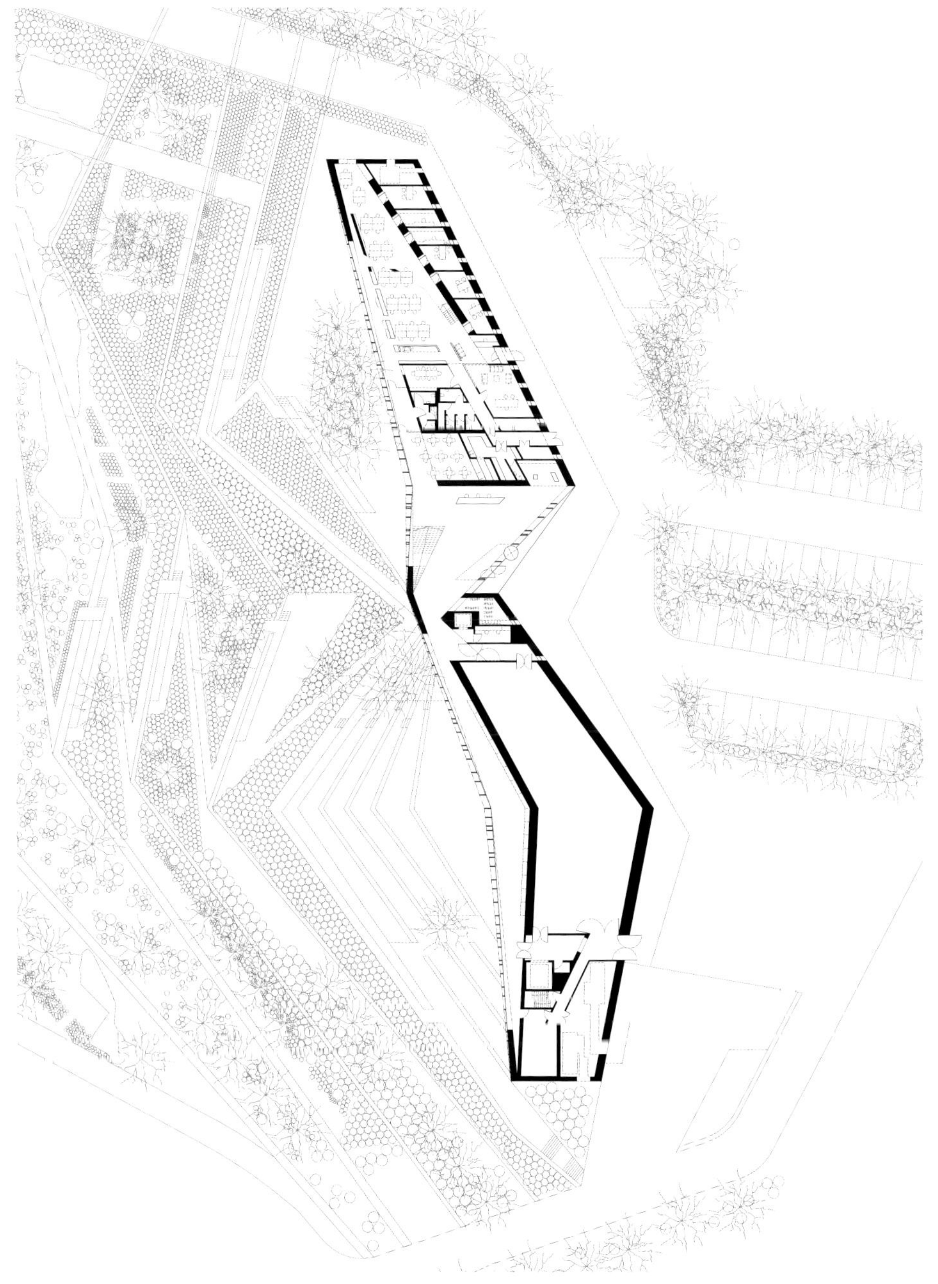

↑ Elevation, looking east.
Cross-section.

→ Ground-floor plan.

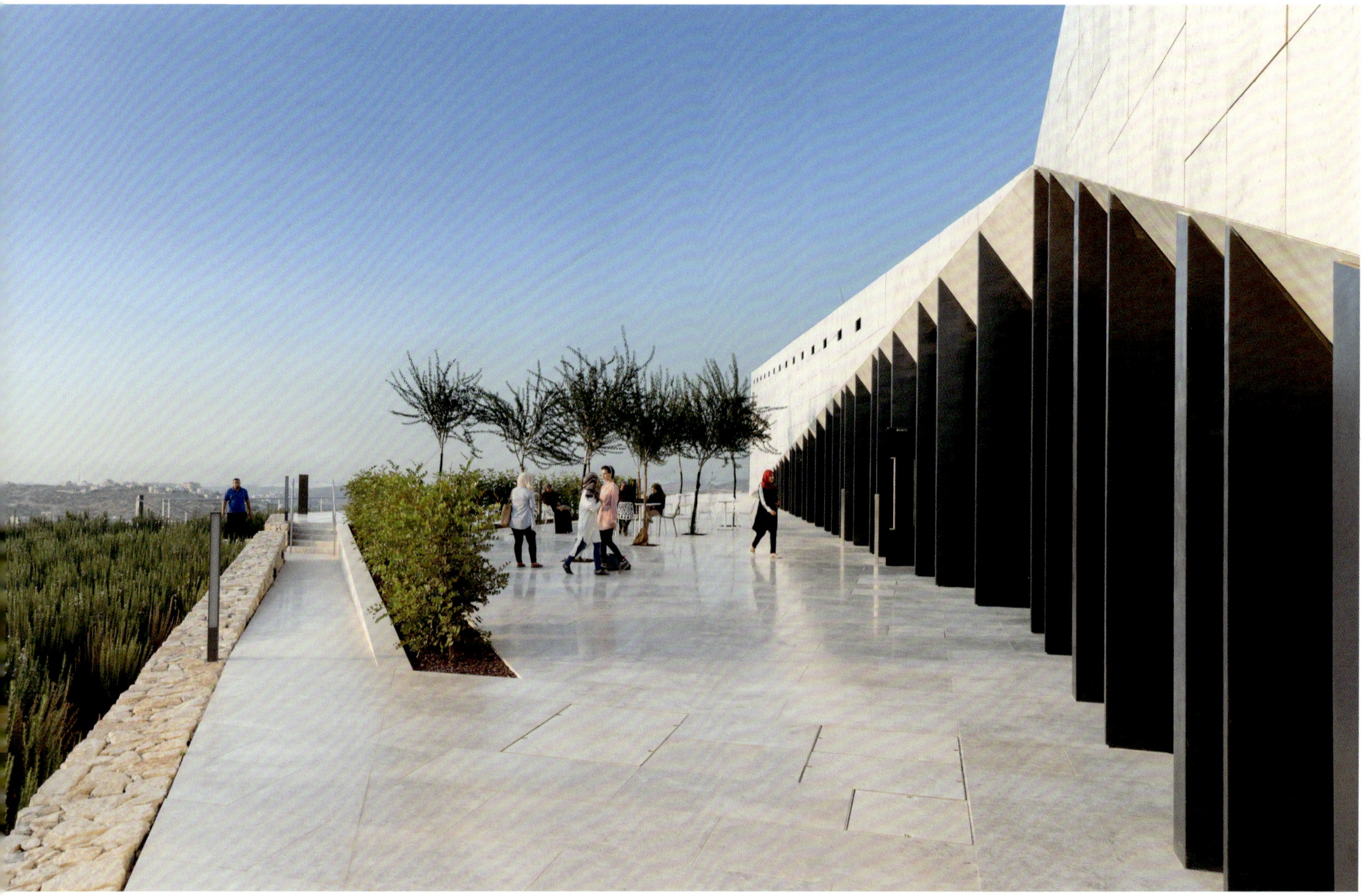

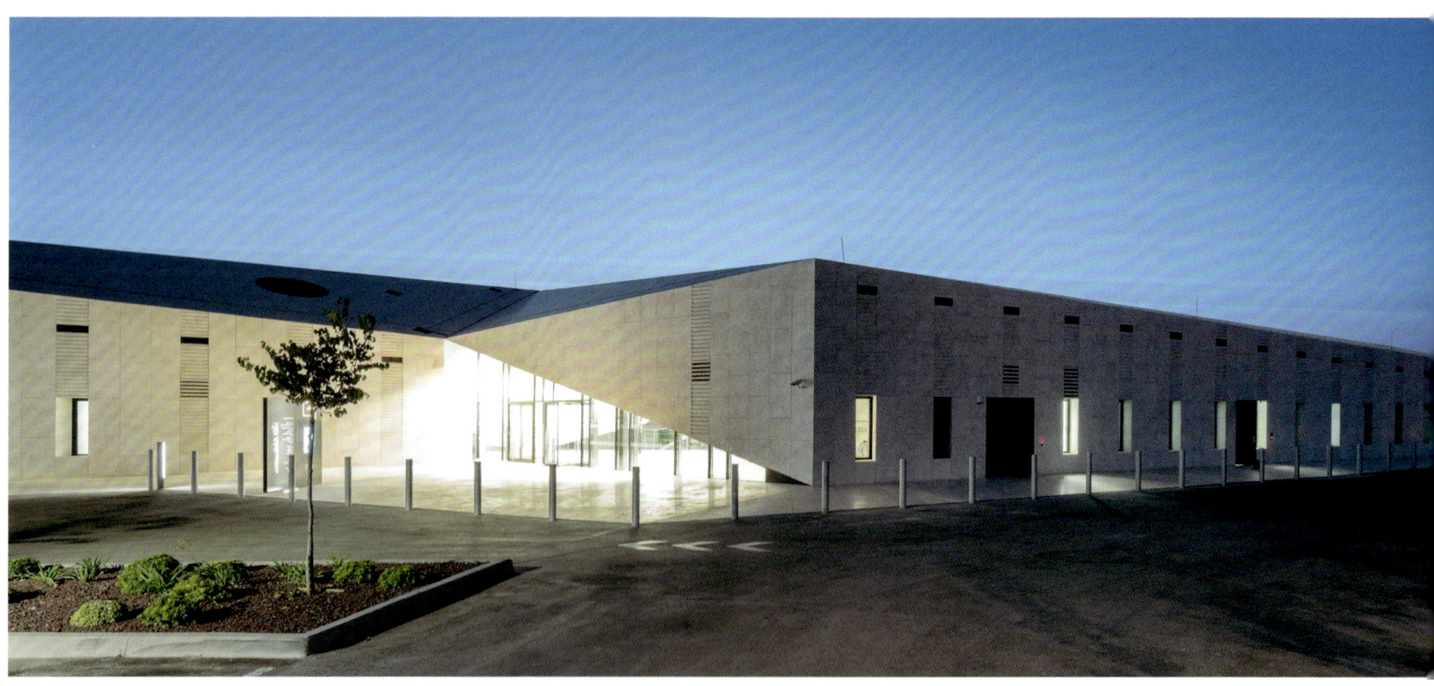

↑   Western terrace.
Eastern façade.

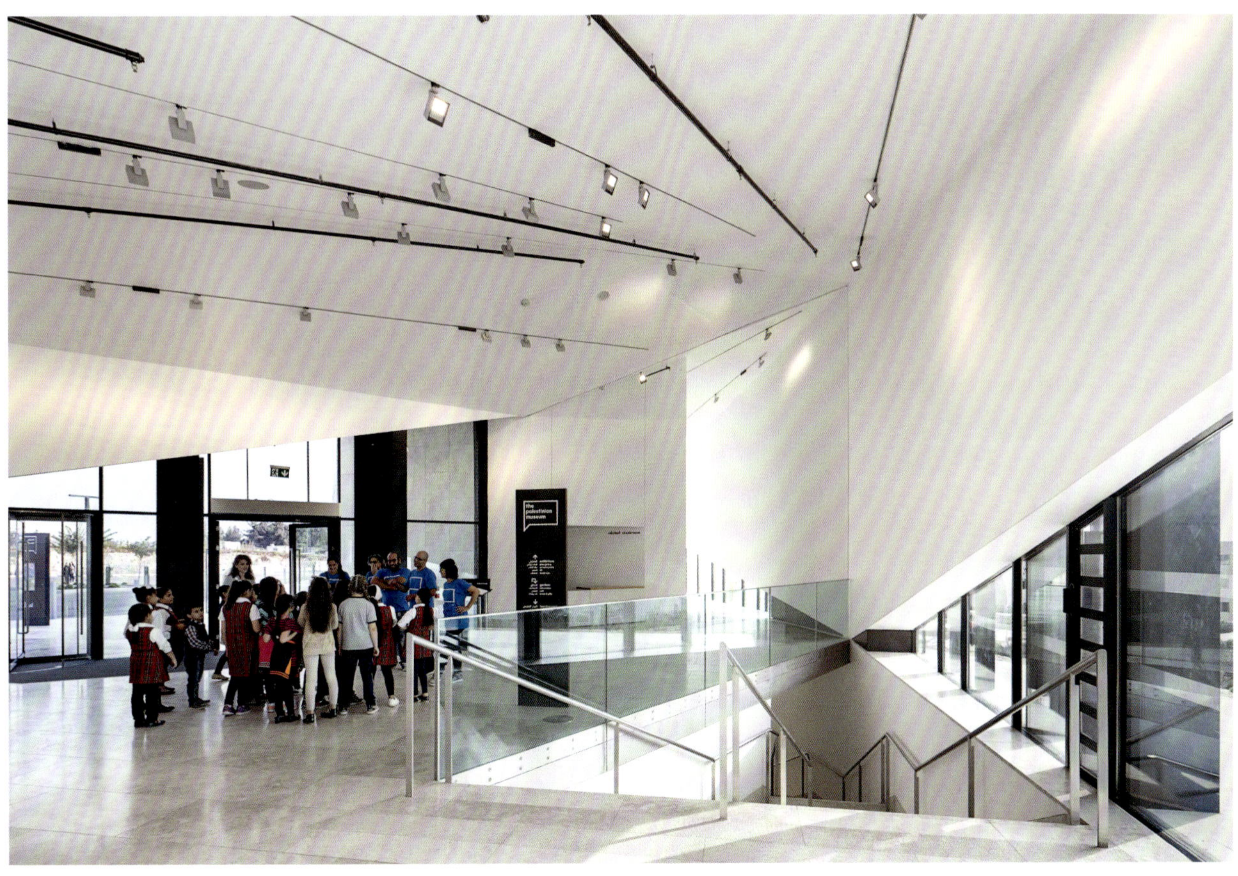

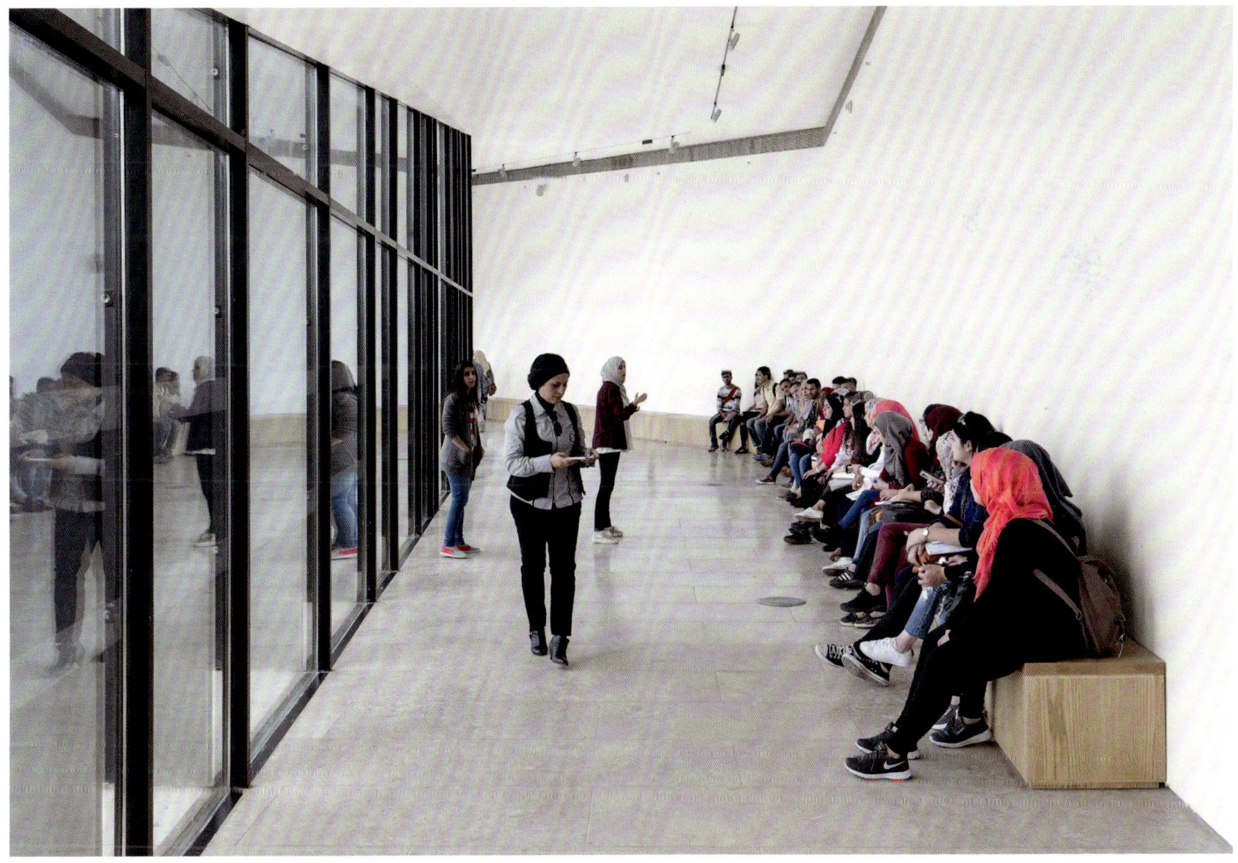

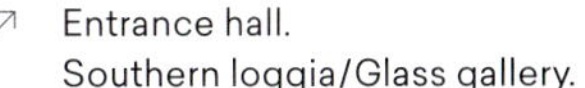

↗ Entrance hall.
Southern loggia/Glass gallery.

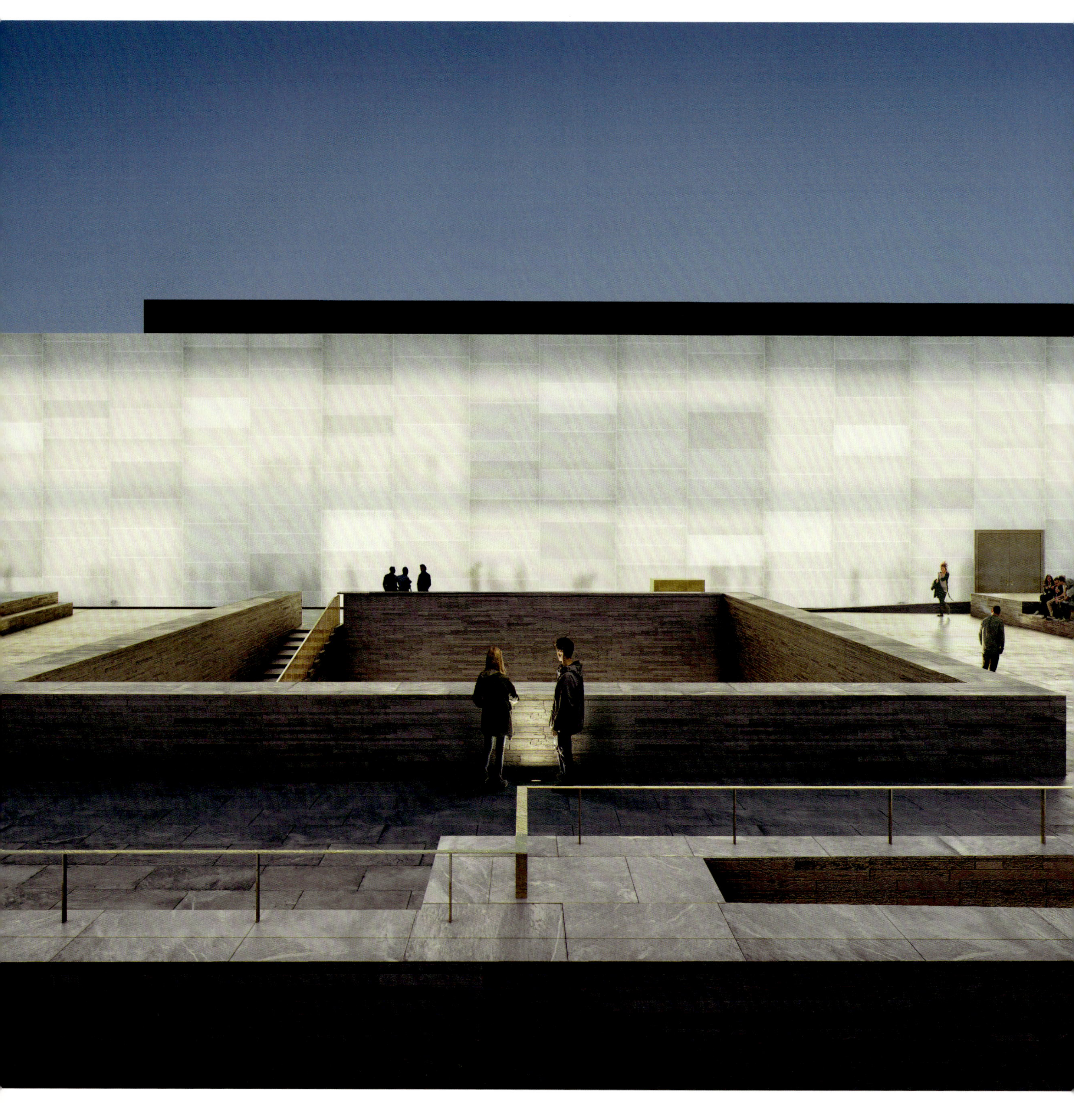

Nasjonalmuseet for kunst, arkitektur og design

Oslo, Norway

Klaus Schuwerk, Kleihues + Schuwerk Architects, Naples
Construction 2014–2019, opening 2020
Building 54,500 sq. m
Art (older and contemporary), arts and crafts, design and architecture

Due for completion in 2019, the Nasjonalmuseet is being built on challenging Oslo terrain. Right next to the water, the former West Station, erected in the historic round-arch style, stands on the future museum site. Farther east is the massive City Hall, built of brick. Also within sight is the medieval Akershus fortress. The architect Klaus Schuwerk therefore decided on a building that will communicate with its neighbours of all different styles and will also add a modern accent next to the pier.

The museum, with its horizontal stone façade, surrounds the old train station and thus creates a new piazza, from which visitors can enter the museum. The window surfaces are designed with sumptuous breadth; they are meant to ensure a pleasant atmosphere inside and at the same time appear inviting from without. From the foyer visitors access the design, art and crafts exhibits, the library, café and bookshop. The display of early, modern and contemporary art begins on the second floor. From the central sculpture courtyard one can enter the terrace and roof gardens.

On the harbour and street sides the height of the base structure matches that of the former West Station, so that the museum is integrated into its surroundings. Above this, set back somewhat, rise the exhibition spaces; their cubic shape echoing the taller neighbouring buildings to the northwest. In front of these floors, facing the water, a very special level is being created – the so-called Alabaster Hall. Klaus Schuwerk refers to it as a kind of temple on the Acropolis. Its double façade, in contrast to that of the massive main building, is clad with thin slabs of alabaster laminated to glass; this hall glows from within like a work of art made of light. The amount of daylight entering can be regulated with vertical blinds. Special installations will be shown here that interact with this semi-transparent, exposed location.

Klaus Schuwerk sees the outer appearance of the museum as a mirror of its content. "This is culture in itself. The paintings inside the museum relate us to the past but they also project us to the future."[1] The new building connects with the older ones on the site and with those near to it – together they create a new, exciting kinship which is what architecture is all about. Museum buildings, especially, depend on the fact that visitors find them attractive and inviting, and that they are not foreign objects in the urban fabric. The new National Museum performs the balancing act of fitting into the existing terrain and at the same time having a look all of its own. This is thanks to an architectural beacon that does not tower upward but extends horizontally, and will beam its cultural message far out across the water.

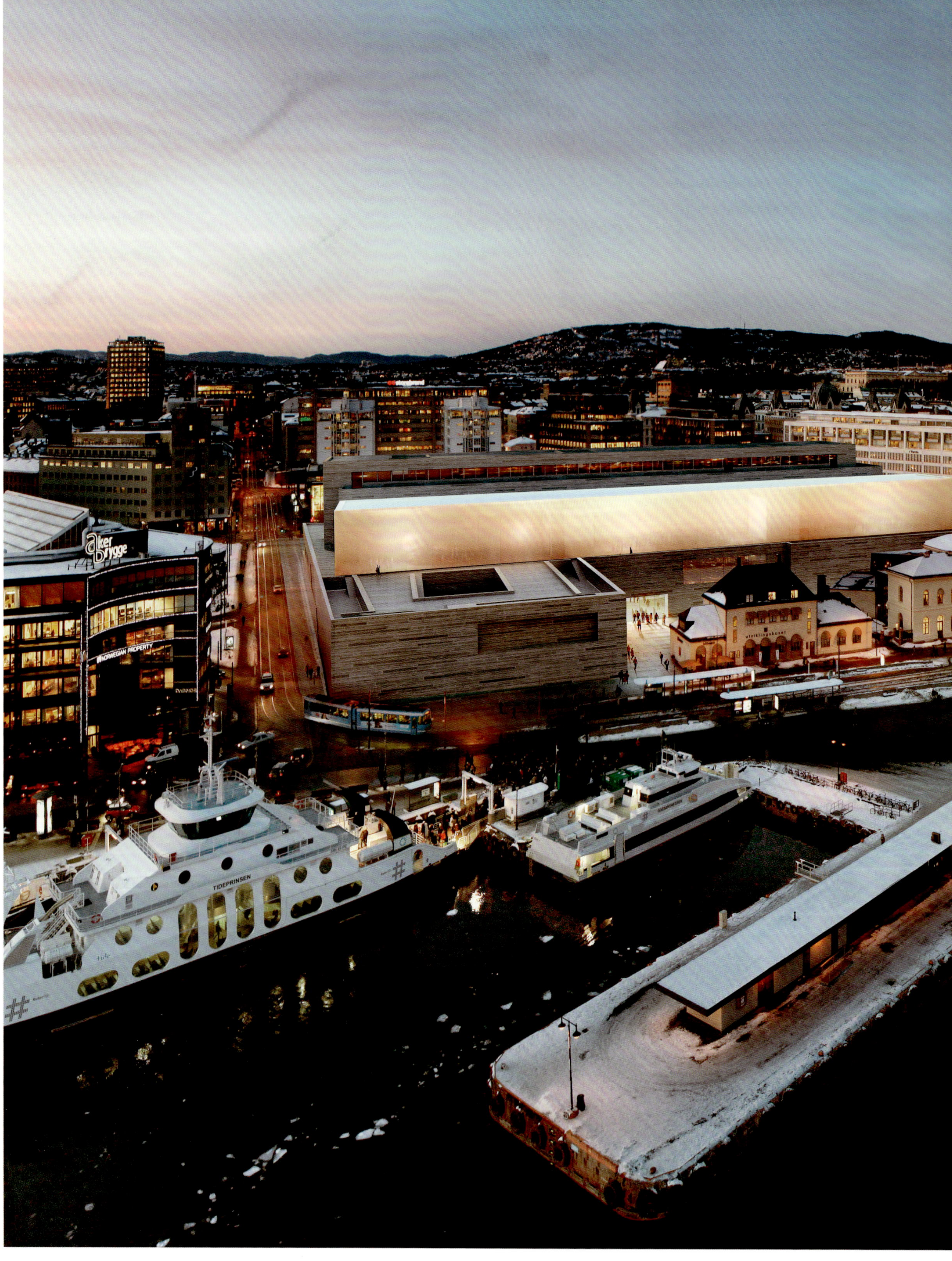

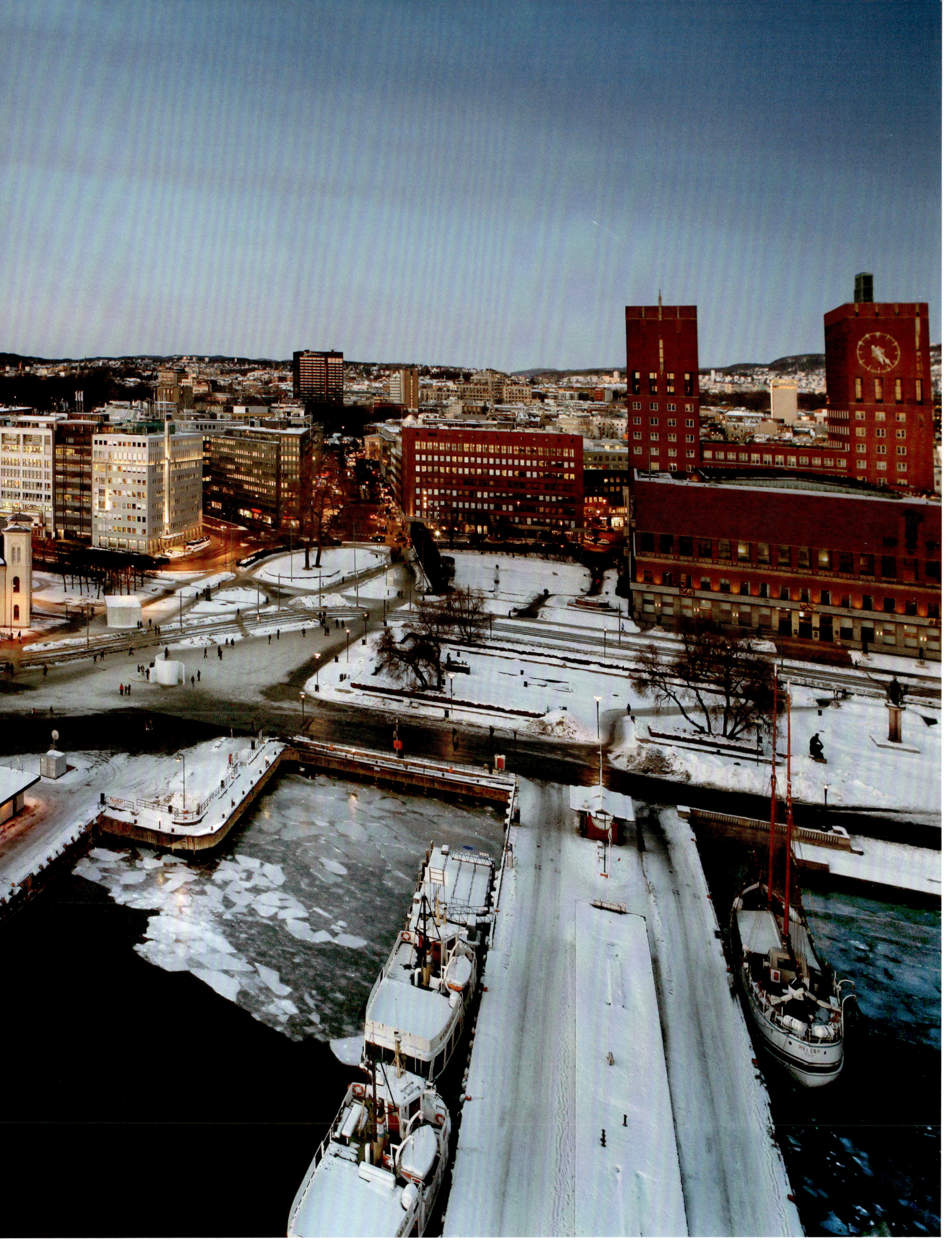

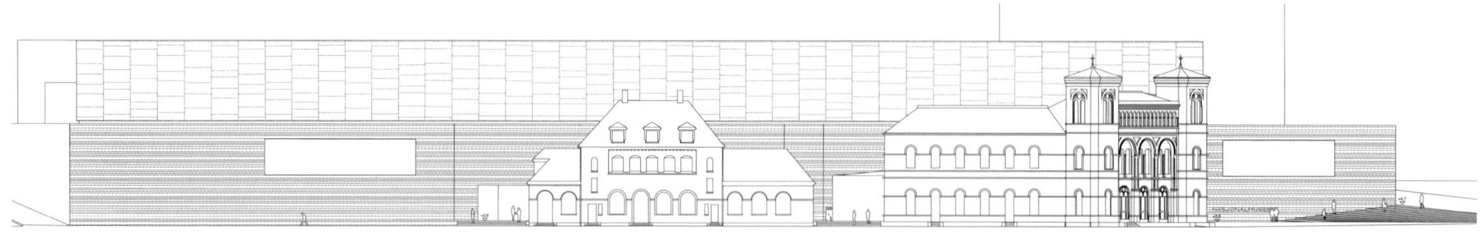

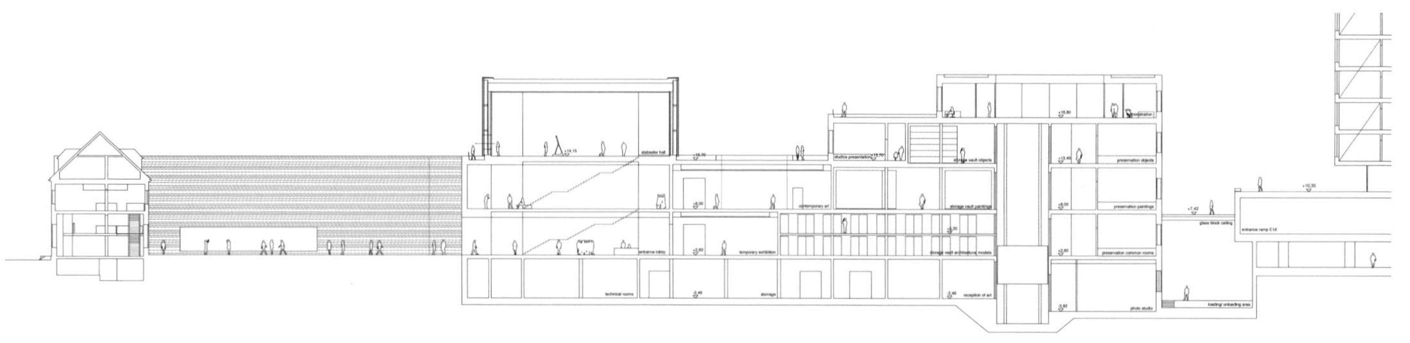

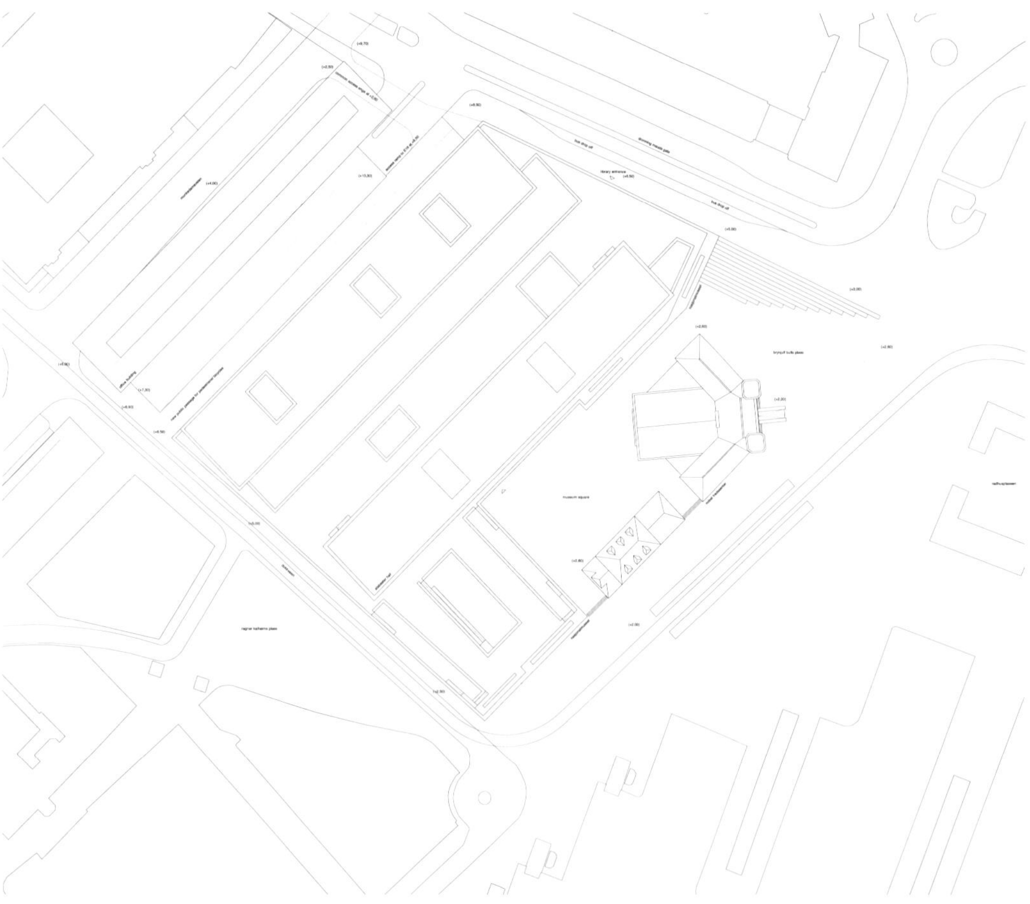

↑ Elevation, from southeast.
Section, southeast–northwest.
Site plan.

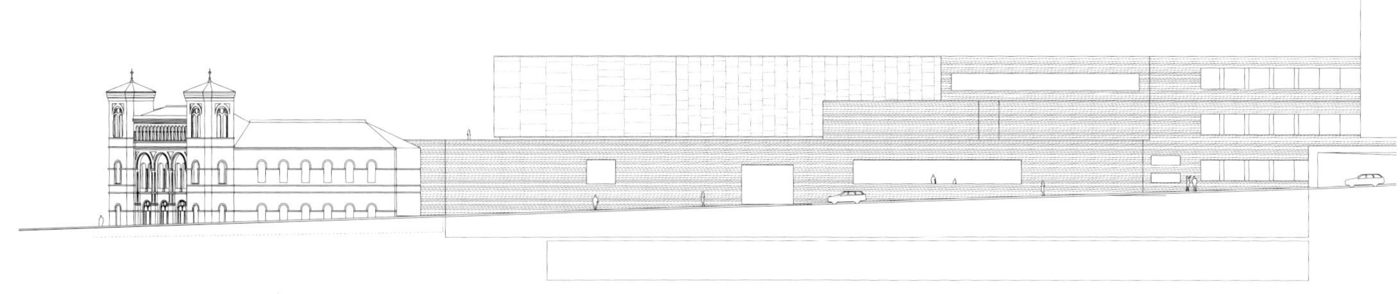

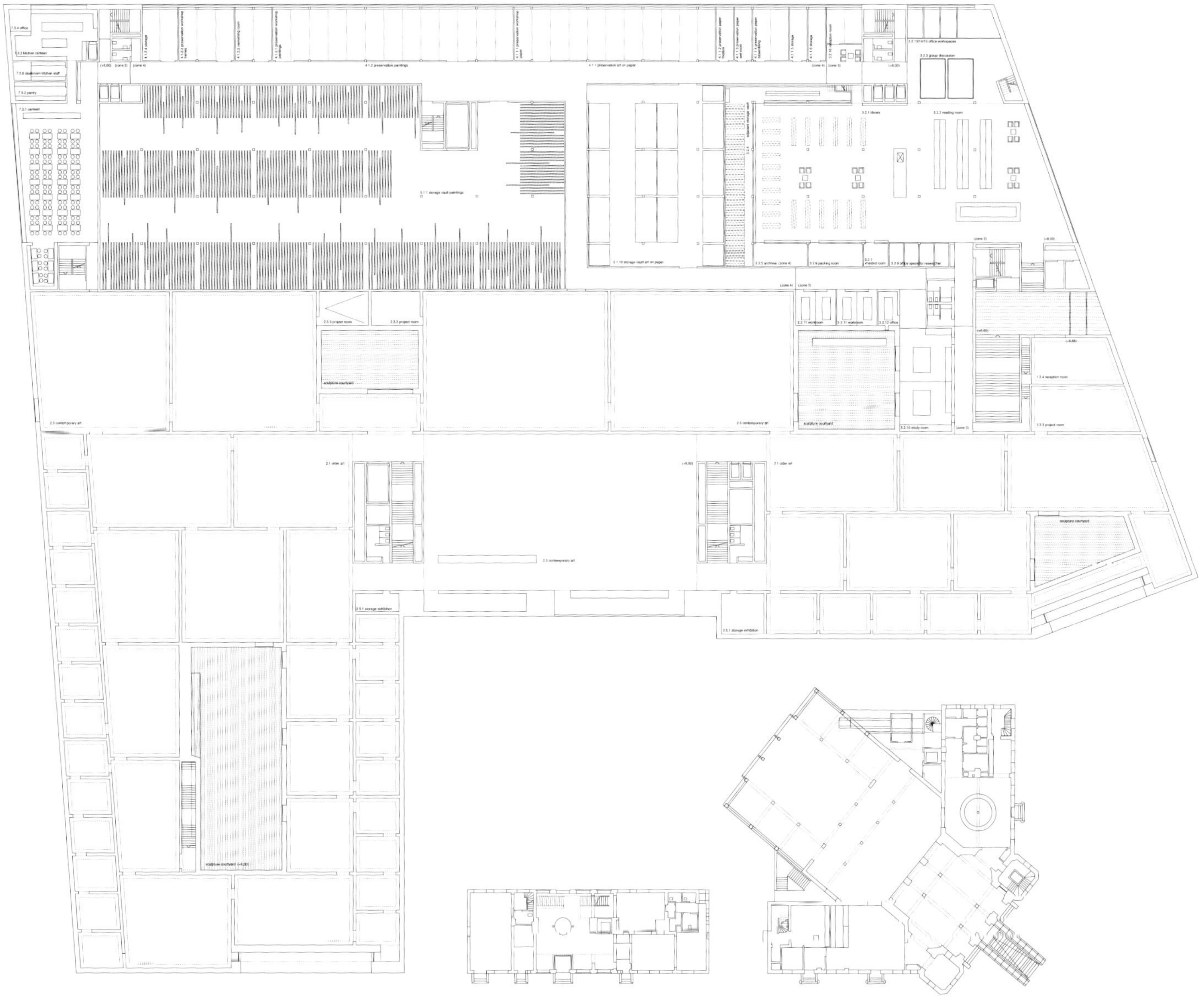

↑ Elevation, from northeast.
Plan: Level +1, permanent exhibition.

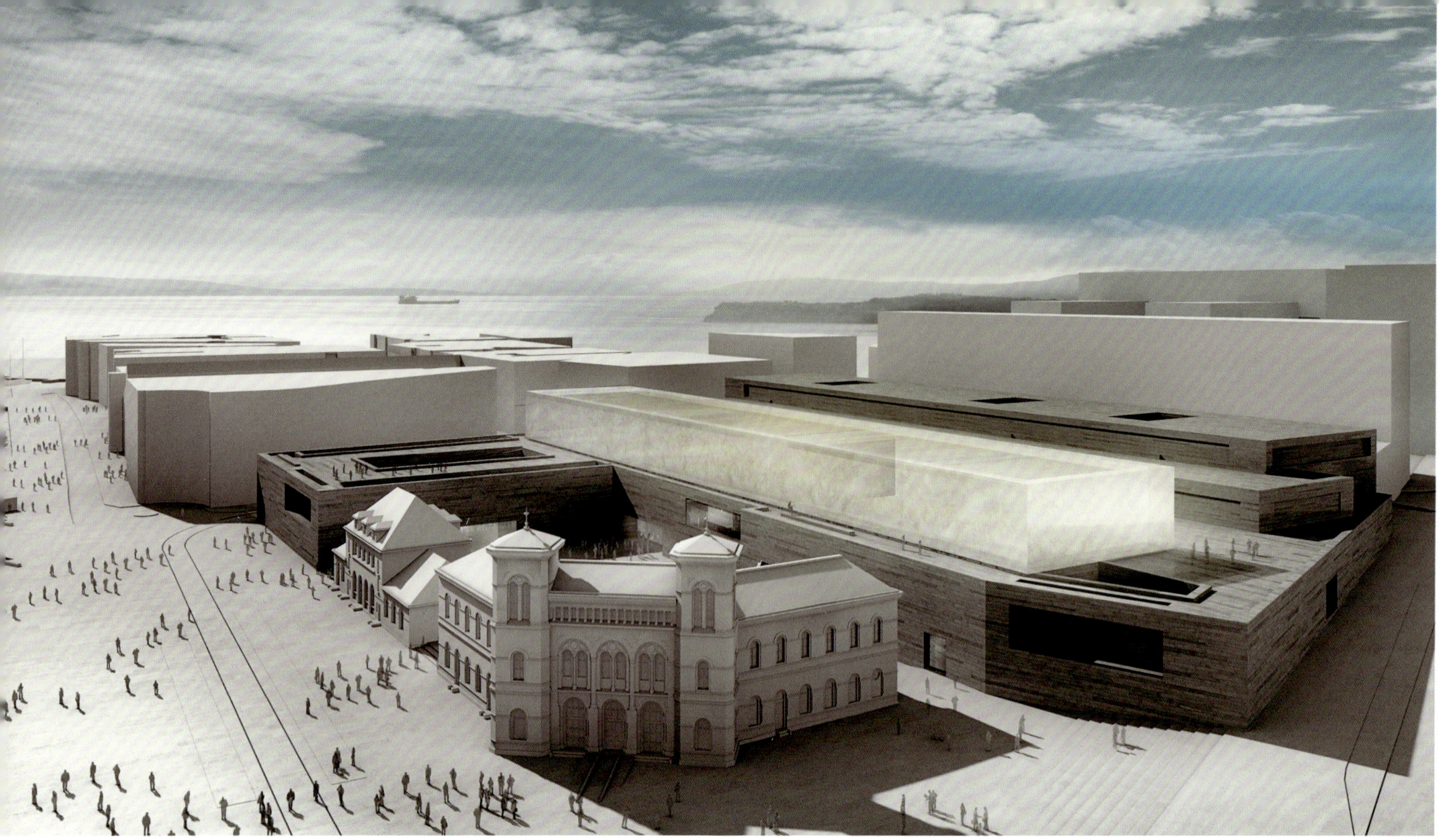

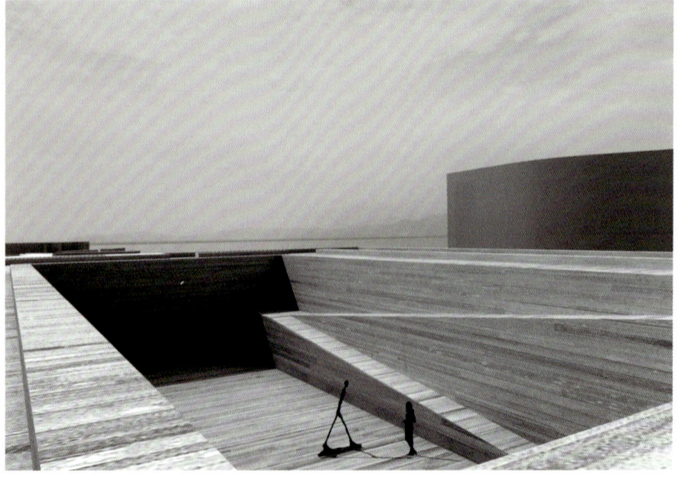

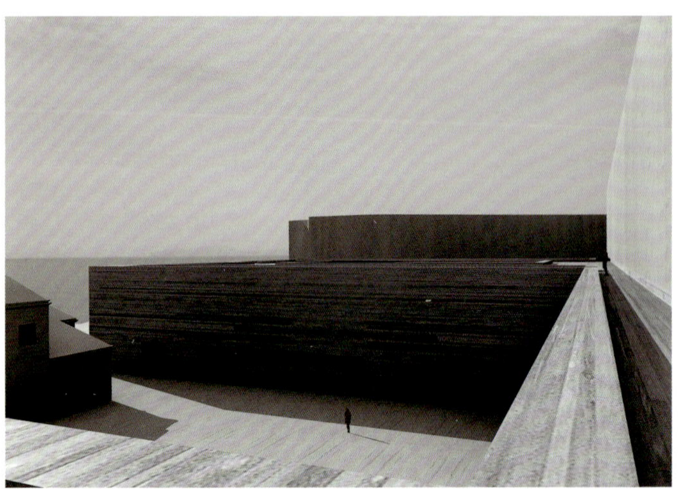

↑ Overview, looking west.

← Sunken Garden.
Entrance Court.

↗ Library "Silent Labyrinth".

→ Gallery "Munch Salen".

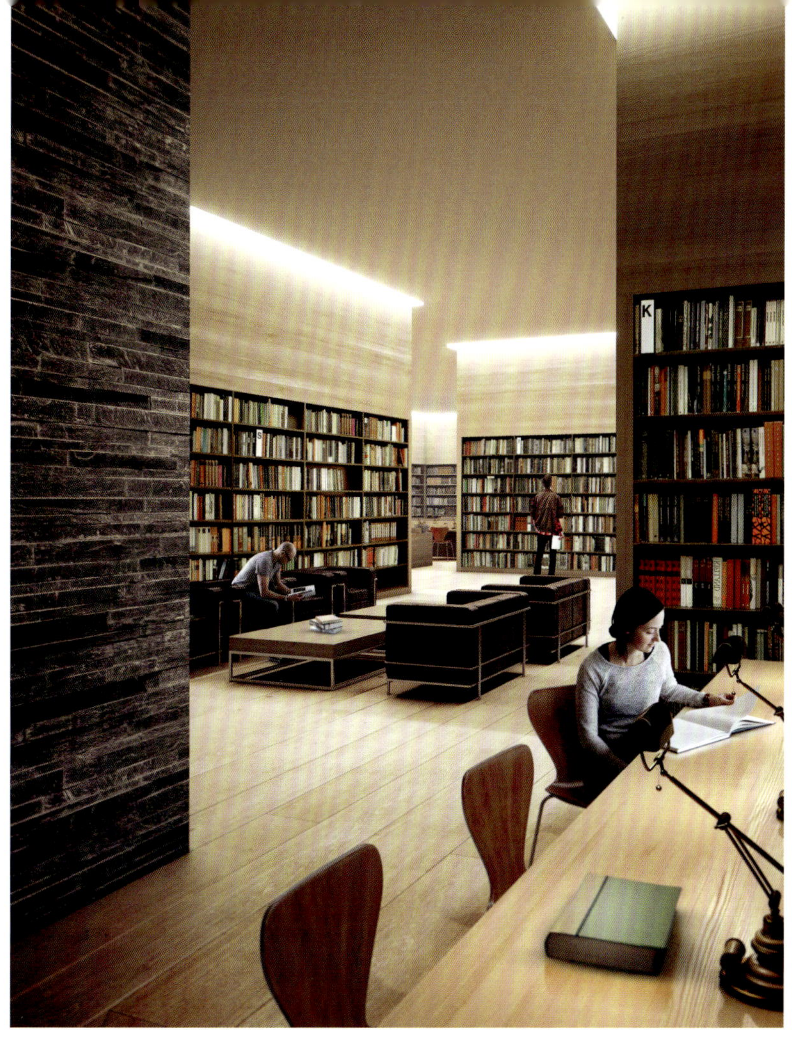

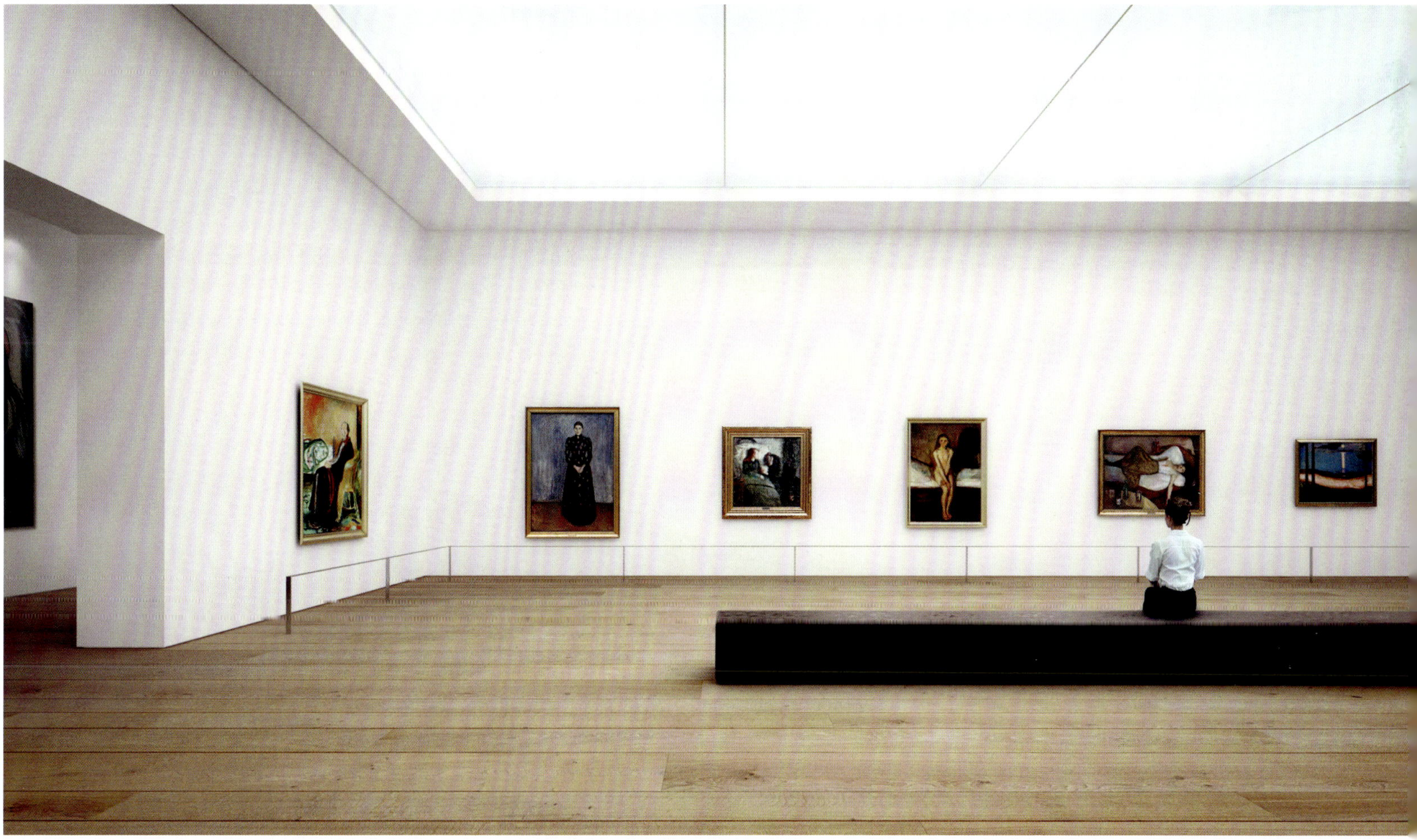

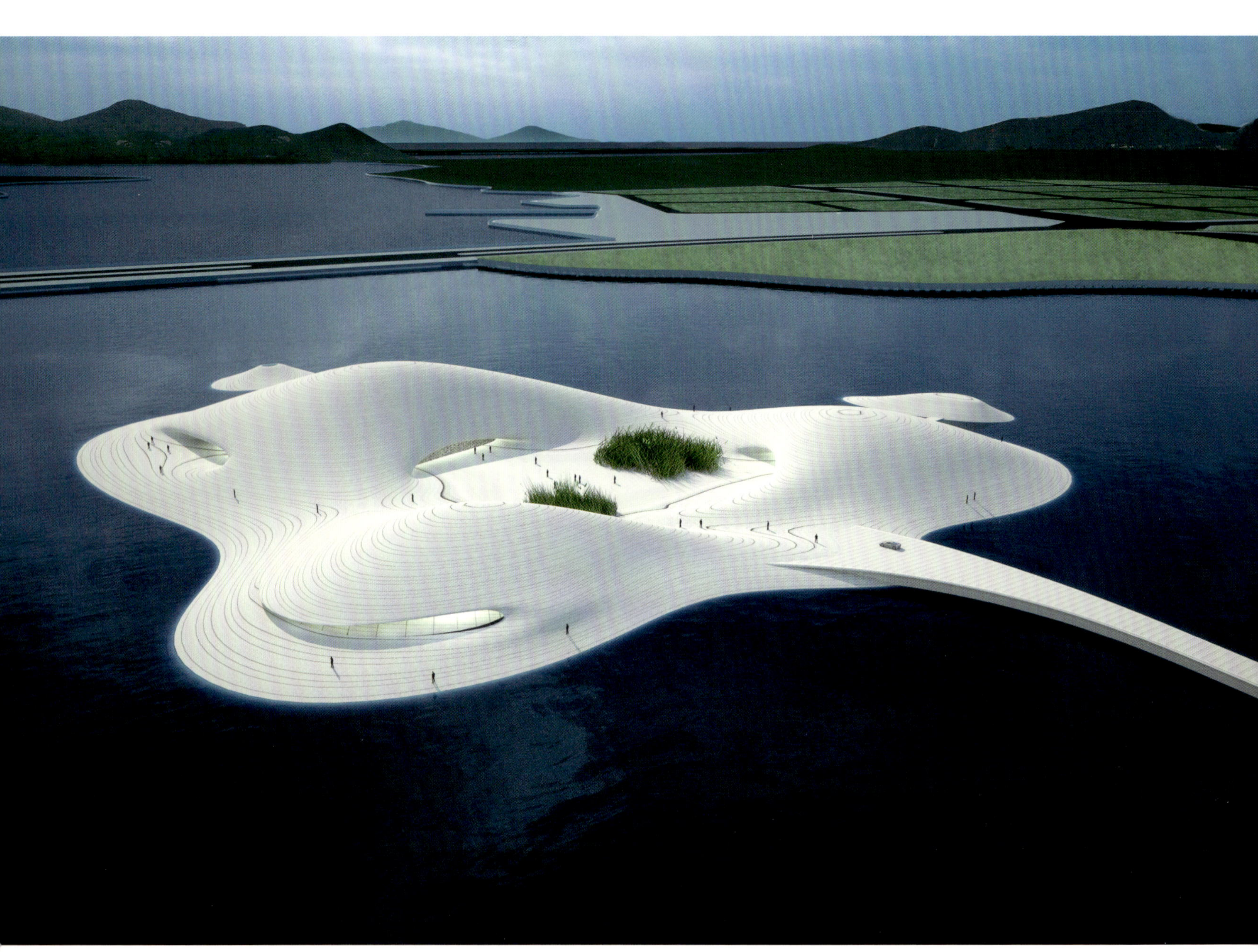

Pingtan Art Museum

Pingtan Island, China

MAD Architects, Beijing
Pending, yet to be realised
Building 40,000 sq. m
Private art collections

In 1988 only five per cent of China's people lived in cities numbering in the millions, but in 2010 it was a fourth of the entire population.[1] More and more so-called central business districts are arising in these cities, generally collaborations between private individuals and the state, which makes land available that is then developed into a new commercial zone.[2] For a few years now additional new zones have been created outside the already densely settled cities. These allow for flexible development, so they are usually not only pure manufacturing sites but also furnished with residential units, shopping opportunities and cultural offerings.[3] For the most part they display a mix of arbitrary architecture that disregards a specifically Chinese point of view.[4]

In 2010 planning for a Comprehensive Experimental Zone, a trading zone symbolic of China's opening out to its neighbour, began on Pingtan, an island belonging to the People's Republic of China across from the northwest coast of Taiwan. In a city that is still under construction, one of Asia's largest private museums is being created. It is being built by the Beijing office of MAD Architects, which works with a unique and innovative repertoire of styles. MAD Architects emphasises both the integration of their buildings in the surrounding landscape and their singularity; they should be more than simply functional – they are meant to inspire.[5] Their unusual appearance can lead to conflict with construction firms and patrons, over whose more traditional concepts MAD is forced to prevail. The firm's founder, Ma Yansong, feels that his office has

to do far more than other architects in order to be able to realise its unique concepts.[6]

The future museum lies on an artificial island in front of the city. A broad causeway, seawater lapping at its sloping sides, leads the visitor to a "floating" white landscape consisting of three gentle hills. Associations with water-worn pebbles, small waves or dune landscapes appear before the mind's eye. All three hills can be entered from a central plaza; inside them visitors move about on several different floors, one of them below sea-level in each case. Art is displayed in two of the hills, the third houses amenities like a café and a library as well as studios for artists. The smallest hill is a full eleven metres tall, the largest just under twenty.

What makes the Pingtan Art Museum so unusual, in addition to its site, is the design of its interiors. Here one won't find classic gallery rooms of the white cube variety – instead, one encounters a kind of landscape of caves that look to have been carved out of the stone by flowing water. Broad paths lead through the organic landscape that seemingly does without corners and sharp edges. Surrounded by sensuous forms, visitors are affected not only by the artworks displayed but also by the building itself.

Of course there's the question of what exactly will be shown in the Pingtan Art Museum. As yet it is uncertain whether the structure will outshine the art or whether the exhibited works can make the building take a back seat to them.

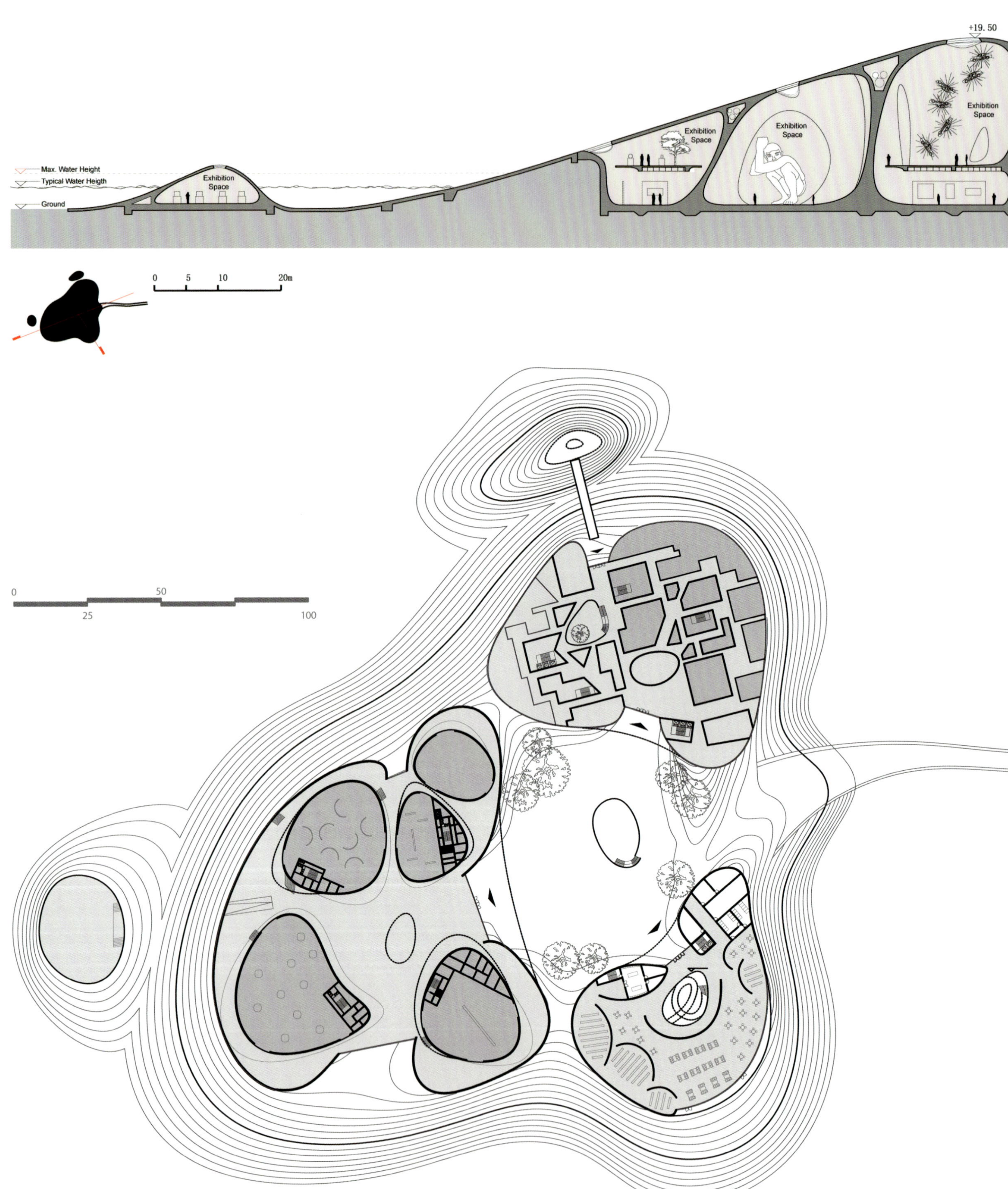

↑ Section, west–east.
Plan, ground floor.

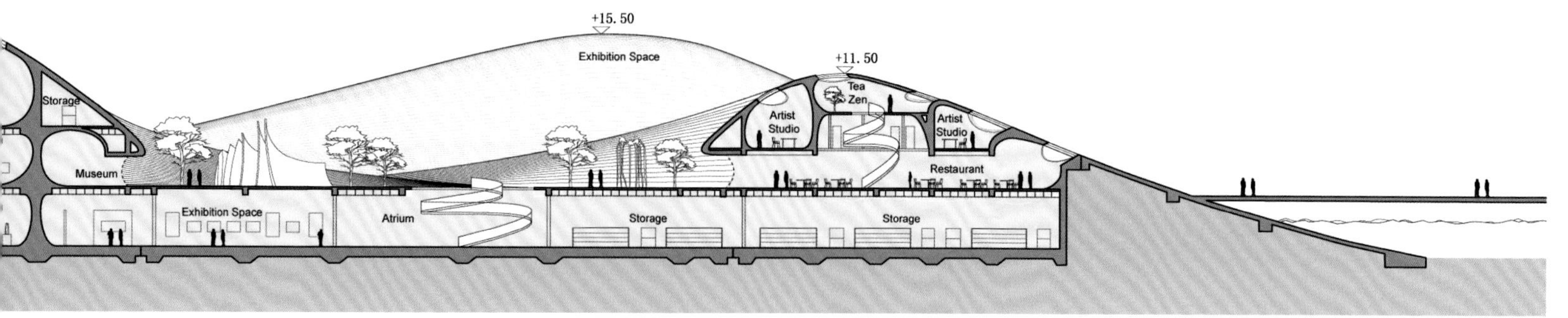

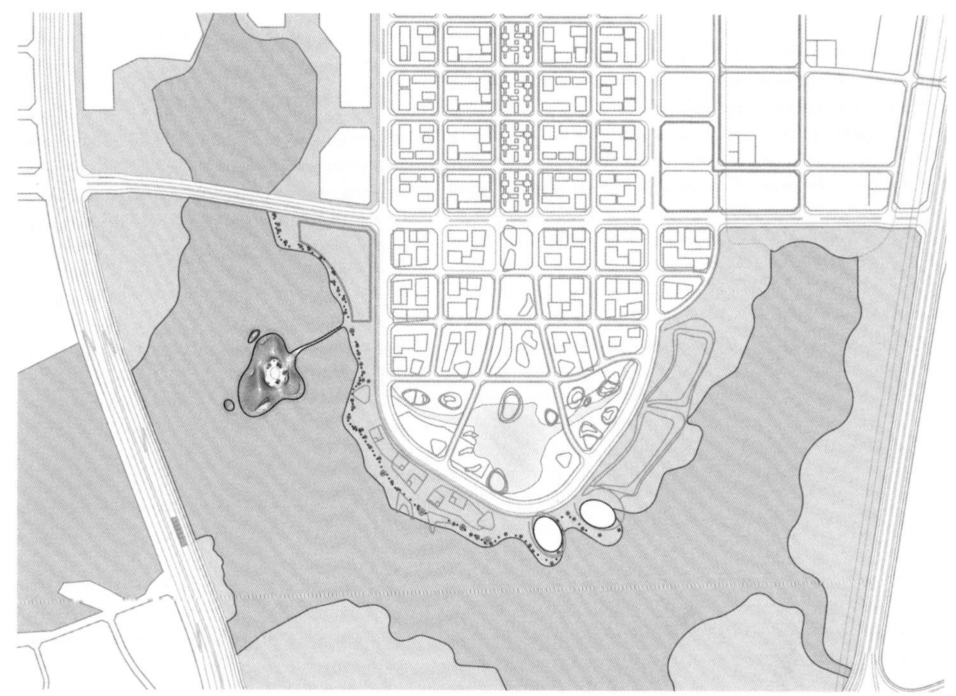

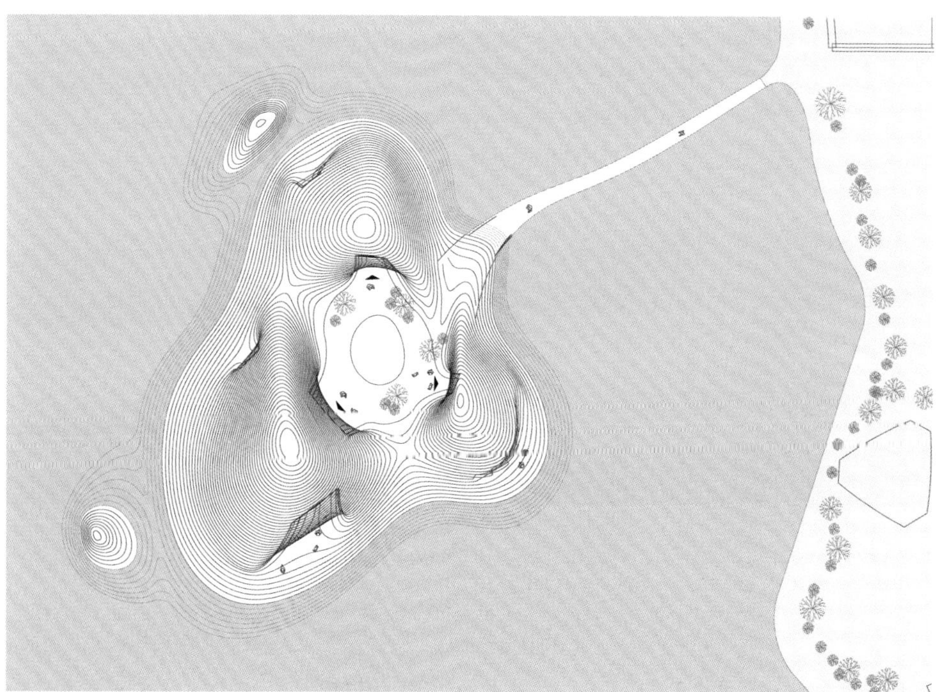

↗ Master plan.
Site plan.

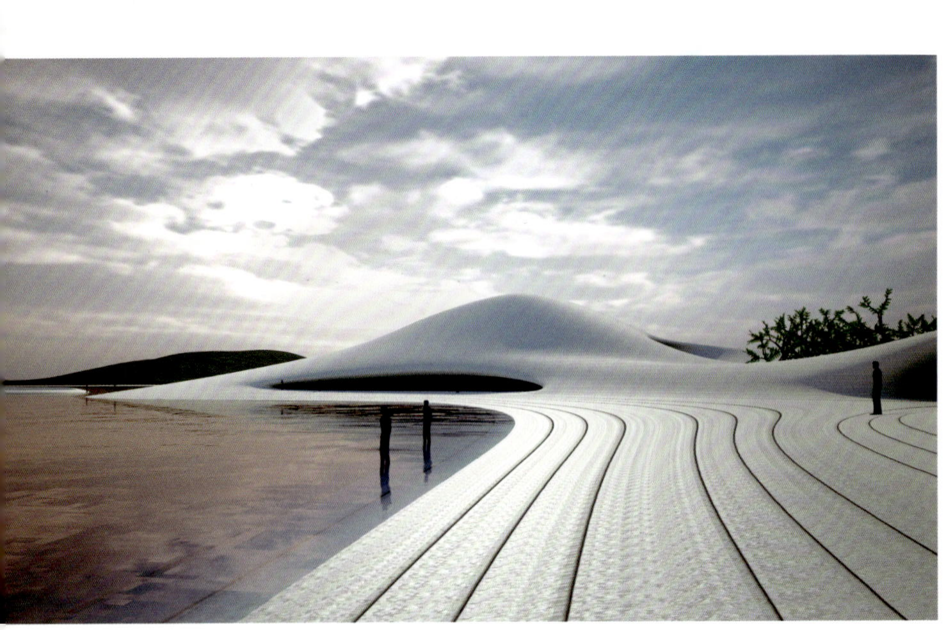

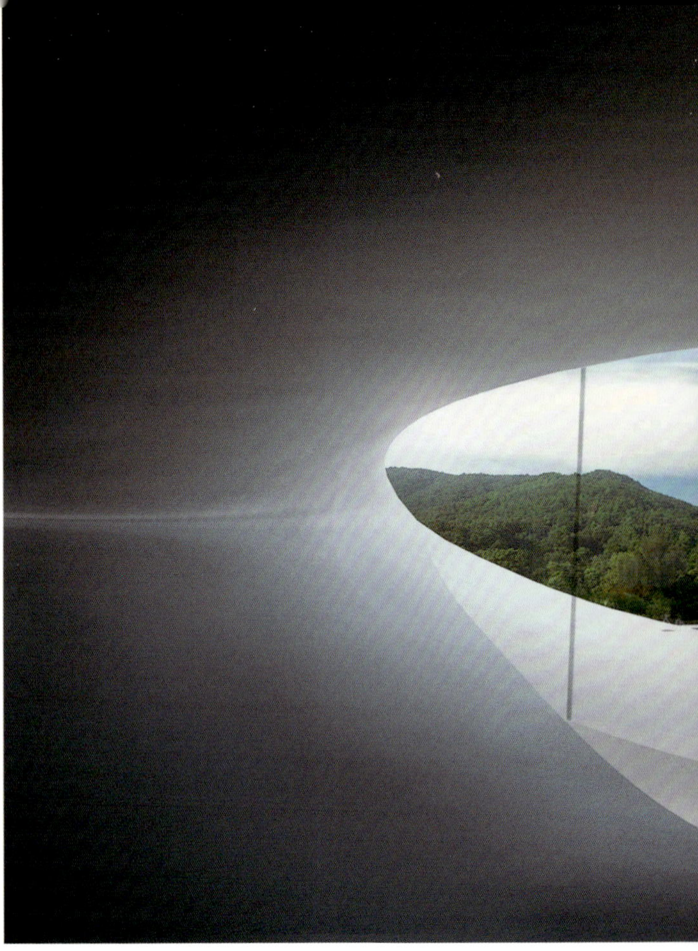

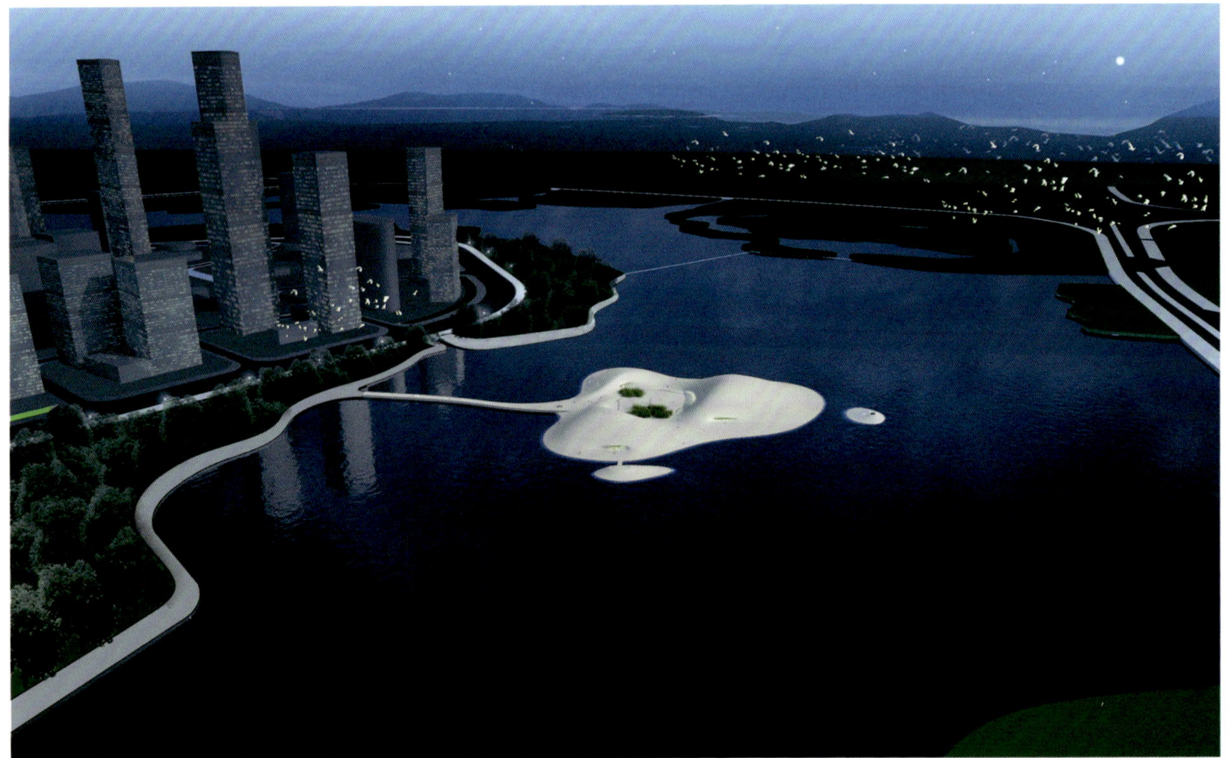

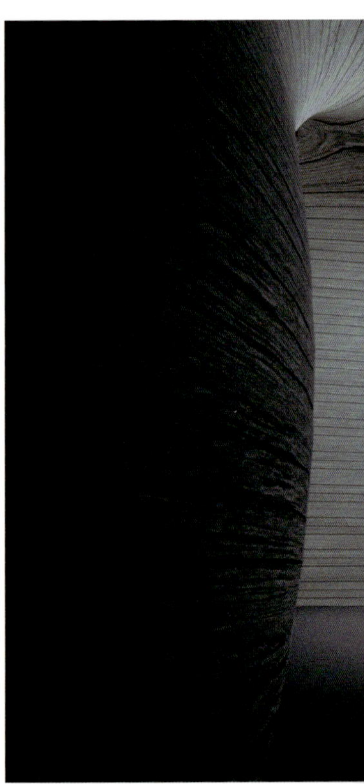

↑ Elevation, from the south.
By night, from the north.

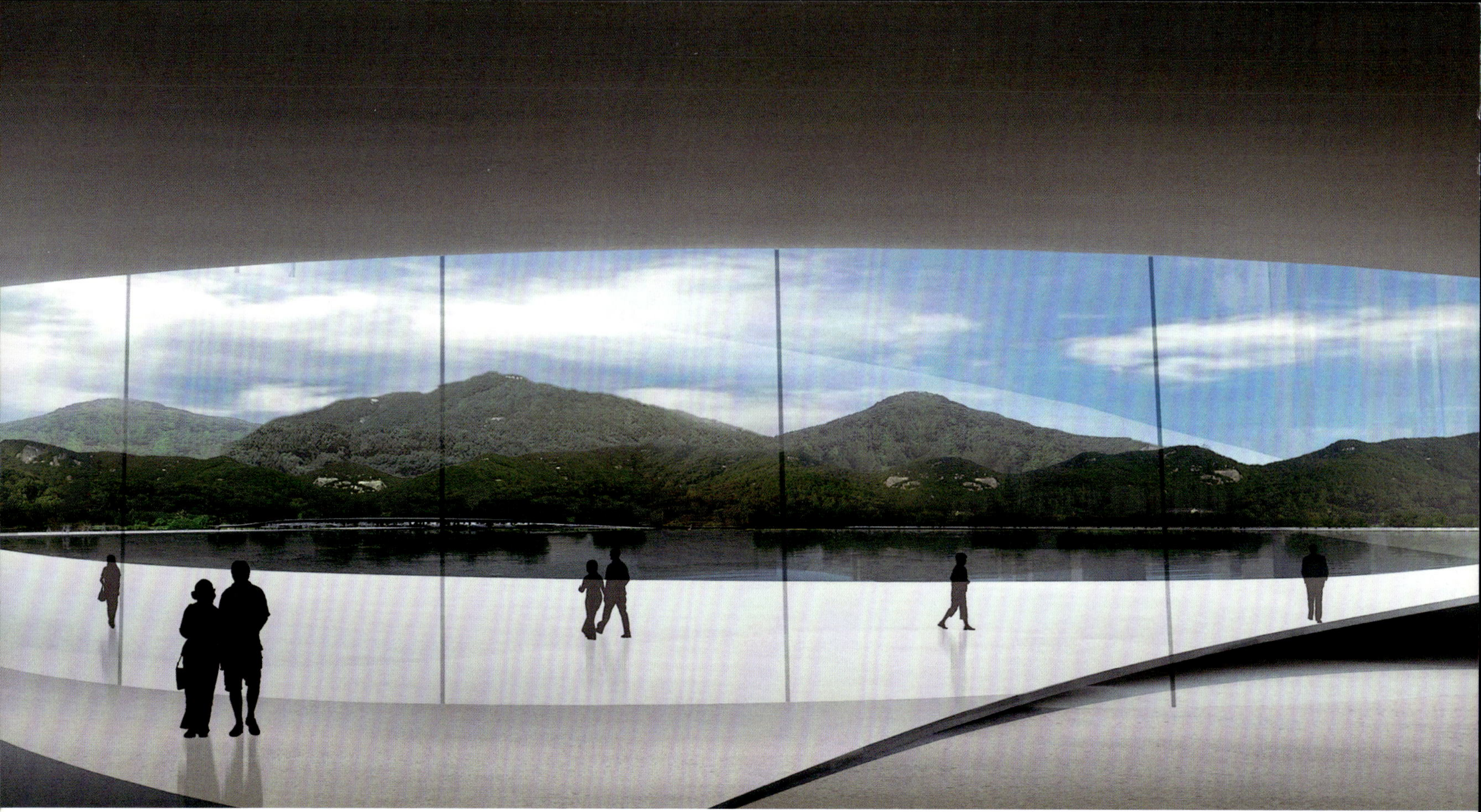

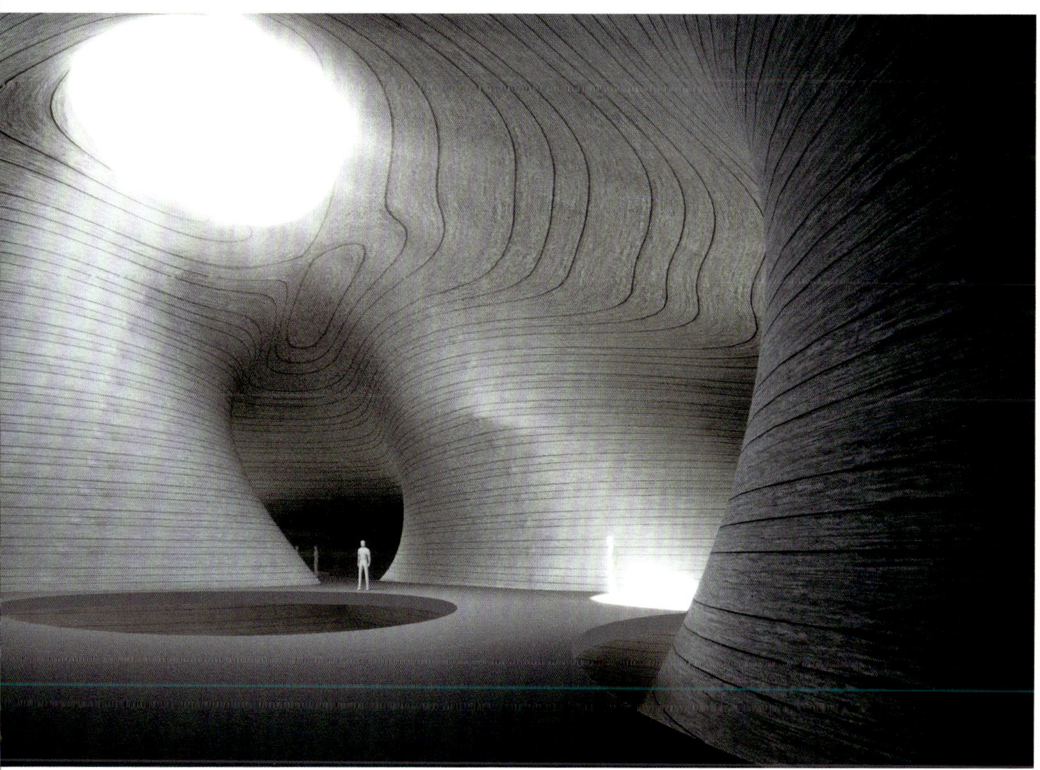

↑   Interior.

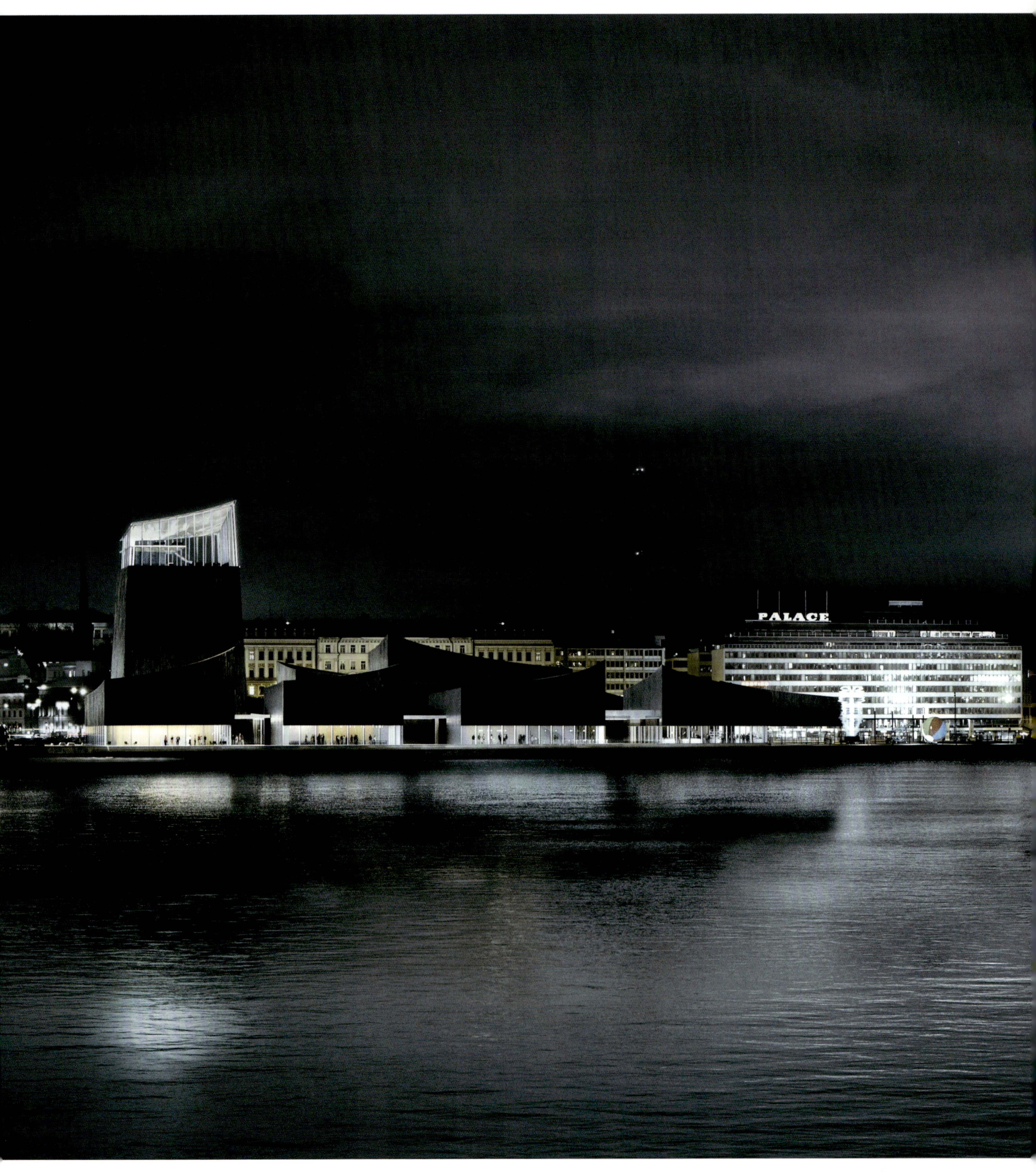
PALACE

Guggenheim Helsinki

Helsinki, Finland

Moreau Kusunoki Architectes, Paris
Pending, yet to be realised
Building 12,437 sq. m
Solomon R. Guggenheim Foundation collection and temporary exhibitions

It is not unusual for architectural competitions to attract hundreds of submitted designs. But it is uncommon for these submissions to be published online[1] and now be available to interested laymen and scholars. The Guggenheim Helsinki made the selection process for its new museum highly transparent from the start, finally settling on the design by Moreau Kusunoki Architectes.

Thanks to this openness, it is possible to compare the various versions of the winning design.[2] For example, already in the first round the distinctive freestanding pavilions were presented with the tower looming above them, together creating the museum complex. For the second round the tower was shifted to the south side, underscoring the flexibility of the design – the collection of structures now seems even more imposing, the accentuation of the heightened pavilion more logical.

Ten slightly separated buildings stand next to Helsinki's harbour. From the sea they look like a fortress protecting the city, and from the land they appear to shield Helsinki from storms and flooding. Instead of being menacing, their dark colour is self-confident and bold, as if they are aware of their cultural importance. Also, the division into separate pavilions relieves the complex of much of its darkness and monumentality; the buildings maintain contact with each other without creating a bulwark. This contact extends to the surroundings: in their wish to make them fit in, Moreau Kusunoki Architectes imitated Helsinki's street grid with the individual structures. Visitors can move freely between the pavilions and cross through them to reach the city from the water and vice versa. The museum adapts to its site, not the site to the museum.

Moreau Kusunoki Architectes is a young firm – founded only in 2011 – that has not subscribed to any specific design philosophy. If one looks at its other designs, however,[3] it is clear that simple geometric forms and gently curving surfaces are typical features. With them they avoid creating time-bound, iconic architecture; instead they strive for timeless structures that exhibit their strength purely by their durability.

The wood sheathing has been charred and then oiled twice, which makes it more durable. A generous use of glass makes the museum visually light and transparent, and the structures do not loom over their surroundings, but rather nestle in among them. There is no visible hierarchy among the separate pavilions: one is not more distinguished than the next, every art genre is given the same importance. The viewing tower is the only element which emerges above the complex, its design corresponding to that of the pavilions. A few of the lower structures have shaded-glass roofs which gently filter natural light from the north to create ideal lighting conditions for the museum pavilions, while others are solid; but all of them sway upwards in a gentle, concave manner. The tower itself is massive and dark at the bottom, while the upper third is entirely glazed and elegantly sets off any sense of heaviness. Its clarity breaks through the darkness. This is especially visible in the evening hours when the pinnacle is lit from within.

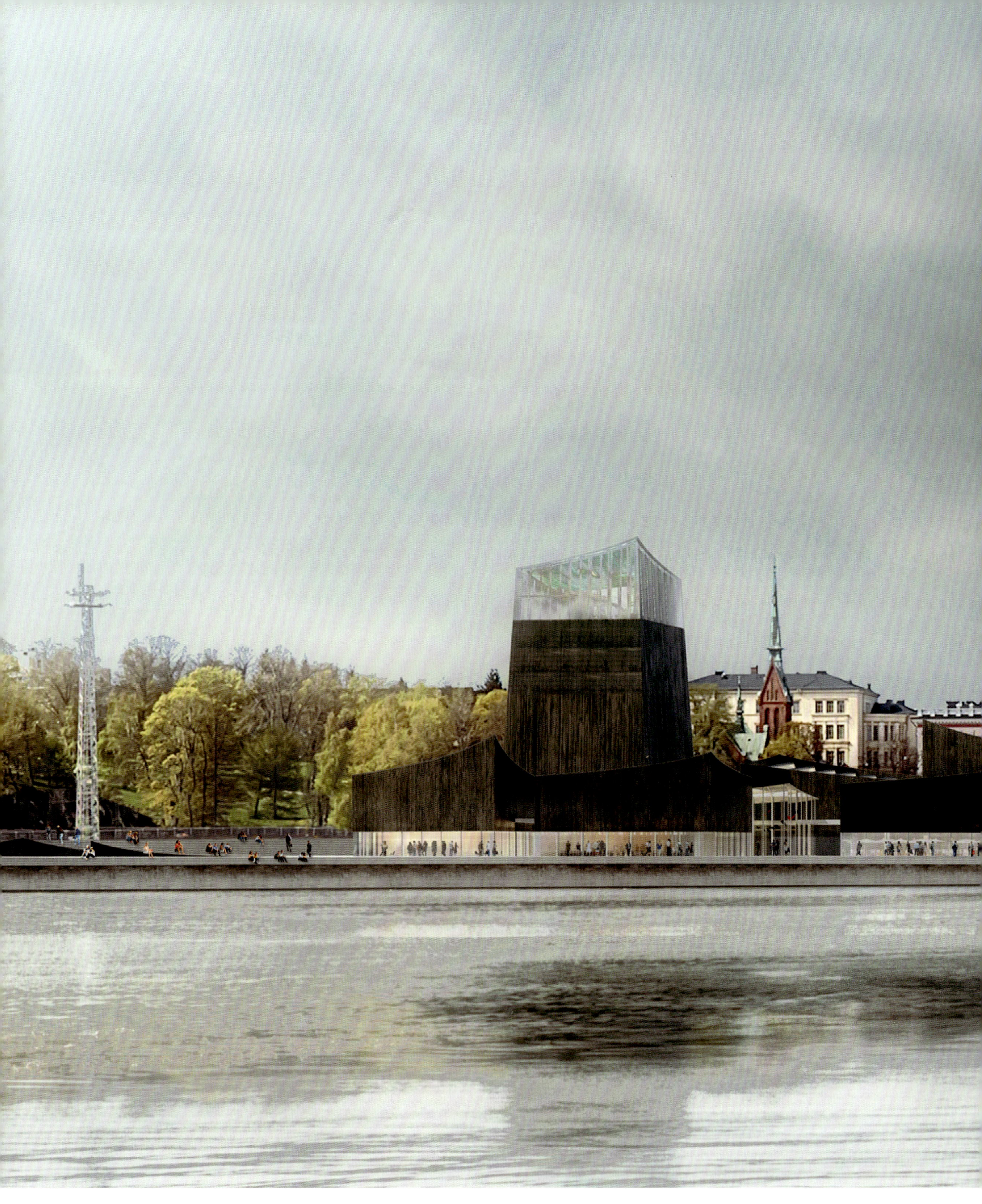

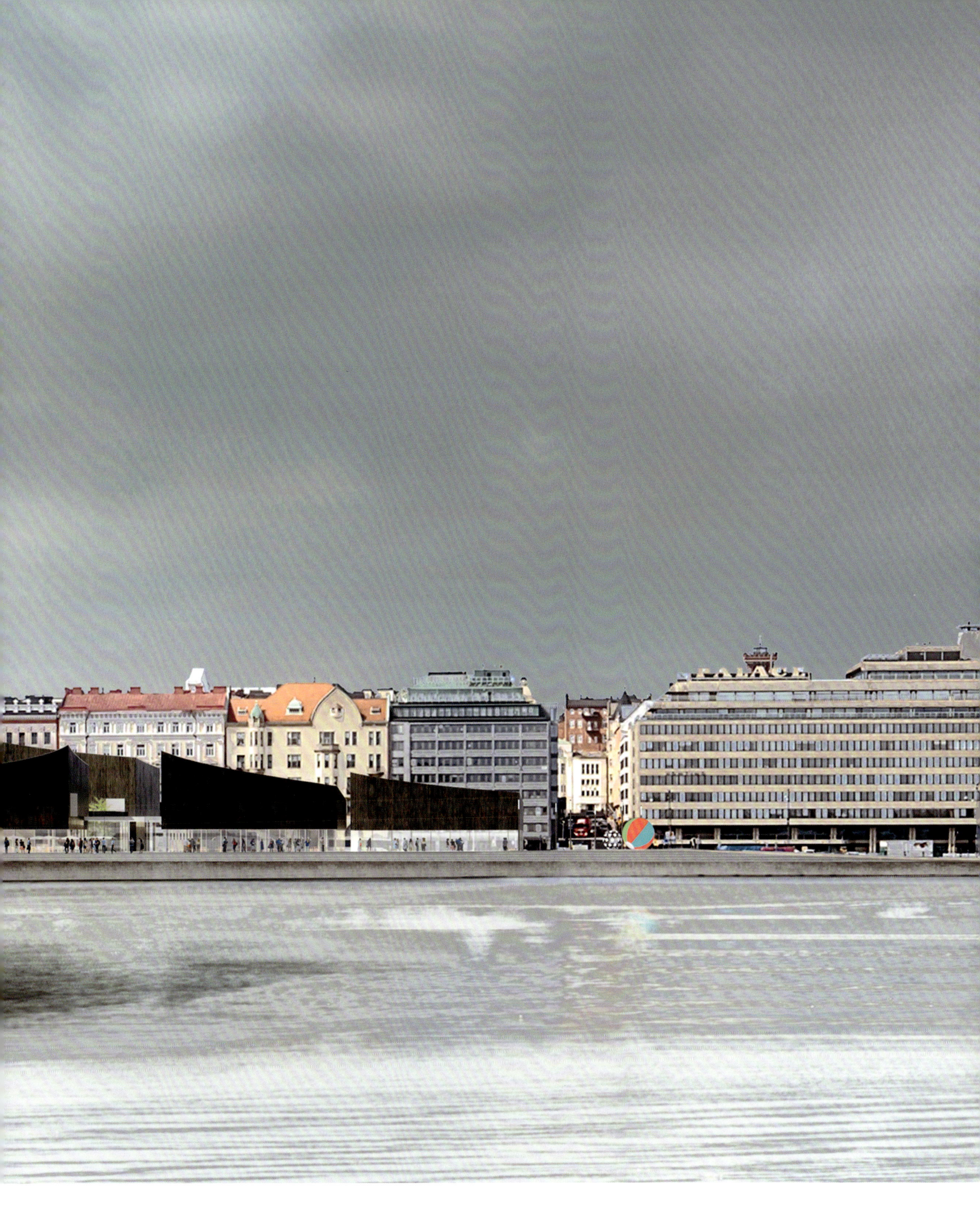

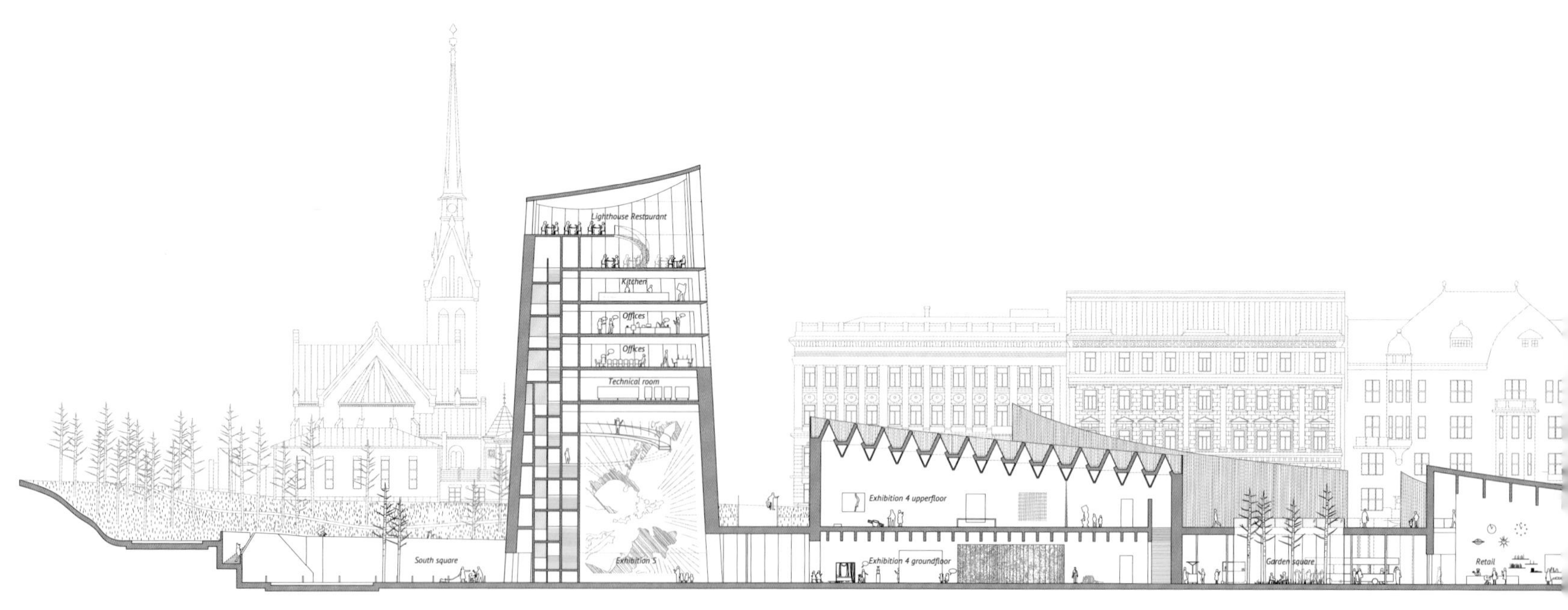

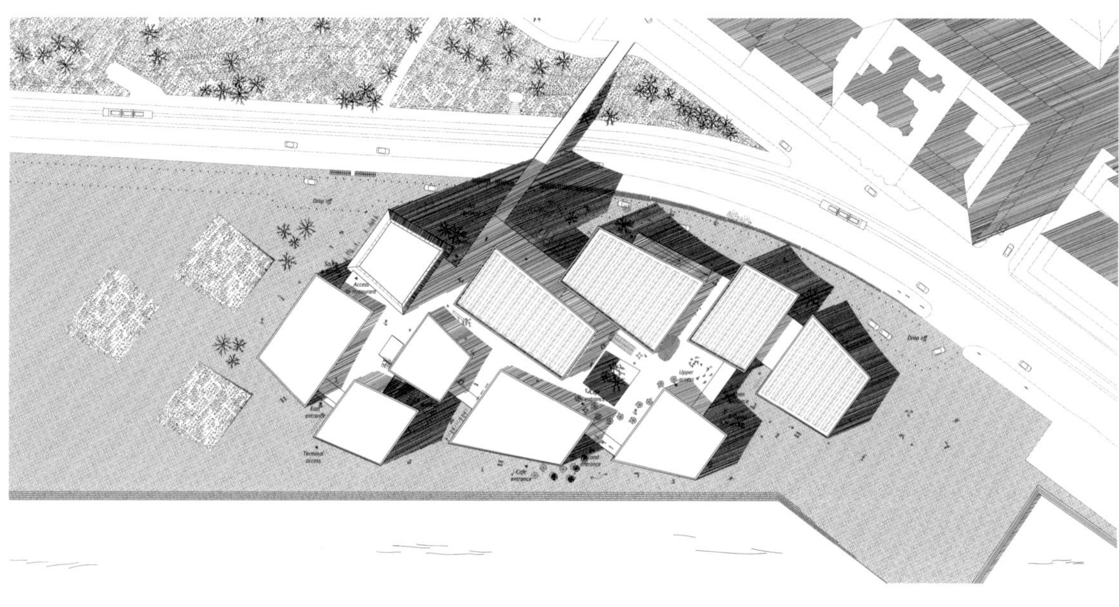

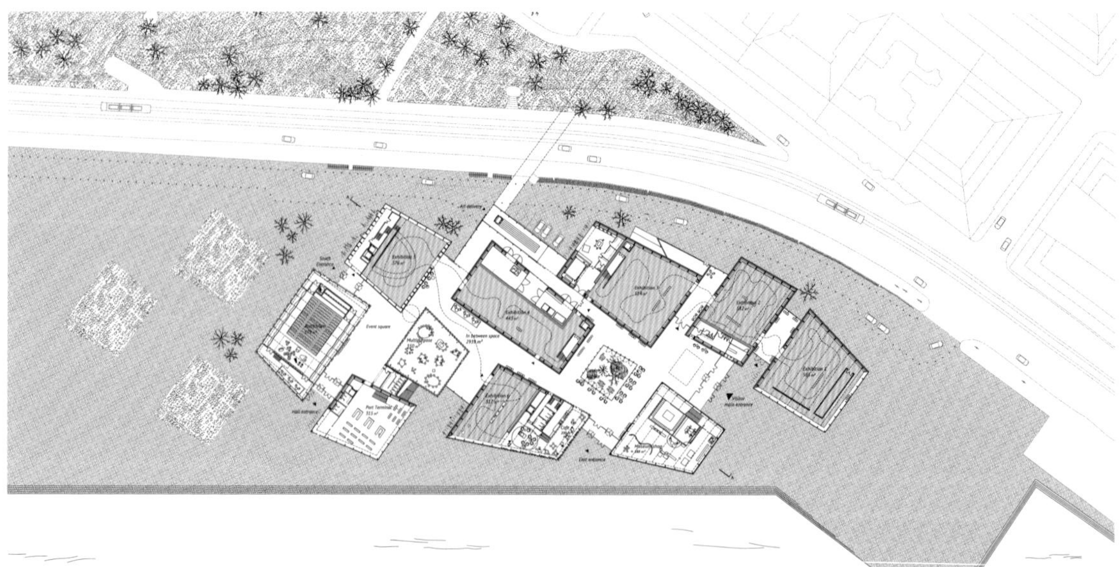

↑   Section, south–north.

↗   Roof plan.
    Site plan.

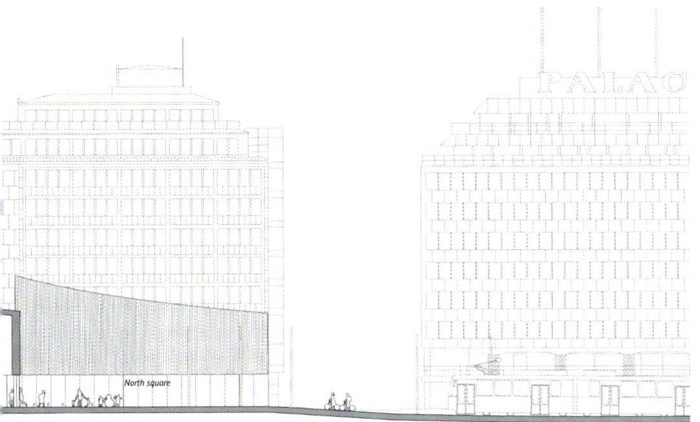

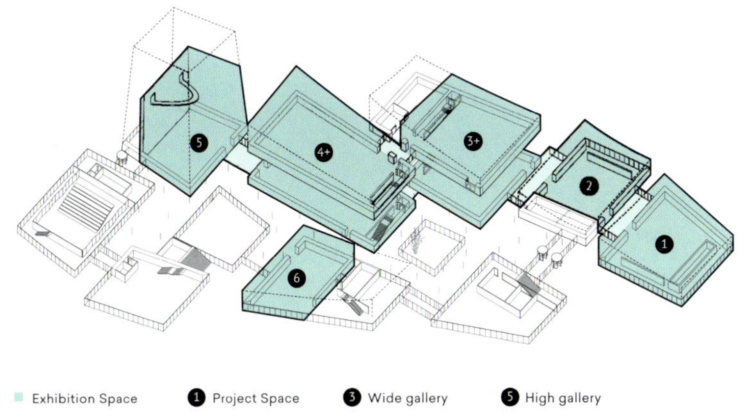

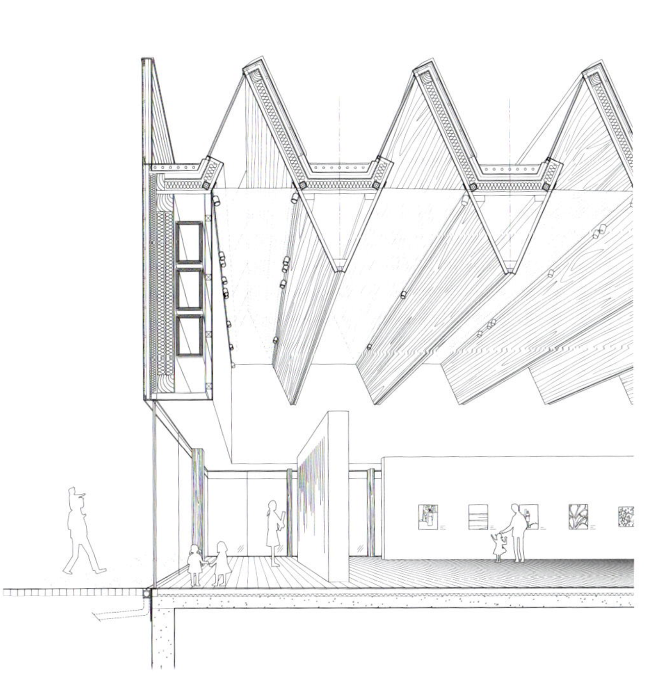

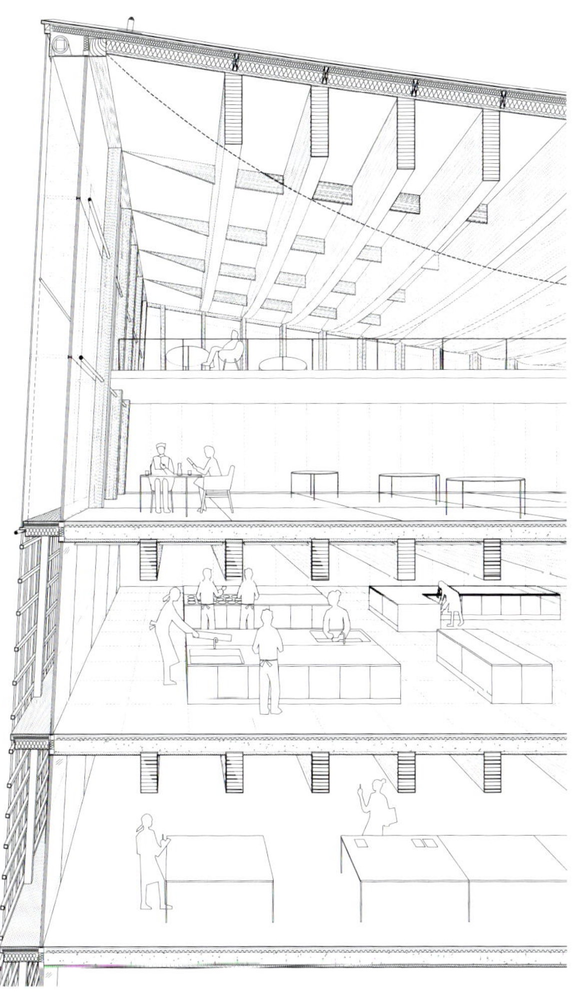

↗ Expo volumetrie.
Sections gallery and tower.

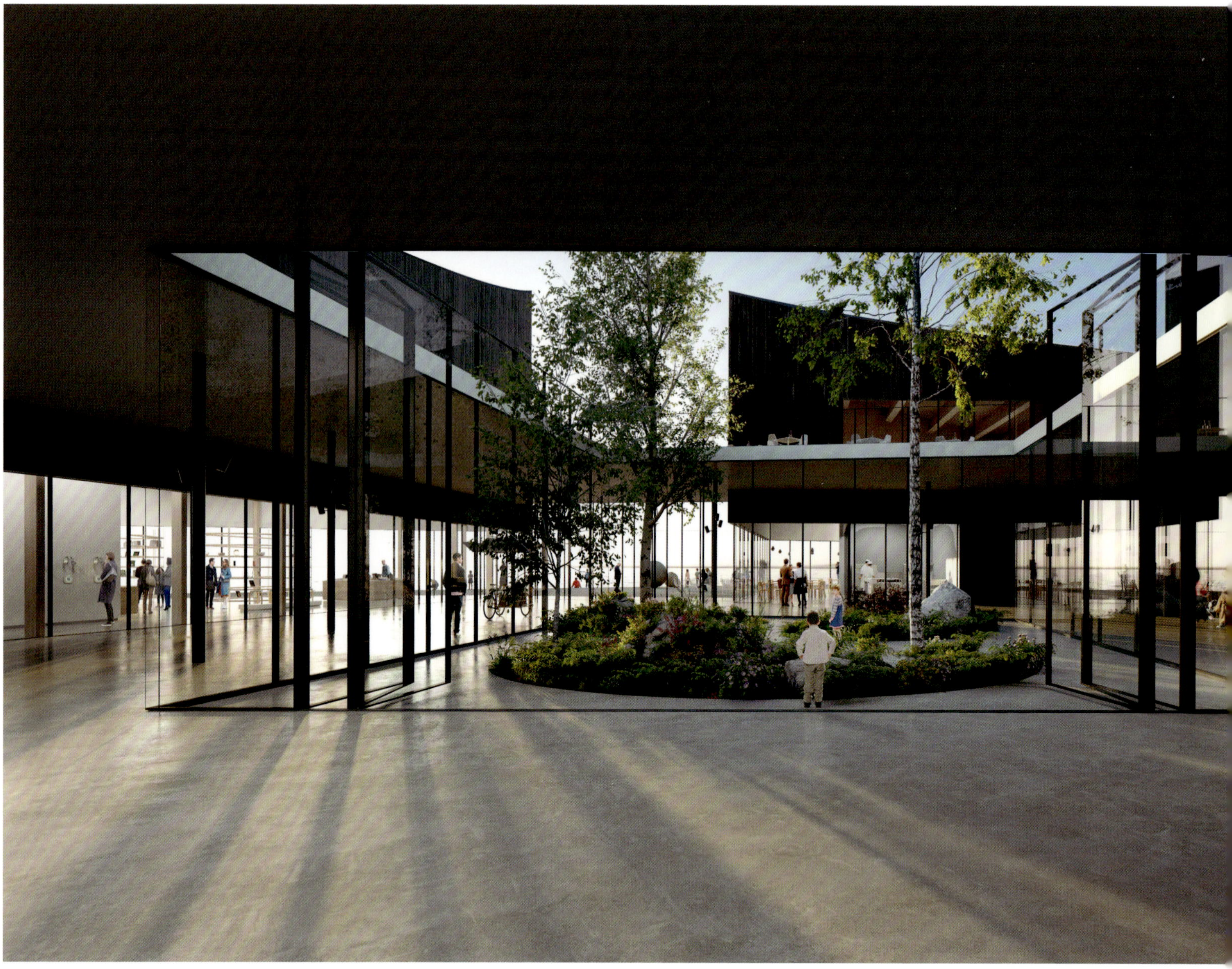

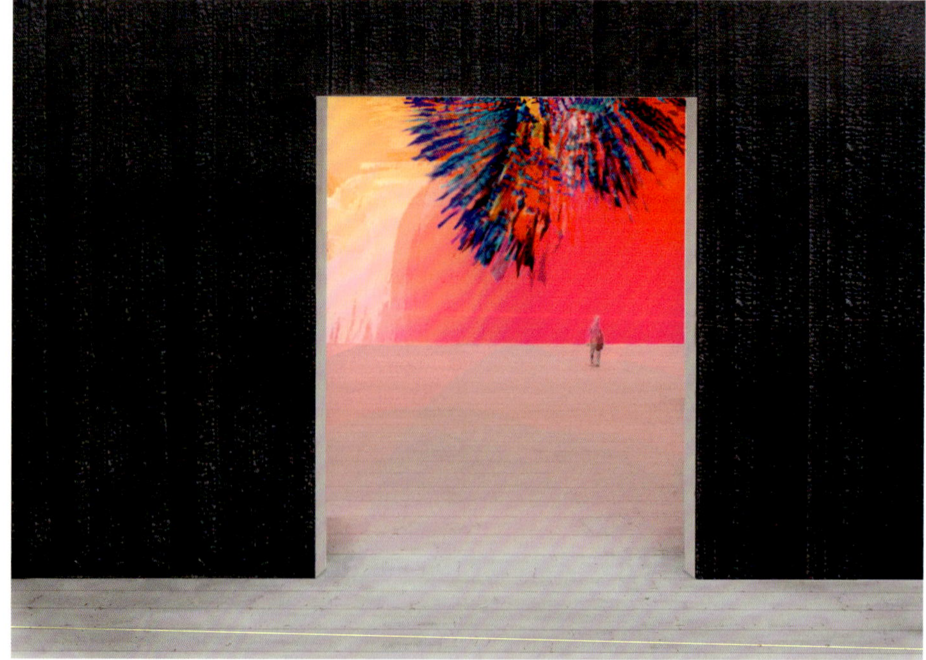

↑ Garden square.

→ Exterior surface.

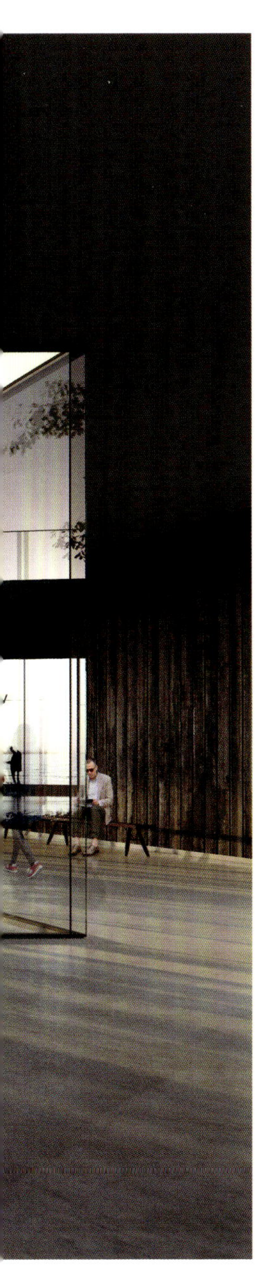

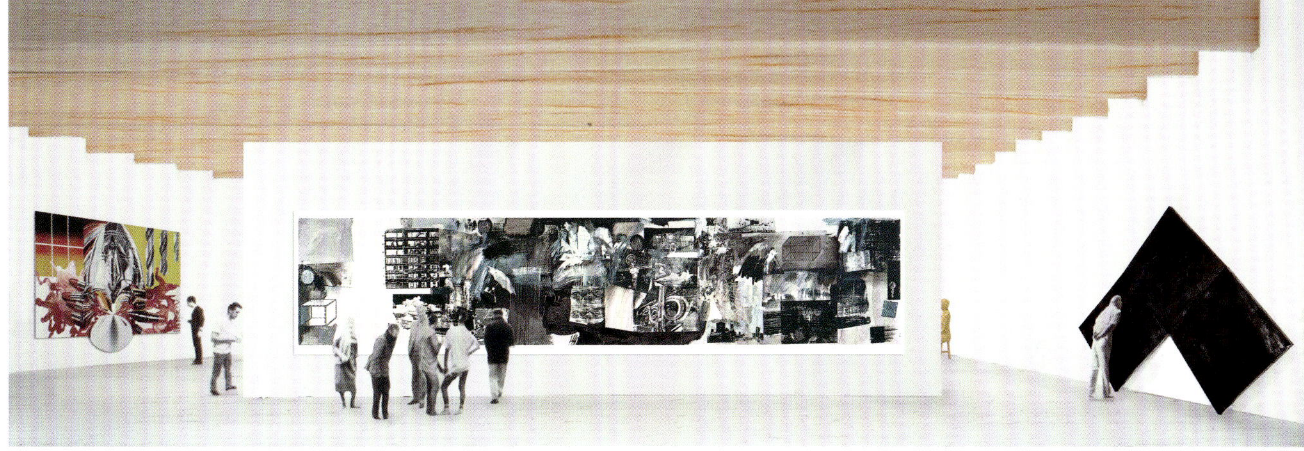

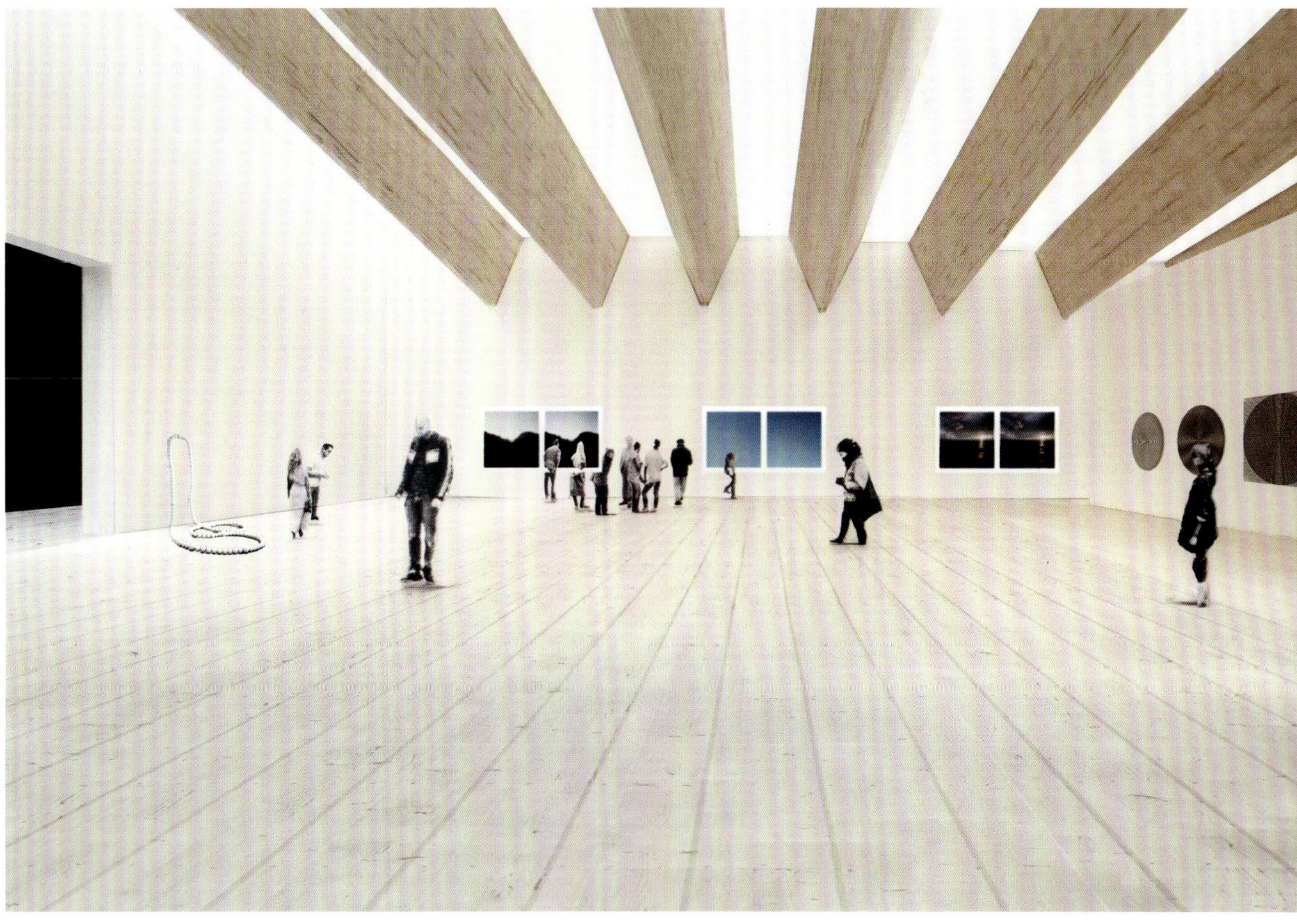

↗ Gallery spaces.

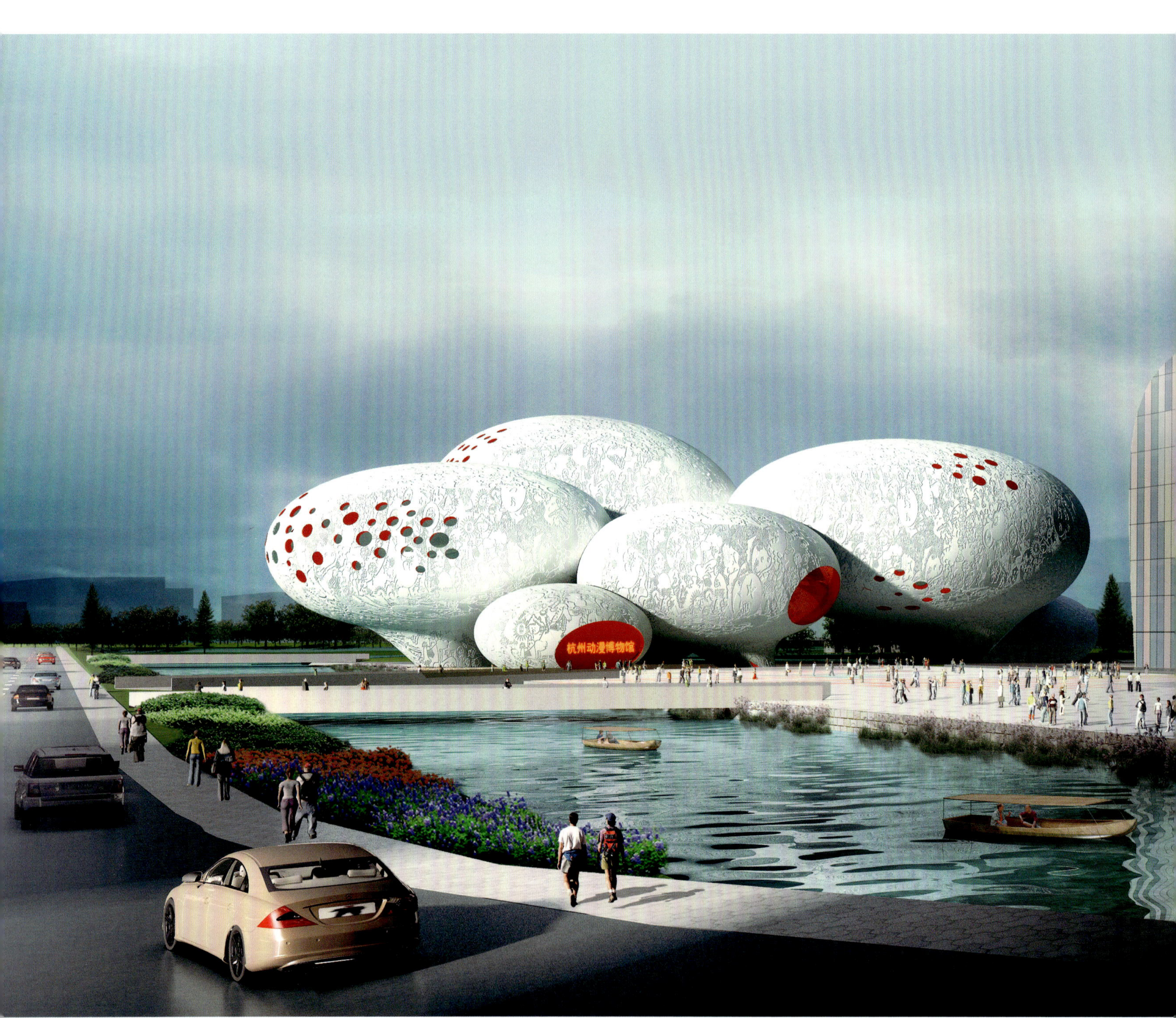

杭州动漫博物馆

China Comic and Animation Museum

Hangzhou, China

MVRDV, Rotterdam
No current plans to progress this design
Building 32,000 sq.m
Private comic collection, animations and multimedia displays

The speech bubble is a distinctive characteristic of comics, even though it doesn't appear in all of them.[1] MVRDV made use of this familiar feature – creating a building complex of separate speech bubbles – when in 2011 they won the competition for the China Comic and Animation Museum. The design consists of six balloon-shaped structures of different sizes that form a sculpture in the artificial island landscape. Around them lie hotels, the new expo building and a great deal of water, so that one can approach the cloud-like design in various ways. The white outer shell is made up of locally produced porcelain tiles[2] onto which films can be projected, so that in summer the setting becomes an open-air cinema. Thus the museum on the tip of the island is not unapproachable; it invites people to linger even when it isn't open. The lush greenery in the midst of the densely built-up office and congress area can be used for recreation by visitors and people who work there.

From the lobby speech bubble, one can already see into the cinema and the so-called Collection Zone. Long escalators leading to the separate zones look like the beginnings of speech bubbles emerging from mouths. And just as figures in comics move the story along with their act of speaking, visitors to the building are active and may design their own tour, for there are no prescribed routes through the bubbles. In the Collection Zone one learns about the history of comics, mangas and graphic novels while surrounded by a bubble that generates a very special sense of space and intensifies one's experience of the objects displayed. In addition to the permanent exhibit, there is an interactive space in another bubble where visitors can create their own comics or multimedia applications. A library and an education space for school classes or groups round off the site.

This complex of buildings is more than a simple shell; it enters the realm of sculpture – and goes even further still, for it unites the sculpture's pretence to artistry with a building's functionality. It combines two things, just as comics combine drawings and text. The comics genre is always aware that it occupies a unique place in literature,[3] for comics are not only read like books, they are also viewed as visual art.[4] By providing its visitors with a chance to look at and understand art and even to set the ball rolling and create art themselves, the museum exceeds the mission of a mere collection.

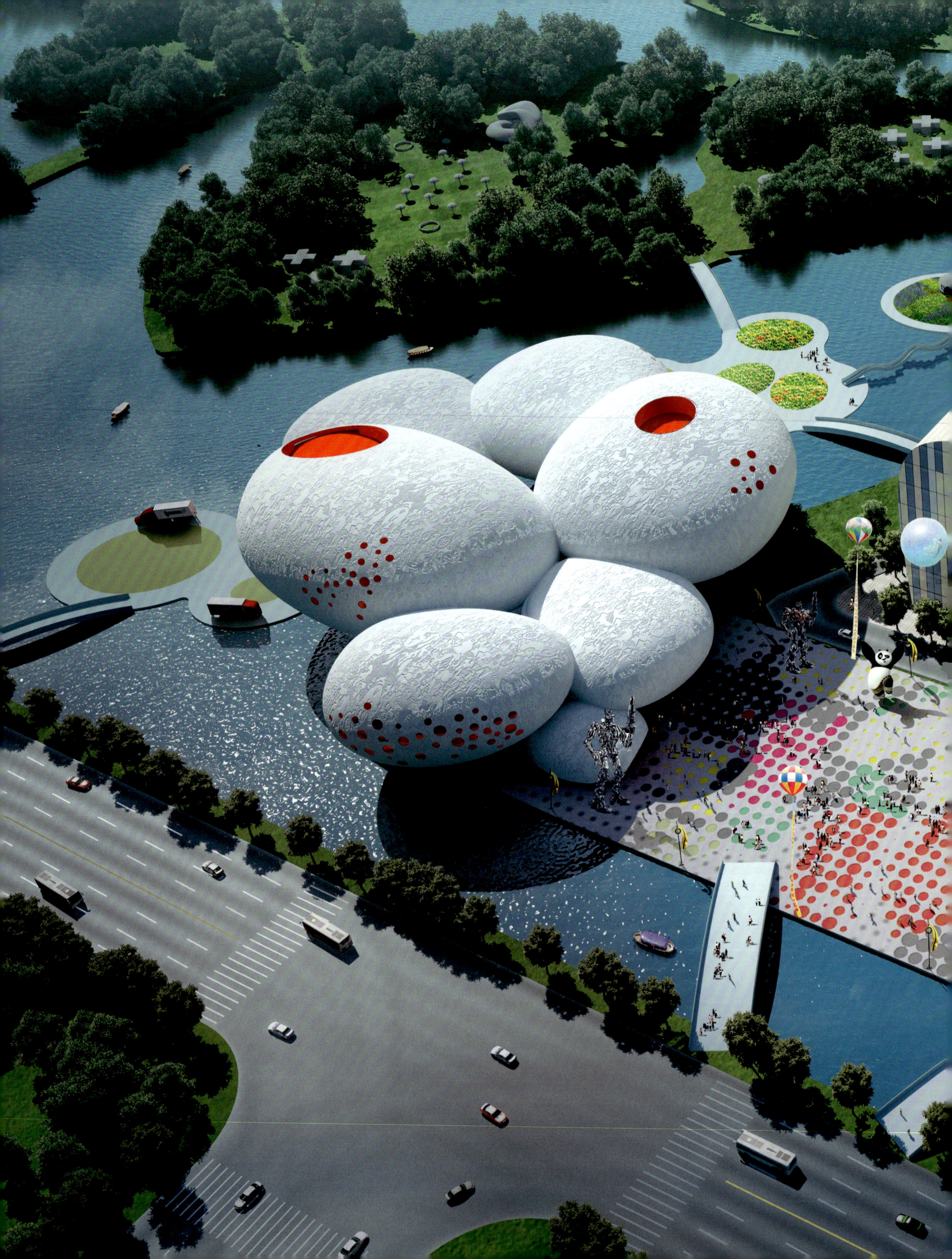

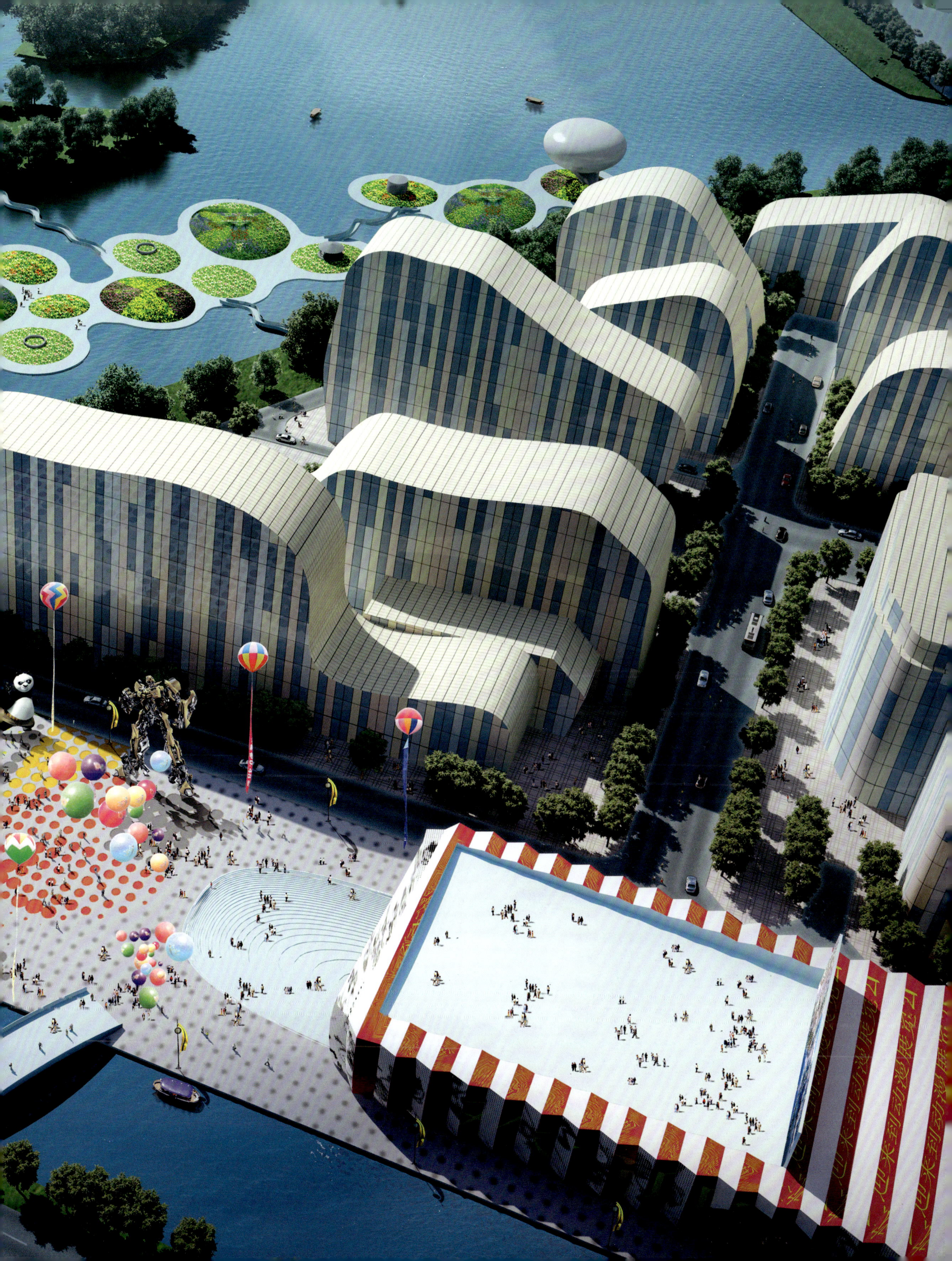

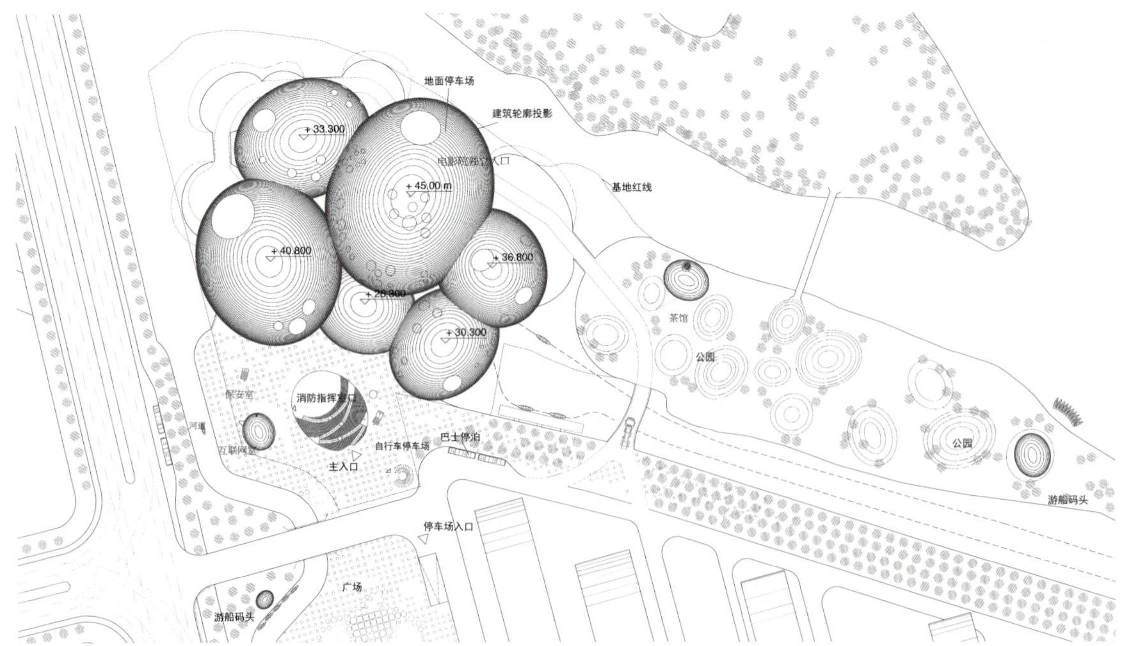

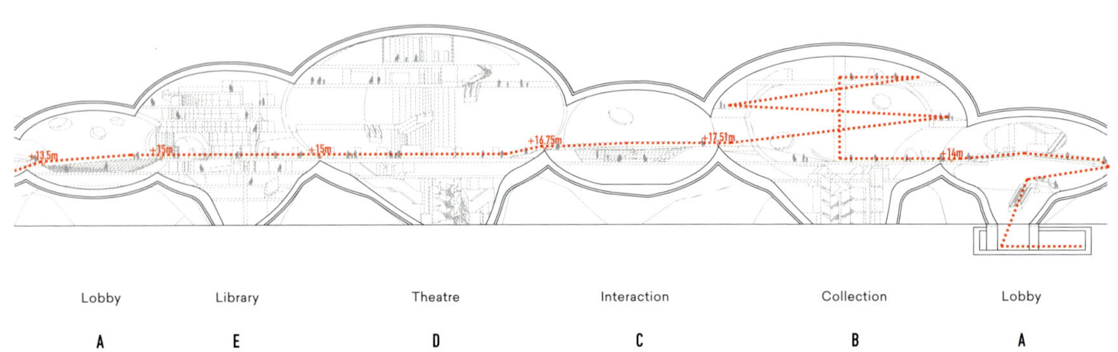

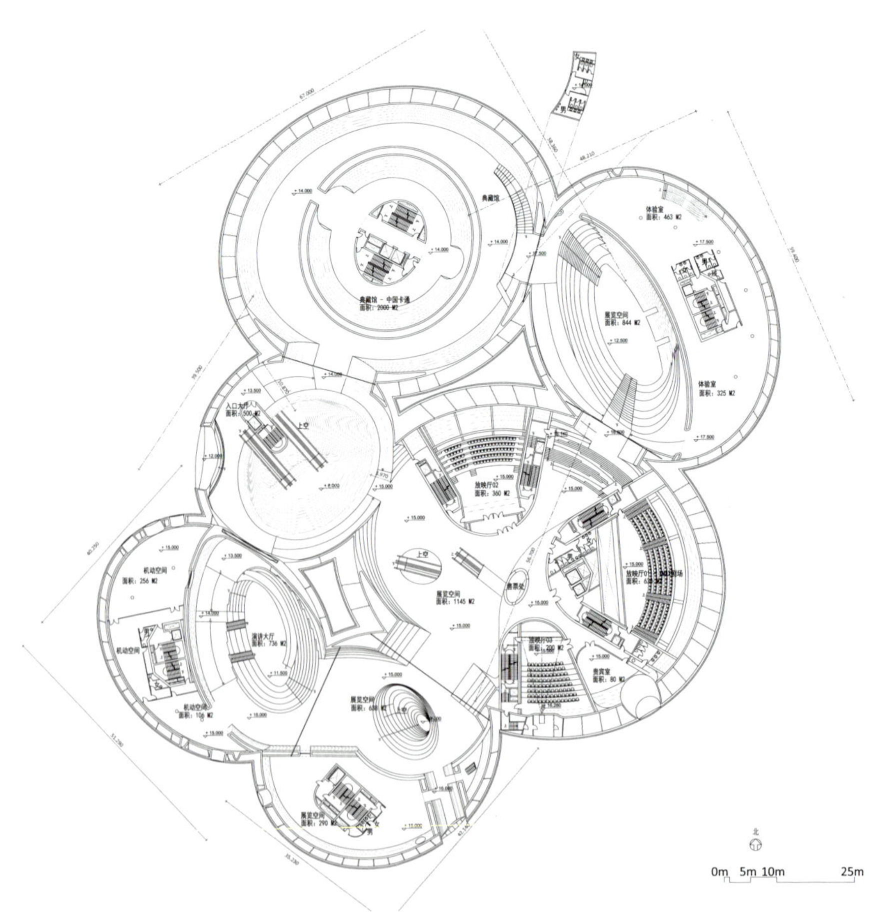

↑ Site plan.
Unfolded section.

→ Floor plan.

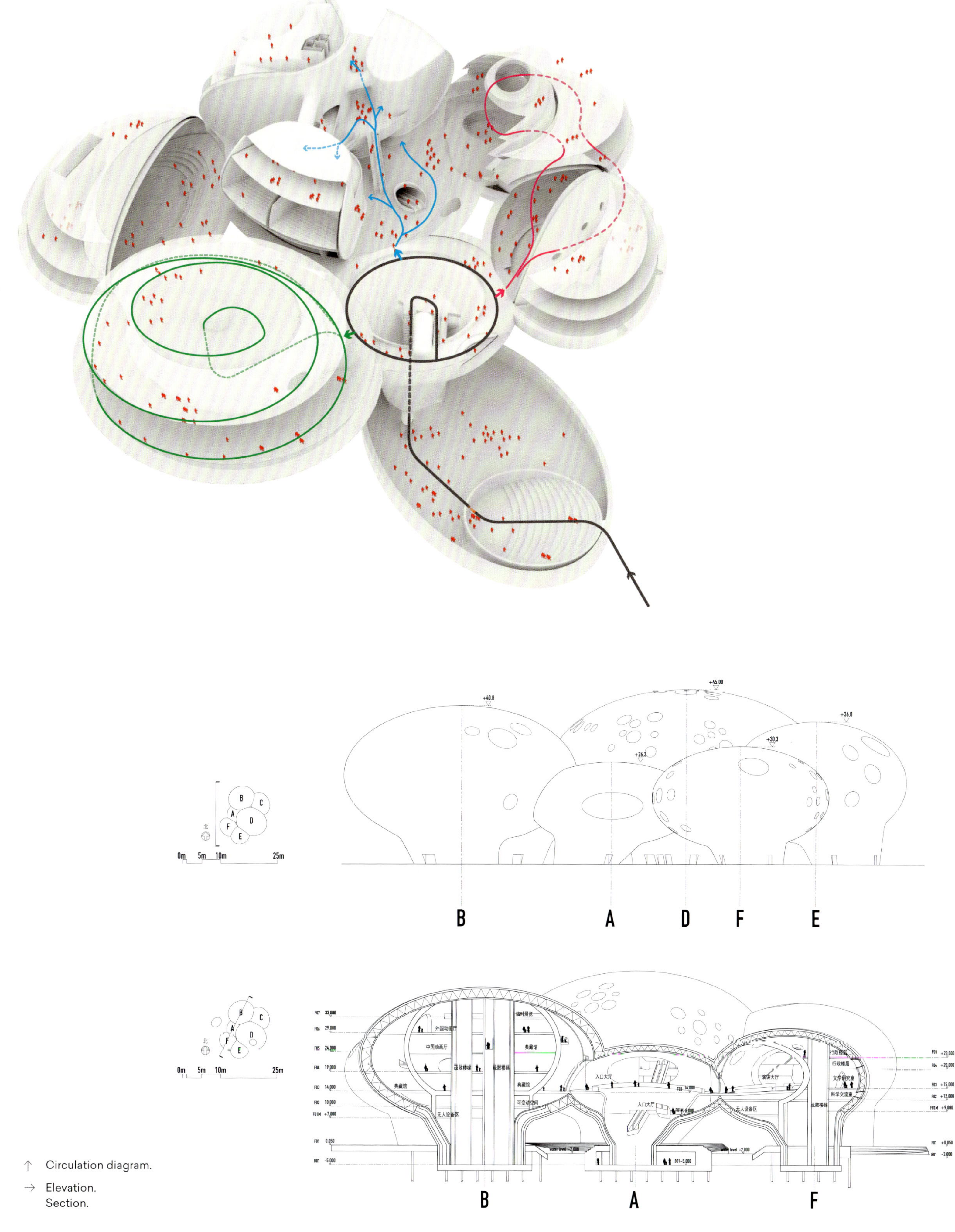

↑ Circulation diagram.

→ Elevation.
Section.

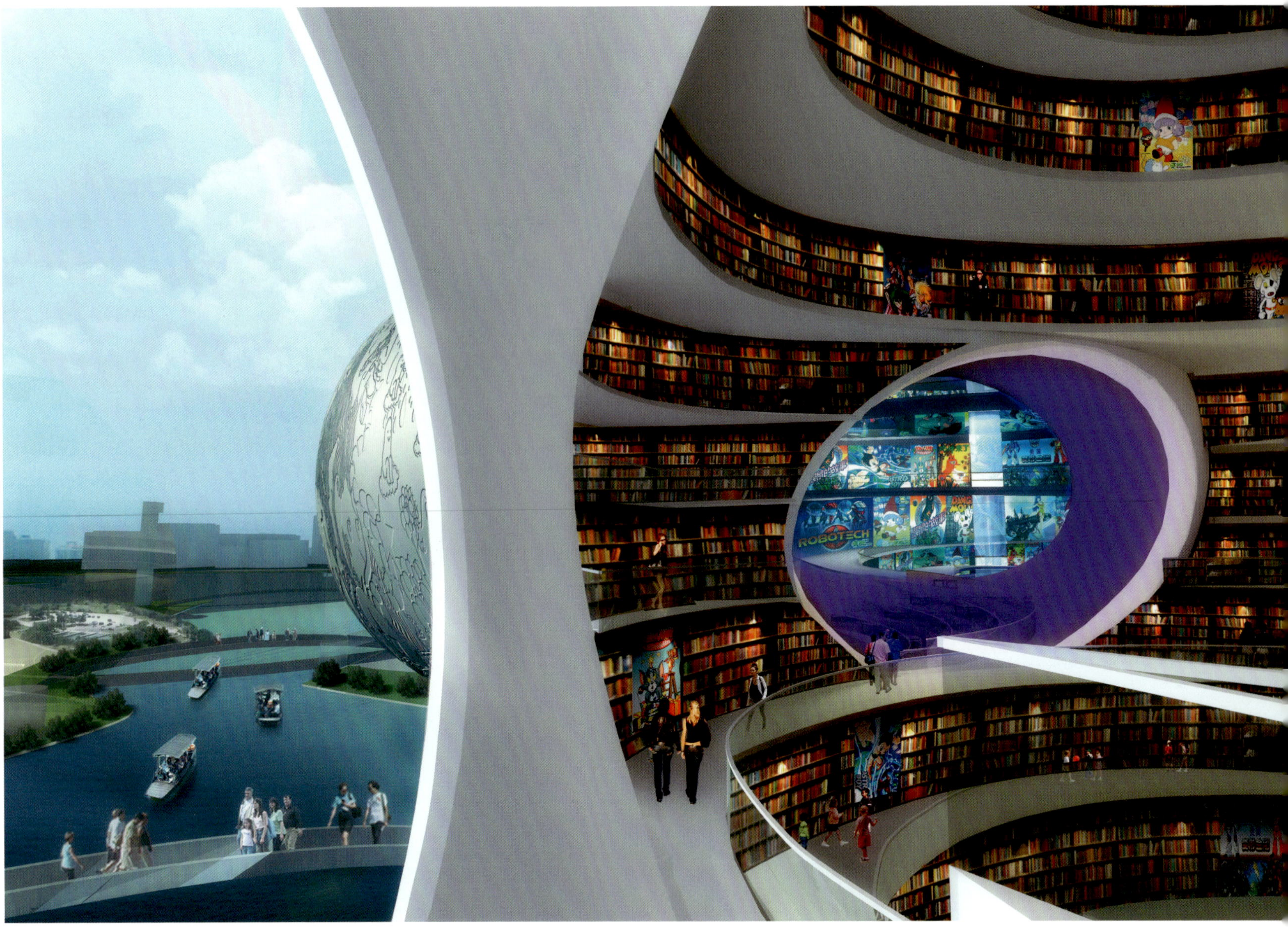

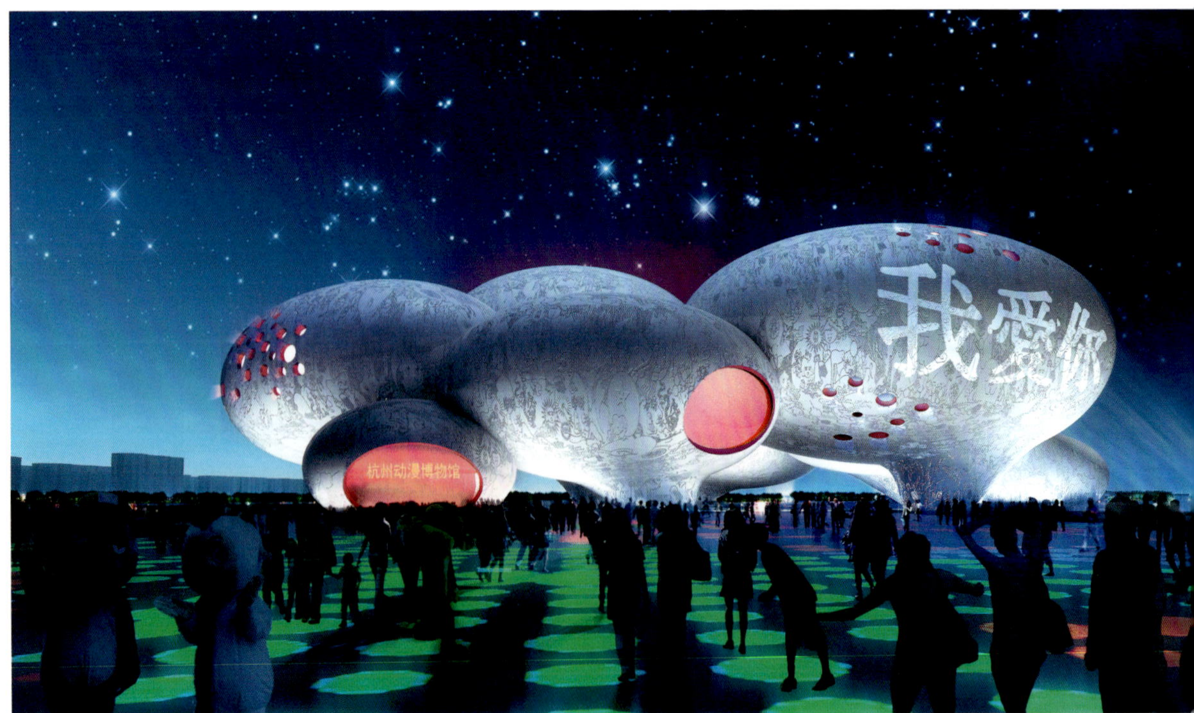

↑   Library.

→   Outside at night.

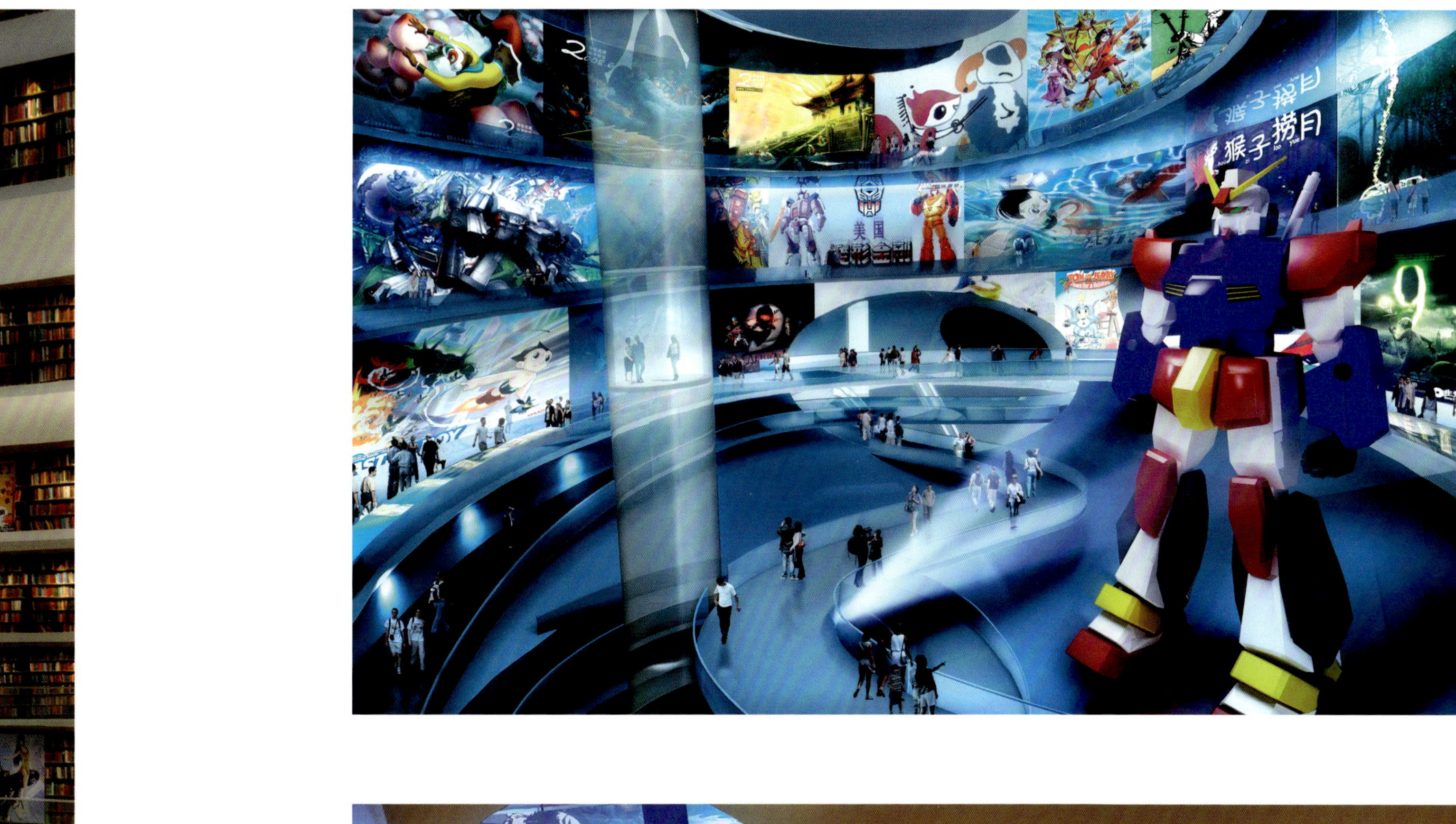

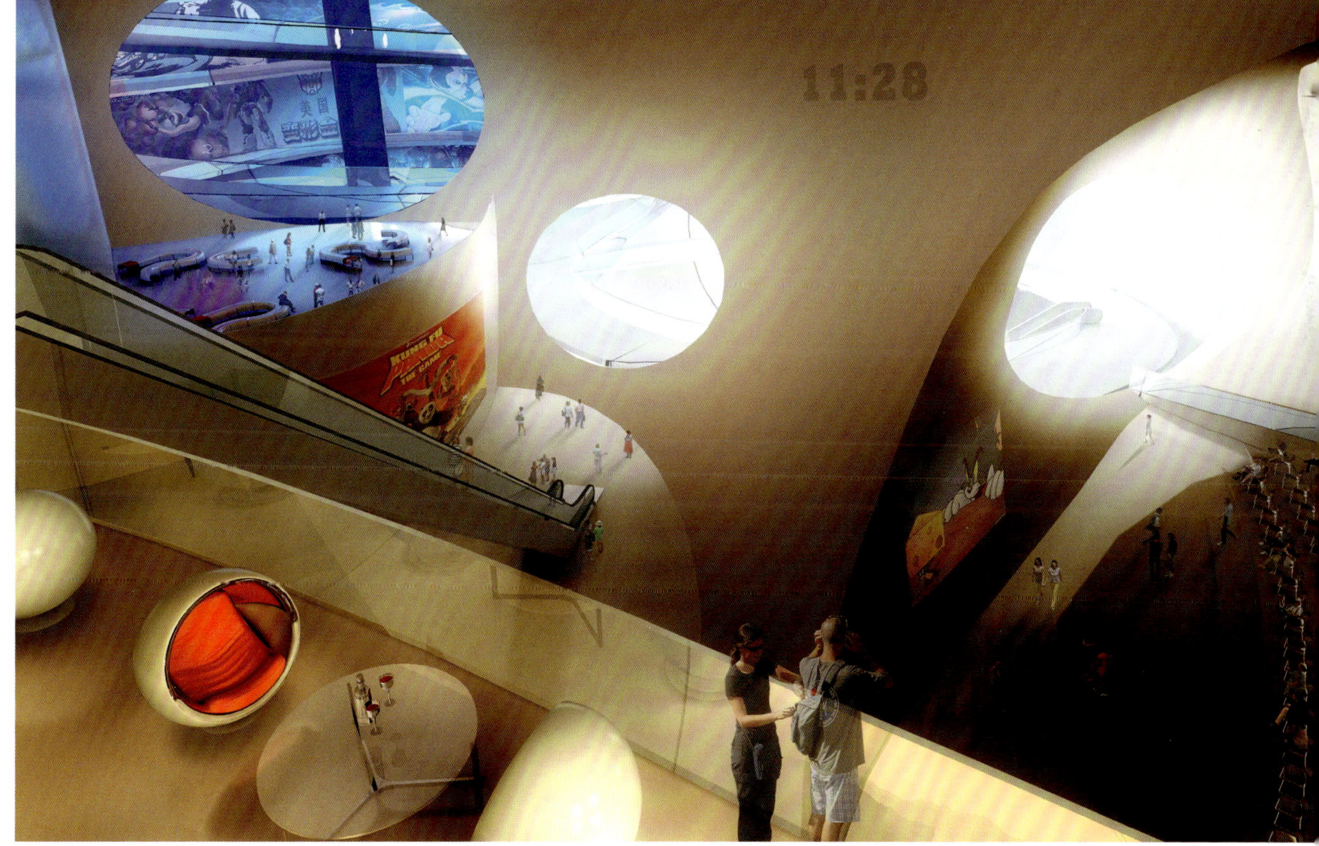

↑ Exhibition.
Theatre.

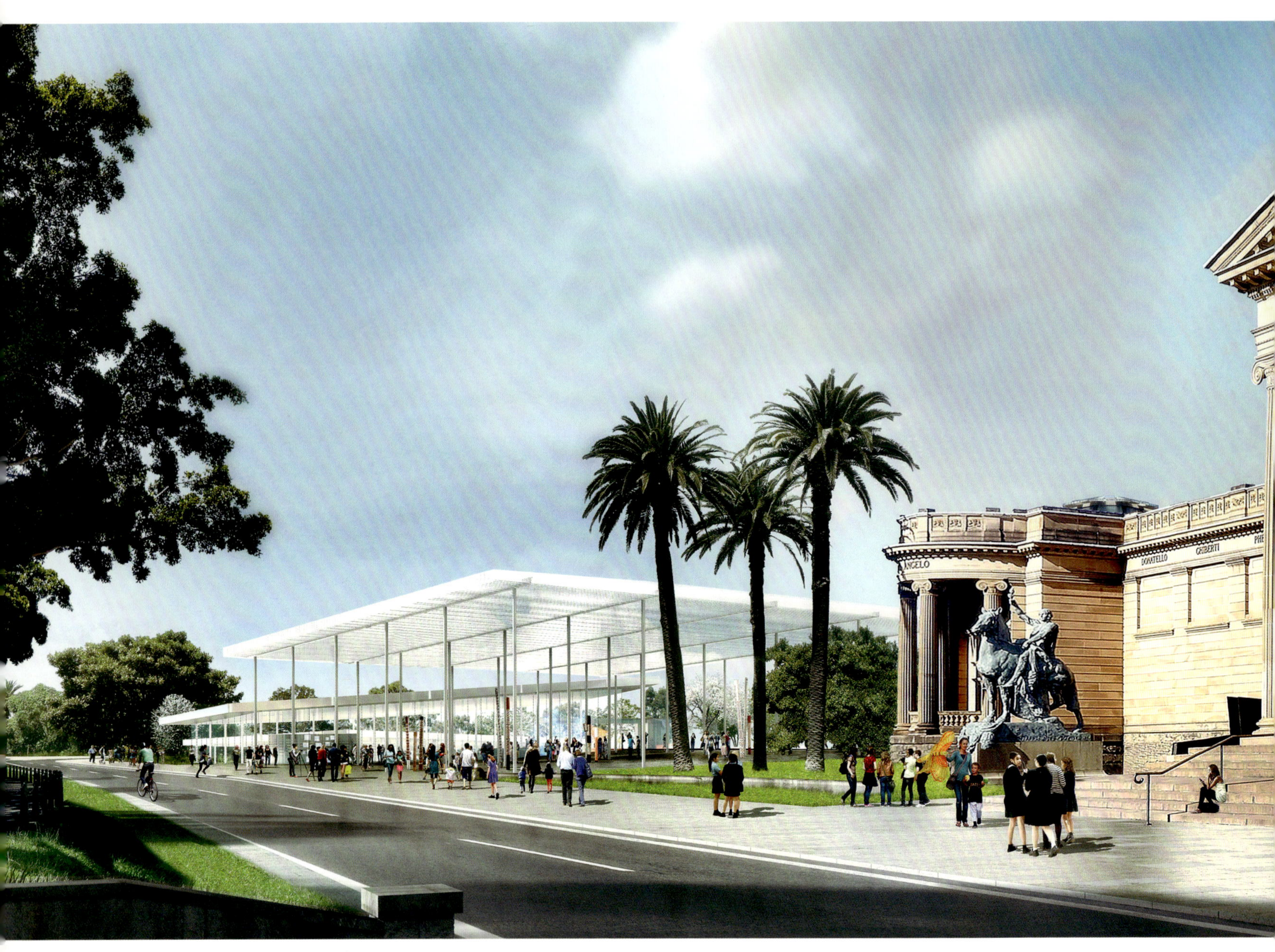

↑ View from Art Gallery Road.

Sydney Modern Project – Art Gallery of New South Wales

Sydney, Australia

SANAA, Tokyo
Construction 2019–2021, opening 2021
Building 20,012 sq. m
Permanent collection and special exhibitions

The Art Gallery of New South Wales is one of Australia's largest museums. The first Walter Vernon section of the Neoclassical building opened in 1897, and since 1972 the museum has been expanded, piece by piece, so as to accommodate the growing collection. By 2008 there had been a total of five additions and expansions.[1] The current extension, by far the largest, will double the previous floor space by 2021.

The architects of the new extension recognised that the former parkland is used to a great extent, so SANAA chose to design a very transparent, airy structure that appears to consist of only slender supports and thin ceilings. The separate pavilions sit gently on the hilly site; they are set at slight angles to each other, and from above it would appear that they have been carefully placed in the landscape with a light hand. Respect for nature is important to SANAA: their architecture is meant to follow the landscape, not vice versa, so as to produce a better relationship between structure and nature, interior and exterior.[2] A strict separation is often even abolished: simple walled structures alternate with roofed ones with open sides that suggest rooms but are not. SANAA is intent on creating a new site where visitors can move about freely, but one that also fosters a sense of community.[3]

On five public levels, distributed over a total of thirty-four metres in height, visitors move between exhibition spaces, cafés and public spaces. The structure's overlapping angled ceiling and floor slabs let light shine in from above in some spaces, which simultaneously heightens the space further and makes it seem airier. The logic of the new extension is most clearly seen when viewed from above: it supplements the historical museum structure with several levels arranged with no attempt to line up with the axes of the original building, which lends the entire complex a sense of lightness, even playfulness. The new building is meant to display Indigenous art as well as contemporary Australian and international art from the last fifty years. It thus adds an important art-historical field to the classical Western European canon housed in the old building. The 21st century museum thus combines old, globally recognised art with new, local art and accords them equal importance – as is visibly expressed by the different but connected levels of the new museum complex.

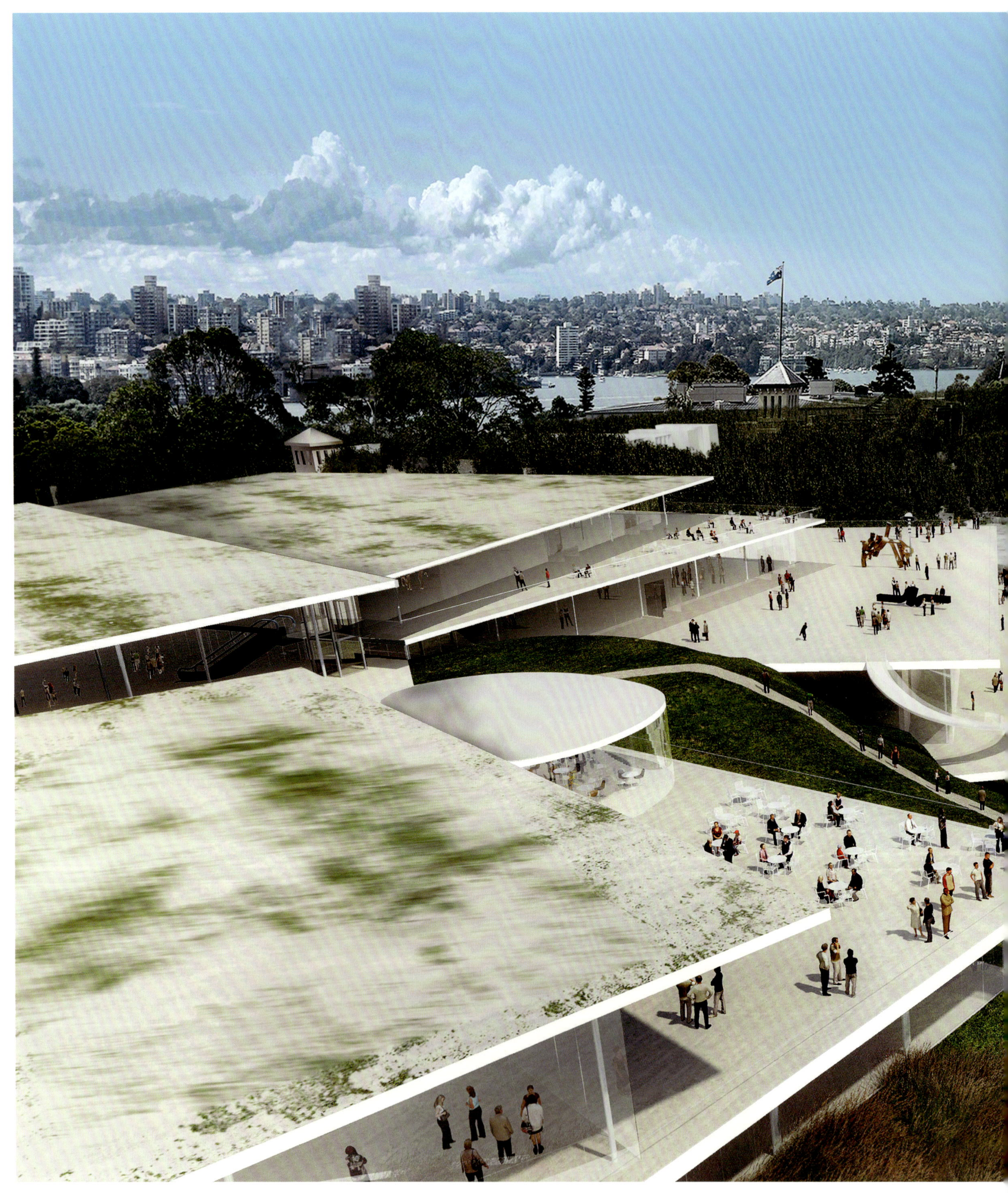

↑ Looking north from the existing building.

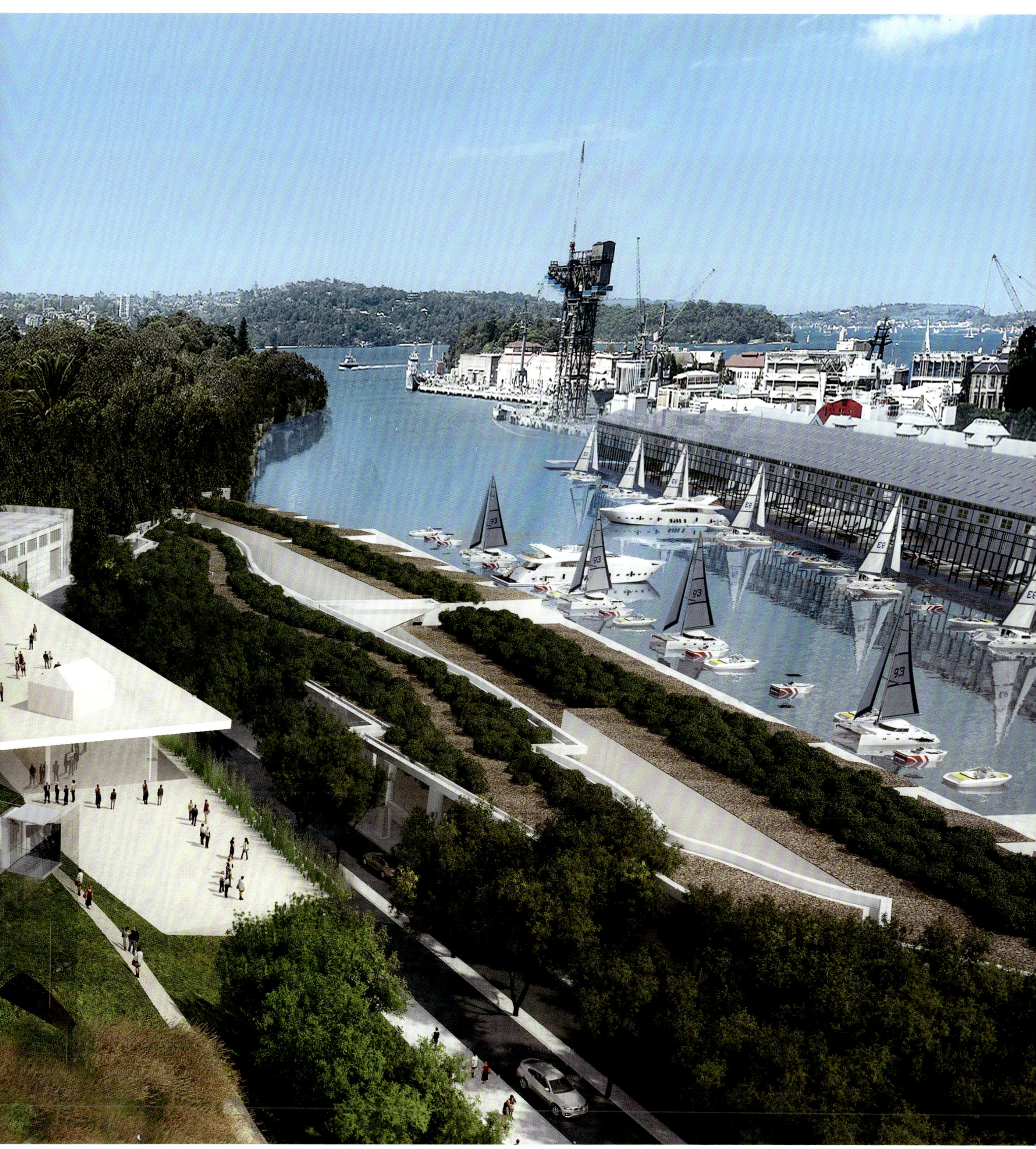

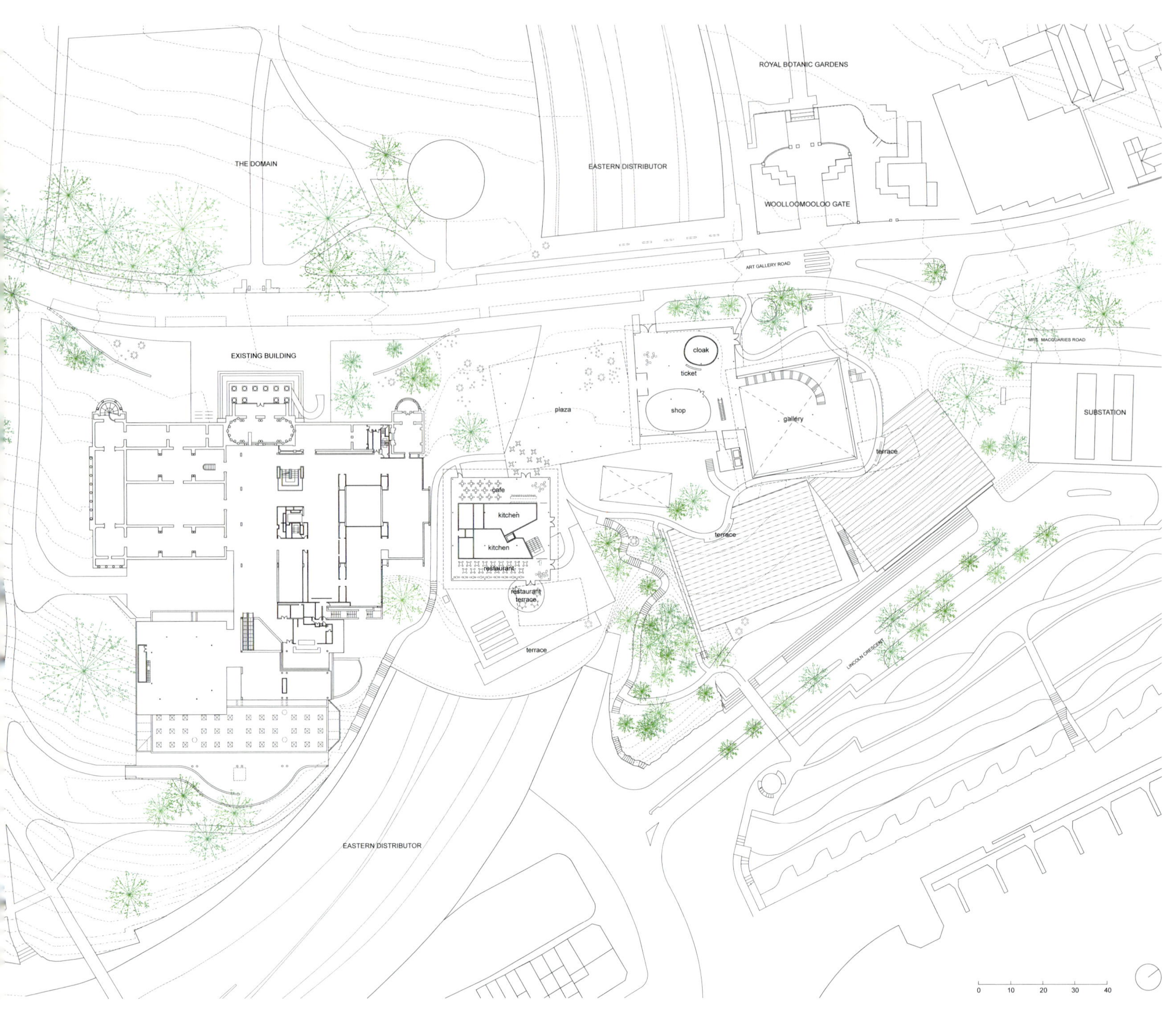

↑   Ground-floor plan.

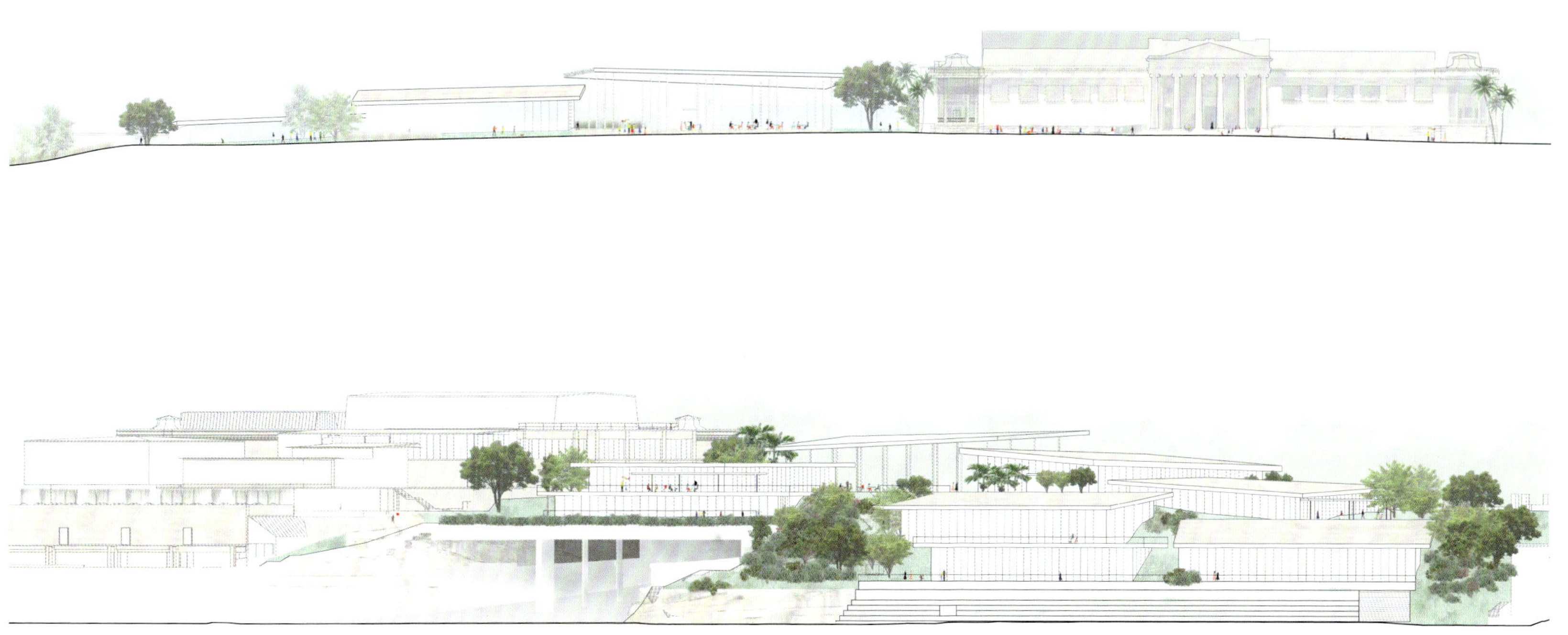

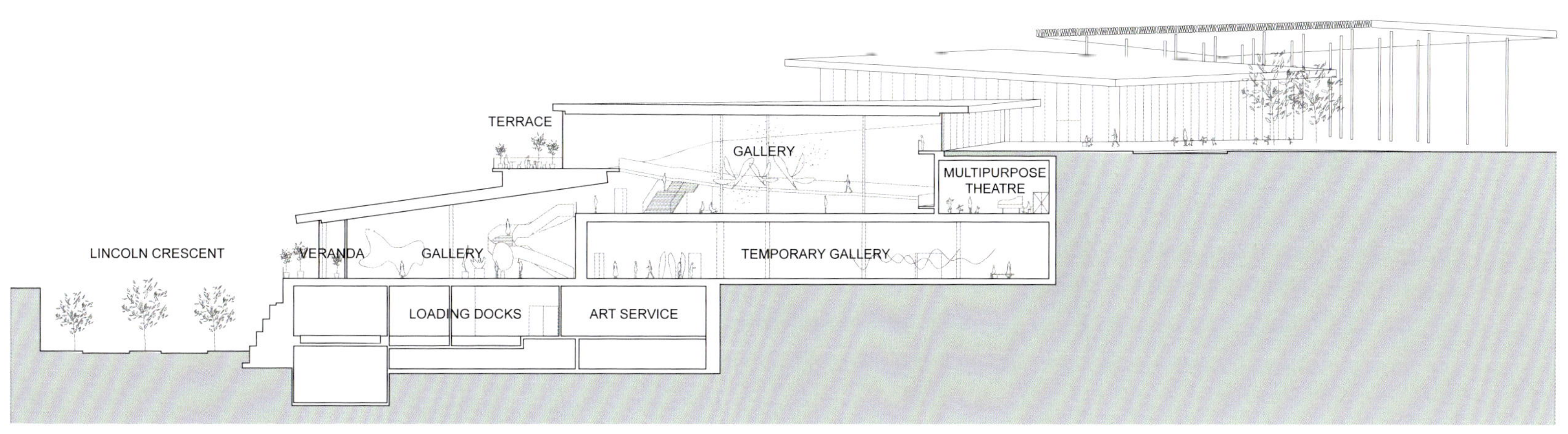

LINCOLN CRESCENT

TERRACE

GALLERY

MULTIPURPOSE
THEATRE

VERANDA GALLERY

LOADING DOCKS ART SERVICE

TEMPORARY GALLERY

↑ Elevation northwest.
Elevation southeast.
Section, west–east.

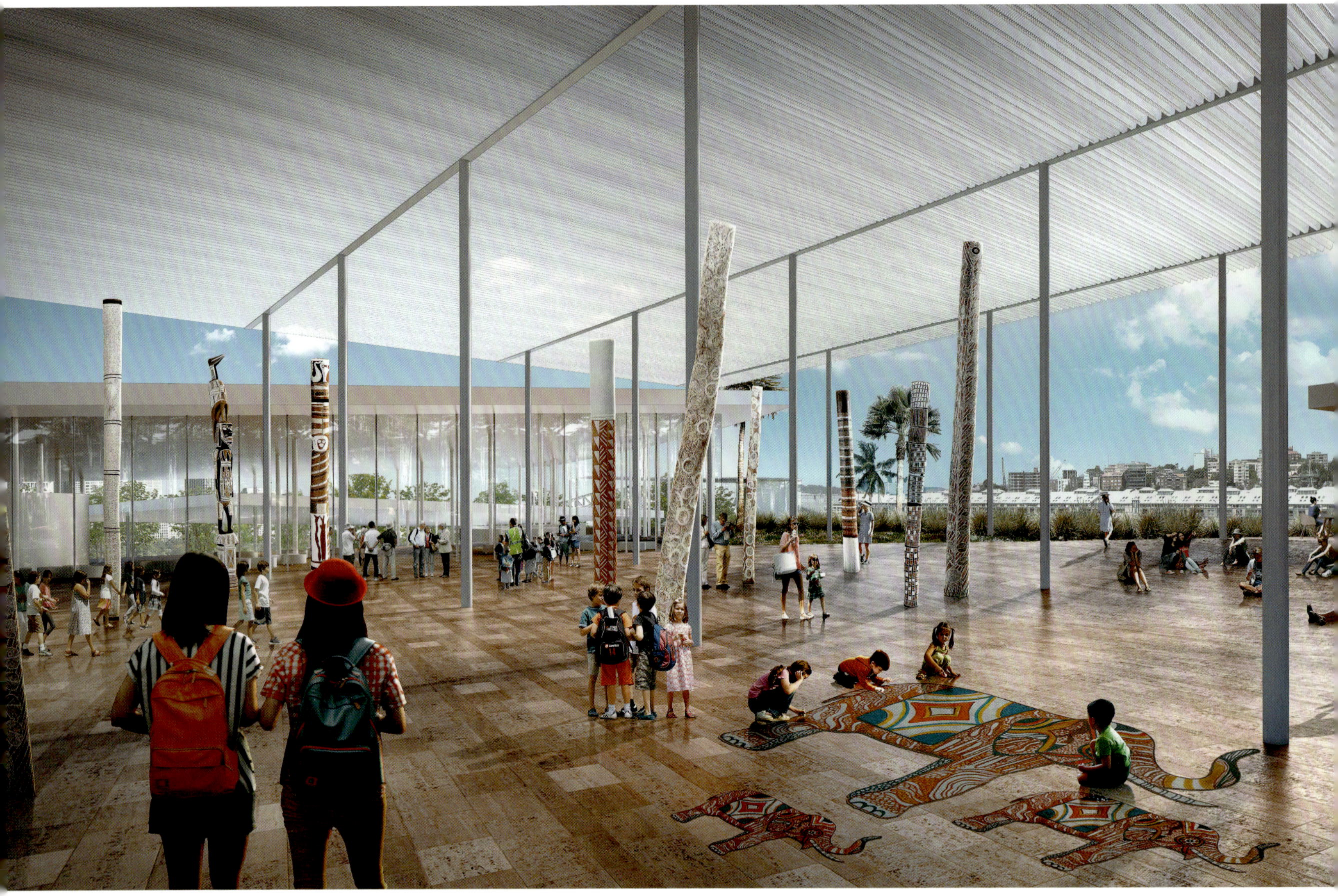

↑ Culture Plaza.

→ Exterior: Public access.
    Interior: Gallery space.

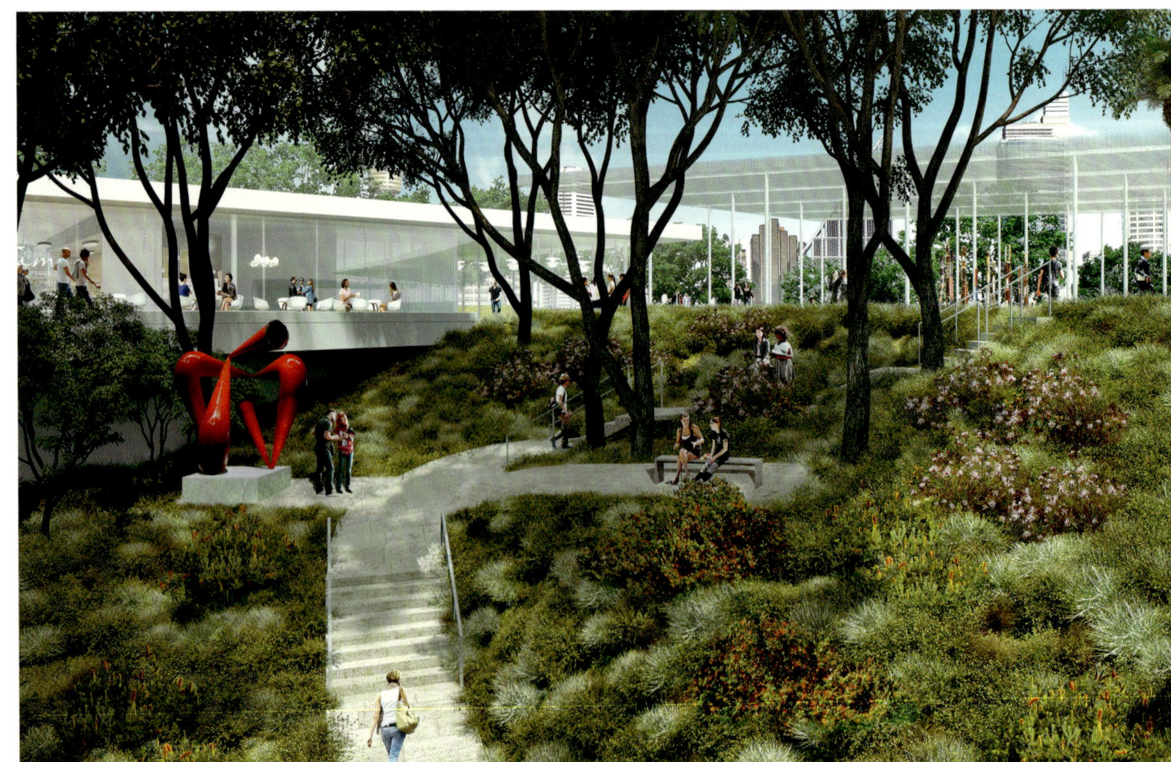

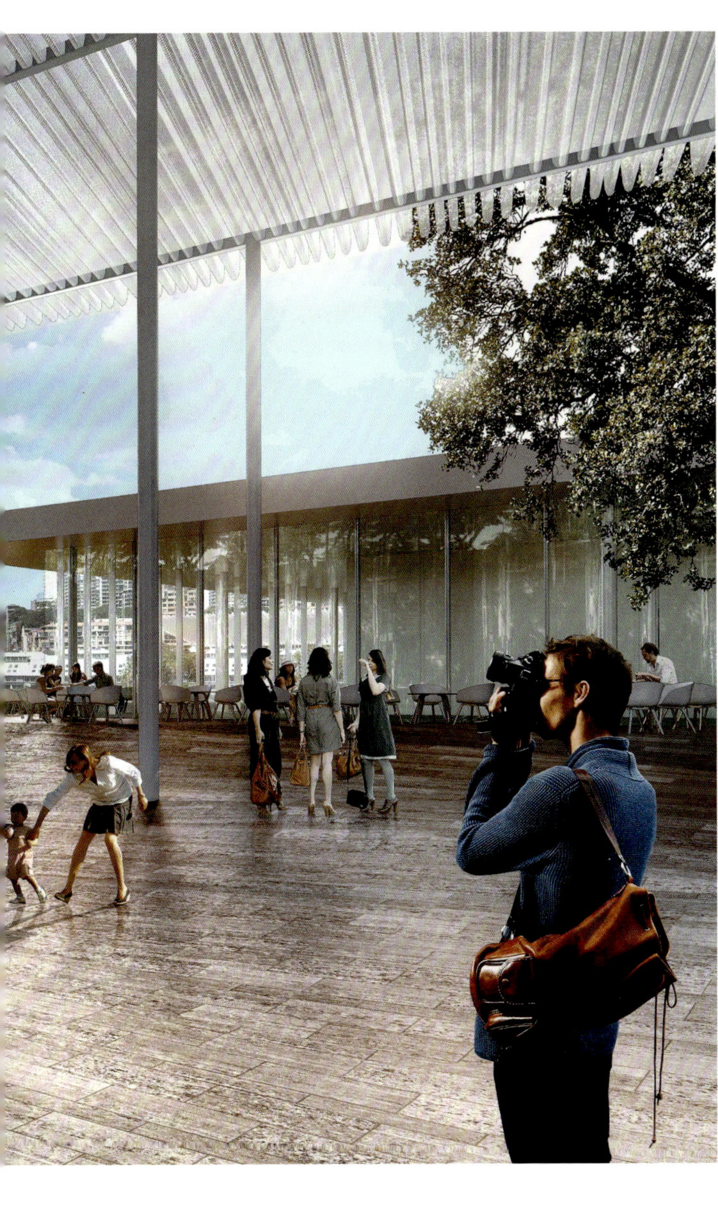

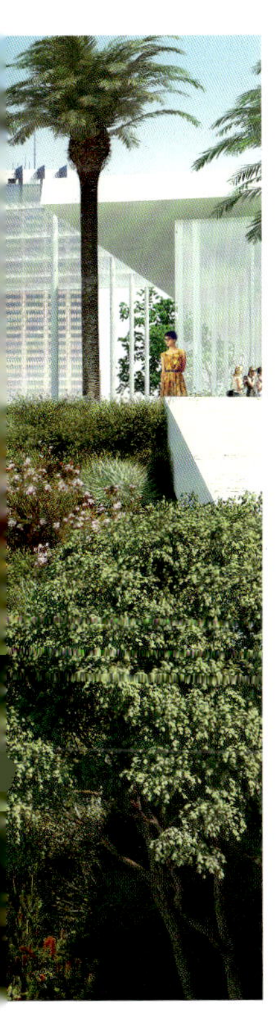

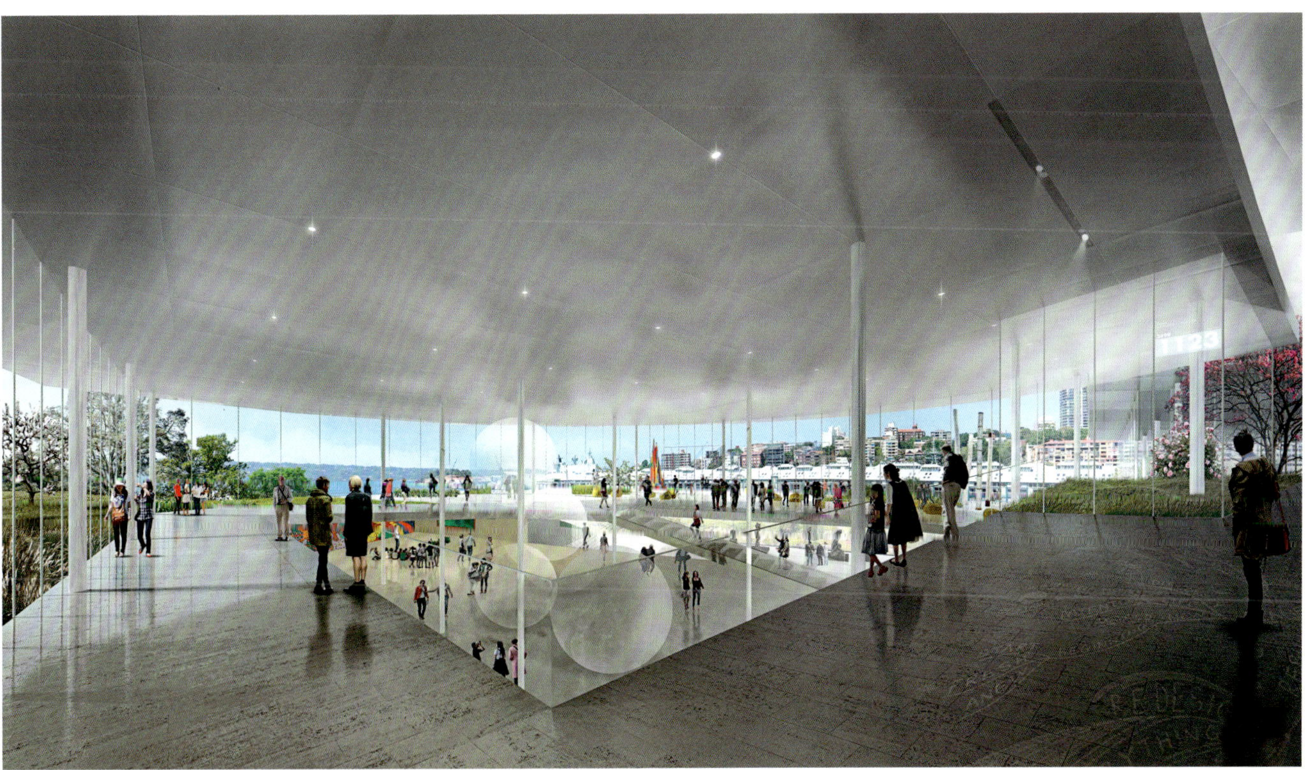

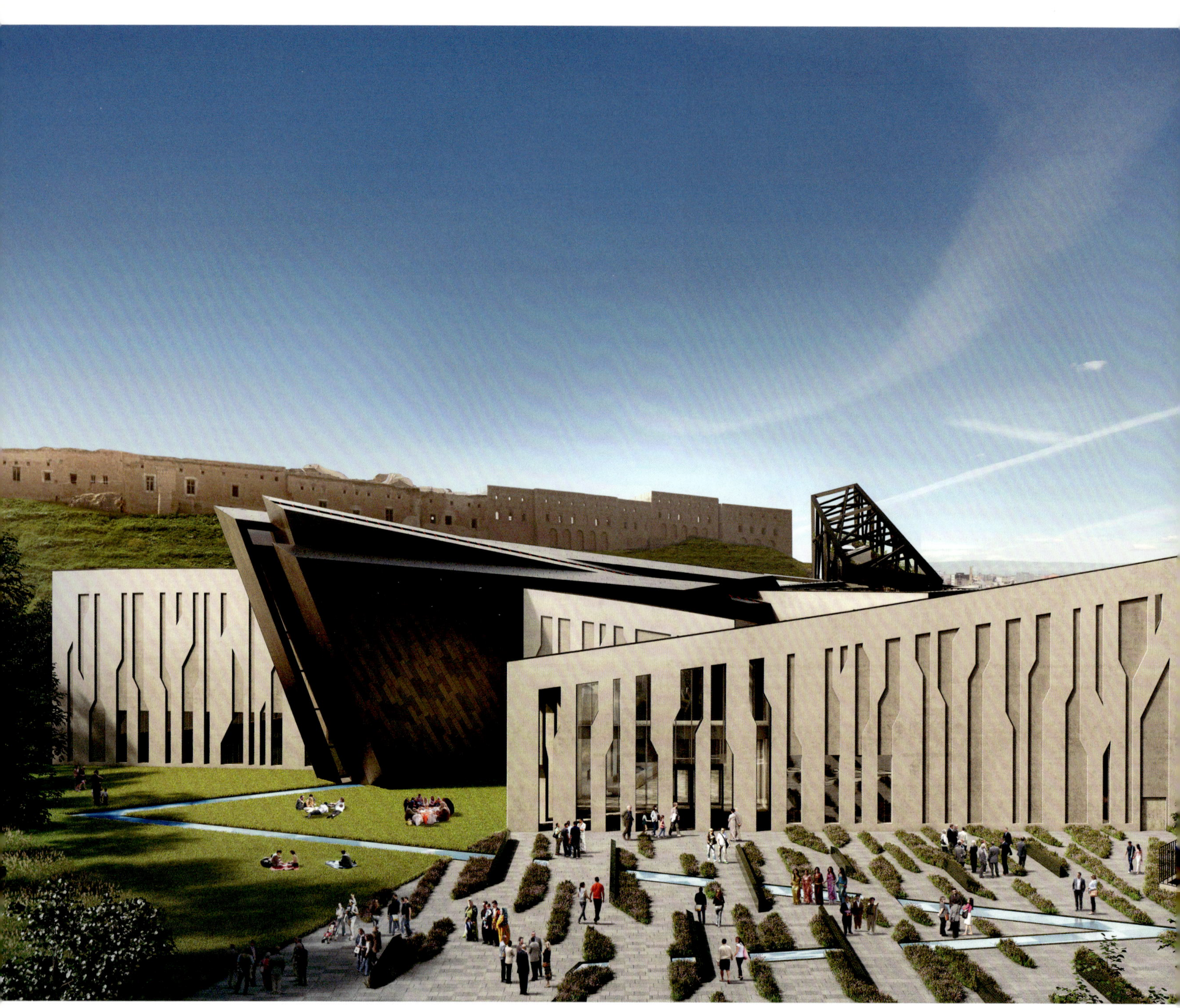

Kurdistan Museum

Erbil, Iraq

Studio Libeskind, New York
In the design phase
Building 19,000 sq. m
Permanent and temporary exhibits about Kurdish art and culture

In the best cases, architecture creates community, uniting what was previously separate. In the realm of museum architecture, especially, it can bring together people, cultures and emotions. It can even capture what doesn't exist, it can tie reality to possibility,[1] and it has a mission. The Kurdistan Museum is one such mission.

The architect Daniel Libeskind designed a museum meant to display the culture of a country that does not exist. The Kurdish homeland extends across four countries: Turkey, Syria, Iran and Iraq. In northern Iraq, at the foot of the historic citadel in Erbil, the capital of the autonomous Iraqi Kurdistan region, a museum will one day stand that unites the Kurdish people – at least metaphorically. After the end of the first phase of the Iraq War in 2003 Erbil had become a favourite tourist destination, thanks to the relative calm and political stability in this region of the country. But that ended with the beginning of the war in Syria in 2011. Libeskind believes that the city will find its way back to its heyday, and for that reason he designed the museum with an eye towards a peaceful future.

Looking down into the valley from the citadel one will then see not a simple roof but a composition, for the roof construction was deliberately planned to be seen from above.[2] Four green-roofed building segments are combined into a large complex fissured by two emphatic straight lines. Each of the four sections of the building represents one of the countries inhabited by the Kurds, and the two straight lines symbolise two decisive events in Kurdish history. The first one, a sombre wedge of concrete, recalls the genocide by Saddam Hussein, who ousted and murdered hundreds of thousands of Iraqi Kurds. The second embodies the opposite: it consists of an airy network of steel striving upward, with growing plants that gradually turn it green, culminating in an eternal flame. This straight line symbolises the freedom the Kurdish people aspire to. For Libeskind architecture is not only a language that provides information about the time in which it was built, but one that also invites further interpretation.[3] With the four pavilions and two notches he indeed leaves little leeway for interpretation;, to be sure, his architectural language is unambiguous and impressive.

For the ochre façade Libeskind took inspiration from Kurdish weaving and pottery. Elongated geometric patterns adorn the wall surfaces; narrow vertical windows are designed in a similar way, and make the building appear upright and self-confident despite the painful wedge. Inside there are none of the usual, clearly arranged exhibition spaces awaiting visitors; the interior is as expressive as the exterior. Narrow corridors alternate with somewhat wider spaces, both of them reminiscent of Libeskind's Jewish Museum in Berlin, which symbolises the dispersion of a people by similar means.[4] Nevertheless, this design seems new and unfamiliar – and will possibly take some time before it is realised.

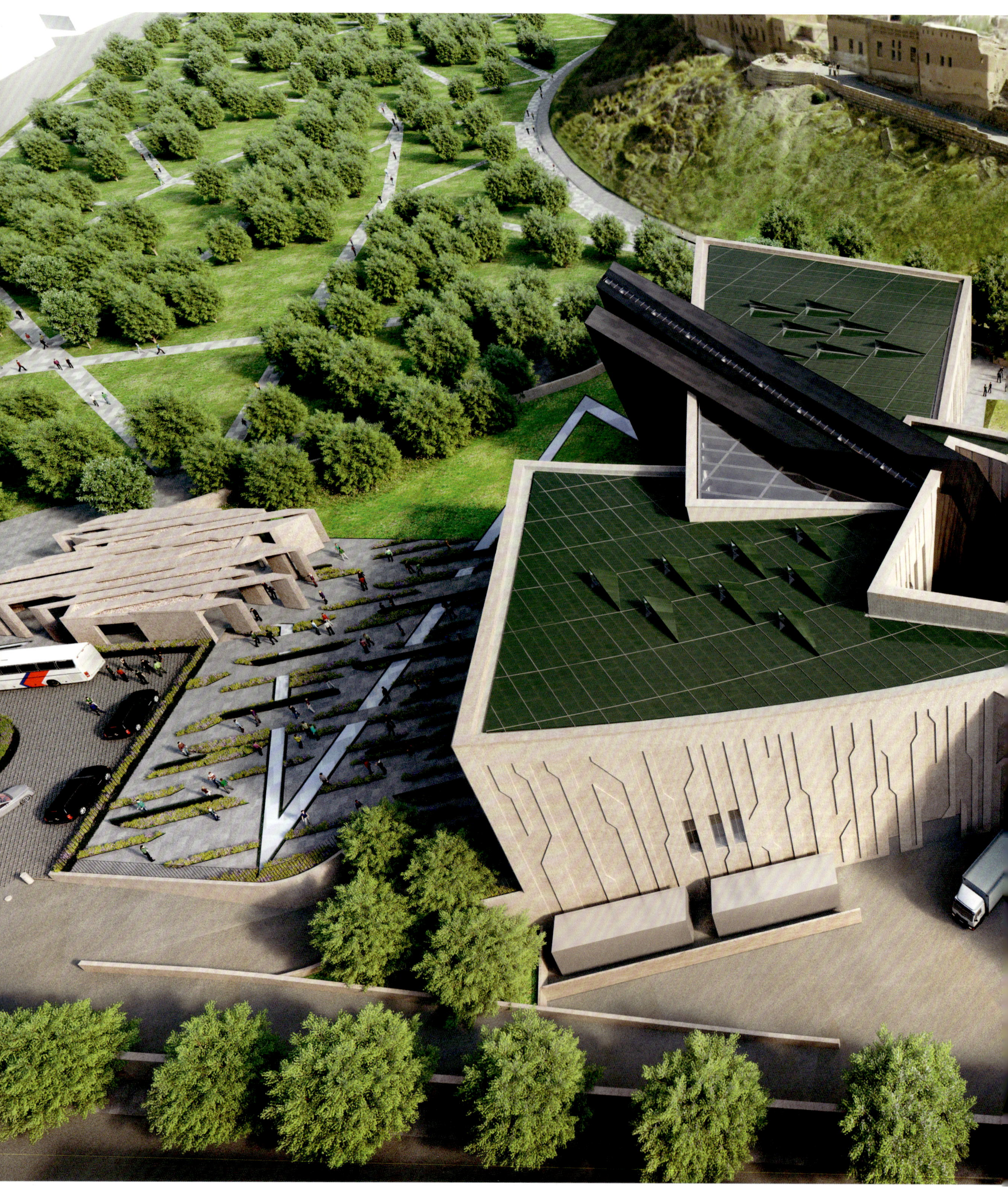

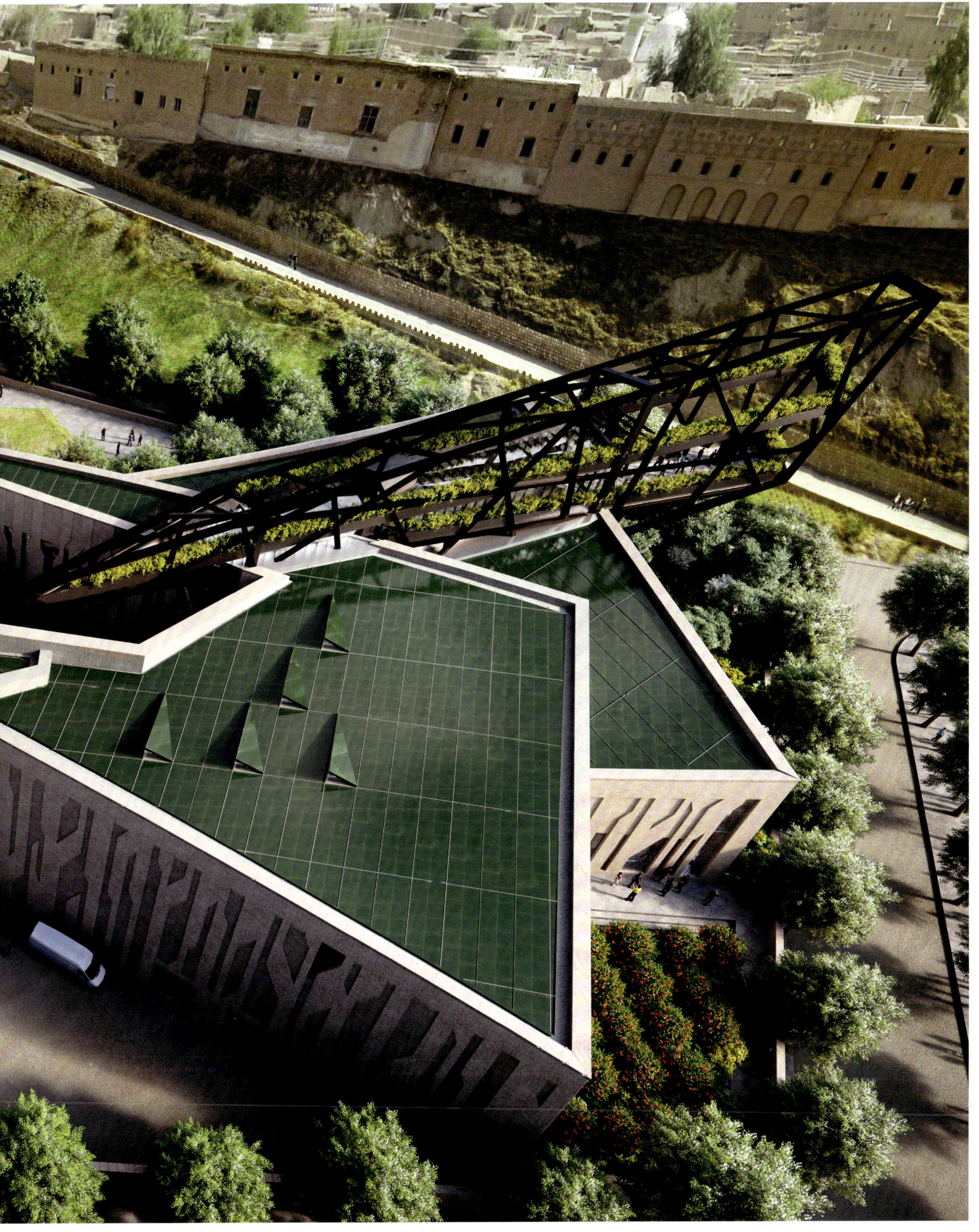

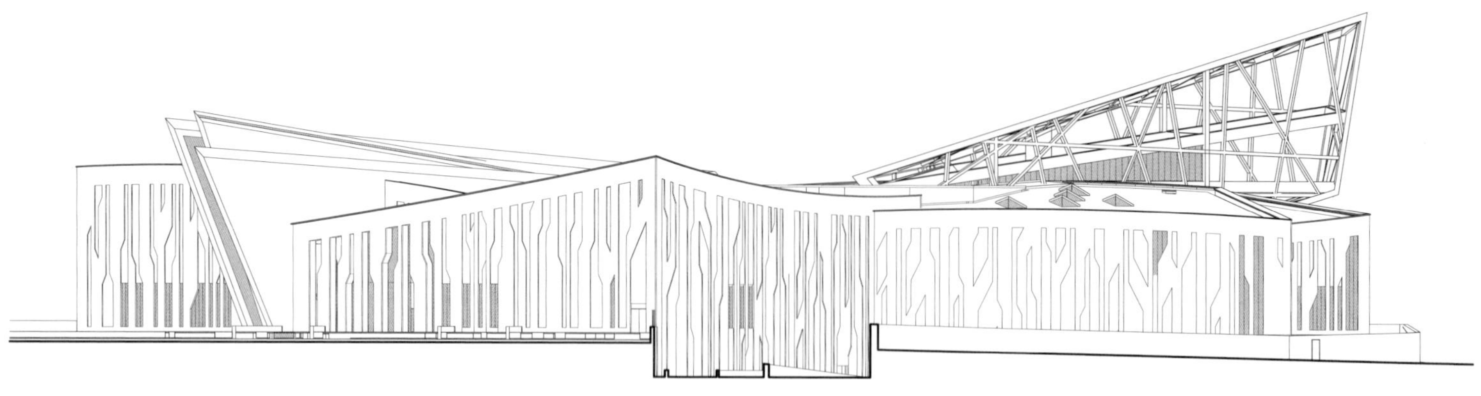

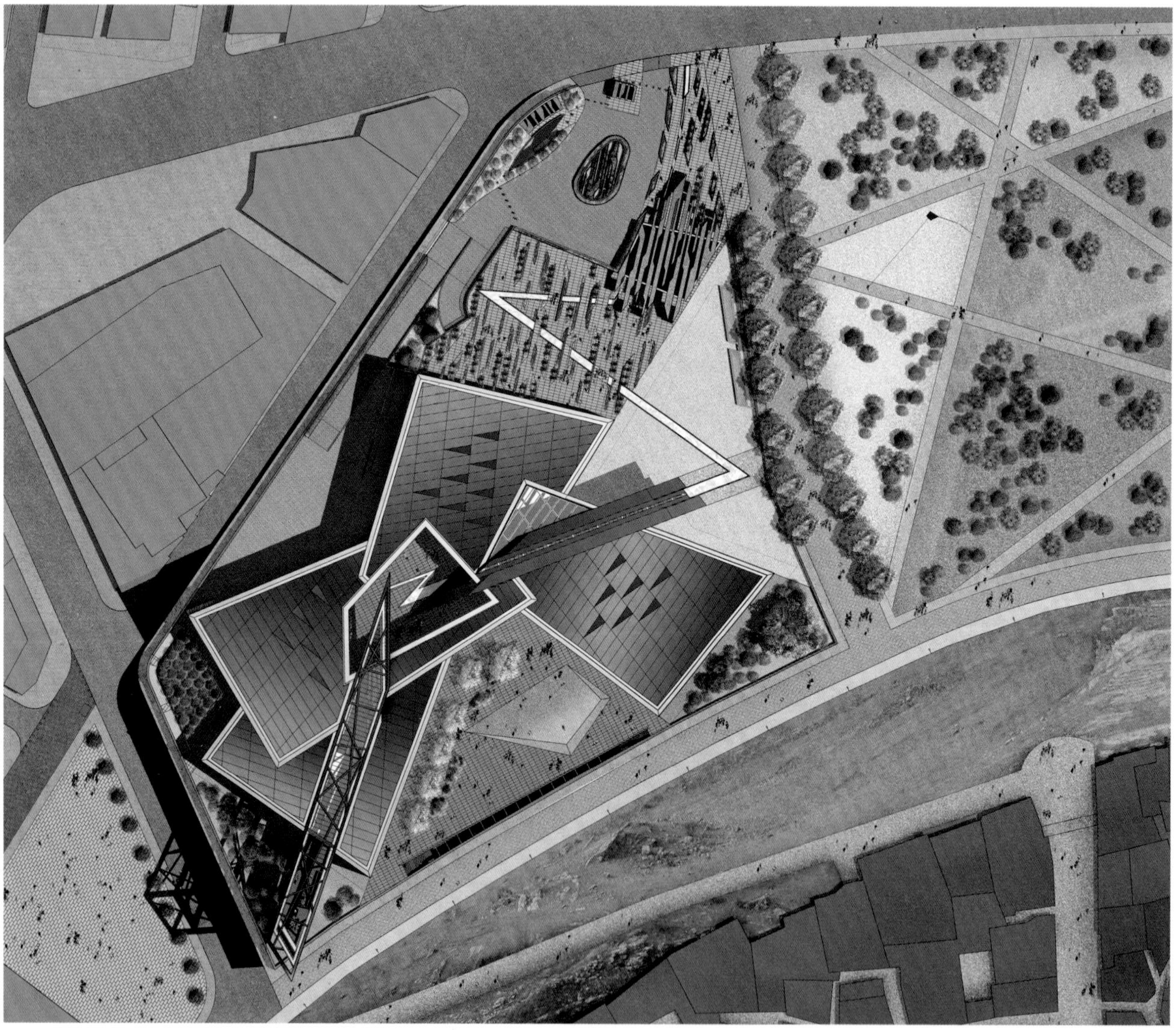

↑ Elevation, from the north.
Site plan.

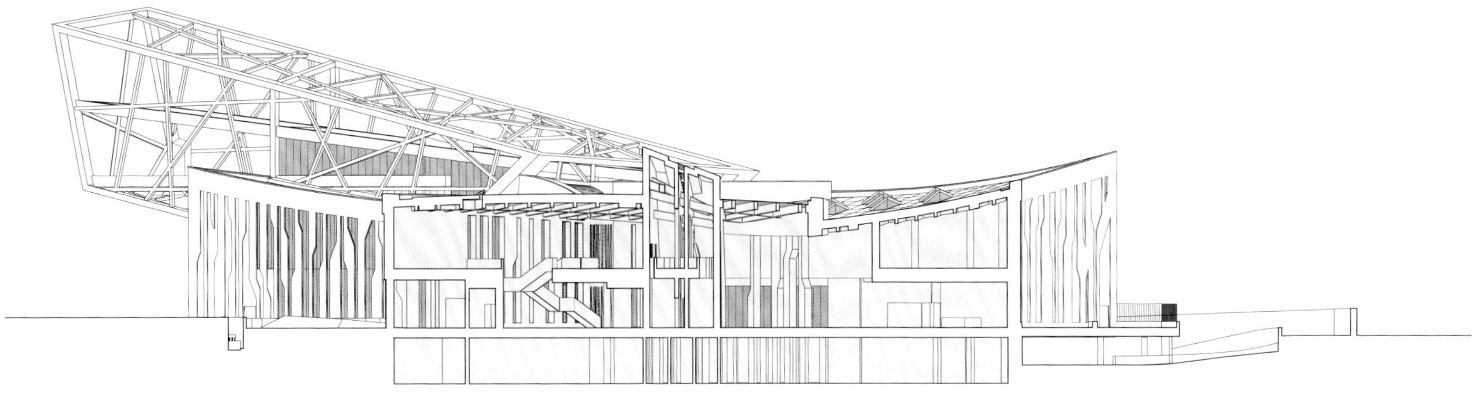

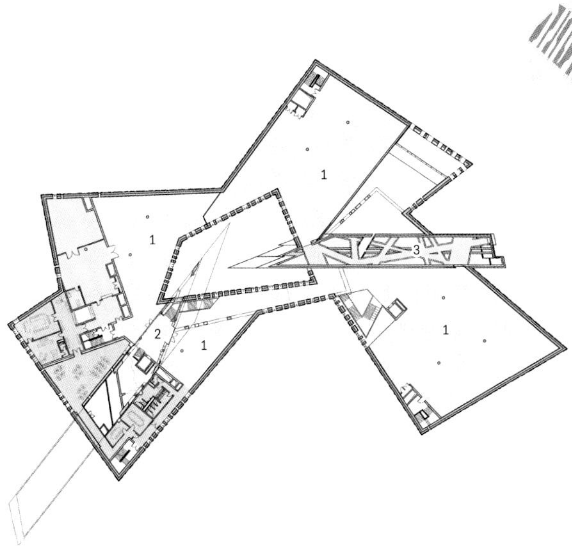

1 Gallery
2 Liberty Line Sky Garden Vestibule
3 Anfal Line

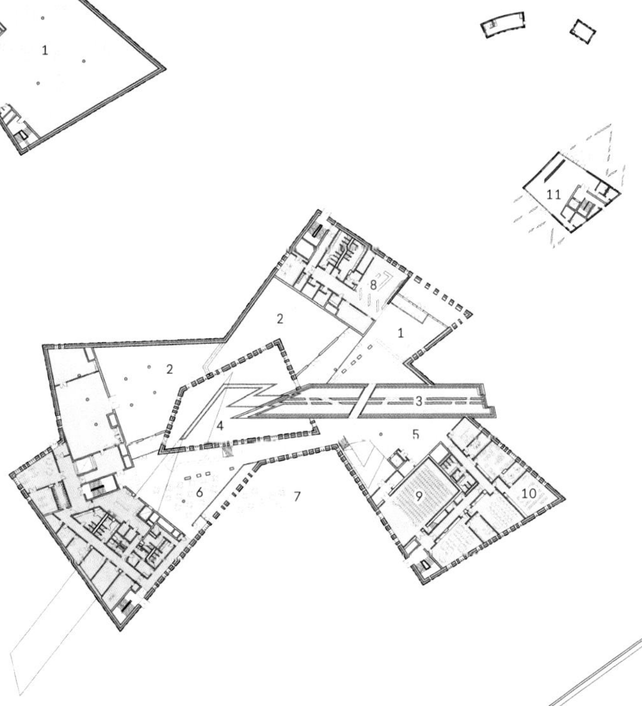

1 Entrance Lobby
2 Special Exhibition
3 Anfal Line
4 Erbil Courtyard
5 Memory Program
6 Café
7 Citadel Plaza
8 Shop
9 Auditorium
10 Education
11 Security Pavilion

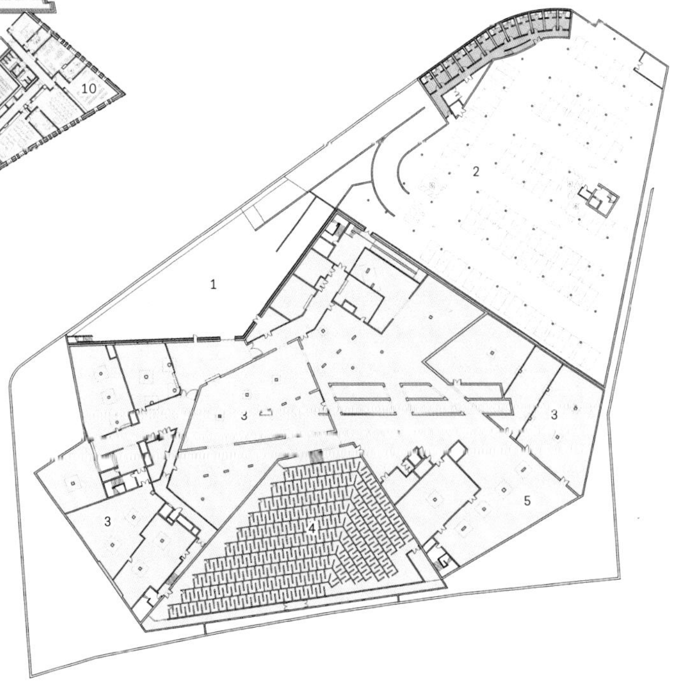

1 Service Yard
2 Parking
3 Mechanical
4 Thermal Labyrinth
5 Storage

↑ Section, south–north.

↗ Floor plans: +1, 0, -1.

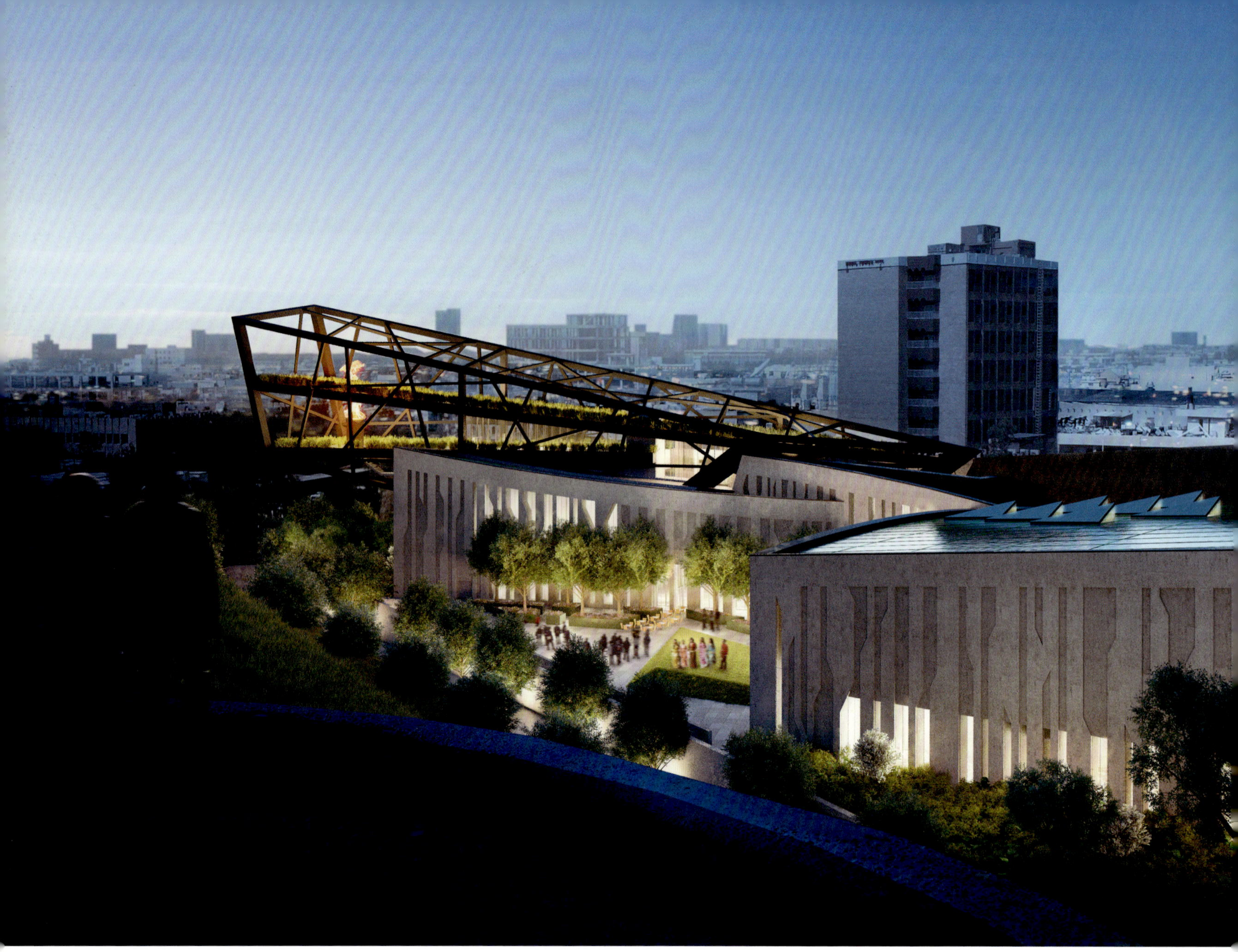

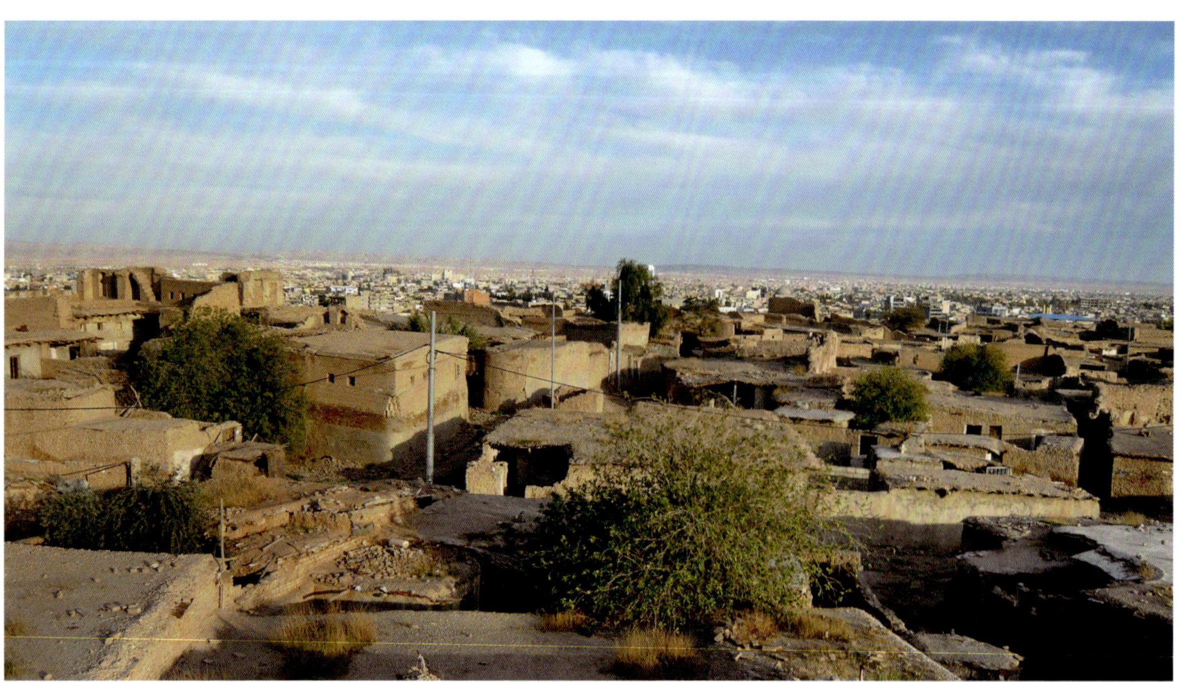

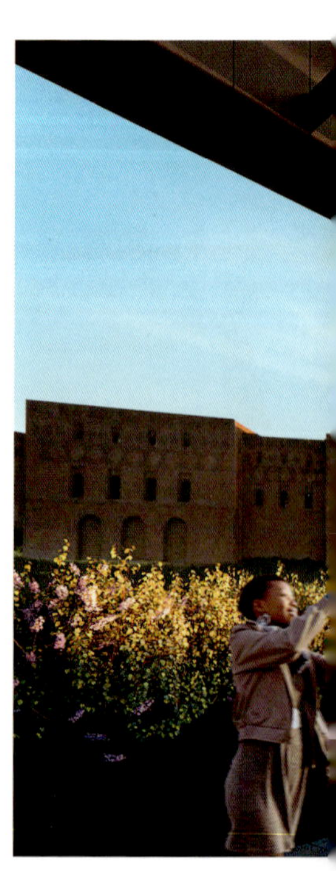

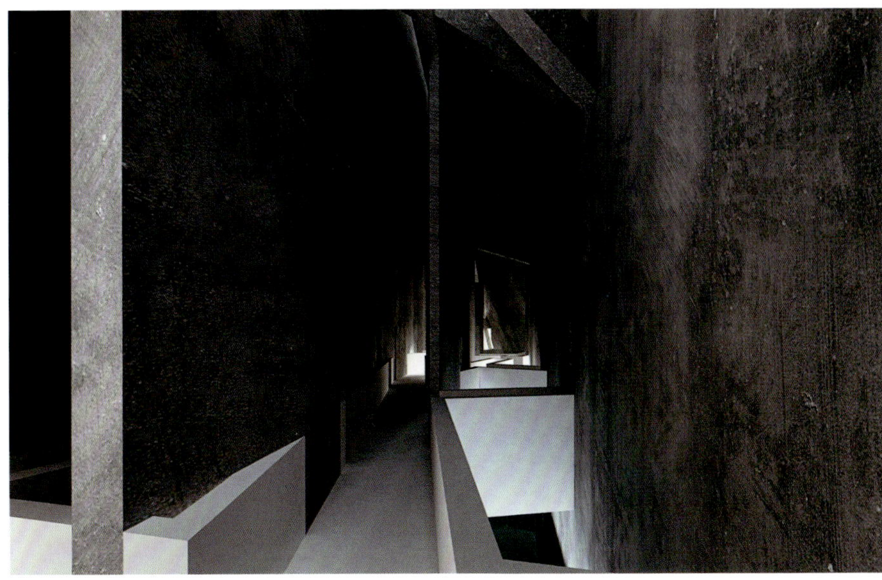

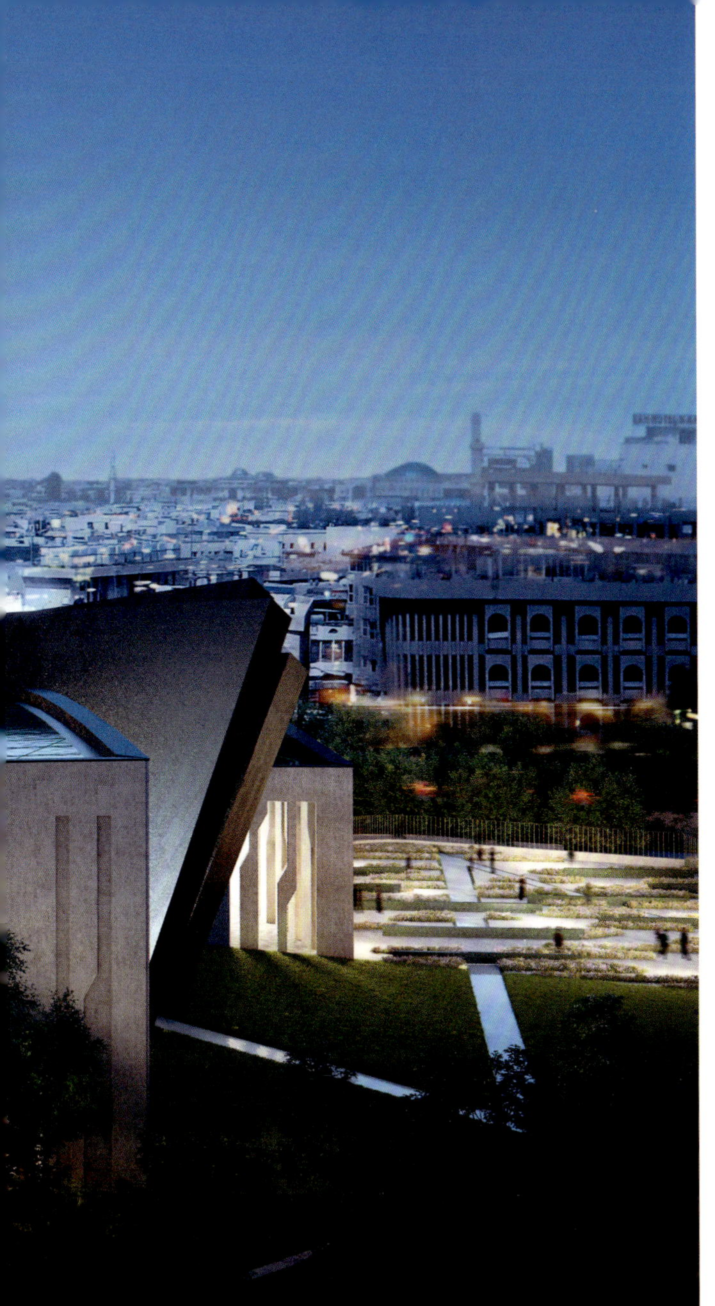

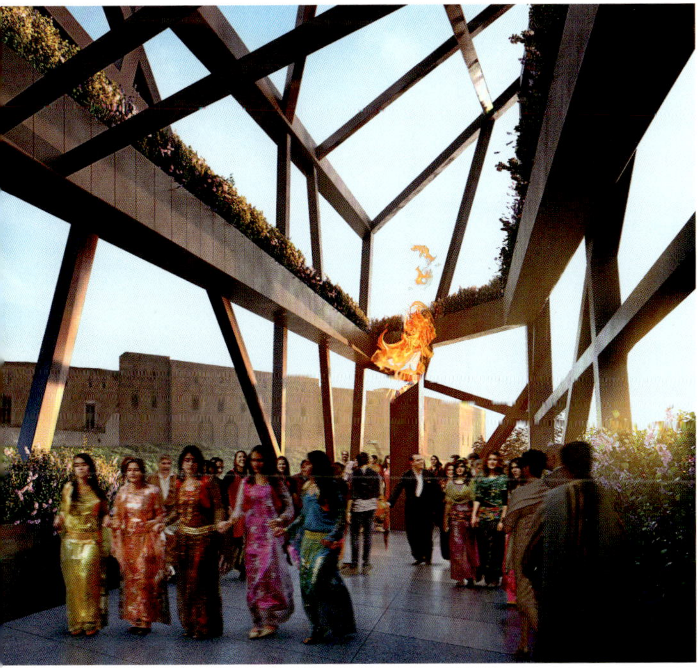

↖ Kurdistan Museum,
looking west from Citadel.

↑ Interior views of Anfal Line.

← Erbil, Citadel.
The Liberty Line.

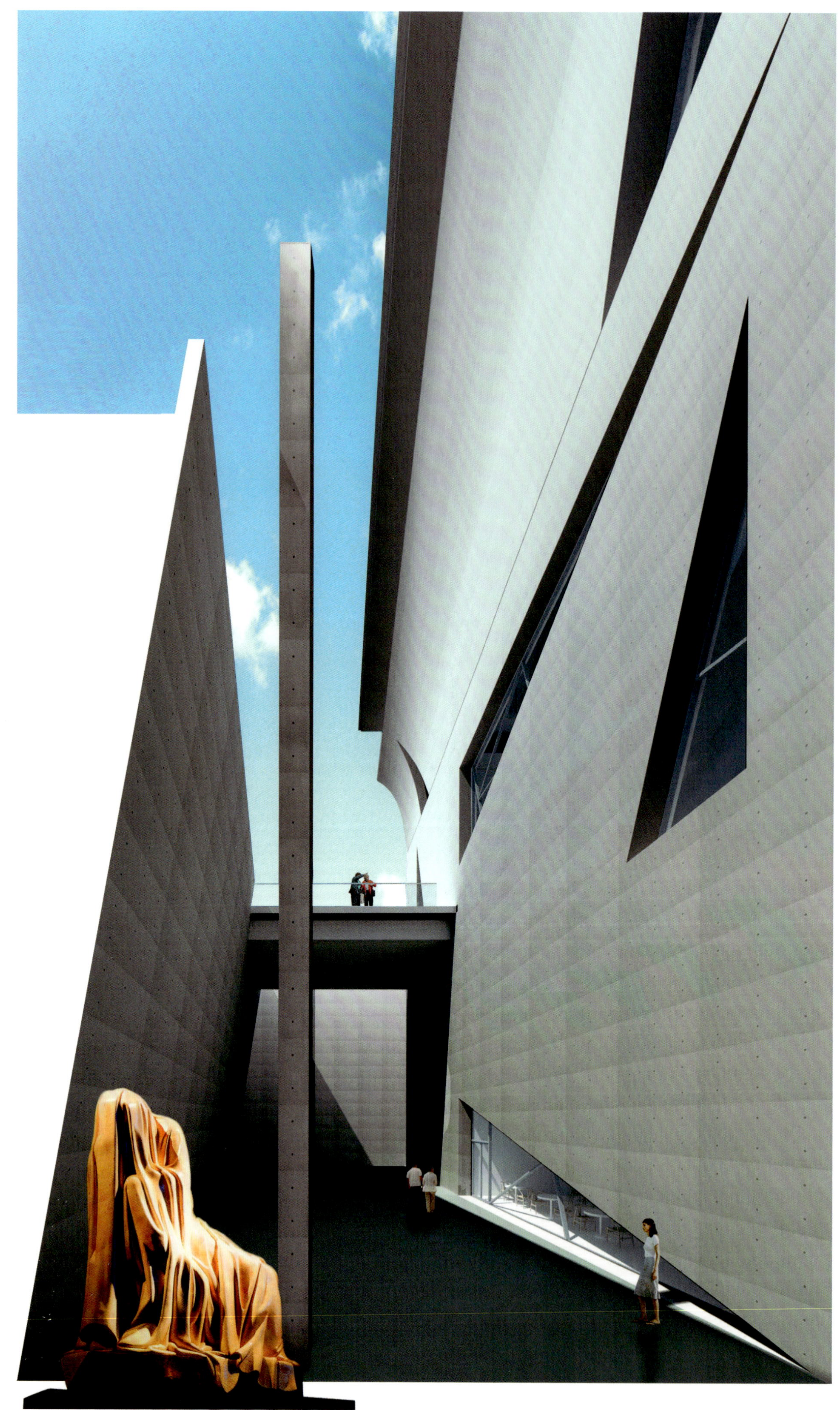

Genesis Museum

Beijing, China

Tadao Ando Architect & Associates, Osaka
Under construction since 2014, opening 2018
Building 8,417 sq. m
Contemporary art

In China, museums cannot look back on a very long history. The first Chinese museum was opened in Nantong in 1905, and by 1936 the country had a mere seventy-two of them. Since the reform policy and opening up to the world market in the late seventies, museums have become fixtures in Chinese cities and experienced an unprecedented building boom.[1] The country's 2000th museum opened in 1999,[2] and by the end of 2012 there were already 3,866 Chinese museums open to visitors.[3]

The building boom also has to do with modern urban development in China. Large cities, especially, are increasingly geared towards those of the West in their layout and in their building tasks. Before the Olympic Games in 2008 Beijing was transformed in record time into a "global city" that has scarcely any resemblance to the old imperial metropolis.[4] In its new commercial and industrial quarters buildings are erected that initially have no function but to provide space – no matter what for.[5] Yet in a different way, the "Genesis Beijing" grew out of this tradition. It does justice to a new development in China in which it is becoming increasingly normal for native Chinese to visit museums and for investors to promote cultural projects. The "Genesis Beijing" lies next to the Third Ring Road, and includes high-priced hotels, and office buildings. In addition, it is the home of a new museum designed by Tadao Ando. The investor owns a major art collection that includes works by Zeng Fanzhi that she would like to share with the populace.

Since Ando was required to take the already existing structures into consideration and follow the overall development plan that specifies how tall buildings are to be, he created a very subtle structure that is nevertheless flexible and, according to the architect, a reflection of Beijing's dynamic art scene.[6] The ground plan was determined by the site: a trapezoid shape extends across several floors, several of them underground. Ando cut a swathe through the aboveground structure and on into the ground, creating a subterranean court onto which the underground floors open. This "sunken court" serves as a deliberately empty space that can be thought of as a counterpart to the increasing density of the surrounding city. Cut into the outside walls bent upward like paper are elongated triangular openings that take up the design of the interior, which also features long, sharp angles – an Ando design tradition; his structures always include geometrical forms. Heavy concrete appears suddenly weightless, and light seems to take on a spiritual quality.[7] Ando's works appear to have been drawn with merely a few strokes, only to then finally stand solidly before us just as convincingly simple. The sculptor Isamu Noguchi advised him: "If you manipulate stone too much, it will never become a sculpture",[8] and Ando has translated that into an architecture that does not appear "overworked." Ando hopes that the Genesis Museum will provide Beijing with a small place of contemplation and silence in the midst of the teeming metropolis.

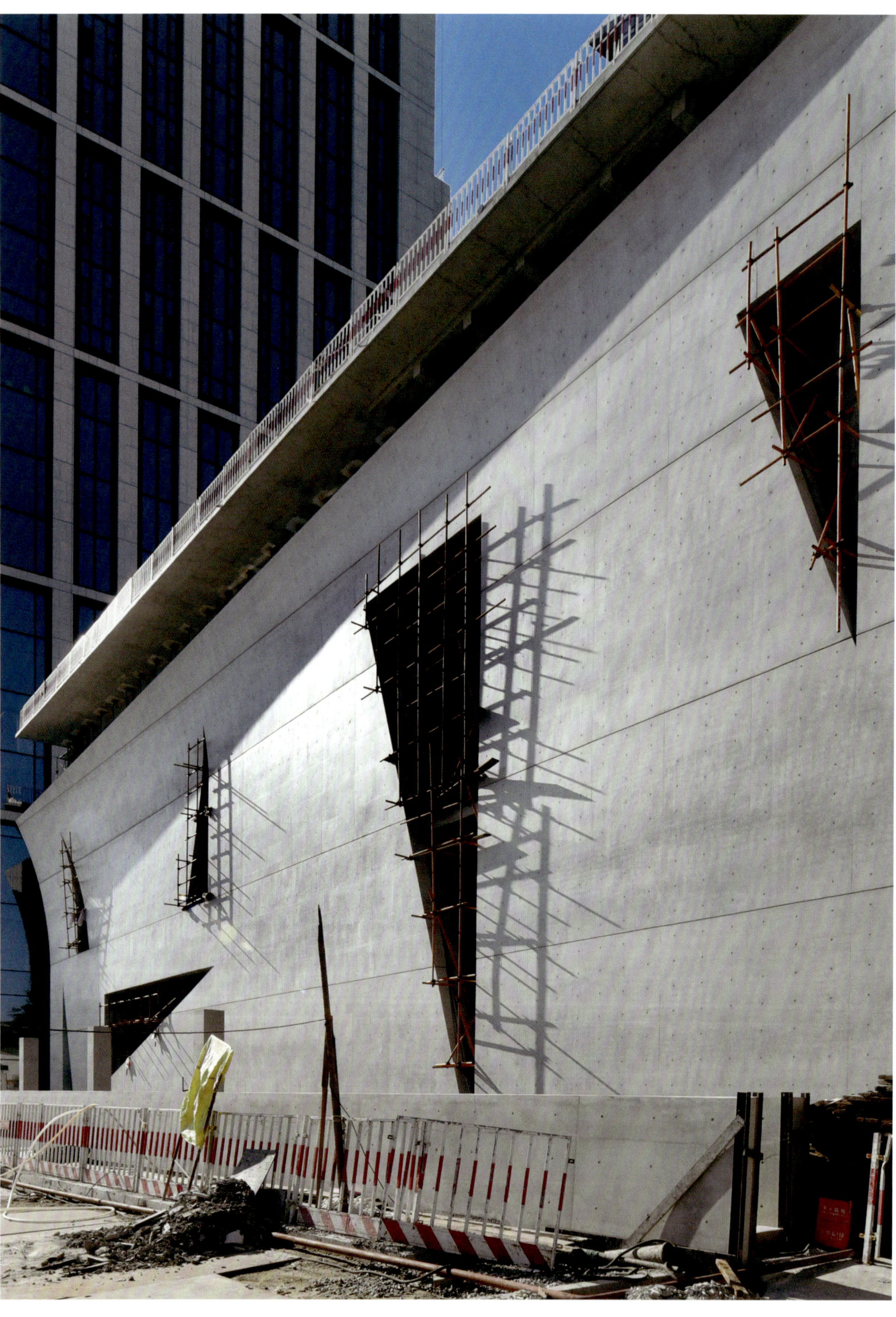

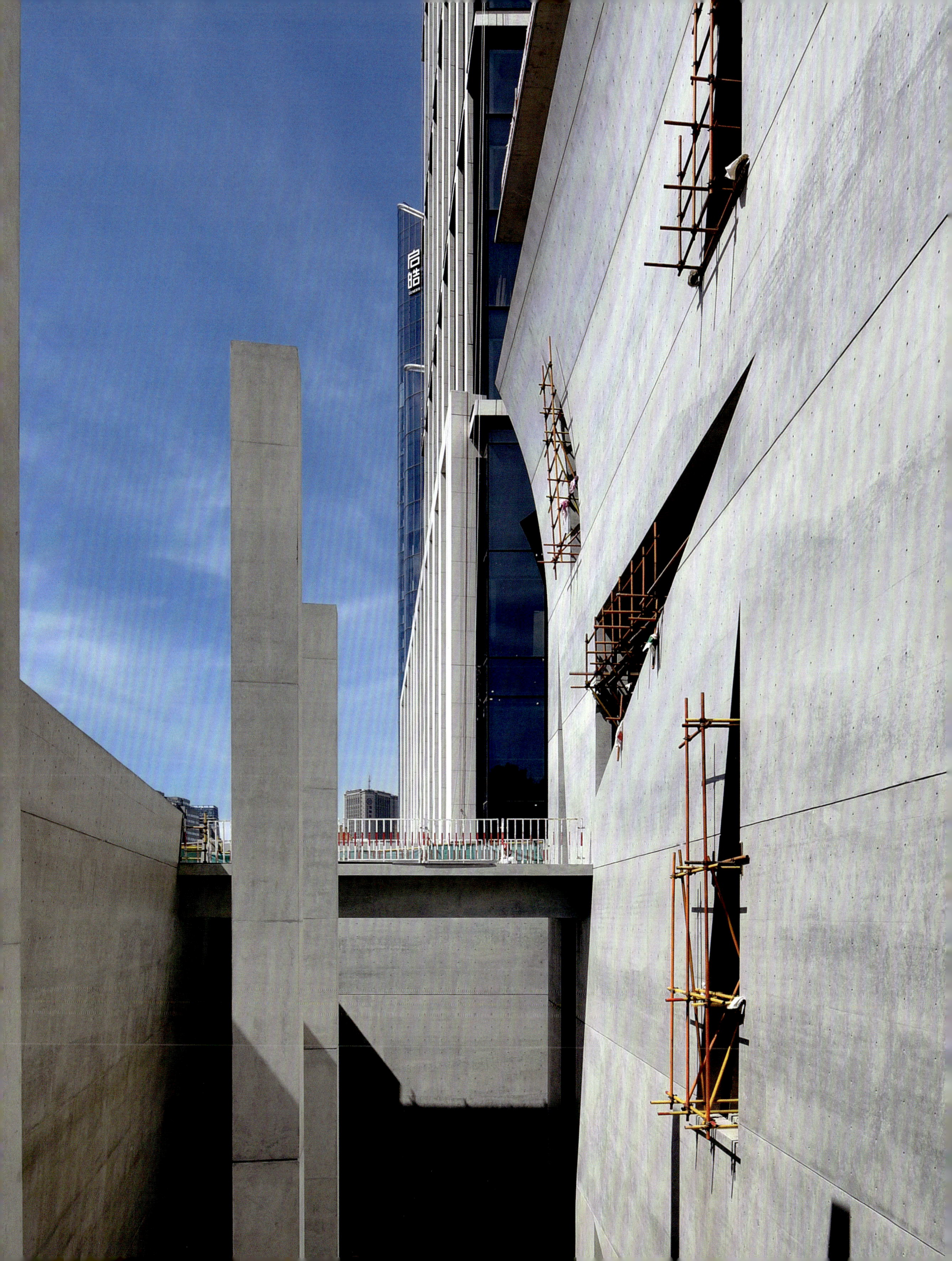

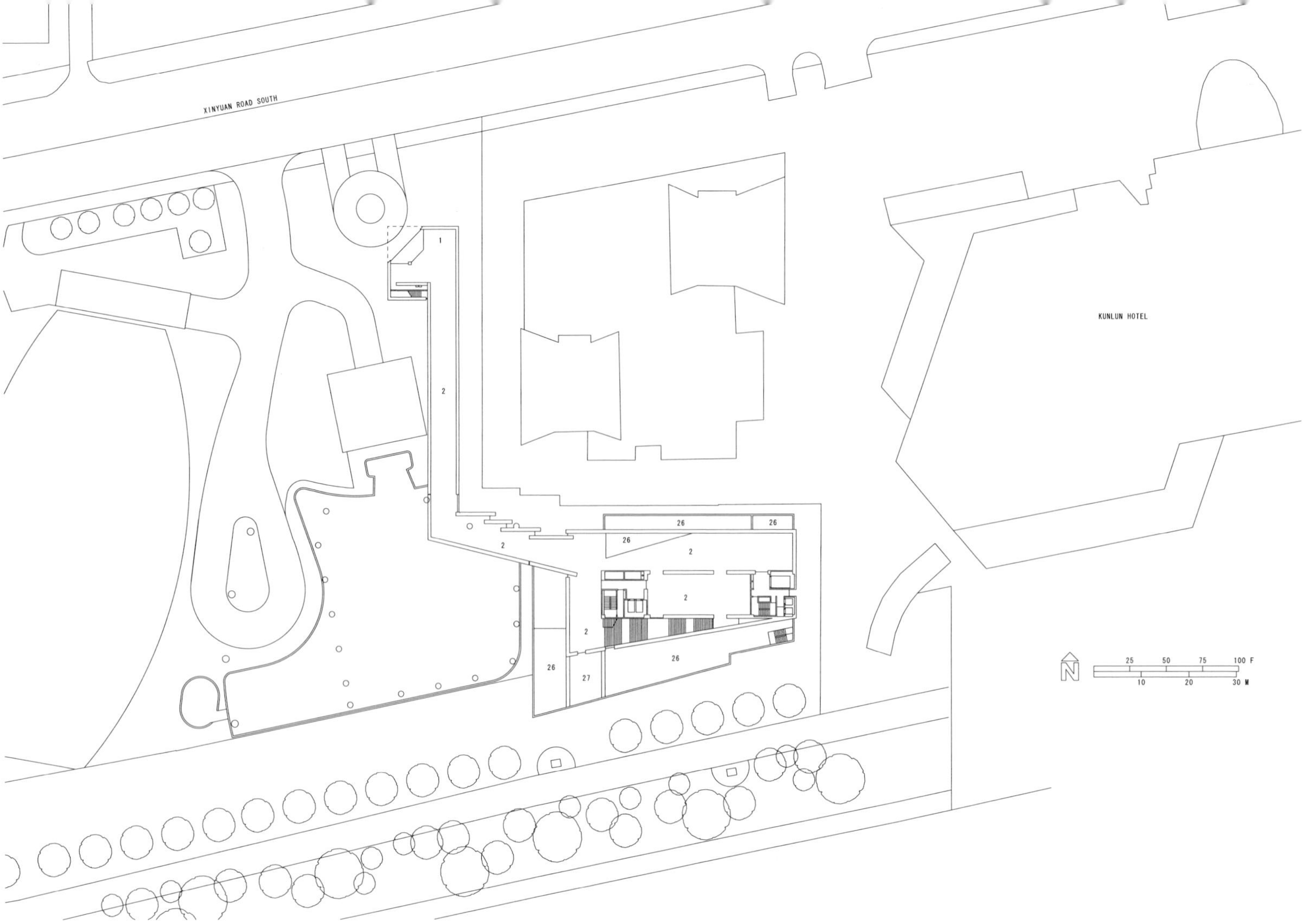

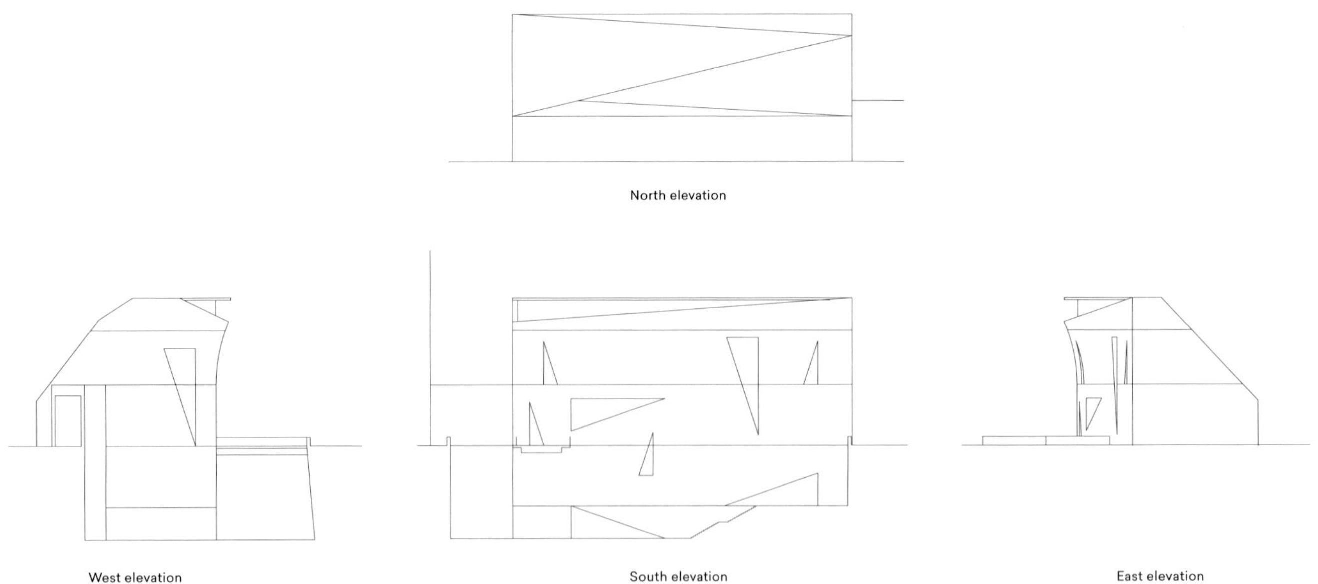

↑ Site plan.

↗ Elevations.

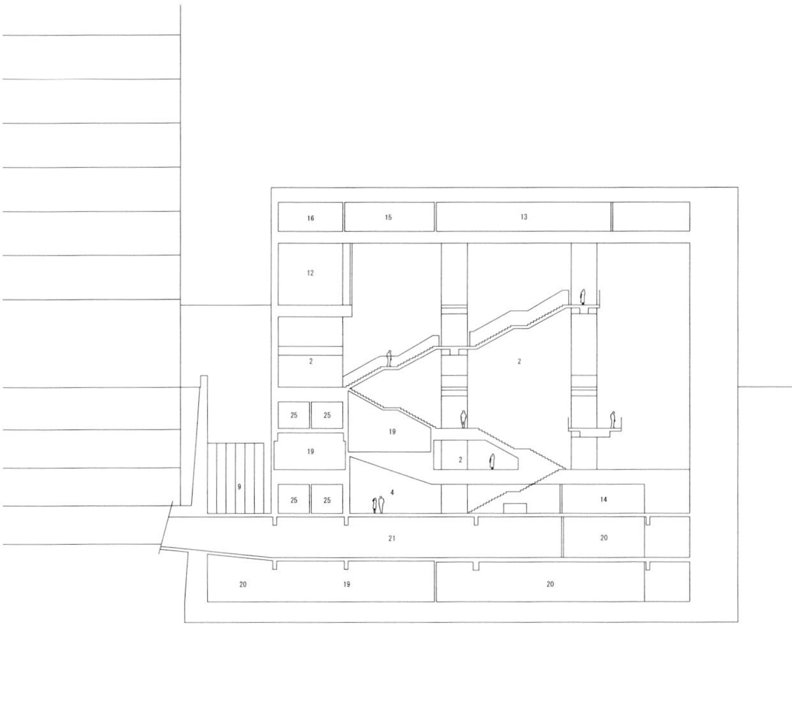
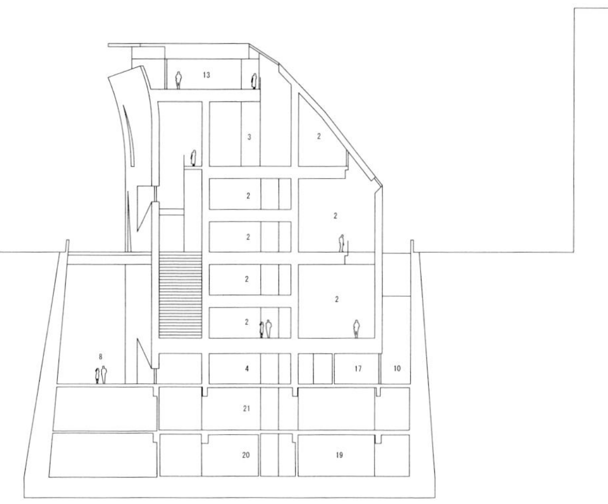
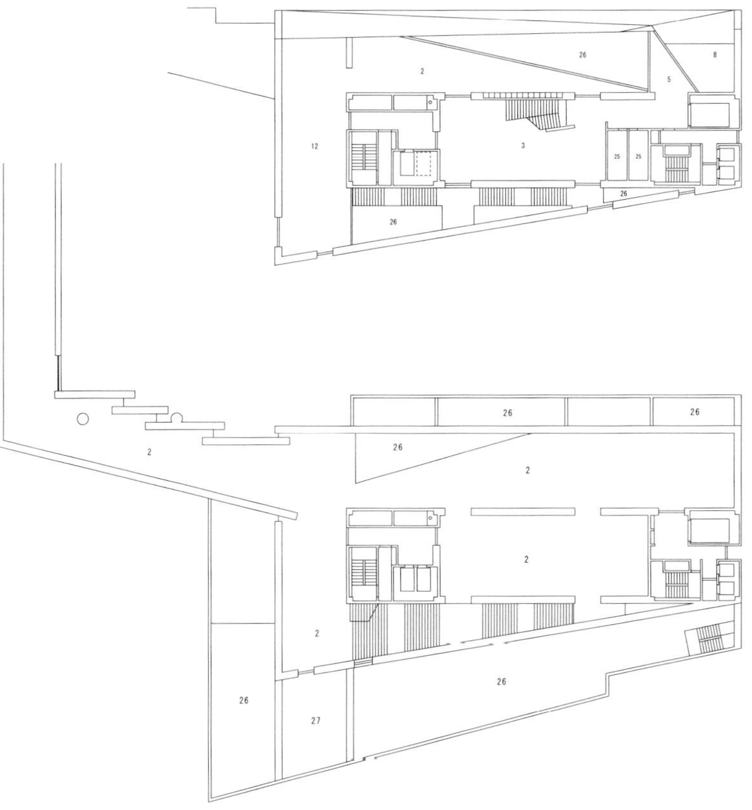

1 Entrance Hall
2 Gallery
3 Living Gallery
4 Café
5 Lounge
8 Terrace
9 Green
10 Sunk Court
12 Studio
13 Dining
14 Kitchen
15 Guest Room
16 Bed Room
17 Office
19 Machine Room
20 Storage
21 Parking
22 Loading
25 WC
26 Void
27 Sculpture Terrace

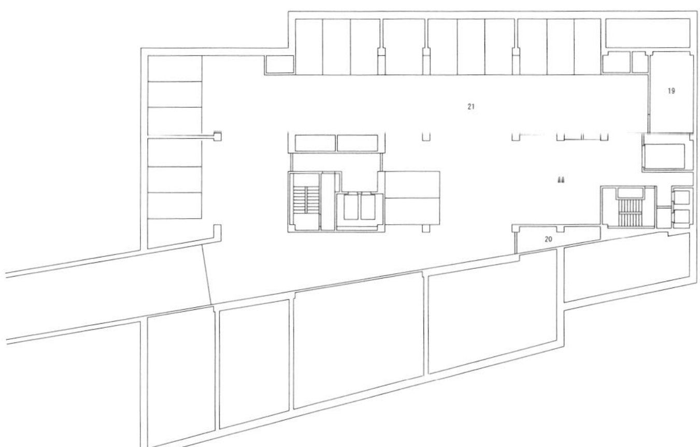

↑   Sections.

↖   Floor plans: +2, +1, –3.

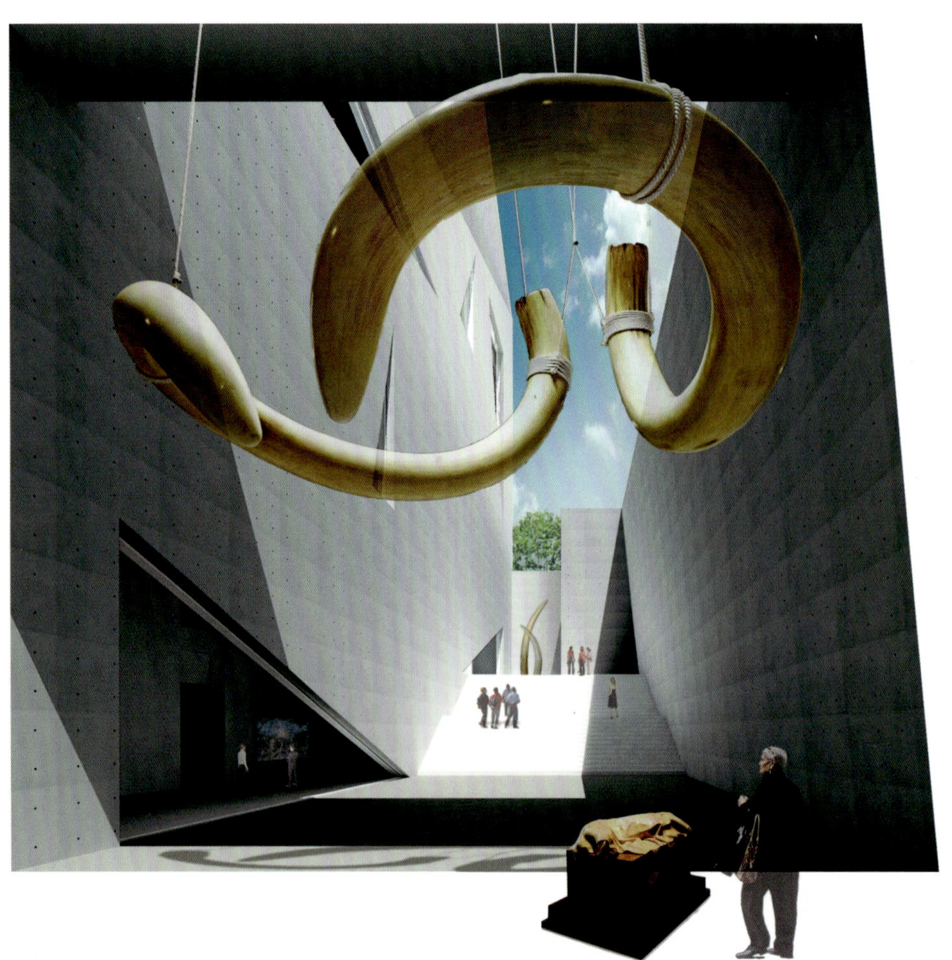

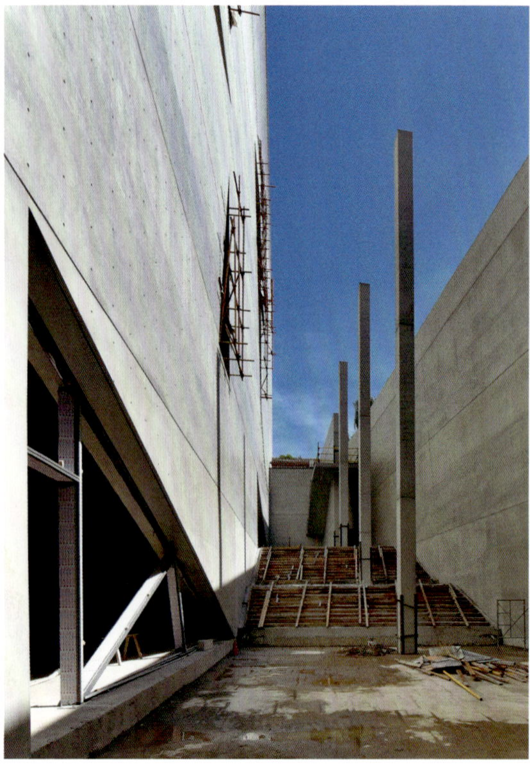

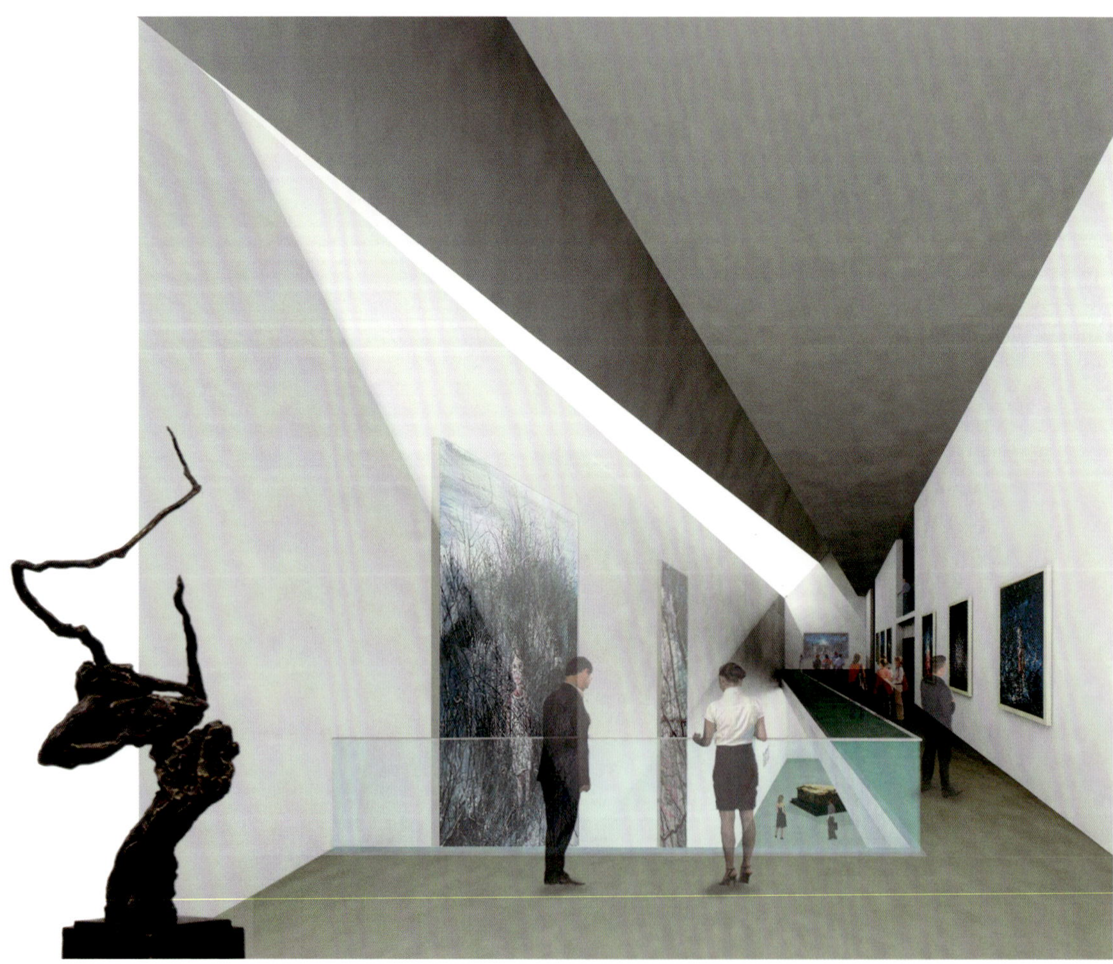

↑   Southern court.

↗   Staircase.

→   Gallery spaces.

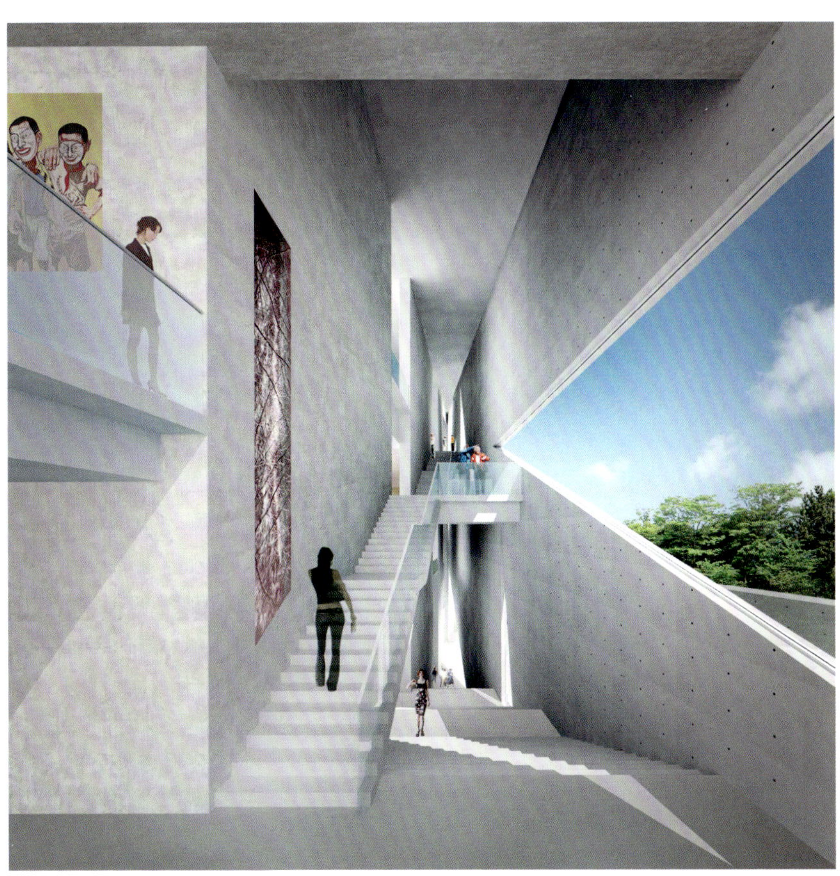

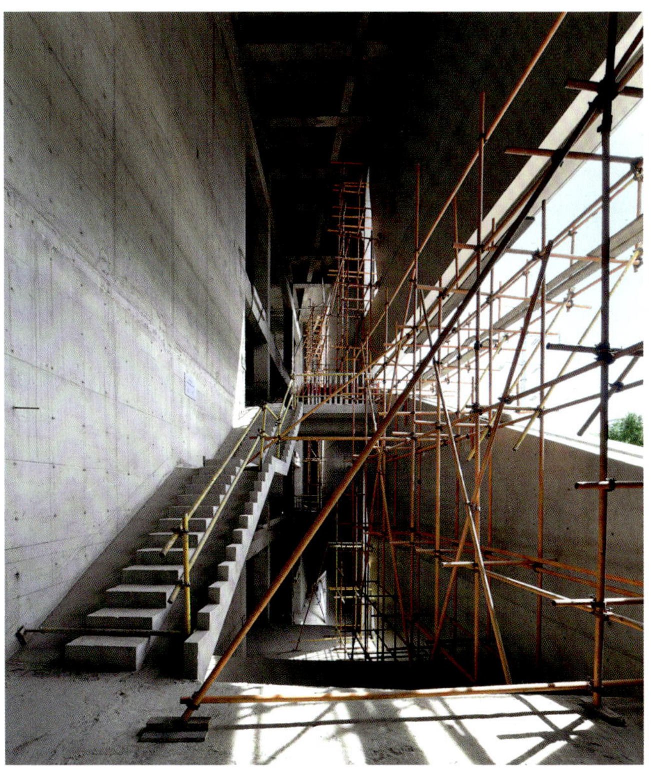

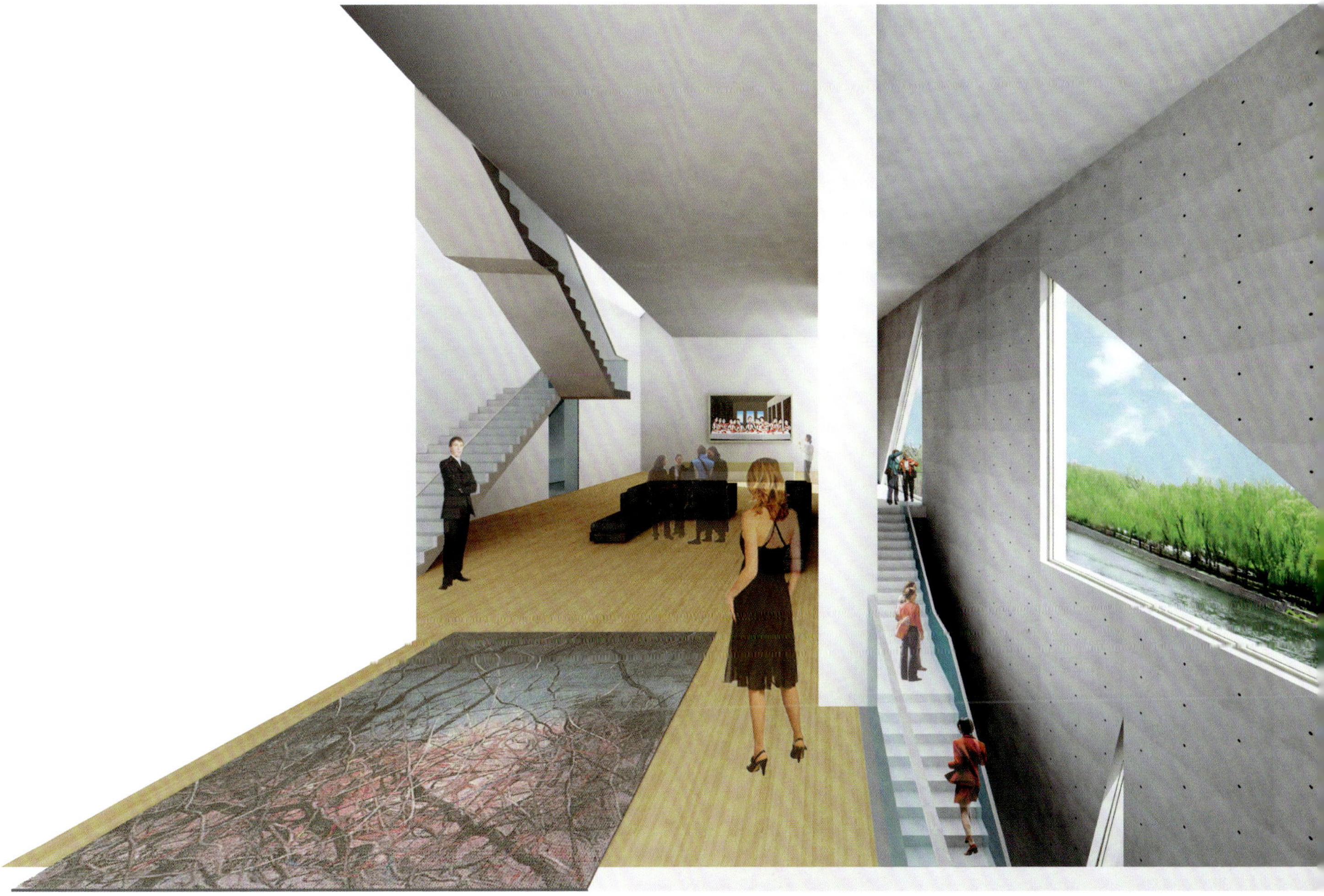

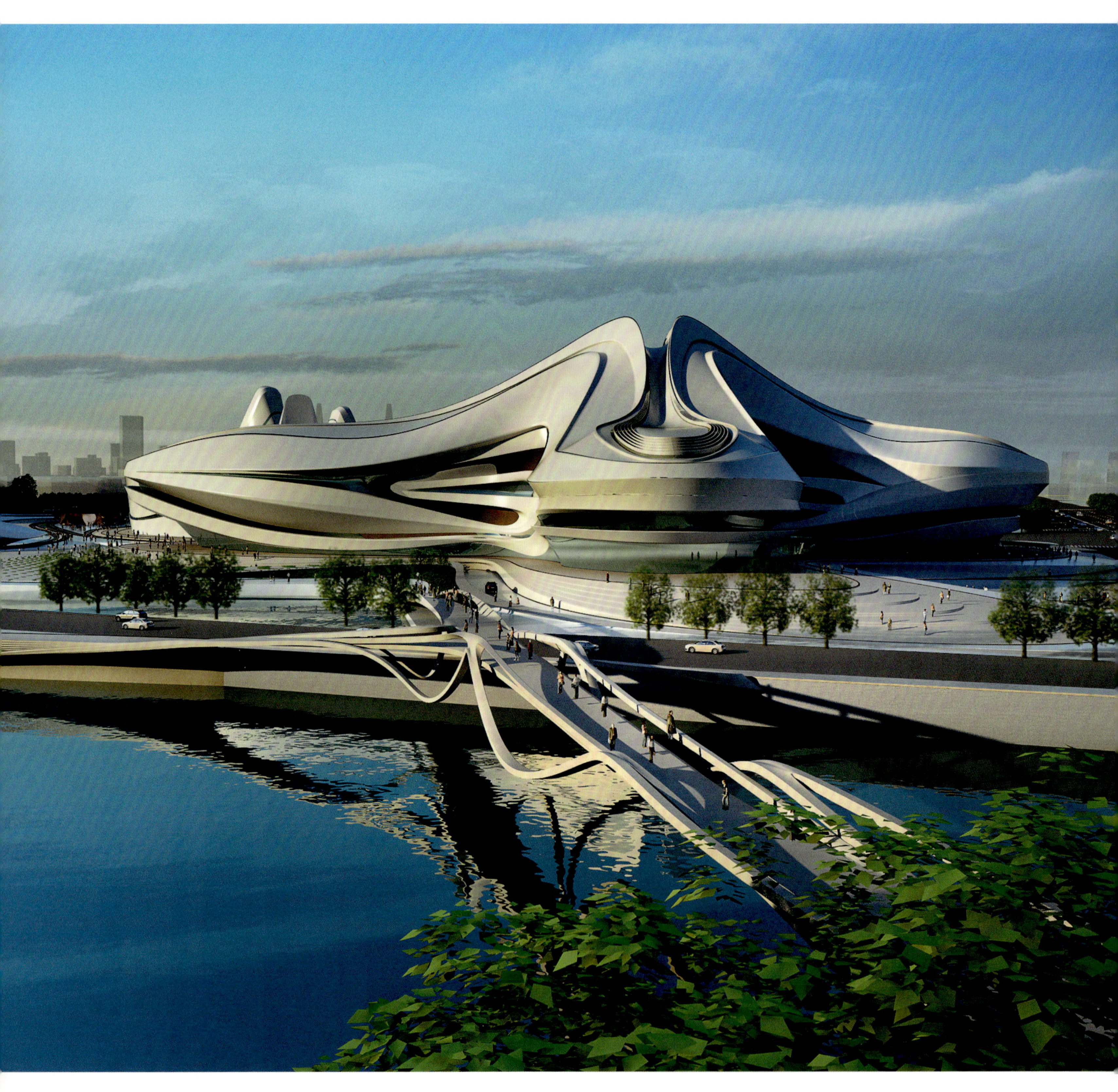

Meixi Lake International Culture & Arts Center

Changsha, China

Zaha Hadid Architects, London
Opening 2017
Building 125,000 sq.m
Contemporary art and cultural objects

To Zaha Hadid, a museum was not only a building in which art is displayed, it was a public place that was meant to be constantly bustling.[1] And it was with that in mind that she designed Meixi Lake International Culture & Arts Center. The collection of buildings contains a 1,800-seat theatre, a museum of contemporary art and a smaller 500-seat hall that can be used for presentations or smaller performances. Arranged around these three central buildings are additional structures with restaurants, shops and plazas accessible around the clock, available at all times to visitors and local residents alike as meeting places and places for communication.[2]

Meixi Lake International Culture & Arts Center will stand to the left of Huan Hu Road and the Xiang River. One first sees the "Small Theatre": an elongated oval with something like its own footprint to the left of it – an additional oval roofless structure that serves as an atrium. It appears as if the one building is the lid of the other, only temporarily set aside; one almost expects that the two pieces will be re-joined, a possibility that lends an exciting dynamism to the entire complex. The hall is several storeys tall, changing back and forth between an open and a closed form – a connection is thus achieved between the different levels of the site. The "Grand Theatre" is reminiscent of a leaf of clover that has been compressed so that it bulges upward; a snow-white mountain that looks like soft-serve ice cream towers over the visitor. The "Art Museum" is a flower, whose three petals are connected by a glass-roofed atrium. With each individually designed structure the undulating site with its many curves picks up on the animated surface of Meixi Lake, which was the

visual inspiration for the complex. The biomorphic forms Hadid loved to work with are clearly identifiable, so the centre seems familiar despite its unique shapes.

What is special about the Meixi Lake International Culture & Arts Center – or about Hadid's architecture in general – is its incorporation of space. Hadid did not build solitary structures with no reference to their surroundings. It was always important to her to develop a new place within an already existing one: she designed not only structures, but also the space surrounding them. This radical approach to spaces, in which we move about, is imposed on both visitors and locals: they have to reorient themselves, can no longer rely on familiar signs and routes.[3] The buildings seem irrational: which element is supporting, which ornamental, where does it begin, where does it end – the viewer has to puzzle this out, just like his route between these structures.[4] This may seem a challenge – but at the same time provides a chance to experience one's surroundings in new ways and develop new associations. This principle is applied inside the museums with particular success: in them, as well, visitors are not meant to follow only the route prescribed by curators, but have an opportunity to make discoveries of their own. The museum in Changsha vaguely recalls the famous spiral in New York's Guggenheim, one of Hadid's favourite museums.[5] In Changsha, too, visitors move about in corridors open to the atrium – a space within the space with enough room for independent interpretations, both of the art exhibited and of the sensuous forms of a building that not only wishes to be functional,[6] but is above all breathtakingly beautiful.

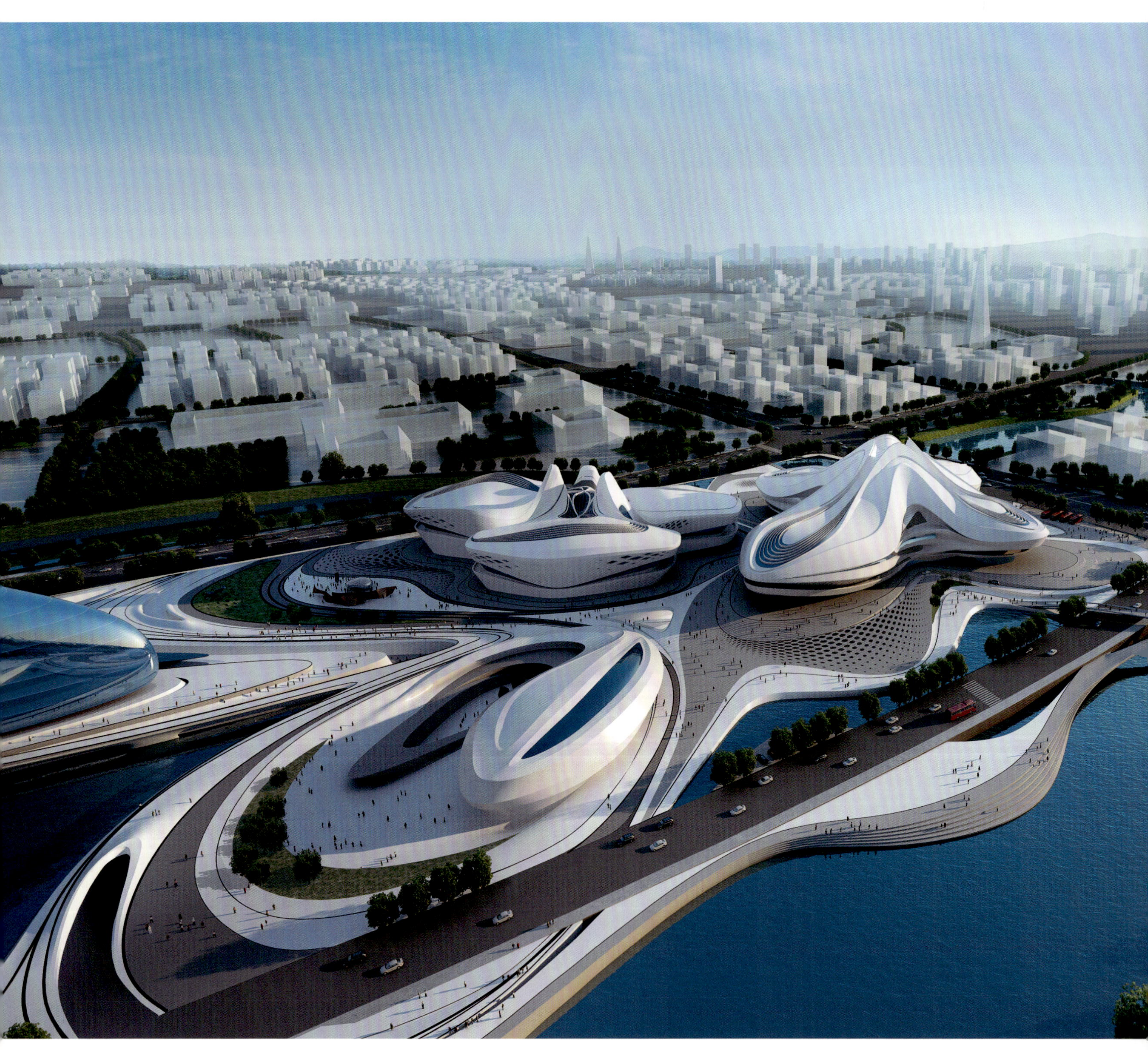

↑ Looking northeast.

→ Roof structure.

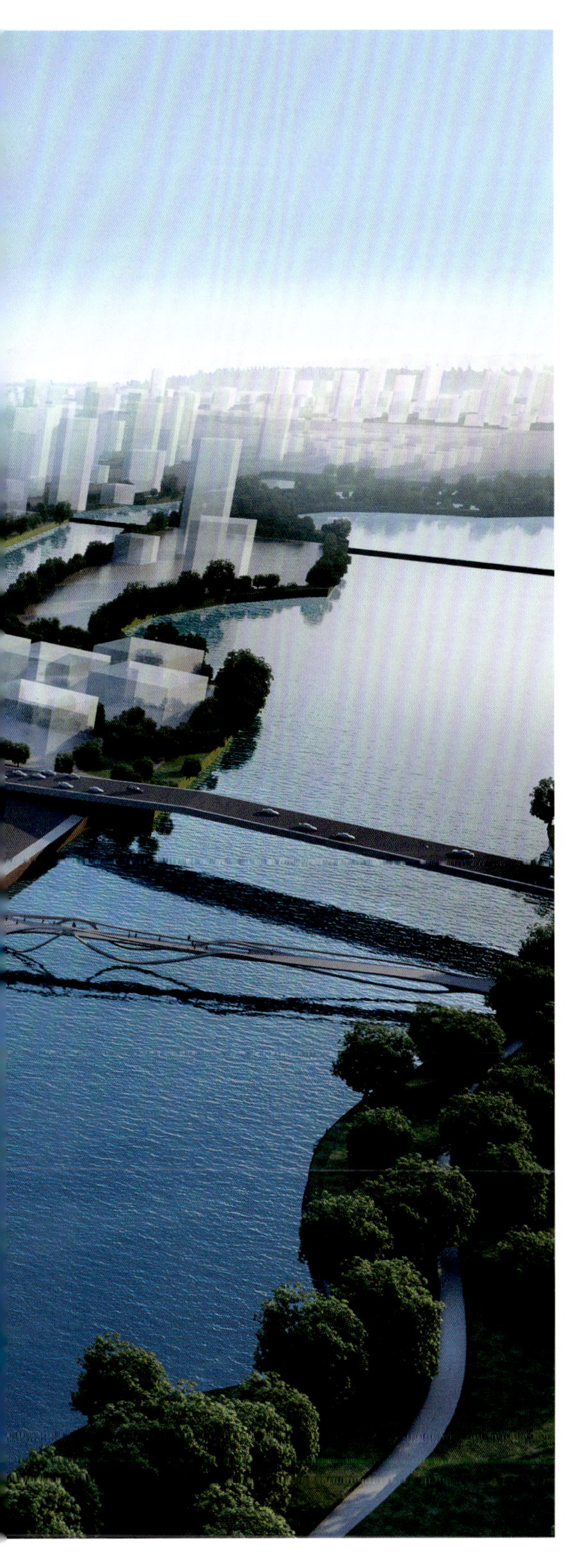

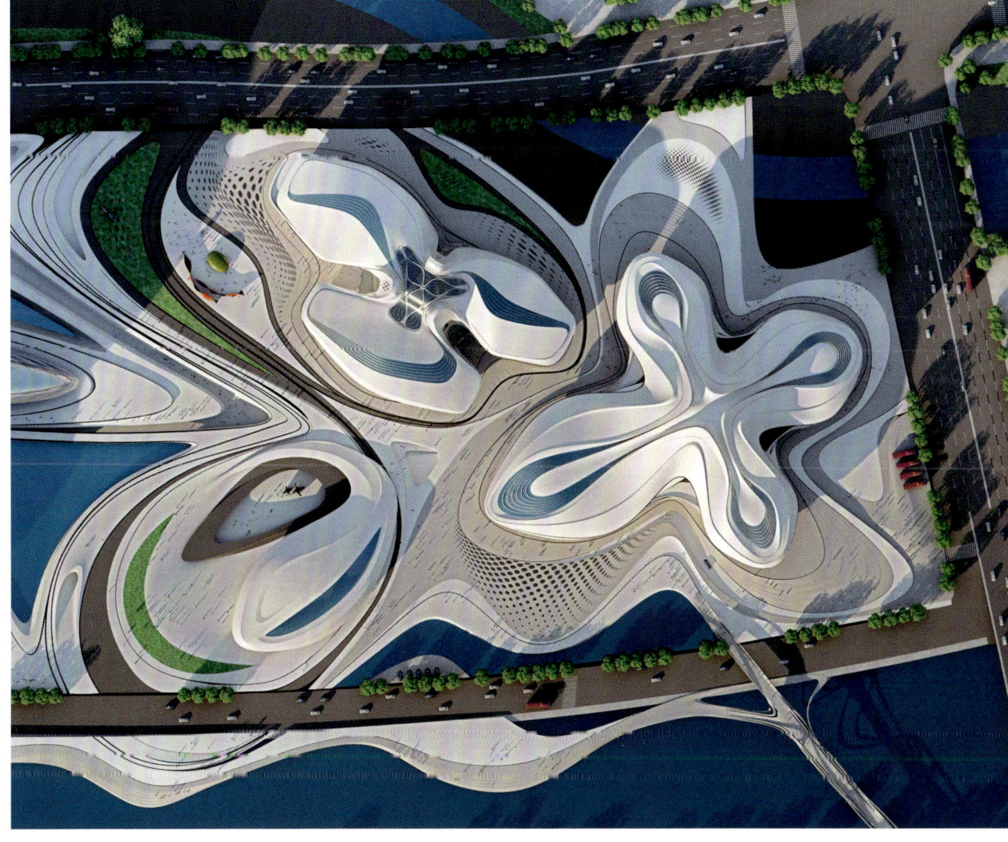

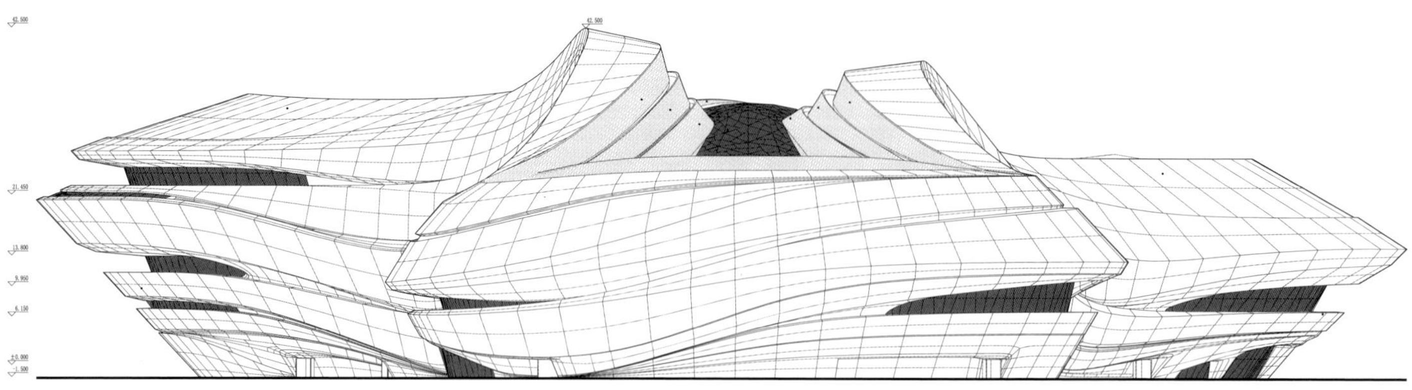

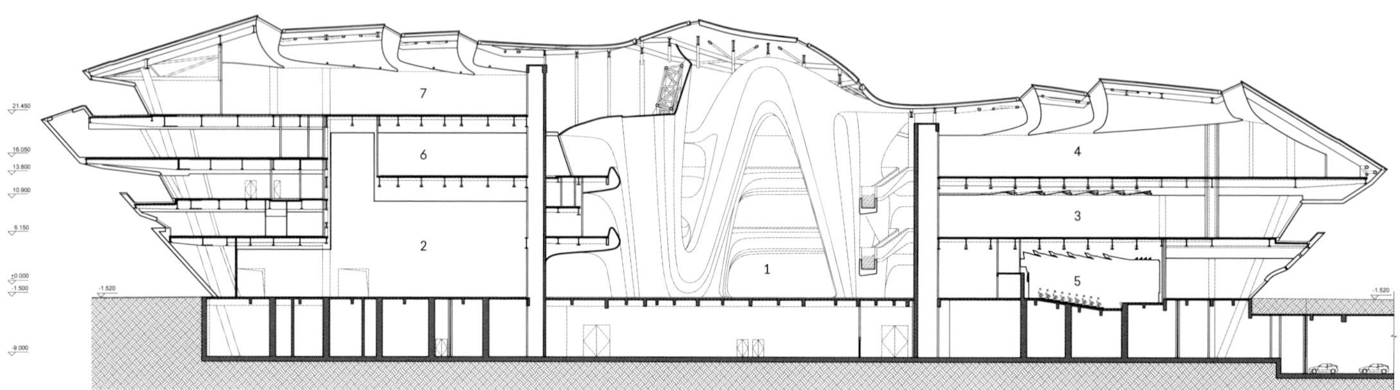

1   Atrium
2   Big Box Exhibition Space
3   Exhibition Space
4   Hunan Exhibition Space
5   Lecture Hall
6   Global Platforms Exhibition Space
7   Permanent Collection

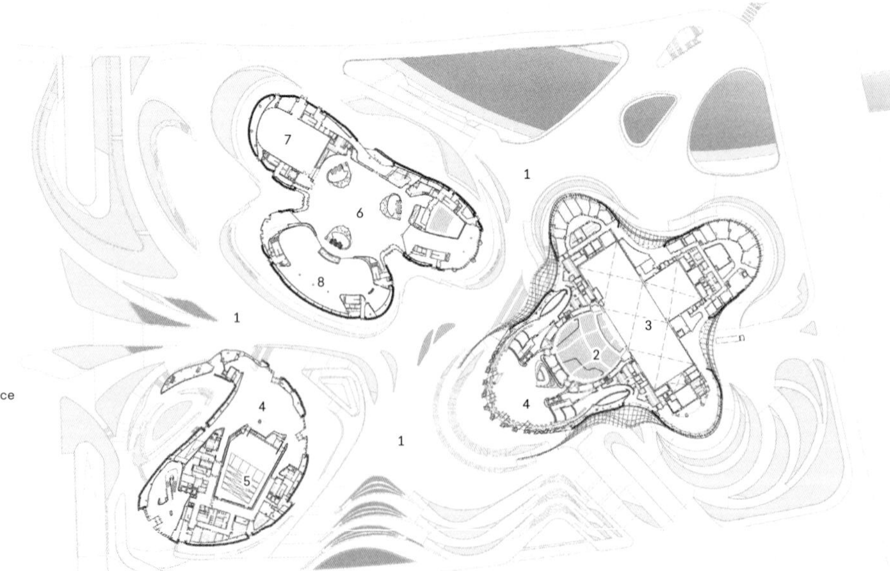

1   Plaza

Grand Theatre:
2   Auditorium
3   Void above Stage

Small Theatre:
4   Foyer
5   Multi-Functional Hall

Art Museum:
6   Atrium
7   Big Box Exhibition Space
8   Applied Art Centre

↑   Art Museum:
    Elevation, looking northeast.
    Section, northwest – southeast.

→   Site plan.

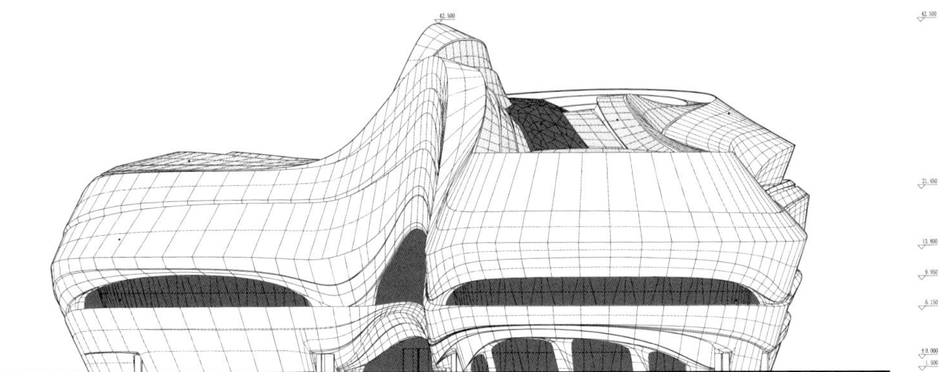

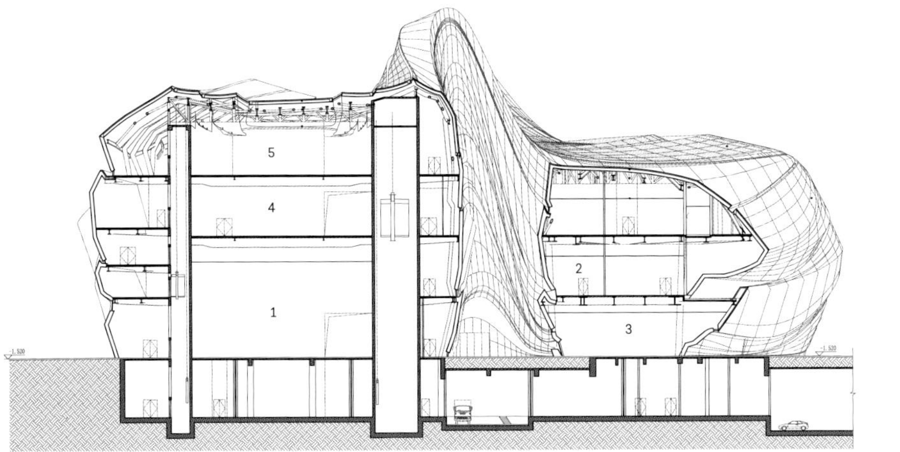

1 Big Box Exhibition Space
2 Class Room
3 Café
4 International Exhibition Space
5 Permanent Collection

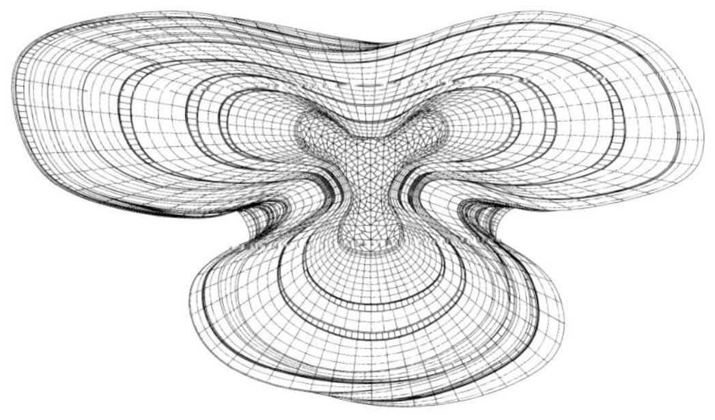

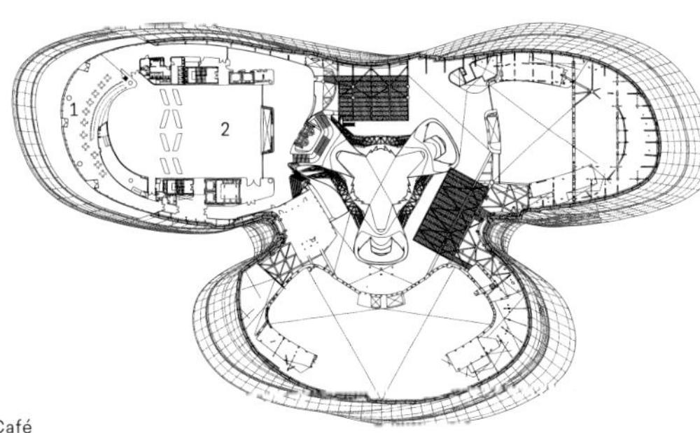

1 Café
2 Permanent Collection Room

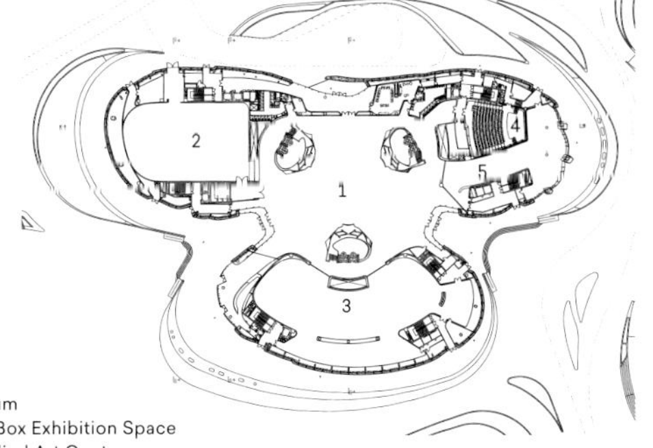

1 Atrium
2 Big Box Exhibition Space
3 Applied Art Centre
4 Lecture Theatre
5 Shop

↑ Art Museum:
Elevation, looking northwest.
Section, northeast–southwest.

→ Plans: Roof, +4, ground floor.

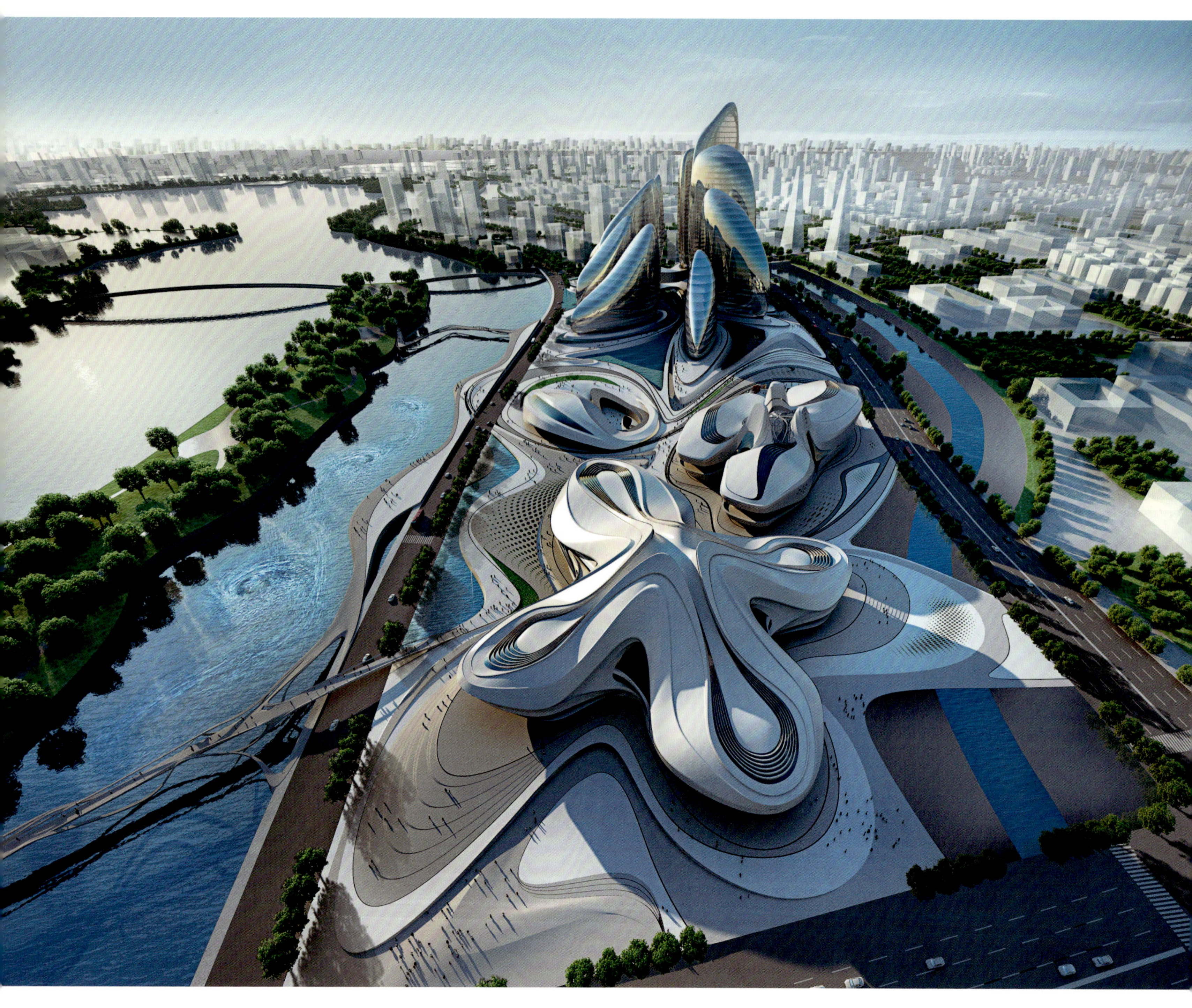

↑ Aerial view, looking west.

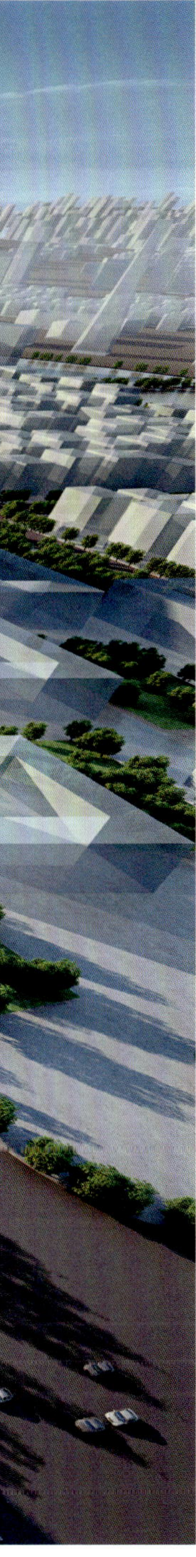

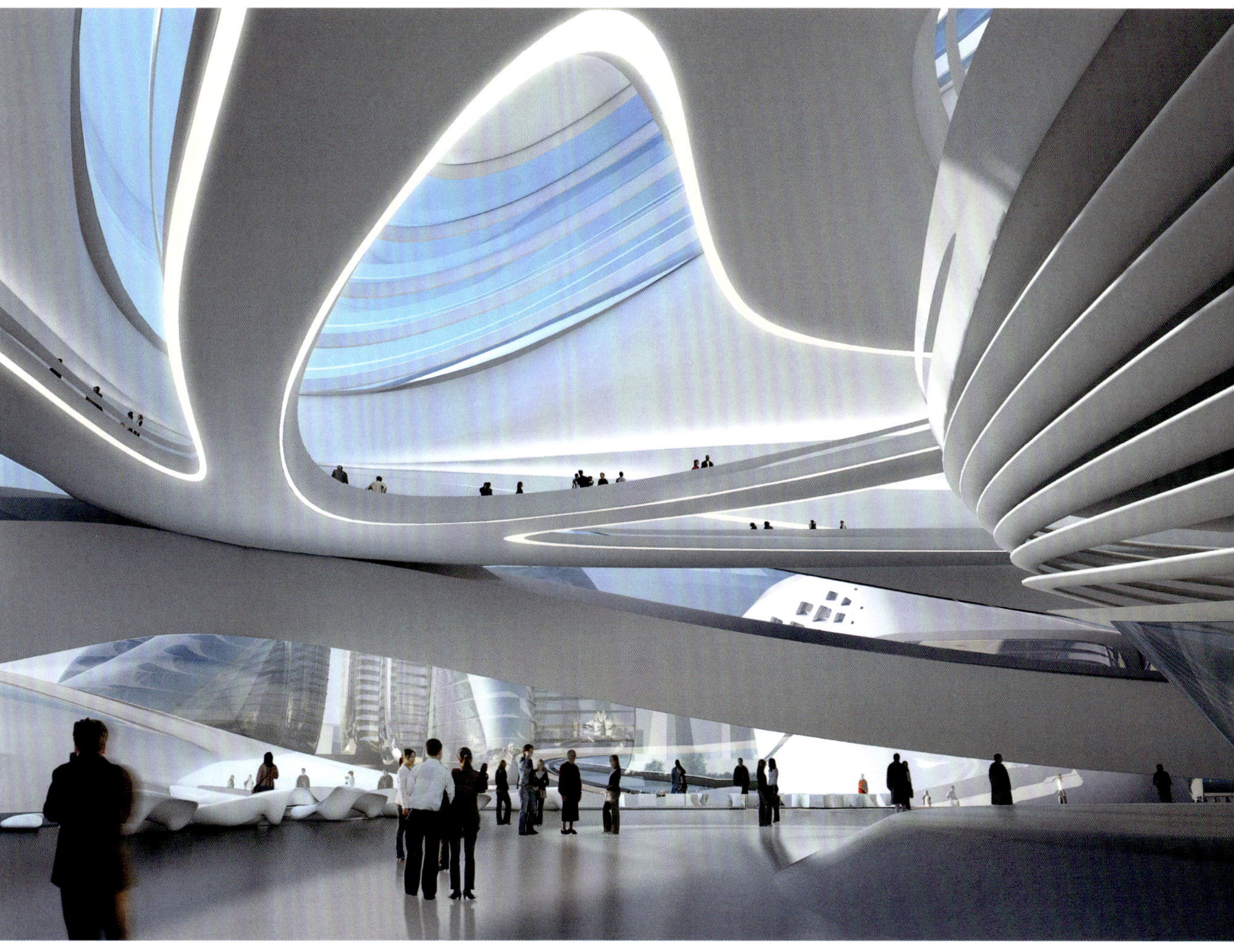

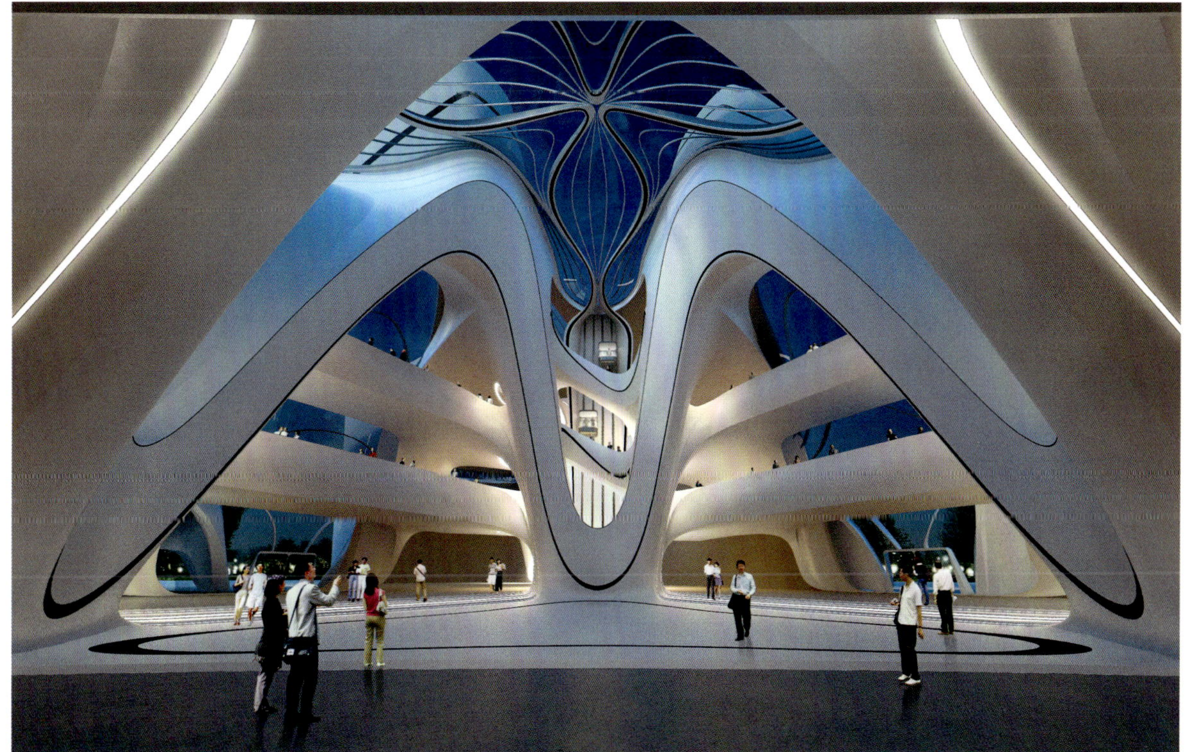

↗ Interior, by day.

→ Art Museum:
The atrium at night.

Notes to the Catalogue

p. 17
National Museum of African American History and Culture (NMAAHC), Washington, D.C.

1 Okwui Enwezor, "Popular Sovereignty and Public Space: David Adjaye's Architecture of Immanence", in *David Adjaye: Making Public Buildings. Specificity, Customization, Imbrication*, ed. Peter Allison (London: Thames & Hudson, 2006), 9.
2 Mabel O. Wilson, "Other Monumentalities", in *David Adjaye: Form, Heft, Material*, ed. Okwui Enwezor et al. (Chicago: Art Institute of Chicago, 2015), 268.
3 Ibid., 279.
4 Kinshasha Holman Conwill, "To Reap the Harvest Wonderful: On Sustainability at the National Museum of African American History and Culture", *American Art* 3 (2014): 24.
5 Ibid., 23.

p. 39
Long Museum West Bund, Shanghai

1 Liu Yichun, Atelier Deshaus, "When Structure Meets a Place: Design Thinking of Long Museum West Bund", 1.
2 Claire Jacobson, *New Museums in China* (New York: Princeton Architectural Press, 2014), ix.
3 Eduard Kögel, "Mit Geschichte aufgeladen. Ein historisches Museum als Reflexion über den Abrisswahn in China", *werk, bauen + wohnen* 5 (2013): 10. In the last few decades China has developed a sense of its own history that had been buried by the Cultural Revolution. One can now assume that an awareness of the more recent past will gradually prevail. See Marzia Varutti, "The Aesthetics and Narratives in National Museums in China", in *National Museums: New Studies from around the World*, ed. Simon J. Knell et al. (London and New York: Routledge, 2011), 307.
4 Liu Yichun, "When Structure Meets a Place", 3–4.
5 Aldo Rossi, *The Architecture of the City* (Cambridge, MA: MIT Press, 1982), 32.

p. 47
Kunstmuseum Basel Extension

1 Nikolaus Meier, *Kunstmuseum Basel. Die Architektur* (Basel: Christoph Merian Verlag, 2003), 23.
2 Bernhard Mendes Bürgi, "Die Wechselwirkung zwischen Kunst und Architektur. Zu den inhaltlichen Aspekten des Neubaus", in *Kunstmuseum Basel, Neubau*, ed. Kunstmuseum Basel (Ostfildern: Hatje Cantz Verlag, 2016), 69.
3 Emanuel Christ, "We look at examples. Ein Gespräch mit Emanuel Christ, Christoph Gantenbein, Diogo Lopes, Kersten Geers und Patricia Barbas", *Baumeister* 8 (2013): 79.

p. 55
Naga Site Museum

1 Jan Hamann, "Naga-Projekt Sudan. Archäologie und Restaurierung im Sudan – Restaurierungsethische Überlegungen zur Hathor-Kapelle", in *Kulturgut erhalten. Standards in der Restaurierungswissenschaft und Denkmalpflege*, ed. Uwe Peltz and Olivia Zorn (Darmstadt: Philipp von Zabern, 2009), 176. This procedure is in accord with UNESCO's policy of wishing to see artefacts exhibited as close to their find spot as possible.
2 Ursula Baus, "David Chipperfield und die Bauherren seiner Museen", in *DAM Jahrbuch*, ed. Deutsches Architektur-Museum (Frankfurt am Main: Prestel, 2005), 22.

3 Fulvio Irace, "Simple, Ordinary, Complex", in *David Chipperfield Architects*, ed. Rik Nys (Cologne: Walther König, 2013), 8.
4 David Chipperfield, *Theoretical Practice* (London: Artemis, 1994), 19.
5 Rafael Moneo, "The Architect's Profession Today: An Alternative in Globalised Times", *El Croquis* 174/175 (2014): 359.

p. 63
Munchmuseet, Oslo

1 Jill Lloyd, "Van Gogh and Munch: A Question of Style", in *Munch: Van Gogh*, ed. Maite van Dijk et al. (Brussels: Mercatorfonds, 2014), 143.
2 For more information about glass as a building material in modern architecture, please see: Iñaki Ábalos and Juan Herreros, *Tower and Office: From Modernist Theory to Contemporary Practice* (Cambridge, MA: MIT Press, 2003), 99.

p. 71
MONA Museum of Old and New Art, Berriedale

1 "Museum of Old and New Art (MONA)", Arney Fender Katsalidis, accessed July 19, 2016, http://www.afkstudios.com/project/museum-for-old-and-new-art-mona/culture.
2 Janice Baker, "Out of the Wilderness (MONA): Critically Engaging with the Profound Art Encounter", in *The Challenge of the Object*, ed. G. Ulrich Grossmann et al. (Nuremberg: Verlag des Germanischen Nationalmuseums, 2013), 395.
3 Sabine Thiel-Silling, "Mut zum Risiko", *Baumeister* 3 (2014): 17.
4 "Museum of Old and New Art", *Australian Design Review*, accessed July 19, 2016, https://www.australiandesignreview.com/architecture/2280-museum-of-old-and-new-art.

p. 79
Zayed National Museum, Abu Dhabi

1 Lawrence Joffe, "Obituary: Sheikh Zayed bin Sultan Al Nahyan", *The Guardian*, November 3, 2004, accessed August 10, 2016, https://www.theguardian.com/news/2004/nov/03/guardianobituaries.israel.
2 Peter Buchanan, "The Urban Room", in *On Foster … Foster On*, ed. David Jenkins (Munich: Prestel, 2000), 429.

p. 83
Zeitz Museum of Contemporary Art Africa (Zeitz MOCAA), Cape Town

1 Corinne Julius, "Making – The World of Thomas Heatherwick", *Craft Arts International* 86 (2012): 18–25.
2 Tom Banks, "Heatherwick to 'Carve Out' Grain Silo in Ambitious African Gallery Project", *Design Week*, February 28, 2014, accessed July 19, 2016, http://www.designweek.co.uk/issues/february-2014/heatherwick-to-carve-out-grain-silo-in-ambitious-african-gallery-project/.

p. 89
The Palestinian Museum, Birzeit

1 "Palestinian Museum", Heneghan Peng, accessed August 9, 2016, http://www.hparc.com/work/palestinian-museum/.
2 Oliver Wainwright, "Palestine Museum review – a Beacon of Optimism on a West Bank Hilltop", *The Guardian*, May 17, 2016, https://www.theguardian.com/artanddesign/2016/may/17/palestine-museum-review-ramallag-west-bank-israel.

3 "Palestinian Journeys – An Interactive Timeline from 1850 to the Modern Day", Palestinian Museum, accessed August 10, 2016, http://www.palmuseum.org/public-programme/palestinian-journeys-an-interactive-timeline-from-1850-to-the-modern-day.

p. 97
Nasjonalmuseet for kunst, arkitektur og design, Oslo

1 Architect Klaus Schuwerk on architecture: https://www.youtube.com/watch?v=Svkl4YdsJO8.

p. 105
Pingtan Art Museum, Pingtan Island

1 Christian Dubrau, *Zeitgenössische Architektur in China. Bauten und Projekte 2000 bis 2020* (Berlin: Dom Publishers, 2010), 10.
2 Fulong Wu, "Re-orientation of the City Plan: Strategic Planning and Design Competition in China", *Geoforum* 38 (2007): 381.
3 Weiping Wu and Piper Gaubatz, *The Chinese City* (London: Routledge, 2013), 158–59.
4 Dubrau, *Zeitgenössische Architektur*, 13.
5 Manon Mollard, "Mad Scene", *Architectural Review* 1425 (2015): 66.
6 Claire Jacobson, *New Museums in China* (New York: Princeton Architectural Press, 2014), 1.

p. 111
Guggenheim Helsinki

1 "Stage One Submissions", Guggenheim Helsinki, accessed July 19, 2016, http://designguggenheimhelsinki.org/stageonegallery/en. More than 1,700 designs were submitted from seventy-seven countries. Of the six finalists the jury finally settled on Moreau Kusunoki Architectes.
2 "Winner", Guggenheim Helsinki, accessed July 19, 2016, http://designguggenheimhelsinki.org/en/finalists/winner.
3 "Homepage", Moreau Kusunoki Architectes, accessed July 19, 2016, http://www.moreaukusunoki.com.

p. 119
China Comic and Animation Museum, Hangzhou

1 Johannes von Müller, "Die Sprechblase", in *Bildlaute und laute Bilder. Die "Audio-Visualität" der Bilderzählungen*, ed. Christian A. Bachmann (Berlin: Christian A. Bachmann Verlag, 2014), 82.
2 Claire Jacobson, *New Museums in China* (New York: Princeton Architectural Press, 2014), 135.
3 W. J. T. Mitchell, "Comics as Media: Afterword", *Critical Inquiry* 40, no. 3 (2014): 259.
4 Tom Gunning, "The Art of Succession: Reading, Writing, and Watching Comics", *Critical Inquiry* 40, no. 3 (2014): 37.

p. 127
Sydney Modern Project – Art Gallery of New South Wales

1 For the museum's building history, see "History of the Building", Art Gallery NSW, accessed July 19, 2016, http://www.artgallery.nsw.gov.au/about-us/history/history-of-the- building/.

2 Inmaculada Maluenda and Enrique Encabo, "Continuity Systems: A Conversation with Kazuyo Sejima & Ryue Nishizawa", *El Croquis* 179/180 (2015): 11.
3 SANAA consider the possibility for communication as a crucial component of their museum buildings. See Hans Ulrich Obrist, *Lives of the Artists, Lives of the Architects* (London: Allen Lane, 2015), 450.

p. 135
Kurdistan Museum, Erbil

1 Alexandra Stara, "Cultivating Architects. History in Architectural Education", in *The Humanities in Architectural Design. A Contemporary and Historical Perspective*, ed. Soumyen Bandyopadhyay et al. (London and New York: Routledge, 2010), 30.
2 Elizabeth Greenspan, "Daniel Libeskind's Secret Museum of the Kurds". *Bloomberg Businessweek*, April 11, 2016, accessed August 19, 2016, http://www.bloomberg.com/features/2016-design/a/daniel-libeskind/.
3 Regine Hess, *Emotionen am Werk. Peter Zumthor, Daniel Libeskind, Lars Spuybroek und die historische Architekturpsychologie* (Berlin: Gebr. Mann Verlag, 2013), 156.
4 Wendy Koenig, *The Phenomenon of Interruption in the Visual Arts* (New York: Edwin Mellen Press, 2009), 55.

p. 143
Genesis Museum, Beijing

1 For museum development in China, see Zhang Gan, "The Modern Museum in China", in *Crossing Cultures: Conflict, Migration and Convergence*, ed. Jaynie Anderson (Carlton: Miegunyah Press, 2009), 1032–35.
2 Claire Jacobson, *New Museums in China* (New York: Princeton Architectural Press, 2014), ix.
3 "Mad about Museums", *The Economist*, December 21, 2013, accessed July 20, 2016, http://www.economist.com/news/special-report/21591710-china-building-thousands-new-museums-how-will-it-fill-them-mad-about-museums.
4 Robert Kaltenbrunner, "Pekings Weg zur globalen Metropole", *Archithese* 4 (2008): 26.
5 Jacobson, *New Museums in China*, x.
6 Tadao Ando, Press kit from Tadao Ando Architect & Associates, "Huadu Museum", June 2016.
7 Philip Jodidio, *Ando: Complete Works* (Cologne: Taschen, 2007), 6.
8 Tadao Ando, *Conversations with Students*, trans. and ed. Matthew Hunter (New York: Princeton Architectural Press, 2012), 60.

p. 151
Meixi Lake International Culture & Arts Center, Changsha

1 Hans Ulrich Obrist, *Zaha Hadid* (Cologne: Walther König, 2007), 11.
2 Jay Landers, "No Title", *Civil Engineering* 5 (2013): 21.
3 Patrik Schumacher, "Design Is Communication", in *Zaha Hadid: Form in Motion*, ed. Kathryn Bloom Hiesinger (New Haven: Yale University Press, 2011), 12.
4 Ulf Meyer, "Gibt es das digital Erhabene?", *Baumeister* 6 (2013): 77.
5 Obrist (as in note 1), 13.
6 Aaron Betsky, "Introduction: Beyond 89 Degrees", in *The Complete Zaha Hadid*, ed. Zaha Hadid and Aaron Betsky (London: Thames & Hudson, 2013), 11.

ESSAYS

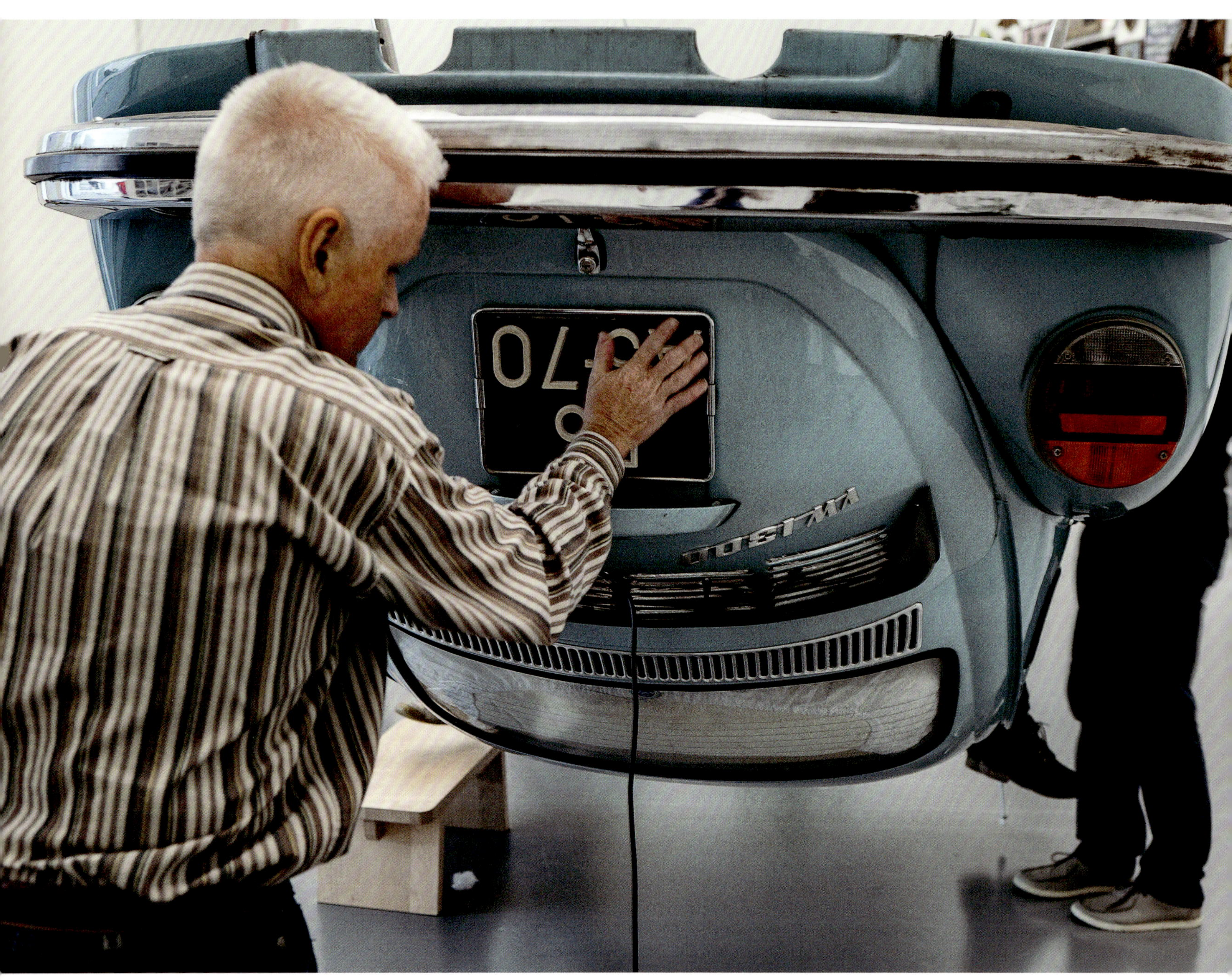

↑ Touching the artwork "Naked Machine" by Surasi
Kusolwong during multi-sensory tour for blind
and partially sighted visitors as part of the Special
Guests program at Van Abbemuseum Eindhoven.

The Idea of the Open Museum: History and Problems

Wolfgang Ullrich

The open museum and the spirit of 1968

There had been plenty of publications on the future of the art museum, but they were never as numerous as in the early 1970s. The sense of a new beginning sparked by the 1968 protests provoked examination of all institutions suspected of being conservative and old-fashioned. It was a time for reflection on how museums might change and have a greater impact on society. In retrospect, it is remarkable how the most important ideas proposed at that time have since become reality. Much of what might have previously appeared to contemporaries as audacious is now practised – or even exceeded – as a matter of course. Whether art education or offerings for visitors unfamiliar with the museum world, the inclusion of new mediums or changing exhibits in addition to the permanent collection, special events, new shops or high-class gastronomy – around 1970 they were all part of thinking for the future, and have since been incorporated in countless new and enlarged venues, also in the restructuring of those rich in tradition. Of all the institutional reforms called for in the spirit of 1968, that of the art museum has thus been particularly successful.

The catchword under which various museum changes were proposed and continued to be implemented since that time was "openness" – openness to new demographics, opening up the boundaries when dealing with art, opening traditional functions to include a concern for the entire society. In a piece in the *Frankfurter Allgemeine Zeitung* in April 1970 the artist Günther Uecker argued that the museum should be "a place of the utmost variety", one that gave people "the greatest latitude".[1] In that same year the collector Peter Ludwig urged that the museum "step outside and play a role in society".[2] And the architect and administrator Paulgerd Jesberg maintained that "the task of the museum of the future [is] to put down roots in the realm of freedom".[3] As for the architecture of new museum buildings, many, like Charles C. Cunningham, former Director of The Art Institute of Chicago, dreamt of "an open plaza for sculptures and other artworks" and as much glass as possible.[4]

Such formulations were not only indebted to the revolutionary, emancipatory spirit of 1968, they were still driven by a feeling of belonging to the cultural avant-garde. They continued to echo the famous and often-varied criticism of the Futurists, who in their 1909 manifesto compared museums to graveyards and mausoleums, describing them as storehouses of dead cultural artefacts.[5]

The image of the museum as a place for the discarded past had so firmly established itself during the first decades of the 20th century, despite a strong museum reform movement – one already initiated in the late 19th century and that especially in the 1920s had experimented with various forms of "openness"[6] – that as the architect Harald Deilmann lamented, "unavoidable associations with building forms of yesterday" accompanied all deliberations about future museum building. Also in 1970 he referred to studies at the University of Munich that had sought to discover what exactly people associated with museums. In the studies the main colours mentioned were "grey, black and violet". Further, the following descriptive terms were common: "solemnity, grandeur, awe, dignity – dust, silence, bad air and chilly atmosphere – guards, barriers and prescribed tours – entrance fees, cloakroom checks and a ban on photography".[7]

These comments so clearly characterised the museum as an institution demanding obsequiousness, one that was boring, run-down and unwelcoming, that the concept that followed from them was inevitable. To attain (or regain) legitimacy in future the museum needed to undergo a thorough renewal, discard the negative qualities attributed to it and attempt where possible to exhibit their opposites. Thus nothing was more self-evident than the widely used, guiding metaphor of "openness".

The power of the bogeyman

In view of the changes made in art museums since 1970 it is nevertheless surprising that the catchword "openness" continues to dominate competition announcements and new museum building designs to this day. Not infrequently, the implication is that it is a novel idea, or at least something that had to be first wrenched away from traditional thinking. Despite all the reforms, the bogeyman of the intimidating walled-off temple to the muses that suppresses all life still haunts people's thinking. This is all the more surprising inasmuch as today – as opposed to shortly after 1968 – there is in fact no longer any sense of an avant-garde that has not been widely criticised, revised or branded as ideological long since. Yet precisely where it was unprecedentedly successful, namely in its assertion of a bogeyman and preconceptions, the avant-garde continues to set the tone in which art museums are planned.

For example, in an application by Nicolas Moreau and Hiroko Kusunoki, who in 2015 won the architectural competition for the Guggenheim Helsinki (see p. 110), one finds the allegation that museums were previously monumentally inflexible, hierarchically structured entities ("solid, monolithic and vertical"), while by contrast the museum of the future has to feature openness and movement – "tomorrow's museum has to be thought of in terms of horizontality, openness, flexibility and public engagement."[8] And a 2014 press release by the Louvre Paris for an exhibition on Jean Nouvel's design for the Louvre Abu Dhabi once again first evokes the negative image of traditional museums, which present their collections strictly chronologically or by genre and are not open and flexible enough to allow appreciation of reciprocal influences between eras, genres and cultures ("Les musées présentent traditionnellement leur collection selon un découpage par école, par techniques et par matériaux qui, s'il permet de reconnaître la singularité d'un ensemble, empêche d'y voir les influences, les échanges et la circulation des idées et des savoir-faire"). By contrast, the new museum is unique in that it presents the multiple influences on artistic creativity ("Il construira sa singularité sur une vision transversale de la création artistique").[9]

This kind of self-praise is not only questionable, it is patently false, for there have been museums that pursue very similar concepts for a long time. One thinks of the Barnes Foundation, for example, established in the small town of Merion, Pennsylvania, in 1922 and at home in its new Philadelphia venue since 2012. From the beginning it has presented its collections in such a way that multiple relationships between epochs, genres and different cultures are evident. Each artefact is treated with the same respect, there are neither hierarchies nor prescribed tour routes; instead, there have always been intensive educational programmes, inspired by the philosopher John Dewey, especially for people who otherwise have little contact with high culture.[10]

That today's museum planners fail to cite such examples from the history of the institution but prefer to try to make points by dredging up the museum bogeyman that was already too one-sided even at the time of the '68 vanguards, is strangely anachronistic, not only in content but also in terms of gesture. How else is one to assess the pathos with which they claim to break with all convention and boast of their own originality decades after postmodernism and deconstruction? Moreover, it is paradoxical that precisely in the planning of museums, which like no other institutions ought to foster a consciousness of genealogy and memory, knowledge of the history of museum

debate need play no role. Instead it is enough to set oneself apart from a negative image of the museum that had long since become a mere cliché.

In fact, there can be few other building assignments carried out in the shadow of negative thinking to the degree that contemporary museum building is: surely architects asked to design a church, an office building, a school or a shopping mall do not first think of what the structure must by no means look like. Instead, they allow themselves to be guided by positive models. The challenge is to update, perfect or vary them.

A contradiction in the paradigm of the open museum

In reaction against that negative image the catchword "openness" is broadly applicable. It is employed not only by architects; museum employees eager to set themselves apart from what they consider the evils of the historical museum – curators, educators, marketing people – resort to it with equal frequency. They wish to be seen as participants in a new beginning, the final legitimisation of the museum after more than 200 years of its

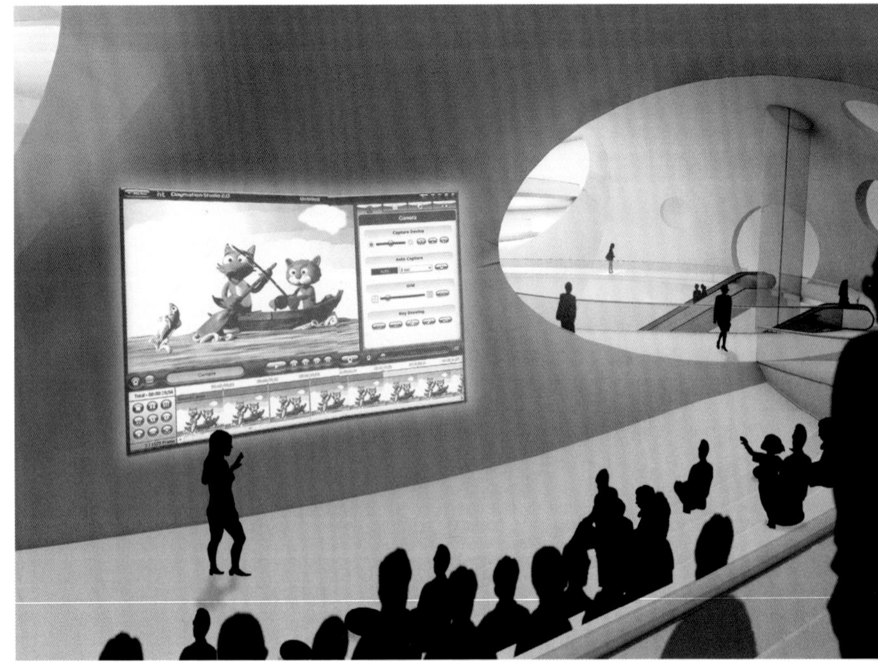

history. For example, like countless similar texts the above-mentioned description of the Guggenheim Helsinki again and again refers to the idea of opening the design in every respect, conjuring up multi-purpose spaces, participatory concepts, heterogeneous public and open discussions: "The multipurpose space with mobile divisions offers manifold opportunities for interactions with and between visitors. It has been developed with the museum team on the basis of a participatory concept opening the museum for a wide and differentiated public, with activities ranging from lunch lectures to discussion of current urban and social debates."[11]

Yet once again one discovers nothing new as compared to the state of the debate in the early 1970s. Then, too, it was said that "mono-functional buildings are to an increasing degree unsuitable", precisely in the case of art museums "that have chances for the future only as integral components of multi-layered contexts".[12] It was demanded that museums "motivate and organise the participation of the individual".[13] And it was postulated that "the populace of an entire city or country should be made to feel at home in museums."[14] At the same time, "in the course of its activities" the art museum was to "act on the objections and suggestions of the public. Exchange of ideas and views regarding what is presented in exhibitions etc. should be stimulated. This is to be done by giving the public an opportunity to add new information to what is presented, express criticism and defend it in public discussions."[15]

These last statements come from Jean Leering, who in 1964, at only thirty years old, had become the Director of the Van Abbemuseum in Eindhoven. His 1970 essay titled "Die künftige Funktion der Kunst" (The Future Function of Art) goes beyond most of what one hears today regarding the programme of the art museum, inasmuch as Leering brings into play historical and sociological viewpoints with which he manages to frame with greater complexity the new paradigm of the open museum and also to analyse it as something contradictory in itself.

Leering points out that the museum originally developed "on the private initiative … of the top echelons of earlier society interested in art", in turn, of "an elitist, urban nature". The museum "hardly needed to be accountable to a broad public". But once that changes, and the museum is to be expressly opened to an entire society, "problems arise": if suddenly art is obliged to serve many – ideally all – levels of society, that same elite no longer identifies with it. And once art loses its ties to a specific segment of society, artists emancipate themselves as well. Since they cannot serve many or all classes at the same time, they feel their responsibility is only to themselves; they are guided by their individual consciences, and as a consequence it becomes less easy to explain art to the general public. Yet it should be more than ever, for now it is required of the museum "that it be truly public, namely that in principle every class, each member of society is offered access to what is shown in the museum as art".

To the same degree that the museum has abandoned its elitist status, art – according to Leering's diagnosis – has abandoned any social role; it is "not up to" any public task "(or refuses to have such a task imposed on it)". Thus a divide between art and its public widens, Leering goes on to say that "the educational activities the museum introduces to bridge this divide are generally destined to fail."[16]

The contradiction Leering identifies in the paradigm of an all-out open museum is somewhat capable of refinement. For example, one must distinguish whether it is earlier art that is exhibited and taught in the museum or modern and contemporary art. While in the former case it is a matter of presenting works once reserved for a specific social class which express its living standard and values in such a way that they can be understood by wholly different classes, not only people of a later century, in the other it is necessary to respond to the idiosyncrasies of the given artist. Whereas the older works were understandable in their time, so that teaching them is mainly a matter of translating, many works of Modernism and the present day have a hermetic, off-putting quality rooted in a private mythology; they are not designed to be readily comprehensible. Teaching them is accordingly not so much a translation as a transformation. Any attempt to help the public share in such works requires changing their character. Opening up the hermetic to all and sundry means treating it in an inappropriate way. Thus art education, and in general a museum appealing to all levels of society, does violence at least to certain forms of art; instead of creating resonance for them it turns them into something they were never meant to be.

At the same time, with the help of Leering's socio-historical analysis it is easier to trace why, even several decades after it was implemented, the paradigm of the open museum can still be depicted as such a positive and major innovation – also why the negative image of the museum as an inflexible, lifeless place continues to predominate. In fact, the hope of making art generally accessible requires so much transformation work that the many endeavours of the last few decades can only seem like baby steps and an awkward beginning. Since it remains the case that only a minority of the populace ever visits museums, and since so much that is incomprehensible to most visitors is shown in them, even with intensified efforts realising the imperative "culture for all" would require several more generations.

The museum as a place for transformation

In 1970, when in his role as Cultural Affairs officer for the city of Frankfurt am Main, Hilmar Hoffmann brought the phrase "culture for all" into circulation, and with it theorised that the museum would only then become democratic and do justice to its role as social "mediator" "when it helps to motivate by an appropriate offering those who are not art-minded, not attuned to art, to pay a visit", he could doubtless not predict what drastic consequences this would have for the entire institution, but also for art.[17] On closer inspection, he did not so much expand the functions of the museum as redefine them. For example, it can be said of an open museum that by way of its educational activities it transforms a part of its holdings in its (hermetic) character, and thus serves the cause of preservation in only a limited way. It is rather seen as a site of endless metamorphoses and is portrayed as such. Only a few years later, in 1977, Pontus Hultén, the founding Director of Paris's Centre Pompidou, expressly admitted this when he wrote that the museum was "no longer a place where works of art are preserved" but rather "a place where the public itself becomes the creator".[18]

In recent texts on museum buildings the change in function is also at times directly addressed. For example, the architects of the Spanish firm estudio Herreros, commissioned to build the new Munchmuseet in Oslo (see p. 62; scheduled for completion in 2019), emphasise in a dossier the advantages of their style of building for conservators ("The collection is protected from direct sunlight, moisture, and art robbers between concrete walls of bunker-like thickness"), yet assert that the museum's most important feature is its flexibility ("flexibility is key in the new Munchmuseet"). Curatorial concepts and exhibition designs are bound to change, after all, as new people join the museum staff; therefore the distribution of spaces and the focus on functions should by no means prescribe anything specific, but rather make everything possible at any time ("to customize space by favouring long-term flexibility over the fixed, the universal over the bespoke, and the multi-functional over the mono-functional").[19]

The ideal museum building is thus to a high degree indeterminate, suitable for as unlimited a number of use scenarios as possible and at the same time stimulating experimentation and transformation. In particular, it offers a mixed public different ways to appreciate the works of art. Since art education is by no means merely a matter of lecturing to visitors in front of exhibits any longer, and it is customary to have them experiment with the given techniques in workshops themselves and be inspired by what they see (in short to become creators), much more space is required for education: workshops are needed, open spaces for performative actions, space in which to display the work produced in workshops by visitors, even storerooms and supply rooms for the materials used in art education.

Hands-on engagement of this kind is beneficial particularly in connection with works that are difficult to understand intellectually and for visitors belonging to marginal social groups or who, like children and young people, are only beginning to learn about art. Such methods make it even clearer that the open museum is a place for transformation, and how it functions. In the old, exclusive museum one was expected to concentrate on masterworks and be moved by them; one was introduced to an approved canon, which is to say that everything was designed for the continuation and preservation of a tradition. By contrast, in today's museum visitors are encouraged to develop their own preferences, to be inspired by the works on display, to experiment creatively themselves and become more self-confident.[20] Some people, like the museologist Kenneth Hudson, even argue for thinking of visitors more as consumers, that is to say as active users.[21]

Instead of ensuring that society remains as stable as possible so that its important holdings are secure, the museum now sees itself obliged to adapt said holdings again and again, to translate them so skilfully and transform them so purposefully that everyone can understand them. Thus art education reduces an artistic approach to a technique that can be learned in practical exercises; in a different educational format works are selected for their specific subject matter, and in yet another they serve to trigger a socio-critical debate or a psychological group therapy session. The paradigm shift to the open museum thus means no less than that the museum's first and last responsibility is no longer to its works but to a heterogeneous public.

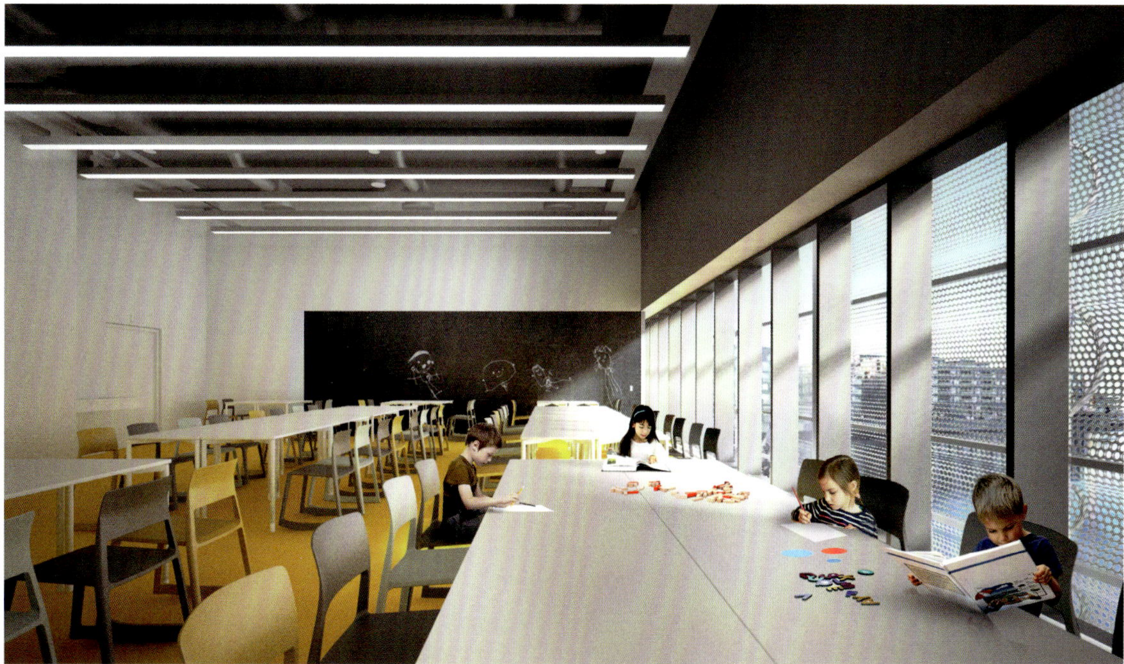

How intent museums are on truly providing access to its works to all is most apparent from their efforts to be inclusive. For example, it has long since become standard practice to schedule events for sufferers of dementia or special guided tours and workshops for the blind. In these, sculptures can be explored by touch, and 3-D models of paintings allow the sightless to feel the objects depicted in them. This alone shows the degree to which its visitors and not its collections are the museum's central focus, for the decisions made by the given artist are no longer respected: that a particular material was selected and a specific style developed for a given work, that specific colours and factures were employed, indeed that above all else the work was to be appreciated as a visual experience – all this is ignored in a desire to appeal to people previously beyond the museum's reach. In obedience to the imperative "culture for all", then, there can be no exceptions; art education recognises no disabilities, only imperfectly transformed works.

That the museum no longer thinks of itself as an advocate for its works becomes still more obvious when tours for the blind are offered, as has now become customary for the seeing as well. They are given black-out glasses, with which the artworks can be appreciated in a wholly different way. To be sure, only in individual cases can it be determined when an educational ploy represents a manipulation that distorts a work beyond recognition and when it is a matter of intensifying certain of its features to facilitate interpretation. As has happened frequently in the history of art, this raises questions; graphic reproductions, for example, represented simplifications of original paintings – owing to the absence of colour – yet they could express the artist's intentions more clearly, or so skilfully translate the original that new insights were provoked and a new circle of recipients created. But interestingly enough questions about the potential and limits of art education are never really raised; the premises according to which every work essentially has to be accessible to every person, that none are to be left out. Hardly anyone,

recognising a work's specific quality, would be prepared to admit that it cannot be taught to specific target groups. And the notion that especially works recognised to be outstanding cannot be translated into other types of sensory stimuli or signs without destroying something, even considerably reducing the aesthetic experience, is held to be altogether absurd.

A museum visit with black-out glasses is not only a side effect of inclusion efforts, but only a variant of the many attempts to offer visitors new, intense, distinctive experiences and adventures. Although there is little debate about the role of art education, there is lively discussion about the "eventification" of the museum; indeed, it is the only issue regarding which the idea of the open museum finds resistance.[22] Yet it is fruitless, for the reorientation of the art museum towards its visitors, or users, also means that the sole mark of its success – and thus at the same time the measure of its legitimacy – is its increased visitor numbers. Formerly, museums concentrated on expanding their collections as much as possible or acquiring works of greater importance, but now the focus is on driving up attendance figures and especially attracting first-time visitors. And this is only possible if the museum is able to produce a variety of different types of experience, from the experience of its architectural substance, vistas and grandiose effects, to its innovative presentations and "special events".

Visual art as a special case

In the last few decades the implementation of the idea of the open museum, one that offers the public much more than simply rooms filled with collections and is truly a public space, even a genuinely democratic institution, has led to an unprecedented boom in museum building. This becomes particularly apparent if one looks at other cultural institutions. There are nowhere near such numbers of new theatres, opera houses, concert halls and libraries.

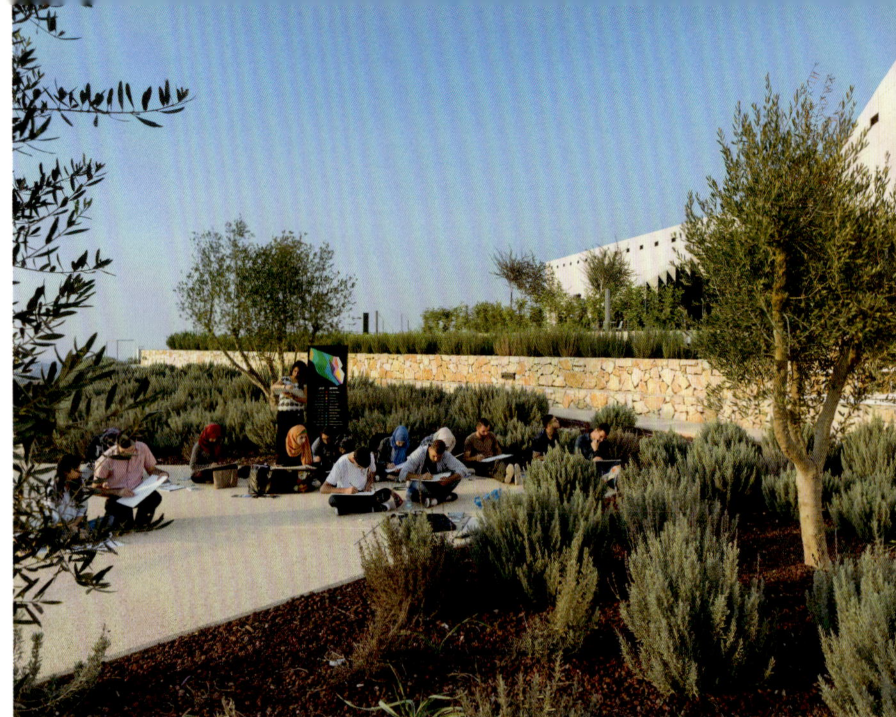

Nor have these undergone any comparable paradigm shift. There's no talk of "open" concert halls or "opera for all", and educational efforts are undertaken in such venues to only a limited degree. For example, there are virtually never sign-language interpreters in theatres making it possible for the deaf and hard of hearing to appreciate a performance, and there is no thought of concerts for the deaf, for whom the music might be translated into colour harmonies.

How to explain this difference between the visual arts and other branches of high culture? It results from the fact that the others have always been more widely accessible, for they are not dealing with unique works owned by single individuals but works that are essentially reproducible at will. Appreciating them has generally been neither too difficult nor all too expensive. Quite the contrary: writers and composers have lived all the better the more editions and performances their works attracted; in order to survive they had to produce something that finds adequate resonance even without additional education.

Thus while literature and music have never been so exclusive that "opening" assuming the dimension of a paradigm shift would have been required of them, the exclusivity of visual art changed only with the founding of museums. Museums were already anti-elitist long before the adoption of the catchword "opening", inasmuch as they were the first places where art was generally accessible independent of ownership, though that was not enough – as we have seen – to interest portions of society with little education and interest in art. But again that had to do with the fact that many earlier works often became less accessible, intellectually or emotionally, in their transfer to museums than they were in the (exclusive) spots for which they were commissioned or in the places where they were owned and lived with. Their public presentation in a museum came at the cost of alienating them from their traditional functions as altarpieces, showpieces, status symbols or heirlooms, and thereby altering their essential character. This alone often made them difficult to understand and in need of explanation.

The topos of the museum as mausoleum – a dead place – that the avant-garde in museum policy was able to propagate so successfully would not even have been possible but for that aspect of alienation. In fact there were already repeated complaints in the 19th century that ultimately the museum – though worthy of praise for liberating art from private ownership – engaged in "vandalism", even "barbarity", for all art was originally created "for a

specific milieu, a given illumination and architecture, for a specific purpose, or at least in the expectation of a specific atmosphere". Such was the lament in 1874 by the cultural scholar Karl Hillebrand, for whom the "poor pictures" in the museum "are freezing" and "robbed of their youthful freshness".[23] Two generations later Martin Heidegger formulated the famous verdict that in the museum works were "torn out of their native habitat" and therefore met with only as "has-beens".[24]

Thus it becomes apparent that the museum bogeyman to which the idea of the open museum was the reaction was the result of a sense of loss. To many the transformation works underwent in their transfer to the museum was tantamount to disfigurement. It was therefore necessary to reconstruct their original contexts through scholarship and pedagogy. A need for art education arose, which in this phase consisted of explaining what was not understood and compensating for the barriers to accessibility created by the transformation. But because it is often necessary to provide explanations even for newer works perhaps expressly made for museums or at least created with their forms of presentation in mind, given that they reflect the artist's more or less hermetic interests, visual art in museums is even doubly predisposed to being and remaining elitist.

This is why far greater education efforts have been initiated in the realm of the visual arts than in other branches of high culture. Ultimately, much as can be seen elsewhere,[25] compensating for what was lacking ended up being overcompensation; the pretence of surmounting the appearance of elitism or exclusivity is taken much more seriously in the case of the visual arts than in the other branches of culture, which are a priori more accessible. The idea of the open museum is an expression of this overcompensation. At the same time, it was an idea already inherent in the original concept of the museum. For from the moment when art was transferred from private ownership to public collections and made accessible to all in a spatial sense, it became possible to think that it would have to be appreciated mind and soul by everyone

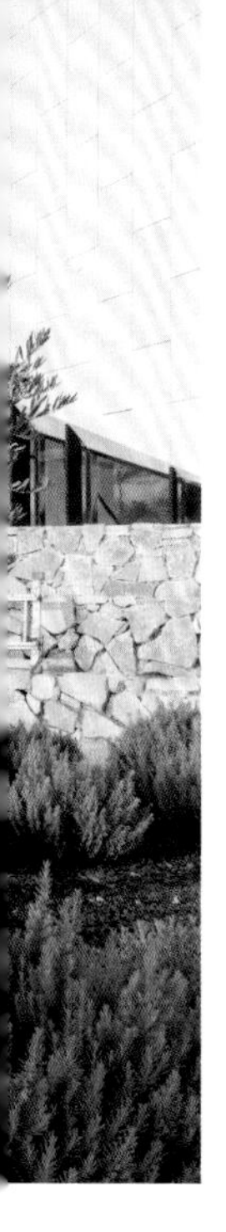

equally – and perhaps even especially by the underprivileged. The more the lower classes, minorities and those with little education visit museums and have artworks explained to them, the more obvious it is that liberating visual art from private ownership by the few represented one of history's few successes. A transformation that was never required or possible to a comparable extent in other branches of culture has here been accomplished.

To the same degree that the museum changed the character of artworks from the beginning, thereby necessitating a certain amount of education, it has now – as an open museum – made transformations routine: the lofty goals of education and the inclusiveness of all people can only be achieved if the works are constantly presented in new ways, if they are reconstructed, reproduced and utilised differently. The open museum is therefore both an active place and one with a social agenda; in it the artworks have been given new functions that can more than make up for the loss of their original purposes and intentions. Thus the open museum is by no means a graveyard for has-beens, rather an institution in which art adapts and changes almost arbitrarily – in which it is not preserved, but experiences continuous metamorphoses.

1 Günther Uecker, "Hat das Museum noch eine Bedeutung, und für wen?" in *Die soziale Dimension der Museumsarbeit. Bericht über ein internationales Seminar der Deutschen UNESCO-Kommission, veranstaltet in Zusammenarbeit mit dem Museum Folkwang vom 20. bis 23. Mai 1974 in Essen* (Cologne: Deutsche UNESCO-Kommission, 1976), 29–30.

2 Peter Ludwig, "Das Museum heute und morgen", in *Das Museum der Zukunft. 43 Beiträge zur Diskussion über die Zukunft des Museums*, ed. Gerhard Bott (Cologne: DuMont, 1970), 175.

3 Paulgerd Jesberg, "Das Museum der Zukunft – Aufgabe, Bau, Einrichtung, Betrieb", in ibid., 139.

4 Charles C. Cunningham, "Das Museum der Zukunft", in ibid., 37.

5 See "Manifest des Futurismus [1909]", in José Pierre, *Futurismus und Dadaismus* (Lausanne: Éditions Rencontres, 1967), 99.

6 See Alexis Joachimides, *Die Museumsreformbewegung in Deutschland und die Entstehung des modernen Museums 1880–1940* (Dresden: Verlag der Kunst, 2001).

7 Harald Deilmann, "Zukunft des Museums?" in *Das Museum der Zukunft*, 41.

8 Nicolas Moreau and Hiroko Kusunoki, *Art in the City*, 2015, accessed July 31, 2016, https://issuu.com/srgf/docs/gh-04380895_a3_booklet_sanitised_-_/1?e=15988582/12215631, 3.

9 Musée du Louvre, Press release, "Louvre Abu Dhabi Contexte, projet architectural et enjeux", 2014, accessed July 31, 2016, http://www.louvre.fr/sites/default/files/presse/fichiers/pdf/louvre-contexte-enjeux-louvre-abu.pdf.

10 See, for example, John Dewey et al., *Art and Education: A Collection of Essays*, 3rd ed. (Collingdale, PA: The Barnes Foundation Press, 1978). Wolfgang Ullrich, "Der Unternehmer als Erzieher. Ein amerikanisches Märchen über den Einsatz von Kunst als Dienstleistung", in *Oeconomenta. Wechselspiele zwischen Kunst und Wirtschaft*, ed. Marc Markowski and Hergen Wöbken (Berlin: Kulturverlag Kadmos, 2007), 123–30.

11 Moreau and Kusunoki, *Art in the City*, 18.

12 Deilmann, "Zukunft des Museums?" in *Das Museum der Zukunft*, 48.

13 Konrad Pfaff, "Das Museum in soziologischer und pädagogischer Sicht", in *Die soziale Dimension der Museumsarbeit*, 21.

14 Dieter Honisch, "Kunst, Museum, Öffentlichkeit", in ibid., 20.

15 Jean Leering, "Die künftige Funktion der Kunst", in *Das Museum der Zukunft*, 165.

16 Ibid., 158.

17 Hilmar Hoffmann, "Das Museum in kulturpolitischer Sicht", in *Die soziale Dimension der Museumsarbeit*, 26.

18 See Nicholas Serota, "Werkerlebnis oder Interpretation? Die Präsentation des Werks", in *Museum 2000. Erlebnispark oder Bildungsstätte?*, ed. Uwe M. Schneede (Cologne: DuMont, 2000), 86.

19 Andreas Ruby and Nathalie Janson, *Civic Icon. The New Munch Museum in Oslo by estudio Herreros* (Madrid: 2012), 5–6.

20 See Wolfgang Ullrich, *Der kreative Mensch. Streit um eine Idee* (Salzburg: Residenz Verlag, 2016), 94–103.

21 See Kenneth Hudson, "Perspektiven für ein Museum des nächsten Jahrhunderts", in *Museen und ihre Besucher. Herausforderungen in der Zukunft*, ed. Annette Noschka-Roos (Berlin: Argon Verlag, 1996), 263–69.

22 See, for example, Uwe M. Schneede, ed., *Museum 2000. Erlebnispark oder Bildungsstätte?*

23 Karl Hillebrand, *Zwölf Briefe eines ästhetischen Ketzers* (Berlin: R. Oppenheim Verlag, 1874), 28.

24 Martin Heidegger, "Der Ursprung des Kunstwerkes [1936]", in idem, *Holzwege*, 6th ed. (Frankfurt am Main: Vittorio Klostermann, 1980), 25–26.

25 See Wolfgang Ullrich, *Siegerkunst. Neuer Adel, teure Lust* (Berlin: Wagenbach, 2016), 25–26.

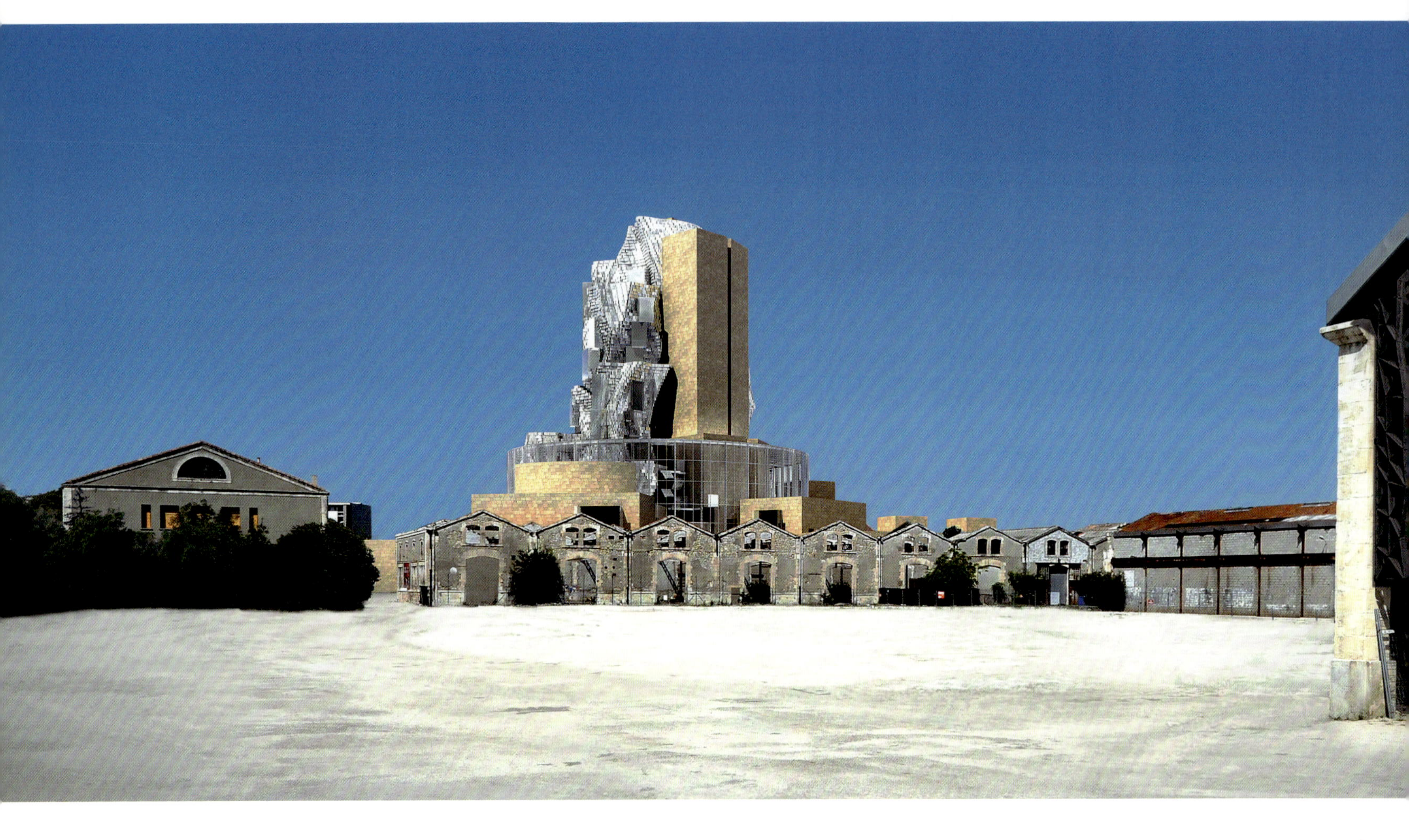

↑ View towards LUMA Arts Resource
Centre from the Grande Halle, Arles,
Gehry Partners.

Why Bother?
or, The Rise of the Private Museum

Chris Dercon

The rise of the private museum has become an inevitable reality, and not just in those regions where public museums hardly exist or are badly equipped. Often insiders need to remind us that many of our grand public institutions began as very private collections or that most private collections will, in the end, enter our public museums anyway. So why bother trying to separate the two? Is there a happy end to it all? There might be.

Nevertheless, it is important to note the differences between the private and the public museum, and thus the issues that are at stake. In China, for instance, hundreds of high-class private museums have been created during the past decade – as a necessity, or a consequence, of intricate financial laws – however the most thriving, professional and visionary museums are those belonging to smaller cities and those in regional provinces. By contrast, were it not for the colourful private "fondazioni" in Italy, international, and even Italian contemporary art, would have remained invisible in Italy, largely ignored by the major publicly funded institutions.

Architecturally, the Long Museum West Bund in Shanghai is an expression of the long-gone international building wave of converting industrial sites into private museums, with some private museums in China closing down already for economic reasons. Meanwhile the private Fondazione Prada by Rem Koolhaas in Milan is a dapper reinterpretation of the "house museum" introduced by radical modernist architectural pioneers, in which style Koolhaas also designed the current home of Moscow's Garage Museum, founded by a pair of oligarchs and gifted to the city. In February 2016 the city of Geneva refused a huge private donation to remake its Musée d'art et d'histoire with a project designed by architect Jean Nouvel, however the French city of Arles cooperated fully together with the visionary international art patron and collector Maja Hoffmann to erect an experimental building by Frank O. Gehry in order to show and produce the newest art.

Due to the rapidly growing, globalised art market the organisational structures of private museums are becoming increasingly complicated. Wim Pijbes, the Director of the fabled Rijksmuseum – the Dutch national public museum par excellence which recently completed a major ten-year renovation – had recently been appointed Director of the private Voorlinden museum, a millionaire's dream in the wealthy Wassenaar suburb of The Hague. However, Pijbes stepped down after only three months. Meanwhile the Fondation Louis Vuitton, a private museum built on public land with special legal exemptions requiring the building to be gifted to the City of Paris after fifty-five years, propagandises itself as a model of the "public institution" for today.

The recently announced Zeitz MOCAA museum in Cape Town was announced as a public museum but could only have been realised by the investment of several well-connected private investors and collectors. African curators and critics alike continue to accuse the Zeitz MOCAA of implicitly ruining artists' careers by buying up their works en masse, thereby monopolising the emerging African contemporary art market. And what of MONA, the "hyper private museum" built and funded by Australian millionaire David Walsh in Tasmania? Can a truly private endeavour offer more than a fickle phantasmagoria of a single individual? Time will tell … yet time is already running out. What will the effect of this paradigm shift be for the future of the fragile production of visual art in itself? Will art continue to change? And is that change for the better?

The purpose of the public museum is to ensure the long-term availability and display of art. Its mission is to create an environment that encourages engagement by the largest audience possible. Consequently, the core responsibility of those in charge of public collections is education. Today education also means making a judgement – a judgement between the portion of contemporary artistic production that parallels the world of luxury goods and the achievements that truly shape culture.

The public museum of today does not exist in a world of its own. It has become one of many environments that comprise a much wider museological project, because of the increasing number of private galleries that call themselves museums, the huge rise in private capital invested in art and the reduction of financial support from the state.

Private collectors make idiosyncratic choices: they collect the good and the bad. Many can also afford purchases that are beyond the reach of public institutions. Nonetheless, we public museums cannot afford to surrender to them the production of memory and the writing of art history.

So what criteria should be weighed when deciding on the acquisition of a work by a public museum? We cannot afford to look at objects in terms of a return on investment, as private collectors can. In this way, public museums are an antidote, not a supplement, to private collections.

At least until recently, most visitors to public museums did not think about works of art as objects that could be

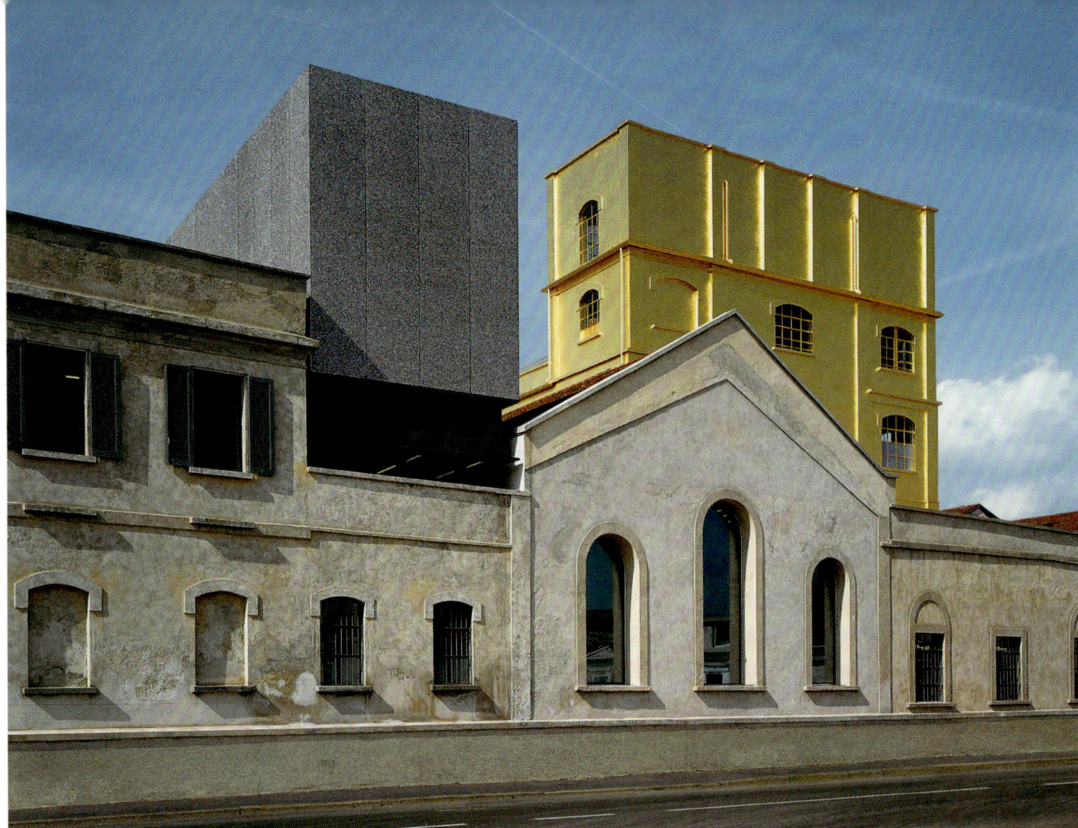

privately owned but as expressions of a culture as a whole. Paradoxically, as we have seen in recent years at the Tate, fewer and fewer visitors to public museums are interested in or even aware of the difference between a display of our own collection and an exhibition of loans: in other words, people are not interested in the distinction between exclusive property and public goods.

The current expansion of the "private museum" phenomenon can also be explained by the way some new pseudo-philanthropists and other risk-based benefactors (including many art dealers) are trying to gain more stature in order to ultimately increase their control over the art market.

Some private museums (whose architecture often reflects the ambitions of their founders) could be seen as the ultimate manifestations of the production of spectacle. Their operators have realised that a new cultural praxis may not necessarily need to rely on many years of experience or historically constructed memory. Moreover, they realise that they can encourage culture to look and feel more like consumerism. And how better to meet this objective than by transposing the model of cultural production into the context of "an architectural event"? It is clear that in an area construed as "a spectacular architectural space" visual art runs the risk of being experienced as a secondary compensation.

Of course there are some private collectors who are reluctant to build their own museums, although they are increasingly rare. They are aware of the complexities of expanded investment and the difficult conditions of such a long-term project. Instead, some of them – such as Dimitris Daskalopoulos, Harald Falckenberg, Ingvild Goetz, Anthony d'Offay or Uli Sigg – seek to create partnerships with the public sector. And public museums recognise the benefits of exploring these forms of public-private partnership.

Finally, to complicate the situation somewhat, the private museum often takes on the role of the failing public cultural sector in cities and regions where public museums are absent. I refer to recent initiatives in Istanbul, Jeddah, Beirut or Delhi, where individuals and private organisations create private museums in the absence of, or as an alternative to, a government cultural axis. This model, even when considered with all the usual precautions, is an example that seems to take the production of memory seriously.

More generally, collectors are beginning to understand that the proper functioning of their own systems and the pragmatic approach to the economic parameters that some of them employ (such as profitability, efficiency of costs, short-term actions and strategies, endless accumulation and expansion of a directionless diversity, discretion about information regarding their assets and costs, the impersonal selection and acquisitions carried out by advisers, insider trading and other aggressive operations) amount to pale imitations of normal museum activities. Moreover, many new and inexperienced collectors seem particularly reluctant to accept (and this is an effect of the art market and global capital flows) that owning contemporary art is, for the most part, a long-term investment, bringing little or no short-term gain.

The private sector almost always adheres to priorities widely different from those of public institutions. It often prefers the production of cultural industry, which, rather than aspiring to sustainability, is characterised by short-term horizons and short-term resources, specialisation and fads. This production is governed by subjective and economic decisions that ultimately lead to more fragmentation, but also to a lack of quality in artistic production. Artists produce more on request, while art criticism has become a kind of creation *ex nihilo*.

There is another corresponding paradox: as there are more private capital owners who invest in art, so serious

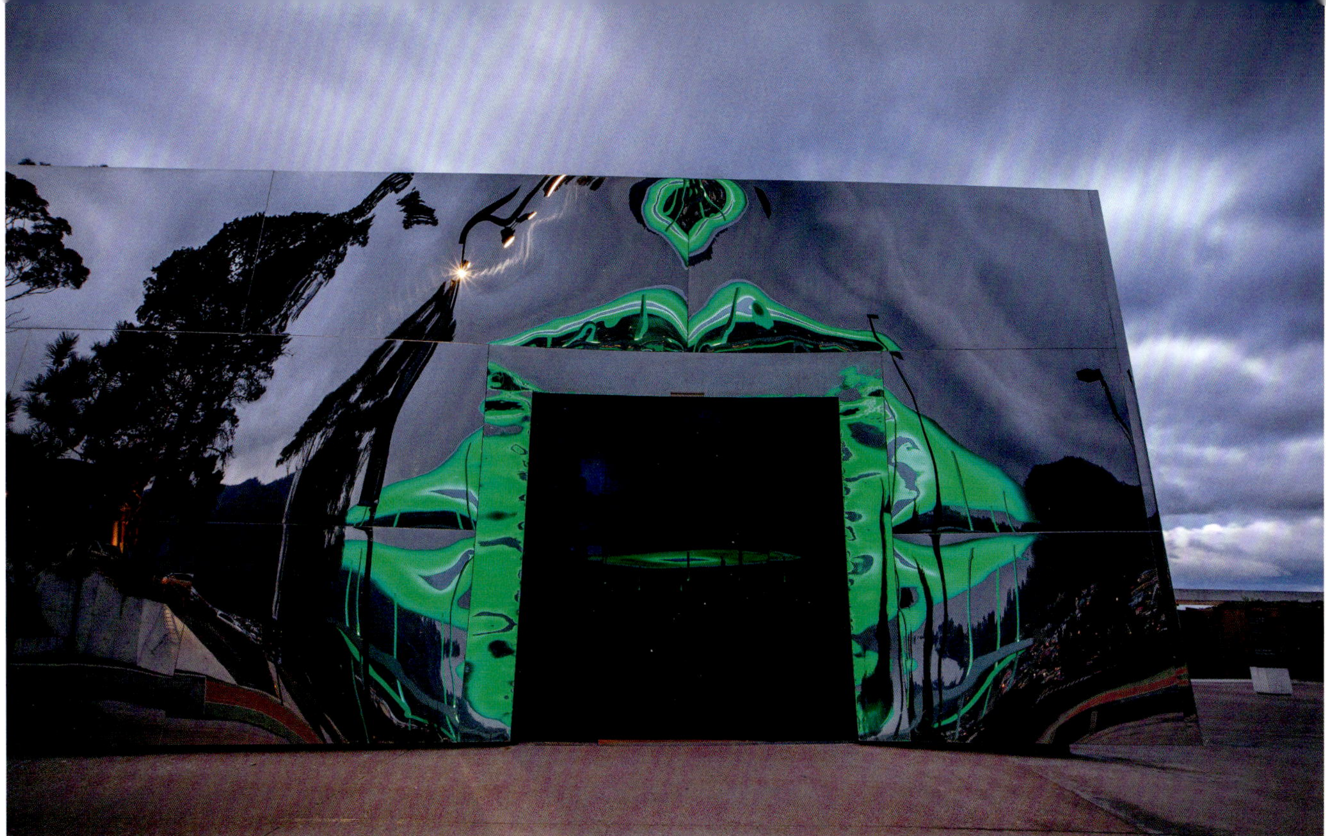

collectors increasingly desire public or critical recognition of what they do. Perhaps I should say that they desire gratitude, not only from their peers and insiders in the art world, but also from a broader audience.

I feel that we must establish new standards for co-operation between private collectors and public museums. And those relationships cannot be based only on gratitude and good faith. The collector who works with a public museum must accept the museum as a place of symbolic value – in the long term – for art. Museums should only approach private collectors who share this conviction. The public museum should cater to the private collector who not only supports the arts and artists but also strengthens the broader culture of public museums. It is this combination of efforts that produces culture.

I want to emphasise that co-operation between public museums and private collectors is fundamentally healthy and constructive. There have been – and still are – many private collectors to whom we are grateful. Nevertheless, we must accept that a division exists between the interests of some private collectors and public museums, between collecting and educating, between the different practices in art and different practices in museography.

Just as object-based art is rooted in a world of material production and manufacture, so the increasingly experiential art of today echoes our new, immaterial social systems and economic networks. We must accept that this will affect the future of public and private collections alike.

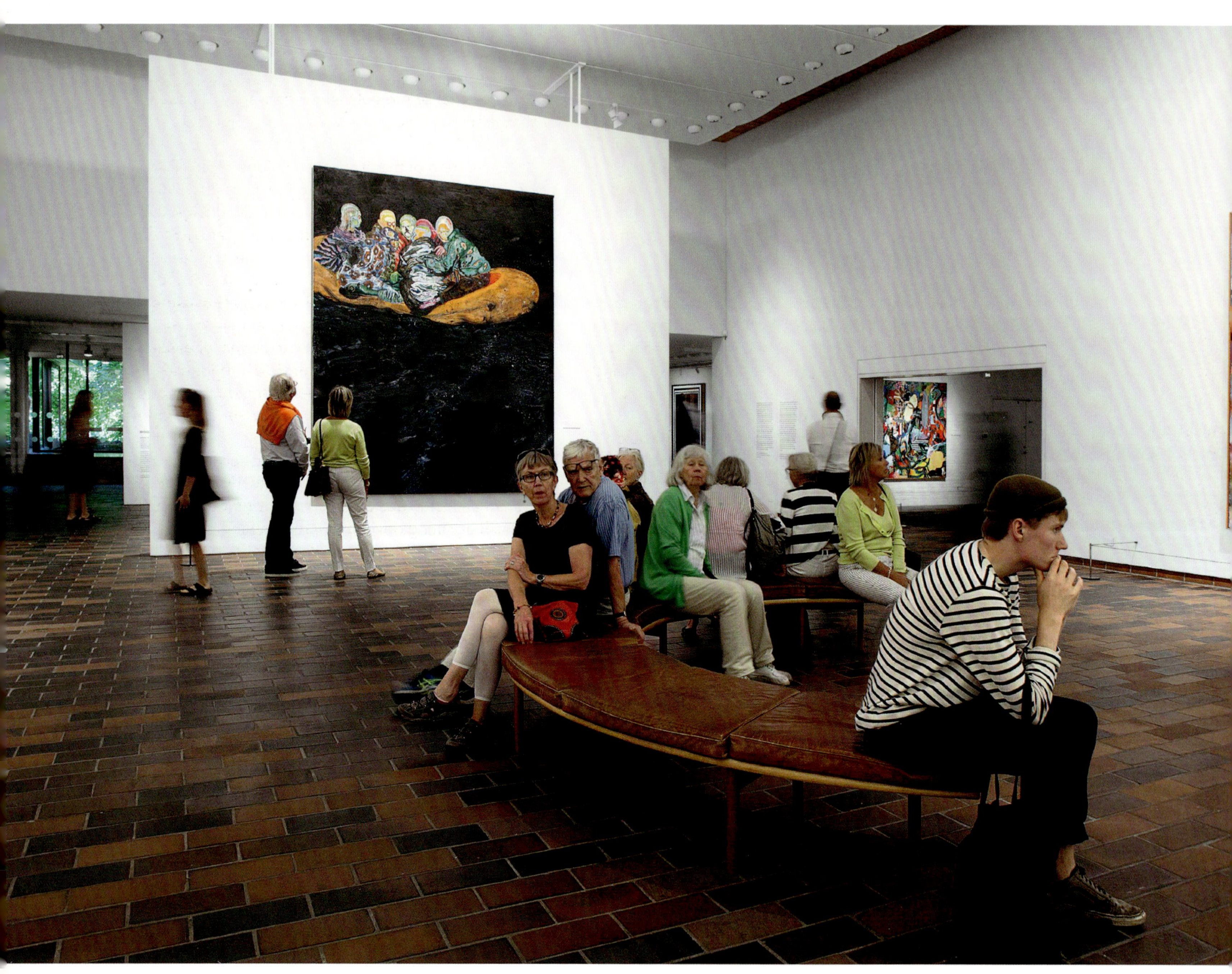

↑ Daniel Richter, *Lonely Old Slogans*, Louisiana Museum of Modern Art,
September 8, 2016–January 8, 2017, installation shot.

Image and Life:
Museum Architecture, Social Sustainability and Design for Creative Lives

Suzanne MacLeod

In 2011 the book *Spatial Agency: Other Ways of Doing Architecture* drew together a series of architectural projects which took as their motivation something other than the market.[1] Driven in part by the philosophical, sociological and urban theories of Henri Lefebvre (1901–1991), the collection drew attention to the possibility of architects taking confident hold of architecture's future social contribution by recognising the inescapable truth of any addition to our built environment: that it will have both intended and unintended social consequences. The projects drawn together were of a particular type – schools, housing schemes, community projects – all of which eschewed purely economic drivers and the concomitant focus on aesthetics, images and form that seem to always accompany buildings driven first and foremost by the production of capital, in order to instead prioritise people, relationships between people and the enabling of a better future for those who will inhabit (and thus produce) the new built forms.

The projects drawn together in *Spatial Agency* couldn't be further from the standard approach to many new museums. New museum projects, especially large iconic ones, are so enmeshed in marketplace economics (most obviously as national and regional icons, magnets for tourism and catalysts for urban and economic regeneration) that they seem to be lost to other, more vital motivations. In these projects, whatever the rhetoric, the articulation of the social value of the project comes lower down the list of priorities and the users of the imagined future museum remain in the fuzzy distance, at best generalised and at worst imagined only within the reductive limits of middle-class consumption described by Andrew Harris.[2] Here museum visitors are invariably consumers of art, coffee, books and high-end design.

This is nothing new for museums. Museum making is an area of practice where it remains incredibly difficult to carve out space for the detailed consideration of potential social impacts (positive and negative). New museum projects tend to be high-profile and their scale and perceived political importance mean that arguments focus on such macro issues as mounting costs or potential contribution to the economy. These debates are at such a high level and so firmly located within a system which benefits the few rather than the many that the everyday lives of most people remain firmly out of view. Other debates relate always to form. Architects and critics will talk about the architectural rigour or intended symbolism of a design more than its social contribution. Again disconnected from everyday life, debates about form operate in a wholly abstract realm,

working to always separate architecture and its discussion from real world concerns. If the debates seem always to be stuck, it is nonetheless no coincidence that political parties rally around some projects and vehemently oppose others. These national projects are statements about the world we want to live in.

The creation of these art destinations, often on iconic waterfront sites, also gets right to the heart of one of the most urgent issues facing museums and galleries: the gradual hollowing out of museums as they are given over to commerce. Implicit in this colonisation of culture by the market, is a concomitant devaluation of civil society and of cultural engagement as a necessary investment in people and that side of their human being that is not about work or consumption. Ironically, a great deal of evidence suggests that if we could alter our view to prioritise citizens over consumers and creative lives over reductive notions of economic prosperity we would be stronger, more innovative and happier as a result.[3]

In the cultural sector, we are used to seeing new museums co-opted by regeneration projects through the application of an iconic design and publicly funded museums used as bargaining devices in large commercial planning developments. Museums here are caught up in city branding, image making and short-term economic development plans. The danger with so many museum developments is that the institution is so formal and museums are so enmeshed in the processes and negative outcomes of capitalism, in processes of what Henri Lefebvre would describe as the production of abstract space, that they fail to notice what is in plain sight – the everyday value of culture, the ways in which different individuals take part in culture, and the positive outcomes that follow from access to diverse cultural experiences. Despite all the evidence, we continue to build incredibly traditional museums. Worse, the increasing emphasis on income generation means that the unique potential of museums to add something vital to our shared life experiences is undermined at every stage.[4]

There is, however, a growing body of opinion which seeks to challenge the sense of weighing down what will always be non-profit organisations with ever larger, revenue-hungry buildings.[5] More than this, the reductive notions of experience upon which many of these projects are based is increasingly open to question. As more and more large-scale art destinations are built in cities rife with division and inequality, it is right that we expect a more detailed and evidenced engagement with notions of public good. But how do architects, museum directors, city governments and others involved in these projects consider questions of public space, public access and public use? How do they think about people and everyday life in projects which are often – unfortunately but invariably – more about property development and the drive for economic growth than nurturing the creative lives of citizens? How do those involved get behind the image making and the solving of symbolic, functional and economic necessities to think deeply about the social impacts of their work?

This essay begins from the idea that it is uncontroversial to expect that the prioritisation of people and the nurturing of our human being is a core responsibility of cultural organisations. It begins from an understanding that museums and galleries are most interesting and valuable for their ability to enable access to that side of ourselves that is not directly related to work and the production of capital. It is built on an argument that positions access to culture and the arts as a human right deeply connected to our health and well-being, sense of belonging, tolerance and ability to engage thoughtfully in a complex world,[6] what we might describe as our creative lives. What might such ideas mean for museum design? And how might such ideas enable us to engage critically with the wealth of new museum developments and image making we see around us today? Are these new museums lost to the market? Or can they carve out a space as genuine enablers of creative lives in ways which begins to utilise these huge investments in all our futures and really lead the way in museum design?

Repositioning architecture as "the anticipation of a future social relationship"[7]

To start, we might, like the authors of *Spatial Agency*, turn to the writings of Henri Lefebvre. Lefebvre's genius was in acknowledging that "(social) space is a (social product)", a view which tells us that people make spaces and spaces make people and that social relations exist – and only exist – in and through space.[8] In this statement Lefebvre challenges the idea of the building as object, broadening our focus to the sociality of space and the relationships and networks in which architecture (as practice and form) is produced. To design structures within this social space is to directly affect people's lives, an observation which has led to the reminder that "every line on an architectural drawing should be sensed as the anticipation of a future social relationship, and not merely as a harbinger of

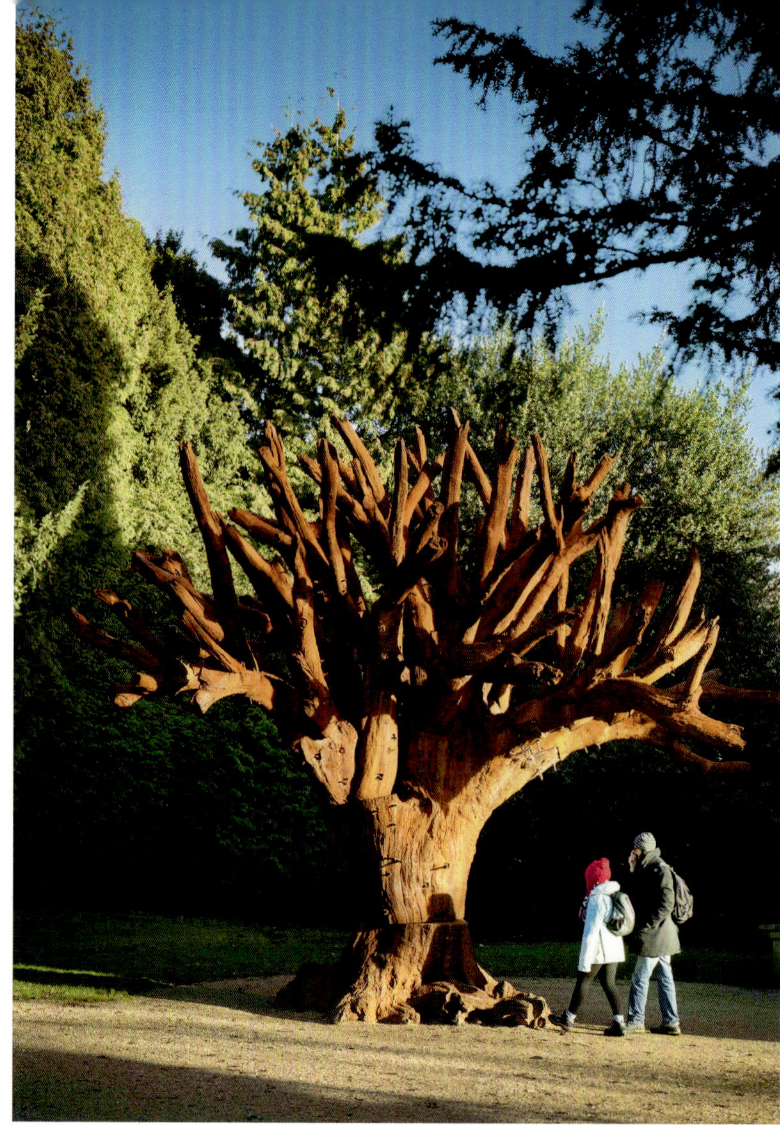

aesthetics or as an instruction to a contractor."[9] In making possible the acknowledgement of the ongoing production of architecture through social practice, Lefebvre both introduces the notion of temporality (architectural production is ongoing) and challenges the myth of the architect as the sole creator of our environments. Architecture here might demand a specialist hand to guide it, but it will also demand detailed understandings of social context, the varying intents of stakeholders and input from an array of potential occupants who will author the space in the future.

As well as encouraging us to think about the production of social space, Lefebvre charted the emergence of abstract space, the space of capitalism.[10] Abstract space is critiqued by Lefebvre for its role in the gradual reduction and flattening of human experience, as social practice is increasingly directed, through space, to labour and the production of capital. Architecture has a role to play in these processes. Here, the reduction of the relations between the social and the spatial to architectural drawings and plans and the tendency to design buildings as an intellectual process separated off from any consideration of use are active, even complicit in, the production of abstract space.[11] These processes of architecture work to influence the ways we think of architecture, so much so that the underlying complexity and politics are masked and users are reduced to passive consumers.[12]

If architecture is susceptible to appropriation by the market (bidding always for the next project),[13] museums are the ultimate malleable cultural institution.

In this abstract space of capitalism time is reduced to "the time of watches and clocks … subordinating to the time of work in space other aspects of the everyday".[14] However, "everyday life remains shot through and traversed by great cosmic and vital rhythms: day and night, the months and the seasons, and still more precisely biological rhythms."[15] From this perspective, the architectural project comes to be about enabling possibilities for human connections to cyclical time, to nature and change, creating the conditions in which social relations and phenomena might not just survive, but multiply. Architecture here is a (potentially) rich experiential environment, linked to our interior world and with the capacity to place us in relation to a past and a future. It is the physical material through which life is lived, and has the capacity to integrate people in the social world.

One final concept can aid our rethinking of architecture. Lefebvre imagined a future in which individuals at the very deepest level of their internalised subjective experience have access to an expressive life. Described as differential space, this is a socialist space, where geniality is prioritised, where difference is celebrated and accentuated, where the body, human needs and social knowledge are recognised and where social practice is reinstated. Interestingly, differential space is defined by what is possible therein, rather than by any particular physical characteristics.[16] Whilst Lefebvre would undoubtedly have dismissed the idea that large cultural developments could encourage the production of differential space (his views on the Centre Pompidou – "a meteorite fallen from another planet, where technocracy reigns untrammelled" – made his thoughts clear),[17] it is nonetheless the case that Lefebvre can help us to ask how these projects can enable our collective and individual creative lives.

Design for creative lives

In the UK the Arts and Humanities Research Council has recently completed a three-year project exploring the value of culture and the "difference to individuals, society and the economy that engagement with arts and culture makes".[18] Recognising that the value of arts and culture is embedded in everyday life and, like Lefebvre, determined to start from the individual, *The Cultural Value Project* sought to identify "a wider and more subtle repertoire" of languages and methodologies for talking about and assessing the value of arts and culture.[19]

Broad in its reach and rigorous in its reassessment of the claims often made for culture, the project drew particular attention to four ways culture is of value to society. First, the role of cultural engagement in *shaping reflective individuals*; "facilitating greater understanding of themselves and their lives, increasing empathy with respect to others, and an appreciation of the diversity of human experience and culture".[20] Second, *producing engaged citizens*. Here, participation in arts and culture can have a role in individual formation, "promoting not only civic behaviours such as voting and volunteering, but also helping articulate alternatives to current assumptions and fuel[ling] a broader political imagination".[21] The arts and culture are rightly recognised here as "fundamental to the effectiveness of democratic political and social systems".[22] Third is the contribution arts and culture make to *improving health and well-being*. The project drew specific attention to Nordic longitudinal studies which have proved particularly effective in capturing the relations between long-term engagement in arts and culture and positive health outcomes. Finally, *arts in education* was highlighted as a field in which cultural participation contributes "in important ways to the factors that underpin learning, such as cognitive abilities, confidence, motivation, problem-solving and communication skills".[23] Recognising these components of cultural value as key aspects of our creative lives, how might this understanding help us to think deeply about museum architecture and its role in the anticipation of future social relationships?

The varied projects drawn together in *Spatial Agency* were assessed against three criteria which provide an excellent starting point for engagement with new museum projects.[24] First, projects considered to prioritise spatial agency would illustrate *spatial judgement* or consideration of the social aspects of space. Rather than the conventional approach of architecture which prioritises form, projects fulfilling the criterion of *spatial judgement* would prioritise the social and ask how formal decisions might initiate empowering social relationships. For museums, we might ask that *spatial judgement* stem from a clear orientation or museum mission which not only drives the project but is actively pursued in its every aspect. As we will see in the discussion below, however, the impetus for spatial judgement does not always come from within the museum!

Second, projects in which architects and architecture become spatial agents would prioritise *mutual knowledge*; architects would value the knowledge of others and share their own openly as a route towards finding solutions. Interestingly, in the context of museums, the gut reactions of the amateur would hold equal sway with the considered view of the expert, and action and use would be valued in equal measure to things. Museums are often criticised for trying to have some kind of impact on different audiences rather than genuinely engaging in dialogue and diverse forms of co-production.[25] How then might the socially responsible museum, genuinely seeking to become a hub for varied forms of cultural engagement and sociality for a diverse public, shape a process based on mutual knowledge?

The third criterion for the authors of *Spatial Agency* is *critical awareness*. That is, those involved would be self-critical and ensure that the project take a research-led stance fully aware of the opportunities and challenges as well as freedoms and restrictions of the site.[26] Crucial to the development of the socially oriented museum, we might also add two additional expectations. One, that a deep consideration of the *integration of engagement with collections* characterise the project with a view to avoiding the phenomenon that we see in so many new museum developments where "public" or multi-use spaces are well occupied but where exhibition galleries are lacking in dynamism. In the most effective, diverse and engaged museums, opportunities for engagement with collections are integrated into experience in increasingly thoughtful and human ways. Finally, and beyond the scope of our project perhaps but vital nonetheless, would be *financial sustainability*; a sophisticated model of resourcing for the project which provides a realistic vision of what investment in the creative lives of human beings will look like in the future.

In the remaining sections, I briefly explore these areas with reference to the Guggenheim Helsinki and the new Munchmuseet in Oslo. Both of these projects make claim to a desire to create a public space which goes beyond the increasingly recognisable international space of art consumption to a more fundamental investment in our shared social world.

Spatial judgement

The idea of the Guggenheim Helsinki project might at first sight suggest a project that is absolutely about image making; a large American brand known for its spectacular architectural projects further establishing its international museum network. However, if we dig a little deeper, there are some surprising qualities emerging in the project which do suggest the potential for the prioritisation of the social over the formal.

In its first iteration, the Guggenheim Helsinki as proposed by the Guggenheim Foundation did not receive approval from the City of Helsinki. According to Sanna-Mari Jäntti, Senior Advisor on the project, from spring 2013, when the Guggenheim Foundation began to work with Helsinki again, "the focus had totally shifted towards the audience and what Helsinki wanted."[27] Embodying the Finnish expectation for a solution which would benefit the people of Finland, an open architectural competition was established, a system of anonymous judging was put in place (avoiding the potential for judges to be swayed by a big name) and a winning design was selected which was considered "deeply respectful of the site and setting, creating a fragmented, non-hierarchical, horizontal campus of linked pavilions where art and society could meet and intermingle".[28] Pressed for more information about why the winning design by Moreau Kusunoki Architectes was successful, Jäntti explained, "the architects were committed to continuing the dialogue with the community."[29]

As Nicolas Moreau and Hiroko Kusunoki describe it, the aim of their proposal is to generate opportunities for a personal experience of art by offering choice, variety and space which is open to appropriation:

> In Finland, people use indoor space in a collective and public way that you don't see so much in France or Japan. Because of that we are allowing significant amounts of gathering space – you can find a sofa, an internet connection, a place to rest … on the one hand having large areas of indoor undefined public space and also having an interface with the plazas and the seashore … the idea of the visitor as the main actor is a real shift. We want people to take the principal role of actor in the drama of their day. … Contemporary art today has a real role in life and so we should feel as a person living in the present time. That's why the void space is necessary for them to make their own dialogue.[30]

The Guggenheim Helsinki project is, in many ways, a surprising place to find the seeds of a social orientation. On the other hand, when one considers the long-established

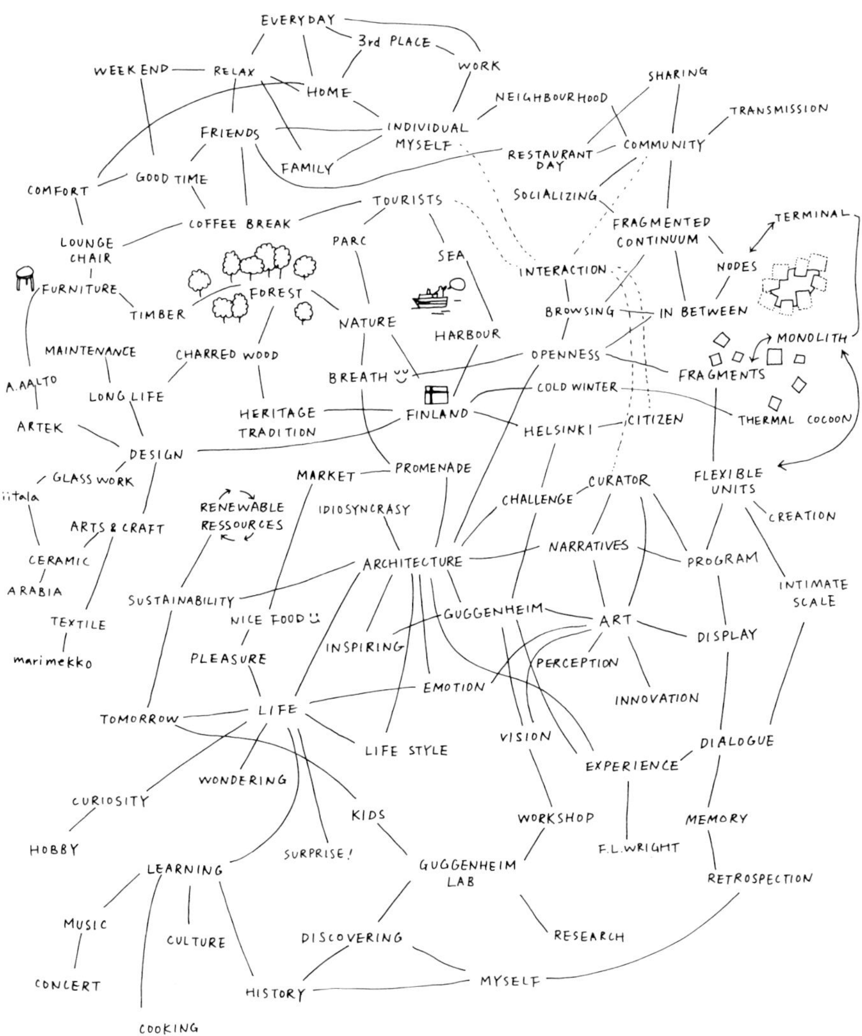

social welfare system in Finland and the deeply rooted notions of equality and dignity for all citizens that continue to shape swathes of Finnish society, one senses that in Helsinki, the Guggenheim could break the tendencies of recent museum building and genuinely illustrate some level of spatial judgement.

In Oslo traces of a prioritisation of the social over the formal are perhaps less readily identified. The story in Oslo is more conventional. The limitations of the existing Munchmuseet in Tøyen were cited as reasons to build a new museum as part of the regeneration of de-industrialised docklands, a project which will see Oslo create a new cultural quarter next to the sea and the new "postcard" of the city. The result of a more recognisable architectural competition to which well-known architectural studios were invited, the winning design is a high-rise statement building by estudio Herreros; the building has a podium containing an assortment of public, leisure and commercial spaces and is topped by seven floors of gallery space, four floors of conservation and administration space as well as the top-floor restaurant and terrace, all linked by a series of vertical circulation spaces.

At first sight then, it is quite difficult to see anything in this project but the requirement for a formal solution. Understanding the project's potential, however, means understanding the different kinds of space that the building, currently under construction, will create. Far from the conventional notion of gallery spaces, orientation spaces and circulation spaces that often comprise new museums, the new Munchmuseet is conceived as containing two covered public squares (an established concept in Norway's often challenging natural environment) at either end of a series of dynamic spaces enabling visitors to move up and down the building and access the self-contained galleries on each floor. Vastly different from Helsinki in its solution, the building nonetheless offers a similar distribution of opportunities to experience art within a broader set of public spaces and social experiences. As Juan Herreros puts it, "This is an everyday life facility."[31]

If the building promises to offer a backdrop to varied social and cultural activities as well as a unique vantage point from which to know the city of Oslo and its past, seeds of a social orientation perhaps also lie elsewhere. In a recent article describing the boost in arts infrastructure in Oslo, Stein Olav Henrichsen, Director of the Munchmuseet, has given some indications of his intentions.

… the important question is how this impact can be used to help build a sound society where democracy, human rights and financial development can prosper, and where conflicts can be discussed and solved in a non-violent order. The answer depends on the ability of institutions to play a relevant part in contemporary core problems.[32]

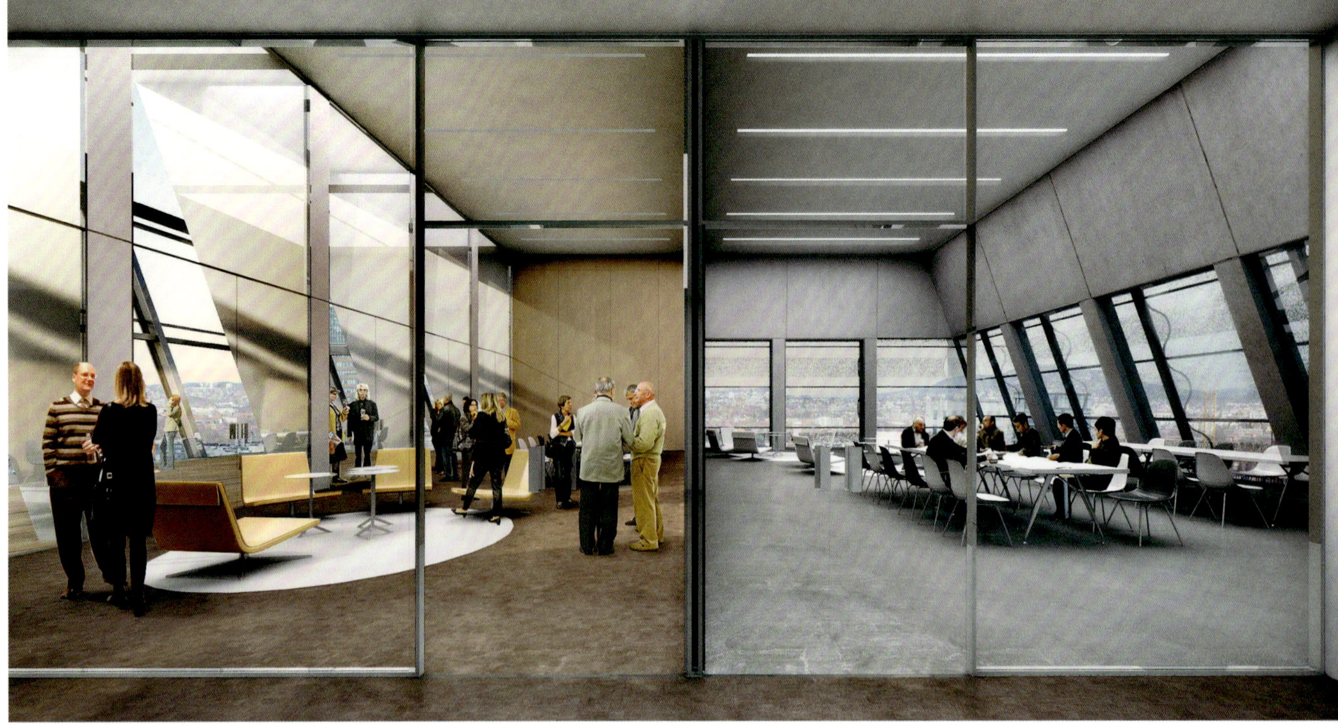

Hidden behind the images, the collections of world-class art, and the claims for some future economic prosperity in the two projects are ambitions to improve life: sophisticated notions of the integration of art in everyday life are traceable in the two projects. Finding ways to prioritise and deepen these ambitions so that they might take priority and genuinely impact the lives of ordinary people seems crucial.

Mutual knowledge

The outward focus and flexibility necessary for a genuine shift to sociality over formality as implied above demands an openness to and respect for diverse forms of knowledge and experience. In Oslo the process of developing the new Munchmuseet is described by Juan Herreros as "a process of intensive dialogue towards the construction of a collective spirit".[33] Interactions with varied stakeholders ("political parties, the media and a range of civic associations as well as individual citizens")[34] included public presentations and exhibitions, round-table discussions and press conferences.

In Helsinki, with the project still at competition stage, it is perhaps too early to comment on what will be a long process of development. That said, the project already shows significant signs of an openness to a participatory approach. Beginning in 2013, once the Guggenheim project found its orientation, a whole series of interactions with community and interest groups and the media was established, opening up dialogue and making all project documentation openly accessible. Expanding the spirit of dialogue and participation, the open competition, in which Juan Herreros was a jury member, generated a phenomenal 1,715 entries and spawned a counter-competition, "The Next Helsinki", which despite its challenge to the Guggenheim project made a significant contribution to generating public debate. In a second stage of the competition, the shortlisted studios were invited to Helsinki

for four "intensive" days of exchanges with project stakeholders, including opponents. For Moreau and Kusunoki the exchanges were significant, resulting in changes to the plans which introduce spaces for local artists close to the waterfront ("more human in scale and more informal in character"[35] than the spaces for the Guggenheim collection). As we will see from our brief consideration of the spatial integration of engagement with collections, these changes may well have very significant impacts beyond the task of ensuring that the perennial tension between international and grass-roots arts is addressed.

When asked about the potential to go further towards the design of spaces where life might play out in its fully embodied and sensory sociality, Moreau and Kusunoki commented, "in Helsinki it has to be that way. … Openness and public participation is in the DNA of Scandinavia. The Finns have changed the rules."[36] Asked the same questions of Oslo, Juan Herreros commented, "Norway leads the way with these questions. In the future, this popular participation or collective mobilisation of social groups to have influence in relation to culture is something we will see more frequently."[37] "Architects need to find new ways of working which respond to these changes."[38]

Critical awareness

Following Lefebvre, we might press for evidence of an even closer engagement with the variables of everyday life in these large-scale interventions in the city. Of course a great deal of research informs architectural developments of this type: research into the geographic locale, social mapping projects, and economic impact studies. To really push for a claim to critical awareness, however, we might supplement the usual approaches to research with Henri Lefebvre's concept of "rhythmanalysis". For Lefebvre, the answer to the production of differential space and challenging abstract space was hidden in plain sight in the everyday. Rhythmanalysis was an attempt to illustrate

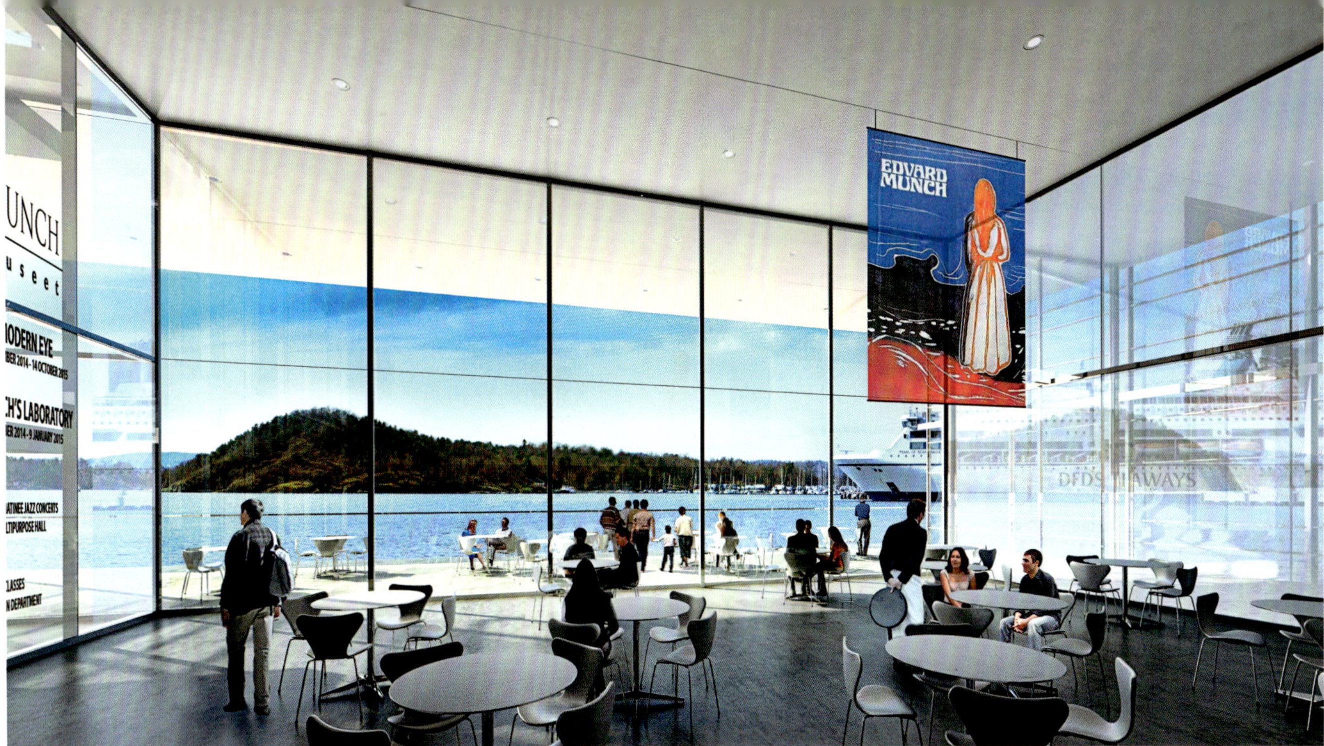

the relationships between time, space and struggles in everyday life.[39] By listening to "a house, a street, a town", the rhythmanalyst might generate a deep understanding of the everyday rhythms of life and build in possibilities for action which responded to or enhanced those existing rhythms, relations and flows.[40] As Nathaniel Coleman has commented, rhythmanalysis offers those involved in capital developments "a method for becoming alive to what is, or ought to be, the object of architects' interests and designs: the lived city and social life, in all of their spatial and temporal richness".[41]

Thinking about the vast interventions into the environments of Oslo and Helsinki that our two projects are making, it is evident that even here there are ample opportunities to listen to "a square, a market, an avenue".[42] As for Moreau and Kusunoki, they imagine a visitor to the Guggenheim Helsinki passing through the site on their way to the nearby market, an idea which necessitates a formal solution which welcomes and facilitates the briefest of cultural encounters as well as the day-long visit. In Oslo the notion that I can engage in contemporary debates through the work and life of Munch along with a visit to the cinema, begins to suggest an attempt to follow and expand the potential embedded within the existing flows of the city. A theory and methodology which demands more exploration than is possible here, rhythmanalysis nonetheless raises the challenge for those involved in cultural developments to cultivate a greater critical awareness towards a closer engagement with the myriad social realities and experiences of everyday life.

The spatial integration of engagement with collections

We have all visited museums where the spectacular parts of the building or displays are well occupied but the gallery spaces, without the same level of spectacle and hyper-reality, are empty. Similarly, we can probably all name museums where significant steps have been taken to try and integrate the space of the museum into everyday life – by making available homework spaces, for example – but where the exhibition spaces are under-utilised, less relevant. More impressively, we probably all know of much-loved museums where collections are integrated successfully into everyday experience and where it feels as though the entire visit nurtures our human being. Some museums, like Louisiana Museum of Modern Art in Denmark and Yorkshire Sculpture Park (YSP) in the UK, build passionate visitor bases who return time and again as part of their everyday lives. Evidence also suggests that when describing their experiences, these audiences talk as much about their personal lives and their loved ones, as they do about art.[43] There are clearly complex forces at play here, but spatial decisions will have a significant impact on the relationship between art and life, and ensure that engagements have the potential to be open to personal and sensory interpretations through an understanding of social and phenomenal experience of the kind encapsulated in Lefebvre's rhythmanalysis.

Both Louisiana and YSP share a number of characteristics worth investigating for their potential to overcome the separation of art from everyday life. Once again, and following Lefebvre, the answer seems to lie in the social and phenomenal human body. Both sites draw heavily on the cyclical time of nature – the seasons, the tides and the minute changes in weather – and the sense of time and unfolding that this enables. Both sites comprise a series of indoor and outdoor spaces configured to offer variety and choice. Visitors are encouraged to venture into the managed space of the museum more fully, though light and the ability to change direction are never far away. Located always in a place through views out of galleries, artworks are also sited in relation to the scale of the human body. The idea of multiple points of approach, and the need to search out or stumble across certain works, result in opportunities for the making personal of the experience. These museums offer their space and contents up for appropriation rather than seeking to impose themselves on visitors. Art here can take centre stage or it can recede into the background, a special backdrop to life. Curation – enchanting placement which also ensures that the spatial integration of varied opportunities for engagement is undertaken here in full awareness of the rhythms (natural, social, biological) that comprise the site – and the buildings and arrangement of the site provide the framework which makes this possible.

Sites like Louisiana and YSP are continuously open to the threat of commercialisation and de-politicisation. Noting the tendency always for abstract space to colonise social space, at their best these sites offer something vital to our understanding of questions of museums, architecture and social sustainability. Our life is given space to continue in these places. More than this, a conscious attempt is made to connect us and our experience of art to nature. If elsewhere we experience museum fatigue – alienation and disruptions to our sense of time – here we have access to our full sense of being.

Inspired by the poetics of Louisiana, in Helsinki the pavilion-like structure with its spaces of varying scale, the outdoor spaces between the pavilions and very direct connection to the waterfront, and the generous gathering spaces with no obvious function "to welcome new programming",[44] suggest that the new Guggenheim Helsinki could offer visitors choice and supported movement into the larger, more institutionalised spaces. Similarly, it feels as though in the new Munchmuseet, the City of Oslo is seeking to create a space through which art and everyday life will come together by offering up moments of engagement as citizens traverse the public spaces of the city. As Juan Herreros noted, "[p]erhaps I am trying to escape the large international museums where you have hundreds of people behind you as you try to view the art."[45]

Financial sustainability

Although beyond the present focus, it is crucial that we include space for our fifth criterion, financial sustainability. The notion of investing in creative lives is something quite different from that of investing in a new cultural quarter or in the creative industries. Arguments for the economic sustainability of a new museum are often made on the basis of reduced revenue costs (perhaps as a result of the building's environmental features) or the potential for income generation. However, models of economic

sustainability which rely on ever larger numbers of tourists or ever more challenging targets for income generation seem antithetical to the embedded, socially driven, not-for-profit arts organisation. As *The AHRC Cultural Value Project* concluded, the value of culture lies in its potential to effect change, to open our minds, to make us feel and think differently.[46] Drawing this unique role of the arts and culture into calculations of value for money and into longer-term planning seems almost impossible, but is perhaps the only way that museums will really move forward and be freed to truly inhabit their social roles and responsibilities.

Conclusion: social sustainability and design for creative lives

A key theme behind all of the concepts and practices discussed in this paper might be summarised as an attempt to bring the variables and multiple realities of everyday life, as it is lived and experienced through the scale and rhythms of the human body, to bear more directly on the shaping of museums. Two iconic and nationally significant new museums might seem to be a rather counter-intuitive place to look for traces of this spatial agency. However, as the analysis suggests, there are discernible traces of our criteria in these very different projects. Both are far from ready for public use and so it remains to be seen how the projects progress and how the various ideas of public use are harnessed. The hope would be that both of these projects could push at the conventions of museum making and try to do something which faces its potential social significance head on.

For museums more broadly, these large projects are incredibly important. They provide models that others will follow. All the evidence suggests that at times culture can nurture, that it can contribute to the building, rather than the dismantling, of communities, and that it can provide an antidote to the alienating conditions of modern life. Architecture, although not the only ingredient, is surely key. But are these large-scale projects lost to the market? Are they, as the sociologists would tell us, unable to escape from the conditions of their making? Is it really accurate to say that architecture's "[e]nclosure by capitalism, with its propensity for destroying communities, presents the biggest obstacle"?[47] Yes and no. On the one hand, these projects are born out of international competition for the memorable postcard and embody ambitions for economic growth.

They will change their surroundings, generating multi-million-pound housing and all the upheaval and destruction that seem always to follow processes of gentrification. There appears little escape from this dilemma, as we are still, as Harris notes, lacking alternative visions of new urban development.[48] What can happen, however, and Lefebvre helps us to see this, is that depending on the willingness of those involved to care about the potential positive and negative social impacts that these projects will have, something other can appear in the gaps and in the everyday. Enabling and engaging with the everyday, then, has to become a priority for museum makers, including architects. Perhaps even these large projects, seemingly lost to capital and the production of art consumers, can be harnessed towards the social, towards improving life as it is lived.

—

Editor's note: 'Since the writing of this essay, the city council of Helsinki voted against the new Guggenheim Helsinki, mainly citing high costs as the reason for their rejection.'

1   Nishat Awan, Tatjana Schneider and Jeremy Till, *Spatial Agency: Other Ways of Doing Architecture* (London and New York: Routledge, 2011).
2   Andrew Harris, "Livingstone versus Serota: The High-rise Battle of Bankside", *The London Journal* 33, no. 3 (2008): 289–99.
3   Geoffrey Crossick and Patrycja Kaszynska, *Understanding the Value of Arts and Culture: The AHRC Cultural Value Project* (Swindon: AHRC, 2016).
4   Robert Janes, "Museums, Corporatism and the Civil Society", *Curator* 50, no. 2 (2007): 219–37.
5   See Robert Janes, *Museums in a Troubled World: Renewal, Irrelevance or Collapse* (London and New York: Routledge, 2009).
6   Richard Sandell and Ethnie Nightingale, *Museums, Equality and Social Justice* (London and New York: Routledge, 2012).
7   Awan, Schneider and Till, *Spatial Agency*, 30.
8   Henri Lefebvre, *The Production of Space*, trans. Donald Nicholson (Oxford, UK, and Cambridge, MA: Blackwell, 1991), 26.
9   Awan, Schneider and Till, *Spatial Agency*, 30.
10 Lefebvre, *The Production of Space*, 49–53.
11 Jeremy Till, *Architecture Depends* (Cambridge, MA: MIT Press, 2013).
12 Lefebvre, *The Production of Space*, 274–75.
13 Awan, Schneider and Till, *Spatial Agency*, 30.
14 Henri Lefebvre, *Rhythmanalysis: Space, Time and Everyday Life*, trans. Stuart Elden (London and New York: Continuum, 2004), 74.
15 Ibid.
16 Lefebvre, *The Production of Space*, 52.
17 Lefebvre, *Rhythmanalysis*, 34.
18 Crossick and Kaszynska, *Understanding*, 6.
19 Ibid., 5.
20 Ibid., 7.
21 Ibid.
22 Ibid.
23 Ibid.
24 Awan, Schneider and Till, *Spatial Agency*, 33.
25 Bernadette Lynch, *Whose Cake Is It Anyway?* (London: Paul Hamlyn Foundation, 2011).
26 Awan, Schneider and Till, *Spatial Agency*, 33.
27 Sanna-Mari Jäntti in telephone interview with author, August 22, 2016.
28 "Winner", Guggenheim Helsinki Design Competition, accessed August 22, 2016, http://designguggenheimhelsinki.org/en/finalists/winner.
29 Sanna-Mari Jäntti in telephone interview with author, August 22, 2016.
30 Nicolas Moreau and Hiroko Kusunoki (architects Guggenheim Helsinki) in telephone interview with author, August 19, 2016.
31 Juan Herreros (architect Munchmuseet) in telephone interview with author, August 22, 2016.
32 Stein Olav Henrichsen, "The Art Museum Propelling City Development – Oslo as a Creative City", *Journal of Urban Culture Research* 9 (2014): 102.
33 Juan Herreros, e-mail message to author, August 25, 2016.
34 Ibid.
35 Nicolas Moreau and Hiroko Kusunoki in telephone interview with author, July 21, 2016.
36 Ibid.
37 Juan Herreros, e-mail message to author, August 25, 2016.
38 Ibid.
39 Stuart Elden, trans., Introduction to *Rhythmanalysis* by Henri Lefebvre, vii–xv.
40 Lefebvre, *Rhythmanalysis*, 87.
41 Nathaniel Coleman, *Lefebvre for Architects* (London and New York: Routledge, 2015), 13.
42 Lefebvre, *Rhythmanalysis*, 89.
43 Suzanne MacLeod, "This Magical Place: The Making of Yorkshire Sculpture Park and the Politics of Landscape, Art and Narrative", in *Museum Making: Narratives, Architectures, Exhibitions*, ed. Suzanne MacLeod, Laure Hanks and Jonathan Hale (London and New York: Routledge, 2012), 48–62.
44 Nicolas Moreau and Hiroko Kusunoki in telephone interview with author, July 21, 2016.
45 Juan Herreros in telephone interview with author, August 22, 2016.
46 Crossick and Kaszynska, *Understanding*.
47 Coleman, *Lefebvre for Architects*, 92.
48 Harris, "Livingstone versus Serota".

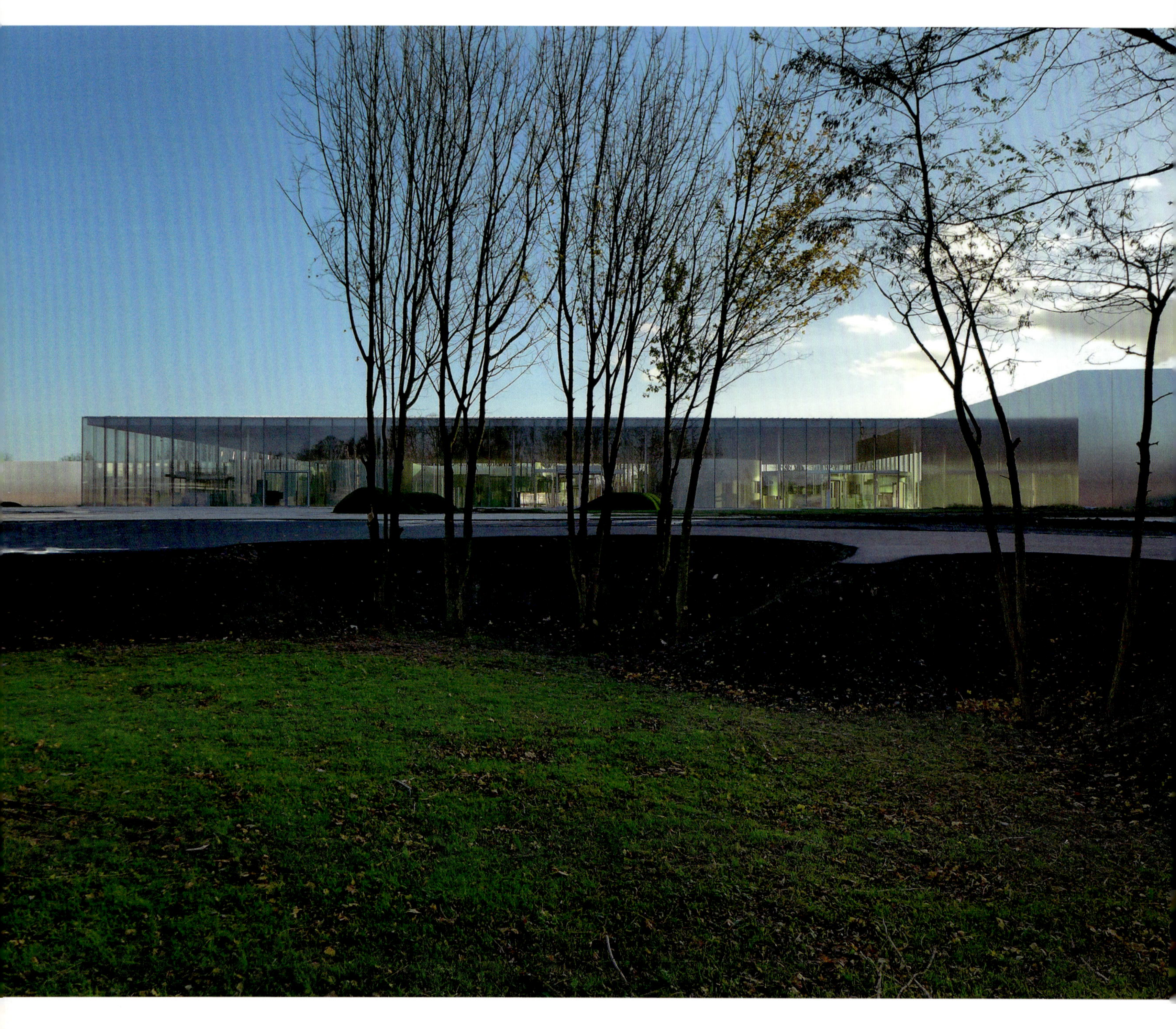

↑ Louvre-Lens, SANAA.

→ Muzej sodobne umetnosti
Metelkova (Museum of
Contemporary Art Metelkova),
Ljubljana, Groleger Arhitekti.

Museum Buildings in the 21st Century: Major Projects and Notes on the Redefinition of the Museum

Karen van den Berg

The new museum apparatus

In many respects the museums of the 21st century face expectations different from those met by their predecessors in previous centuries. New are museums's display methods, their types of spaces, their architecture and rules of behaviour, and the phenomenon that new museums even outside the Western world are being established at a great rate. Whereas traditional museum buildings of the 19th and 20th centuries served the bourgeoisie as temples of high culture and places in which to flaunt one's taste,[1] present-day museums increasingly see themselves as mass media and tourist magnets.[2] Many of the new museum buildings planned in the last two decades no longer serve as showcases and historical storehouses for young nation-states or regions, but instead pursue multi-dimensional strategies. In the words of Michel Foucault, one can speak of an altered apparatus (*dispositif*),[3] which is to say that present-day museum architecture is a response to concepts, rankings, propositions and social functions, which was not the case twenty years ago.

In the process, different types of museums have arisen. One type thinks of itself as a critical platform, a place for cultural and political discourse. Claire Bishop recently described this type in her book *Radical Museology*.[4] It is concerned with debates on democratisation, and subscribes to the so-called "institutional critique", a self-examination on the part of museums that since the 1960s has sought to disenthral the museum's bourgeois *illusio* and transform it into an open, critical, post-colonial institution.[5] In this sense museums have been designed – in the words of the Belgian political scientist Chantal Mouffe – as "anti-hegemonic places for escaping from the dominance of the market", and in which "alternative identities" can be constructed.[6] The corresponding architectural structures needed to be open to dialogue formats. One example is the Muzej sodobne umetnosti Metelkova (Museum for Contemporary Art Metelkova), which was opened in 2011 in Ljubljana, designed by Groleger Arhitekti, a third of whose façade is used as a writing surface. The whole new structure seems like a single large portal opening onto the adjacent square.[7] Characteristic of this type is a clear communication with public space coupled with a large amount of it allotted to education, discussions and events. Another example is the BALTIC Centre for Contemporary Art in Newcastle, a repurposed industrial building in which an entire floor above the large entrance space with its shop and cafeteria is dedicated to the mediation of the art on display.

In addition to these "art centres" and museums seeking dialogue with the public,[8] there are also a number of younger museums that are conceived as retreats, places to slow down, and are often found in out-of-the-way places. They generally open out into the landscape. This type is especially favoured in rural regions in the United States, Europe and Japan. It is not uncommon for them to be private foundations. One thinks of the Teshima Art Museum (2010) designed by Ryue Nishizawa or DIA:Beacon's industrial building near New York, redesigned by Robert Irwin and OpenOffice (2003).[9]

The major museum has evolved as a third and currently predominant type. Its location is essentially determined by political considerations and global competition for attention worldwide. It is the very opposite of what critical "museum studies" and the above-named "institutional critique" have attempted to realise over the past few decades.[10] The major museum does anything but represent the politics of a self-critical post-colonialist identity. Instead, its mission is defined by the term "universal museums", which lays its claim to global significance. In 2002 a number of long-established major museums – among them the Louvre in Paris, the Staatliche Museen zu Berlin, the Metropolitan Museum of Art in New York and the State Hermitage Museum in Saint

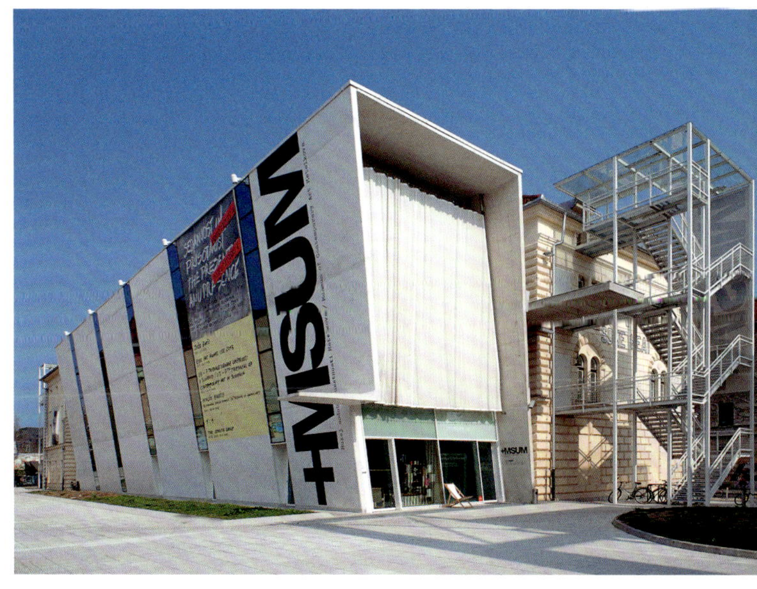

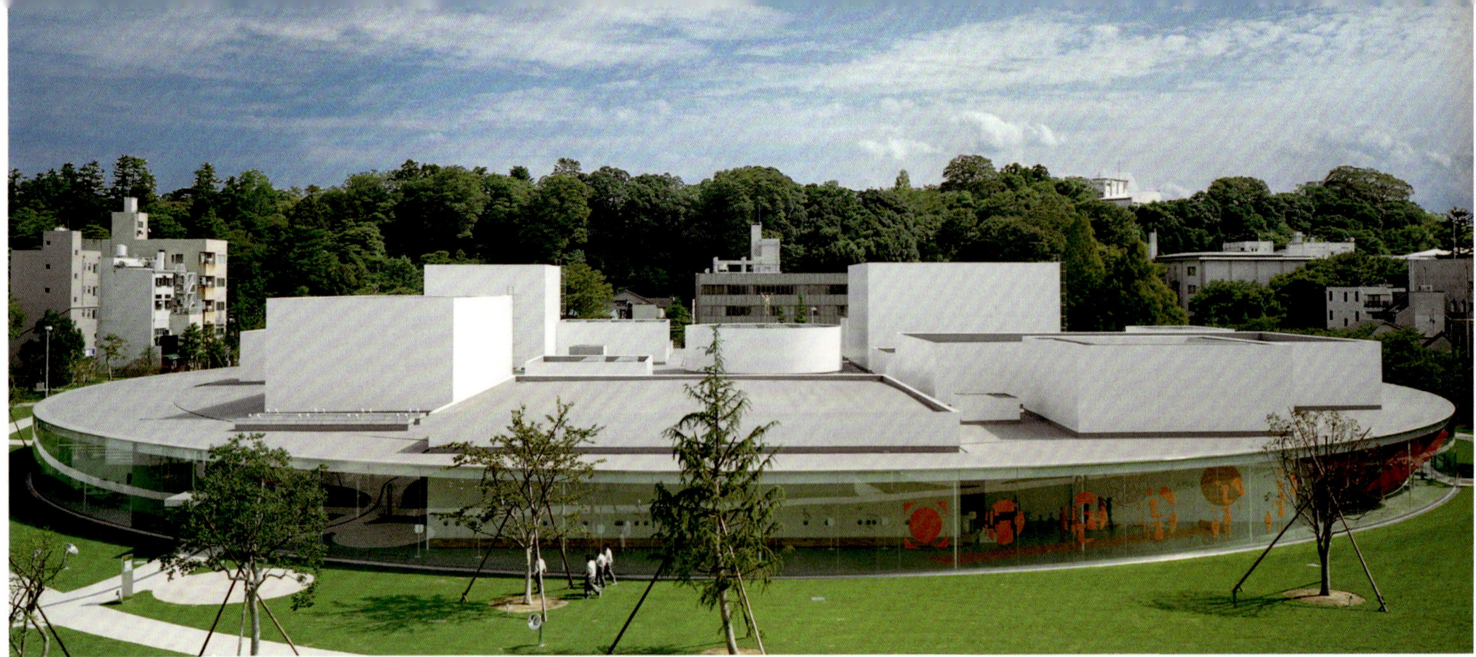

Petersburg – published a declaration that emphasised their unique importance.[11] This is based above all on the fact that they house artefacts from various different cultures. In part under pressure from restitution demands, in their declaration they refer to the fact that they help to cultivate a more expansive, universal view of a multifaceted human history and thus to promote greater tolerance and cultural openness.[12] The highly controversial branch of the Louvre currently under construction in Abu Dhabi is also advertising itself as the kind of "universal museum" described in that declaration. Criticised in the press as a megalomaniacal undertaking,[13] that project is worth looking at more closely, for it is one of the largest known museum building projects of our day and because in its principles, problems and convictions it is virtually a textbook example of this third museum type.

It is striking that in all the varieties of new museums architecture plays an increasingly important role. Although so very different in their sense of themselves, they thus share this one characteristic that shows them to be museums of the 21st century. Before I discuss the giant project in the Gulf more fully, I would therefore like to highlight five features they have in common.

The museum as contemporary landmark

Many eccentric, photogenic new museum buildings stress one thing above all else: the fact that they are contemporary, which encompasses both their presence as well as their newness. Even the minimalist structures of the Japanese architectural duo SANAA present themselves as startlingly "new". In the past few years SANAA has realised some of the most notable projects in this spate of new museum building. Following their 21st Century Museum of Contemporary Art in Kanazawa (2004), they have built the Glass Pavilion for the Toledo Museum of Art (2006), the New Museum in New York (2007) and the Louvre-Lens (2012). And in 2014 they won the competition for a major expansion of the Art Gallery of New South Wales in Sydney (see p. 127). With their transparency, their dominance of light and white and their simple industrial

materials, even these buildings designed in the simple forms of Modernism have an aura of contemporaneity. SANAA's structures have an immaterial radiance precisely because of their clarity and loose, non-hierarchical spatial arrangement.[14]

Other examples are the buildings of Zaha Hadid. The late Iraqi architect's startling, dynamic formal idiom is based entirely on physically appreciable "presence effect".[15] Examples are MAXXI Museo nazionale delle arti del XXI secolo in Rome (2010), the Eli and Edythe Broad Art Museum at Michigan State University (2012), and the capricious, loop-shaped design for the Meixi Lake International Culture & Arts Center in China from 2012 (see p. 151). Angled walls, open staircases only for visitors with no fear of heights and protruding structural elements highlight the physical experience of architecture. The same can be said of the deconstructivist museum buildings of Daniel Libeskind – the Denver Art Museum (2006), the Royal Ontario Museum in Toronto (2007) and the Kurdistan Museum not yet under construction in the Iraqi city Erbil – which offer similarly dizzying walkways and theatrical spaces (see p. 135). The last building's expressive form has a special significance, for the four parts of the structure wedged into each other represent the four countries – Turkey, Iraq, Iran and Syria – inhabited by Kurds.

Slanted walls that challenge one's sense of balance can also be seen in many more recent designs, such as that of Oslo's Munchmuseet by estudio Herreros, for example, scheduled for completion in 2019 (see p. 63).[16]

Whereas the 19th-century museum presented itself as a place of identity formation and in its generally Neoclassical structure provided its bourgeois visitors with historical narratives and collective memories, the 21st-century museum building relies on the display of the expressly new. This is often affected with highly symbolic imagery. Many new designs are unmistakably pictorial, and rely on iconography for their success. For example, the renderings by MVRDV for the futuristic bubbles of the China Comic and Animation Museum in Hangzhou obviously look like speech balloons (see p. 119), and with its decorative façade pattern the design by Adjaye Associates for the National Museum of African American History and Culture in Washington, D.C., recalls African handicrafts (see p. 17). Building shapes and façades thus become unmistakable instruments of communication.

All in all, the 21st-century museum no longer poses as a guardian of cultural traditions, but rather as an iconic, hip and innovative destination – as though designed to be featured in the media. Even museums planned in historic structures concur with this trend, as for example the Zeitz Museum of Contemporary Art Africa now being built in Cape Town by Heatherwick Studio, which in its monumentality is reminiscent of Tate Modern and which will doubtless be the largest museum on the African continent (see p. 83) for the near future. Precisely because of its exposed, vintage appearance, the building has a powerful presence. The raw surfaces of this industrial ruin underscore the fact that a new, post-industrial age has dawned.

The tendency to highlight the structure's physical presence is furthered by the creation of new types of museum-specific displays. This is an innovation not only in museums for contemporary art. Opulent displays are also being created in historical collections by a young generation of professional scenographers. These are produced not only for changing exhibitions but also as redesigns of permanent collections. In addition, varied programme offerings ensure that the museum's primary focus is the presentation of a highly contemporary view of the past wholly in tune with present-day thinking. The museum is concerned not so much with preservation, commemoration and archiving but more and more with exhibits that are emphatically contemporary.

Experiential spaces for fragile identities

Related to architectural style and the design of displays, a second innovation in the museum apparatus is the fact that a collection's objects and the taxonomy of the displays no longer stand in the foreground, their arrangement reflecting scholarly principles and historical narrative. Instead, what matters is the architecture itself. In many newer houses the experience of space, the reputation of the architect, and the creation of atmosphere appear to be almost more important than the objects displayed. In the course of this development museums have been created for every kind of subject matter imaginable. This trend has gone hand in hand with the popularisation and heteronomous encryption of the museum, which indeed no longer represents an autonomous sphere of culture. Every

self-assured car maker invites a star architect to design an "automobile museum". The BMW Welt in Munich, for example, which opened in 2007 and was designed by Coop Himmelb(l)au, shows how fluid the boundaries can be between museum, sales office and event venue.

Like the above-mentioned China Comic and Animation Museum, the Musée Hergé, dedicated to the famous comic draftsman, designed by Christian de Portzamparc and opened in 2009 in Louvain-la-Neuve, shows that museums are no longer simply places for the preservation of sanctioned high culture or treasuries housing rare to irreplaceable unica, as Theodor W. Adorno called them.[17] The idea that museums preserve unique cultural treasures and venerable objects that are part of a cosmos of knowledge was abandoned by many institutions long ago. It no longer seems to be a matter of making exhibits in need of explanation and worth protecting accessible to as broad a public as possible, for now museums are elevating goods of mass consumption – not even historical ones – into objects of cultural value, and turning more and more towards pop culture. To succeed at this, it is even more important that they have prestigious, attention-getting buildings that do not merely attest to the value of the exhibits but in fact create it.

If present-day museums do indeed contain unique, unwieldy, unusual cultural artefacts requiring commentary, it is expected that they should create readily accessible and consumer-friendly contexts for them. A few years ago the Romanian artist Dan Perjovschi sketched a cartoon that perfectly illustrates this development:

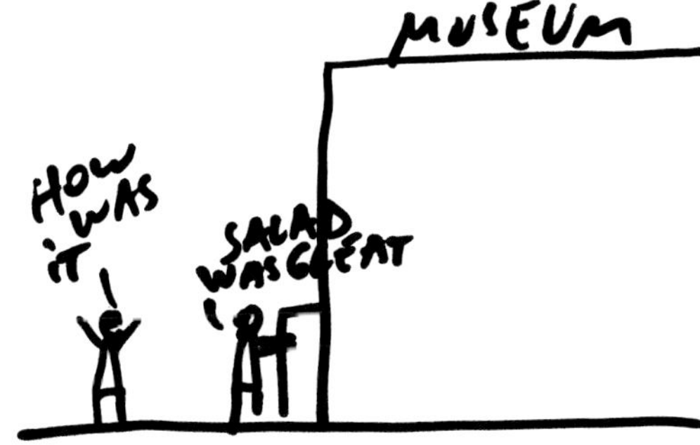

Dan Perjovschi, museum drawing (Salad Was Great), 2005.

Public service areas – the cafeteria, the bookshop, the gift shop, the lecture room, the VIP lounge and spaces for museum pedagogy and the like – have expanded enormously as compared to the exhibition galleries. In the case

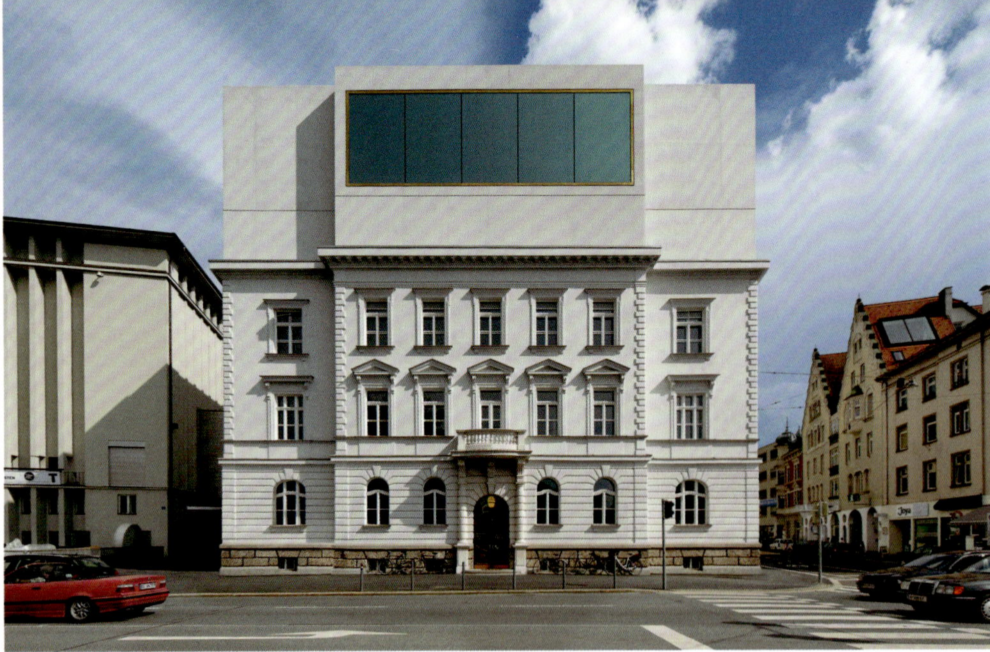

of the Louvre Abu Dhabi, for example, only 9,200 square metres of the total 64,000 square metres are to be used as exhibition space.[18]

This new focus on the space and its atmosphere, coupled with the fact that Japanese architects are building in New York and Sydney and French and American ones in the Persian Gulf, produces a further, third consideration that typifies the new museum apparatus along with its focus on its building and emphasis on contemporaneity: now very few new foundations are geared toward their local culture. Most look to global horizons. Accordingly, the presentation of a specific local material culture and identifiable local style is thrust into the background. It is therefore typical of the museum apparatus of the 21st century that its building and displays serve less and less to create specific cultural narratives. It seems to be much more important to adorn cities and communities with startling new buildings and thus, in the global race for attention, get listed on the map of "places to be".

Virtually no one would head to Bilbao to see the works displayed in the Guggenheim Museum, but many people do so in order to admire Frank O. Gehry's striking building as a site of new urbanism. And one would hardly set out for Lens for the chance to look at a Peter Paul Rubens painting. But pictures of SANAA's unusually light, airy staging of the history of world art in Louvre-Lens's Galerie du Temps were seen around the world, and in the first year it was open the museum lured 900,000 visitors to this little town in northern France.

It is thus worth noting that these new structures attract more attention than the artefacts housed in them. As a result, architecture and the museum's concept are increasingly unconcerned with the assertion and preservation of a local identity. If at all, individual identity is presented in only two variants: the first consists of a post-colonial, self-critical view of the fragile local culture and how it relates to the wider world. A successful example of this is the vorarlberg museum in Bregenz, opened in 2013 – another stunning, sumptuous house with rich interactive media displays planned by Cukrowicz Nachbaur Architekten. The second variant subscribes to the notion of the "universal museum", and claims to provide an

experience of the universal and abstract idea of mankind in the 21st century. These houses think of themselves as expressions of a global contemporary culture, which means – as in the Louvre Abu Dhabi, for example – being able to present "the" history of mankind unsullied by colonialist, nationalist or religious views – hardly a convincing claim in the case of this mega-museum dedicated to cultural tourism in the Gulf, as discussed further below.

Dismissal of the bourgeois subject

A fourth feature common to many new museums is a revised political orientation, coupled in that context with new considerations as to how potential visitors can be envisaged and anticipated.

The museum of the 21st century no longer thinks of the education of the individual as a cornerstone of bourgeois society, but rather of demographic issues. A few decades ago the ritual of silent contemplation of a museum's displays was still seen as an emancipatory exercise for the individual bourgeois. Now, however, the political considerations regarding culture which are behind the founding of new museums tend to emphasise an interest in "the public", or even "the population", and a desire to influence immigration and emigration and demographic developments.

As late as the 1980s there was a bitter fight to preserve the museum as a bastion of intellectual and aesthetic autonomy, one reserved for the individual visitor's subjective experience.[19] One was supposed to cultivate an informed, self-reliant encounter with its displays.[20] Independent study – presupposing a great deal – was encouraged. The museum was a place of cultivation where one honed one's independent judgement. And an ability to judge, in turn, was considered essential to decision making in an enlightened democratic society. In this context Peter Sloterdijk described the museum as a place for the "bourgeois process of global appropriation as the simultaneous identification and mobilization of all assets" and a "School of Alienation"[21] in which the individual finds his judgement challenged in his study of extraordinary exhibits. The presentation of a work's uniqueness at the same time provokes an invocation of the viewer as an idiosyncratic individual.

Criticism of this concept was as old as the concept itself. Yet in the 1960s it became increasingly heated. Museums were above all accused of being the sacred temples of a privileged bourgeoisie and of shutting out other population groups.[22]

Also, with the beginning of postmodernism the aura of the unique object and the idea of originality, with its assumption of an author who was unique if not a genius, was increasingly discredited, and with it the call for its counterpart: the informed or active viewer. The German literature theorist Jürgen Fohrmann described this process: "Originality can no longer be seen as its own sole justification, as the indispensable prerequisite."[23] He was simultaneously referring to a loss that accompanied the farewell to the author, to genius and originality, for the notion of originality implied a resistance to and hostility towards prevailing power relationships, inasmuch as the genius and the original avoid any kind of subservience, considering themselves exceptional.

In the museum of the 21st century star architects take the place of outstanding works and heroic creators. And the star is distinguished from the genius by the fact that he becomes one thanks to the public's adulation. In any event, the idea of the strong bourgeois subject has been shown the door.

This and the increased demand for inclusivity have brought about changes: the museum has become discursive, popularised and economised. What these three contradictory tendencies have in common is the fact that it is no longer the single (bourgeois) visitor who is addressed but rather plural visitors. Thus efforts to be inclusive have among other things the paradoxical, by no means emancipatory, effect that henceforth attendance figures become the decisive criterion in terms of cultural policy, and the individual visitor's museum experience is no longer a chief concern.

The redistribution of cultural capital

Today museums are therefore seen less and less as places to cultivate an emancipated viewpoint. For some two decades now the new foundations and monumental expansions of existing houses have been responses to wholly different considerations. And here we have the

fifth innovation: since the museum is considered a mass medium, publicly financed new museums have highlighted demographic issues, settlement policies of shrinking cities, job creation and positioning in the global competition for attention. The idea of opening up the museum instead of concentrating on the cultivated bourgeois individual had been achieved with great effort, and now underwent a neoliberal reinterpretation. The inauguration of the Guggenheim Museum Bilbao in 1997 can serve as the decisive turning point for this change in museum history.[24] There for the first time the function of the museum was seen to be blatantly economic: the museum building was celebrated as a local landmark. Pictures of Frank O. Gehry's eccentric structure in the Basque metropolis became the icons of a new era, and the so-called "Bilbao effect" became the mantra of a competition-oriented cultural policy that soon adopted the theories of the American economist and urbanist Richard Florida with his talk of the "creative economy".[25] Hence the rise of the pompous bogeymen of the neoliberal museum empires.

What had happened? Shortly before the turn of the century Thomas Krens, then the Director of New York's Guggenheim Museum, transformed one of the great American private art collections into the largest art consortium in the world. The trained art historian and economist devised a branch system with an aggressive brand policy, with headquarters in New York and branches in Venice, Bilbao and Berlin. Krens's strategy for the Basque branch entailed an established, prestigious museum providing its name and know-how to the creation of new museums even in cultural backwaters. Thomas Krens's speech about the "five rides", which claims that successful museums need "a great permanent collection, great exhibitions, great architecture, excellent places to eat and drink, and numerous shopping opportunities", was understood to be the new museum business model.[26] Krens's model of the successful museum has in many places been understood as a new business model. His recipe for Bilbao was to invite a world-famous architect to design the museum, to give a few "high-calibre works" as loans so that then the museum could start building collections of its own following the standards of the main house.[27] In the case of Bilbao the region invested millions in extraordinary architecture – in the mid-1990s the Basque country paid 100 million dollars for the Gehry structure. In return Thomas Krens provided a concept for the museum's direction and future expansion, making assurances that its collection would be supplemented by loans from the Guggenheim's holdings.[28] Such open propagation of the museum as economic factor was immediately met with fierce criticism. Both cultural conservatives and critics of capitalism decried what they saw as the "McDonald-isation" of the museum.[29] Many critics repudiated the new Guggenheim Museum inasmuch as it had appropriated the thinking of retail chains with their licensed outlets. A few years later came talk of the "Bilbao defect", for in many places competition-driven local politics and the engagement of cultural institutions in gentrification processes had become increasingly obvious.[30] Nonetheless, inspired by the "Bilbao effect" there was soon a demand for new museum buildings worldwide. With increasing frequency, whether in Rome, Denver, Tokyo or Ningbo, structures were designed to be distinctive, high-end, photogenic and eccentric, all with the hope they might contribute to the revaluation of their respective urban surroundings and to their economies.

How greatly cultural policies have changed in recent years is also evident from the example of the Louvre-Lens. In the autumn of 2004 the French state decided to erect a branch of the Louvre in one of France's poorest municipalities, the mining town of Lens with a mere 32,000 residents; in a competition it had been given the nod because it was culturally the most remote.[31] It was immediately apparent that what was going on was above all – to use the words of the French sociologist Pierre Bourdieu – a redistribution of "cultural capital" and a regional revitalisation.[32] That the Tokyo architectural duo SANAA then received the go-ahead over 125 competitors[33] was because its museums are extremely unpretentious, accessible, transparent structures in which interior and exterior spaces flow into each other, so that they seemed suited even for a public with little contact with art. At least as important was the fact that for all their accessibility, they nevertheless exude the aura of contemporaneity required of a true public magnet meant to contribute to a region's revitalisation. And this was precisely what the house in northern France would accomplish, for from the beginning it was assumed that it would attract half a million visitors a year, so that the project would be financially viable. In any case, the building, financed by the region, the commune, the European Regional Development Fund (ERDF), the state and private sponsors, cost 150 million euros.[34]

Behind projects like this there is a whole tangle of new cultural policy considerations affecting the museum in the early 21st century; they operate with such phrases as "Bilbao effect", "creative city" and "cultural capital".[35] This development becomes dubious when public institutions are guided primarily by free-market considerations – which cannot be said of Louvre-Lens, by the way. As the political scientist Colin Crouch convincingly explained in his book *The Knowledge Corrupters*, every unabated reduction in costs is a form of erosion although "the market is itself a highly elaborate form of knowledge, heavy reliance on it undermines other forms of knowledge." [36]

Museum temples in the Gulf

Today, twenty years after Bilbao, the population policy and competitive approach is culminating in a museum quarter of superlatives: Abu Dhabi's Saadiyat Cultural District, currently under construction.[37] This monster project is highly controversial for any number of reasons. Here we are clearly dealing with a new era in museum history, for behind this endeavour is a concept of the museum that has only very little to do with the former memory-oriented place in which the bourgeois might learn about the past – especially since there is no bourgeois tradition in the Gulf. Here, by contrast, the notion of the museum as bourgeois behaviour pattern has itself become a luxury article. The Louvre and the Guggenheim have become luxury brands signalling a new level of cultural appropriation beyond the importation of Bentleys and Louis Vuitton handbags. Compared to the Abu Dhabi branch the highly criticised traditional museum aggregate as manifested in the old Louvre Paris seems like a virtual enclave of humanism. In the Gulf state the idea of the museum as a local attraction, export brand and luxury commodity has triumphed as never before.

On the twenty-seven square kilometres of the previously undeveloped sandy island of Saadiyat on the outskirts of the capital of the United Arab Emirates, what has to be the most spectacular collection of new museum buildings in the world is being erected – literally from scratch. In 2004 the young Gulf state's Tourism & Culture Authority commissioned the Tourism Development & Investment Company (TDIC) to develop a new urban quarter, and in 2007 asked the American landscape planners EDAW [38] to develop a master plan for the siting of more than two dozen hotels, four museums and a theatre complex.[39] No less than five Pritzker Prize architects were invited to design the prestigious cultural buildings. The first structure, a branch of the Louvre designed by Jean Nouvel, is now slated for completion in 2017. To the north

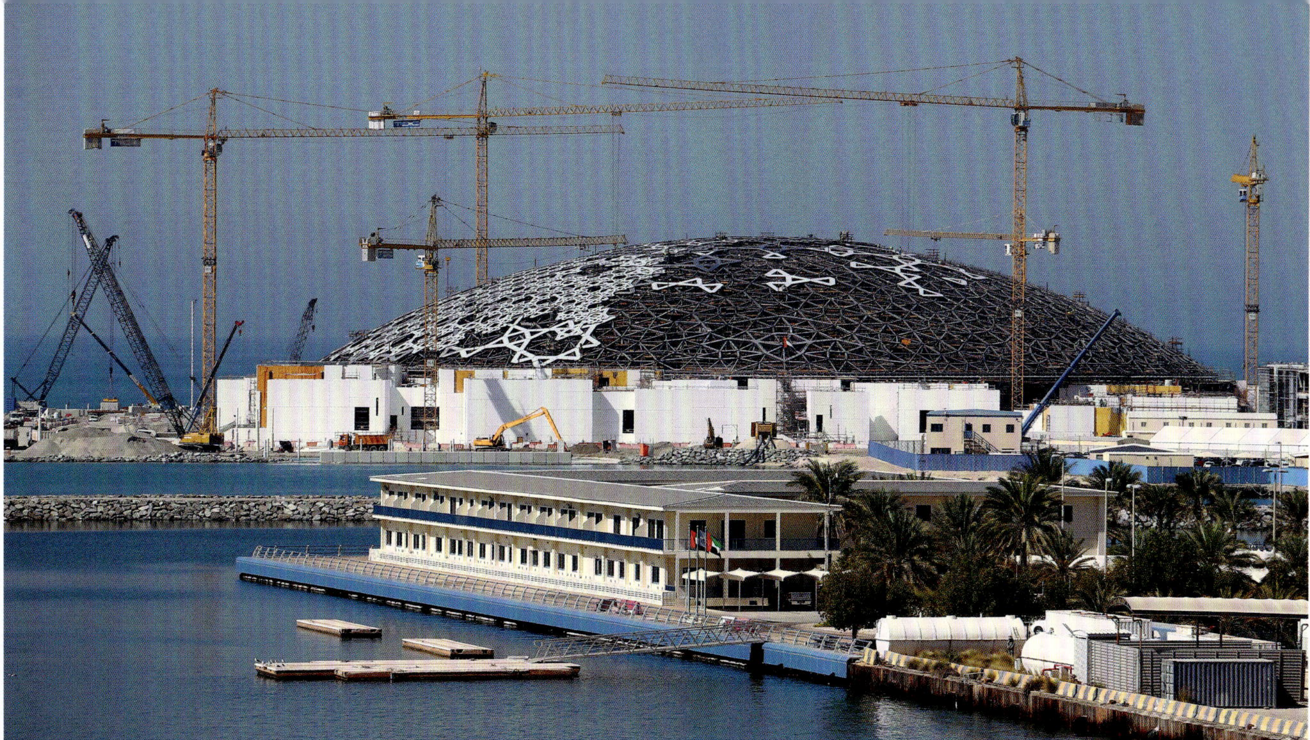

of it there are plans to build the largest Guggenheim Museum in the world – designed, as in Bilbao, by Frank O. Gehry.[40] To the south of the two art museums a Performing Arts Centre is projected that was designed by Zaha Hadid, and next to it there is to be a Maritime Museum planned by Tadao Ando. Finally, a bit farther east the island is to be crowned by the Zayed National Museum, for which Norman Foster provided the design.

The promotional publications of the branch of the Louvre Paris on the Persian Gulf make it clear that Paris's "museum of museums" thinks of itself as an institution that is creating a new, pluralistic narrative of world culture. The strategy of displaying in Paris cultural artefacts from looting campaigns in the Orient and around the world has been turned around. Now the institutional know-how and premium brand name "Louvre" are being exported. So a satellite museum is taking shape in the capital of the United Arab Emirates, one that has landed in a world in which as yet there has been no fine art tradition. More-over, there's the fact that the Louvre's location in the Gulf follows an agreement at state level involving the westward flow of just under a billion euros. The *Neue Zürcher Zeitung* has reported: "In exchange, by 2026 the emirate is to pay 164 million euros for 'construction assistance,' 190 mil-lion euros for the permanent exhibitions and 195 million euros for the changing ones, as well as 400 million for the use of the name 'Louvre' until 2037."[41] The French govern-ment made this deal over the objections of 4,650 signato-ries from France's cultural community and several dozen curators of the Louvre itself.[42] The experts had expressed concerns about whether works would be damaged by the extreme climate in the Gulf.

But the concept of the universal museum supposed to exhibit "masterpieces from all civilizations" and thus intended to combat intolerance and promote intercultural dialogue is also problematic. This is how Mubarak Hamad Al Muhairi, Director General of Abu Dhabi Tourism & Culture Authority, described it in the catalogue of the pre-opening exhibition in 2013.[43] The curator responsible

for that show, Laurence des Cars, claimed that a universal museum could represent a multipolar world, and create a "unifying narrative",[44] but this seems far from convincing in view of the conditions under which the mega-museum is being built. On the international mega building site immigrant workers are labouring under wholly unac-ceptable safety standards. The project, so dedicated to enlightenment and humanism, has earned sharp criticism for its poor working conditions, listed by Human Rights Watch as degrading.[45] According to reports, the work-ers, mostly from India, Pakistan, Bangladesh, Sri Lanka and Nepal, are not only stripped of their passports, but they have few or no legal rights, and as the human rights organisation claims, they have highly unsatisfactory basic medical care.[46]

Against this background, in 2011 a group of inter-national artists and activists formed the Gulf Labour Coalition. It initiated a series of protests demanding better working conditions and fair pay for the migrant workers. They staged repeated actions in the Guggen-heim Museum in New York, and were invited to the 56th Biennale in Venice to call attention to the problem. A few months ago the Director of New York's Guggen-heim Museum ended the long-lasting dialogue with the Gulf Labour Coalition and accused the group of false statements.[47]

Such accusations will not prevent the opening of the entire district and the Louvre with its large, impos-ing cupola the size of five football fields. Instead, the advance hype will ensure that all eyes will be directed at the finished project. With its opening it can be expected that it will become clear to a broader public that a new era has dawned in the history of the museum. And the impressive building by Jean Nouvel greatly contributes to this change. The museum now has a new function; indeed it will no longer be used by Western democra-cies as an important medium of communication. The art critic Jonathan Jones makes it clear that this is a turning point in museum history that is important for Europe:

"To create a new global museum in the Arab world with an Arab perspective is a revolutionary subversion of the old European imperialism of knowledge."[48] In the case of the Louvre, it remains to be seen whether this new orientation becomes a success story or whether the museum strays into a cul-de-sac. Enthusiasm for Jean Nouvel's structure, unmatched for its futuristic design, will possibly sweep away any political discussion about human rights issues and conceptual flaws. Shimmering surfaces of water, islands dotted with palms and an impressive play of light and shadow will lure visitors into what amounts to a dream world. Beneath the flat, monumental dome, made up of a complex network of steel beams and overlapping layers of aluminium plates and reminiscent of the canopies over Arab bazaars, a dizzying rain of light will unfold. Beneath an umbrella that mitigates the heat of the desert state there will be a variegated parcours of alleys, canals and exhibition spaces.

Since a part of the all-white architecture stands in water and opens out onto the sea, the building invites strolling and browsing. The renderings already have the iconic look of postcard motifs.

The staged setting – only a very small percentage of the space is to be used for exhibits – recalls the upbeat, relaxed atmosphere of the shopping arcades found in luxury hotels in the Gulf with their interaction of open spaces, dining options, and book and souvenir shops. In the blistering heat of the Gulf metropolis these are the few spaces that are semi-public. This idea of a semi-public space is perhaps a minor sensation for the Gulf state. From the perspective of the Western museum tradition the Louvre Abu Dhabi will seem like a gallery of the most refined taste, one meeting the demands of a wealthy consumer society and custom-made for future cultural tourism, in which visitors are treated as sophisticated customers.

1 See Carol Duncan, "Art Museums and the Ritual of Citizenship", in *Exhibiting Cultures: The Poetics and Politics of Museum Display*, ed. Steven D. Lavine and Ivan Karp (Washington and London: Smithsonian Institution Press, 1991), 88–103.
2 See Andreas Huyssen, *Twilight Memories: Making Time in a Culture of Amnesia* (London and New York: Routledge, 1995), 15.
3 For the term *"dispositif"*, here translated as "apparatus", see Michel Foucault, "The Confession of the Flesh", in *Power/Knowledge: Selected Interviews and Other Writings*, ed. Colin Gordon (New York: Pantheon Books, 1980), 194–98.
4 Claire Bishop, *Radical Museology or, What's "Contemporary" in Contemporary Museums of Contemporary Art?* (London: König Books, 2014).
5 For the term *"illusio"*, see Pierre Bourdieu, *The Rules of Art: Genesis and Structure of the Literary Field* (Stanford, CA: Stanford University Press, 1996), 227.
6 Chantal Mouffe, *Agonistics: Thinking the World Politically* (London: Verso, 2013), 93, 101.
7 See Bishop, *Radical Museology*, 47 ff.
8 See Christian Kravagna, ed., *The Museum as Arena: Artists on Institutional Critique* (Cologne: Walther König, 2001).
9 Other examples would be the Chinati Foundation in Marfa, the Museum Insel Hombroich near Düsseldorf, Situation Kunst in Bochum, Benesse Art Site in Naoshima Island (Japan) and the Aomori Museum of Art (Japan). See also Karen van den Berg, "The Unconditional Museum and the Fragile Logic of the Ensemble", in *Situation Kunst for Max Imdahl. The Extension 2006; a publication of the Stiftung Situation Kunst*, ed. Silke von Berswordt Wallrabe and Friederike Wappler (Düsseldorf: Richter, 2008), 9–29.
10 See Mieke Bal, "Telling, Showing, Showing Off", *Critical Inquiry* 18, no. 3 (1992): 556–94.
11 "Declaration on the Importance and Value of Universal Museums 2002", in *Witnesses to History: A Compendium of Documents and Writings on the Return of the Cultural Objects*, ed. Lyndel V. Prott (Paris: UNESCO, 2009), 116–117.
12 See also Mark O'Neill, "Enlightenment Museums: Universal or Merely Global?" *Museum and Society* 2, no. 3 (2004): 197.
13 See Vincent Noce, "Work on Louvre Abu Dhabi goes into overdrive", *The Art Newspaper*, March 4, 2015, accessed October 4, 2016, http://old.theartnewspaper.com/articles/Work-on-Louvre-Abu-Dhabi-agoes-into-overdrive/37118; and Benjamin Sutton, "Breaking Down ArtReview's 2014 Power 100 List", *Hyperallergic*, October 23, 2014, accessed October 4, 2016, http://hyperallergic.com/157870/breaking-down-artreviews-2014-power-100-list/.
14 See Benoît Vandenbulcke, "Concretion, Abstraction: The Place of Design Processes in Today's Architecture Practice. Case Study: Sanaa", in *Proceedings from the 1st International Conference on Architecture & Urban Design* (Tirana: Epoka University, 2012), 28.
15 For the term "presence effect", see Hans Ulrich Gumbrecht, *Production of Presence: What Meaning Cannot Convey* (Stanford, CA: Stanford University Press, 2004).
16 See Nina Berglund, "Majority Hails New Munch Museum", *News in English*, accessed October 4, 2016, http://www.newsinenglish.no/2013/05/29/majority-cheers-new-munch-museum/.
17 Theodor W. Adorno, "Valéry Proust Museum", in idem, *Prisms*, trans. Shierry Weber Nicholsen and Samuel Weber (Cambridge, MA: MIT Press, 1982), 175–85, 177.
18 See Musée du Louvre, Press Release, "Birth of a Museum: Louvre Abu Dhabi", 2014, accessed October 4, 2016, http://www.louvre.fr/sites/default/files/Louvre%20Abu%20Dhabi%20exhibition%20Press%20Kit_v2.pdf.
19 See Achim Preiss, Karl Stamm and Frank Günther Zehnder, eds, *Das Museum. Die Entwicklung in den 80er Jahren. Festschrift Hugo Borger zum 65. Geburtstag* (Munich: Klinkhardt & Biermann, 1990).
20 See Harald Szeemann, *Museum der Obsessionen* (Berlin: Merve, 1981), 20.

21 Peter Sloterdijk, "Museum – School of Alienation", *Art in Translation* 6, no. 4 (2014): 437–48, 440, 443.

22 Most prominently by Paul Valéry and Walter Benjamin. Valéry referred to the powerful and awe-inspiring dimensions of the ritual of silent contemplation. He recognised in the museum behaviour code primarily suppressive, anti-emancipatory effects (Paul Valéry, "The Problem with Museums", in idem, *Degas, Manet, Morisot*, [London and New York: Routledge, 2007], 202–06). Benjamin's discomfort had to do with the cult of the original, or unique work, a cult that – in his opinion – could take on uncritical and desocialising features (Walter Benjamin, "The Work of Art in the Age of Its Technological Reproducibility", in *The Work of Art in the Age of Its Technological Reproducibility and Other Writings on Media*, ed. Michael W. Jennings, Brigid Doherty and Thomas Y. Levin [Cambridge, MA, and London: Belknap Press of Harvard University Press, 2008], 39). See also Pierre Bourdieu, *Distinction* (London and New York: Routledge, 2013), 67.

23 See Jürgen Fohrmann, "'Dichter heißen so gerne Schöpfer'. Über Genies und andere Epigonen", *Merkur* 39 (1985): 988.

24 See Hilmar Hoffmann, ed., *Das Guggenheim Prinzip* (Ostfildern: DuMont Reiseverlag, 1999).

25 Richard L. Florida, *The Rise of the Creative Class and How It's Transforming Work, Leisure, Community and Everyday Life* (New York: Basic Books, 2004).

26 Joy Sperling, "Popular Genres in the Visual Arts", in *A Companion to Popular Culture*, ed. Gary Burns (Chichester: Wiley, 2016), 160.

27 Jean-Christoph Ammann, "Das 'Guggenheim Syndrom' oder das Erstarren der Maus vor der Schlange", in Hoffmann, *Das Guggenheim-Prinzip*, 32.

28 Hilmar Hoffmann, "Das Prinzip Guggenheim", in ibid., 11–31.

29 See Peter Noever, ed., *The Discursive Museum* (Ostfildern: Hatje Cantz Verlag, 2001) and Tobias Wall, *Das unmögliche Museum. Zum Verhältnis von Kunst und Kunstmuseen der Gegenwart* (Bielefeld: Transcript, 2006).

30 See Robert Kaltenbrunner, "Urbanität mit Bilbao-Defekt. Was braucht die Stadt an 'Baukultur'?" *Neue Gesellschaft – Frankfurter Hefte* 12 (2012): 92–95; and Laura C. Mallonee, "Marfa's Art World Gentrification Is Pushing out Long-time Residents", *Hyperallergic*, August 11, 2014, accessed October 4, 2016, http://hyperallergic.com/142955/marfas-art-world-gentrification-is-pushing-out-long-time-residents/.

31 Susanne Stacher, "Der Louvre Lens, Frankreich – Architektur als Land Art, Landschaft als Kunst", *Architektur Aktuell* 396, no. 3 (2013): 98.

32 Pierre Bourdieu, "The Forms of Capital", in *Handbook of Theory and Research for the Sociology of Education*, ed. John Richardson (New York: Greenwood, 1986), 241–58.

33 See Stacher, "Der Louvre Lens", 98.

34 Specifically, the financing was put together from the Regional Council Nord-Pas-de-Calais (59 %), local sponsors (12 %), as well as the Conseil Général (Pas-de-Calais Département), the city of Lens, Lens Metropolitan authorities, the ERDF (altogether 20 %) and additional private sponsors (5 %) and the state (4 %) (see Guy Baudelle and Gerhard Krauss, "The Governance Model of Two French National Museums of Fine Arts Relocated in the Province: Centre Pompidou Metz and Louvre-Lens", *Belgeo*, published online December 15, 2014, accessed October 4, 2016. doi: 10.4000/belgeo.12765; Peter Popp and Emilia Margaretha, "Integrative Transparency: Louvre-Lens by SANAA", *Detail*, published September 1, 2013, accessed October 4, 2016, http://www.detail-online.com/article/integrative-transparency-louvre-lens-by-sanaa-16498/; Elena Borin and Ivan Paunović, "The Case of Louvre-Lens: Regional

Regeneration through Cultural Innovation", in *Sitcon: Singidunum International Tourism Conference* (Belgrade: Univerzitet Singidunum, 2015), 250.

35 Borin and Paunović (ibid.) write: "[The] Louvre-Lens was used as a driver for the relaunch of the area on the basis of culture. … One of the most relevant critical points identified at the beginning of the project was the lack of local creative industries." See also Baudelle and Krauss, "The Governance Model", 8.

36 Colin Crouch, *The Knowledge Corrupters: Hidden Consequences of the Financial Takeover of Public Life* (Cambridge, UK: Polity Press, 2015), 130.

37 For a more extensive discussion, see Karen van den Berg, "Das ausgestellte Museum. Von Abu Dhabi nach Teshima", *Paragrana* 1 (2017): 57–72.

38 Taken over by AECOM in 2005, and absorbed as the firm name in 2009.

39 Adrian Hornsby, "Saadiyat Island", *The Architect's Journal*, November 3, 2008, accessed October 4, 2016, http://www.architectsjournal.co.uk/news/saadiyat-island/1914047.fullarticle.

40 As yet there is no definite date for the completion of the museum and no contractual agreement. See Amy Frearson, "Construction of Gehry's Guggenheim Abu Dhabi yet to start", *Dezeen*, February 12, 2016, accessed November 4, 2016, http://www.dezeen.com/2016/02/12/construction-guggenheim-frank-gehry-abu-dhabi-still-yet-to-start/.

41 Marc Zitzmann, "Fata Morgana am Meer", *Neue Zürcher Zeitung*, May 7, 2014, accessed October 4, 2016, http://www.nzz.ch/feuilleton/kunst_architektur/fata-morgana-am-meer-1.18296931.

42 Gerhard Mack, "Kunst aus Europa, Geld vom Golf", *Neue Zürcher Zeitung*, March 11, 2007, accessed October 4, 2016, http://www.nzz.ch/articleEZPoB-1.125922.

43 Mubarak Hamad Al Muhairi, "A Bridge to the World", in *Louvre Abu Dhabi: Birth of a Museum*, ed. Laurence des Cars (Paris: Musée du Louvre Éditions/ Tourism and Culture Authority (TCA)/Skira Flammarion, 2013), 15.

44 Laurence des Cars, "The Louvre Abu Dhabi, a Universal and Singular Museum", in ibid., 31.

45 Sarah Leah Whitson, "Foreword", in *The Gulf: High Culture/Hard Labor*, ed. Andrew Ross (New York and London: OR Books, 2015), 7–10.

46 Journalists from *The Guardian* and Gulf labour activists held more than one hundred interviews with workers (see David Batty, "Migrants Building UAE Cultural Hub 'Risk Abuse If They Complain'", *The Guardian*, February 10, 2015, accessed October 4, 2016, https://www.theguardian.com/global-development/2015/feb/10/migrants-united-arab-emirates-human-rights-watch. See also Andrew Ross, "Leveraging the Brand: A History of Gulf Labor", in *The Gulf. High Culture/Hard Labor*, 12.

47 In an open letter he writes: "The Guggenheim is and always will be a champion for art and for artists. We respect activism and recognize its value. We welcome dialogue and accept criticism. But we cannot stand silent in the face of deliberate falsehoods", in Hrag Vartanian, "Guggenheim Breaks Off Negotiations with Gulf Labor over Migrant Rights", *Hyperallergic*, April 17, 2016, accessed October 4, 2016, http://hyperallergic.com/291594/guggenheim-breaks-off-negotiations-with-gulf-labor-over-migrant-rights/.

48 Jonathan Jones, "Why the Louvre Abu Dhabi Is Worth Celebrating, Despite Its Dark Side", *The Guardian*, March 9, 2015, accessed October 4, 2016, https://www.the guardian.com/artanddesign/jonathanjonesblog/2015/mar/09/louvre-abu-dhabi-worth-celebrating-jean-nouvel-human-rights.

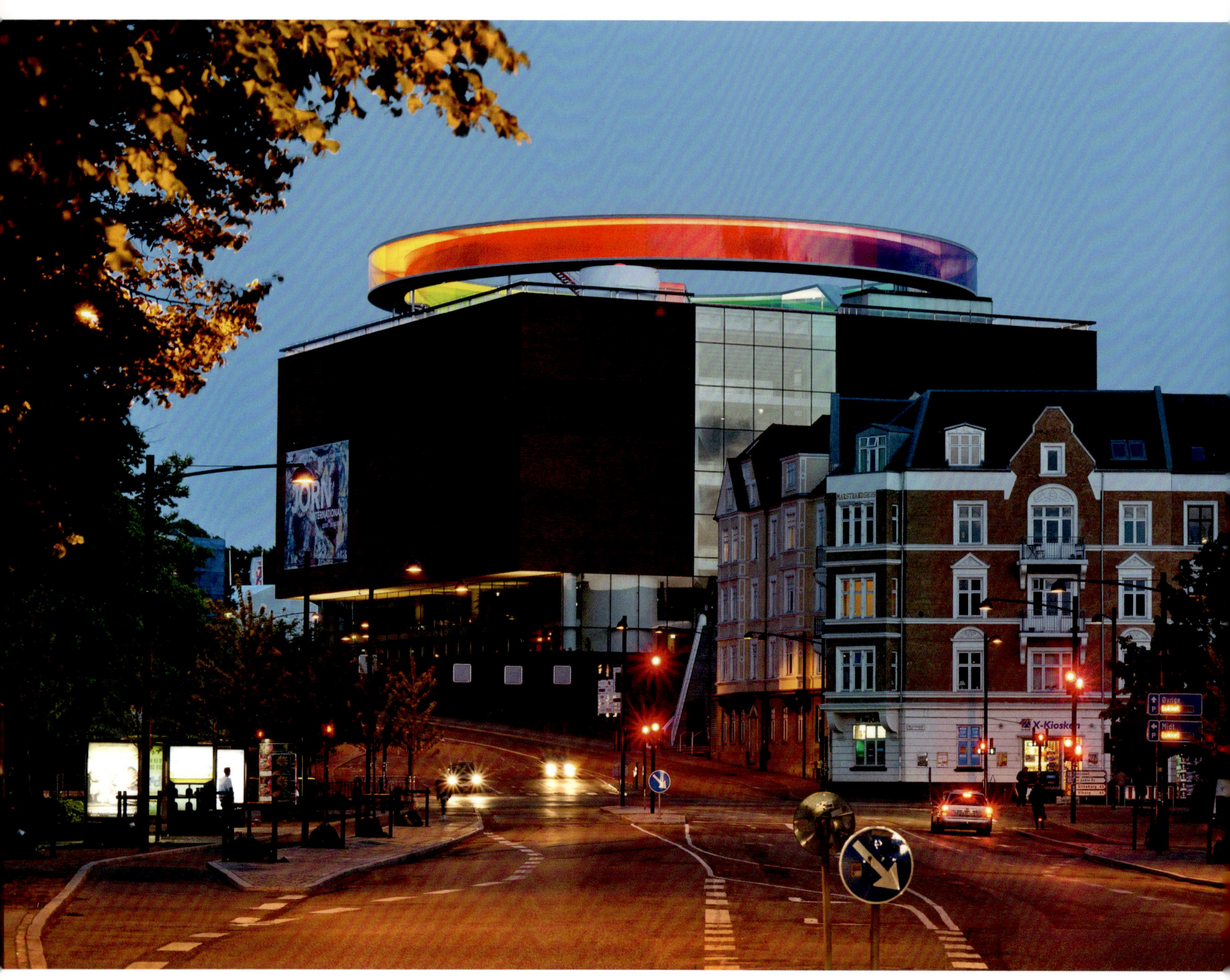

↑ Olafur Eliasson, *Your rainbow panorama*, 2006–2011.
ARoS Aarhus Kunstmuseum.

The Museum, a Building in and for the City: An Exploration from a Spatial Point of View

Kali Tzortzi

Museums are among the iconic buildings of the start of the 21st century. Through the architectural heterogeneity of their structures and the curatorial inventiveness of their exhibitions, these "powerful symbolic cultural institutions"[1] can become an inseparable part of the identity of a city. The relationship between the museum and the city is of course not new, but rather permeates museum history. Today it is a central theme in museum architecture, from the tangibles of the physical design to the intangibles of symbolic and cultural meanings, and relates to current tendencies in the museum's role as a staging of display narratives and as a place for sociability.[2] Here we intend to look at the interaction between museum and city from a spatial point of view. We see space both as the common ground between the museum building and its display, and as the technology through which the museum connects to its urban setting. In this sense space offers us a unifying framework within which we can examine museums – mainly of art – both those recently built (21st Century Museum of Contemporary Art, Kanazawa; Acropolis Museum, Athens; Museum aan de Stroom (MAS), Antwerp; Louvre-Lens; Tate Modern, London) as well as new projects at the design stage (Nasjonalmuseet for kunst, arkitektur og design, Oslo; Munchmuseet, Oslo; Guggenheim Helsinki; Musée cantonal des Beaux-Arts [mcb-a], Musée de l'Elysée [Musée cantonal de la photographie], and Musée de design et d'arts appliqués contemporains [mudac], Lausanne; Art Gallery of New South Wales – Sydney Modern Project), where the relation of the museum to the city is seen as a key parameter in the museum experience, affecting spatial structure, visual presence, display and social function.

The museum as a spatial structure in the city

In terms of the larger scale of the urban setting, historical overviews emphasise that the beginning of the relation between the museum and the city can be traced to the creation of the Altes Museum, Berlin (1830). Occupying a key urban site, opposite the royal palace and next to the cathedral and the armoury, it established the theme of the museum as one of the buildings that constitute the city's image[3] and represent its social structure. In parallel, through the design of the upper-floor loggia that offered a panoramic view of the "new Berlin", including the Lustgarten – now an urban square – Karl Friedrich Schinkel introduced the idea of a museum creating positions from which the city can be seen. With the Neues Museum that followed (1855), the museum became a central theme in the creation of part of the city, the part that is now Museum Island.[4]

Spatial links between the museum and the city are today a recurrent theme in museum architecture, one which is being developed, reinterpreted and combined in experimental designs, with close interaction as the common discursive aim. In general, museums seek to establish continuity with their immediate environment and to stress the building's permeability and approachability by multiple routes and entrances. The pioneering 21st Century Museum of Contemporary Art in the centre of Kanazawa (by Kazuyo Sejima and Ryue Nishizawa of SANAA, 2004), was given a transparent façade and a circular form allowing approach equally from any direction and through different entrances, based on the concept that it should be open to the city like a park. The new project of the Guggenheim Helsinki (by Nicolas Moreau and Hiroko Kusunoki of Moreau Kusunoki Architectes) creatively synthesises a range of techniques so as to seamlessly relate the museum's spatial structure to its urban context. Located in the working port of the South Harbour area, and close to the Market Hall, it takes the form not of a single-volume building but of a carefully arranged cluster of pavilions. It is accessed by eight "entrances" linking different directions and levels, and served by a promenade along the South Harbour, while its upper-floor terrace is the prolongation of a new pedestrian footbridge connecting it to the adjacent Observatory Park and, through this, to the quay. More interestingly, it constitutes a "Fragmented Continuum" (as defined by the title of the project) that continues the urban space by allowing routes to pass through rather than simply leading to the museum, rendering its interior an open space for both museum visitors and urban explorers.

In addition to constructing connections to and from parts of the city to generate movement, museums create continuity with the city through the design of urban spaces adjacent to or within the building, where visitors' paths converge and informal encounters occur. The Centre Pompidou can be seen as their precursor. In 1977 it marked a large-scale urban project, one in which "the building occupied half of the Beaubourg Plateau, the other half being covered by a long plaza" gently sloping downward to the foot of the building to create "a meeting place, a place of assembly, […] a constant focus of life and movement."[5] The ground floor was conceived as an interior courtyard – though it was not a totally open space as in

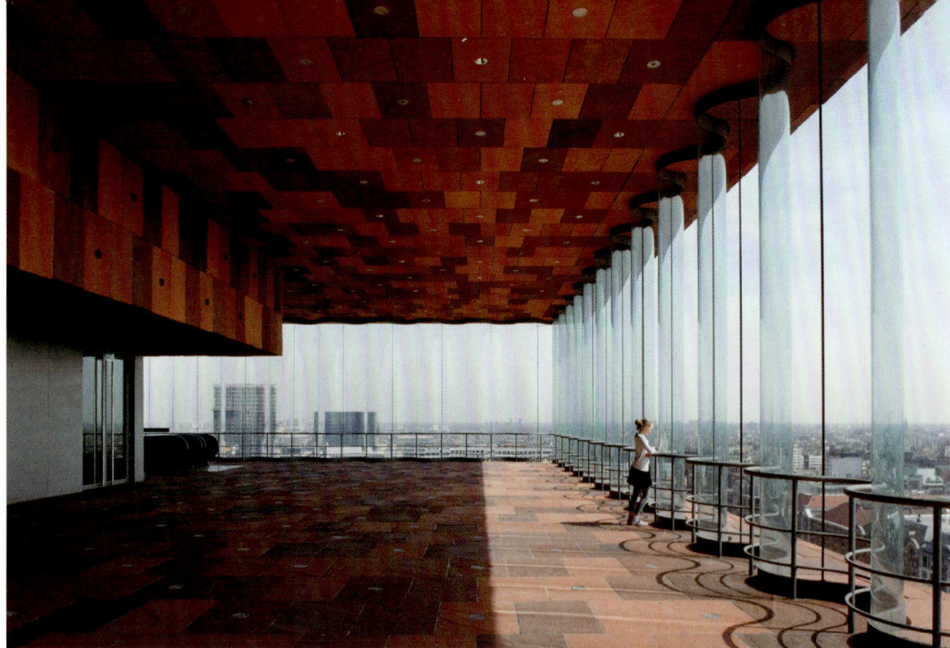

the original design – and was accompanied by a "vertical plaza" on the façade. The vertical plaza was created by the escalator hanging diagonally across the building (which became the Centre Pompidou's signature), in combination with open and glazed circulation spaces on each floor, making the flow of visitors visible as they discovered panoramic views of the city. Inspired perhaps by the complex of public and movement spaces of the Centre Pompidou, in 2000 Tate Modern transformed its main space, the Turbine Hall, into a "covered street",[6] as well as a vast display space, inviting interpretation at that scale by artists. By provoking thinking and "asking questions", the art displayed through a series of commissions of site-specific works (2000–2012) enhanced the social nature of the space and contributed to new forms of community and sociability.

Both the new Nasjonalmuseet for kunst, arkitektur og design (by Klaus Schuwerk, Kleihues + Schuwerk Architects) and the Munchmuseet (by estudio Herreros), in Oslo's waterfront areas, place emphasis on public space. In the new Nasjonalmuseet, the space created by the museum and adjacent buildings serves as a piazzetta (described through its relation with the neighbouring piazza of the city hall), combining art and restaurants and working as an extension of the urban space. In the Munchmuseet, the "covered plaza" of the ground floor is seen as a prolongation of public space, while its transparency enhances its visual continuity with adjacent outdoor spaces. It is extended to the "vertical plaza", along the translucent west façade, with its escalators and circulation areas. As in the Centre Pompidou, visitors' movement becomes a powerful visual theme. In the new Art Gallery of New South Wales, Sydney, designed by SANAA as "a gallery in the gardens", the "Cultural Plaza", a public activity zone, will mediate with the existing building and create "a destination even for those who do not intend to journey inside the Gallery".[7] In Lausanne, the whole project of Plateforme 10 is aimed at creating urbanity: the two new buildings are related to each other and to the existing street pattern to create a complex of public spaces that can be explored in themselves quite apart from the museums.

But museums can also structure their own internal spaces so that they work like the street network of a city. The layout of the 21st Century Museum of Contemporary Art, Kanazawa, is organised as a system of independent galleries forming the museum's core and a system of public spaces as the outer zone, with glazed interior courtyards between them. They are all arranged so that corridor-like linear spaces, connected at right angles, pass among them, creating lines of sight. Some lines traverse the whole building, others are more localised, while the longest lines link to the main entrance space. The "urban" nature of this network facilitates orientation and allows visitors to explore and choose at will. A different interpretation of the idea of structuring museum space so that it works like a city, both in terms of spatial layout and function, is provided by the Guggenheim Helsinki. The continuous space between the pavilions takes the form of squares and routes, shaping a system linking key origins and destinations. It is arranged so as to create two main spatial complexes that are closely connected to each other by the principal route in the layout, while each complex is also visible from the entrances to the pavilions and directly served by two museum entrances. These frequent relations of the "in-between" space both to the pavilions and to the outside suggest that museum space will be used by a mix of people coming with different goals and interests. Intriguingly, by being inspired by the form of cities, the museum acknowledges the alternation, during the visit, of motivation, interest and fatigue; visitors can move about, pause and start again. The layout seems like an explorable urban space, implying informality and the museum visit as a relaxed activity.

The museum as a social space

These design choices affect the social meaning of museum space. The realised and new projects we have discussed allow us to see how the spatial organisation of the museum can affect the way visitors become aware of each other, a key social dimension of museum experience. At a basic level, they suggest a distinction between the intentionally designed public spaces of the museum, and the unprogrammed social effects of its arrangement of space. The public or "gathering" spaces can assume key functions, from playing the role of reference points so as to provide orientation, to working as large-scale circulation spaces that organise visitors' exploration sequences to and from the galleries, and acting as focal points of the visit experience. Also, by being close to the entrance of the building, they relate in and out movement with circulation in the museum, contributing to its sense of liveliness. A particularly clear example of this is the shared ground-floor space of the new building of the Musée de l'Elysée and the mudac, Lausanne, by Manuel and Francisco Aires Mateus. The social and unifying space of the building is shaped as an extension to the urban space, open on all four sides.

Over and above encounters in the public spaces, spatial configuration in itself can have social effects. The layout, by shaping movement patterns in the museum as a whole, creates varying degrees of co-presence among visitors in the different spaces, and so affects the way they become aware of one another throughout the building. In that sense, space generates its own form of community, a "virtual community" based on mutual awareness, prior to active interaction.[8] This is most clearly shown in the urban-type layouts (like the 21st Century Museum of Contemporary Art and the Guggenheim Helsinki): the complex of routes and paths through spaces and pavilions does not simply gather and distribute movement, but empowers visitors by allowing alternative paths, and increases the probability of informal encounter and re-encounter as a by-product of the exploration of space. The more exploratory visitors' movement pattern, the more random their pattern of encounter and the more variable their pattern of co-presence, rendering the whole experience intensely social.

But in many of the cases we have seen there is an additional way in which the spatial configuration acts on the "virtual community": the transparency of spaces and rich cross-visibility make visitors constantly aware of people in other spaces as they move around and explore the museum. Thus, the visibility structure of the layout enhances visual co-awareness, rather than simply spatial co-presence, and so sustains a dense pattern of visual encounter. This intensifies the "theatrical" element of the contemporary museum, where "the 'mise en scène' of visitors becomes part of the 'mise en exposition' of the works of art".[9]

In all these ways, museum space becomes the physical expression of the key museological concepts of openness,

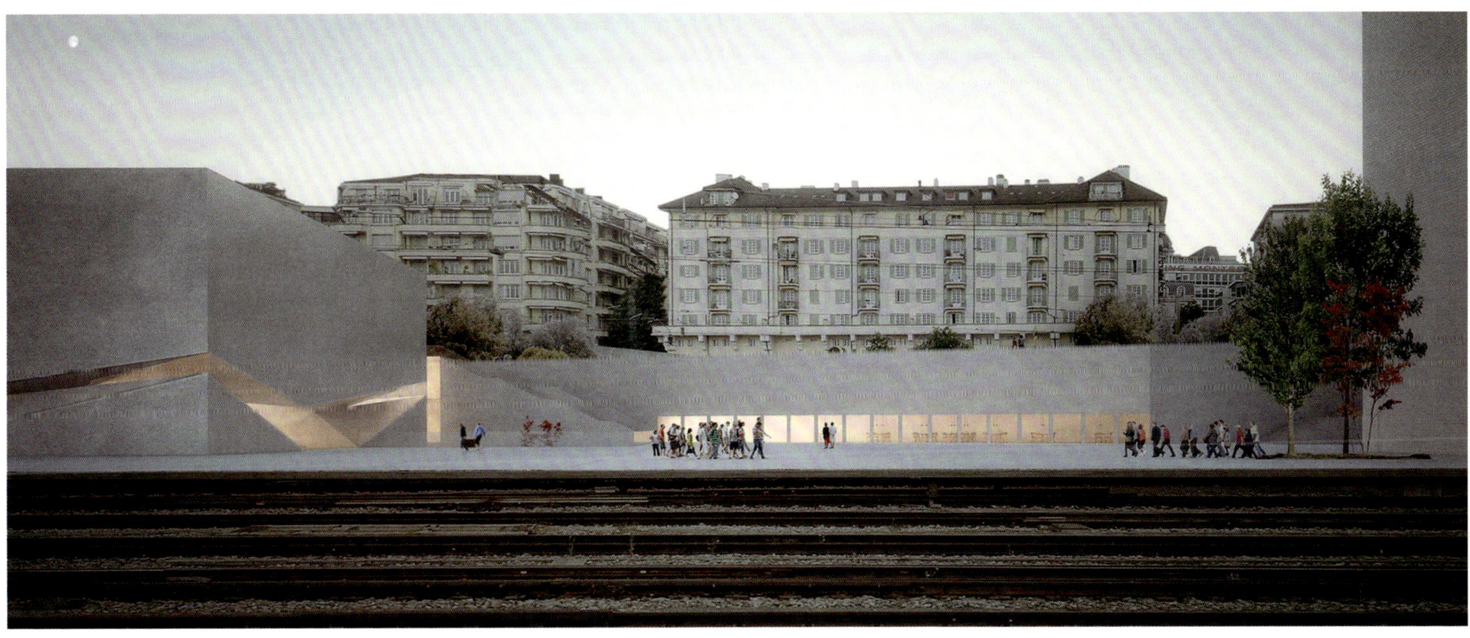

accessibility and "being-in-the-world", in the sense of the museum's being integrated into everyday urban life. It also emphasises the role of the museum as a public building, a social space, rendering dominant collective and shared experiences. As was said of Tate Modern, "the people visiting it and the works of art combine in an interesting dance of value creation: people are moved by what they see and hear in the galleries, while the very fact that there are so many visitors itself contributes to the experience."[10] In this context, it is interesting to reflect that while the Altes Museum was designed as part of the city's "symbolic geography of power",[11] contemporary museums seek to integrate the life of the streets. The social experience of the museum becomes richer in the manner of city space.

The museum as visual symbol and as city "lantern"

No less striking than the spatial relations between the museum and the city are the visual links, both in the sense of the visibility of the museum from the city and of the city from the museum. At the most elementary level, a new museum tends to be today a visually exceptional building, unlike any other, so that it has the potential to act as a symbol of the city. In more subtle ways, its architectural form can make correspondences with other landmark buildings, and act as part of the background to urban life. The new Nasjonalmuseet, Oslo, relates at two levels to its urban context: the lower with the adjacent station buildings (the site was one of Oslo's main train stations), and the higher level with key "monuments", the City Hall and the Akershus fortress. In a similar way, the tower of the Guggenheim Helsinki echoes the city's strong vertical elements such as factory chimneys and the Assumption and Lutheran cathedrals' bell towers. In contrast, the Munchmuseet creates a tension with the neighbouring Opera House through visual themes: its vertical form and the movement of visitors along its façade oppose the horizontal silhouette of the Opera and the movement of people on its roof.

In terms of the inverse relation, the museum constructs positions from which the city can be seen and understood using dedicated upper floors with open visibility as viewing platforms. In Tate Modern, the 360-degree view of London from the top floor of the new Switch House, accessed independently of the galleries, is intended to be a key attraction. In both the new Nasjonalmuseet and the Munchmuseet, Oslo, specially designed spaces are devoted to the panoramic view of the urban and natural landscape. More unexpectedly, the concept of mutual visibility is extended in the new Nasjonalmuseet by way of a large upper-level space designed to be a highly distinctive exhibition setting, which, at the same time, becomes visible to the city as a "lantern". Interestingly, both the Guggenheim Helsinki tower and the Munchmuseet are described as "lighthouses". This architectural idea brings to mind the mediating experience between the visitor, the museum and the city, created by Ofalur Eliasson's permanent work of art, *Your rainbow panorama* (2006–2011), a circular walkway in glass in all the colours of the rainbow, at the top of the ARoS Aarhus Kunstmuseum building. While offering a collective sensory experience for visitors moving along the walkway and perceiving the surrounding urban landscape through changing colour zones, it transforms the museum into "a beacon, visible throughout the city" and "a compass in time and space for its citizens".[12]

The museum as display

Shifting attention from the museum visit as social event to the museum visit as an experience of viewing art, and from the generic function of buildings to organise users' movement to the specific function of museums to display objects, it is of interest first to note that new museum buildings (or extensions of existing ones) often become the starting point for bringing together different collections and proposing new connections and relations. In 2011 a new museum, the Museum aan de Stroom (by Neutelings Riedijk Architects), was created in the port area of Antwerp as part of a major urban renewal project by unifying the collections of three former museums (Ethnographic, Folk and Maritime) and an art collection, with the aim of presenting a synthetic view of the city's history. Treating the collections as one permitted their presentation through universal themes – Display of Power, Metropolis, World Port, Life and Death – and so a fresh reading in terms of the city. Similarly, the new building of the Nasjonalmuseet, Oslo, will bring together the collections of four institutions that merged in 2003 (Nasjonalgalleriet, Museet for samtidskunst, Kunstindustrimuseet, and Nasjonalmuseet – Arkitektur), creating a *"forum artis"*, and the Munchmuseet will integrate both the Munch and the Stenersen collections. At a larger urban scale, the project of Plateforme 10 marks the gathering together of

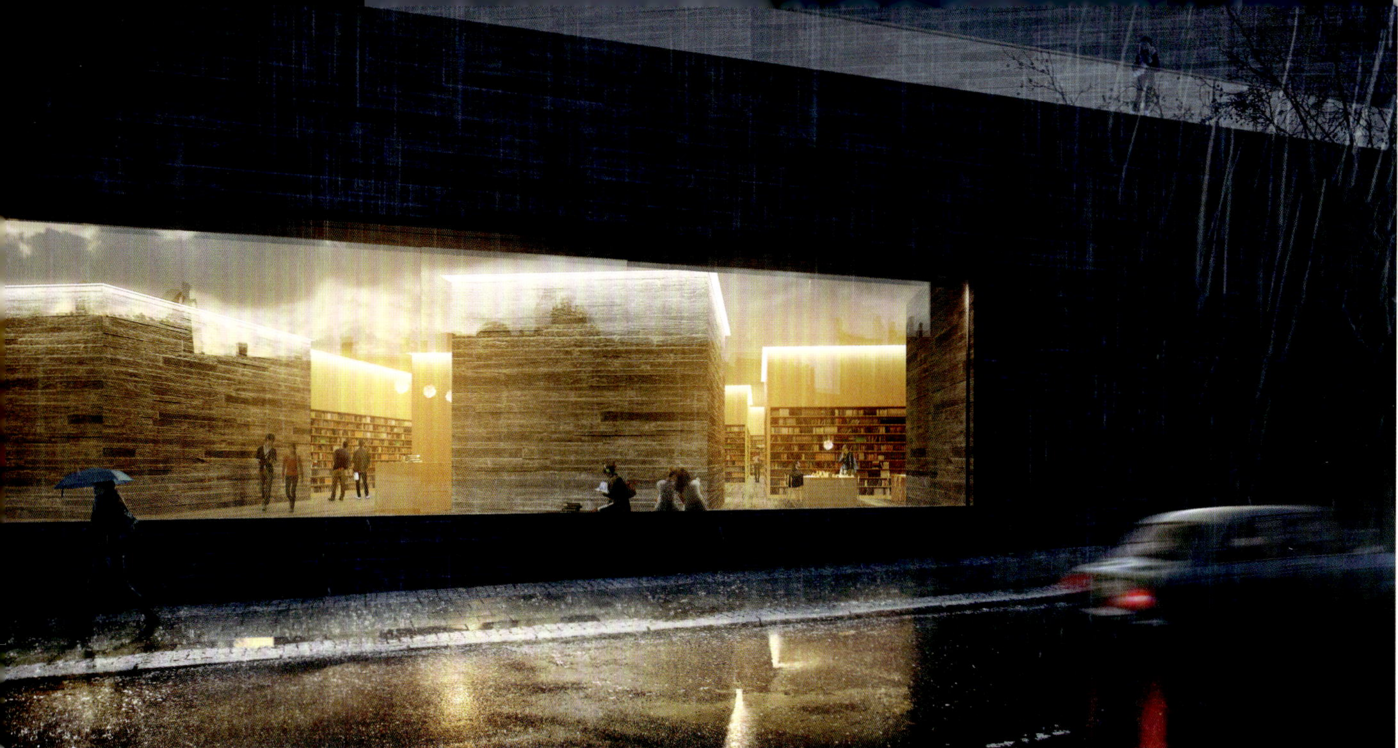

two foundations (Fondation Félix Vallotton and Fondation Toms Pauli) with no fixed exhibition space, and three institutions (mcb-a, Musée de l'Elysée, mudac) that had previously been dispersed in the city of Lausanne.

New buildings are also seen as opportunities for experimenting with novel ways of presenting art, a complementary expression of the way museums address urban communities. With the intention that "meaning can be communicated and experience can be felt by audiences of every kind",[13] displays seek to open up alternative perspectives rather than reflecting well-established knowledge and interpretations, and to involve the viewer in making the links between works. During the gallery's first five years (2000–2005), Tate Modern's displays dispensed with "chronological" progression, and opted for an overview of 20th-century art by adopting four broad themes – Landscape, Still Life, The Nude, History. A shift from the "curatorial" to the "visual" has also marked the new displays of the extended Tate Modern (2016),[14] a mode of grouping which, by handing interpretative initiative to the viewer, can be more exploratory intellectually. The creation of the Louvre-Lens (2012) also was described as "a formidable source of experimentation and inspiration" in that it sought to create "another Louvre" and address new audiences by offering "new keys for understanding".[15] The museum presents highlights of the Louvre collection organised not by departments and schools, as in the Louvre Paris, but under the theme of time. By grouping, in an open space, contemporary works of different cultures and techniques, it "offers the visitor the freedom and pleasure of establishing dialogue with the works of art, a discussion without end, since it is constantly reinvented by his/her patterns of movements".[16]

There is another sense in which visitors are invited to create their own story. Displays are characterised by emphasis on discrete experiences, rather than a global narrative, and the museum itinerary tends to be a non-complex structure, interrelating shorter independent sequences with their own entries and exits. In the new

Tate Modern, several complexes of galleries, bigger or smaller, coexist in parallel, offering different perspectives on art – In the Studio, Artist and Society, Between Object and Architecture, Living Cities – and a degree of choice for viewers. In the Museum aan de Stroom, each floor accommodates a different theme, and so a different approach to the collections and a different local experience for visitors. In the Guggenheim Helsinki, the display space is not a continuous space but pavilions linked to each other in potential sequences, suggested by the positioning of entrances. The new building for the Art Gallery of New South Wales consists of a complex of pavilion-like units. In the mcb-a, Lausanne (by Fabrizio Barozzi and Alberto Veiga) the spaces for both the permanent collections and temporary exhibitions are organised vertically, on two different floors. The new Nasjonalmuseet, Oslo, will accommodate distinct viewing sequences for the collections of art, architecture and design. In all these cases, the architecture of the museum can provide an intelligible framework to facilitate choices and give viewers the power to select what to see.

To the diversity of object arrangements is added the plurality of spatial forms and atmospheres of galleries (as for example in the Guggenheim Helsinki and the Sydney Modern Project), aiming to generate different types of experience in parallel for the visitor. Large spaces interchange with intimate ones, while circulation spaces (as in the new Tate Modern) or other "accidental" places (as in the Sydney Modern Project) are planned as display spaces, expanding our sense of the possibilities for experiencing art. Galleries where visual insulation governs the relationship to the outside are combined with exhibition spaces bringing urban or landscape views indoors, and displaying them in juxtaposition to art.

What seems increasingly consistent is the idea that the experience of the museum location as a *place* tends to become integral to that of viewing art. In certain cases, visual experience of the place becomes part of the display narrative and triggers new modes for interpreting the

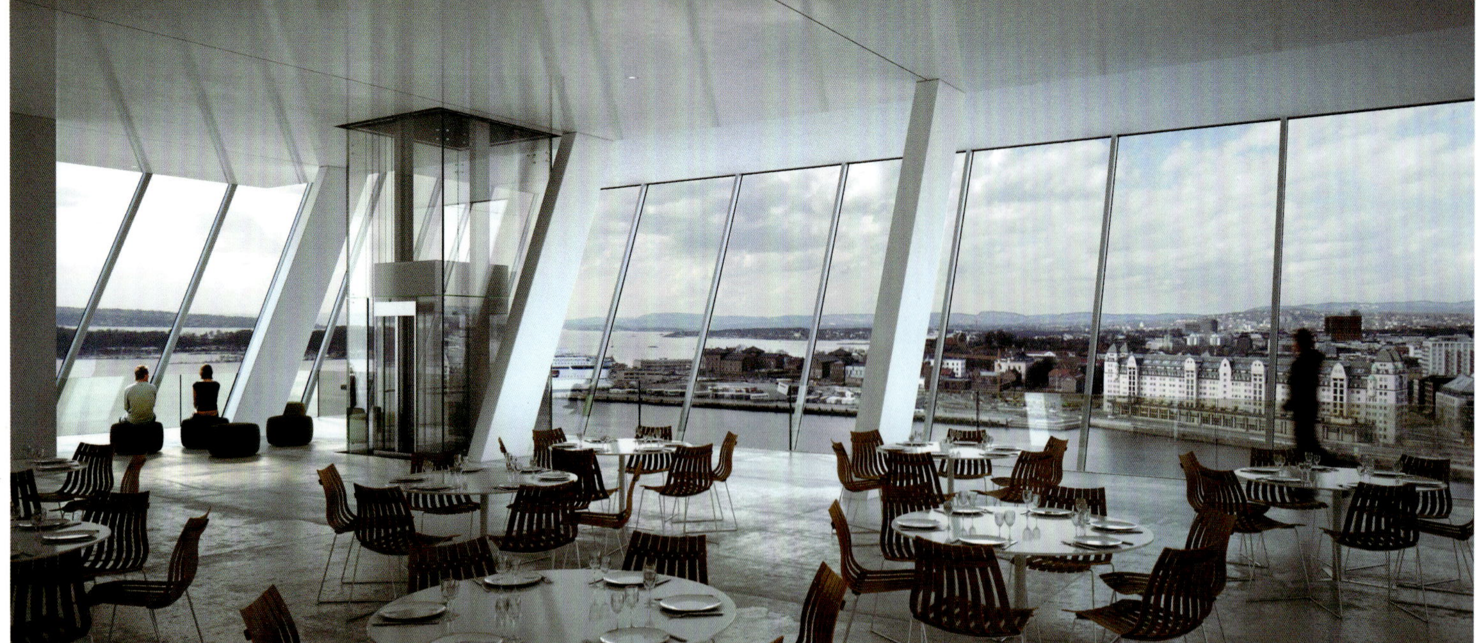

city and its history. In the Acropolis Museum (by Bernard Tschumi Architects, 2009) the design of the building integrates into its lower part archaeological remains of the city from different time periods, which are visible in the museum through transparent floors. In the galleries above, recurrent open views outside merge the experience of objects with the experience of the city. Most powerfully, the top "Parthenon Gallery", through its transparency, makes the Parthenon itself visible, in combination with panoramic views of the contemporary city, rendering it the key exhibit of the museum. So, rather than accentuating the contrast between past and present, the Acropolis Museum brings them together as a place, and creates a sense of history experienced as the present. The Museum aan de Stroom also links the experience of the past with that of the present, but in a different way, complementing and interchanging the stories of objects about the city with the visual experience of the living city itself. The display spaces, described as black boxes because of their visual and spatial isolation, are separated from the public circulation spaces, which are characterised by transparency, openness and light. Organised in a continuous route from the entrance of the building to the top floor, they create the rising spiral "MAS Boulevard", offering changing views of the city, the port and the river, as each floor alters the viewer's visual field by ninety degrees. Thus, visitors can perceive the contemporary urban landscape as the empirical reality against which to co-ordinate the display. These images are then synthesised at the top level of the building, which is devoted only to a panoramic view of the whole city.

In other cases the architecture of the museum alternates the viewing experience of the display with the experience of the physical dimensions and atmosphere of the place, independently of narrative. The linear volume of the new building of the mcb-a takes the place of the early 20th-century locomotive shed of the neighbouring station. At the same time, it maintains key characteristic elements of the shed and integrates them into the new structure, most notably the big window of the façade of the original central nave, which will lie on the axis of the museum entrance. Through its physical form, the museum building recalls the past, so that the visitor's experience of the new museum and its setting is constantly charged by symbolic references to the history of the site's function. In the Sydney Modern Project, the place also plays a pervasive role in the museum experience, but here it takes the form of a natural site. While the existing Art Gallery of New South Wales was entirely surrounded by the Royal Botanic Garden and the Domain, the new Gallery is based on the idea of the interpenetration of the two: art and activities will be extended into the landscape, blurring the boundary between museum and nature, and within the museum display spaces will be linked to the landscape. Views of nature thus become part of the visual aesthetic and so of the total experience of the visit.

All these strategies show that the architecture of the museum can play a key role in the ways art is experienced and meanings are created by and for visitors. This role of museum architecture can be best illuminated by the distinction between the two types of information a cultural message contains: the *semantic information*, meaning its logical content, and the *aesthetic information*, meaning the way the message is expressed.[17] It could be argued that in museums, over and above the semantic information of displays, the visit can become meaningful also through the aesthetic information that the museum adds through the arrangement of objects in the particular exhibition setting, and through the richness of experience generated by the existence of the specific museum. In our cases, meanings arise from different kinds of visual, spatial and conceptual relations created by the museum, and from interactions between visitors and the city, history, ideas, other visitors. These fields of possible meanings are specific to the museum that communicates them, and form a key part of its spatial identity.

Thoughts for the museum of the future

Looking at recent cases and new projects through the lens of the relationship between the museum and the city can perhaps suggest some directions for the museum of the future. Drawing on Manuel Castells's ideas,[18] it could

←   Munchmuseet, Oslo,
    estudio Herreros. Restaurant.

↓   Guggenheim Helsinki,
    Moreau Kusunoki
    Architectes. Restaurant.

be argued that what we are witnessing is the challenge for new museum buildings to contribute to "the reconstruction of public space" and become "spaces of cultural innovation and centres of experimentation", where people learn to communicate through shared experiences. In the contemporary network society, marked, he proposes, by the separation between the "space of flows", the global system of worldwide hyper-communication, and "the space of places", that is of physical localities, characterised by "the individualisation of messages, the fragmentation of societies and a lack of shared codes of communication between particular identities", we could see museums playing a key role as "cultural connectors".

From a museological point of view, this extension of the social role of museums resonates with changes in the idea of the museum as a locus of knowledge: not only with the observation that in museum practice there has been a pervasive shift of focus from the transmission of culturally established knowledge to the creation of new perspectives, but also with recent advances in our understanding that "it is through our bodily perceptions, movements, emotions, and feelings that meaning becomes possible and takes the form it does."[19] As we have seen, over and above what is explicitly presented, meanings are generated by the interaction of visitor and museum, through embodied experiences that engage the senses, in particular sight, in significant ways. This "embodied cognition" approach in museums can be seen in the wider theoretical context of human experience in general. As argued by Mark Johnson in his "embodied theory of meaning", "mind and body are not two things"; "it is the bodily engagement with our environment that makes thought possible."[20]

In this, museum architecture can play a critical role by seeking to create, through physical and spatial design, a layered experience, in which the "proprioceptive, sensory, intellectual, aesthetic and social"[21] are interrelated for the visitor. It is in this sense that the experience of the spaces in the museum can echo that of the city. In conclusion, perhaps unexpectedly, the museum of the future could be paralleled to Aldo Rossi's *Teatro del Mondo* (created for the Venice Biennale 1979), where "the window allowed a constant view of the city and the interior becomes, in this way, part of the city."[22]

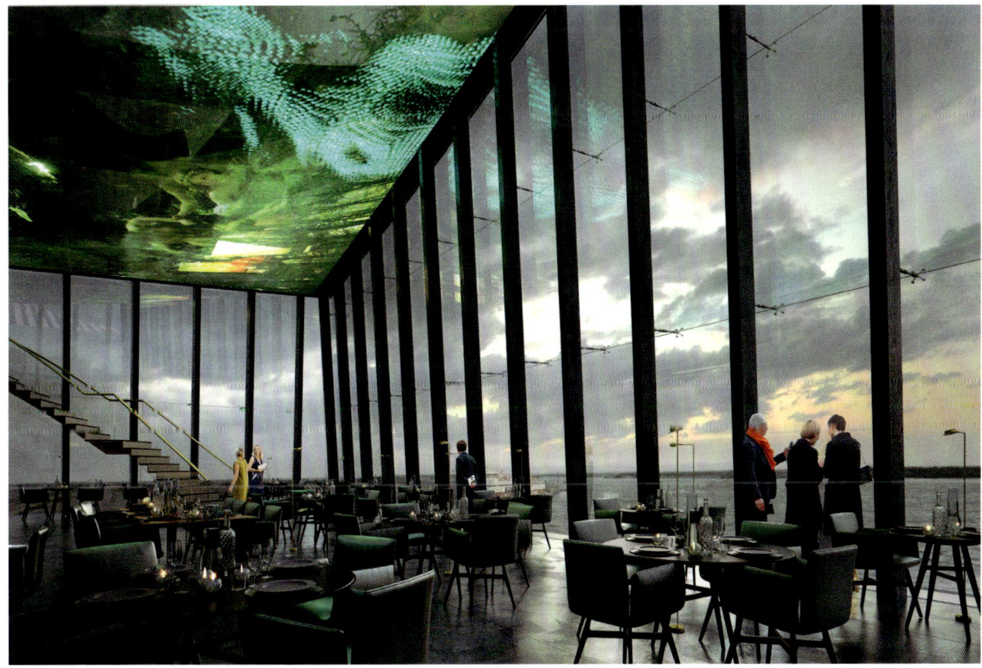

1   Manuel Castells, "Museums in the Information Era: Cultural Connectors of Time and Space", *ICOM News* (2001): 7.

2   See Luca Basso Peressut, "Envisioning 21st Century Museums for Transnational Societies", in *Museums in an Age of Migrations: Questions, Challenges, Perspectives*, ed. Luca Basso Peressut and Clelia Pozzi (Milan: Politecnico di Milano, 2012), 44–45, accessed September 26, 2016, http://www.mela-project.polimi.it/publications/845.htm. Also: Luca Basso Peressut, "Contemporary Museums between Theory and Practice", in *Advancing Museum Practices*, ed. Francesca Lanz and Elena Montanari (Turin: Allemandi, 2014), 148, accessed September 26, 2016, http://www.mela-project.polimi.it/publications/1185.htm.

3   Adrian von Buttlar, "The Museum Island: An Architectural-Historical Overview", in *Museum Island Berlin*, ed. Michael Eissenhauer, Astrid Bähr and Elisabeth Rochau-Shalem (Berlin: Hirmer Publishers, 2012), 100.

4   Gino Malacarne, "Il museo come parte di città", in *L'Architettura del museo con scritti e progetti di Aldo Rossi*, ed. Patricia Montini Zimolo (Milano: CittàStudi, 1995), 102.

5   Quoted in Laurence Castany, ed., *Centre Pompidou, Creation in the Heart of Paris* (Paris: Éditions du Centre Pompidou, 2011), 45.

6   Nicholas Serota, "Tate Modern: The First Decade", in *Tate Modern: The Handbook*, ed. Matthew Gale (London: Tate Publishing, 2012), 12.

7   Sydney Modern Project, *Stage 2 Competition Brief*, Commercial-in-Confidence (January 2015), 62.

8   Bill Hillier et al., "Creating Life: Or Does Architecture Determine Anything?", *Architecture and Comportment/Architecture and Behaviour* 3, no. 3 (1987): 248.

9   Luca Basso Peressut, *Musei: architetture, 1990–2000* (Milan: Motta, 1999), 29.

10 John Holden, "The Cultural Value of Tate Modern", in *Tate Modern: The First Five Years*, ed. Martin Gayford (London: Tate Publishing, 2005), 35.

11 Michaela Giebelhausen, "Introduction: The Architecture of the Museum – Symbolic Structures, Urban Contexts", in *The Architecture of the Museum: Symbolic Structures, Urban Contexts*, ed. Michaela Giebelhausen (Manchester: Manchester University Press, 2003), 5.

12 Olafur Eliasson, "The Future Is Curved", *Architectural Design* 84, no. 5 (2014): 90–91.

13 Francis Morris, "From Then to Now and Back Again: Tate Modern Collection Displays", in *Tate Modern: The Handbook*, 23.

14 Laura Cumming, "Tate Modern's Switch House: Art Comes First", *The Guardian*, June 19, 2016, accessed September 26, 2016, https://www.theguardian.com/artanddesign/2016/jun/19/tate-modern-switch-house-extension-art-comes-first.

15 "Louvre-Lens", Ministère de la Culture et de la Communication, published May 12, 2005, accessed September 26, 2016, http://www.culture.gouv.fr/culture/actualites/dossiers-presse/louvre-lens/louvre-lens.pdf.

16 Adrien Gardère, "La muséographie", in *Louvre Lens*. Press release, 51.

17 The distinction between semantic and aesthetic information is proposed by Abraham A. Moles in *Information Theory and Esthetic Perception* (London and Urbana: University of Illinois Press, 1996), 129–33.

18 Castells, "Museums in the Information Era", 4–7.

19 Mark Johnson, *The Meaning of the Body. Aesthetics of Human Understanding* (Chicago and London: The University of Chicago Press, 2007), ix.

20 Ibid., 278.

21 Nina Levent and Alvaro Pascual-Leone, "Introduction", in *The Multisensory Museum: Cross-disciplinary Perspectives on Touch, Sound, Smell, Memory, and Space*, ed. Nina Levent and Alvaro Pascual-Leone (Lanham: Rowman & Littlefield, 2014), xiii.

22 The *Teatro del Mondo* was a floating pavilion created for the Biennale, based on the idea of the 16th-century floating pavilions, and towed by sea to the Punta della Dogana. See Aldo Rossi, "Teatro del Mondo, 1979", in *Aldo Rossi, Opera Grafica 1973–1995*, ed. Umberto S. Barbieri and Giovanni Bertolotto (Maastricht: Bonnefantenmuseum, 1995), 10.

APPENDIX

Profiles

The information in this section has been provided by the architects.

p. 16
**Smithsonian National Museum of African American History
and Culture (NMAAHC)**

Location: Washington, D.C., USA
Architects: Adjaye Associates, New York/London, USA/UK
Architects in charge: Adjaye Associates (Lead Designer);
    Perkins+Will (Architect of Record)
Design team:
    Freelon Adjaye Bond/SmithGroup
    Structural engineer: Guy Nordeson and Associates, Robert Silman
    Associates; Mechanical engineer: WSP Flack + Kurtz; Sustainability
    consultant: Rocky Mountain Institute; Landscape architect:
    Gustafson Guthrie Nichol; Lighting consultants: Fisher Marantz
    Stone; Acoustics/AV/Theatre/Multi-Media consultants: Shen Milson
    Wilke; Façade consultant: R. A. Heintges & Associates; Security
    consultants: ARUP North America
Type: new museum
Building area: 39,000 sq. m
Exhibition area: 10,815 sq. m
Site area: 20,234 sq. m
Construction period: April 2009–September 2016
Opening date: September 24, 2016
Status: complete
Construction budget: 540 M. USD (about 512 M. EUR)
Owner: Smithsonian Institution
Client: Smithsonian Institution
Number of visitors expected per year: 3 M.
What is displayed in the museum?
    Items reflecting the vast array of African American History
    and Culture
Other museum projects:
    Museum of Contemporary Art (MCA), Denver, USA
    Nobel Peace Centre, Oslo, Norway
    Ethelbert Cooper Gallery of African & African American Art,
    Cambridge, USA
    Studio Museum in Harlem, New York, USA
    Latvian Museum of Contemporary Art, Latvia
Other significant projects:
    Sugar Hill Affordable Housing, New York, USA
    Moscow School of Management SKOLKOVO,
    Francis Gregory and Bellevue Neighbourhood Libraries,
    Washington, D.C., USA

p. 24
Plateforme10

Construction budget of Plateforme10: 180 M. CHF (about 168 M. EUR)

**First phase:
mcb-a (Musée cantonal des Beaux-Arts)**

Location: Lausanne, Switzerland
Architects: Barozzi/Veiga, Barcelona, Spain
Architects in charge: Fabrizio Barozzi, Alberto Veiga, Pieter Janssens
Design team:
    Roi Carrera, Eleonora Maccari, Shin Hye Kwang, Agniezska Samsel,
    Agniezska Suchocka, Verena Recla, Arnau Sastre, Cecilia Vielba,
    Laura Rodriguez, Cristina Porta, Maria Ubach, Marta Grządziel

Type: new building for an existing museum
Building area: 12,450 sq. m
Exhibition area: 3,220 sq. m
Site area: 25,800 sq. m
Project year: 2011
Construction period: 2016–2019
Opening date: 2019
Status: under construction
Owner: État de Vaud/Plateforme10
Client: État de Vaud/Plateforme10
What will be displayed in the museum?
    Permanent art collection of the museum (10,000 pieces)
    and temporary art exhibitions
Other museum projects:
    Graubünden Museum of Fine Arts, Chur, Switzerland
Other significant projects:
    Philharmonic Hall, Szczecin, Poland
    Regulatory Council for the D.O. Ribera del Duero, Roa, Spain
    Auditorium and Congress Centre, Águilas, Spain

**Second phase: "One Museum, Two Museums"
mudac (Musée de design et d'arts appliqués contemporains) and
Musée de l'Elysée (Musée cantonal de la photographie)**

Location: Lausanne, Switzerland
Architects: Manuel Aires Mateus e Francisco Aires Mateus,
    Lisbon, Portugal
Architects in charge: Manuel Aires Mateus, Francisco Aires Mateus,
    Francisco Caseiro
Design team:
    Daniel Lopez, Bernardo Sousa, Luz Jimenez, Christophe Gourdier,
    Nicole Addati, Andrea Auerbach, Diogo Castro Guimaraes,
    Leonardo Marchesi, Vega Solaz Soler, João Ramos, Charles
    Cossement, Olga Sanina, Mariana Mayer
Type: new building for two existing museums
Building area: 14,056 sq. m
Exhibition area: 3,200 sq. m
Site area: 25,800 sq. m
Project year: 2015
Construction period: 2017–2021
Opening date: 2021
Status: under construction
Owner: État de Vaud/Plateforme10
Client: État de Vaud/Plateforme10
What will be displayed in the museums?
    Design and photography permanent collections of the museums
    and temporary exhibitions
Other museum projects:
    Centre de Création contemporaine Olivier Debré, Tours, France
    Library and Cultural Centre, Sines, Portugal
    "Storytelling Museum" restoration and extension of Convento
    de la Trinidad, Málaga, Spain
    Grand Egyptian Museum, Cairo, Egypt
Other significant projects:
    EDP headquarters, Lisbon, Portugal
    Muslim Centre, Bordeaux, France
    Architecture Faculty – Catholic University of Louvain, Belgium
    Houses for eldery people, Alcácer do Sal, Portugal

p. 38
Long Museum West Bund

Location: Xuhui District, Shanghai, China
Architects: Atelier Deshaus, Shanghai, China
Architect in charge: Liu Yichun
Design team:
    Liu Yichun, Chen Yifeng, Wang Longhai, Wang Weishi,
    Wu Zhenghui, Wang Xuepei, Chen Kun
Type: new museum
Building area: 33,007 sq. m
Exhibition area: 8,020 sq. m
Site area: 19,337 sq. m
Project year: 2011
Construction period: April 2012–March 2014
Opening date: March 28, 2014
Status: complete
Construction budget: 58 M. USD (about 55 M. EUR)
Owner: Long Museum
Client: Shanghai Xuhui Waterfront Development Investment Co. Ltd
Number of visitors: 48,530 from January 2016 to July 2016
What is displayed in the museum?
    Contemporary art and Chinese ancient art
Other museum projects:
    Taizhou Contemporary Art Museum, Taizhou, China
    Qintai Art Museum, Wuhan, China
    Jingmen Art Museum, Jingmen, China
Other significant projects:
    Xiayu Kindergarden, Qingpu, Shanghai, China
    Kindergarten of Jiading New Town, Jiading, Shanghai, China
    Yachang Art Centre, Shanghai, China

p. 46
Kunstmuseum Basel Extension

Location: Basel, Switzerland
Architects: Christ & Gantenbein, Basel, Switzerland
Architects in charge: Emanuel Christ, Christoph Gantenbein
Project leaders: Julia Tobler, Michael Bertschmann,
    Stephanie Hirschvogel
Design team:
    Cloé Gattigo, Thomas Gläss, Thomas Grahammer, Christoph
    Hiestand, Petra Jossen, Daan Koch, Astrid Kühn, Marcus Müller,
    Patrick Reuter, Anette Schick, Louis Schiess, Jennifer Schmachten-
    berg, Anne Katharina Schulze, Kai Timmermann, Francisco Moura
    Veiga, Christina Wendler, Jan Zachmann
Type: extension
Building surface: 1,582 sq. m
Gross floor area: 11,481 sq. m
Exhibition area: 2,555 sq. m
Site area: 3,636 sq. m
Project year: 2010
Construction period: 2012–2016
Opening date: April 2016
Status: complete
Construction budget: 100 M. CHF (about 93.9 M. EUR)
Owner: Municipality of the City of Basel, Immobilien Basel-Stadt
Client: Construction and Transport Department of the Canton Basel-
    Stadt, Town Planning and Architecture, Building Department
Number of visitors expected per year: 300,000
What is displayed in the museum?
    Fine arts (special exhibitions and permanent display)
Other museum projects:
    Swiss National Museum extension and renovation, Zurich,
    Switzerland
    Wallraf-Richartz-Museum extension, Cologne, Germany
    Lindt Chocolate Competence Centre, Kilchberg, Switzerland

Other significant projects:
    Ancient Tree, Jinhua, China
    Swiss Church, London, UK
    Cerro del Obispo Lookout Point, Ruta del Peregrino, Mexico

p. 54
Naga Site Museum

Location: Naga, Sudan
Architect: David Chipperfield Architects Berlin, Germany
Design team:
    Partners in charge: David Chipperfield, Martin Reichert, Alexander
    Schwarz (design lead); Project architects: Thomas Benk, Michael
    Freytag; Project team: Felix Buschinger, Elisa Giusti, Pascal Maas,
    Antonia Schlegel
Type: new museum
Building area: 1,400 sq. m
Exhibition hall: 278.5 sq. m
Inner courtyard: 410 sq. m
Loggia: 110.5 sq. m
Project year: 2008
Status: in the planning phase
Client: Verein zur Förderung des Ägyptischen Museums Berlin e.V.
What will be displayed in the museum?
    Excavations from the site. Naga was a religious centre during the
    Meriotic Empire (approximately 300 BC–AD 300).
Other museum projects:
    Gallery building "Am Kupfergraben 10", Berlin, Germany
    Museum of Modern Literature, Marbach am Neckar, Germany
    Neues Museum, Museum Island, Berlin, Germany
    Museum Folkwang, Essen, Germany
    River and Rowing Museum, Henley-on-Thames, UK
    Turner Contemporary, Margate, UK
    The Hepworth Wakefield, West Yorkshire, UK
    Museo Jumex, Mexico City, Mexico
    Saint Louis Art Museum, Saint Louis, Missouri, USA
    Liangzhu Museum, Liangzhu Cultural Village, China
Other significant projects:
    America's Cup Building "Veles e Vents", Valencia, Spain
    Ninetree Village, Hangzhou, China
    James-Simon-Galerie, Museum Island, Berlin, Germany

p. 62
Munchmuseet (The New Munch Museum)

Location: Bjørvika, Oslo, Norway
Architects: estudio Herreros, Madrid, Spain
Architects in charge: Juan Herreros, Jens Richter
Design team:
    Architecture: estudio Herreros
    Consultants: Local architect: LPO ARKITEKTER; Project managers:
    ÅF ADVANSIA, Jard Bringedal, Nina Dillingøen, Geir Arne Hansen,
    Anders Fjeld, Toralf Hystad, Per Daniel Pedersen; General engineer:
    KULTURPLAN BJØRVIKA [MULTICONSULT, HJELLNES CONSULT,
    BREKKE & STRAND AKUSTIKK], Nils Erik Forsén, Svein Nielsen;
    BIM manager: Joakim Rud Nilsen; Structure: Pål A Thomas, Florian
    Kosche, Morten Ødegård; MEP: Anders Netland, Jonas Aune,
    Gunnar Brevig, Finn Lysnæs-Larsen, Bente Hauknes; Lighting:
    Jan Helge Drabløs, Silje Thorsager Østby, Maria Carmen Øfsthus;
    Fire safety: Lars Erik Sothe, Eivind Løken; Building physics: Erik
    Algaard, Grete Kjeldsen; Acoustics: Jannicke Olshausen; Logistics:
    Rolv Lea; Façade: IDOM (competition), ARUP (schematic design),
    BOLLINGER + GROHMAN (construction documents), Daniel Pfanner,
    Tobias Jarosch; Sustainability: ASPLAN VIAK, Per F Jørgensen,
    Espen Løken; ICT: RAMBØLL NORGE, Sigrun Vaage, Knut Bojer-
    Letrud, Jørgen Kirvang Johansen; Event consultant: Nils Gunnerud;

Security: COWI, Randmod Omarhaug, Geir Sjøtner; Kitchens: VIDAR
BØE; Doors: DØRTEKNIKK AS, Tor Erik Sandvik; Façade maintenance:
HØYDEN, Niclas Risvoll; Cost Consultant: AS BYGGANALYSE, Jens
Røren Strand; Interiors: SCENARIO, Trine Vibeke Roald, Cathrine
Beatrix Andreassen, Bjørn Fredrik Gjerstad; Landscape: Thor-
björn Andersson (competition), SLA (design development), Hanne
Bruun Møller
Type: new building for an existing museum
Building area: 26,300 sq.m
Exhibition area: 4,455 sq.m
Site area: 6,800 sq.m
Project year: 2008–2009
Construction period: August 2015–2019
Opening date: 2019
Status: under construction
Construction budget: 2,012 M. NOK (about 226 M. EUR)
Owner: Oslo municipality
Client: Oslo municipality
Number of visitors expected: 500,000
    (for the first year after opening of the new building)
What will be displayed in the museum?
    28,000 original works of art from Edvard Munch, altogether about
    45,000 museum objects included in the permanent collection of the
    Munch Museum
Other museum projects:
    Museo Nacional Centro de Arte Reina Sofía's Exhibition Spaces,
    Madrid, Spain
    MALBA Museo de Arte Latinoamericano de Buenos Aires, Argentina
    Carreras Múgica Contemporary Art, Bilbao, Spain
    SOLO Space for Contemporary Art, Madrid, Spain
Other significant projects:
    Ágora Congress Centre, Bogotá, Colombia
    Intermodal Station, Santiago de Compostela, Spain
    Ecocite, Marseilles, France

p. 70
MONA Museum of Old and New Art

Location: Berriedale, Tasmania
Architects: Fender Katsalidis Architects, Australia, Melbourne
Architect in charge: Nonda Katsalidis
Design team:
    Karl Fender, James Pearce, Kathie Hall, Roland Catalani, Andrew
    Walker, Falk Peuser, Wayne King, Jessica Lee, Shem Kelder, Eve
    Sayer, Daniel Coldin, Tom Robertson, Robyn Bartley, Nicolina Iuliano
Type: new museum
Building area: 9,500 sq.m
Exhibition area: 6,500 sq.m
Site area: 95,050 sq.m
Project year: 2007
Construction period: three years
Opening date: January 21, 2011
Status: complete
Owner: David Walsh AO
Client: MONA Museum of Old and New Art
Number of visitors per year: 350,000
What is displayed in the museum?
    Antiquities and contemporary artwork from around the world
Other museum projects:
    Bendigo Art Gallery, Victoria, Australia
    Ian Potter Museum of Art, Melbourne, Victoria, Australia
Other significant projects:
    Eureka Tower, Melbourne, Victoria, Australia
    NewActon Precinct, Canberra, ACT, Australia
    Merdeka PNB118, Kuala Lumpur, Malaysia

p. 78
Zayed National Museum

Location: Abu Dhabi, United Arab Emirates
Architects: Foster + Partners, London, UK
Architect in charge: Gerard Evenden
Design team: Norman Foster, David Nelson, Gerard Evenden,
    Toby Blunt, Martin Castle, Ross Palmer, Marilu Sicoli, Dara Towhidi,
    Andrew King, Munehiko Yokomatsu, Florian Rieger
Type: new museum
Gross floor area: 38,000 sq.m
Net internal museum area: 19,483 sq.m
Project year: 2007
Construction period: 2009–2020 (expected completion year)
Opening date: 2020 (expected completion year)
Status: under construction
Owner: Tourism Development + Investment Company
Client: Tourism Development + Investment Company
What will be displayed in the museum?
    The history, culture and social and economic transformation
    of the Emirates
Other museum projects:
    Sainsbury Centre for Visual Arts, Norwich, UK
    American Air Museum, Cambridge, UK
    Addition to Joslyn Art Museum, Omaha, USA
    Great Court at the British Museum, London, UK
    Museum of Fine Arts, Boston, USA
    Imperial War Museum, London, UK
    Smithsonian Institution, National Portrait Gallery, Washington, D.C.,
    USA
Other significant projects:
    30 St. Mary Axe, London, UK
    Millau Viaduct, Millau, France
    Reichstag, New German Parliament, Berlin, Germany

p. 82
Zeitz Museum of Contemporary Art Africa

Location: Cape Town, South Africa
Architects: Heatherwick Studio, London, UK
Project architect: Stepan Martinovsky
Design team:
    Thomas Heatherwick, Stepan Martinovsky, Mat Cash, Simona Auteri,
    Ruggero Bruno Chialastri, Yao Jen Chuang, Francis Field, Sarah Gill,
    Xuanzhi Huang, Changyeob Lee, Julian Liang, Débora Mateo, Stefan
    Ritter, Luke Snow, Ondrej Tichý
Type: renovation and new museum
Building area: 9,500 sq.m
Exhibition area: 6,000 sq.m
Project year: 2013
Construction period: expected three years
Opening date: expected 2017
Status: under construction
Construction budget: 500 M. ZAR (about 36 M. EUR)
Owner: V&A Waterfront
Client: V&A Waterfront
What will be displayed in the museum?
    The Zeitz Collection, the museum's permanent collection
    and travelling exhibitions
Other significant projects:
    Garden Bridge, London, UK
    Pier55, New York, USA
    Google Mountain View, California, USA

p. 88
The Palestinian Museum

Location: Birzeit, West Bank, Palestine
Architects: Heneghan Peng Architects, Dublin, Ireland
Director in charge: Roisin Heneghan
Project architect: Conor Sreenan
Design team:
    Concept/Scheme design:
    Architecture: Heneghan Peng Architects; Landscape architect:
    Lara Zureikat; Project managers: Projacs International; CS/MEP/Fire:
    ARUP; QS: Davis Langdon/AECOM; Concept façade: T/E/S/S;
    Concept lighting: Bartenbach Lichtlabor
    Tender/Construction stage:
    Architecture: Heneghan Peng Architects; Landscape architect: Lara
    Zureikat; Project managers: Projacs International; CS/MEP/Fire/QS:
    Arabtech Jardaneh
Type: new museum
Building area: 3,500 sq.m
Exhibition area: 475 sq.m (Black Box), 165 sq.m (Glass Gallery),
    30,000 sq.m (Garden Gallery)
Site area: 40,000 sq.m
Project year: 2011
Construction period: January 2014–May 2016
Opening date: 18 May 2016
Status: complete
Construction budget: 18 M. USD (about 17 M. EUR) +
Owner: Palestinian Museum & Welfare Association/Taawon
Client: Palestinian Museum & Welfare Association/Taawon
Number of visitors expected per year: 100,000
What is displayed in the museum?
    Permanent and temporary exhibitions with archaeological,
    ethnographic and contemporary art collections.
Other museum projects:
    Grand Egyptian Museum, Giza, Cairo, Egypt
    National Centre for Contemporary Arts, Moscow, Russia
    Canadian Canoe Museum – Peterborough, Ontario, Canada
Other significant projects:
    National Gallery of Ireland, Dublin, Ireland
    Giant's Causeway Visitor Centre, Antrim, Northern Ireland
    Greenwich Library and School of Architecture, London, UK

p. 96
**Nasjonalmuseet for kunst, arkitektur og design
(The National Museum of Art, Architecture and Design)**

Location: Oslo, Norway
Architect: Klaus Schuwerk, Kleihues + Schuwerk Architects, Naples, Italy
Design team:
    Anna Zeuthen Andersen, Carl Johan Andersson, Maria Chiara
    Baldassarre, Hans Bennetzen, Daniela Büter, Paolo Casaburi, Jan
    Dinnebier, Helge Garke, Claudia Gheorge, Dirk Hagenow, Markus
    Helbach, Martim Enes Dias, Benjamin Hummitzsch, Jan Kleihues,
    Anna Kostreva, Johannes Kressner, Giampiero Lagnese, Oyvind
    Ljosland, Oystein Lovholt, Stephan Märker, Siri Meisal, Joana Morim,
    Massimo Negri, Nils Nüchter, Inés Oliveira, Peter Osburg, Alexander
    Perackis, Arne Qvenild, Martin Reichenbach, Eduardo Caetano Reis,
    Arnstein Sande, Claudia Sasso, Klaus Schuwerk, Astrid Seeberg,
    Cecilie Simonsen, Andreas Steinmann, Robert Stüdemann, Hermann
    Sturmberger, Veronika Weber, Alexander Waimer, Nicolas Winklmair,
    Philipp Zora
Type: new building for several existing museums
Building area: 54,600 sq.m
Exhibition area: 13,000 sq.m
Site area: 18,100 sq.m
Project year: 2010

Construction period: 2014–2019
Opening date: 2020
Status: under construction
Construction budget: 720 M. EUR
Owner: State of Norway
Client: Statsbygg
Number of visitors expected per year: 1 M.
What will be displayed in the museum?
    Art (older and contemporary), arts and crafts, design and architecture
Other museum projects:
    Depot of the Museum of Labour and Industry, Rodengo Saiano, Italy
    Museo dell'Industria e del Lavoro, Brescia, Italy
    Betile – Museo dell'art nuragica e dell'arte contemporanea,
    Cagliari, Italy
    Museum of Polish History, Warsaw, Poland
Other significant projects:
    Mystetskyi Arsenal, Kiev, Ukraine
    Nuovo Impianto Natatorio, Brescia, Italy

p. 104
Pingtan Art Museum

Location: Pingtan, China
Architects: MAD Architects, Beijing, China
Architects in charge: Ma Yansong, Dang Qun, Yosuke Hayano
Design team:
    Zhao Wei, Huang Wei, Liu Jiansheng, Jei Kim, Li Jian,
    Li Guangchong, Alexandre Sadeghi
Type: new museum
Building area: 40,000 sq.m
Site area: 32,000 sq.m
Project year: 2011
Status: pending, yet to be realised
What would have been displayed in the museum?
    Private art collections
Other museum projects:
    Ordos Art & City Museum, Ordos, Inner Mongolia, China
    China Wood Sculpture Museum, Harbin, China
Other significant projects:
    Absolute Towers, Mississauga, Ontario, Canada
    Harbin Opera House, Harbin, Heilongjiang, China
    Lucas Museum of Narrative Art, Chicago, USA

p. 110
Guggenheim Helsinki, Art in the City

Location: Helsinki, Finland
Architects: Moreau Kusunoki Architectes, Paris, France
Design team:
    Lead architect: Moreau Kusunoki
    Directors: Nicolas Moreau, Hiroko Kusunoki
    Sammy Vormus, Clement Talbot, Patrick Kouaghu,
    Nicolas Delmas, Maxime Kreiter, Mariana Duarte,
    Risako Sekine, Jules Giraudeau, Elise Laudet, Nare Shin
    Associated architect (for stage 1): Tomoyo Arimoto
Consultants:
    Museum and art consultant: Bogner.cc, Dieter Bogner; Engineering:
    Arup Germany, Team lead: Jan Wurm; Structure: Carsten Hein, MEP:
    Mikal Ahmed, Façade and material: Charlotte Heesbeen, Light-
    ing: Paula Longato; Local architect (for stage 2): Huttunen Lipasti
    Pakkanen Architects, Pekka Pakkanen; Fire consultant: KK-Palokon-
    sultti; Quantity surveyor: A insinoorit; Acoustic: Theater project,
    Sebastien Jouan
Type: new museum
Building area: 12,437 sq.m

Exhibition area: 4,168 sq. m
Site area: 13,000 sq. m
Project year: 2014
Opening date: undefined at this stage
Status: undefined at this stage
Construction budget: 130 M. EUR
Owner: City of Helsinki, State of Finland
Client: City of Helsinki, State of Finland, Guggenheim Helsinki
    Supporting Foundation
Number of visitors expected per year: 500,000 to 550,000
What will be displayed in the museum?
    Guggenheim Foundation's art collection and local artists' work
Other museum projects:
    House of Culture and Memories, Cayenne, French Guiana
    Contemporary Art Centre, the FRAC in Marseilles
    (with Kengo Kuma), France
    Contemporary Art Centre, the FRAC in Besançon
    (with Kengo Kuma), France
Other significant projects:
    Paris High Court Plaza, Paris, France
    University of Savoie, Polytech Annecy-Chambéry, France
    Beauvais Theatre, Beauvais, France

p. 118
China Comic and Animation Museum

Location: Hangzhou, China
Architects: MVRDV, Netherlands, Rotterdam
Architects in charge: Winy Maas, Jacob van Rijs, Nathalie de Vries
Design team:
    Wenchian Shi, Nacho Velasco, Wing Yun, Pepijn Bakker, Monika
    Kowaluk, Javier Gigosos, Renske van der Stoep, Stefan de Koning,
    Hui Hsin Liao, Rune Veile, Doris Strauch, Maria Lopez, Arjen Ketting,
    John Tsang, Aser Gimenez, Juras Lasovsky and Suchi Vora
Type: new museum
Building area: 32,000 sq. m
Exhibition area: 10,000 sq. m
Site area: 13.7 ha
Project year: 2011
Status: no current plans to progress this design
Construction budget: 92 M. EUR
Client: Hangzhou White Horse Lake Creative Town, Hangzhou, China
What would have been displayed in the museum?
    Various forms of comics and animations
Other museum projects:
    Ragnarock Museum for Rock Music, Roskilde, Denmark
    Depot Boijmans van Beuningen, Rotterdam, Netherlands
    Cultural Centre Matsudai, Japan
    Entrance Stedelijk Museum Schiedam, Netherlands
Other significant projects:
    Markthal, Rotterdam, Netherlands
    EXPO 2000 Netherlands Pavilion, Hannover, Germany
    Villa VPRO, Hilversum, Netherlands

p. 126
Sydney Modern Project

Location: Sydney, Australia
Architects: SANAA, Japan, Tokyo
Architects in charge: Kazuyo Sejima, Ryue Nishizawa
Design team:
    Asano Yagi, Yumiko Yamada, Ichio Matsuzawa, Hyunsoo Kim
Type: extension
Building area: 20,012 sq. m

Exhibition area: 8,973 sq. m
Site area: 31,417 sq. m
Project year: 2015
Construction period: 2019–2021
Opening date: December 2021
Status: in the design phase
Client: Art Gallery of New South Wales
Number of visitors expected per year: 2 M.
What will be displayed in the museum?
    Indigenous art as well as contemporary Australian and
    international art from the last fifty years
Other museum projects:
    21st Century Museum of Contemporary Art Kanazawa,
    Kanazawa, Japan
    Toledo Museum of Art, Glass Pavilion, Toledo, Ohio, USA
    New Museum of Contemporary Art, New York, USA
    Louvre-Lens, France
Other significant projects:
    Serpentine Pavilion, London, UK
    Rolex Learning Centre, EPFL, Lausanne, Switzerland
    Grace Farms, New Canaan, Connecticut, USA

p. 134
Kurdistan Museum

Location: Erbil, Iraq
Architects: Studio Libeskind, New York, USA
Architect in charge: Daniel Libeskind
Design team:
    Architect: Studio Libeskind; Exhibition designer: Haley Sharpe
    Design; Structural engineer: Expedition, mechanical and environ-
    mental engineer: Atelier Ten; Project managers: Jackson Coles;
    Consultants for landscape and botany: Royal Botanic Gardens, Kew;
    Development, management and content production: RWF World;
    Project director: Tim Renwick
Type: new museum
Building area: 19,000 sq. m
Exhibition area: 4,700 sq. m
Site area: 16,600 sq. m
Project year: 2009
Opening date: undefined at that stage
Status: in the design phase
Construction budget: 126 M. USD (about 119 M. EUR)
Owner: Kurdistan Regional Government
Client: Kamko
Number of visitors expected per year: 500,000
What will be displayed in the museum?
    Permanent and temporary exhibitions about Kurdish history,
    art and culture
Other museum projects:
    Denver Art Museum, Denver, Colorado, USA
    Jewish Museum, Berlin, Germany
    Imperial War Museum, Manchester, United Kingdom
    Royal Ontario Museum, Toronto, Canada
    Felix Nussbaum Haus, Osnabruck, Germany
    Danish Jewish Museum, Copenhagen, Denmark
    Military History Museum, Dresden, Germany
    Comtemporary Jewish Museum, San Francisco, California, USA
    Modern Art Centre, Vilinus, Lithuania
    Zhang Zhidong and Modern Industrial Museum, Wuhan, China
    The Wohl Centre, Ramat-Gan, Israel
    Studio Weil, Mallorca, Spain
Other significant projects:
    World Trade Center Masterplan, New York, USA
    Reflections, Keppel Bay, Singapore

p. 142
Genesis Museum

Location: Beijing, China
Architects: Tadao Ando Architect & Associates, Osaka, Japan
Architect in charge: Tadao Ando
Design team: Masataka Yano, Kazutoshi Miyamura
Type: new museum
Building area: 8,417 sq.m
Site area: 27,310 sq.m
Project year: 2012
Construction period: from September 2014
Opening date: 2018
Status: under construction
Owner: Genesis Property (Beijing) Co., Ltd.
Client: Genesis Property (Beijing) Co., Ltd.
What will be displayed in the museum?
    Contemporary art
Other museum projects:
    Pinault Collection – Bourse de Commerce, Paris, France
    He Museum, Foshan, China
    Century Museum, Beijing, China
Other significant projects:
    I.S.A. Project, Bologna, Italy
    Valser Path, Vals, Switzerland
    Art gallery in Chicago, USA

p. 150
Meixi Lake International Culture and Arts Centre

Location: Changsha, Hunan Province, China
Architects: Zaha Hadid Architects, London, UK
Architects in charge:
Design: Zaha Hadid, Patrik Schumacher
Project directors: Simon Yu, Woody Yao
Project associate: Eddie Can

Design team:
    Zhenjiang Guo, Charles Kwan, Jinqi Huang, Neil Sansom, Pravin
    Ghosh, Thomas Jensen, Wandy Mulia, Uli Schifferdecker, Fei Wang,
    Justin Kelly, Adrian Aguirre Herrera, Aurora Santana, Koren Sin,
    Johanna Huang, Yifan Zhang Collin Spelts, Fei Liang, Adam Fingrut
    Yitzhak Samun, Mono Tung, Wei You
Museum design:
    Tariq Khayyat, Kutbuddin Nadiadi, Diego Rossel, Gerry Cruz, Matteo
    Melioli, Xiaosheng Li, Yuxi Fu, Thomas Jensen, Matthew Johnson,
    Justin Kelly, Drew Merkle
Competition team:
    Project architect: Tiago Correia
    Victor Orive, Fabiano Continanza, Zhenjiang Guo, Danilo Arsic,
    Ines Fontoura, Rafael González, Alejandro Díaz, Jimena Araiza
Concept development:
    Hannes Schafelner, Philipp Ostermaier, Jakub Klaska, Maren Klasing,
    Saman Saffarian, Martin Krcha, Maria Tsironi, Spyridon Kaprinis
Type: new museum
Building area (for all three buildings, including the art museum):
    125,000 sq.m
Exhibition area: 8,650 sq.m
Site area: 99,400 sq.m
Project year: 2012
Construction period: 2013–2017
Opening date: late 2017
Status: in construction
Construction budget: 2.35 Billion RMB (about 323 M. EUR)
Owner: Changsha
Client: Meixihu Investment (Changsha) Co. Ltd.
What will be displayed in the museum?
    Contemporary and cultural arts
Other museum projects:
    Rosenthal Center for Contemporary Art, Cincinnati, USA
    MAXXI: Museum of XXI Century Arts, Rome, Italy
    Riverside Museum, Glasgow, Scotland
    Messner Mountain Museum Corones (MMM Corones), Kronplatz,
    South Tyrol, Italy

Bibliography

Articles and Essays

"Declaration on the Importance and Value of Universal Museums 2002".
In *Witnesses to History: A Compendium of Documents and Writings
on the Return of the Cultural Objects*, edited by Lyndel V. Prott,
116–17. Paris: UNESCO, 2009.

Adorno, Theodor W. "Valéry Proust Museum". In idem, *Prisms*, translated
by Shierry Weber Nicholsen and Samuel Weber, 175–85. Cambridge,
MA: MIT Press, 1982.

Avery, Jill. "The Tate's Digital Transformation". *Harvard Business School
Case* 314-122, April 2014.

Baker, Janice. "Out of the Wilderness (MONA): Critically Engaging with
the Profound Art Encounter". In *The Challenge of the Object*, edited
by G. Ulrich Grossmann and Petra Krutisch, 394–97. Nuremberg:
Verlag des Germanischen Nationalmuseums, 2013.

Bal, Mieke. "Telling, Showing, Showing Off". *Critical Inquiry* 18, no. 3
(1992): 556–94.

Baus, Ursula. "David Chipperfield und die Bauherren seiner Museen".
In *DAM Jahrbuch*, edited by Deutsches Architektur-Museum, 18–25.
Munich: Prestel, 2005.

Benjamin, Walter. "The Work of Art in the Age of Its Technological
Reproducibility". In *The Work of Art in the Age of Its Technological
Reproducibility and Other Writings on Media*, edited by Michael W.
Jennings, Brigid Doherty and Thomas Y. Levin, 19–55. Cambridge,
MA, and London: Belknap Press of Harvard University Press, 2008.

Betsky, Aaron. "Introduction: Beyond 89 Degrees". In *The Complete
Zaha Hadid*, edited by Zaha Hadid and Aaron Betsky. London:
Thames & Hudson, 2013.

Borin, Elena, and Ivan Paunović. "The Case of Louvre-Lens: Regional
Regeneration through Cultural Innovation". In *Sitcon: Singidunum
International Tourism Conference*, 248–51. Belgrade: Singidunum
University, 2015.

Bourdieu, Pierre. "The Forms of Capital". In *Handbook of Theory and
Research for the Sociology of Education*, edited by John Richardson,
241–58. New York: Greenwood, 1986.

Buchanan, Peter. "The Urban Room". In *On Foster … Foster On*, edited
by David Jenkins, 428–37. Munich: Prestel, 2000.

Bürgi, Bernhard Mendes. "Die Wechselwirkung zwischen Kunst und
Architektur. Zu den inhaltlichen Aspekten des Neubaus". In *Kunst-
museum Basel*, Neubau, edited by Kunstmuseum Basel, 66–70.
Ostfildern: Hatje Cantz Verlag, 2016.

Castells, Manuel. "Museums in the Information Era: Cultural Connectors
of Time and Space". *ICOM News* (2001): 4–7.

Christ, Emanuel. "We Look at Examples. Ein Gespräch mit Emanuel
Christ, Christoph Gantenbein, Diogo Lopes, Kersten Geers, und
Patricia Barbas". *Baumeister* 8 (2013): 68–89.

Duncan, Carol. "Art Museums and the Ritual of Citizenship". In *Exhibiting
Cultures. The Poetics and Politics of Museum Display*, edited by
Steven D. Lavine and Ivan Karp, 88–103. Washington and London:
Smithsonian Institution Press, 1991.

Elden, Stuart, trans. Introduction to *Rhythmanalysis: Space, Time and
Everyday Life*, by Henri Lefebvre, vii–xv. London and New York:
Continuum, 2004.

Eliasson, Olafur. "The Future Is Curved". *Architectural Design* 84, no. 5
(2014): 86–93.

Enwezor, Okwui. "Popular Sovereignty and Public Space: David Adjaye's
Architecture of Immanence". In *David Adjaye: Making Public Buildings. Specificity, Customization, Imbrication*, edited by Peter Allison,
8–12. London: Thames & Hudson, 2006.

Fohrmann, Jürgen. "'Dichter heißen so gerne Schöpfer'. Über Genies
und andere Epigonen". *Merkur* 39 (1985): 980–89.

Foucault, Michel. "The Confession of the Flesh". In *Power/Knowledge.
Selected Interviews and Other Writings*, edited by Colin Gordon,
194–98. New York: Pantheon Books, 1980.

Gan, Zhang. "The Modern Museum in China". In *Crossing Cultures:
Conflict, Migration and Convergence*, edited by Jaynie Anderson,
1032–35. Carlton: Miegunyah Press, 2009.

Gunning, Tom. "The Art of Succession: Reading, Writing and Watching
Comics". *Critical Inquiry* 40, no. 3 (2014): 36–51.

Hamann, Jan. "Naga-Projekt Sudan. Archäologie und Restaurierung im
Sudan – Restaurierungsethische Überlegungen zur Hathor-Kapelle".
In *Kulturgut erhalten. Standards in der Restaurierungswissenschaft
und Denkmalpflege*, edited by Uwe Peltz and Olivia Zorn, 171–77.
Darmstadt: Philipp von Zabern, 2009.

Harris, Andrew. "Livingstone versus Serota: The High-rise Battle of
Bankside". *The London Journal* 33, no. 3 (2008): 289–99.

Heidegger, Martin. "Der Ursprung des Kunstwerkes". In idem, *Holzwege*,
1–70. Sixth ed. Frankfurt am Main: Vittorio Klostermann, 1980.

Henrichsen, Stein Olav. "The Art Museum Propelling City Development:
Oslo as a Creative City". *Journal of Urban Culture Research* 9 (2014):
102–10.

Hillier, Bill, Richard Burdett, John Peponis and Alan Penn. "Creating Life:
Or, Does Architecture Determine Anything?" *Architecture and
Comportment/Architecture and Behaviour* 3, no. 3 (1987): 233–50.

Holden, John. "The Cultural Value of Tate Modern". In *Tate Modern:
The First Five Years*, edited by Martin Gayford, 33–38. London: Tate
Publishing, 2005.

Holman Conwill, Kinshasha. "To Reap the Harvest Wonderful: On
Sustainability at the National Museum of African American History
and Culture". *American Art* 3 (2014): 20–27.

Hudson, Kenneth. "Perspektiven für ein Museum des nächsten Jahr-
hunderts". In *Museen und ihre Besucher. Herausforderungen in der
Zukunft*, edited by Annette Noschka-Roos, 263–69. Berlin: Argon
Verlag, 1996.

Irace, Fulvio. "Simple, Ordinary, Complex". In *David Chipperfield Architects*, edited by Rik Nys, 8–14. Cologne: Walther König, 2013.

Janes, Robert. "Museums, Corporatism and the Civil Society". *Curator*
50, no. 2 (2007): 219–37.

Julius, Corinne. "Making: The World of Thomas Heatherwick". *Craft Arts
International* 86 (2012): 18–25.

Kaltenbrunner, Robert. "Pekings Weg zur globalen Metropole". *Archithese* 4 (2008): 22–27.

Kaltenbrunner, Robert. "Urbanität mit Bilbao-Defekt. Was braucht die
Stadt an 'Baukultur'?" *Neue Gesellschaft – Frankfurter Hefte* 12 (2012):
92–95.

Kögel, Eduard. "Mit Geschichte aufgeladen. Ein historisches Museum
als Reflexion über den Abrisswahn in China". *werk, bauen + wohnen*
5 (2013): 8–15.

Landers, Jay. "No Title". *Civil Engineering* 5 (2013): 20–21.
Lloyd, Jill. "Van Gogh and Munch: A Question of Style". In *Munch: Van Gogh*, edited by Maite van Dijk, Magne Bruteig, and Leo Jansen, 124–47. Brussels: Mercatorfonds, 2014.

MacLeod, Suzanne. "This Magical Place: The Making of Yorkshire Sculpture Park and the Politics of Landscape, Art and Narrative". In *Museum Making: Narratives, Architectures, Exhibitions*, edited by Suzanne MacLeod, Laura Hanks and Jonathan Hale, 48–62. London and New York: Routledge, 2012.
Malacarne, Gino. "Il museo come parte di città". In *L'Architettura del museo con scritti e progetti di Aldo Rossi*, edited by Patricia Montini Zimolo, 97–110. Milan: CittàStudi, 1995.
Maluenda, Inmaculada, and Enrique Encabo. "Continuity Systems: A Conversation with Kazuyo Sejima & Ryue Nishizawa". *El Croquis* 179/180 (2015): 7–25.
Meyer, Ulf. "Gibt es das digital Erhabene?" *Baumeister* 6 (2013): 76–79.
Mitchell, W. J. T. "Comics as Media: Afterword". *Critical Inquiry* 40, no. 3 (2014): 255–65.
Mollard, Manon. "Mad Scene". *Architectural Review* 1425 (2015): 66–77.
Moneo, Rafael. "The Architect's Profession Today: An Alternative in Globalised Times". *El Croquis* 174/175 (2014): 356–73.

O'Neill, Mark. "Enlightenment Museums: Universal or Merely Global?" *Museum and Society* 2, no. 3 (2004): 190–202.

Ritzer, George. "The Globalization of Nothing". *SAIS Review* 23, no. 2 (2003): 189–200.
Rossi, Aldo. "Teatro del Mondo, 1979". In *Aldo Rossi, Opera Grafica 1973–1995*, edited by Umberto S. Barbieri and Giovanni Bertolotto, 10–11. Maastricht: Bonnefantenmuseum, 1995.

Schumacher, Patrik. "Design Is Communication". In *Zaha Hadid. Form in Motion*, edited by Kathryn Bloom Hiesinger, 11–13. New Haven: Yale University Press, 2011.
Sloterdijk, Peter. "Museum: School of Alienation". *Art in Translation* 6, no. 4 (2014): 437–48.
Sperling, Joy. "Popular Genres in the Visual Arts". In *A Companion to Popular Culture*, edited by Gary Burns, 144–83. Chichester: Wiley, 2016.
Stacher, Susanne. "Der Louvre Lens, Frankreich – Architektur als Land Art, Landschaft als Kunst". *Architektur Aktuell* 396, no. 3 (2013): 96–107.
Stara, Alexandra. "Cultivating Architects: History in Architectural Education". In *The Humanities in Architectural Design: A Contemporary and Historical Perspective*, edited by Soumyen Bandyopadhyay, Jane Lomholt, Nicholas Temple and Renee Tobe, 28–35. London and New York: Routledge, 2010.

Thiel-Silling, Sabine. "Mut zum Risiko". *Baumeister* 3 (2014): 16–18.

Ullrich, Wolfgang. "Der Unternehmer als Erzieher. Ein amerikanisches Märchen über den Einsatz von Kunst als Dienstleistung". In *Oeconomenta. Wechselspiele zwischen Kunst und Wirtschaft*, edited by Marc Markowski and Hergen Wöbken, 123–30. Berlin: Kulturverlag Kadmos, 2007.

Valéry, Paul. "The Problem with Museums". In idem, *Degas, Manet, Morisot*, 202–06. London and New York: Routledge, 2007.
Van den Berg, Karen. "The Unconditional Museum and the Fragile Logic of the Ensemble". In *Situation Kunst for Max Imdahl: The Extension 2006; a publication of the Stiftung Situation Kunst*, edited by Silke von Berswordt Wallrabe and Friederike Wappler, 9–29. Düsseldorf: Richter, 2008.
Van den Berg, Karen. "Das ausgestellte Museum. Von Abu Dhabi nach Teshima". *Paragrana* 1 (2017): 57–72.
Vandenbulcke, Benoît. "Concretion, Abstraction: The Place of Design Processes in Today's Architecture Practice. Case Study: Sanaa".

In *Proceedings from the 1st International Conference on Architecture & Urban Design*, 25–35. Tirana: Epoka University, 2012.
Varutti, Marzia. "The Aesthetics and Narratives in National Museums in China". In *National Museums: New Studies from around the World*, edited by Simon J. Knell, Peter Aronsson and Arne Bugge Amundsen, 302–12. London and New York: Routledge, 2011.
Von Buttlar, Adrian. "The Museum Island: An Architectural-Historical Overview". In *Museum Island Berlin*, edited by Michael Eissenhauer, Astrid Bähr and Elisabeth Rochau-Shalem, 94–117. Munich: Hirmer Publishers, 2012.
Von Müller, Johannes. "Die Sprechblase". In *Bildlaute und laute Bilder. Die "Audio-Visualität" der Bilderzählungen*, edited by Christian A. Bachmann, 75–93. Berlin: Christian A. Bachmann Verlag, 2014.

Wilson, Mabel O. "Other Monumentalities". In *David Adjaye: Form, Heft, Material*, edited by Okwui Enwezor and Zoë Ryan in consultation with Peter Allison, 265–84. Chicago: Art Institute of Chicago, 2015.
Wu, Fulong. "Re-orientation of the City Plan: Strategic Planning and Design Competition in China". *Geoforum* 38 (2007): 379–92.

Monographs

Die soziale Dimension der Museumsarbeit. Bericht über ein internationales Seminar der Deutschen UNESCO-Kommission, veranstaltet in Zusammenarbeit mit dem Museum Folkwang vom 20. bis 23. Mai 1974 in Essen. Cologne: Deutsche UNESCO-Kommission, 1976.

Ábalos, Iñaki, and Juan Herreros. *Tower and Office: From Modernist Theory to Contemporary Practice*. Cambridge, MA: MIT Press, 2003.
Ando, Tadao. *Conversations with Students*. Translated and edited by Matthew Hunter. New York: Princeton Architectural Press, 2012.
Awan, Nishat, Tatjana Schneider and Jeremy Till. *Spatial Agency: Other Ways of Doing Architecture*. London and New York: Routledge, 2011.

Basso Peressut, Luca. *Musei: architetture, 1990–2000*. Milan: Motta, 1999.
Bishop, Claire. *Radical Museology or, What's "Contemporary" in Contemporary Museums of Contemporary Art?* London: König Books, 2014.
Bott, Gehrard, ed. *Das Museum der Zukunft. 43 Beiträge zur Diskussion über die Zukunft des Museums*. Cologne: DuMont, 1970.
Bourdieu, Pierre. *The Rules of Art: Genesis and Structure of the Literary Field*. Stanford, CA: Stanford University Press, 1996.
Bourdieu, Pierre. *Distinction*. London and New York: Routledge, 2013.

Castany, Laurence, ed. *Centre Pompidou: Creation in the heart of Paris*. Paris: Éditions du Centre Pompidou, 2011.
Chipperfield, David. *Theoretical Practice*. London: Artemis, 1994.
Coleman, Nathaniel. *Lefebvre for Architects*. London and New York: Routledge, 2015.
Crossick, Geoffrey, and Patrycja Kaszynska. *Understanding the Value of Arts and Culture: The AHRC Cultural Value Project*. Swindon: AHRC, 2016.
Crouch, Colin. *The Knowledge Corrupters: Hidden Consequences of the Financial Takeover of Public Life*. Cambridge, UK: Polity Press, 2015.

Des Cars, Laurence, ed. *Louvre Abu Dhabi: Birth of a Museum*. Paris: Musée du Louvre Éditions/Tourism and Culture Authority (TCA)/Skira Flammarion, 2013.
Dewey, John, Albert C. Barnes, Laurence Buermeyer, Mary Mullen and Violette de Mazia. *Art and Education: A Collection of Essays*. Third ed. Collingdale, PA: The Barnes Foundation Press, 1978.
Dubrau, Christian. *Zeitgenössische Architektur in China. Bauten und Projekte 2000 bis 2020*. Berlin: DOM Publishers, 2010.

Florida, Richard L. *The Rise of the Creative Class and How It's Transforming Work, Leisure, Community and Everyday Life*. New York: Basic Books, 2004.

Gale, Matthew, ed. *Tate Modern: The Handbook*. London: Tate Publishing, 2012.
Giebelhausen, Michaela, ed. *The Architecture of the Museum: Symbolic Structures, Urban Contexts*. Manchester: Manchester University Press, 2003.
Gumbrecht, Hans Ulrich. *Production of Presence: What Meaning Cannot Convey*. Stanford CA: Stanford University Press, 2004.

Hess, Regine. *Emotionen am Werk. Peter Zumthor, Daniel Libeskind, Lars Spuybroek und die historische Architekturpsychologie*. Berlin: Gebr. Mann Verlag, 2013.
Hillebrand, Karl. *Zwölf Briefe eines ästhetischen Ketzers*. Berlin: R. Oppenheim Verlag, 1874.
Hoffmann, Hilmar, ed. *Das Guggenheim Prinzip*. Cologne: DuMont Reiseverlag, 1999.
Huyssen, Andreas. *Twilight Memories: Making Time in a Culture of Amnesia*. London and New York: Routledge, 1995.

Jacobson, Claire. *New Museums in China*. New York: Princeton Architectural Press, 2014.
Janes, Robert. *Museums in a Troubled World: Renewal, Irrelevance or Collapse*. London and New York: Routledge, 2009.
Joachimides, Alexis. *Die Museumsreformbewegung in Deutschland und die Entstehung des modernen Museums 1880–1940*. Dresden: Verlag der Kunst, 2001.
Jodidio, Philip. *Ando. Complete Works*. Cologne: Taschen, 2007.
Johnson, Mark. *The Meaning of the Body: Aesthetics of Human Understanding*. Chicago and London: The University of Chicago Press, 2007.

Koenig, Wendy. *The Phenomenon of Interruption in the Visual Arts*. New York: Edwin Mellen Press, 2009.
Kravagna, Christian, ed. *The Museum as Arena: Artists on Institutional Critique*. Cologne: Walther König, 2001.

Lefebvre, Henri. *The Production of Space*. Translated by Donald Nicholson. Oxford, UK, and Cambridge, MA: Blackwell, 1991.
Lefebvre, Henri. *Rhythmanalysis: Space, Time and Everyday Life*. Translated by Stuart Elden. London and New York: Continuum, 2004.
Levent, Nina, and Alvaro Pascual-Leone, eds. *The Multisensory Museum: Cross-disciplinary Perspectives on Touch, Sound, Smell, Memory, and Space*. Lanham: Rowman & Littlefield, 2014.
Lynch, Bernadette. *Whose Cake Is It Anyway?* London: Paul Hamlyn Foundation, 2011.

Meier, Nikolaus. *Kunstmuseum Basel. Die Architektur*. Basel: Christoph Merian Verlag, 2003.
Moles, Abraham A. *Information Theory and Esthetic Perception*. Urbana: University of Illinois Press, 1996.
Mouffe, Chantal. *Agonistics: Thinking the World Politically*. London: Verso, 2013.

Noever, Peter, ed. *The Discursive Museum*. Ostfildern: Hatje Cantz Verlag, 2001.

Obrist, Hans Ulrich. *Zaha Hadid*. Cologne: Walther König, 2007.
Obrist, Hans Ulrich. *Lives of the Artists, Lives of the Architects*. London: Allen Lane, 2015.

Pierre, José. *Futurismus und Dadaismus*. Lausanne: Éditions Rencontres, 1967.
Preiss, Achim, Karl Stamm and Frank Günter Zehnder, eds. *Das Museum. Die Entwicklung in den 80er Jahren. Festschrift Hugo Borger zum 65. Geburtstag*. Munich: Klinkhardt & Biermann, 1990.

Ross, Andrew, ed. *The Gulf: High Culture/Hard Labor*. New York and London: OR Books, 2015.
Rossi, Aldo. *The Architecture of the City*. Cambridge, MA: MIT Press, 1982.

Sandell, Richard, and Ethnie Nightingale. *Museums, Equality and Social Justice*. London and New York: Routledge, 2012.
Schneede, Uwe M., ed. *Museum 2000. Erlebnispark oder Bildungsstätte?* Cologne: DuMont , 2000.
Szeemann, Harald. *Museum der Obsessionen*. Berlin: Merve, 1981.

Till, Jeremy. *Architecture Depends*. Cambridge, MA: MIT Press, 2013.

Ullrich, Wolfgang. *Der kreative Mensch. Streit um eine Idee*. Salzburg: Residenz Verlag, 2016.
Ullrich, Wolfgang. *Siegerkunst. Neuer Adel, teure Lust*. Berlin: Wagenbach, 2016.

Wall, Tobias. *Das unmögliche Museum. Zum Verhältnis von Kunst und Kunstmuseen der Gegenwart*. Bielefeld: Transcript, 2006.
Wu, Weiping, and Piper Gaubatz. *The Chinese City*. London: Routledge, 2013.

Online Publications

"Leading Art Expert Says Finland Too Coy About Its Visual Culture". *Yle*, October 4, 2014. Accessed September 16, 2016. http://yle.fi/uutiset/leading_art_expert_says_finland_too_coy_about_its_visual_culture/7508772.
"Mad about Museums". *The Economist*, December 21, 2013. Accessed July 20, 2016. http://www.economist.com/news/special-report/21591710-china-building-thousands-new-museums-how-will-it-fill-them-mad-about-museums.

Banks, Tom. "Heatherwick to 'Carve Out' Grain Silo in Ambitious African Gallery Project". *Design Week*, February 28, 2014. Accessed July 19, 2016. http://www.designweek.co.uk/issues/february-2014/heatherwick-to-carve-out-grain-silo-in-ambitious-african-gallery-project/.
Basso Peressut, Luca. "Envisioning 21st Century Museums for Transnational Societies". In *Museums in an Age of Migrations. Questions, Challenges, Perspectives*, edited by Luca Basso Peressut and Clelia Pozzi, 19-54. Milan: Politecnico di Milano, 2012. Accessed September 26, 2016. http://www.mela-project.polimi.it/publications/845.htm.
Basso Peressut, Luca. "Contemporary Museums between Theory and Practice". In *Advancing Museum Practices*, edited by Francesca Lanz and Elena Montanari, 148–62. Turin: Allemandi, 2014. Accessed September 26, 2016. http://www.mela-project.polimi.it/publications/1185.htm.
Batty, David. "Migrants Building UAE Cultural Hub 'Risk Abuse If They Complain'". *The Guardian*, February 10, 2015. Accessed October 4, 2016. https://www.theguardian.com/global-development/2015/feb/10/migrants-united-arab-emirates-human-rights-watch.
Baudelle, Guy, and Gerhard Krauss. "The Governance Model of Two French National Museums of Fine Arts Relocated in the Province: Centre Pompidou Metz and Louvre-Lens". *Belgeo*, published online December 15, 2014. Accessed October 4, 2016. doi: 10.4000/belgeo.12765.
Berglund, Nina. "Majority Hails New Munch Museum". *News in English*. Accessed October 4, 2016. http://www.newsinenglish.no/2013/05/29/majority-cheers-new-munch-museum/.

Cumming, Laura. "Tate Modern's Switch House: Art Comes First". *The Guardian*, June 19, 2016. Accessed September 26, 2016. https://www.theguardian.com/artanddesign/2016/jun/19/tate-modern-switch-house-extension-art-comes-first.

Davis, Ben. "How the Rich Are Hurting the Museums They Fund". *The New York Times*, July 22, 2016. Accessed September 15, 2016. http://www.nytimes.com/2016/07/24/opinion/sunday/how-the-rich-are-hurting-the-museums-they-fund.html?_r=0.

Flanagan, Richard. "Tasmanian Devil". *The New Yorker*, January 21, 2013. Accessed September 15, 2016. http://www.newyorker.com/magazine/2013/01/21/tasmanian-devil.

Frearson, Amy. "Construction of Gehry's Guggenheim Abu Dhabi Yet to Start". Dezeen, February 12, 2016. Accessed November 4, 2016. http://www.dezeen.com/2016/02/12/construction-guggenheim-frank-gehry-abu-dhabi-still-yet-to-start/.

Greenspan, Elizabeth. "Daniel Libeskind's Secret Museum of the Kurds". *Bloomberg Businessweek*, April 11, 2016. Accessed August 10, 2016. http://www.bloomberg.com/features/2016-design/a/daniel-libeskind/.

Hornsby, Adrian. "Saadiyat Island". *The Architect's Journal*, November 3, 2008. Accessed October 4, 2016. http://www.architectsjournal.co.uk/news/saadiyat-island/1914047.fullarticle.

Joffe, Lawrence. "Obituary: Sheikh Zayed bin Sultan Al Nahyan". *The Guardian*, November 3, 2004. Accessed August 10, 2016. https://www.theguardian.com/news/2004/nov/03/guardianobituaries.israel.

Jones, Jonathan. "Why the Louvre Abu Dhabi Is Worth Celebrating, Despite Its Dark Side". *The Guardian*, March 9, 2015. Accessed October 4, 2016. https://www.the guardian.com/artanddesign/jonathanjonesblog/2015/mar/09/louvre-abu-dhabi-worth-celebrating-jean-nouvel-human-rights.

Mack, Gerhard. "Kunst aus Europa, Geld vom Golf". *Neue Zürcher Zeitung*, March 11, 2007. Accessed October 4, 2016. http://www.nzz.ch/articleEZP0B-1.125922.

Mallonee, Laura C. "Marfa's Art World Gentrification Is Pushing out Long-time Residents". *Hyperallergic*, August 11, 2014. Accessed October 4, 2016. http://hyperallergic.com/142955/marfas-art-world-gentrification-is-pushing-out long-time-residents/.

Mann, Stephan. "Die Lage der Museen. Neue Hierarchie Fallen". *Frankfurter Allgemeine Zeitung*, November 5, 2015. Accessed September 15, 2016. http://www.faz.net/aktuell/feuilleton/kunst/die-lage-der-museen-in-der-hierarchiefalle-13891625.html.

Ministère de la Culture et de la Communication. "Louvre-Lens", published May 12, 2005. Accessed September 26, 2016. http://www.culture.gouv.fr/culture/actualites/dossiers-presse/louvre-lens/louvre-lens.pdf.

Moreau, Nicolas, and Hiroko Kusunoki. *Art in the City*, 2015. Accessed July 31, 2016. https://issuu.com/srgf/docs/gh-04380895_a3_booklet_sanitised_-_/1?e=15988582/12215631.

Müller, Felix. "Historische Museen in der Krise. Die Eventfalle". *Neue Zürcher Zeitung*, June 3, 2016. Accessed September 15, 2016. http://www.nzz.ch/feuilleton/aktuell/historische-museen-in-der-krise-die-eventkultur-fordert-ihren-preis-ld.86606.

Musée du Louvre. Press Release. "Birth of a Museum: Louvre Abu Dhabi", 2014. Accessed October 4, 2016. http://www.louvre.fr/sites/default/files/Louvre%20Abu%20Dhabi%20exhibition%20Press%20Kit_v2.pdf.

Noce, Vincent. "Work on Louvre Abu Dhabi Goes into Overdrive". *The Art Newspaper*, March 4, 2015. Accessed October 4, 2016. http://old.theartnewspaper.com/articles/Work-on-Louvre-Abu-Dhabi-goes-into-overdrive/37118.

Popp, Peter, and Emilia Margaretha. "Integrative Transparency: Louvre-Lens by SANAA". *Detail*, published September 1, 2013. Accessed October 4, 2016. http://www.detail-online.com/article/integrative-transparency-louvre-lens-by-sanaa-16498/.

Report by Britain Thinks for Museums Association, March 2013. Accessed September 15, 2016. https://www.museumsassociation.org/download?id=954916.

Rothman, Joshua. "The Meaning of Culture". *The New Yorker*, December 26, 2014. Accessed September 15, 2016. http://www.newyorker.com/books/joshua-rothman/meaning-culture.

Stack, John. "Tate Online Strategy, 2010–12". *Tate Papers* 13 (Spring 2010). Accessed September 15, 2016. http://www.tate.org.uk/research/publications/tate-papers/13/tate-online-strategy-2010-12.

Sutton, Benjamin. "Breaking Down ArtReview's 2014 Power 100 List". *Hyperallergic*, October 23, 2014. Accessed October 4, 2016. http://hyperallergic.com/157870/breaking-down-artreviews-2014-power-100-list/.

Tourism Tasmania. "Mona Visitor Profile, March 2016". Accessed September 15, 2016. http://www.tourismtasmania.com.au/__data/assets/pdf_file/0010/39772/MONA-Visitor-Profile-YE-Dec-2015.pdf.

Vartanian, Hrag. "Guggenheim Breaks Off Negotiations with Gulf Labor Over Migrant Rights". *Hyperallergic*, April 17, 2016. Accessed October 4, 2016. http://hyperallergic.com/291594/guggenheim-breaks-off-negotiations-with-gulf-labor-over-migrant-rights/.

Wainwright, Oliver. "Palestine Museum Review: A Beacon of Optimism on a West Bank Hilltop". *The Guardian*, May 17, 2016. Accessed August 9, 2016. https://www.theguardian.com/artanddesign/2016/may/17/palestine-museum-review-ramallah-west-bank-israel.

Zitzmann, Marc. "Fata Morgana am Meer". *Neue Zürcher Zeitung*, May 7, 2014. Accessed October 4, 2016. http://www.nzz.ch/feuilleton/kunst_architektur/fata-morgana-am-meer-1.18296931.

Websites

Architect Klaus Schuwerk on architecture: https://www.youtube.com/watch?v=Svkl4YdsJO8.

Arney Fender Katsalidis. "Museum of Old and New Art (MONA)". Accessed July 19, 2016. http://fkaustralia.com/projects#project-1.

Art Gallery NSW. "History of the Building". Accessed July 19, 2016. http://www.artgallery.new.gov.au/about-us/history/history-of-the-building/.

Australian Design Review. "Museum of Old and New Art". Accessed July 19, 2016. https://www.australiandesignreview.com/architecture/2280-museum-of-old-and-new-art.

Guggenheim Helsinki Design Competition. Accessed July 19, 2016. http://designguggenheimhelsinki.org.

Heneghan Peng Architects. "Palestinian Museum". Accessed August 9, 2016. http://www.hparc.com/work/palestinian-museum/.

MONA. "Cemetery". Accessed September 15, 2016. https://www.mona.net.au/mona/Cemetery.

Moreau Kusunoki Architectes. "Homepage". Accessed July 19, 2016. http://www.moreaukusunoki.com.

The Palestinian Museum. "Palestinian Journeys: An Interactive Timeline from 1850 to the Modern Day". Accessed August 10, 2016. http://www.palmuseum.org/public-programme/palestinian-journeys-an-interactive-timeline-from-1850-to-the-modern-day.

Photo Credits

© 2015 Getty Images. Photography by Dan Kitwood, p. 191

© Adjaye Associates, pp. 20–21

© AFL / estudio Herreros, p. 200

© Aires Mateus, Plateforme 10, Lausanne, pp. 28 (bottom), 32–37, 197

© Alan Karchmer / Adjaye Associates, pp. 22 (bottom), 23 (top left)

© Atelier Deshaus, pp. 42–43

© Barozzi/Veiga, Plateforme 10, Lausanne, pp. 24, 26–31

Carl André, *10 × 10 Altstadt Square*, 1967 © 2017, Prolitteris, Zurich, photography by Stefano Graziani, p. 53 (bottom right)

© Christ & Gantenbein, pp. 50–51

Courtesy of ARoS Aarhus Kunstmuseum, Denmark, 2011, photography by Ole Hein Pedersen © Olafur Eliasson, p. 194

Courtesy Fondazione Prada, New Milan venue of Fondazione Prada, Architectural project by OMA, photography by Bas Princen, 2015, p. 172

Courtesy of Gehry Partners, LLP, p. 170

Courtesy of Louisiana, photography by Poul Buchard, p. 174

Courtesy of MONA Museum of Old and New Art, Hobart, Tasmania, Australia, photography by Brett Boardman, pp. 76 (bottom right), 77 (bottom left)

Courtesy of MONA Museum of Old and New Art, Hobart, Tasmania, Australia, photography by Rémi Chauvin, pp. 8, 70, 76 (top left, top right and bottom left), 77 (top and bottom right), 173

Courtesy Yorkshire Sculpture Park © Jonty Wilde (Photo), p. 176

Courtesy of Zaha Hadid Architects © pp. 150, 152–157

© Dan Perjovschi, p. 187

© David Chipperfield Architects, pp. 54, 56–60 (top), 61

Donald Judd, *Untitled*, 1969 © Judd Foundation / 2017, Prolitteris, Zurich, photography by Stefano Graziani, p. 53 (bottom left)

© estudio Herreros, pp. 66–69, 167, 180–181

© Fender Katsalidis Architects, pp. 74–75

© Foster + Partners, pp. 78, 80–81

Günther Förg, *Villa Malaparte, Capri*, 1983/2005 © 2017, Prolitteris, Zurich, photography by Stefano Graziani, p. 53 (top left)

© Hanspeter Schiess for cukrowicz nachbaur architekten, p. 188

© Heatherwick Studio, pp. 82, 84–87

© Hufton+Crow, p. 12

© James Turrell / Courtesy of MONA Museum of Old and New Art, Hobart, Tasmania, Australia, photography by Rémi Chauvin, pp. 72–73

© Kazuyo Sejima + Ryue Nishizawa / SANAA, pp. 184, 186

© Kazuyo Sejima + Ryue Nishizawa / SANAA (Architect); Art Gallery of New South Wales (Client), pp. 130–131

© Kazuyo Sejima + Ryue Nishizawa / SANAA (Architect); Art Gallery of New South Wales (Client); Doug&Wolf (Rendering), pp. 126, 132–133 (Process images, 2016)

© Kazuyo Sejima + Ryue Nishizawa / SANAA (Architect); Art Gallery of New South Wales (Client); Studio Cyrille Thomas (Rendering), pp. 128–129 (Competition scheme, 2015)

© Klaus Schuwerk, p. 102 (centre and bottom)

© Klaus Schuwerk, Kleihues + Schuwerk, pp. 100–101

© Kleihues + Schuwerk, MIR, pp. 96, 98–99, 103, 199

© Kleihues + Schuwerk, Neumeyer Treese, p. 102 (top)

© MAD Architects, pp. 104, 106–109

© MIR / estudio Herreros, pp. 62, 64–65

© Moderna galerija, Ljubljana, photography by Dejan Habicht, p. 185

© Moreau Kusunoki, pp. 112–115, 116 (bottom), 117, 179, 201

© Moreau Kusunoki, ArteFactory (rendering), p. 116 (top)

© Moreau Kusunoki, ArteFactory (rendering), Maris Mezulis (photography), p. 110

© MVRDV, pp. 118, 120–125, 164 (Competition renderings)

© Neutelings Riedijk Architects, photography by Sarah Blee, p. 196

© Palestinian Museum, Heneghan Peng Architects, pp. 92–93

© Palestinian Museum, photography by Iwan Baan, pp. 88, 90–91, 94–95, 168

© Perry van Duijnhoven (2014), Van Abbemuseum p. 162

© Stefano Graziani / Christ & Gantenbein, pp. 48, 49, 52, 53 (top right)

© Steve Hall, Hedrich Blessing, p. 22 (top)

© Studio Libeskind, pp. 134, 136–141

© Susheng Liang / Atelier Deshaus, pp. 38, 44 (bottom right)

© Tadao Ando Architect & Associates, pp. 142, 144–149

© Tate, London 2017, p. 10

© TrigonArt Bauer Praus GbR, p. 60 (bottom)

© Wade Zimmerman, pp. 16, 18–19, 23 (top right, bottom)

© Walter Mair / Christ & Gantenbein, p. 46

© Xia Zhi / Atelier Deshaus, pp. 40–41, 44 (top left, top right and bottom left), 45

Imprint

This catalogue is published on the occasion of the exhibition

**New Museums: Intentions, Expectations, Challenges /
Musées du XXIᵉ siècle: visions, ambitions, défis**

at Musée d'art et d'histoire de Genève,
May 11–August 20, 2017

An exhibition created and curated by Art Centre Basel,
on behalf of Musées d'art et d'histoire de Genève.

For Art Centre Basel
Suzanne Greub, Director
Katharina Beisiegel, Deputy Director,
    Editor and Exhibition Curator
Marie Gaitzsch, Curatorial and Editorial Assistant
Julie Bachmann, Editorial Assistant

For Musées d'art et d'histoire de Genève
Jean-Yves Marin, Director
Silvia Iuorio, Administrator
Bertrand Mazeirat, Exhibition Curator, Head of Exhibitions
David Meier, Exhibition Designer
Cédric Siegenthaler, Graphic Designer
And the whole team of Musées d'art et d'histoire
    involved in the project

Project Management: Jürgen Kleidt, Hirmer Verlag
Translations: Russell Stockman, Robert Scot McInnes (Preface)
Copy-editing: Vanessa Magson-Mann (English),
    Russell Stockman (English), Gunnar Musan (German)
Design: Akademischer Verlagsservice Gunnar Musan
Fonts: Sailec by Type Dynamic, Overpass by Delve Fonts
Lithography: Reproline Genceller, Munich
Paper: GardaMatt Art 170 g/sq. m
Printing and binding: Printer Trento S.r.l., Trento
Printed in Italy

Bibliographic information published by the Deutsche
Nationalbibliothek. The Deutsche Nationalbibliothek
lists this publication in the Deutsche Nationalbibliografie;
detailed bibliographic data are available at http://dnb.de.

ISBN 978-3-7774-2724-9 (English Edition)
ISBN 978-3-7774-2726-3 (French Edition)

http://www.artcentrebasel.com
http://institutions.ville-geneve.ch/fr/mah
http://www.hirmerpublishers.com